An Introduction to Econometrics

An Introduction to Econometrics

A Self-contained Approach

Frank Westhoff

The MIT Press
Cambridge, Massachusetts
London, England

MIT Press books may be purchased at special quantity discounts for business or sales promotional use. For information, please email special_sales@mitpress.mit.edu or write to Special Sales Department, The MIT Press, 55 Hayward Street, Cambridge, MA 02142.

This book was set in Times and Syntax by Toppan Best-set Premedia Limited. Printed and bound in the United States of America.

Library of Congress Cataloging-in-Publication Data

Westhoff, Frank, 1946–
   An introduction to econometrics : a self-contained approach / Frank Westhoff.
      pages   cm
   Includes index.
   ISBN 978-0-262-01922-4 (hardcover : alk. paper)
   1. Econometrics.   I. Title.
   HB139.W475 2013
   330.01′5195–dc23

2012049424

10 9 8 7 6 5 4 3 2 1

Contents

How to Use This Textbook

This textbook utilizes many empirical examples and Java simulations that play a critical role. The empirical examples show you how we use statistical software to analyze real world data. The Java simulations confirm the algebraic equations that are derived in the chapters, providing you with a better appreciation of what the equations mean, and also demonstrate important econometric concepts without delving into complicated mathematics. The simulations are called Econometrics Labs. The textbook calls your attention to the empirical examples and labs by denoting them with a ⌨ icon.

To gain the most benefit from the textbook, you should read the textbook while seated at a computer to take advantage of the empirical examples and labs. Connect to the following url: http://mitpress.mit.edu/westhoffeconometrics

This takes you to the first page of our textbook website. You will now be asked to select a data format for the empirical examples. All the data used in the textbook are available on the website stored as EViews workfiles, State workfiles, and Excel spreadsheets. If you will be using the EViews statistical software, click on EViews, or if you will be using Stata, click on Stata; otherwise, click on Excel. After doing so, bookmark this page. In the future, whenever you see the ⌨ icon in the textbook, connect to your bookmarked page to avoid specifying your statistical software repeatedly.

Next click on the chapter you are reading. A list of the empirical examples and labs for the chapter will now appear. Click on the appropriate one. To gain the most from the textbook, you should perform the empirical analysis and complete the labs for yourself as well as read the results that are presented in the textbook. The textbook includes many "Getting Started in EViews" sections to guide you through the empirical examples if you are using EViews. Also note that the labs are Java applets; consequently the computer you use must have the Java Runtime Environment installed to run the labs. Each lab may take a few seconds to load. (If you have trouble viewing the applets, be certain you are running an up-to-date version of Java.) Shortly thereafter instructions will appear and the lab will pose questions. You can navigate from question to question clicking **Next Question** and, if need be, **Previous Question**. You should work your way through each empirical example and lab as you read along in the textbook. By doing so, you will gain a better appreciation of the concepts that are introduced.

1 Descriptive Statistics

Chapter 1 Prep Questions

1. Look at precipitation data for the twentieth century. How would you decide which month of the year was the wettest?

2. Consider the monthly growth rates of the Dow Jones Industrial Average and the Nasdaq Composite Index.

    a. In most months, would you expect the Nasdaq's growth rate to be high or low when the Dow's growth rate is high?

    b. In most months, would you expect the Nasdaq's growth rate to be high or low when the Dow's growth rate is low?

c. Would you describe the Dow and Nasdaq growth rates as being correlated or uncorrelated?

1.1 Describing a Single Data Variable

Descriptive statistics allow us to summarize the information inherent in a data variable. The weather provides many examples of how useful descriptive statistics can be. Every day we hear people making claims about the weather. "The summer of 2012 was the hottest on record," "April is the wettest month of the year," "Last winter was the coldest ever," and so on. To judge the validity of such statements, we need some information, some data.

We will focus our attention on precipitation in Amherst, Massachusetts, during the twentieth century. Table 1.1 reports the inches of precipitation in Amherst for each month of the twentieth century.[1]

1.1.1 Introduction to Distributions

What is the wettest month of the summer in Amherst? How can we address this question? While it is possible to compare the inches of precipitation in June, July, and August by carefully studying the numerical values recorded in table 1.1, it is difficult, if not impossible, to draw any conclusions. There is just too much information to digest. In some sense, the table includes too much detail; it overwhelms us. For example, we can see from the table that July was the wettest summer month in 1996, August was the wettest summer month in 1997, June was the wettest summer month in 1998, August was again the wettest summer month in 1999, and finally, June was again the wettest summer month in 2000. We need a way to summarize the information contained in table 1.1. Descriptive statistics perform this task. By describing the distribution of the values, descriptive statistics distill the information contained in many observations into single numbers. Summarizing data in this way has both benefits and costs. Without a summary, we can easily "lose sight of the forest for the trees." In the process of summarizing, however, some information will inevitably be lost.

First, we will discuss the two most important types of descriptive statistics that describe a single data variable: measures of the **distribution center** and measures of the **distribution spread**. Next we will introduce **histograms**. A histogram visually illustrates the distribution of a single data variable.

---

1. With the exception of two months, March 1950 and October 1994, the data were obtained from NOAA's National Climate Data Center. Data for these two months were missing from the NOAA center and were obtained from the Phillip T. Ives records that are stored in the Amherst College archives.

1.1.2 Measure of the Distribution Center: Mean (Average)

No doubt the most commonly cited descriptive statistic is the **mean** or **average**.[2] We use the mean to denote the center of the distribution all the time in everyday life. For example, we use the mean or average income earned by individuals in states, per capita income, to denote how much a typical state resident earns. Massachusetts per capita income in 2000 equaled $25,952. This means that some Massachusetts residents earned more than $25,952 and some less, but $25,952 lies at the center of the income distribution of Massachusetts residents. A typical or representative state resident earned $25,952. A baseball player's batting average is also a mean: the number of hits the player gets per official at bat.

Since the mean represents the center of the distribution, the representative value, why not simply calculate the mean amount of precipitation in June, July, and August to decide on the wettest summer month? The month with the highest mean would be deemed the wettest. To calculate the mean (average) precipitation for June in the twentieth century, we sum the amount of precipitation in each June and divide the total by the number of Junes, 100 in this case:

$$\text{Mean for June} = \frac{0.75 + 4.54 + \ldots + 7.99}{100} = \frac{377.76}{100} = 3.78$$

The mean precipitation for June is 3.78 inches. More formally, we can let x represent the data variable for monthly precipitation in June:

x_1 = value for the first observation (June 1901) = 0.75

x_2 = value for the second observation (June 1902) = 4.54

$$\vdots$$

x_T = value for the Tth or last observation (June 2000) = 7.99

The following equation expresses the mean generally:

$$\text{Mean}[x] = \bar{x} = \frac{x_1 + x_2 + \ldots + x_T}{T} = \frac{\sum_{t=1}^{T} x_t}{T}$$

where

T = total number of observations

The mean of a data variable is often denoted by a bar above the symbol, $\bar{x}$, pronounced "x bar." $\sum_{t=1}^{T} x_t / T$ is a concise way to describe the arithmetic used to compute the mean. Let us now "dissect" the numerator of this expression:

---

2. The median and mode are other measures of the center. They are presented in chapter 25.

Table 1.1
Monthly precipitation in Amherst, Massachusetts, 1901 to 2000 (inches)

Year	Jan	Feb	Mar	Apr	May	Jun	Jul	Aug	Sep	Oct	Nov	Dec
1901	2.09	0.56	5.66	5.80	5.12	0.75	3.77	5.75	3.67	4.17	1.30	8.51
1902	2.13	3.32	5.47	2.92	2.42	4.54	4.66	4.65	5.83	5.59	1.27	4.27
1903	3.28	4.27	6.40	2.30	0.48	7.79	4.64	4.92	1.66	2.72	2.04	3.95
1904	4.74	2.45	4.48	5.73	4.55	5.35	2.62	4.09	5.45	1.74	1.35	2.75
1905	3.90	1.70	3.66	2.56	1.28	2.86	2.63	6.47	6.26	2.27	2.06	3.15
1906	2.18	2.73	4.90	3.25	4.95	2.82	3.45	6.42	2.59	5.69	1.98	4.49
1907	2.73	1.92	1.82	1.98	4.02	2.61	3.87	1.44	8.74	5.00	4.50	3.89
1908	2.25	3.53	2.86	1.97	4.35	0.76	3.28	4.27	1.73	1.57	1.06	3.05
1909	3.56	5.16	3.01	5.53	3.36	2.24	2.24	3.80	4.99	1.23	1.06	2.95
1910	6.14	5.08	1.37	3.07	2.67	2.65	1.90	4.03	2.86	0.93	3.69	1.72
1911	2.36	2.18	3.80	1.87	1.37	2.02	4.21	5.92	3.41	8.81	3.84	4.42
1912	2.18	3.16	5.70	3.92	4.34	0.77	2.61	3.22	2.52	2.07	4.03	4.04
1913	3.98	2.94	6.30	3.30	4.94	0.90	1.59	2.26	2.56	5.16	2.11	3.38
1914	3.72	3.36	5.52	6.59	3.56	2.32	3.53	5.11	0.52	2.09	2.62	2.89
1915	6.52	7.02	0.12	3.99	1.20	3.00	9.13	8.28	1.37	2.89	2.20	5.86
1916	2.56	5.27	3.97	3.69	3.21	4.97	6.85	2.49	5.08	1.01	3.29	2.85
1917	3.30	1.98	4.08	1.83	4.13	5.27	3.36	7.06	2.42	6.60	0.63	2.56
1918	4.11	2.99	2.91	2.78	2.47	4.01	1.84	2.22	7.00	1.32	2.87	2.95
1919	2.02	2.80	4.22	2.37	6.20	1.09	4.17	4.80	4.45	1.81	6.20	1.48
1920	2.74	4.45	2.90	4.71	3.65	6.26	2.06	3.62	6.74	1.54	4.62	6.02
1921	2.00	2.38	3.57	6.47	4.56	3.87	6.00	2.35	1.84	1.08	6.20	1.90
1922	1.56	3.02	5.34	2.81	5.47	9.68	4.28	4.25	2.27	2.55	1.56	3.15
1923	6.02	1.81	1.98	3.19	3.26	2.24	1.77	2.55	1.89	5.50	5.05	4.23
1924	3.85	2.56	1.05	4.54	2.21	1.28	1.75	3.11	5.87	0.01	2.57	2.16
1925	3.42	3.64	4.12	3.10	2.55	4.28	6.97	1.93	3.09	4.74	3.23	3.56
1926	3.23	5.01	3.95	3.62	1.19	2.03	3.24	3.97	1.50	5.02	5.38	2.78
1927	2.50	2.62	1.96	1.60	4.83	3.37	3.40	5.01	2.79	4.59	8.65	5.66
1928	2.19	2.90	1.17	4.16	3.25	6.97	6.23	8.40	3.07	0.87	1.79	0.97
1929	4.33	3.92	3.20	6.89	4.17	3.06	0.70	1.54	3.62	2.75	2.73	4.05
1930	2.59	1.39	3.95	1.41	3.34	4.47	4.50	1.82	2.08	2.24	3.42	1.63
1931	3.58	1.80	3.79	2.95	7.44	4.24	3.87	6.57	2.50	3.06	1.55	3.83
1932	3.68	2.70	4.24	2.33	1.67	2.62	3.83	2.67	3.96	3.69	6.05	1.99
1933	2.44	3.48	4.79	5.03	1.69	3.68	2.25	6.63	12.34	3.90	1.19	2.81
1934	3.50	2.82	3.60	4.44	3.42	4.67	1.73	3.02	9.54	2.35	3.50	2.99
1935	4.96	2.50	1.48	2.54	2.17	5.50	3.10	0.82	4.67	0.88	4.41	1.05
1936	6.47	2.64	7.04	4.07	1.76	3.28	1.45	4.85	3.80	4.80	2.02	5.96
1937	5.38	2.22	3.38	4.03	6.09	5.72	2.88	4.91	3.24	4.33	4.86	2.44
1938	6.60	1.77	2.00	3.07	3.81	8.45	7.45	2.04	14.55	2.49	3.02	3.95
1939	2.21	3.62	4.49	4.56	2.15	3.21	2.30	3.89	2.97	4.55	0.98	3.89
1940	2.63	2.72	5.58	6.37	5.67	2.46	4.69	1.56	1.53	1.04	6.31	3.01

Table 1.1
(continued)

Year	Jan	Feb	Mar	Apr	May	Jun	Jul	Aug	Sep	Oct	Nov	Dec
1941	2.21	1.59	1.63	0.55	2.87	6.13	4.04	1.79	2.88	2.13	4.29	3.82
1942	3.54	1.66	7.89	0.96	2.98	3.63	4.95	2.93	3.94	3.27	6.07	6.03
1943	2.92	1.63	3.07	3.66	5.62	2.38	6.18	2.49	2.40	3.88	4.64	0.58
1944	1.24	2.34	4.36	3.66	1.35	4.70	3.88	4.33	5.31	1.74	4.21	2.18
1945	3.07	3.33	2.16	5.43	6.45	7.67	7.36	2.79	3.57	2.18	3.54	3.91
1946	2.72	3.52	1.60	2.16	5.41	3.30	5.30	4.00	4.88	1.51	0.70	3.51
1947	3.37	1.96	3.29	4.59	4.63	3.22	2.73	1.69	2.84	2.04	5.63	2.33
1948	2.63	2.45	2.92	2.87	5.83	5.67	2.95	3.56	1.92	1.14	5.22	2.87
1949	4.52	2.47	1.67	2.70	4.76	0.72	3.41	3.64	3.55	2.58	1.79	2.44
1950	4.33	3.99	2.67	3.64	2.77	3.65	2.83	2.93	2.24	1.87	6.60	4.64
1951	3.28	4.61	5.13	3.63	2.96	3.05	4.15	3.56	2.63	4.66	4.64	4.35
1952	4.02	1.97	3.17	3.40	4.00	4.97	4.99	3.98	4.05	1.07	0.89	4.10
1953	6.24	2.97	8.24	5.36	6.81	2.41	1.95	1.87	1.88	5.15	2.36	4.53
1954	2.45	1.94	3.93	4.24	4.80	2.68	3.00	3.91	6.14	1.89	5.07	3.19
1955	0.81	3.73	4.39	4.76	3.00	4.06	1.99	16.10	3.80	7.57	4.46	0.79
1956	1.75	3.52	4.94	4.49	2.02	2.86	2.90	2.71	5.55	1.64	3.10	4.83
1957	1.38	1.10	1.55	2.75	3.89	4.50	1.67	0.94	1.57	2.19	5.54	6.39
1958	4.03	2.21	2.62	4.58	2.98	1.64	5.13	5.19	3.90	3.79	3.79	1.57
1959	3.81	2.32	3.84	3.80	1.04	5.65	5.07	6.70	1.03	7.81	4.33	3.85
1960	2.35	3.90	3.32	4.30	3.44	4.73	6.84	3.74	6.75	2.43	3.13	2.71
1961	2.52	3.16	3.00	4.72	3.20	6.05	2.82	2.86	2.02	2.33	3.79	3.27
1962	3.01	3.59	1.84	2.69	2.03	1.06	2.16	3.33	3.74	4.16	2.11	3.30
1963	2.95	2.62	3.61	2.00	1.97	3.98	1.92	2.54	3.56	0.32	3.92	2.19
1964	5.18	2.32	2.71	2.72	0.83	1.84	3.02	3.01	0.94	1.32	1.68	3.98
1965	1.57	2.33	1.10	2.43	2.69	2.41	3.97	3.43	3.68	2.32	2.36	1.88
1966	1.72	3.43	2.93	1.28	2.26	3.30	5.83	0.67	5.14	4.51	3.48	2.22
1967	1.37	2.89	3.27	4.51	6.30	3.61	5.24	3.76	2.12	1.92	2.90	5.14
1968	1.87	1.02	4.47	2.62	3.02	7.19	0.73	1.12	2.64	3.10	5.78	5.08
1969	1.28	2.31	1.97	3.93	2.73	3.52	6.89	5.20	2.94	1.53	5.34	6.30
1970	0.66	3.55	3.52	3.69	4.16	4.97	2.17	5.23	3.05	2.45	3.27	2.37
1971	1.95	3.29	2.53	1.49	3.77	2.68	2.77	4.91	4.12	3.60	4.42	3.19
1972	1.86	3.47	4.85	4.06	4.72	10.25	2.42	2.25	1.84	2.51	6.92	6.81
1973	4.26	2.58	3.45	6.40	5.45	4.43	3.38	2.17	1.83	2.24	2.30	8.77
1974	3.35	2.42	4.34	2.61	5.21	3.40	3.71	3.97	7.29	1.94	2.76	3.67
1975	4.39	3.04	3.97	2.87	2.10	4.68	10.56	6.13	8.63	4.90	5.08	3.90
1976	5.23	3.30	2.15	3.40	4.49	2.20	2.20	6.21	2.74	4.31	0.71	2.69
1977	2.24	2.21	5.88	4.91	3.57	3.83	4.04	5.94	7.77	5.81	4.37	5.22
1978	8.16	0.88	2.65	1.48	2.53	2.83	1.81	4.85	0.97	2.19	2.31	3.93
1979	11.01	2.49	3.00	5.37	4.78	0.77	6.67	5.14	4.54	5.79	3.84	4.00
1980	0.50	0.99	6.42	3.84	1.47	3.94	2.26	1.43	2.33	2.23	3.63	0.91

Table 1.1
(continued)

Year	Jan	Feb	Mar	Apr	May	Jun	Jul	Aug	Sep	Oct	Nov	Dec
1981	0.49	7.58	0.24	4.48	2.99	3.81	3.11	1.36	3.53	6.10	1.57	4.41
1982	3.92	3.65	2.26	4.39	2.54	8.07	4.20	2.00	2.81	2.29	3.55	1.85
1983	4.82	4.42	4.95	8.99	5.54	2.42	3.10	2.39	1.82	5.47	7.05	6.40
1984	1.75	6.42	3.68	4.30	11.95	1.69	4.66	1.34	1.02	3.13	3.97	2.84
1985	1.73	1.97	2.65	1.55	4.53	3.59	2.16	4.29	2.88	3.50	6.27	1.78
1986	5.86	2.83	3.69	1.43	2.36	5.02	7.32	1.99	1.07	2.43	5.32	5.52
1987	4.32	0.08	4.58	4.76	1.44	4.16	1.51	3.84	7.65	4.16	3.27	2.31
1988	2.40	3.40	2.13	3.59	2.58	1.28	6.37	4.71	2.45	1.72	5.83	1.52
1989	0.94	2.55	2.00	4.29	8.79	5.74	3.81	5.97	5.99	8.10	3.21	1.06
1990	4.32	3.15	3.13	4.35	6.79	1.49	1.70	8.05	1.42	6.40	3.64	5.07
1991	2.37	1.67	4.73	3.66	5.40	2.03	1.39	9.06	7.10	4.21	5.01	3.20
1992	2.12	1.78	3.25	2.95	2.32	3.34	4.28	7.63	2.47	2.18	4.43	3.76
1993	2.18	2.31	5.44	4.69	0.88	2.53	2.99	3.04	4.59	3.79	4.35	3.86
1994	5.76	1.87	5.60	3.19	6.34	2.70	6.87	4.39	3.72	1.34	3.87	5.06
1995	3.66	3.00	1.68	2.15	2.09	2.10	3.75	2.38	3.04	10.93	4.66	2.20
1996	6.68	4.01	2.19	8.30	3.62	4.50	6.94	0.70	6.01	4.11	3.59	6.09
1997	3.56	2.27	3.19	3.68	3.56	1.30	3.99	4.69	1.30	2.27	4.67	1.38
1998	4.19	2.56	4.53	2.79	3.50	8.60	2.06	1.45	2.31	5.70	1.78	1.24
1999	5.67	1.89	4.82	0.87	3.83	2.78	1.65	5.45	13.19	3.48	2.77	1.84
2000	3.00	3.40	3.82	4.14	4.26	7.99	6.88	5.40	5.36	2.29	2.83	4.24

- The uppercase Greek sigma, Σ, is an abbreviation for the word summation.
- The $t = 1$ and T represent the first and last observations of the summation.
- The x_t represents observation t of the data variable.

Consequently the expression $\sum_{t=1}^{T} x_t$ says "calculate the sum of the x_t's from t equals 1 to t equals T"; that is,

$$\sum_{t=1}^{T} x_t = x_1 + x_2 + \ldots + x_T$$

Note that the x in Mean[$\boldsymbol{x}$] is in a bold font. This is done to emphasize the fact that the mean describes a specific characteristic, the distribution center, of the entire collection of values, the entire distribution.

Suppose that we want to calculate the precipitation mean for each summer month. We could use the information in tables and a pocket calculator to compute the means. This would not only be laborious but also error prone. Fortunately, econometric software provides us with an easy and reliable alternative. The Amherst weather data are posted on our website.

Amherst precipitation data: Monthly time series precipitation in Amherst, Massachusetts from 1901 to 2000 (inches)

Precip_t   Monthly precipitation in Amherst, MA, for observation t (inches)

Getting Started in EViews

Access the Amherst weather data online:

To access this online material, go to http://mitpress.mit.edu/westhoffeconometrics and select Amherst Weather

Then:

• In the File Download window: Click **Open.** (Note that different browsers may present you with a slightly different screen to open the workfile.)

Next instruct EViews to calculate the means:

• In the Workfile window: Highlight **year** by clicking on it; then, while depressing <Ctrl>, click on **month** and **precip** to highlight them also.

• In the Workfile window: Double click on any of the highlighted variables.

• A new list now pops up: Click **Open Group**. A spreadsheet including the variables Year, Month, and Precip for all the months appears.

• In the Group window: Click **View**; then click **Descriptive Stats**, and then **Individual Samples.**[3] Descriptive statistics for all the months of the twentieth century now appear. We only want to consider one month at a time. We want to compute the mean for June and then for July and then for August. Let us see how to do this.

• In the Group window: Click **Sample**. In the Sample window: Enter **month = 6** in the "If condition (optional)" text area to restrict the sample to the sixth month, June, only.

• Click **OK**. Descriptive statistics for the 100 Junes appear in the Group window. Record the mean.

• In the Group window: Click **Sample**. In the Sample window: Enter **month = 7** in the "If condition (optional)" text area to restrict the sample to July only. Click **OK**. Descriptive statistics for the 100 Julys appear in the Group window. Record the mean.

• In the Group window: Click **Sample**. In the Sample window: Enter **month = 8** in the "If condition (optional)" text area to restrict the sample to August only. Click **OK**. Descriptive statistics for the 100 Augusts appear in the Group window. Record the mean.

---

3. Common sample eliminates all observations in which there is one or more missing values in one of the variables; the individual samples option does not do so. Since no values are missing for June, July, and August, the choice of common or individual has no impact.

- **This last step is critical.** In the Group window: Click **Sample**.

- In the Sample window: Clear the "If condition (optional)" text area by deleting **month = 8**; otherwise, the restriction, **month = 8**, will remain in effect if you ask EViews to perform any more computations.

Now, do not forget to close the file:

- In the EViews window: Click **File**, then **Exit.**

- In the Workfile window: Click **No** in response to the save changes made to workfile.

Table 1.2 summarizes the information. August has the highest mean. Based on the mean criterion, August was the wettest summer month in the twentieth century; the mean for August equals 3.96, which is greater than the mean for June or July.

1.1.3   Measures of the Distribution Spread: Range, Variance, and Standard Deviation

While the center of the distribution is undoubtedly important, the spread can be crucial also. On the one hand, if the spread is small, all the values of the distribution lie close to the center, the mean. On the other hand, if the spread is large, some of the values lie far below the mean and some lie far about the mean. Farming provides a good illustration of why the spread can be important. Obviously the mean precipitation during the growing season is important to the farmer. But the spread of the precipitation is important also. Most crops grow best when they get a steady amount of moderate rain over the entire growing season. An unusually dry period followed by an unusually wet period, and vice versa, is not welcome news for the farmer. Both the center (mean) and the spread are important. The years 1951 and 1998 illustrate this well (see table 1.3).

In reality, 1951 was a better growing season than 1998 even though the mean for 1998 was a little higher. Precipitation was less volatile in 1951 than in 1998. Arguably, the most straightforward measure of distribution spread is its **range**. In 1951, precipitation ranged from a minimum of 2.96 to a maximum of 4.15. In 1998, the range was larger from 1.45 to 8.60.

While the range is the simplest, it is not the most sensitive. The most widely cited measure of spread is the **variance** and its closely related cousin, the **standard deviation**. The variance equals the average of the squared deviations of the values from the mean. While this definition may sound a little overwhelming when first heard, it is not as daunting as it sounds. We can use the following three steps to calculate the variance:

Table 1.2
Mean monthly precipitation for the summer months in Amherst, Massachusetts, 1901 to 2000

	Jun	Jul	Aug
Mean	3.78	3.79	3.96

Table 1.3
Growing season precipitation in Amherst, Massachusetts, 1951 and 1998

Year	Apr	May	Jun	Jul	Aug	Mean
1951	3.63	2.96	3.05	4.15	3.56	3.47
1998	2.79	3.50	8.60	2.06	1.45	3.68

• For each month, calculate the amount by which that month's precipitation deviates from the mean.

• Square each month's deviation.

• Calculate the average of the squared deviations; that is, sum the squared deviations and divide by the number of months, 5 in this case.

Let us first calculate the variance for 1998:

Month	Precipitation	Mean	Deviation from mean	Squared deviation
Apr	2.79	3.68	$2.79 - 3.68 = -0.89$	0.7921
May	3.50	3.68	$3.50 - 3.68 = -0.18$	0.0324
Jun	8.60	3.68	$8.60 - 3.68 = 4.92$	24.2064
Jul	2.06	3.68	$2.06 - 3.68 = -1.62$	2.6244
Aug	1.45	3.68	$1.45 - 3.68 = -2.23$	<u>4.9729</u>

Sum of squared deviations = 32.6282

$$\text{Variance} = \frac{\text{Sum of squared deviations}}{T} = \frac{32.6282}{5} = 6.5256$$

Note that the mean and the variance are expressed in different units; the mean is expressed in inches and the variance in inches squared. Often it is useful to compare the mean and the measure of spread directly, in terms of the same units. The standard deviation allows us to do just that. The standard deviation is the square root of the variance; hence the standard deviation is expressed in inches, just like the mean:

$$\text{Standard deviation} = \sqrt{\text{Variance}} = \sqrt{6.5256 \text{ in}^2} = 2.55 \text{ in}$$

We can use the same procedure to calculate the variance and standard deviation for 1951:

Month	Precipitation	Mean	Deviation from mean	Squared deviation
Apr	3.63	3.47	$3.63 - 3.47 = 0.16$	0.0256
May	2.96	3.47	$2.96 - 3.47 = -0.51$	0.2601
Jun	3.05	3.47	$3.05 - 3.47 = -0.42$	0.1764
Jul	4.15	3.47	$4.15 - 3.47 = 0.68$	0.4624
Aug	3.56	3.47	$3.56 - 3.47 = 0.09$	<u>0.0081</u>

Sum of squared deviations $= 0.9326$

$$\text{Variance} = \frac{\text{Sum of squared deviations}}{T} = \frac{0.9326}{5} = 0.1865$$

$$\text{Standard deviation} = \sqrt{\text{Variance}} = \sqrt{0.1865 \text{ in}^2} = 0.43 \text{ in}$$

When the spread is small, as it was in 1951, all observations will be close to the mean. Hence the deviations will be small. The squared deviations, the variance, and the standard deviation will also be small. However, if the spread is large, as it was in 1998, some observations must be far from the mean. Hence some deviations will be large. Some squared deviations, the variance, and the standard deviation will also be large. Let us summarize:

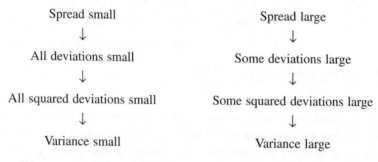

We can concisely summarize the steps for calculating the variance with the following equations:

$$\text{Var}[x] = \frac{(x_1 - \text{Mean}[x])^2 + (x_2 - \text{Mean}[x])^2 + \ldots + (x_T - \text{Mean}[x])^2}{T}$$

$$= \frac{(x_1 - \overline{x})^2 + (x_2 - \overline{x})^2 + \ldots + (x_T - \overline{x})^2}{T}$$

where

$T = $ total number of observations

$\overline{x} = \text{Mean}[x] = $ mean of x

We can express the variance more concisely using "summation" notation:

$$\text{Var}[\boldsymbol{x}] = \frac{\sum_{t=1}^{T}(x_t - \text{Mean}[\boldsymbol{x}])^2}{T} = \frac{\sum_{t=1}^{T}(x_t - \bar{x})^2}{T}$$

The standard deviation is the square root of the variance:

$$\text{SD}[\boldsymbol{x}] = \sqrt{\text{Var}[\boldsymbol{x}]}$$

Again, let us now "dissect" the summation expressions $\sum_{t=1}^{T}(x_t - \text{Mean}[\boldsymbol{x}])^2$ and $\sum_{t=1}^{T}(x_t - \bar{x})^2$:

- The uppercase Greek sigma, Σ, is an abbreviation for the word summation.
- The $t = 1$ and T represent the first and last observations of the summation.
- The x_t represents observation t of the data variable.

$\sum_{t=1}^{T}(x_t - \text{Mean}[\boldsymbol{x}])^2$ and $\sum_{t=1}^{T}(x_t - \bar{x})^2$ equal the sum of the squared deviations from the mean. Note that the x in Var[$\boldsymbol{x}$] and in SD[$\boldsymbol{x}$] is in a bold font. This emphasizes the fact that the variance and standard deviation describe one specific characteristic, the distribution spread, of the entire distribution.

1.1.4 Histogram: Visual Illustration of a Data Variable's Distribution

A **histogram** is a bar graph that visually illustrates how the values of a single data variable are distributed. Figure 1.1 is a histogram for September precipitation in Amherst. Each bar of the histogram reports on the number of months in which precipitation fell within the specified range.

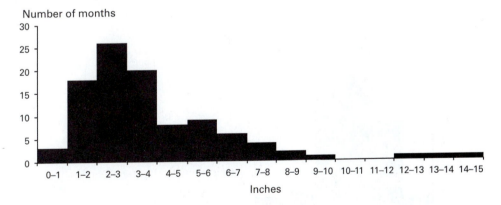

Figure 1.1
Histogram—September precipitation in Amherst, Massachusetts, 1901 to 2000

The histogram provides a visual illustration of the distribution of September precipitation in Amherst during the twentieth century. That is, figure 1.1 illustrates how frequently there was less than 1 inch of precipitation, how frequently there was between 1 and 2 inches, and so on. In September there was

- less than 1 inch of rain in 3 years
- between 1 and 2 inches of rain in 18 years
- between 2 and 3 inches of rain in 26 years
- between 3 and 4 inches of rain in 19 years
- between 4 and 5 inches of rain in 8 years
- between 5 and 6 inches of rain in 9 years
- between 6 and 7 inches of rain in 7 years
- between 7 and 8 inches of rain in 4 years

- between 8 and 9 inches of rain in 2 years
- between 9 and 10 inches of rain in 1 year
- between 10 and 11 inches of rain in 0 years
- between 11 and 12 inches of rain in 0 years
- between 12 and 13 inches of rain in 1 year
- between 13 and 14 inches of rain in 1 year
- between 14 and 15 inches of rain in 1 year

We can use histograms to illustrate the differences between two distributions. For example, compare the histogram for September (figure 1.1) and the histogram for February precipitation (figure 1.2):

The obvious difference in the two histograms is that the September histogram has a longer "right-hand tail." The center of September's distribution lies to the right of February's; consequently we would expect September's mean to exceed February's. Also the distribution of precipitation in September is more "spread out" than the distribution in February; hence we would expect September's variance to be larger. Table 1.4 confirms quantitatively what we observe visually. September has a higher mean: 3.89 for September versus 2.88 for February. Also the variance for September is greater.

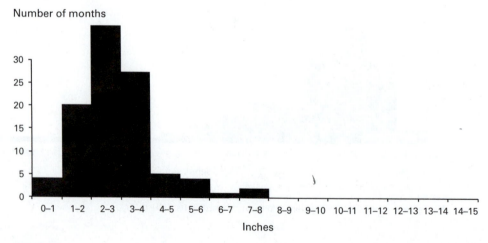

Figure 1.2
Histogram—February precipitation in Amherst, Massachusetts, 1901 to 2000

Table 1.4
Means and variances of precipitation for February and September, 1901 to 2000

	Mean	Variance
February	2.88	1.49
September	3.89	6.50

1.2 Describing the Relationship between Two Data Variables

1.2.1 Scatter Diagram: Visual Illustration of How Two Data Variables Are Related

We will use the Dow Jones and Nasdaq data appearing in tables 1.5a and 1.5b to introduce another type of useful graph, the **scatter diagram**, which visually illustrates the relationship between two variables.

We will focus on the relationship between the Dow Jones and Nasdaq growth rates. Figure 1.3 depicts their scatter diagram by placing the Dow Jones growth rate on the horizontal axis and the Nasdaq growth rate on the vertical axis.

1.2.2 Correlation of Two Variables

On the scatter diagram in figure 1.3, each point illustrates the Dow Jones growth rate and the Nasdaq growth rate for one specific month. For example, the top left point labeled Feb 2000 represents February 2000 when the Dow fell by 7.42 percent and the Nasdaq grew by 19.19 percent. Similarly the point in the first quadrant labeled Jan 1987 represents January 1987 when the Dow rose by 13.82 percent and the Nasdaq rose by 12.41 percent.

The Dow Jones and Nasdaq growth rates appear to be **correlated**. Two variables are correlated when information about one variable helps us predict the other. Typically, when the Dow Jones growth rate is positive, the Nasdaq growth rate is also positive; similarly, when the Dow Jones growth rate is negative, the Nasdaq growth rate is usually negative. Although there are exceptions, February 2000, for example, knowing one growth rate typically helps us predict the other. For example, if we knew that the Dow Jones growth rate was positive in one specific month, we would predict that the Nasdaq growth rate would be positive also. While we would not always be correct, we would be right most of the time.

1.2.3 Measure of Correlation: Covariance

Covariance quantifies the notion of correlation. We can use the following three steps to calculate the covariance of two data variables, x and y:

1. For each observation, calculate the amount by which variable x deviates from its mean and the amount by which variable y deviates from its mean.

Table 1.5a
Monthly percentage growth rate of Dow Jones Industrial Index, 1985 to 2000

Year	Jan	Feb	Mar	Apr	May	Jun	Jul	Aug	Sep	Oct	Nov	Dec
1985	6.21	-0.22	-1.34	-0.69	4.55	1.53	0.90	-1.00	-0.40	3.44	7.12	5.07
1986	1.57	8.79	6.41	-1.90	5.20	0.85	-6.20	6.93	-6.89	6.23	1.94	-0.95
1987	13.82	3.06	3.63	-0.79	0.23	5.54	6.35	3.53	-2.50	-23.22	-8.02	5.74
1988	1.00	5.79	-4.03	2.22	-0.06	5.45	-0.61	-4.56	4.00	1.69	-1.59	2.56
1989	8.01	-3.58	1.56	5.46	2.54	-1.62	9.04	2.88	-1.63	-1.77	2.31	1.73
1990	-5.91	1.42	3.04	-1.86	8.28	0.14	0.85	-10.01	-6.19	-0.42	4.81	2.89
1991	3.90	5.33	1.10	-0.89	4.83	-3.99	4.06	0.62	-0.88	1.73	-5.68	9.47
1992	1.72	1.37	-0.99	3.82	1.13	-2.31	2.27	-4.02	0.44	-1.39	2.45	-0.12
1993	0.27	1.84	1.91	-0.22	2.91	-0.32	0.67	3.16	-2.63	3.53	0.09	1.90
1994	5.97	-3.68	-5.11	1.26	2.08	-3.55	3.85	3.96	-1.79	1.69	-4.32	2.55
1995	0.25	4.35	3.65	3.93	3.33	2.04	3.34	-2.08	3.87	-0.70	6.71	0.84
1996	5.44	1.67	1.85	-0.32	1.33	0.20	-2.22	1.58	4.74	2.50	8.16	-1.13
1997	5.66	0.95	-4.28	6.46	4.59	4.66	7.17	-7.30	4.24	-6.33	5.12	1.09
1998	-0.02	8.08	2.97	3.00	-1.80	0.58	-0.77	-15.13	4.03	9.56	6.10	0.71
1999	1.93	-0.56	5.15	10.25	-2.13	3.89	-2.88	1.63	-4.55	3.80	1.38	5.69
2000	-4.84	-7.42	7.84	-1.72	-1.97	-0.71	0.71	6.59	-5.03	3.01	-5.07	3.59

Table 1.5b
Monthly percentage growth rate of Nasdaq Index, 1985 to 2000

Year	Jan	Feb	Mar	Apr	May	Jun	Jul	Aug	Sep	Oct	Nov	Dec
1985	12.79	1.97	-1.76	0.50	3.64	1.86	1.72	-1.19	-5.84	4.35	7.35	3.47
1986	3.35	7.06	4.23	2.27	4.44	1.32	-8.41	3.10	-8.41	2.88	-0.33	-3.00
1987	12.41	8.39	1.20	-2.86	-0.31	1.97	2.40	4.62	-2.35	-27.23	-5.60	8.29
1988	4.30	6.47	2.07	1.23	-2.35	6.59	-1.87	-2.76	2.95	-1.34	-2.88	2.66
1989	5.22	-0.40	1.75	5.14	4.35	-2.44	4.25	3.42	0.77	-3.66	0.11	-0.29
1990	-8.58	2.41	2.28	-3.54	9.26	0.72	-5.21	-13.01	-9.63	-4.27	8.88	4.09
1991	10.81	9.39	6.44	0.50	4.41	-5.97	5.49	4.71	0.23	3.06	-3.51	11.92
1992	5.78	2.14	-4.69	-4.16	1.15	-3.71	3.06	-3.05	3.58	3.75	7.86	3.71
1993	2.86	-3.67	2.89	-4.16	5.91	0.49	0.11	5.41	2.68	2.16	-3.19	2.97
1994	3.05	-1.00	-6.19	-1.29	0.18	-3.98	2.29	6.02	-0.17	1.73	-3.49	0.22
1995	0.43	5.10	2.96	3.28	2.44	7.97	7.26	1.89	2.30	-0.72	2.23	-0.67
1996	0.73	3.80	0.12	8.09	4.44	-4.70	-8.81	5.64	7.48	-0.44	5.82	-0.12
1997	6.88	-5.13	-6.67	3.20	11.07	2.98	10.52	-0.41	6.20	-5.46	0.44	-1.89
1998	3.12	9.33	3.68	1.78	-4.79	6.51	-1.18	-19.93	12.98	4.58	10.06	12.47
1999	14.28	-8.69	7.58	3.31	-2.84	8.73	-1.77	3.82	0.25	8.02	12.46	21.98
2000	-3.17	19.19	-2.64	-15.57	-11.91	16.62	-5.02	11.66	-12.68	-8.25	-22.90	-4.90

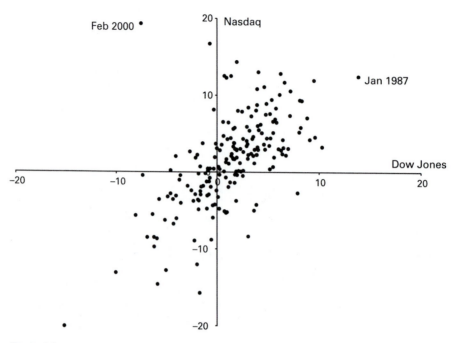

Figure 1.3
Scatter diagram—Dow Jones growth rate versus Nasdaq growth rate

2. Multiply each observation's x deviation by its y deviation.

3. Calculate the average of these products; that is, sum the products of the deviations and divide by the number of observations.

We can express these steps concisely with an equation:

$$\text{Cov}[x, y] = \frac{(x_1 - \bar{x})(y_1 - \bar{y}) + (x_2 - \bar{x})(y_2 - \bar{y}) + \ldots + (x_T - \bar{x})(y_T - \bar{y})}{T}$$

$$= \frac{\sum_{t=1}^{T}(x_t - \bar{x})(y_t - \bar{y})}{T}$$

where

T = total number of observations

$\bar{x} = \text{Mean}[x]$ = mean of x

$\bar{y} = \text{Mean}[y]$ = mean of y

Let us calculate the covariance for the Dow and Nasdaq monthly growth rates. The average monthly increase for the Dow Jones Industrial average was 1.25 percent and the average increase for the Nasdaq Composite was 1.43 percent. Their covariance equals 19.61:

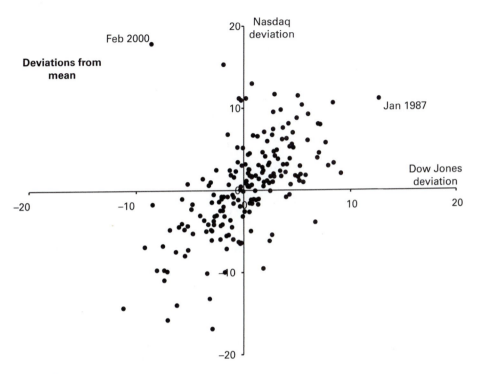

Figure 1.4
Scatter diagram—Dow Jones growth rate less its mean versus Nasdaq growth rate less its mean

$$\text{Cov}[x, y] = \frac{(x_1 - \bar{x})(y_1 - \bar{y}) + \ldots + (x_T - \bar{x})(y_T - \bar{y})}{T}$$

$$= \frac{(6.21 - 1.25)(12.79 - 1.43) + \ldots + (3.59 - 1.25)(-4.90 - 1.43)}{192}$$

$$= 19.61$$

A nonzero variance suggests that the variables are correlated. To understand why, consider a scatter diagram of the deviations. As seen in figure 1.4, we place the deviation of the Dow Jones growth rate from its mean on the horizontal axis and the deviation of the Nasdaq growth rate from its mean on the vertical axis. This scatter diagram allows us to motivate the relationship between the covariance and correlation.[4]

The covariance equation and the scatter diagram are related. The numerator of the covariance equation equals the sum of the products of each month's deviations, $(x_t - \bar{x})(y_t - \bar{y})$:

---

4. The discussion that follows is not mathematically rigorous because it ignores the magnitude of the deviation products. Nevertheless, it provides valuable insights. Chapter 25 provides a more rigorous discussion of covariance.

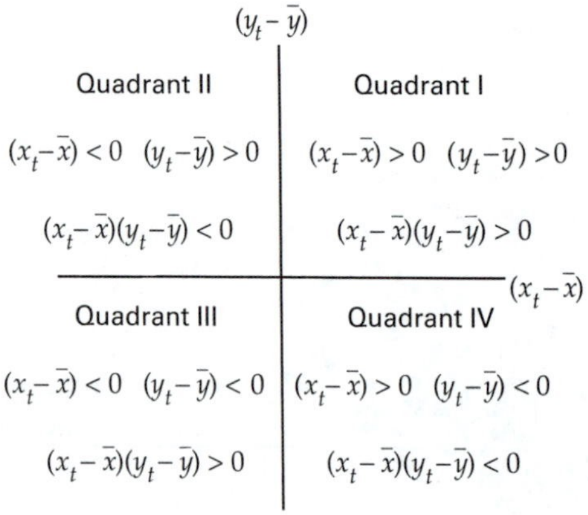

$$(y_t - \bar{y})$$

Quadrant II	Quadrant I
$(x_t - \bar{x}) < 0$ $(y_t - \bar{y}) > 0$	$(x_t - \bar{x}) > 0$ $(y_t - \bar{y}) > 0$
$(x_t - \bar{x})(y_t - \bar{y}) < 0$	$(x_t - \bar{x})(y_t - \bar{y}) > 0$

$$(x_t - \bar{x})$$

Quadrant III	Quadrant IV
$(x_t - \bar{x}) < 0$ $(y_t - \bar{y}) < 0$	$(x_t - \bar{x}) > 0$ $(y_t - \bar{y}) < 0$
$(x_t - \bar{x})(y_t - \bar{y}) > 0$	$(x_t - \bar{x})(y_t - \bar{y}) < 0$

Figure 1.5
Scatter diagram—Deviations and covariance terms

$$\text{Cov}[x, y] = \frac{\sum_{t=1}^{T} (x_t - \bar{x})(y_t - \bar{y})}{T}$$

What can we say about the sign of each observation's deviations and their product, $(x_t - \bar{x})(y_t - \bar{y})$, in each quadrant of the scatter diagram (figure 1.5)?

• First quadrant. Dow growth rate is greater than its mean and Nasdaq growth is greater than its mean. Both deviations are positive; hence the product of the deviations is positive in the first quadrant:

$$(x_t - \bar{x}) > 0 \quad \text{and} \quad (y_t - \bar{y}) > 0 \rightarrow (x_t - \bar{x})(y_t - \bar{y}) > 0$$

• Second quadrant. Dow growth rate is less than its mean and Nasdaq growth is greater than its mean. One deviation is positive and one negative; hence the product of the deviations is negative in the second quadrant:

$$(x_t - \bar{x}) < 0 \quad \text{and} \quad (y_t - \bar{y}) > 0 \rightarrow (x_t - \bar{x})(y_t - \bar{y}) < 0$$

• Third quadrant. Dow growth rate is less than its mean and Nasdaq growth is less than its mean. Both deviations are negative; hence the product of the deviations is positive in the third quadrant:

$$(x_t - \bar{x}) < 0 \quad \text{and} \quad (y_t - \bar{y}) < 0 \rightarrow (x_t - \bar{x})(y_t - \bar{y}) > 0$$

• Fourth quadrant. Dow growth rate is greater than its mean and Nasdaq growth is less than its mean. One deviation is positive and one negative; hence, the product of the deviations is negative in the fourth quadrant:

$$(x_t - \bar{x}) > 0 \quad \text{and} \quad (y_t - \bar{y}) < 0 \rightarrow (x_t - \bar{x})(y_t - \bar{y}) < 0$$

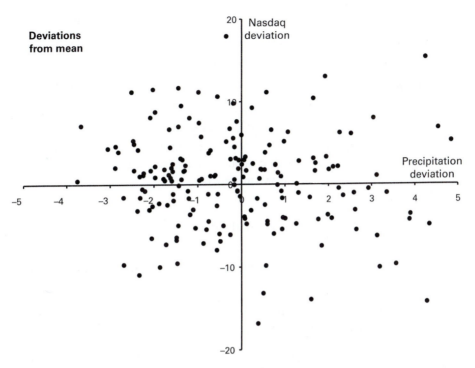

Figure 1.6
Scatter diagram—Amherst precipitation less its mean versus Nasdaq growth rate less its mean

Compare figures 1.4 and 1.5. In the Dow Jones and Nasdaq deviation scatter diagram (figure 1.4), the points representing most months lie in the first and third quadrants. Consequently the product of the deviations, $(x_t - \overline{x})(y_t - \overline{y})$, is positive in most months. This explains why the covariance is positive.[5] A positive covariance means that the variables are positively correlated. When one variable is above average, the other is typically above average as well. Similarly, when one variable is below average, the other is typically below average.

1.2.4   Independence of Two Variables

Two variables are **independent** or **uncorrelated** when information about one variable does not help us predict the other. The covariance of two independent (uncorrelated) data variables is approximately zero. To illustrate two independent variables, consider the precipitation in Amherst and the Nasdaq growth rate. The scatter diagram in figure 1.6 plots the deviation of Amherst precipitation from its mean versus the deviation of the Nasdaq growth rate from its mean: Recall what we know about the sign of the deviation in each quadrant:

---

5. As mentioned above, we are ignoring how the magnitude of the products affects the sum.

- First quadrant: $(x_t - \bar{x}) > 0$ and $(y_t - \bar{y}) > 0 \rightarrow (x_t - \bar{x})(y_t - \bar{y}) > 0$
- Second quadrant: $(x_t - \bar{x}) < 0$ and $(y_t - \bar{y}) > 0 \rightarrow (x_t - \bar{x})(y_t - \bar{y}) < 0$
- Third quadrant: $(x_t - \bar{x}) < 0$ and $(y_t - \bar{y}) < 0 \rightarrow (x_t - \bar{x})(y_t - \bar{y}) > 0$
- Fourth quadrant: $(x_t - \bar{x}) > 0$ and $(y_t - \bar{y}) < 0 \rightarrow (x_t - \bar{x})(y_t - \bar{y}) < 0$

Since the points are distributed more or less evenly across all four quadrants, the products of the deviations, $(x_t - \bar{x})(y_t - \bar{y})$, are positive in about half the months and negative in the other half.[6] Consequently the covariance will be approximately equal to 0. In general, if variables are independent, the covariance will be about 0. In reality, the covariance of precipitation and the Nasdaq growth rate is −0.91, approximately 0:

$$\text{Cov}[x, y] = \frac{\sum_{t=1}^{T}(x_t - \bar{x})(y_t - \bar{y})}{T} = -0.91 \approx 0$$

We can use EViews to calculate the covariance. The stock market data are posted on our website.

Stock market data: Monthly time series growth rates of the Dow Jones Industrial and Nasdaq stock indexes from January 1985 to December 2000

DJGrowth_t   Monthly growth rate of the Dow Jones Industrial Average based on the monthly close for observation t (percent)

NasdaqGrowth_t   Monthly growth rate of the Nasdaq Composite based on the monthly close for observation t (percent)

Precip_t   Monthly precipitation in Amherst, MA, for observation t (inches)

Getting Started in EViews

Access the stock market data online:

[To access this online material, go to http://mitpress.mit.edu/westhoffeconometrics and select Stock Market.]

Then:

- In the File Download window: Click **Open.** (Note that different browsers may present you with a slightly different screen to open the workfile.)

Next instruct EViews to calculate the covariance of Amherst precipitation and the Nasdaq growth rate:

---

6. Again, note that this explanation ignores the magnitude of the products.

- In the Workfile window: Highlight **precip** by clicking on it; then, while depressing <Ctrl>, click on **nasdaqgrowth** to highlight it.
- In the Workfile window: Double click on any of the highlighted variables.
- A new list now pops up: Click **Open Group**. A spreadsheet including the variables Precip and NasdaqGrowth appears.
- In the Group window: Click **View**, and then click **Covariance Analysis**. . . .
- In the Covariance Analysis window: Be certain that the Covariance checkbox is selected; then click **OK**.

Last, close the file:

- In the EViews window: Click **File**, then **Exit**.
- In the Workfile window: Click **No** in response to the save changes made to the workfile.

Both the variances and the covariances are reported in table 1.6. The variances are reported in the diagonal cells: the variance for Amherst precipitation is 4.17 and the variance for the Nasdaq growth rate is 43.10. Their covariance appears in the off diagonal cells: the covariance is −0.91. Note that the two off-diagonal cells report the same number. This results from a basic arithmetic fact. When we multiply two numbers together, the order of the multiplication does not matter:

$$(x_t - \bar{x})(y_t - \bar{y}) = (y_t - \bar{y})(x_t - \bar{x})$$

Let us summarize the relationship between correlation, independence, and covariance:

Variables are correlated	Variables are independent
↓	↓
The value of one variable does help predict the value of the other	The value of one variable does not help predict the value of the other
↓	↓
$\text{Cov}[x, y] \neq 0$	$\text{Cov}[x, y] = 0$

Table 1.6
Amherst precipitation and Nasdaq growth rate covariance matrix

	Covariance matrix	
	Precip	*NasdaqGrowth*
Precip	4.170426	−0.911125
NasdaqGrowth	−0.911125	43.09910

1.2.5 Measure of Correlation: Correlation Coefficient

There is no natural range for the covariance; its magnitude depends on the units used. To appreciate why, suppose that we measured Amherst precipitation in centimeters rather than inches. Consequently all precipitation figures appearing in table 1.1 would be multiplied by 2.54 to convert from inches to centimeters. Now consider the covariance equation:

$$\text{Cov}[\boldsymbol{x}, \boldsymbol{y}] = \frac{(x_1 - \bar{x})(y_1 - \bar{y}) + (x_2 - \bar{x})(y_2 - \bar{y}) + \ldots + (x_T - \bar{x})(y_T - \bar{y})}{T}$$

The covariance for Amherst precipitation would rise by a factor of 2.54. To understand why, let the variable x represent Amherst precipitation and y the Nasdaq growth rate:

x_t's up by a   → $\bar{x}$ up by a
factor of 2.54   factor of 2.54

$(x_t - \bar{x})'s$ up by a
factor of 2.54

$$\text{Cov}[\boldsymbol{x}, \boldsymbol{y}] = \frac{(x_1 - \bar{x})(y_1 - \bar{y}) + (x_2 - \bar{x})(y_2 - \bar{y}) + \ldots + (x_T - \bar{x})(y_T - \bar{y})}{T}$$

Cov[$\boldsymbol{x}, \boldsymbol{y}$] up by a
factor of 2.54

Our choice of which units to use in measuring rainfall, inches or centimeters, is entirely arbitrary. The arbitrary choice affects the magnitude of the covariance. How, then, can we judge the covariance to be large or small when its size is affected by an arbitrary decision?

Unit Insensitivity
To address this issue, we introduce the correlation coefficient that is not affected by the choice of units:

$$\text{CorrCoef}[\boldsymbol{x}, \boldsymbol{y}] = \frac{\text{Cov}[\boldsymbol{x}, \boldsymbol{y}]}{\sqrt{\text{Var}[\boldsymbol{x}]}\sqrt{\text{Var}[\boldsymbol{y}]}}$$

To appreciate why this resolves the problem, again let x represent Amherst precipitation. We know that measuring rainfall in centimeters rather than inches causes the covariance to increase by a factor of 2.54. But how does the use of centimeters affect the variance of precipitation and its square root?

x_t's up by a
factor of 2.54 $\rightarrow$ $\bar{x}$ up by a
factor of 2.54

$(x_t - \bar{x})$'s up by a
factor of 2.54

$$\text{Var}[x] = \frac{\sum_{t=1}^{T}(x_t - \bar{x})^2}{T}$$

Var[x] up by a
factor of 2.54^2

$\sqrt{\text{Var}[x]}$ up by a
factor of 2.54

We will now consider the correlation coefficient equation. When we use centimeters rather than inches, both Cov[x, y] and $\sqrt{\text{Var}[x]}$ increase by a factor of 2.54; consequently both the numerator and the denominator of the correlation coefficient equation increase by a factor of 2.54:

Cov[x, y] up by
a factor of 2.54

$$\text{CorrCoef}[x, y] = \frac{\text{Cov}[x, y]}{\sqrt{\text{Var}[x]}\sqrt{\text{Var}[y]}}$$

$\sqrt{\text{Var}[x]}$ up by
a factor of 2.54

The value of the correlation coefficient is unaffected by the choice of units.

Natural Range

The correlation coefficient also has another important property; it must lie between −1.00 and +1.00. Therefore it provides us with a sense of how strongly two variables are correlated. A correlation coefficient of +1.00 represents perfect positive correlation and −1.00 represents perfect negative correlation (figure 1.7).

To understand why, consider the two polar cases of perfect positive and perfect negative correlation.

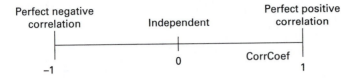

Figure 1.7
Range of correlation coefficients

Let us begin by reviewing the definitions of variance and covariance:

$$\text{Var}[x] = \frac{\sum_{t=1}^{T}(x_t - \bar{x})^2}{T}, \quad \text{Var}[y] = \frac{\sum_{t=1}^{T}(y_t - \bar{y})^2}{T}$$

$$\text{Cov}[x, y] = \frac{\sum_{t=1}^{T}(x_t - \bar{x})(y_t - \bar{y})}{T}$$

Perfect Positive Correlation   Consider an example of perfect positive correlation. Suppose that two variables are identical; that is, suppose that

$$y_t = x_t \quad \text{for each } t = 1, 2, \ldots, T$$

In this case the variables exhibit perfect positive correlation. If we know the value of x, we can perfectly predict the value of y, and vice versa. Let us compute their correlation coefficient. To do so, first note that x and y have identical means

$$\bar{y} = \bar{x}$$

and that each observation's deviation from the means is the same for x and y

$$y_t - \bar{y} = x_t - \bar{x} \quad \text{for each } t = 1, 2, \ldots, T$$

Consider the equations above for the variances and covariance; both the variance of y and the covariance equal the variance of x:

$$\text{Var}[y] = \text{Var}[x] \quad \text{and} \quad \text{Cov}[x, y] = \text{Var}[x]$$

It is easy to understand why:

$$\text{Var}[y] = \frac{\sum_{t=1}^{T}(y_t - \bar{y})^2}{T} = \frac{\sum_{t=1}^{T}(x_t - \bar{x})^2}{T} = \text{Var}[x]$$

$$\qquad\quad\uparrow \qquad\qquad\quad \uparrow \qquad\qquad\quad \uparrow$$

Definition $y_t - \bar{y} = x_t - \bar{x}$ Definition

and

$$\text{Cov}[x, y] = \frac{\sum_{t=1}^{T}(x_t - \bar{x})(y_t - \bar{y})}{T} = \frac{\sum_{t=1}^{T}(x_t - \bar{x})^2}{T} = \text{Var}[x]$$

$\uparrow$ $\uparrow$ $\uparrow$

Definition $y_t - \bar{y} = x_t - \bar{x}$ Definition

Now apply the correlation coefficient equation. The correlation coefficient equals 1.00:

$$\text{CorrCoef}[x, y] = \frac{\text{Cov}[x, y]}{\sqrt{\text{Var}[x]}\sqrt{\text{Var}[y]}} = \frac{\text{Var}[x]}{\sqrt{\text{Var}[x]}\sqrt{\text{Var}[x]}} = \frac{\text{Var}[x]}{\text{Var}[x]} = 1.00$$

$\uparrow$ $\uparrow$

Definition $\text{Cov}[x, y] = \text{Var}[x]$

Perfect Negative Correlation   Next consider an example of perfect negative correlation; suppose that

$$y_t = -x_t \quad \text{for each } t = 1, 2, \ldots, T$$

In this case the variables exhibit perfect negative correlation. Clearly, y's mean is the negative of x's:

$$\bar{y} = -\bar{x}$$

and y's deviation from its mean equals the negative of x's deviation from its mean for each observation

$$y_t - \bar{y} = -(x_t - \bar{x}) \quad \text{for each } t = 1, 2, \ldots, T$$

The variance of y equals the variance of x and the covariance equals the negative of the variance of x:

$$\text{Var}[y] = \text{Var}[x] \quad \text{and} \quad \text{Cov}[x, y] = -\text{Var}[x]$$

Let us show why:

$$\text{Var}[y] = \frac{\sum_{t=1}^{T}(y_t - \bar{y})^2}{T} = \frac{\sum_{t=1}^{T}(x_t - \bar{x})^2}{T} = \text{Var}[x]$$

$\uparrow$ $\uparrow$ $\uparrow$

Definition $y_t - \bar{y} = -(x_t - \bar{x})$ Definition

and

$$\text{Cov}[x, y] = \frac{\sum_{t=1}^{T}(x_t - \bar{x})(y_t - \bar{y})}{T} = \frac{\sum_{t=1}^{T}(x_t - \bar{x})^2}{T} = -\text{Var}[x]$$

$\uparrow$ $\uparrow$ $\uparrow$

Definition $y_t - \bar{y} = -(x_t - \bar{x})$ Definition

Applying the correlation coefficient equation, the correlation coefficient equals -1.00:

$$\text{CorrCoef}[x, y] = \frac{\text{Cov}[x, y]}{\sqrt{\text{Var}[x]}\sqrt{\text{Var}[y]}} = \frac{-\text{Var}[x]}{\sqrt{\text{Var}[x]}\sqrt{\text{Var}[x]}} = \frac{-\text{Var}[x]}{\text{Var}[x]} = -1.00$$

$\uparrow$ $\uparrow$

Definition $\text{Cov}[x, y] = -\text{Var}[x]$

Getting Started in EViews

Access the stock market data online:

[To access this online material, go to http://mitpress.mit.edu/westhoffeconometrics and select Stock Market.]

Then:

• In the File Download window: Click **Open.** (Note that different browsers may present you with a slightly different screen to open the workfile.)

• In the Workfile window: Highlight **precip** by clicking on it; then, while depressing <Ctrl>, click on **nasdaqgrowth** and **djgrowth** to highlight them also.

• In the Workfile window: Double click on any of the highlighted variables.

• A new list now pops up: Click **Open Group**. A spreadsheet including the variables Precip, NasdaqGrowth, and DJGrowth appears.

• In the Group window: Click **View** and then click **Covariance Analysis**. . . .

• In the Covariance Analysis window: Clear the Covariance box and select the Correlation box; then click **OK**.

All diagonal elements must equal 1.00. This reflects the fact that when two variables are identical, perfect positive correlation results. Each off-diagonal cell reports the correlation coefficient for the two different variables, as shown in table 1.7.

Table 1.7

Amherst precipitation, Nasdaq growth rate, and Dow Jones growth rate correlation matrix

	Correlation matrix		
	Precip	*NasdaqGrowth*	*DJGrowth*
Precip	1.000000	−0.067960	−0.128425
NasdaqGrowth	−0.067960	1.000000	0.669061
DJGrowth	−0.128425	0.669061	1.000000

Note that all the correlation coefficients fall within the −1.00 to +1.00 range. Each correlation coefficient provides us with a sense of how correlated two variables are:

CorrCoef[**Dow Jones Growth Rate**, **Nasdaq Growth Rate**] = 0.67

CorrCoef[**Nasdaq Growth Rate**, **Amherst Precipitation**] = −0.07

The correlation coefficient for the Dow and Nasdaq growth rate is positive. On the one hand, this illustrates that they are positively correlated. On the other hand, the correlation coefficient for Nasdaq growth rate and Amherst precipitation is approximately 0, indicating that the Nasdaq growth rate and Amherst precipitation are independent (figure 1.8).

1.2.6 Correlation and Causation

The fact that two variables are highly correlated does not necessarily indicate that one variable is causing the other to rise and fall. For example, the Dow Jones and Nasdaq growth rates are indeed positively correlated. This does not imply that a rise in the Dow Jones causes the Nasdaq to rise or that a rise in the Nasdaq causes the Dow Jones to rise, however. It simply means that when one rises, the other tends to rise, and when one falls, the other tends to fall. One reason that these two variables tend to move together is that both are influenced by similar factors. For example, both are influenced by that the general health of the economy. On the one hand, when the economy prospers, both Dow Jones stocks and Nasdaq stocks tend to rise; therefore both indexes tend to rise. On the other hand, when the economy falters, both indexes tend to fall. While the indexes are correlated, other factors are responsible for the causation.

1.3 Arithmetic of Means, Variances, and Covariances

Elementary algebra allows us to derive the following relationships for means, variances, and covariances:[7]

---

7. See appendix 1.1 at the end of this chapter for the algebraic proofs.

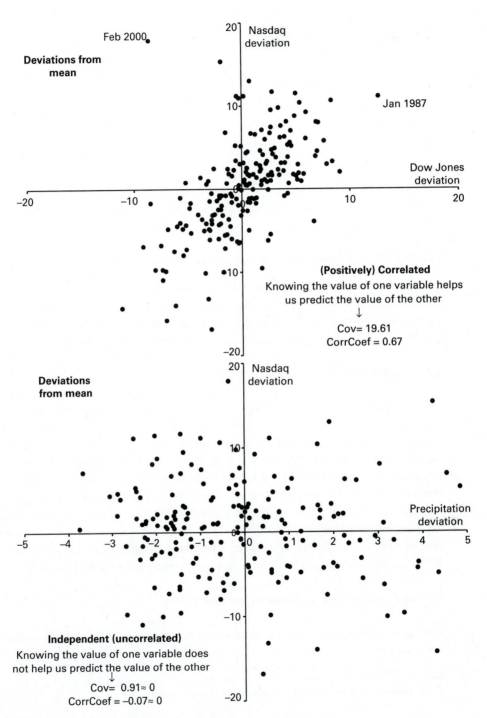

Figure 1.8
Scatter diagrams—Comparison of correlated and independent variables

- **Mean of a constant plus a variable:** $\text{Mean}[c + x] = c + \text{Mean}[x]$

The mean of a constant plus a variable equals the constant plus the mean of the variable.

- **Mean of a constant times a variable:** $\text{Mean}[cx] = c\,\text{Mean}[x]$

The mean of a constant times a variable equals the constant times the mean of the variable.

- **Mean of the sum of two variables:** $\text{Mean}[x + y] = \text{Mean}[x] + \text{Mean}[y]$

The mean of the sum of two variables equals the sum of the means of the variables.

- **Variance of a constant plus a variable:** $\text{Var}[c + x] = \text{Var}[x]$

The variance of a constant plus a variable equals the variance of the variable.

- **Variance of a constant times a variable:** $\text{Var}[cx] = c^2\,\text{Var}[x]$

The variance of a constant times a variable equals the constant squared times the variance of the variable.

- **Variance of the sum of two variables:** $\text{Var}[x + y] = \text{Var}[x] + 2\,\text{Cov}[x, y] + \text{Var}[y]$

The variance of the sum of two variables equals the sum of the variances of the variables plus twice the variables' covariance.

- **Variance of the sum of two independent (uncorrelated) variables:** $\text{Var}[x + y] = \text{Var}[x] + \text{Var}[y]$

The variance of the sum of two independent (uncorrelated) variables equals the sum of the variances of the variables.

- **Covariance of the sum of a constant and a variable:** $\text{Cov}[c + x, y] = \text{Cov}[x, y]$

The covariance of two variables is unaffected when a constant is added to one of the variables.

- **Covariance of the product of a constant and a variable:** $\text{Cov}[cx, y] = c\,\text{Cov}[x, y]$

Multiplying one of the variables by a constant increases their covariance by a factor equal to the constant.

Chapter 1 Review Questions

1. Focus on the mean.

    a. In words, what does the mean describe?

    b. What is the equation for the mean?

2. Focus on the variance.

    a. In words, what does the variance describe?

    b. What is the equation for the variance?

3. What does a histogram illustrate?

4. What does a scatter diagram illustrate?

5. Does the value of one variable help you predict the value of a second variable when the two variables are

    a. correlated?

    b. independent (uncorrelated)?

6. What is the equation for the

    a. covariance?

    b. correlation coefficient?

7. What will the covariance and correlation coefficient equal when two variables are

    a. positively correlated?

    b. negatively correlated?

    c. independent (uncorrelated)?

Chapter 1 Exercises

1. Consider the inches of precipitation in Amherst, MA, during 1964 and 1975:

Year	Jan	Feb	Mar	Apr	May	Jun	Jul	Aug	Sep	Oct	Nov	Dec
1964	5.18	2.32	2.71	2.72	0.83	1.84	3.02	3.01	0.94	1.32	1.68	3.98
1975	4.39	3.04	3.97	2.87	2.10	4.68	10.56	6.13	8.63	4.90	5.08	3.90

    a. For each year, record the number of months that fall into the following categories:

Inches of precipitation	1964	1975
0–1	_____	_____
1–2	_____	_____
2–3	_____	_____
3–4	_____	_____
4–5	_____	_____
5–6	_____	_____
6–7	_____	_____
7–8	_____	_____
8–9	_____	_____
9–10	_____	_____
10–11	_____	_____

    b. Using your answers to part a, construct two histograms, one for 1964 and one for 1975. Be certain that your horizontal and vertical scales are the same on the two histograms.

2. Consider the inches of precipitation in Amherst, MA, during 1964 and 1975.

a. Focus on the two histograms you constructed in exercise 1. Based on the histograms, in which of the two years is the

  i. center of the distribution greater (further to the right)? _____

  ii. spread of the distribution greater? _____

b. For each of the two years, use your statistical software to find the mean and the sum of squared deviations. Report your answers in the table below:

	1964	1975
Mean	_____	_____
Sum of squared deviations	_____	_____

Getting Started in EViews

Access the Amherst weather data online:

[To access this online material, go to http://mitpress.mit.edu/westhoffeconometrics and select Amherst Weather.]

Then:

• In the File Download window: Click **Open**. (Note that different browsers may present you with a slightly different screen to open the workfile.)

Instruct EViews to calculate the means and sum of squared deviations:

• In the Workfile window: Highlight **year** by clicking on it; then, while depressing <Ctrl>, click on **month** and **precip** to highlight them also.

• In the Workfile window: Double click on any of the highlighted variables.

• A new list now pops up: Click **Open Group**. A spreadsheet including the variables Year, Month, and Precip for all the months appears.

• In the Group window: Click **View**; next click **Descriptive Stats** and then **Individual Samples**.[8] Descriptive statistics for all the months of the twentieth century now appear. We only want to consider one year at a time. We want to compute the statistics for 1964 and then for 1975. Let us see how to do this:

---

8. Common sample eliminates all observations in which there is one or more missing value in one of the variables; the individual samples option does not do so. Since no values are missing for 1964 and 1975, the choice of common or individual has no impact.

In the Group window: Click **Sample**.

· In the Sample window: Enter **year = 1964** in the "If condition (optional)" text area to restrict the sample to 1964 only.

· Click **OK**. Descriptive statistics for 1964 appear in the Group window. Record the mean and sum of squared deviations for 1964.

In the Group window: Click **Sample**.

· In the Sample window: Enter **year = 1975** in the "If condition (optional)" text area to restrict the sample to 1975 only.

· Click **OK**. Descriptive statistics for 1975 appear in the Group window. Record the mean and sum of squared deviations for 1975.

Last, do not forget to close the file:

· In the EViews window: Click **File**, then **Exit**.

· In the Workfile window: Click **No** in response to the save changes made to workfile.

---

c. Using your answers to part b and some simple arithmetic (division), compute the variance for each year:

            1964   1975

Variance   _____   _____

d. Are your answers to parts b and c consistent with your answer to part a? Explain.

3. Focus on precipitation in Amherst, MA in 1975. Consider a new variable, *TwoPlusPrecip*, which equals two plus each month's precipitation: *TwoPlusPrecip* = 2 + *Precip*.

a. Fill in the blanks in the table below:

1975	Jan	Feb	Mar	Apr	May	Jun	Jul	Aug	Sep	Oct	Nov	Dec
Precip	4.39	3.04	3.97	2.87	2.10	4.68	10.56	6.13	8.63	4.90	5.08	3.90
TwoPlusPrecip	___	___	___	___	___	___	___	___	___	___	___	___

b. Construct a histogram for *TwoPlusPrecip* and compare it to the histogram for *Precip* in 1975 that you constructed in problem 1.

  i. How are the histograms related?

  ii. What happened to the distribution center?

  iii. What happened to the distribution spread?

c. Consider the equations that describe mean and variance of a constant plus a variable:

$$\text{Mean}[c + x] = c + \text{Mean}[x] \quad \text{Var}[c + x] = \text{Var}[x]$$

Based on these equations and the mean and variance of **Precip** in 1975, what is the

   i. mean of **TwoPlusPrecip** in 1975? _____

   ii. variance of **TwoPlusPrecip** in 1975? _____

d. Using your statistical package, generate a new variable: *TwoPlusPrecip* = 2 + *Precip*. What is the

   i. mean of **TwoPlusPrecip** in 1975? _____

   ii. sum of squared deviations of **TwoPlusPrecip** in 1975? _____

Getting Started in EViews

Access the Amherst weather data online:

[To access this online material, go to http://mitpress.mit.edu/westhoffeconometrics and select Amherst Weather.]

Then:

• In the File Download window: Click **Open**. (Note that different browsers may present you with a slightly different screen to open the workfile.)

Instruct EViews to generate the new variable:

• In the Workfile window: Click **Genr** in the toolbar.

• In the Generate Series by Equation window; enter the formula for the new variable:

TwoPlusPrecip* = 2 + *Precip

• Click **OK**.

Instruct EViews to calculate the mean and sum of squared deviations of *TwoPlusPrecip*:

• In the Workfile window: Double click on **TwoPlusPrecip**.

• A spreadsheet displaying the value of *TwoPlusPrecip* for all the months appears.

• In the Series window: Click **View**; next click **Descriptive Statistics & Tests** and then **Stats Table**. Descriptive statistics for all the months of the twentieth century now appear.

• In the Series window: Click **Sample**. In the Sample window: Enter **year = 1975** in the "If condition (optional)" text area to restrict the sample to 1975 only.

• Click **OK**. Descriptive statistics for 1975 appear in the Group window. Record the mean and sum of squared deviations for 1975.

iii. Using the sum of squared deviations and a calculator, compute the variance of *TwoPlus-Precip* in 1975. _____

e. Are your answers to parts b, c, and d consistent? Explain.

4. Focus on precipitation in Amherst, MA, in 1975. Suppose that we wish to report precipitation in centimeters rather than inches. To do this, just multiply each month's precipitation by 2.54. Consider a new variable, *PrecipCm*, which equals 2.54 times each month's precipitation as measured in inches: *PrecipCm* = 2.54 × *Precip*.

a. Consider the equations that describe mean and variance of a constant times a variable:

$$\text{Mean}[cx] = c \, \text{Mean}[x], \quad \text{Var}[cx] = c^2 \, \text{Var}[x]$$

Based on these equations and the mean and variance of **Precip** in 1975, what is the

i. mean of *PrecipCm* in 1975? _____

ii. variance of *PrecipCm* in 1975? _____

b. Using your statistical package, generate a new variable: *PrecipCm* = 2.54 × *Precip*. What is the

i. mean of *PrecipCm* in 1975? _____

ii. sum of squared deviations of *PrecipCm* in 1975? _____

Getting Started in EViews

Access the Amherst weather data online:

[To access this online material, go to http://mitpress.mit.edu/westhoffeconometrics and select Amherst Weather.]

Then:

• In the File Download window: Click **Open**. (Note that different browsers may present you with a slightly different screen to open the workfile.)

Instruct EViews to generate the new variable:

• In the Workfile window: Click **Genr** in toolbar.

• In the Generate Series by Equation window; enter the formula for the new variable:

PrecipCm* = 2.54 * *Precip

NB: The asterisk, *, is the EViews multiplication symbol.

• Click **OK**.

Instruct EViews to calculate the mean and sum of squared deviations of *PrecipCm*:

• In the Workfile window: Double click on **PrecipCm**.

• A spreadsheet now appears.

• In the Series window: Click **View**; next click **Descriptive Statistics & Tests** and then **Stats Table**.

• In the Group window: Click **Sample**. In the Sample window: Enter **year = 1975** in the "If condition (optional)" text area to restrict the sample to 1975 only.

• Click **OK**. Descriptive statistics for 1975 appear in the Group window. Record the mean and sum of squared deviations for 1975.

---

    iii. Using the sum of squared deviations and a calculator, compute the variance of *PrecipCm* in 1975. _____

    c. Are your answers to parts a and b consistent? Explain.

Focus on thirty students who enrolled in an economics course during a previous semester.

Student SAT data: Cross-sectional data of student math and verbal high school SAT scores from a group of 30 students.

$SatMath_t$	Math SAT score for student t
$SatVerbal_t$	Verbal SAT score for student t
$SexM1_t$	1 if student t is male; 0 if female

The table below reports their SAT scores and sex:

Student	SatMath	SatVerbal	SexM1	Student	SatMath	SatVerbal	SexM1
1	670	760	0	16	680	580	1
2	780	700	0	17	750	730	1
3	720	700	0	18	630	610	1
4	770	750	0	19	700	730	1
5	610	620	0	20	730	650	1
6	790	770	0	21	760	730	1
7	740	800	0	22	650	650	1
8	720	710	0	23	800	800	1
9	700	680	0	24	680	750	1
10	750	780	0	25	800	740	1
11	800	750	1	26	800	770	1
12	770	690	1	27	770	730	1
13	790	750	1	28	750	750	1
14	700	620	1	29	790	780	1
15	730	700	1	30	780	790	1

5. Consider the equations that describe the mean and variance of the sum of two variables:

$\text{Mean}[x + y] = \text{Mean}[x] + \text{Mean}[y]$

$\text{Var}[x + y] = \text{Var}[x] + 2\,\text{Cov}[x, y] + \text{Var}[y]$

a. Focus on *SatMath* and *SatVerbal*. On a sheet of graph paper, construct the scatter diagram.

b. Based on the scatter diagram, do *SatMath* and *SatVerbal* appear to be correlated? Explain.

c. Use your statistical package to compute the following descriptive statistics for *SatMath* and *SatVerbal*; then fill in the blanks:

	SatMath	*SatVerbal*
Mean	_____	_____
Variance	_____	_____
Covariance	_____	
Correlation coefficient	_____	

Getting Started in EViews

Access the student SAT data online:

[To access this online material, go to http://mitpress.mit.edu/westhoffeconometrics and select Student Data.]

Then:

• In the File Download window: Click **Open**. (Note that different browsers may present you with a slightly different screen to open the workfile.)

• In the Workfile window: Highlight **satmath** by clicking on it; then, while depressing <Ctrl>, click on **satverbal** to highlight it also.

• In the Workfile window: Double click on any of the highlighted variables.

• A new list now pops up: Click **Open Group**. A spreadsheet including the variables *SatMath* and *SatVerbal* for all the students appears.

Now, instruct EViews to calculate the means:

• In the Group window: Click **View**; next click **Descriptive Stats** and then **Individual Samples**.[9] Descriptive statistics now appear. Record the *SatMath* and *SatVerbal* means.

---

9. Common sample eliminates all observations in which there is one or more missing value in one of the variables; the individual samples option does not do so. Since no values are missing, the choice of common or individual has no impact.

Next instruct EViews to calculate the variances and covariance:

· In the Group window: Click **View** and then click **Covariance Analysis**. . . .

· In the Covariance Analysis window: Note that the Covariance checkbox is selected; then click **OK**. The covariance matrix now appears. Record the variances and covariance.

Last, instruct EViews to calculate the correlation coefficient:

· In the Group window: Click **View** and then click **Covariance Analysis**. . . .

· In the Covariance Analysis window: Clear the Covariance box and select the Correlation box; then click **OK**. The correlation matrix now appears. Record the correlation coefficient.

· Close the Group window to return to the Workfile window.

Note: Copying and Pasting EViews Text   It is often convenient to copy and paste EViews results into a word processing document such as Microsoft Word. In the long run this can save you much time because you can reproduce your results quickly and accurately:

· In EViews, highlight the text you wish to copy and paste.

· Right click on the highlighted area.

· Unless you have a good reason to do otherwise, accept the default choice by clicking **OK**.

· In your word processor: click **Paste**.

Do these calculations support your answer to part b?

Focus on the sum of each student's SAT scores: *SatSum = SatMath + SatVerbal*

d. Consider the equations that describe mean and variance of the sum of two variables:

$$\text{Mean}[x + y] = \text{Mean}[x] + \text{Mean}[y]$$

$$\text{Var}[x + y] = \text{Var}[x] + 2\,\text{Cov}[x, y] + \text{Var}[y]$$

Based on these equations and the mean and variance of *SatMath* and *SatVerbal*, what is the

i. mean of *SatSum*? _____

ii. variance of *SatSum*? _____

e. Using your statistical package, generate a new variable:

SatSum = SatMath + SatVerbal. What is the

i. mean of *SatSum*? _____

ii. sum of squared deviations of *SatSum*? _____

Getting Started in EViews

Generate *SatSum* in EViews:

· In the Workfile window: Click **Genr** in toolbar

· In the Generate Series by Equation window. Enter the formula for the new variable:

SatSum = SatMath + SatVerbal

· Click **OK**.

---

f. Using a calculator compute the variance of *SatSum*. _____

Are your answers to parts d and e consistent?

6. Continue to focus on the student SAT data.

[To access this online material, go to http://mitpress.mit.edu/westhoffeconometrics and select Student Data.]

a. If student 1 drops the course, would the mean Math SAT score of the 29 remaining students increase or decrease?

b. More generally, if a student drops the course, what determines whether the mean Math SAT score of the remaining students would increase or decrease?

c. If a student adds the course, what determines whether the mean Math SAT would increase or decrease?

d. Evaluate the following statement:

"A student transfers from College A to College B. The mean Math SAT scores at both colleges increase."

Could this statement possibly be true? If so, explain how; if not, explain why not.

7. Again, focus on the student SAT data. Consider the equation for the mean Math SAT score of the students:

$$\text{Mean}[SatMath] = \frac{x_1 + x_2 + \ldots + x_{30}}{30}$$

where x_i = student i's Math SAT score

Next consider the mean Math SAT score of just the female students and the mean of the just the male students. Since students 1 through 10 are female and students 11 through 30 are male:

$$\text{Mean}[SatMathFemale] = \frac{x_1 + x_2 + \ldots + x_{10}}{10}$$

$$\text{Mean}[SatMathMale] = \frac{x_{11} + x_{12} + \ldots + x_{30}}{20}$$

a. Using algebra, show that the mean for all students equals the weighted average of the mean for female students and the mean for male students where the weights equal the proportion of female and male students; that is,

Mean[***SatMath***] = Wgt_{Female}Mean[***SatMathFemale***] + Wgt_{Male}Mean[***SatMathMale***]

where

$$Wgt_{Female} = \frac{\text{Number of female students}}{\text{Total number of students}}$$

$\qquad$ = Weight given to female students

and

$$Wgt_{Male} = \frac{\text{Number of male students}}{\text{Total number of students}}$$

$\qquad$ = Weight given to male students

b. Do the weights sum to 1? Explain.

c. Find the means all students, for females, and for males. Are your results consistent with the weighted average equation you just derived? Explain.

[To access this online material, go to http://mitpress.mit.edu/westhoffeconometrics and select Student Data.]

Mean[***SatMath***] = _____

Mean[***SatMathFemale***] = _____   Mean[***SatMathMale***] = _____

8. The following data from the 1995 and 1996 baseball seasons illustrate what is known as Simpson's paradox.

Hits and at bats

	1995		1996		Combined	
	Hits	AB	Hits	AB	Hits	AB
Derek Jeter	12	48	183	582	____	____
David Justice	104	411	45	140	____	____

Batting averages

	1995	1996	Combined
Derek Jeter	____	____	____
David Justice	____	____	____

a. Compute the batting average for both players in 1995. Fill in the appropriate blanks. In 1995, who had the higher average?

b. Compute the batting average for both players in 1996. Fill in the appropriate blanks. In 1996, who had the higher average?

c. Next combine the hits and at bats for the two seasons. Fill in the appropriate blanks. Compute the batting average for both players in the combined seasons. Fill in the appropriate blanks. In the combined seasons, who had the higher average?

d. Explain why the batting average results appear paradoxical.

e. Resolve the paradox. Hint: Jeter's combined season average can be viewed as a weighted average of his two seasons, weighted by his at bats. Similarly Justice's combined season average can be viewed as a weighted average also. Apply the equation you derived in problem 7.

Appendix 1.1: The Arithmetic of Means, Variances, and Covariances

Let us begin by quickly reviewing the mathematical definitions:

$$\text{Mean}[x] = \bar{x} = \frac{x_1 + x_2 + \ldots + x_T}{T} = \frac{\sum_{t=1}^{T} x_t}{T}$$

$$\text{Var}[x] = \frac{(x_1 - \bar{x})^2 + (x_2 - \bar{x})^2 + \ldots + (x_T - \bar{x})^2}{T} = \frac{\sum_{t=1}^{T}(x_t - \bar{x})^2}{T}$$

$$\text{Cov}[x, y] = \frac{(x_1 - \bar{x})(y_1 - \bar{y}) + (x_2 - \bar{x})(y_2 - \bar{y}) + \ldots + (x_T - \bar{x})(y_T - \bar{y})}{T} = \frac{\sum_{t=1}^{T}(x_t - \bar{x})(y_t - \bar{y})}{T}$$

where T = total number of observations.

Mean of a Constant Plus a Variable: Mean[c + x] = c + Mean[x]

The mean of a constant plus a variable equals the constant plus the mean of the variable:

$$\text{Mean}[c + x] = \frac{c + x_1 + c + x_2 + \ldots + x_T + c}{T}$$

$$= \frac{c + c + \ldots + c}{T} + \frac{x_1 + x_2 + \ldots + x_T}{T}$$

$$= \frac{Tc}{T} + \frac{x_1 + x_2 + \ldots + x_T}{T}$$

$$= c + \text{Mean}[x] = c + \bar{x}$$

Mean of a Constant Times a Variable: Mean[cx] = c Mean[x]

The mean of a constant times a variable equals the constant times the mean of the variable:

$$\text{Mean}[cx] = \frac{cx_1 + cx_2 + \ldots + cx_T}{T}$$

$$= c \frac{x_1 + x_2 + \ldots + x_T}{T}$$

$$= c \, \text{Mean}[x] = c\bar{x}$$

Mean of the Sum of Two Variables: Mean[x + y] = Mean[x] + Mean[y]

The mean of the sum of two variables equals the sum of the means of the variables:

$$\text{Mean}[x + y] = \frac{x_1 + y_1 + x_2 + y_2 + \ldots + x_T + y_T}{T}$$

$$= \frac{(x_1 + x_2 + \ldots + x_T) + (y_1 + y_2 + \ldots + y_T)}{T}$$

$$= \frac{x_1 + x_2 + \ldots + x_T}{T} + \frac{y_1 + y_2 + \ldots + y_T}{T}$$

$$= \bar{x} + \bar{y}$$

Variance of a Constant Plus a Variable: Var[c + x] = Var[x]

The variance of a constant plus a variable equals the variance of the variable:

$$\text{Var}[c + x] = \frac{[(c + x_1) - (c + \bar{x})]^2 + [(c + x_2) - (c + \bar{x})]^2 + \ldots + [(c + x_T) - (c + \bar{x})]^2}{T}$$

$$= \frac{[(c - c) + (x_1 - \bar{x})]^2 + [(c - c) + (x_2 - \bar{x})]^2 + \ldots + [(c - c) + (x_T - \bar{x})]^2}{T}$$

$$= \frac{(x_1 - \bar{x})^2 + (x_2 - \bar{x})^2 + \ldots + (x_T - \bar{x})^2}{T}$$

$$= \text{Var}[x]$$

Variance of a Constant Times a Variable: Var[cx] = c² Var[x]

The variance of a constant times a variable equals the constant squared times the variance of the variable:

$$\mathrm{Var}[cx] = \frac{(cx_1 - c\bar{x})^2 + (cx_2 - c\bar{x})^2 + \ldots + (cx_T - c\bar{x})^2}{T}$$

$$= \frac{c^2(x_1 - \bar{x})^2 + c^2(x_2 - \bar{x})^2 + \ldots + c^2(x_T - \bar{x})^2}{T}$$

$$= c^2 \frac{(x_1 - \bar{x})^2 + (x_2 - \bar{x})^2 + \ldots + (x_T - \bar{x})^2}{T}$$

$$= c^2 \mathrm{Var}[x]$$

Variance of the Sum of Two Variables: Var[x + y] = Var[x] + 2 Cov[x, y] + Var[y]

The variance of the sum of two variables equals the sum of the variances of the variables plus twice the variables' covariance:

$$\mathrm{Var}[x + y]$$

$$= \frac{[(x_1 + y_1) - (\bar{x} + \bar{y})]^2 + \ldots + [(x_T + y_T) - (\bar{x} + \bar{y})]^2}{T}$$

$$= \frac{[(x_1 - \bar{x}) + (y_1 - \bar{y})]^2 + \ldots + [(x_T - \bar{x}) + (y_T - \bar{y})]^2}{T}$$

$$= \frac{[(x_1 - \bar{x})^2 + 2(x_1 - \bar{x})(y_1 - \bar{y}) + (y_1 - \bar{y})^2] + \ldots + [(x_T - \bar{x})^2 + 2(x_T - \bar{x})(y_T - \bar{y}) + (y_T - \bar{y})^2]}{T}$$

$$= \frac{[(x_1 - \bar{x})^2 + \ldots + (x_T - \bar{x})^2] + 2[(x_1 - \bar{x})(y_1 - \bar{y}) + \ldots + (x_T - \bar{x})(y_T - \bar{y})] + [(y_1 - \bar{y})^2 + \ldots + (y_T - \bar{y})^2]}{T}$$

$$= \frac{(x_1 - \bar{x})^2 + \ldots + (x_T - \bar{x})^2}{T} + 2\frac{(x_1 - \bar{x})(y_1 - \bar{y}) + \ldots + (x_T - \bar{x})(y_T - \bar{y})}{T}$$

$$+ \frac{(y_1 - \bar{y})^2 + \ldots + (y_T - \bar{y})^2}{T}$$

$$= \mathrm{Var}[x] + 2 \mathrm{Cov}[x, y] + \mathrm{Var}[y]$$

Variance of the Sum of Two Independent (Uncorrelated) Variables: Var[x + y] = Var[x] + Var[y]

The variance of the sum of two independent (uncorrelated) variables equals the sum of the variances of the variables:

$$\mathrm{Var}[x + y] = \mathrm{Var}[x] + 2 \mathrm{Cov}[x, y] + \mathrm{Var}[y]$$

$$= \mathrm{Var}[x] + \mathrm{Var}[y]$$

(since x and y are independent, $\mathrm{Cov}[x, y] = 0$).

Covariance of the Sum of a Constant and a Variable: Cov[c + x, y] = Cov[x, y]

The covariance of two variables is unaffected when a constant is added to one of the variables:

$\text{Cov}[c+x, y]$

$$= \frac{[(c+x_1)-(c+\bar{x})](y_1-\bar{y})+[(c+x_2)-(c+\bar{x})](y_2-\bar{y})+\ldots+[(c+x_T)-(c+\bar{x})](y_T-\bar{y})}{T}$$

$$= \frac{[(c-c)+(x_1-\bar{x})](y_1-\bar{y})+[(c-c)+(x_2-\bar{x})](y_2-\bar{y})+\ldots+[(c-c)+(x_T-\bar{x})](y_T-\bar{y})}{T}$$

$$= \frac{(x_1-\bar{x})(y_1-\bar{y})+(x_2-\bar{x})(y_2-\bar{y})+\ldots+(x_T-\bar{x})(y_T-\bar{y})}{T}$$

$$= \text{Cov}[x, y]$$

Covariance of the Product of a Constant and a Variable: Cov[cx, y] = c Cov[x, y]

Multiplying a variable by a constant increases the covariance by a factor equal to the constant:

$$\text{Cov}[cx, y] = \frac{(cx_1-c\bar{x})(y_1-\bar{y})+(cx_2-c\bar{x})(y_2-\bar{y})+\ldots+(cx_T-c\bar{x})(y_T-\bar{y})}{T}$$

$$= \frac{c(x_1-\bar{x})(y_1-\bar{y})+c(x_2-\bar{x})(y_2-\bar{y})+\ldots+c(x_T-\bar{x})(y_T-\bar{y})}{T}$$

$$= c\frac{(x_1-\bar{x})(y_1-\bar{y})+(x_2-\bar{x})(y_2-\bar{y})+\ldots+(x_T-\bar{x})(y_T-\bar{y})}{T}$$

$$= c\text{Cov}[x, y]$$

2 Essentials of Probability and Estimation Procedures

Chapter 2 Prep Questions

1. Consider a standard deck of 52 cards: 13 spades, 13 hearts, 13 diamonds, and 13 clubs. Thoroughly shuffle the deck and then randomly draw one card. Do not look at the card. Fill in the following blanks:

a. There are ____ chances out of _____ that the card drawn is a heart; that is, the probability that the card drawn will be a heart equals _____.

b. There are ____ chances out of _____ that the card drawn is an ace; that is, the probability that the card drawn will be an ace equals _____.

c. There are ____ chances out of _____ that the card drawn is a red card; that is, the probability that the card drawn will be a red card equals _____.

2. Consider the following experiment: Thoroughly shuffle a standard deck of 52 cards. Randomly draw one card and note whether or not it is a heart. Replace the card drawn.

a. What is the probability that the card drawn will be a heart? _____

b. If you were to repeat this experiment many, many times, what portion of the time would you expect the card drawn to be a heart? _____

3. Review the arithmetic of means and variances and then complete the following equations:

a. Mean[cx] = _____

b. Mean[$x + y$] = _____

c. Var[cx] = _____

d. Var[$x + y$] = _____

e. When x and y are independent: Var[$x + y$] = _____

4. Using algebra, show that the expression:

$$(1 - p)^2 p + p^2(1 - p)$$

simplifies to

$$p(1 - p)$$

2.1   Random Processes and Probability

2.1.1   Random Process: A Process Whose Outcome Cannot Be Predicted with Certainty

The outcome of a **random process** is uncertain. Tossing a coin is a random process because you cannot tell beforehand whether the coin will land heads or tails. A baseball game is a random process because the outcome of the game cannot be known beforehand, assuming of course that the game has not been fixed. Drawing a card from a well-shuffled deck of fifty-two cards is a random process because you cannot tell beforehand whether the card will be the ten of hearts, the six of diamonds, the ace of spades, and so on.

2.1.2 Probability: The Likelihood of a Particular Outcome of a Random Process

The **probability** of an outcome tells us how likely it is for that outcome to occur. The value of a probability ranges from 0 to 1.0. A probability of 0 indicates that the outcome will never occur; 1.0 indicates that the outcome will occur with certainty. A probability of one-half indicates that the chances of the outcome occurring equals the chances that it will not. For example, if the experts believe that a baseball game between two teams, say the Red Sox and Yankees, is a toss-up, then the experts believe that

- the probability of a Red Sox win (and a Yankee loss) is one-half and
- the probability of a Red Sox loss (and a Yankee win) is also one-half.

An Example: A Deck of Four Cards

We will use a card draw as our first illustration of a random process. While we could use a standard deck of fifty-two cards as the example, the arithmetic can become cumbersome. Consequently, to keep the calculations manageable, we will use a deck of only four cards, the 2 of clubs, the 3 of hearts, the 3 of diamonds, and the 4 of hearts:

2♣, 3♥, 3♦, 4♥

Experiment 2.1: Random Card Draw

- Shuffle the 2♣, 3♥, 3♦, and 4♥ thoroughly.
- Draw one card and record its value.
- Replace the card.

This experiment represents one repetition of a random process because we cannot determine which card will be drawn before the experiment is conducted. Throughout this textbook, we will continue to use the word experiment to represent one repetition of a random process. It is easy to calculate the probability of each possible outcome for our card draw experiment.

Question: What is the probability of drawing the 2 of clubs?

Answer: Since the cards are well shuffled, each card is equally likely to be drawn. There is one chance in four of drawing the 2 of clubs, so the probability of drawing the 2 of clubs is 1/4.

Question: What is the probability of drawing the 3 of hearts?

Answer: There is one chance in four of drawing the 3 of hearts, so the probability of drawing the 3 of hearts is 1/4.

Similarly the probability of drawing the 3 of diamonds is 1/4 and the probability of drawing the 4 of hearts is 1/4. To summarize,

$$\text{Prob}[2\clubsuit] = \frac{1}{4}, \quad \text{Prob}[3\heartsuit] = \frac{1}{4}, \quad \text{Prob}[3\diamondsuit] = \frac{1}{4}, \quad \text{Prob}[4\heartsuit] = \frac{1}{4}$$

2.1.3   Random Variable: A Variable That Is Associated with an Outcome of a Random Process

A **random variable** is a variable that is associated with a random process. The value of a random variable cannot be determined with certainty before the experiment is conducted. There are two types of random variables:

· A **discrete random variable** can only take on a countable number of discrete values.

· A **continuous random variable** can take on a continuous range of values; that is, a continuous random variable can take on a continuum of values.

2.2   Discrete Random Variables and Probability Distributions

To illustrate a discrete random variable, consider our card draw experiment and define v:

v = the value of the card drawn

That is, v equals 2, if the 2 of hearts were drawn; 3, if the 3 of hearts or the 3 of diamonds were drawn; and 4, if the 4 of hearts were drawn.

Question: Why do we call v a discrete random variable?

Answer:

· v is discrete because it can only take on a countable number of values; v can take on three values: 2 or 3 or 4.

· v is a random variable because we cannot determine the value of v before the experiment is conducted.

2.2.1   Probability Distribution Describes the Probability for All Possible Values of a Random Variable

While we cannot determine v's value beforehand, we can calculate the probability of each possible value:

· v equals 2 whenever the 2 of clubs is drawn; since the probability of drawing the 2 of clubs is 1/4, the probability that v will equal 2 is 1/4.

Table 2.1
Probability distribution of random variable v

Card drawn	v	Prob[v]
2♣	2	$\frac{1}{4} = 0.25$
3♥ or 3♦	3	$\frac{1}{4} + \frac{1}{4} = \frac{1}{2} = 0.50$
4♥	4	$\frac{1}{4} = 0.25$

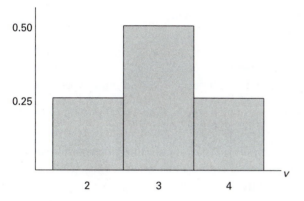

Figure 2.1
Probability distribution of the random variable v

• v equals 3 whenever the 3 of hearts or the 3 of diamonds is drawn; since the probability of drawing the 3 of hearts is 1/4 and the probability of drawing the 3 of diamonds is 1/4, the probability that v will equal 3 is 1/2.

• v equals 4 whenever the 4 of hearts is drawn; since the probability of drawing the 4 of hearts is 1/4, the probability that v will equal 4 is 1/4.

Table 2.1 describes the probability distribution of the random variable v. The probability distribution is sometimes called the probability density function of the random variable or simply the distribution of the random variable. Figure 2.1 illustrates the probability distribution with a graph that indicates how likely it is for the random variable to equal each of its possible values. Note that the probabilities must sum to 1 because one of the four cards must be drawn; v must equal either 2 or 3 or 4. This illustrates a general principle: The sum of the probabilities of all possible outcomes must equal 1.

2.2.2   A Random Variable's Bad News and Good News

In general, a random variable brings both bad and good news. Before the experiment is conducted:

Bad news: What we do not know: on the one hand, we cannot determine the numerical value of the random variable with certainty.

Good news: What we do know: on the other hand, we can often calculate the random variable's probability distribution telling us how likely it is for the random variable to equal each of its possible numerical values.

2.2.3   Relative Frequency Interpretation of Probability

We can interpret the probability of a particular outcome as the **relative frequency** of the outcome after the random process, the experiment, is repeated many, many times. We will illustrate the relative frequency interpretation of probability using our card draw experiment:

Question: If we repeat the experiment many, many times, what portion of the time would we draw a 2?

Answer: Since one of the four cards is a 2, we would expect to draw a 2 about one-fourth of the time. That is, when the experiment is repeated many, many times, the relative frequency of a 2 should be about 1/4, its probability.

Question: If we repeat the experiment many, many times, what portion of the time would we draw a 3?

Answer: Since two of the four cards are 3's, we would expect to draw a 3 about one-half of the time. That is, when the experiment is repeated many, many times, the relative frequency of a 3 should be about 1/2 its probability.

Question: If we repeat the experiment many, many times, what portion of the time would we draw a 4?

Answer: Since one of the four cards is a 4, we would expect to draw a 4 about one-fourth of the time. That is, when the experiment is repeated many, many times, the relative frequency of a 4 should be about 1/4, its probability.

Econometrics Lab 2.1: Card Draw—Relative Frequency Interpretation of Probability

We could justify this interpretation of probability "by hand," but doing so would be a very time-consuming and laborious process. Computers, however, allow us to simulate the experiment quickly and easily. The Card Draw simulation in our econometrics lab does so (figure 2.2).

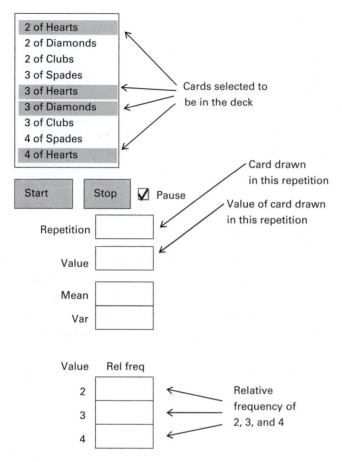

Figure 2.2
Card Draw simulation

[To access this online material, go to http://mitpress.mit.edu/westhoffeconometrics and select Lab 2.1.]

We first specify the cards to include in our deck. By default, the 2♣, 3♥, 3♦, and 4♥ are included. When we click **Start**, the simulation randomly selects one of our four cards. The card drawn and its value are reported. To randomly select a second card, click **Continue**. A table reports on the relative frequency of each possible value and a histogram visually illustrates the distribution of the numerical values.

Click **Continue** repeatedly to convince yourself that our experiment is indeed a random process; that is, convince yourself that there is no way to determine which card will be drawn beforehand. Next uncheck the Pause checkbox and click **Continue**. The simulation no longer

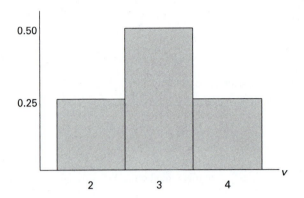

Figure 2.3
Histogram of the numerical values of v

pauses after each card is selected. It will now repeat the experiment very rapidly. What happens as the number of repetitions becomes large? The relative frequency of a 2 is approximately 0.25, the relative frequency of a 3 is approximately 0.50, and the relative frequency of a 4 is approximately 0.25 as illustrated by the histogram appearing in figure 2.3. After many, many repetitions click **Stop**. Recall the probabilities that we calculated for our random variable v:

$\text{Prob}[v = 2] = 0.25$

$\text{Prob}[v = 3] = 0.50$

$\text{Prob}[v = 4] = 0.25$

This simulation illustrates the relative frequency interpretation of probability.

2.2.4   Relative Frequency Interpretation of Probability Summary

When the experiment is repeated many, many times, the relative frequency of each outcome equals its probability. After many, many repetitions the distribution of the numerical values from all the repetitions mirrors the probability distribution:

Distribution of the
numerical values

                              After many,
        $\downarrow$ many
                              repetitions

Probability distribution

2.3 Describing a Probability Distribution of a Random Variable

2.3.1 Center of the Probability Distribution: Mean (Expected Value) of the Random Variable

We have already defined the mean of a data variable in chapter 1. That is, the mean is the average of the numerical values. We can extend the notion of the mean to a random variable by applying the relative frequency interpretation of probability. The mean of a random variable equals the average of the numerical values after the experiment is repeated many, many times. The mean is often called the expected value because that is what we would expect the numerical value to equal on average after many, many repetitions of the experiment.[1]

Question: On average, what would we expect v to equal if we repeated our experiment many, many times? About one-fourth of the time v would equal 2, one-half of the time v would equal 3, and one-fourth of the time v would equal 4:

$\frac{1}{4}$ of the time $\frac{1}{2}$ of the time $\frac{1}{4}$ of the time

↓   ↓   ↓

$v = 2$ $v = 3$ $v = 4$

Answer: On average, v would equal 3. Consequently the mean of the random variable v equals 3.

More formally, we can calculate the mean of a random variable using the following two steps:

· Multiply each value by the value's probability.
· Sum the products.

The mean equals the sum of these products. The following equation describes the steps more concisely:[2]

$$\text{Mean}[\mathbf{v}] = \sum\nolimits_{\text{All } v} v \, \text{Prob}[v]$$

In words, it states that for each possible value, multiply the value and its probability; then sum the products.

Let us now "dissect" the right-hand side of the equation:

---

1. The mean and expected value of a random variable are synonyms. Throughout this textbook we will be consistent and always use the term "mean." You should note, however, that the term "expected value" is frequently used instead of "mean."

2. Note that the v in Mean[$\mathbf{v}$] is in a bold font. This is done to emphasize the fact that the mean refers to the entire probability distribution. Mean[$\mathbf{v}$] refers to the center of the entire probability distribution, not just a single value. When v does not appear in a bold font, we are referring to a specific value that v can take on.

- "v" represents the numerical value of the random variable.
- "Prob[v]" represents the probability of v.
- The uppercase sigma, Σ, is the summation sign; it indicates that we should sum the product of v and its probability, Prob[v].
- The "All v" indicates that we should sum over all numerical values of v.

In our example, v can take on three values: 2, 3, and 4. Applying the equation for the mean obtains

$$
\begin{array}{ccccccc}
 & v = 2 & & v = 3 & & v = 4 & \\
 & \downarrow & & \downarrow & & \downarrow & \\
\mathrm{Mean}[v] = & 2 \times \dfrac{1}{4} & + & 3 \times \dfrac{1}{2} & + & 4 \times \dfrac{1}{4} & \\
= & \dfrac{1}{2} & + & \dfrac{3}{2} & + & 1 & = 3
\end{array}
$$

2.3.2   Spread of the Probability Distribution: Variance of the Random Variable

Next let us turn our attention to the variance. Recall from chapter 1 that the variance of a data variable describes the spread of a data variable's distribution. The variance equals the average of the squared deviations of the values from the mean. Just as we used the relative frequency interpretation of probability to extend the notion of the mean to a random variable, we will now use it to extend the notion of the variance. The variance of a random variable equals the average of the squared deviations of the values from its mean after the experiment is repeated many, many times.

Begin by calculating the deviation from the mean and then the squared deviation for each possible value of v:

Card drawn	v	Mean[v]	Deviation from Mean[v]	Squared deviation	Prob[v]
2♣	2	3	$2 - 3 = -1$	1	$\dfrac{1}{4} = 0.25$
3♥ or 3♦	3	3	$3 - 3 = 0$	0	$\dfrac{1}{2} = 0.50$
4♥	4	3	$4 - 3 = 1$	1	$\dfrac{1}{4} = 0.25$

If we repeat our experiment many, many times, what would the squared deviations equal on average?

• About one-fourth of the time v would equal 2, the deviation would equal −1, and the squared deviation 1.

• About one-half of the time v would equal 3, the deviation would equal 0, and the squared deviation 0.

• About one-fourth of the time v would equal 1, the deviation would equal 1, and the squared deviation 1.

That is, after many, many repetitions,

$\frac{1}{4}$ of the time	$\frac{1}{2}$ of the time	$\frac{1}{4}$ of the time
↓	↓	↓
$v = 2$	$v = 3$	$v = 4$
↓	↓	↓
Deviation = −1	Deviation = 0	Deviation = 1
↓	↓	↓
Squared deviation = 1	Squared deviation = 0	Squared deviation = 1

Half of the time the squared deviation would equal 1 and half of the time 0. On average, the squared deviations from the mean would equal 1/2.

More formally, we can calculate the variance of a random variable using the following four steps:

• For each possible value of the random variable, calculate the deviation from the mean.

• Square each value's deviation.

• Multiply each value's squared deviation by the value's probability.

• Sum the products.

We use an equation to state this more concisely:

$$\text{Var}[v] = \sum_{\text{All } v} (v - \text{Mean}[v])^2 \text{Prob}[v]$$

For each possible value, multiply the squared deviation and its probability; then sum the products. In our example there are three possible values for v: 2, 3, and 4:

$$
\begin{array}{ccccc}
v = 2 & & v = 3 & & v = 4 \\
\downarrow & & \downarrow & & \downarrow \\
\end{array}
$$

$$
\mathrm{Var}[v] \;=\; 1 \times \frac{1}{4} \;+\; 0 \times \frac{1}{2} \;+\; 1 \times \frac{1}{4}
$$

$$
\;=\; \frac{1}{4} \;+\; 0 \;+\; \frac{1}{4} \;=\; \frac{1}{2} \;=\; 0.5
$$

Econometrics Lab 2.2: Card Draw Simulation—Checking the Mean and Variance Calculations

It is useful to use our simulation to check our mean and variance calculations. We will exploit the relative frequency interpretation of probability to do so. Recall our experiment:

- Shuffle the 2♣, 3♥, 3♦, and 4♥ thoroughly.
- Draw one card and record its value.
- Replace the card.

The relative frequency interpretation of probability asserts that when an experiment is repeated many, many times, the relative frequency of each outcome equals its probability. After many, many repetitions the distribution of the numerical values from all the repetitions mirrors the probability distribution:

Distribution of the
numerical values

$$\downarrow$$
After many,
many
repetitions

Probability distribution

If our equations are correct, what should we expect when we repeat our experiment many, many times?

- The mean of a random variable's probability distribution should equal the average of the numerical values of the variable obtained from each repetition of the experiment after the experiment is repeated many, many times. Consequently after many, many repetitions the mean should equal about 3.

- The variance of a random variable's probability distribution should equal the average of the squared deviations from the mean obtained from each repetition of the experiment after the experiment is repeated many, many times. Consequently after many, many repetitions the variance should equal about 0.5.

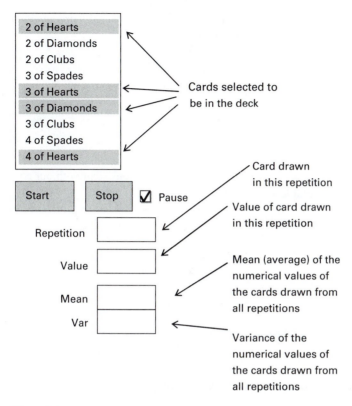

Figure 2.4
Card Draw simulation

The Card Draw simulation in our econometrics lab allows us to confirm this:

[To access this online material, go to http://mitpress.mit.edu/westhoffeconometrics and select Lab 2.2.]

As before, the 2♣, 3♥, 3♦, and 4♥ are selected by default (figure 2.4); so just click **Start**. Recall that the simulation now randomly selects one of the four cards. The numerical value of the card selected is reported. Note that the mean and variance of the numerical values are also reported. You should convince yourself that the simulation is calculating the mean and variance correctly by clicking **Continue** and calculating the mean and variance yourself. You will observe that the simulation is indeed performing the calculations accurately. If you are still skeptical, click **Continue** again and perform the calculations. Do so until you are convinced that the mean and variance reported by the simulation are indeed correct.

Next uncheck the Pause checkbox and click **Continue**. The simulation no longer pauses after each card is selected. It will now repeat the experiment very rapidly. After many, many repetitions click **Stop**. What happens as the number of repetitions becomes large?

· The mean of the numerical values is about 3. This is consistent with our equation for the mean of the random variable's probability distribution:

$$\text{Mean}[v] = \sum_{\text{All } v} v \, \text{Prob}[v]$$

$$
\begin{aligned}
\text{Mean}[v] \;\; &= \;\; 2 \times \frac{1}{4} \;\; + \;\; 3 \times \frac{1}{2} \;\; + \;\; 4 \times \frac{1}{4} \\[2mm]
&= \;\; \frac{1}{2} \;\; + \;\; \frac{3}{2} \;\; + \;\; 1 \;\; = \;\; 3
\end{aligned}
$$

· The variance of the numerical values is about 0.5. This is consistent with our equation for the variance of the random variable's probability distribution:

$$\text{Var}[v] = \sum_{\text{All } v} (v - \text{Mean}[v])^2 \, \text{Prob}[v]$$

$$
\begin{aligned}
\text{Var}[v] \;\; &= \;\; 1 \times \frac{1}{4} \;\; + \;\; 0 \times \frac{1}{2} \;\; + \;\; 1 \times \frac{1}{4} \\[2mm]
&= \;\; \frac{1}{4} \;\; + \;\; 0 \;\; + \;\; \frac{1}{4} \;\; = \;\; \frac{1}{2} \;\; = \;\; 0.5
\end{aligned}
$$

The simulation illustrates that the equations we use to compute the mean and variance are indeed correct.

2.4   Continuous Random Variables and Probability Distributions

A **continuous random variable**, unlike a discrete random variable, can take on a continuous range of values, a continuum of values. To learn more about these random variables, consider the following example. Dan Duffer consistently hits 200 yard drives from the tee. A diagram of the eighteenth hole appears in figure 2.5. The fairway is 32 yards wide 200 yards from the tee. While the length of Dan's drives is consistent (he always drives the ball 200 yards from the tee), he is not consistent "laterally." That is, his drives sometimes go to the left of where he aims and sometimes to the right. Despite all the lessons Dan has taken, his drive can land up to 40 yards to the left and up to 40 yards to the right of his target point. Suppose that Dan's target point is the center of the fairway. Since the fairway is 32 yards wide, there are 16 yards of fairway to the left of Dan's target point and 16 yards of fairway to the right.

The probability distribution appearing below the diagram of the eighteenth hole describes the probability that his drive will go to the left and right of his target point. v equals the lateral distance from Dan's target point. A negative v represents a point to the left of the target point and a positive v a point to the right. Note that v can take an infinite number of values between -40 and $+40$: v can equal 10 or 16.002 or -30.127, and so on. v is a continuous rather than a discrete random variable. The probability distribution at the bottom of figure 2.5 indicates how likely it is for v to equal each of its possible values.

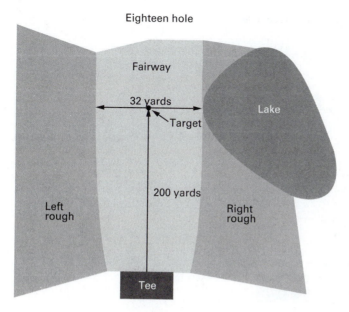

Eighteen hole

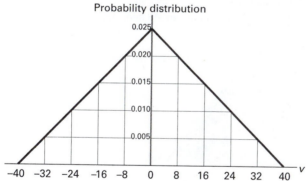

Probability distribution

Figure 2.5
A continuous random variable

What is the area beneath the probability distribution? Applying the equation for the area of a triangle obtains

$$\text{Area beneath} = \frac{1}{2} \times 0.025 \times 40 + \frac{1}{2} \times 0.025 \times 40$$
$$= 0.5 + 0.5 = 1$$

The area equals 1. This is not accidental. Dan's probability distribution illustrates the property that all probability distributions must exhibit:

· The area beneath the probability distribution must equal 1.

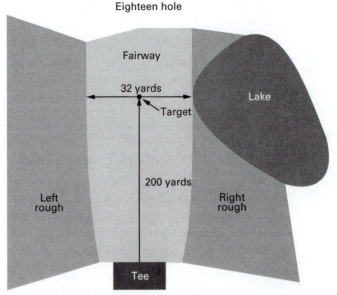

Eighteen hole

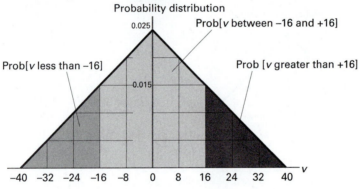

Figure 2.6
A continuous random variable—Calculating probabilities

The area equaling 1 simply means that a random variable must always take on one of its possible values (see figure 2.6). In Dan's case the area beneath the probability distribution must equal 1 because Dan's ball must land somewhere.

Let us now calculate some probabilities:

· What is the probability that Dan's drive will land in the lake? The shore of the lake lies 16 yards to the right of the target point; hence the probability that his drive lands in the lake equals the probability that v will be greater than 16:

Prob[Drive in lake] = Prob[v greater than +16]

This just equals the area beneath the probability distribution that lies to the right of 16. Applying the equation for the area of a triangle:

$$\text{Prob[Drive in lake]} = \frac{1}{2} \times 0.015 \times 24 = 0.18$$

• What is the probability that Dan's drive will land in the left rough? The left rough lies 16 yards to the left of the target point; hence, the probability that his drive lands in the left rough equals the probability that v will be less than or equal to -16:

Prob[Drive in left rough] = Prob[v less than -16]

This just equals the area beneath the probability distribution that lies to the left of -16:

$$\text{Prob[Drive in left rough]} = \frac{1}{2} \times 0.015 \times 24 = 0.18$$

• What is the probability that Dan's drive will land in the fairway? The probability that his drive lands in the fairway equals the probability that v will be within 16 yards of the target point:

Prob[Drive in fairway] = Prob[v between -16 and $+16$]

This just equals the area beneath the probability distribution that lies between -16 and 16. We can calculate this area by dividing the area into a rectangle and triangle:

$$\begin{aligned}
\text{Prob[Drive in fairway]} &= 0.015 \times 32 + \frac{1}{2} \times 0.010 \times 32 \\
&= 0.015 \times 32 + 0.005 \times 32 \\
&= (0.015 + 0.005) \times 32 \\
&= 0.020 \times 32 = 0.64
\end{aligned}$$

As a check let us sum these three probabilities:

Prob[Drive in lake] + Prob[Drive in left rough] + Prob[Drive in fairway] = 0.18 + 0.18 + 0.64 = 1.0

The sum equals 1.0, illustrating the fact that Dan's drive must land somewhere. This example illustrates how we can use probability distributions to compute probabilities.

2.5   Estimation Procedures: Populations and Samples

We will now apply what we have learned about random variables to gain insights into statistics that are cited in the news every day. For example, when the Bureau of Labor Statistics calculates the unemployment rate every month, it does not interview every American, the entire American **population**; instead, it gathers information from a subset of the population, a **sample**. More specifically, data are collected from interviews with about 60,000 households. Similarly political pollsters do not poll every American voter to forecast the outcome of an election, but rather they query only a sample of the voters. In each case a sample of the population is used to draw inferences about the entire population. How reliable are these inferences? To address this question, we consider an example.

2.5.1   Clint's Dilemma: Assessing Clint's Political Prospects

A college student, Clinton Jefferson Williams, is running for president of his student body. On the day before the election, Clint must decide whether or not to hold a pre-election beer tap rally:

• If he is comfortably ahead, he will not hold the beer tap rally; he will save his campaign funds for a future political endeavor (or perhaps a Caribbean vacation in January).

• If he is not comfortably ahead, he will hold the beer tap rally to try to sway some voters.

There is not enough time to interview every member of the student body, however. What should Clint do? He decides to conduct a poll.

Clint's Opinion Poll
• **Questionnaire:**   Are you voting for Clint?

• **Procedure:**   Clint selects 16 students at random and poses the question. That is, each of the 16 randomly selected students is asked who he/she supports in the election.

• **Results:**   12 students report that they will vote for Clint and 4 against Clint.

Econometrician's philosophy
If you lack the information to determine the value directly, estimate the value to the best of your ability using the information you do have. By conducting the poll, Clint has adopted the philosophy of the econometrician. Clint uses the information collected from the 16 students, the sample, to draw inferences about the entire student body, the population. Seventy-five percent, 0.75, of the sample support Clint:

Estimate of the actual population fraction supporting Clint = $EstFrac$ = 12/16 = 3/4 = 0.75

This suggests that Clint leads, does it not? But how confident should Clint be that he is in fact ahead. Clint faces a dilemma.

Clint's Dilemma
Should Clint be confident that he has the election in hand and save his funds or should he finance the beer tap rally?

We will now pursue the following project to help Clint resolve his dilemma.

Project

Use Clint's opinion poll to assess his election prospects.

2.5.2 Usefulness of Simulations

In reality, Clint only conducts one poll. How, then, can a simulation of the polling process be useful? The relative frequency interpretation of probability provides the answer. We can use a simulation to conduct a poll many, many times. After many, many repetitions the simulation reveals the probability distribution of the possible outcomes for the one poll that Clint conducts:

Distribution of the
numerical values

$\downarrow$ After many,
many
repetitions

Probability distribution

We will now illustrate how the probability distribution might help Clint decide whether or not to fund the beer tap rally.

Econometrics Lab 2.3: Simulating Clint's Opinion Poll

The Opinion Poll simulation in our Econometrics Lab can help Clint address his dilemma. In the simulation, we can specify the sample size. To mimic Clint's poll, a sample size of 16 is selected by default (shown in figure 2.7). Furthermore we can do something in the simulation that we cannot do in the real world. We can specify the actual fraction of the population that supports Clint, *ActFrac*. By default, the actual population fraction is set at 0.5; half of all voters support Clint and half do not. In other words, we are simulating an election that is a toss-up.

[To access this online material, go to http://mitpress.mit.edu/westhoffeconometrics and select Lab 2.3.]

When we click the **Start** button, the simulation conducts a poll of 16 people and reports the fraction of those polled that support Clint:

$$EstFrac = \frac{\text{Number for Clint}}{\text{Sample size}}$$

$$= \frac{\text{Number for Clint}}{16}$$

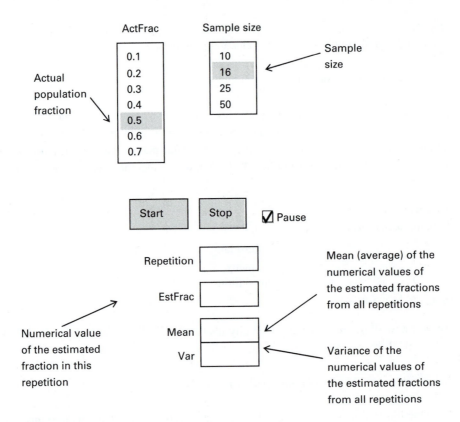

Figure 2.7
Opinion Poll simulation

EstFrac equals the estimated fraction of the population supporting Clint. To conduct a second poll, click the **Continue** button. Do this several times. What do you observe? Sometimes the estimated fraction, *EstFrac*, may equal the actual population fraction, 0.5, but usually it does not. Furthermore *EstFrac* is a random variable; we cannot predict its value with certainty before the poll is conducted. Next uncheck the **Pause** checkbox and click **Continue**. After many, many repetitions click **Stop**.

The simulation histogram illustrates that sometimes 12 or more of those polled support Clint even though only half the population actually supports him. So it is entirely possible that the election is a toss-up even though 12 of the 16 individuals supported Clint in his poll. In other words, Clint cannot be completely certain that he is leading, despite the fact that 75 percent of the 16 individuals polled supported him. And where does Clint stand? The poll results do not allow him to conclude he is leading with certainty. What conclusions can Clint justifiably draw from his poll results?

To address this question, we should first do some "groundwork." We begin by considering a very simple experiment. While this experiment may appear naïve or even silly, it provides the foundation that will allow us to help Clint address his dilemma. So please be patient.

Experiment 2.2: Opinion Poll with a Sample Size of 1—An Unrealistic but Instructive Experiment

Write the name of each student in the college, the population, on a 3×5 card; then:

· Thoroughly shuffle the cards.
· Randomly draw one card.
· Ask that individual if he/she supports Clint and record the answer.
· Replace the card.

Next define the variable, v:

$$v = \begin{cases} 1 & \text{if the individual polled supports Clint} \\ 0 & \text{otherwise} \end{cases}$$

v is a random variable. We cannot determine the numerical value of v before the experiment is conducted because we cannot know beforehand whether or not the randomly selected student will support Clint or not (see figure 2.8).

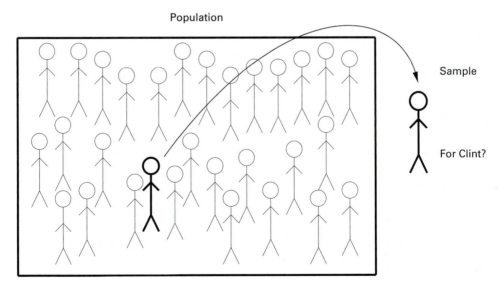

Figure 2.8
Opinion Poll simulation—Sample size of one

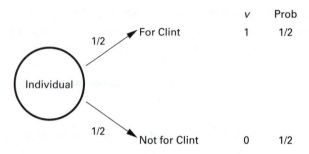

v	Prob
1	1/2
0	1/2

Figure 2.9
Probabilities for a sample size of one

Question: What, if anything, can we say about the random variable v?

Answer: We can describe its probability distribution.

To explain how we can do so, assume for the moment that the election is actually a toss-up as we did in our simulation; that is, assume that half the population supports Clint and half does not. We make this hypothetical assumption only temporarily because it will help us understand the polling process. With this assumption we can easily determine v's probability distribution. Since the individual is chosen at random, the chances that the individual will support Clint equal the chances he/she will not (see figure 2.9):

Individual's response	v	Prob[v]
For Clint	1	$\dfrac{1}{2}$
Not for Clint	0	$\dfrac{1}{2}$

We describe v's probability distribution by calculating its center (mean) and spread (variance).

2.5.3   Center of the Probability Distribution: Mean of the Random Variable

Recall the equation for the mean of a random variable:

$$\text{Mean}[v] = \sum_{\text{All } v} v \, \text{Prob}[v]$$

For each possible value, multiply the value and its probability; then sum the products. There are two possible values for v, 1 and 0:

$$v = 1 \qquad v = 0$$
$$\downarrow \qquad \downarrow$$
$$\text{Mean}[v] \;=\; 1 \times \frac{1}{2} \;+\; 0 \times \frac{1}{2}$$
$$=\; \frac{1}{2} \;+\; 0 \;=\; \frac{1}{2}$$

This makes sense, does it not? In words, the mean of a random variable equals the average of the values of the variable after the experiment is repeated many, many times. Recall that we have assumed that the election is a toss-up. Consequently after the experiment is repeated many, many times we would expect v to equal

· 1, about half of the time.
· 0, about half of the time.

After many, many repetitions of the experiment, the numerical value of v should average out to equal 1/2.

2.5.4 Spread of the Probability Distribution: Variance of the Random Variable

Recall the equation and the four steps we used to calculate the variance:

$$\text{Var}[v] = \sum_{\text{All } v} (v - \text{Mean}[v])^2 \, \text{Prob}[v]$$

For each possible value, multiply the squared deviation and its probability; then sum the products.

· For each possible value, calculate the deviation from the mean;
· Square each value's deviation;
· Multiply each value's squared deviation by the value's probability;
· Sum the products.

Individual's response	v	Mean[v]	Deviation from Mean[v]	Squared deviation	Prob[v]
For Clint	1	$\dfrac{1}{2}$	$1 - \dfrac{1}{2} = \dfrac{1}{2}$	$\dfrac{1}{4}$	$\dfrac{1}{2}$
Not for Clint	0	$\dfrac{1}{2}$	$0 - \dfrac{1}{2} = -\dfrac{1}{2}$	$\dfrac{1}{4}$	$\dfrac{1}{2}$

There are two possible values for v, 1 and 0:

$$v = 1 \qquad v = 0$$
$$\downarrow \qquad\quad \downarrow$$

$$\text{Var}[v] \;=\; \frac{1}{4} \times \frac{1}{2} \;+\; \frac{1}{4} \times \frac{1}{2}$$

$$\;=\; \frac{1}{8} \;+\; \frac{1}{8} \;=\; \frac{1}{4}$$

The variance equals 1/4.

Econometrics Lab 2.4: Polling—Checking the Mean and Variance Calculations

We will now use our Opinion Poll simulation to check our mean and variance calculations by specifying a sample size of 1. In this case the estimated fraction, *EstFrac*, and v are identical:

$$EstFrac = \frac{\text{Number for Clint}}{\text{Sample size}} = \frac{\text{Number for Clint}}{1} = v$$

Once again, we exploit the relative frequency interpretation of probability. After many, many repetitions of the experiment the distribution of the numerical values from the experiment mirrors the random variable's probability distribution:

Distribution of the
  numerical values

                        After many,
        $\downarrow$ many
                      repetitions

Probability distribution

If our calculations for the mean and variance of v's probability distribution are correct, the mean of the numerical values should equal about 0.50 and the variance about 0.25 after many, many repetitions:

Mean of the numerical   Variance of numerical values
        values

        $\downarrow$ After many, many repetitions $\downarrow$

Mean of probability   Variance of probability

distribution $= \dfrac{1}{2} = 0.50$ distribution $= \dfrac{1}{4} = 0.25$

Table 2.2
Opinion Poll simulation results—sample size of one

Actual population fraction = $ActFrac = p = \dfrac{1}{2} = 0.50$				
Equations:			Simulation:	
Mean of v's probability distribution	Variance of v's probability distribution	Simulation repetitions	Mean of numerical values of v from the experiments	Variance of numerical values of v from the experiments
$\dfrac{1}{2} = 0.50$	$\dfrac{1}{4} = 0.25$	$>1{,}000{,}000$	≈ 0.50	≈ 0.25

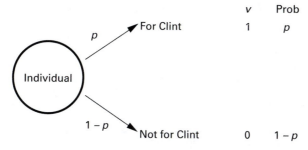

	v	Prob
For Clint	1	p
Not for Clint	0	$1 - p$

Figure 2.10
Probabilities for a sample size of one

[To access this online material, go to http://mitpress.mit.edu/westhoffeconometrics and select Lab 2.4.]

Table 2.2 confirms that after many, many repetitions the mean numerical value is about 0.50 and the variance about 0.25, which is consistent with our calculations.

Generalization

Thus far we have assumed that the portion of the population supporting Clint is 1/2. Let us now generalize our analysis by letting p equal the actual fraction of the population supporting Clint's candidacy: $ActFrac = p$. The probability that that the individual selected will support Clint just equals p, the actual fraction of the population supporting Clint (see figure 2.10):

Individual's Response	v	Prob(v)
For Clint	1	p
Not for Clint	0	$1 - p$

where

$$p = ActFrac = \text{Actual fraction of population supporting Clint}$$

$$= \frac{\text{Number of Clint supporters in student body}}{\text{Total number of students in student body}}$$

We can derive an equation for the mean of v's probability distribution and the variance of v's probability distribution.

Center of the Probability Distribution: Mean of the Random Variable

Once again, recall the equation we use to compute the mean:

$$\text{Mean}[v] = \sum\nolimits_{\text{All } v} v \, \text{Prob}[v]$$

For each possible value, multiply the value and its probability; then sum the products. As before, there are two possible values for v, 1 and 0:

$$
\begin{array}{ccc}
v = 1 & & v = 0 \\
\downarrow & & \downarrow \\
\end{array}
$$

$$
\begin{aligned}
\text{Mean}[v] &= 1 \times p \;\; + \;\; 0 \times (1 - p) \\
&= \quad p \;\;\; + \quad\;\; 0 \quad\;\; = p
\end{aligned}
$$

The mean equals p, the actual fraction of the population supporting Clint.

Spread of the Probability Distribution: Variance of the Random Variable

The equation and the four steps we used to calculate the variance are the same as before.

$$\text{Var}[v] = \sum\nolimits_{\text{All } v} (v - \text{Mean}[v])^2 \, \text{Prob}[v]$$

For each possible value, multiply the squared deviation and its probability, and sum the products—in four steps:

- For each possible value, calculate the deviation from the mean.
- Square each value's deviation.
- Multiply each value's squared deviation by the value's probability.
- Sum the products.

Individual's response	v	Mean[v]	Deviation from Mean[v]	Squared deviation	Prob[v]
For Clint	1	p	$1 - p$	$(1 - p)^2$	p
Not for Clint	0	p	$-p$	p^2	$1 - p$

Again, there are two possible values for v, 1 and 0:

$$v = 1 \qquad v = 0$$
$$\downarrow \qquad \quad \downarrow$$

$$\mathrm{Var}[v] = (1 - p)^2 \times p + p^2(1 - p)$$
$$= \qquad\qquad\qquad\qquad \text{factoring out } p(1 - p)$$
$$= \quad p(1 - p)[(1 - p) + p]$$
$$\qquad\qquad\qquad \text{simplifying}$$
$$= \qquad\quad p(1 - p)$$

The variance equals $p(1 - p)$.

Experiment 2.3: Opinion Poll with Sample Size of 2—Another Unrealistic but Instructive Experiment

In reality, we would never use a poll of only two individuals to estimate the actual fraction of the population supporting Clint. Nevertheless, analyzing such a case is instructive. Therefore let us consider an experiment in which two individuals are polled (figure 2.11). Remember, we have written the name of each student enrolled in the college on a 3×5 card.

   In the first stage:

· Thoroughly shuffle the cards.

· Randomly draw one card.

· Ask that individual if he/she supports Clint and record the answer; this yields a specific numerical value of v_1 for the random variable. v_1 equals 1 if the first individual polled supports Clint; 0 otherwise.

· Replace the card.

   In the second stage, the procedure is repeated:

· Thoroughly shuffle the cards.

· Randomly draw one card.

· Ask that individual if he/she supports Clint and record the answer; this yields a specific numerical value of v_2 for the random variable. v_2 equals 1 if the second individual polled supports Clint; 0 otherwise.

· Replace the card.

Last, calculate the fraction of those polled supporting Clint.

Estimated fraction of population supporting Clint $= EstFrac = \dfrac{v_1 + v_2}{2} = \dfrac{1}{2}(v_1 + v_2)$

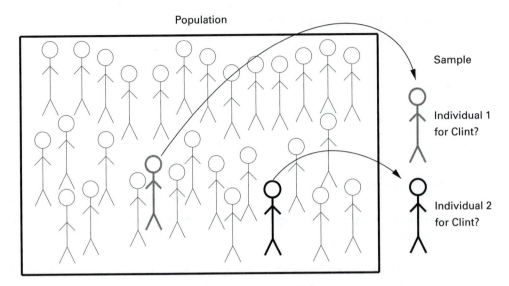

Population

Sample

Individual 1
for Clint?

Individual 2
for Clint?

Figure 2.11
Opinion Poll simulation—Sample size of two

The estimated fraction of the population supporting Clint, *EstFrac*, is a random variable. We cannot determine with certainty the numerical value of the estimated fraction, *EstFrac*, before the experiment is conducted.

Question: What can we say about the random variable *EstFrac*?

Answer: We can describe its probability distribution.

The probability distribution reports the likelihood of each possible outcome. We can describe the probability distribution by calculating its center (mean) and spread (variance).

Center of the Probability Distribution: Mean of the Random Variable
Recall that

$$\text{Mean}[\textbf{\textit{EstFrac}}] = \text{Mean}\left[\frac{1}{2}(v_1 + v_2)\right]$$

What do we know that would help us calculate the mean? We know the means of v_1 and v_2; also we know about the arithmetic of means.

That is, we already have the means of the random variables v_1 and v_2:

• The first stage of the experiment is identical to the previous experiment in which only one card is drawn; consequently

$$\text{Mean}[v_1] = \text{Mean}[v] = p$$

where

$p = ActFrac =$ Actual fraction of population supporting Clint

$$= \frac{\text{Number of Clint supporters in student body}}{\text{Total number of students in student body}}$$

• Since the first card drawn is replaced, the second stage of the experiment is also identical to the previous experiment:

$\text{Mean}[v_2] = \text{Mean}[v] = p$

Next let us review the arithmetic of means:

• $\text{Mean}[cx] = c\ \text{Mean}[x]$
• $\text{Mean}[x + y] = \text{Mean}[x] + \text{Mean}[y]$

We will focus on

$$\text{Mean}\left[\frac{1}{2}(v_1 + v_2)\right]$$

and apply the arithmetic of means:

$$\text{Mean}[cx] = c\ \text{Mean}[x] \quad \text{Mean}[x + y] = \text{Mean}[x] + \text{Mean}[y]$$

$$\downarrow \qquad\qquad\qquad\qquad \downarrow$$

$$\text{Mean}\left[\frac{1}{2}(v_1 + v_2)\right] = \frac{1}{2}\text{Mean}[(v_1 + v_2)] = \frac{1}{2}[\text{Mean}[v_1] + \text{Mean}[v_2]]$$

$\text{Mean}[v_1] = \text{Mean}[v_2] = p$

$$= \frac{1}{2}[p + p]$$

simplifying

$$= \frac{1}{2}[2p]$$

$$= p$$

Spread of the Probability Distribution: Variance of the Random Variable

What do we know that would help us calculate the variance? We know the variances of v_1 and v_2; also we know about the arithmetic of variances:

$$\text{Var}[\boldsymbol{EstFrac}] = \text{Var}\left[\frac{1}{2}(v_1 + v_2)\right]$$

That is, we already have the variances of the random variables v_1 and v_2:

• The first stage of the experiment is identical to the previous experiment in which only one card was drawn; consequently

$$\text{Var}[v_1] = \text{Var}[v] = p(1-p)$$

• Since the first card drawn is replaced, the second stage of the experiment is also identical to the previous experiment:

$$\text{Var}[v_2] = \text{Var}[v] = p(1-p)$$

Let us review the arithmetic of variances:

• $\text{Var}[cx] = c^2 \, \text{Var}[x]$

• $\text{Var}[x+y] = \text{Var}[x] + 2\,\text{Cov}[x,y] + \text{Var}[y]$

Now focus on the covariance of v_1 and v_2, $\text{Cov}[v_1, v_2]$. The covariance tells us whether the variables are correlated or independent. On the one hand, when two variables are correlated their covariance is nonzero; knowing the value of one variable helps us predict the value of the other. On the other hand, when two variables are independent their covariance equals zero; knowing the value of one does not help us predict the other.

In this case, v_1 and v_2 are independent and their covariance equals 0. Let us explain why. Since the first card drawn is replaced, whether or not the first voter polled supports Clint does not affect the probability that the second voter will support Clint. Regardless of whether or not the first voter polled supported Clint, the probability that the second voter will support Clint is p, the actual population fraction:

$$p = \textit{ActFrac} = \text{Actual fraction of population supporting Clint}$$

$$= \frac{\text{Number of Clint supporters in student body}}{\text{Total number of students in student body}}$$

More formally, the numerical value of v_1 does not affect v_2's probability distribution, and vice versa. Consequently the two random variables, v_1 and v_2, are independent and their covariance equals 0:

$$\text{Cov}[v_1, v_2] = 0$$

Focus on

$$\text{Var}\left[\frac{1}{2}(v_1 + v_2)\right]$$

and apply all this:

$$\text{Var}[cx] = c^2 \, \text{Var}[x] \qquad \text{Var}[x+y] = \text{Var}[x] + 2 \, \text{Cov}[x,y] + \text{Var}[y]$$

$$\downarrow \qquad\qquad\qquad\qquad \downarrow$$

$$\text{Mean}\left[\frac{1}{2}(v_1+v_2)\right] = \frac{1}{4}\text{Var}[(v_1+v_2)] = \frac{1}{4}[\text{Var}[v_1] + 2\,\text{Cov}[v_1+v_2] + \text{Var}[v_2]]$$

$$\text{Cov}[v_1, v_2] = 0$$

$$= \frac{1}{4}[\text{Var}[v_1] + \text{Var}[v_2]]$$

$$\text{Var}[v_1] = \text{Var}[v_2] = p(1-p)$$

$$= \frac{1}{4}[p(1-p) + p(1-p)]$$

simplifying

$$= \frac{1}{4}[2p(1-p)]$$

$$= \frac{p(1-p)}{2}$$

Econometrics Lab 2.5: Polling—Checking the Mean and Variance Calculations

As before, we can use the simulation to check the equations we just derived by exploiting the relative frequency interpretation of probability. When the experiment is repeated many, many times, the relative frequency of each outcome equals its probability. After many, many repetitions the distribution of the numerical values from all the repetitions mirrors the probability distribution:

Distribution of the
numerical values

After many,
$$\downarrow$$
many
repetitions

Probability distribution

Applying this to the mean and variance obtains

Mean of the numerical
values

Variance of numerical values

After many,
↓   many   ↓
repetitions

Mean of probability
distribution $= p$

Variance of probability
distribution $= \dfrac{p(1-p)}{2}$

To check the equations, we will specify a sample size of 2 and select an actual population fraction of 0.50. Using the equations we derived, the mean of the estimated fraction's probability distribution should be 0.50 and the variance should be 0.125:

$$\text{Mean}[\textbf{\textit{EstFrac}}] = p = 0.50$$

$$\text{Var}[\textbf{\textit{EstFrac}}] = \frac{p(1-p)}{2} = \frac{\frac{1}{2}\left(1-\frac{1}{2}\right)}{2} = \frac{\frac{1}{2}\times\frac{1}{2}}{2} = \frac{1}{8} = 0.125$$

[To access this online material, go to http://mitpress.mit.edu/westhoffeconometrics and select Lab 2.5.]

Be certain the simulation's Pause checkbox is cleared. Click **Start** and then, after many, many repetitions, click **Stop**.

The simulation results (table 2.3) suggest that our equations are correct. After many, many repetitions the mean (average) of the numerical values equals the mean of the probability distribution, 0.50. Similarly, the variance of the numerical values equals the variance of the probability distribution, 0.125.

Table 2.3
Opinion Poll simulation results—sample size of two

Actual population fraction $= ActFrac = p = \dfrac{1}{2} = 0.50$					
	Equations			Simulation	
Sample size	Mean of EstFrac's probability distribution	Variance of EstFrac's probability distribution	Simulation repetitions	Mean of numerical values of EstFrac from the experiments	Variance of numerical values of EstFrac from the experiments
2	$\dfrac{1}{2} = 0.50$	$\dfrac{1}{8} = 0.125$	>1,000,000	≈0.50	≈0.125

2.6   Mean, Variance, and Covariance: Data Variables and Random Variables

In this chapter we extended the notions of mean, variance, and covariance that we introduced in chapter 1 from data variables to random variables. The mean and variance describe the distribution of a single variable. The mean depicts the center of a variable's distribution; the variance depicts the distribution spread. In the case of a data variable, the distribution is illustrated by a histogram; consequently the mean and variance describe the center and spread of the data variable's histogram. In the case of a random variable, mean and variance describe the center and spread of the random variable's probability distribution.

Covariance quantifies the notion of how two variables are related. When two data variables are uncorrelated, they are independent; the value of one variable does not help us predict the value of the other. In the case of independent random variables, the value of one variable does not affect the probability distribution of the other variable and their covariance equals 0.

Chapter 2 Review Questions

1. What is a random process?
2. What information does the probability of an outcome provide?
3. What is a random variable?
4. What information does a random variable's probability distribution provide?
5. When dealing with a random variable what is the
    a. bad news; that is, what do we not know about the random variable?
    b. good news; that is, what do we often know about the random variable?
6. What is the relative frequency interpretation of probability?
7. Focus on the probability distribution of a random variable. What information does its
    a. mean provide?
    b. variance provide?

Chapter 2 Exercises

1. Suppose that you have a deck composed of the following 10 cards:

2♠   2♥   2♦   2♣   3♠

3♥   3♦   4♠   4♥   5♦

Consider the following experiment:

· Thoroughly shuffle the deck of 10 cards.

· Draw one card.

· Replace the card drawn.

a. Let v equal the value on the card drawn. Define the term "random variable." Is v a random variable? Explain.

b. What is the probability distribution of the random variable v? That is, what is the probability that v equals

i. 2?

ii. 3?

iii. 4?

iv. 5?

c. Recall the equation for the mean and variance of the random variable v's probability distribution:

$$\text{Mean}[v] = \sum\nolimits_{\text{All } v} v \, \text{Prob}[v], \quad \text{Var}[v] = \sum\nolimits_{\text{All } v} (v - \text{Mean}[v])^2 \text{Prob}[v]$$

Using these equations, calculate the mean (expected value) and variance of the random variable v's probability distribution.

Use the relative frequency interpretation of probability to check your answers to parts b and c by clicking on the following link:

[To access this online material, go to http://mitpress.mit.edu/westhoffeconometrics and select Lab 2E.1.]

d. After the experiment is repeated many, many times, does the distribution of numerical values from the experiments mirror the random variable v's probability distribution?

e. After the experiment is repeated many, many times, how are the mean and variance of the random variable v's probability distribution related to the mean and variance of the numerical values?

2. Consider the following experiment. Using the same deck from question 1,

· Thoroughly shuffle the deck of 10 cards.

· Draw one card and record its value.

· Replace the card drawn.

· Thoroughly shuffle the deck of 10 cards.

· Draw a second card and record its value.

Let

v_1 = value of the first card drawn

v_2 = value of the second card drawn

   a. What are the mean and variance of the random variable v_1? What are the mean and variance of the random variable v_2?

   b. Are the random variables v_1 and v_2 independent? That is, would knowing the value of the first card drawn affect the probability distribution for the value of the second card drawn?

   c. Review the arithmetic of means and variances. Using your answers to part a, calculate the mean (expected value) and variance of the sum of the two random variables, $v_1 + v_2$.

   d. What are the mean (expected value) and variance of the average of the two random variables, $(v_1 + v_2)/2$?

3. Consider the following experiment. Using the same deck from questions 1 and 2,

· Thoroughly shuffle the deck of 10 cards.

· Draw one card and record its value.

· Do *not* replace the card drawn.

· Thoroughly shuffle the remaining 9 cards.

· Draw a second card and record its value.

(Note: This experiment differs from the earlier one in that the first card drawn is not replaced.) As before, let

v_1 = value of the first card drawn

v_2 = value of the second card drawn

   a. Calculate the following probabilities:

      i. Prob[$v_2 = 2$ if $v_1 = 2$]: _____

      ii. Prob[$v_2 = 2$ if $v_1 \neq 2$]: _____

   b. Are the random variables v_1 and v_2 independent? Explain.

Next suppose that instead of 10 cards, the deck contains 10,000 cards: 4,000 2's, 3,000 3's, 2,000 4's, and 1,000 5's. Consider this new experiment:

· Thoroughly shuffle the deck of 10,000 cards.

· Draw one card and record its value.

· Do *not* replace the card drawn.

· Thoroughly shuffle the remaining 9,999 cards.

· Draw a second card and record its value.

c. Calculate the following probabilities:

   i. $\text{Prob}[v_2 = 2 \text{ IF } v_1 = 2]$: _____

   ii. $\text{Prob}[v_2 = 2 \text{ IF } v_1 \neq 2]$: _____

Compare the consequences of not replacing the first card drawn with the deck of 10 cards versus the deck of 10,000.

d. Compare your answers to parts a and c. As the population size increases (i.e., as the number of cards in the deck increases), is the probability of drawing a 2 on the second draw affected more or less by whether or not a 2 is drawn on the first draw?

e. Suppose that a student assumes v_1 and v_2 to be independent even though the first card is not replaced. As the population size increases, would this assumption become a better or worse approximation of reality?

f. In view of the fact that there are more than 100 million American voters, should a professional pollster of American sentiments worry about "the replacement issue?"

4. A European roulette wheel has 37 slots around its perimeter (see figure 2.12). The slots are numbered 1 through 36 and 0. You can place a bet on the roulette board.

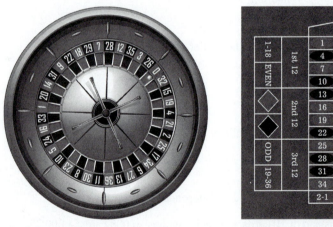

Figure 2.12
Game of roulette (© Can Stock Photo Inc./RaStudio and © Can Stock Photo Inc./oorka)

Many different types of bets can be made. You can bet on a single number, a row of numbers, a column of numbers, a set of twelve numbers, all red numbers, all black numbers, all even numbers, or all odd numbers. (Note: The rows, columns, twelves, reds, blacks, evens, and odds do not include 0.) Once all bets are placed, the roulette wheel is spun and a ball is dropped into the spinning wheel. Initially, the ball bounces wildly around the wheel, but eventually, it settles into one of the 37 slots. If this is a slot that you bet on, you win; the amount of winnings depends on the type of bet you made:

Type of bet	Gross winnings from a $1 bet
Single number	$36
Single row	$12
Single column	$3
Set of twelve	$3
All reds	$2
All blacks	$2
All evens	$2
All odds	$2

If the ball does not settle into a slot you bet on, you lose your bet. Suppose that you always place a $1 bet. Let

v = Your net winnings = Your gross winnings − $1

Roulette wheels are precisely balanced so that the ball is equally likely to land in each of the 37 slots.

a. Suppose that you place a $1 bet on the first set of twelve numbers.

i. If the ball ends up in one of the first 12 slots, what will v equal? What is the probability of this scenario?

ii. If the ball does not end up in one of the first 12 slots, what will v equal? What is the probability of this scenario?

iii. In this scenario, what are the mean (expected value) and variance of v?

b. Suppose that you place a $1 bet on red.

i. If the ball ends up in one of the 18 red slots, what will v equal? What is the probability of this scenario?

ii. If the ball does not end up in one of the 18 red slots, what will v equal? What is the probability of this scenario?

iii. In this scenario, what are the mean (expected value) and variance of v?

c. Compare the two bets. How are they similar? How are they different?

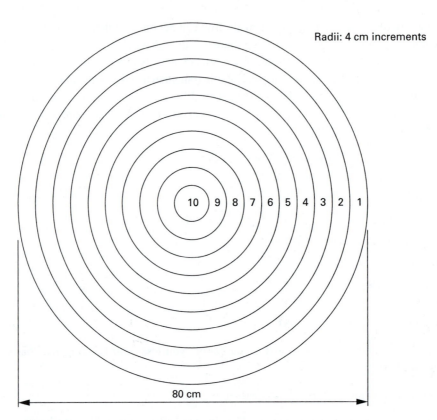

Radii: 4 cm increments

10 9 8 7 6 5 4 3 2 1

80 cm

Figure 2.13
Assignment of archery points

5. The International Archery Federation establishes the rules for archery competitions. The Federation permits the distance between the competitor and the target as well as the size of the target to vary from competition to competition. Distance varies from 18 to 90 meters; the size of the target varies from 40 to 122 centimeters in diameter. Say a friend, Archie, is participating in a 60-meter contest. At a distance of 60 meters, the Federation specifies a target 80 centimeters in diameter. At this distance Archie, an excellent archer, always shoots his arrows within 20 centimeters of the target's center. Figure 2.13 described how points are assigned:

· 10 points if the arrow strikes within 4 centimeters of the target's center.

· 9 points if the arrow strikes between 4 and 8 centimeters of the target's center.

· 8 points if the arrow strikes between 8 and 12 centimeters of the target's center.

· 7 points if the arrow strikes between 12 and 16 centimeters of the target's center.

· 6 points if the arrow strikes between 16 and 20 centimeters of the target's center.

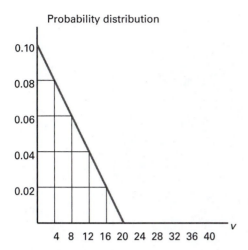

Figure 2.14
Probability distribution of v, the distance of Archie's arrow from the target center

- 5 points if the arrow strikes between 20 and 24 centimeters of the target's center.
- 4 points if the arrow strikes between 24 and 28 centimeters of the target's center.
- 3 points if the arrow strikes between 28 and 32 centimeters of the target's center.
- 2 points if the arrow strikes between 32 and 36 centimeters of the target's center.
- 1 points if the arrow strikes between 36 and 40 centimeters of the target's center.

Figure 2.14 describes the probability distribution of v, the distance of Archie's arrow from the target center; v is the distance of Archie's arrow from the target's center.

    a. Explain why the area beneath Archie's probability distribution must equal 1.

    b. What is the probability that Archie will score at least 6 points?

    c. What is the probability that Archie will score 10 points?

    d. What is the probability that Archie will score 9 points?

    e. What is the probability that Archie will score 7 or 8 points?

6. Recall our friend Dan Duffer who consistently hits 200 yard drives from the tee. Also recall that Dan is not consistent "laterally"; his drive can land as far as 40 yards to the left or right of his target point. Here v is the distance from Dan's target point (see figure 2.15).

Dan has had a tough day on the course and has lost many golf balls. He only has one ball left and wants to finish the round. Accordingly he wants to reduce the chances of driving his last ball into the lake. So, instead of choosing a target point at the middle of the fairway, as indicated in the figure to the right, he contemplates aiming his drive 8 yards to the left of the fairway midpoint.

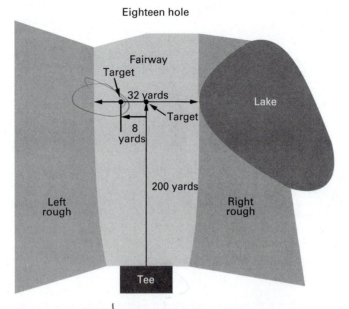

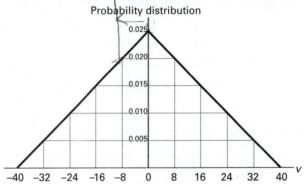

Figure 2.15
Dan Duffer's eighteenth hole

a. Revise and realign the figure to the right to reflect the new target point that Dan is contemplating.

Based on this new target point:

b. What is the probability that his drive will land in the lake? _____

c. What is the probability that his drive will land in the left rough? _____

d. What is the probability that his drive will land in the fairway? _____

7. Joe passes through one traffic light on his daily commute to work. The traffic department has set up the traffic light on a one minute cycle:

Red   30 seconds

Yellow   5 seconds

Green   25 seconds

Joe, a safe driver, decides whether or not to brake for the traffic light when he is 10 yards from the light. If the light is red or yellow, he brakes; otherwise, he continues on.

   a. When Joe makes his brake/continue decision next Monday, what is the probability that the light will be

      i. Red? _____

      ii. Yellow? _____

      iii. Green? _____

   b. What is the probability that his brake/continue decision next Monday will be

      i. Brake? _____

      ii. Continue? _____

   c. What is the probability that Joe will not stop at the light for the next five workdays during his daily commute to work?

8. To avoid studying, you and your roommate decide to play the following game:

• Thoroughly shuffle your roommate's standard deck of fifty-two cards: 13 spades, 13 hearts, 13 diamonds, and 13 clubs.

• Draw one card.

• If the card drawn is red, you win $1 from your roommate; if the card drawn is black, you lose a $1.

• Replace the card drawn.

   Let v equal your net winnings from the game:

• If a red card is drawn, v will equal +1.

• If a black card is drawn, v will equal −1.

   a. What are the following probabilities?

      i. $\text{Prob}[v = +1] =$ _____

      ii. $\text{Prob}[v = -1] =$ _____

   b. What do the mean and variance of v equal?

      i. $\text{Mean}[v] =$ _____

      ii. $\text{Var}[v] =$ _____

After you play the game once, you both decide to play it again. Let us modify the notation to reflect this:

v_1 = your net winnings from the first repetition of the game

v_2 = your net winnings from the second repetition of the game

v_3 = your net winnings from the third repetition of the game

$\vdots$

    c. Are the random variables v_1 and v_2 correlated or independent? Explain.

    d. Is any one v_t correlated with another?

You and your roommate play the game eighteen times. Let TNW equal your total net winnings; that is,

$$TNW = v_1 + v_2 + \ldots + v_{18}$$

    e. What do the mean and variance of *TNW* equal?

      i. Mean[***TNW***] = ____

      ii. Var[***TNW***] = ____

3 Interval Estimates and the Central Limit Theorem

Chapter 3 Outline

Chapter 3 Prep Questions

1. Consider a random process and the associated random variable.

    a. What do we mean by a random variable?

    b. When dealing with a random variable:

        i. What do we never know?

        ii. What can we hope to know?

2. Apply the arithmetic of means to show that

$$\text{Mean}\left[\frac{1}{T}(v_1 + v_2 + \ldots + v_T)\right] = p$$

whenever $\text{Mean}[v_t] = p$ for each t; that is, $\text{Mean}[v_1] = \text{Mean}[v_2] = \ldots = \text{Mean}[v_T] = p$.

3. Apply the arithmetic of variances to show that

$$\text{Var}\left[\frac{1}{T}(v_1 + v_2 + \ldots + v_T)\right] = \frac{p(1-p)}{T}$$

Whenever

• $\text{Var}[v_t] = p(1-p)$ for each t; that is, $\text{Var}[v_1] = \text{Var}[v_2] = \ldots = \text{Var}[v_T] = p(1-p)$

and

• v_t's are independent; that is, all the covariances equal 0.

4. What is the relative frequency interpretation of probability?

5. What two concepts have we introduced to describe a probability distribution?

6. Would you have more confidence in a poll that queries a small number of individuals or a poll that queries a large number?

3.1   Review

3.1.1   Random Variables

Remember, random variables bring both bad and good news. Before the experiment is conducted:

Bad news: What we do not know: on the one hand, we cannot determine the numerical value of the random variable with certainty.

Good news: What we do know: on the other hand, we can often calculate the random variable's probability distribution telling us how likely it is for the random variable to equal each of its possible numerical values.

3.1.2   Relative Frequency Interpretation of Probability

After many, many repetitions of the experiment the distribution of the numerical values from the experiments mirrors the random variable's probability distribution.

3.2   Populations, Samples, Estimation Procedures, and the Estimate's Probability Distribution

Polling procedures use information gathered from a sample of the population to draw inferences about the entire population. In the previous chapter we considered two unrealistic samples sizes, a sample size of 1 and a sample size of 2. Common sense suggests that such small samples would not be helpful in drawing inferences about an entire population. We considered these unrealistic sample sizes to lay the groundwork for realistic ones. We are now prepared to analyze the general case in which the sample size equals T. Let us return to our friend Clint who is running for president of his student body. Consider the following experiment:

Experiment 3.1: Opinion Poll with a Sample Size of T

Write the names of every individual in the population on a card. Perform the following procedure T times:

· Thoroughly shuffle the cards.

· Randomly draw one card.

· Ask that individual if he/she supports Clint; the individual's answer determines the numerical value of v_t: v_t equals 1 if the tth individual polled supports Clint; 0 otherwise.

· Replace the card.

Calculate the fraction of those polled supporting Clint:

$$EstFrac = \frac{v_1 + v_2 + \ldots + v_T}{T}$$

$$= \frac{1}{T}(v_1 + v_2 + \ldots + v_T)$$

where T = sample size. The estimated fraction of the population supporting Clint, *EstFrac*, is a random variable. We cannot determine the numerical value of the estimated fraction, *EstFrac*, with certainty before the experiment is conducted.

Question: What can we say about the random variable *EstFrac*?

Answer: We can describe the center and spread of *EstFrac*'s probability distribution by calculating its mean and variance.

Using the same logic as we applied in chapter 2, we know the following:

- $\text{Mean}[v_t] = p$ for each t; that is, $\text{Mean}[v_1] = \text{Mean}[v_2] = \ldots = \text{Mean}[v_T] = p$.
- $\text{Var}[v_t] = p(1-p)$ for each t; that is, $\text{Var}[v_1] = \text{Var}[v_2] = \ldots = \text{Var}[v_T] = p(1-p)$, where $p = ActFrac$ = actual fraction of the population supporting Clint.
- v_t's are independent; hence their covariances equal 0.

3.2.1   Measure of the Probability Distribution Center: Mean of the Random Variable

First, consider the mean. Apply the arithmetic of means and what we know about the v_t's:

$$\text{Mean}[\boldsymbol{EstFrac}] = \text{Mean}\left[\frac{1}{T}(v_1 + v_2 + \ldots + v_T)\right]$$

since $\text{Mean}[c\boldsymbol{x}] = c\,\text{Mean}[\boldsymbol{x}]$

$$= \frac{1}{T}\text{Mean}[(v_1 + v_2 + \ldots + v_T)]$$

since $\text{Mean}[\boldsymbol{x} + \boldsymbol{y}] = \text{Mean}[\boldsymbol{x}] + \text{Mean}[\boldsymbol{y}]$

$$= \frac{1}{T}(\text{Mean}[v_1] + \text{Mean}[v_2] + \ldots + \text{Mean}[v_T])$$

$$= \frac{1}{T}(p + p + \ldots + p)$$

How many p terms are there? A total of T.

$$= \frac{1}{T}(T \times p)$$

Simplifying obtains

$$= p$$

3.2.2   Measure of the Probability Distribution Spread: Variance of the Random Variable

Next, focus on the variance. Apply the arithmetic of variances and what we know about the v_t's:

$$\text{Var}[\textbf{\textit{EstFrac}}] = \text{Var}\left[\frac{1}{T}(v_1 + v_2 + \ldots + v_T)\right]$$

since $\text{Var}[cx] = c^2\text{Var}[x]$

$$= \frac{1}{T^2}\text{Var}\left[(v_1 + v_2 + \ldots + v_T)\right]$$

since $\text{Var}[x + y] = \text{Var}[x] + \text{Var}[y]$ when x and y are independent; hence the covariances are all 0.

$$= \frac{1}{T^2}(\text{Var}[v_1] + \text{Var}[v_2] + \ldots + \text{Var}[v_T])$$

since $\text{Var}[v_1] = \text{Var}[v_2] = \ldots = \text{Var}[v_T] = p(1 - p)$

$$= \frac{1}{T^2}\left[p(1-p) + p(1-p) + \ldots + p(1-p)\right]$$

How many $p(1 - p)$ terms are there? A total of T.

$$= \frac{1}{T^2}\left[T \times p(1-p)\right]$$

Simplifying obtains

$$= \frac{p(1-p)}{T}$$

To summarize:

$$\text{Mean}[\textbf{\textit{EstFrac}}] = p, \quad \text{Var}[\textbf{\textit{EstFrac}}] = \frac{p(1-p)}{T}$$

where $p = ActFrac$ = actual fraction of the population supporting Clint and T = sample size.

Econometrics Lab 3.1: Polling—Checking the Mean and Variance Equations

Once again, we will exploit the relative frequency interpretation of probability to check the equations for the mean and variance of the estimated fraction's probability distribution:

Distribution of the
numerical values

After many,

$\downarrow$ many

repetitions

Probability distribution

We just derived the mean and variance of the estimated fraction's probability distribution:

$$\text{Mean}[\textit{EstFrac}] = p, \quad \text{Var}[\textit{EstFrac}] = \frac{p(1-p)}{T}$$

where $p = \textit{ActFrac}$ and T = sample size. Consequently after many, many repetitions the mean of these numerical values should equal approximately p, the actual fraction of the population that supports Clint, and the variance should equal approximately $p(1-p)/T$.

In the simulation we begin by specifying the fraction of the population supporting Clint. We could choose any actual population fraction; for purposes of illustration we choose 1/2 here.

$$\text{Actual fraction of the population supporting Clint} = \textit{ActFrac} = \frac{1}{2} = 0.50$$

$$\text{Mean}[\textit{EstFrac}] = p = \frac{1}{2} = 0.50, \quad \text{Var}[\textit{EstFrac}] = \frac{\frac{1}{2}\left(1-\frac{1}{2}\right)}{T} = \frac{\frac{1}{2}\times\frac{1}{2}}{T} = \frac{\frac{1}{4}}{T} = \frac{1}{4T}$$

We will now use our simulation to consider different sample sizes, different T's.

[To access this online material, go to http://mitpress.mit.edu/westhoffeconometrics and select Lab 3.1.]

Our simulation results appearing in table 3.1 are consistent with the equations we derived. After many, many repetitions the means of the numerical values equal the means of the estimated fraction's probability distribution. The same is true for the variances.

Public opinion polls use procedures very similar to that described in our experiment. A specific number of people are asked who or what they support and then the results are reported. We can think of a poll as one repetition of our experiment. Pollsters use the numerical value of the estimated fraction from one repetition of the experiment to estimate the actual fraction. But how reliable is such an estimate? We will now show that the reliability of an estimate depends on the mean and variance of the estimate's probability distribution.

Table 3.1
Opinion Poll simulation results with selected sample sizes

	Actual population fraction = *ActFrac* = *p* = 0.50				
	Equations			Simulation	
Sample size	Mean of *EstFrac*'s probability distribution	Variance of *EstFrac*'s probability distribution	Simulation repetitions	Mean (average) of numerical values of *EstFrac* from the experiments	Variance of numerical values of *EstFrac* from the experiments
1	$\frac{1}{2} = 0.50$	$\frac{1}{4} = 0.25$	>1,000,000	≈0.50	≈0.25
2	$\frac{1}{2} = 0.50$	$\frac{1}{8} = 0.125$	>1,000,000	≈0.50	≈0.125
25	$\frac{1}{2} = 0.50$	$\frac{1}{100} = 0.01$	>1,000,000	≈0.50	≈0.01
100	$\frac{1}{2} = 0.50$	$\frac{1}{400} = 0.0025$	>1,000,000	≈0.50	≈0.0025
400	$\frac{1}{2} = 0.50$	$\frac{1}{1,600} = 0.000625$	>1,000,000	≈0.50	≈0.000625

3.2.3   Why Is the Mean of the Estimate's Probability Distribution Important? Biased and Unbiased Estimation Procedures

Recall Clint's poll in which 12 of the 16 individuals queried supported him. The estimated fraction, *EstFrac*, equaled 0.75:

$$EstFrac = \frac{12}{16} = 0.75$$

In chapter 2 we used our Opinion Poll simulation to show that this poll result did not prove with certainty that the actual fraction of the population supporting Clint exceeded 0.50. In general, we observed that while it is possible for the estimated fraction to equal the actual population fraction, it is more likely for the estimated fraction to be greater than or less than the actual fraction. In other words, we cannot expect the estimated fraction from a single poll to equal the actual population fraction.

What then can we conclude? We know that the estimated fraction is a random variable. While we cannot determine its numerical value with certainty before the experiment is conducted, we can describe its probability distribution. A random variable's mean describes the center of its probability distribution. Using a little algebra, we showed that the mean of the estimated fraction's probability distribution equals the actual fraction of the population supporting Clint. Whenever the mean of an estimate's probability distribution equals the actual value, the estimation procedure is **unbiased** as illustrated in figure 3.1:

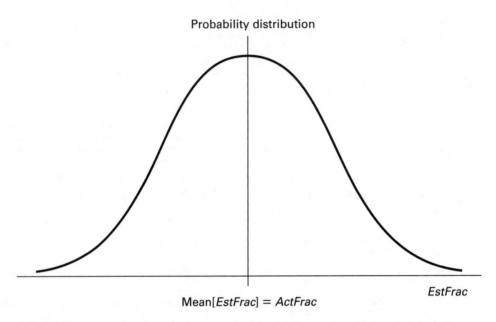

Probability distribution

Mean[*EstFrac*] = *ActFrac*

EstFrac

Figure 3.1
Probability distribution of *EstFrac* values

Unbiased estimation procedure

↓

Mean[**EstFrac**] = Actual population fraction = *ActFrac*

Being unbiased is a very desirable property. An unbiased procedure does not systematically underestimate or overestimate the actual fraction of the population supporting Clint.

By exploiting the relative frequency interpretation of probability we can use the simulations we just completed to confirm that Clint's estimation procedure is unbiased.

Relative frequency interpretation of probability:
After many, many repetitions, the distribution of the
numerical values mirrors the probability distribution.

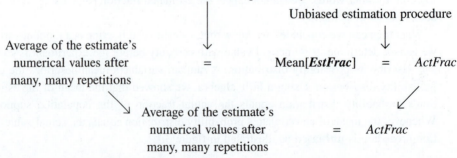

Unbiased estimation procedure

Average of the estimate's
numerical values after   =   Mean[**EstFrac**]   =   *ActFrac*
many, many repetitions

Average of the estimate's
numerical values after   =   *ActFrac*
many, many repetitions

When the estimation procedure is unbiased, the average of the numerical values of the estimated fractions equaled the actual population fraction after many, many repetitions. Table 3.1 reports that this is true.

We can obtain even more intuition about unbiased estimation procedures when the probability distribution of the estimate is symmetric. In this case the chances that the estimated fraction will be less than the actual population fraction in one repetition equal the chances that the estimated fraction will be greater than the actual fraction. We will use a simulation to illustrate this.

Econometrics Lab 3.2: Polling—Illustrating the Importance of the Mean

[To access this online material, go to http://mitpress.mit.edu/westhoffeconometrics and select Lab 3.2.]

Figure 3.2 illustrates the defaults. An actual population fraction of 0.50 and a sample size of 100 are specified. Two new lists appear in the lower left of the window: a From list and a To

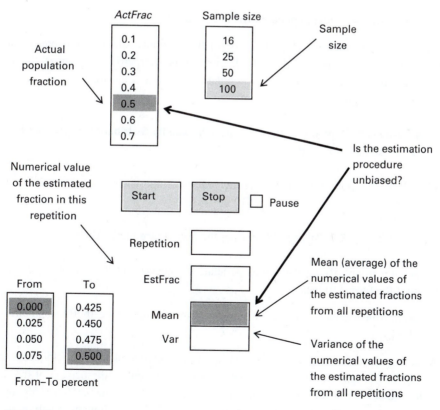

Figure 3.2
Opinion Poll simulation

list. By default, a From value of .000 and a To value of .500 are selected. The From–To Percent line reports the percentage of repetitions in which the estimated fraction lies between the From value, .000, and the To value, .500.

Check to be certain that the simulation is calculating the From–To Percent correctly by clicking **Start** and then **Continue** a few times. Then clear the Pause box and click **Continue**. After many, many repetitions click **Stop**. The From–To Percent equals approximately 50 percent. The estimates in approximately 50 percent of the repetitions are less than 0.5, the actual value; consequently approximately 50 percent of the repetitions are greater than 0.5, the actual value. The chances that the estimated fraction will be less than the actual population fraction in one repetition equal the chances that the estimated fraction will be greater than the actual fraction.

To summarize, there are two important points to make about Clint's poll:

Bad news: We cannot expect the estimated fraction from Clint's poll, 0.75, to equal the actual population fraction.

Good news: The estimation procedure that Clint used is unbiased. The mean of the estimated fraction's probability distribution equals the actual population fraction:

Mean[*EstFrac*] = Actual population fraction = *ActFrac*

The estimation procedure does not systematically underestimate or overestimate the actual population fraction. If the probability distribution is symmetric, the chances that the estimated fraction will be less than the actual population fraction equal the chances that the estimated fraction will be greater.

3.2.4   Why Is the Variance of the Estimate's Probability Distribution Important? Reliability of Unbiased Estimation Procedures

We will use the polling simulation to illustrate the importance of the probability distribution's variance.

Econometrics Lab 3.3: Polling—Illustrating the Importance of the Variance

In addition to specifying the actual population fraction and the sample size, the simulation includes the From–To lists.

[To access this online material, go to http://mitpress.mit.edu/westhoffeconometrics and select Lab 3.3.]

As before, the actual population fraction equals 0.50 by default. Select 0.450 from the From list and 0.550 from the To list. The simulation will now calculate the percent of the repetitions in which the numerical value of the estimated fraction lies within the 0.450 to 0.550 interval. Since we have specified the actual population fraction to be 0.50, the simulation will report the percent

Table 3.2
Opinion Poll From–To simulation results

	Actual population fraction = ActFrac = p = 0.50 ⇒ Mean[EstFrac] = 0.50		
Sample Size	Variance of *EstFrac*'s probability distribution	Simulation repetitions	Simulation: Percent of repetitions in which the numerical value of *EstFrac* lies between 0.45 and 0.55
25	0.01	>1,000,000	≈39
100	0.0025	>1,000,000	≈69
400	0.000625	>1,000,000	≈95

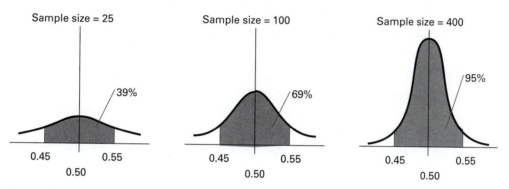

Figure 3.3
Histograms of estimated fraction numerical values

of repetitions in which the numerical value of the estimate fraction lies within 0.05 of the actual fraction. Initially a sample size of 25 is selected. Note that the Pause checkbox is cleared. Click **Start** and then after many, many repetitions click **Stop**. Next consider sample sizes of 100 and 400. Table 3.2 reports the results for the three sample sizes:

When the sample size is 25, the numerical value of the estimated fraction falls within 0.05 of the actual population fraction in about 39 percent of the repetitions. When the sample size is 100, the numerical value of the estimated fraction falls within 0.05 of the actual population fraction in about 69 percent of the repetitions. When the sample size is 400, the numerical value of the estimated fraction falls within 0.05 of the actual population fraction in about 95 percent of the repetitions (see figure 3.3).

The variance plays the key role here. On the one hand, when the variance is large, the distribution is "spread out"; the numerical value of the estimated fraction falls within 0.05 of the actual fraction relatively infrequently. On the other hand, when the variance is small, the distribution is tightly "cropped" around the actual population fraction, 0.50; consequently the numerical value of the estimated fraction falls within 0.05 of the actual population fraction more frequently.

3.3   Interval Estimates

We can now exploit the relative frequency interpretation of probability to obtain a quantitative sense of how much confidence we should have in the results of a single opinion poll. We do so by considering the following interval estimate question:

Interval estimate question: What is the probability that the numerical value of the estimated fraction, *EstFrac*, from one repetition of the experiment lies within ___ of the actual population fraction, *ActFrac*? _____

Since we are focusing on the interval from 0.450 to 0.550 and the actual population fraction is specified as 0.50, we can enter 0.05 in the first blank:

Interval estimate question: What is the probability that the numerical value of the estimated fraction, *EstFrac*, from one repetition of the experiment lies within **<u>0.05</u>** of the actual population fraction, *ActFrac*? _____

   Begin by focusing on a sample size of 25. In view of what we just learned from the simulation, we can now answer the interval estimate question. After many, many repetitions of the experiment, the numerical value of the estimated fraction falls within 0.05 of the actual value about 39 percent of the time. Now apply the relative frequency interpretation of probability.

3.4   Relative Frequency Interpretation of Probability

When the experiment is repeated many, many times, the relative frequency of each outcome equals its probability. Consequently, when the sample size is 25, the probability that the numerical value of the estimated fraction in one repetition of the experiment falls within 0.05 of the actual value is about 0.39. By the same logic, when the sample size is 100, the probability that the numerical value of the estimated fraction in one repetition of the experiment will fall within 0.05 of the actual value is about 0.69. When the sample size is 400, the probability that the numerical value of the estimated fraction in one repetition of the experiment will fall within 0.05 of the actual value is about 0.95 (see table 3.3 and figure 3.4).

   As the sample size becomes larger, it becomes more likely that the estimated fraction resulting from a single poll will be close to the actual population fraction. This is consistent with our intuition, is it not? When more people are polled, we have more confidence that the estimated fraction will be close to the actual value.

   We can now generalize what we just learned (shown in figure 3.5). When an estimation procedure is unbiased, the variance of the estimate's probability distribution is important because it determines the likelihood that the estimate will be close to the actual value. When the probability distribution's variance is large, it is unlikely that the estimated fraction from one poll will be close to the actual population fraction; consequently the estimated fraction is an unreliable estimate of the actual population fraction. However, when the probability distribution's variance

Table 3.3
Interval estimate question and Opinion Poll simulation results

		Actual population fraction = $ActFrac = p = 0.50 \Rightarrow$ Mean[$EstFrac$] = 0.50	
Sample Size	Variance of *EstFrac's* probability distribution	After many, many repetitions, the percent of repetitions in which *EstFrac* falls within the interval from 0.45 to 0.55	In a single poll, the probability that *EstFrac* falls within the interval from 0.45 to 0.55
25	0.01	≈39%	≈0.39
100	0.0025	≈69%	≈0.69
400	0.000625	≈95%	≈0.95

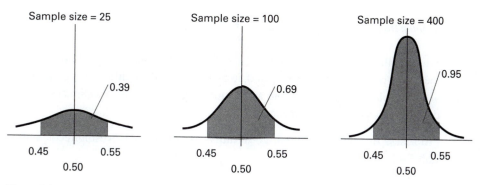

Figure 3.4
Probability distribution of estimated fraction values

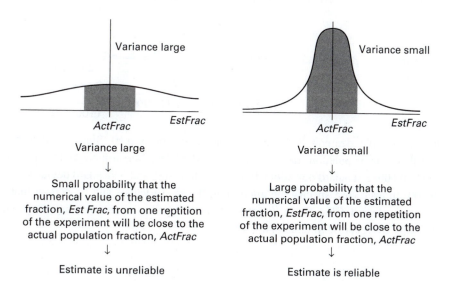

Figure 3.5
Probability distribution of estimated fraction values

is small, it is likely that the estimated fraction from one poll will be close to the actual population fraction; in this case the estimated fraction is a reliable estimate of the actual population fraction.

3.5 Central Limit Theorem

You might have noticed that the distributions of the numerical values produced by the simulation for the samples of 25, 100, and 400 look like bell-shaped curves. Although we do not provide a proof, it can be shown that as the sample size increases, the distribution gradually approaches what mathematicians and statisticians call the normal distribution. Formally, this result is known as the **Central Limit Theorem**.

Econometrics Lab 3.4: The Central Limit Theorem

We will illustrate the Central Limit Theorem by using our Opinion Poll simulation. Again, let the actual population fraction equal 0.50 and consider three different sample sizes: 25, 100, and 400. In each case we will use our simulation to calculate interval estimates for 1, 2, and 3 standard deviations around the mean.

[To access this online material, go to http://mitpress.mit.edu/westhoffeconometrics and select Lab 3.4.]

First consider a sample size of 25:

$$\text{Sample size} = T = 25, \quad \text{Actual population fraction} = ActFrac = \frac{1}{2} = 0.50$$

$$\text{Mean}[\textbf{\textit{EstFrac}}] = p = \frac{1}{2} = 0.50, \quad \text{Var}[\textbf{\textit{EstFrac}}] = \frac{p(1-p)}{T} = \frac{\frac{1}{2} \times \frac{1}{2}}{25} = \frac{\frac{1}{4}}{25} = \frac{1}{100}$$

$$\text{SD}[\textbf{\textit{EstFrac}}] = \sqrt{\text{Var}[\textbf{\textit{EstFrac}}]} = \sqrt{\frac{1}{100}} = \frac{1}{10} = 0.10$$

When the sample size equals 25, the standard deviation is 0.10. Since the distribution mean equals the actual population fraction, 0.50, 1 standard deviation around the mean would be from 0.400 to 0.600, 2 standard deviations from 0.300 to 0.700, and 3 standard deviations from 0.200 to 0.800. In each case specify the appropriate From–To values and be certain that the Pause checkbox is cleared. Click **Start**, and then after many, many repetitions click **Stop**. The simulation results are reported in table 3.4.

Table 3.4
Interval percentages for a sample size of 25

Interval: Standard deviations within random variable's mean	From	To	Simulation: Percent of repetitions within interval
1	0.400	0.600	69.25
2	0.300	0.700	96.26
3	0.200	0.800	99.85

Table 3.5
Interval percentages for a sample size of 100

Interval: Standard deviations within random variable's mean	From	To	Simulation: Percent of repetitions within interval
1	0.450	0.550	68.50
2	0.400	0.600	95.64
3	0.350	0.650	99.77

Next consider a sample size of 100 (table 3.5):

$$\text{Sample size} = T = 100, \quad \text{Actual population fraction} = ActFrac = \frac{1}{2} = 0.50$$

$$\text{Mean}[\textbf{\textit{EstFrac}}] = p = \frac{1}{2} = 0.50, \quad \text{Var}[\textbf{\textit{EstFrac}}] = \frac{p(1-p)}{T} = \frac{\frac{1}{2} \times \frac{1}{2}}{100} = \frac{\frac{1}{4}}{100} = \frac{1}{400}$$

$$\text{SD}[\textbf{\textit{EstFrac}}] = \sqrt{\text{Var}[\textbf{\textit{EstFrac}}]} = \sqrt{\frac{1}{400}} = \frac{1}{20} = 0.05$$

When the sample size equals 100, the standard deviation is 0.05. Since the distribution mean equals the actual population fraction, 0.50, 1 standard deviation around the mean would be from 0.450 to 0.550, 2 standard deviations from 0.400 to 0.600, and 3 standard deviations from 0.350 to 0.650.

Table 3.6
Interval percentages for a sample size of 400

Interval: Standard deviations within distribution mean	From	To	Simulation: Percent of repetitions within interval
1	0.475	0.525	68.29%
2	0.450	0.550	95.49%
3	0.425	0.575	99.73%

Last, consider a sample size of 400 (table 3.6):

$$\text{Sample size} = T = 400, \quad \text{Actual population fraction} = ActFrac = \frac{1}{2} = 0.50$$

$$\text{Mean}[\textbf{\textit{EstFrac}}] = p = \frac{1}{2} = 0.50, \quad \text{Var}[\textbf{\textit{EstFrac}}] = \frac{p(1-p)}{T} = \frac{\frac{1}{2} \times \frac{1}{2}}{400} = \frac{\frac{1}{4}}{400} = \frac{1}{1,600}$$

$$\text{SD}[\textbf{\textit{EstFrac}}] = \sqrt{\text{Var}[\textbf{\textit{EstFrac}}]} = \sqrt{\frac{1}{1,600}} = \frac{1}{40} = 0.025$$

When the sample size equals 400, the standard deviation is 0.025. Since the distribution mean equals the actual population fraction, 0.5, 1 standard deviation around the mean would be from 0.475 to 0.525; 2 standard deviations from 0.450 to 0.550, and 3 standard deviations from 0.425 to 0.575.

Let us summarize the simulation results in a single table (table 3.7). Clearly, standard deviations play a crucial and consistent role here. Regardless of the sample size, approximately 68 or 69 percent of the repetitions fall within one standard deviation of the mean, approximately 95 or 96 percent within two standard deviations, and more than 99 percent within three. The normal distribution exploits the key role played by standard deviations.

3.6   The Normal Distribution: A Way to Calculate Interval Estimates

The **normal distribution** is a symmetric, bell-shaped curve with the midpoint of the bell occurring at the distribution mean (figure 3.6). The total area lying beneath the curve is 1.0. As mentioned before, it can be proved rigorously that as the sample size increases, the probability distribution of the estimated fraction approaches the normal distribution. This fact allows us to use the normal distribution to estimate probabilities for interval estimates.

Nearly every econometrics and statistics textbook includes a table that describes the normal distribution. We will now learn how to use the table to estimate the probability that a random variable will lie between any two values. The table is based on the "normalized value" of the random variable. By convention, the normalized value is denoted by the letter z (figure 3.7):

Table 3.7
Summary of interval percentages results

	Sample sizes		
Mean[*EstFrac*]	25	100	400
SD[*EstFrac*]	0.100	0.050	0.025
Interval: 1 SD			
From–To values	0.400–0.600	0.450–0.550	0.475–0.525
Percent of repetitions	69.25%	68.50%	68.29%
Interval: 2 SD			
From–To values	0.300–0.700	0.400–0.600	0.450–0.550
Percent of repetitions	96.26%	95.64%	95.49%
Interval: 3 SD			
From–To values	0.200–0.800	0.350–0.650	0.425–0.575
Percent of repetitions	99.85%	99.77%	99.73%

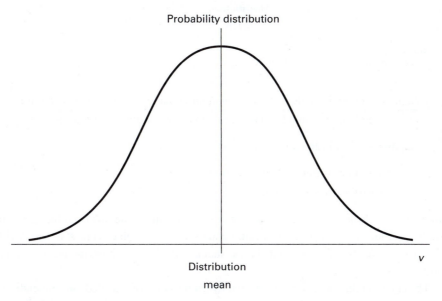

Probability distribution

Distribution
mean

v

Figure 3.6
Normal distribution

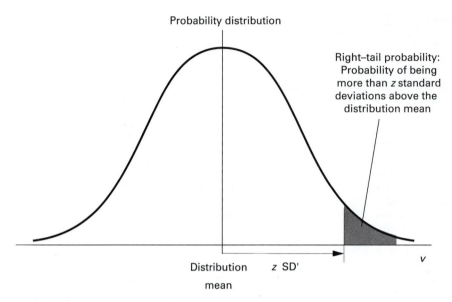

Figure 3.7
Normal distribution right-tail probabilities

$$z = \frac{\text{Value of random variable} - \text{Mean of random variable's probability distribution}}{\text{Standard deviation of random variable's probability distribution}}$$

Let us express this a little more concisely:

$$z = \frac{\text{Value of random variable} - \text{Distribution mean}}{\text{Distribution standard deviation}}$$

In words, z tells us by how many standard deviations the value lies from the mean. If the value of the random variable equals the mean, z equals 0.0; if the value is one standard deviation above the mean, z equals 1.0; if the value is two standard deviations above the mean, z equals 2.0; and so on.

The equation that describes the normal distribution is complicated (see appendix 3.1). Fortunately, we can avoid using the equation because tables are available that describe the distribution. The entire normal distribution table appears in appendix 3.1; an abbreviated portion appears in table 3.8.

In the table the normal distribution row specifies the z value's whole number and its tenths; the column the z-value's hundredths. The numbers within the body of the table estimate the probability that the random variable lies more than z standard deviations above its mean.

Table 3.8
Right-tail probabilities for the normal distribution

z	0.00	0.01	0.02	0.03	0.04	0.05	0.06	0.07	0.08	0.09
⋮										
0.4	0.3446	0.3409	0.3372	0.3336	0.3300	0.3264	0.3228	0.3192	0.3156	0.3121
0.5	0.3085	0.3050	0.3015	0.2981	0.2946	0.2912	0.2877	0.2843	0.2810	0.2776
0.6	0.2743	0.2709	0.2676	0.2643	0.2611	0.2578	0.2546	0.2514	0.2483	0.2451
⋮										
1.4	0.0808	0.0793	0.0778	0.0764	0.0749	0.0735	0.0721	0.0708	0.0694	0.0681
1.5	0.0668	0.0655	0.0643	0.0630	0.0618	0.0606	0.0594	0.0582	0.0571	0.0559
1.6	0.0548	0.0537	0.0526	0.0516	0.0505	0.0495	0.0485	0.0475	0.0465	0.0455
⋮										

3.6.1 Properties of the Normal Distribution

- The normal distribution is bell shaped.
- The normal distribution is symmetric around its mean (center).
- The area beneath the normal distribution equals 1.0.

3.6.2 Using the Normal Distribution Table: An Example

For purposes of illustration, suppose that we want to use the normal distribution to calculate the probability that the estimated fraction from one repetition of the experiment would fall between 0.525 and 0.575 when the actual population fraction was 0.50 and the sample size was 100 (figure 3.8). We begin by calculating the probability distribution's mean and standard deviation:

$$\text{Sample size} = T = 100, \text{Actual population fraction} = ActFrac = \frac{1}{2} = 0.50$$

$$\text{Mean}[\textbf{\textit{EstFrac}}] = p = \frac{1}{2} = 0.50 \quad \text{Var}[\textbf{\textit{EstFrac}}] = \frac{p(1-p)}{T} = \frac{\frac{1}{2} \times \frac{1}{2}}{100} = \frac{\frac{1}{4}}{100} = \frac{1}{400}$$

$$\text{SD}[\textbf{\textit{EstFrac}}] = \sqrt{\text{Var}[\textbf{\textit{EstFrac}}]} = \sqrt{\frac{1}{400}} = \frac{1}{20} = 0.05$$

To calculate the probability that the estimated fraction lies between 0.525 and 0.575, we first calculate the z-values for 0.525 and 0.575; that is, we calculate the number of standard deviations

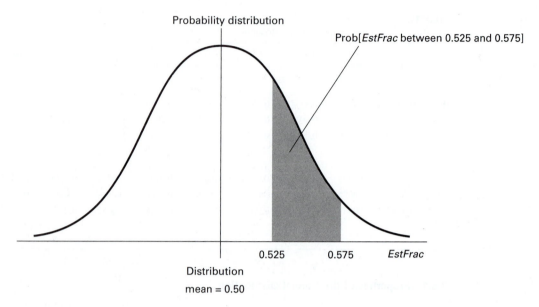

Figure 3.8
Interval estimate from 0.525 to 0.575

that 0.525 and 0.575 lie from the mean. Since the mean equals 0.500 and the standard deviation equals 0.05,

• z-value for 0.525 equals 0.50:

$$z = \frac{0.525 - 0.500}{0.05} = \frac{0.025}{0.05} = \frac{1}{2} = 0.50$$

0.525 lies a half standard deviation above the mean.

• z-value for 0.575 equals 1.50:

$$z = \frac{0.575 - 0.500}{0.05} = \frac{0.075}{0.05} = \frac{3}{2} = 1.50$$

0.575 lies one and a half standard deviations above the mean.

Next consider the right-tail probabilities for the normal distribution in table 3.9. When we use this table we implicitly assume that the normal distribution accurately describes the estimated fraction's probability distribution. For the moment, assume that this is true. The entry corresponding to z equaling 0.50 is 0.3085; this tells us that the probability that the estimated fraction lies above 0.525 is 0.3085 (figure 3.9a).

Prob[*EstFrac* greater than 0.525] = 0.3085

Table 3.9
Selected right-tail probabilities for the normal distribution

z	0.00	0.01
0.4	0.3446	0.3409
0.5	**0.3085**	0.3050
0.6	0.2743	0.2709
1.4	0.0808	0.0793
1.5	**0.0668**	0.0655

The entry corresponding to z equaling 1.50 is 0.0668; this tells us that the probability that the estimated fraction lies above 0.525 is 0.0668 (figure 3.9b).

Prob[*EstFrac* greater than 0.575] = 0.0668

It is now easy to calculate the probability that the estimated fraction will lie between 0.525 and 0.575:

Prob[*EstFrac* between 0.525 and 0.575]

Just subtract the probability that the estimated fraction will be greater than 0.525 from the probability that the estimated fraction will be greater than 0.575:

Prob[*EstFrac* greater than 0.525] = 0.3085

Prob[*EstFrac* greater than 0.575] = <u>0.0668</u>

Prob[*EstFrac* between 0.525 and 0.575] = 0.2417

With a sample size of 100, the probability that *EstFrac* will lie between 0.525 and 0.575 equals 0.2417. This, of course, assumes that the normal distribution describes *EstFrac*'s probability distribution accurately.

3.6.3   Justifying the Use of the Normal Distribution

To justify using the normal distribution to calculate the probabilities, reconsider our simulations in which we calculated the percentages of repetitions that fall within one, two, and three standard deviations of the mean after many, many repetitions. Now use the normal distribution to calculate these percentages.

We can now calculate the probability of being within one, two, and three standard deviations of the mean by reviewing two important properties of the normal distribution:

· The normal distribution is symmetric about its mean.

· The area beneath the normal distribution equals 1.0.

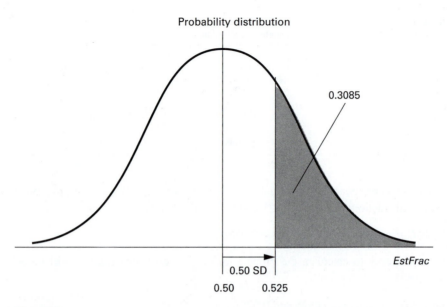

Figure 3.9a
Probability of *EstFrac* greater than 0.525

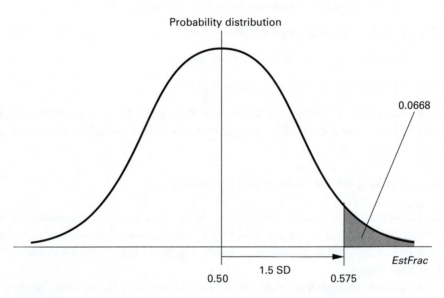

Figure 3.9b
Probability of *EstFrac* greater than 0.575

Table 3.10
Right-tail probabilities for the normal distribution

z	0.00	0.01	z	0.00	0.01	z	0.00	0.01
0.9	0.1841	0.1814	**1.9**	0.0287	0.0281	**2.9**	0.0019	0.0018
1.0	**0.1587**	0.1562	**2.0**	**0.0228**	0.0222	**3.0**	**0.0013**	0.0013
1.1	0.1357	0.1335	**2.1**	0.0179	0.0174			

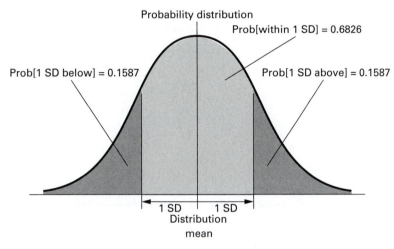

Figure 3.10
Normal distribution calculations

We begin with the one standard deviation (SD) case. Table 3.10 reports that the right-hand tail probability for $z = 1.00$ equals 0.1587:

Prob[1 SD above] = 0.1587

We will now use that to calculate the probability of being within one standard deviation of the mean as illustrated in figure 3.10:

• Since the normal distribution is symmetric, the probability of being more than one standard deviation above the mean equals the probability of being more than one standard deviation below the mean.

Prob[1 SD below] = Prob[1 SD above]

$$= 0.1587$$

• Since the area beneath the normal distribution equals 1.0, the probability of being within one standard deviation of the mean equals 1.0 less the sum of the probabilities of being more than one standard deviation above the mean and the probalibity of being more than one standard deviation below the mean.

$$\text{Prob}[1 \text{ SD within}] = 1.0 - (\text{Prob}[1 \text{ SD below}] + \text{Prob}[1 \text{ SD above}])$$

$$= 1.0 - 0.1587 + 0.1587$$

$$= 1.0 - 0.3174$$

$$= 0.6826$$

We apply the same to two and three standard deviations:

· Two standard deviations. As table 3.10 reports, the right-hand tail probability for $z = 2.00$ equals 0.0228:

$$\text{Prob}[2 \text{ SDs within}] = 1.0 - (\text{Prob}[2 \text{ SDs below}] + \text{Prob}[2 \text{ SDs above}])$$

$$= 1.0 - 0.0228 + 0.0228$$

$$= 1.0 - 0.0456$$

$$= 0.9544$$

· Three standard deviations. As table 3.10 reports, the right-hand tail probability for $z = 3.00$ equals 0.0026:

$$\text{Prob}[3 \text{ SDs within}] = 1.0 - (\text{Prob}[3 \text{ SDs below}] + \text{Prob}[3 \text{ SDs above}])$$

$$= 1.0 - 0.013 + 0.0013$$

$$= 1.0 - 0.0026$$

$$= 0.9974$$

Table 3.11 compares the percentages calculated from our simulations with the percentages that would be predicted by the normal distribution.

Table 3.11 reveals that the normal distribution percentages are good approximations of the simulation percentages. Furthermore, as the sample size increases, the percentages of repetitions within each interval gets closer and closer to the normal distribution percentages. This is precisely what the Central Limit Theorem states. We use the normal distribution to calculate interval estimates because it provides estimates that are close to the actual values.

3.6.4   Normal Distribution's Rules of Thumb

Table 3.12 illustrates what are sometimes called the normal distribution's "rules of thumb." In round numbers, the probability of being within one standard deviation of the mean is 0.68, the

Table 3.11
Interval percentages results and normal distribution percentages

Interval: Standard deviations within distribution mean	Simulation: Percent of repetitions within interval sample size			Normal distribution percentages
	25	100	400	
1	69.25%	68.50%	68.29%	**68.26%**
2	96.26%	95.64%	95.49%	**95.44%**
3	99.85%	99.77%	99.74%	**99.74%**

Table 3.12
Normal distribution rules of thumb

Standard deviations from the mean	Probability of being within
1	≈ 0.68
2	≈ 0.95
3	> 0.99

probability of being within two standard deviations is 0.95, and the probability of being within three standard deviations is more than 0.99.

Clint's Dilemma and His Opinion Poll

We will now return to Clint's dilemma. The election is tomorrow and Clint must decide whether or not to hold a pre-election beer tap rally designed to entice more students to vote for him. If Clint is comfortably ahead, he could save his money and not hold the beer tap rally. But with the election so close, the beer tap rally could be critical. Ideally, Clint would like to contact each individual in the student body, which time does not permit to happen.

In view of the lack of time, Clint decides to poll a sample of 16 students in the population. Clint has adopted the philosophy of econometricians:

Econometrician's philosophy: If you lack the information to determine the value directly, estimate the value to the best of your ability using the information you do have.

More specifically, he wrote the name of each student on a 3×5 card and repeated the following procedure 16 times:

- Thoroughly shuffle the cards.
- Randomly draw one card.
- Ask that individual if he/she supports Clint and record the answer.
- Replace the card.

After conducting his poll, Clint learns that 12 of the 16 students polled support him. That is, the estimated fraction of the population supporting Clint is 0.75:

Estimated fraction of the population supporting Clint: $EstFrac = \dfrac{12}{16} = \dfrac{3}{4} = 0.75$

Based on the results of the poll, it looks like Clint is ahead. But how confident should he be that this is in fact true? We will address this question in the next chapter.

Chapter 3 Review Questions

1. Consider an estimate's probability distribution:

    a. Why is the mean of the probability distribution important? Explain.

    b. Why is the variance of the probability distribution important? Explain.

2. What is an interval estimate?

3. What is the Central Limit Theorem?

Chapter 3 Exercises

1. During the 1994 to 1995 academic year, the mean Math and Verbal SAT scores in Ohio were 515 and 460. The standard deviation for both scores was 100. Consider the following two variables:

SatSum = SatMath + SatVerbal

SatDiff = SatMath − SatVerbal

    a. What is the mean of

    i. *SatSum?* _____

    ii. *SatDiff?* _____

    b. Assume that *SatMath* and *SatVerbal* are independent. What is the variance of

    i. *SatSum?* _____

    ii. *SatDiff?* _____

    c. Assume that *SatMath* and *SatVerbal* exhibit perfect positive correlation. What is the variance of

    i. *SatSum?* _____

    ii. *SatDiff?* _____

d. Assume that the correlation coefficient for *SatMath* and *SatVerbal* equals 0.50. What is the variance of

   i. *SatSum?* _____

   ii. *SatDiff?* _____

e. Assume that the correlation coefficient for *SatMath* and *SatVerbal* equals −0.50. What is the variance of

   i. *SatSum?* _____

   ii. *SatDiff?* _____

f. Using your knowledge of the real world, which of the following do you find most likely. That is, would you expect the correlation coefficient for *SatMath* and *SatVerbal* to be

0.0_____   1.0_____   between 0.0 and 1.0_____   less than 0.0 _____ Explain.

2. Assume that the correlation coefficient for Math and Verbal SAT scores in Ohio is 0.5. Suppose that an Ohio student is randomly chosen. What is the probability that his/her

   a. SAT sum, *SatSum*, exceeds 1,000? _____

   b. SAT Math and Verbal difference, *SatDiff*, exceeds 100? _____

Hint: Apply the normal distribution.

3. During the 1994 to 1995 academic year the mean Math SAT score for high school students in Alaska was 489; in Michigan, the mean was 549. The standard deviation in both states equaled 100. A college admission officer must decide between one student from Alaska and one from Michigan. Both students have taken the SAT, but the admission office has lost their scores. All else being equal, the admission officer would like to admit the Alaska student for reasons of geographic diversity, but he/she is a little concerned that the average math SAT score in Alaska is lower.

   a. Would knowledge of the Alaskan student's Math SAT score help you predict the Michigan student's score, and vice versa?

   b. Are the Alaskan student's and Michigan student's Math SAT scores independent?

   c. The admission officer asks you to calculate the probability that the student from Michigan has a higher score than the student from Alaska. Assuming that the applicants from each state mirror that state's Math SAT distribution, what is this probability?

4. The Wechsler Adult Intelligence Scale is a well-known IQ test. The test results are scaled so that the mean score is 100 and the standard deviation is 15. There is no systematic difference between the IQs of men and women. A dating service is matching male and female subscribers whose IQs mirror the population as a whole.

   a. What is the probability that a male subscriber will have an IQ exceeding 110? _____

   b. What is the probability that a female subscriber will have an IQ exceeding 110? _____

c. Assume that the dating service does not account for IQ when matching its subscribers; consequently the IQs of the men and women who are matched are independent. Consider a couple that has been matched by the dating service. What is the probability that both the male and female will have an IQ exceeding 110? _____

d. Suppose instead that the dating service does consider IQ; the service tends to match high IQ men with high IQ women, and vice versa. Qualitatively, how would that affect your answer to part c? _____

5. Consider the automobiles assembled at a particular auto plant. Even though the cars are the same model and have the same engine size, they obtain slightly different gas mileages. Presently the mean is 32 miles per gallon with a standard deviation of 4.

a. What portion of the cars obtains at least 30 miles per gallon? Hint: Apply the normal distribution.

A rental car company has agreed to purchase several thousand cars from the plant. The contract demands that at least 90 percent of the autos achieve at least 30 miles per gallon. Engineers report that there are two ways in which the plant can be modified to achieve this goal:

Approach 1:   Increase the mean miles per gallon leaving the standard deviation unaffected; the cost of increasing the mean is $100,000 for each additional mile.

Approach 2:   Decrease the standard deviation leaving the mean unaffected; the cost of decreasing the standard deviation is $200,000 for each mile reduction.

b. If approach 1 is used to achieve the objective, by how much must the mean be increased?

c. If approach 2 is used to achieve the objective, by how much must the standard deviation be decreased?

d. Assuming that the plant owner wishes to maximize profits, which approach should be used?

6. Recall the game described in the problems for chapter 2 that you and your roommate played:

· Thoroughly shuffle your roommate's standard deck of fifty-two cards: 13 spades, 13 hearts, 13 diamonds, and 13 clubs.

· Draw one card.

· If the card drawn is red, you win $1 from your roommate; if the card drawn is black, you lose a $1.

· Replace the card drawn.

TNW equals your total net winnings after you played the game eighteen times:

$$TNW = v_1 - v_2 + \ldots + v_{18}$$

where v_i = your net winnings from the ith repetition of the game. Recall that the mean of *TNW*'s probability distribution equals 0 and the variance equals 18. Use the normal distribution to estimate the probability of:

a. winning something: *TNW* greater than 0. _____

b. winning more than $2: *TNW* greater than 2. _____

c. losing more than $6: *TNW* less than −6. _____

d. losing more than $12: *TNW* less than −12. _____

7. Suppose that you and a friend each decide to play roulette fifty times, each time placing a $1 bet. Focus on the total net winnings of you and your friend after you played the game fifty times:

$$TNW = v_1 - v_2 + \ldots + v_{50}$$

where v_i = Your net winnings from the ith spin of the roulette wheel.

a. You decide to always bet on the first set of twelve numbers.

i. Calculate the mean and variance of *TNW*'s probability distribution.

Mean[*TNW*] = _____   Var[*TNW*] = _____

Using the normal distribution, estimate the probability that in net, you will

ii. win $10 or more. _____

iii. lose $10 or more. _____

b. Your friend decides to always bet on red.

i. Calculate the mean and variance of *TNW*'s probability distribution.

Mean[*TNW*] = _____   Var[*TNW*] = _____

Using the normal distribution, estimate the probability that in net, he will

ii. win $10 or more. _____

iii. lose $10 or more. _____

c. A risk averse individual attempts to protect him/herself from losses. Who would be using a more risk averse strategy, you or your friend?

8. Consider the following polls that were conducted in 2004:

	Reuters/ Zogby	ABC News/ Wash Post	CBS News	CNN/USA Today/Gallop
Date	Oct 12–14	Oct 11–13	Oct 9–11	Oct 9–10
Bush–Cheney	48%	48%	48%	48%
Kerry–Edwards	44%	48%	45%	49%
Nader–Camejo	1%	1%	2%	1%
Other/unsure	8%	3%	5%	2%
Number polled	1,220	1,202	760	793
Margin of error	±3%	±3%	±4%	±4%

Focus on the number of individuals polled. Let us do some "back of the envelope" calculations. For the calculations, consider only two major candidates, Bush and Kerry, and assume that the election is a tossup; that is,

$$ActFrac = p = \frac{1}{2} = 0.50$$

a. Complete the following table:

	Reuters/ Zogby	ABC News/ Wash Post	CBS News	CNN/USA Today/Gallop
Var[*EstFrac*]	_____	_____	_____	_____
SD[*EstFrac*]	_____	_____	_____	_____
2 × SD[*EstFrac*]	_____	_____	_____	_____
3 × SD[*EstFrac*]	_____	_____	_____	_____

b. Compare the numbers in the table to the margins of error. What do you suspect that the margin of error equals? _____

Hint: Round off your "table numbers" to the nearest percent.

c. Recall that the polling procedure is unbiased. Using the normal distribution's rules of thumb interpret the margin of error.

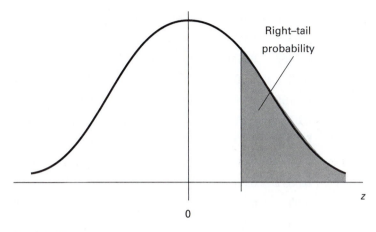

Figure 3.11
Right-tail probability

Appendix 3.1: Normal Distribution Right-Tail Probabilities

z	0.00	0.01	0.02	0.03	0.04	0.05	0.06	0.07	0.08	0.09
0.0	0.5000	0.4960	0.4920	0.4880	0.4840	0.4801	0.4761	0.4721	0.4681	0.4641
0.1	0.4602	0.4562	0.4522	0.4483	0.4443	0.4404	0.4364	0.4325	0.4286	0.4247
0.2	0.4207	0.4168	0.4129	0.4090	0.4052	0.4013	0.3974	0.3936	0.3897	0.3859
0.3	0.3821	0.3783	0.3745	0.3707	0.3669	0.3632	0.3594	0.3557	0.3520	0.3483
0.4	0.3446	0.3409	0.3372	0.3336	0.3300	0.3264	0.3228	0.3192	0.3156	0.3121
0.5	0.3085	0.3050	0.3015	0.2981	0.2946	0.2912	0.2877	0.2843	0.2810	0.2776
0.6	0.2743	0.2709	0.2676	0.2643	0.2611	0.2578	0.2546	0.2514	0.2483	0.2451
0.7	0.2420	0.2389	0.2358	0.2327	0.2296	0.2266	0.2236	0.2206	0.2177	0.2148
0.8	0.2119	0.2090	0.2061	0.2033	0.2005	0.1977	0.1949	0.1922	0.1894	0.1867
0.9	0.1841	0.1814	0.1788	0.1762	0.1736	0.1711	0.1685	0.1660	0.1635	0.1611
1.0	0.1587	0.1562	0.1539	0.1515	0.1492	0.1469	0.1446	0.1423	0.1401	0.1379
1.1	0.1357	0.1335	0.1314	0.1292	0.1271	0.1251	0.1230	0.1210	0.1190	0.1170
1.2	0.1151	0.1131	0.1112	0.1093	0.1075	0.1056	0.1038	0.1020	0.1003	0.0985
1.3	0.0968	0.0951	0.0934	0.0918	0.0901	0.0885	0.0869	0.0853	0.0838	0.0823
1.4	0.0808	0.0793	0.0778	0.0764	0.0749	0.0735	0.0721	0.0708	0.0694	0.0681
1.5	0.0668	0.0655	0.0643	0.0630	0.0618	0.0606	0.0594	0.0582	0.0571	0.0559
1.6	0.0548	0.0537	0.0526	0.0516	0.0505	0.0495	0.0485	0.0475	0.0465	0.0455

1.7	0.0446	0.0436	0.0427	0.0418	0.0409	0.0401	0.0392	0.0384	0.0375	0.0367
1.8	0.0359	0.0351	0.0344	0.0336	0.0329	0.0322	0.0314	0.0307	0.0301	0.0294
1.9	0.0287	0.0281	0.0274	0.0268	0.0262	0.0256	0.0250	0.0244	0.0239	0.0233
2.0	0.0228	0.0222	0.0217	0.0212	0.0207	0.0202	0.0197	0.0192	0.0188	0.0183
2.1	0.0179	0.0174	0.0170	0.0166	0.0162	0.0158	0.0154	0.0150	0.0146	0.0143
2.2	0.0139	0.0136	0.0132	0.0129	0.0125	0.0122	0.0119	0.0116	0.0113	0.0110
2.3	0.0107	0.0104	0.0102	0.0099	0.0096	0.0094	0.0091	0.0089	0.0087	0.0084
2.4	0.0082	0.0080	0.0078	0.0075	0.0073	0.0071	0.0069	0.0068	0.0066	0.0064
2.5	0.0062	0.0060	0.0059	0.0057	0.0055	0.0054	0.0052	0.0051	0.0049	0.0048
2.6	0.0047	0.0045	0.0044	0.0043	0.0041	0.0040	0.0039	0.0038	0.0037	0.0036
2.7	0.0035	0.0034	0.0033	0.0032	0.0031	0.0030	0.0029	0.0028	0.0027	0.0026
2.8	0.0026	0.0025	0.0024	0.0023	0.0023	0.0022	0.0021	0.0021	0.0020	0.0019
2.9	0.0019	0.0018	0.0018	0.0017	0.0016	0.0016	0.0015	0.0015	0.0014	0.0014
3.0	0.0013	0.0013	0.0013	0.0012	0.0012	0.0011	0.0011	0.0011	0.0010	0.0010

$$z = \frac{\text{Value of random variable} - \text{Distribution mean}}{\text{Distribution standard deviation}} = \frac{x - \text{Mean}[x]}{\text{SD}[x]}$$

Normal distribution probability density function: $\dfrac{1}{\text{SD}[x]\sqrt{2\pi}} e^{-\{(x - Mean[x])/SD[x]\}/2}$

4 Estimation Procedures, Estimates, and Hypothesis Testing

Chapter 4 Prep Questions

1. Consider an estimate's probability distribution:

    a. Why is the mean of the probability distribution important? Explain.

    b. Why is the variance of the probability distribution important? Explain.

2. After collecting evidence from a crime scene, the police identified a suspect. The suspect provides the police with a statement claiming innocence. The district attorney is deciding whether or not to charge the suspect with a crime. The district attorney asks a forensic expert to examine the evidence and compare it to the suspect's personal statement. After the expert completes his/her work, the district attorney poses the following the question to the expert:

Question: What is the probability that similar evidence would have arisen IF the suspect were in fact innocent?

Initially, the forensic expert assesses this probability to be 0.50. A week later, however, more evidence is uncovered and the expert revises the probability to 0.01. In light of the new evidence, is it more or less likely that the suspect is telling the truth?

3. The police charge a seventeen-year-old male with a serious crime. History teaches us that no evidence can ever prove that a defendant is guilty beyond all doubt. In this case, however, the police do have strong evidence against the young man suggesting that he is guilty, although the possibility that he is innocent cannot be completely ruled out. You have been impaneled on a jury to decide this case. The judge instructs you and your fellow jurors to find the young man guilty if you determine that he committed the crime "beyond a reasonable doubt."

    a. The following table illustrates the four possible scenarios:

	Jury finds defendant guilty		**Jury finds defendant innocent**	
Defendant actually innocent	Jury is correct__	incorrect__	Jury is correct__	incorrect__
Defendant actually guilty	Jury is correct__	incorrect__	Jury is correct__	incorrect__

For each scenario, indicate whether the jury would be correct or incorrect.

    b. Consider each scenario in which the jury errs. In each of these cases, what are the consequences (the "costs") of the error to the young man and/or to society?

4. Suppose that two baseball teams, Team RS and Team Y, have played 185 games against each other in the last decade. Consider the following statement made by Mac Carver, a self-described baseball authority:

Carver's view: "Over the last decade, Team RS and Team Y have been equally strong."
Now consider two hypothetical scenarios:

       Hypothetical scenario A   Hypothetical scenario B
Team RS wins 180 of the 185 games   Team RS wins 93 of the 185 games

    a. For the moment, assume that Carver's is correct. Comparatively speaking, which scenario would be likely (high probability) and which scenario would be unlikely (low probability)?

Assuming that Carver's view is correct

Would scenario A be   Would scenario B be

Likely? ___   Unlikely? ___   Likely? ___   Unlikely? ___

↓   ↓

Would   Would

Prob[Scenario A IF Carver correct] be   Prob[Scenario B IF Carver correct] be

High? ___   Low? ___   High? ___   Low? ___

b. Next suppose that scenario A actually occurs. Would you be inclined to reject Carver's view or not reject it? If instead scenario B actually occurs, what would you be inclined to do?

Scenario A actually occurs   **Scenario B actually occurs**

↓   ↓

Reject Carver's view?   Reject Carver's view?

Yes___   No___   Yes___   No___

4.1   Clint's Dilemma and Estimation Procedures

We will now return to Clint's dilemma. The election is tomorrow and Clint must decide whether or not to hold a pre-election beer tap rally designed to entice more students to vote for him. On the one hand, if Clint is comfortably ahead, he could save his money by not holding the beer tap rally. On the other hand, if the election is close, the beer tap rally could prove critical. Ideally Clint would like to poll each member of the student body, but time does not permit this. Consequently Clint decides to conduct an opinion poll by selecting 16 students at random. Clint adopts the philosophy of econometricians:

Econometrician's philosophy: If you lack the information to determine the value directly, estimate the value to the best of your ability using the information you do have.

4.1.1   Clint's Opinion Poll and His Dilemma

Clint wrote the name of each student on a 3 × 5 card and repeated the following procedure 16 times:

· Thoroughly shuffle the cards.

· Randomly draw one card.

- Ask that individual if he/she supports Clint and record the answer.
- Replace the card.

Twelve of the 16 students polled support Clint. That is, the estimated fraction of the population supporting him is 0.75:

$$\text{Estimated fraction of population supporting Clint}: EstFrac = \frac{12}{16} = \frac{3}{4} = 0.75$$

Based on the results of the poll, it looks like Clint is ahead. But how confident should Clint be that he is in fact ahead. Clint faces a dilemma:

Clint's dilemma: Should Clint be confident that he has the election in hand and save his funds or should he finance the beer tap rally?

Our project is to use the poll to help Clint resolve his dilemma:

Project: Use Clint's poll to assess his election prospects.

   Our Opinion Poll simulation taught us that while the numerical value of the estimated fraction from one poll could equal the actual population fraction, it typically does not. The simulations showed that in most cases the estimated fraction will be either greater than or less than the actual population fraction. Accordingly Clint must accept the fact that the actual population fraction probably does not equal 0.75. So Clint faces a crucial question:

Crucial question: How much confidence should Clint have in his estimate? More to the point, how confident should Clint be in concluding that he is actually leading?

To address the confidence issue, it is important to distinguish between the general properties of Clint's estimation procedure and the one specific application of that procedure, the poll Clint conducted.

4.1.2   Clint's Estimation Procedure: The General and the Specific

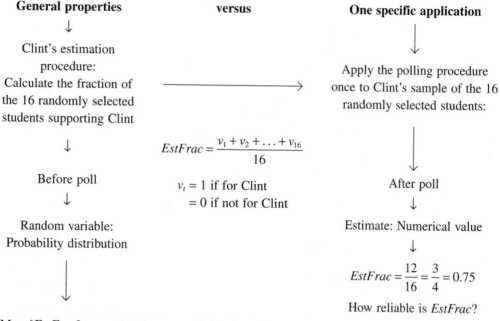

General properties   versus   **One specific application**

↓

Clint's estimation
procedure:
Calculate the fraction of   ⟶   Apply the polling procedure
the 16 randomly selected   once to Clint's sample of the 16
students supporting Clint   randomly selected students:

↓

$$EstFrac = \frac{v_1 + v_2 + \ldots + v_{16}}{16}$$

Before poll $v_t = 1$ if for Clint   After poll
↓ $= 0$ if not for Clint   ↓

Random variable: Estimate: Numerical value
Probability distribution   ↓

↓ $$EstFrac = \frac{12}{16} = \frac{3}{4} = 0.75$$

How reliable is *EstFrac*?

Mean[*EstFrac*] = p = *ActFrac* = actual fraction of the population supporting Clint

Var[*EstFrac*] = $\dfrac{p(1-p)}{T} = \dfrac{p(1-p)}{16}$,   where T = sample size

↓

Mean and variance describe the center and spread of the estimate's probability distribution

4.1.3   Taking Stock and Our Strategy to Assess the Reliability of Clint's Poll Results

Let us briefly review what we have done thus far. We have laid the groundwork required to assess the reliability of Clint's poll results by focusing on what we know before the poll is conducted; that is, we have focused on the general properties of the estimation procedure, the probability distribution of the estimate. In chapter 3 we derived the general equations for the mean and variance of the estimated fraction's probability distribution algebraically and then checked our algebra by exploiting the relative frequency interpretation of probability in our Opinion Poll simulation:

What can we deduce before the poll is
conducted?

General properties of the polling
procedure described by *EstFrac*'s
probability distribution

Probability distribution as described by
its mean (center) and variance (spread)

Use algebra to derive the equations for
the probability distribution's
mean and variance

$$\text{Mean}[\textbf{\textit{EstFrac}}] = p$$

$$\text{Var}[\textbf{\textit{EstFrac}}] = \frac{p(1-p)}{T}$$

$\longrightarrow$ Check the algebra with a simulation
by exploiting the relative frequency
interpretation of probability

Let us review the importance of the mean and variance of the estimated fraction's probability
distribution.

4.1.4 Importance of the Mean (Center) of the Estimate's Probability Distribution

Clint's estimation procedure is unbiased because the mean of the estimated fraction's probability
distribution equals the actual fraction of the population supporting Clint (figure 4.1):

$$\text{Mean}[\textit{EstFrac}] = p = \textit{ActFrac} = \text{actual population fraction}$$

His estimation procedure does not systematically underestimate or overestimate the actual value.
If the probability distribution is symmetric, the chances that the estimated fraction will be too
high in one poll equal the chances that it will be too low.

We used our Opinion Poll simulation to illustrate the unbiased nature of Clint's estimation
procedure by exploiting the relative frequency interpretation of probability. After the experiment
is repeated many, many times, the average of the estimates obtained from each repetition of the
experiment equaled the actual fraction of the population supporting Clint:

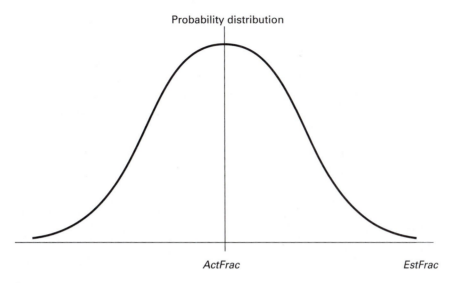

Probability distribution

ActFrac   EstFrac

Figure 4.1
Probability distribution of *EstFrac,* estimated fraction values—Importance of the mean

Relative frequency interpretation of probability:
After many, many repetitions, the distribution of the
numerical values mirrors the probability distribution

Average of the estimate's   Unbiased estimation procedure
numerical values after
many, many repetitions   =   Mean[***EstFrac***]   =   *ActFrac*

Average of the estimate's
numerical values after   =   *ActFrac*
many, many repetitions

4.1.5   Importance of the Variance (Spread) of the Estimate's Probability Distribution for an Unbiased Estimation Procedure

How confident should Clint be that his estimate is close to the actual population fraction? Since the estimation procedure is unbiased, the answer to this question depends on the variance of the estimated fraction's probability distribution (see figure 4.2). As the variance decreases, the likelihood of the estimate being "close to" the actual value increases; that is, as the variance decreases, the estimate becomes more reliable.

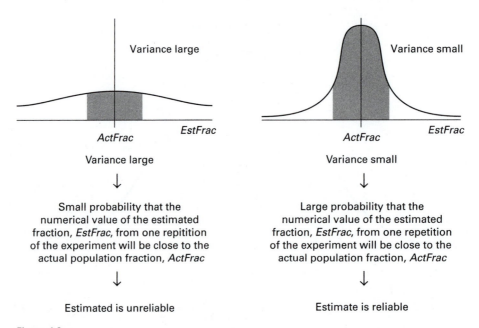

Figure 4.2
Probability distribution of *EstFrac,* estimated fraction values—Importance of variance

4.2   Hypothesis Testing

Now we will apply what we have learned about the estimate's probability distribution, the estimation procedure's general properties, to assess how confident Clint should be in concluding that he is ahead.

4.2.1   Motivating Hypothesis Testing: The Evidence and the Cynic

Hypothesis testing allows us to accomplish this assessment. The hypothesis-testing technique has a wide variety of applications. For example, it was used to speculate on the relationship between Thomas Jefferson and Sally Hemings as described by Joseph J. Ellis in his book, *American Sphinx: The Character of Thomas Jefferson* (p. 21):

The results, published in the prestigious scientific magazine *Nature* . . . showed a match between Jefferson and Eston Hemings, Sally's last child. The chances of such a match occurring randomly are less than one in a thousand.

We will motivate the rationale behind hypothesis testing by considering a cynical view.

Playing the Cynic: The Election Is a Toss-Up

In the case of Clint's poll, a cynic might say "Sure, a majority of those polled supported Clint, but the election is actually a toss-up. The fact that 75 percent of those polled supported Clint was just the luck of the draw."

Cynic's view: Despite the poll results, the election is actually a toss-up.

Econometrics Lab 4.1: Polling—Could the Cynic Be Correct?

Could the cynic be correct? Actually we have already shown that the cynic could be correct when we introduced our Opinion Poll simulation. Nevertheless, we will do so again for emphasis.

[To access this online material, go to http://mitpress.mit.edu/westhoffeconometrics and select Lab 4.1.]

The Opinion Poll simulation clearly shows that 12 or even more of the 16 students selected could support Clint in a single poll when the election is a toss-up. Accordingly we cannot simply dismiss the cynic's view as nonsense. We must take the cynic seriously. To assess his view, we pose the following question. It asks how likely it would be to obtain a result like the one that actually occurred if the cynic is correct.

Question for the cynic: What is the probability that the result from a single poll would be like the one actually obtained (or even stronger), if the cynic is correct and the election is a toss-up?

More specifically,

Question for the cynic: What is the probability that the estimated fraction supporting Clint would equal 0.75 or more in one poll of 16 individuals, if the cynic is correct (i.e., if the election is actually a toss-up and the fraction of the actual population supporting Clint equals 0.50)?

We denote the answer to this question as Prob[Results IF cynic correct]:

Prob[Results IF cynic correct = Probability that the result from a single poll would be like the one actually obtained (or even stronger), IF the cynic is correct (if the election is a toss-up)

When the probability is small, it would be unlikely that the election is a toss-up, and hence we could be confident that Clint actually leads. When the probability is large, it is likely that the election is a toss-up even though the poll suggests that Clint leads:

Prob[Results IF cynic correct] small	Prob[Results IF cynic correct] large
↓	↓
Unlikely that the cynic is correct	Likely that the cynic is correct
↓	↓
Unlikely that the election is a toss-up	Likely that the election is a toss-up

Assessing the Cynic's View Using the Normal Distribution: Prob[Results IF cynic correct]

How can we answer the question for the cynic? That is, how can we calculate this probability, Prob[Results IF cynic correct]? To understand how, recall Clint's estimation procedure, his poll:

Write the names of every individual in the population on a separate card, then perform the following procedure 16 times:

• Thoroughly shuffle the cards.

• Randomly draw one card.

• Ask that individual if he/she supports Clint and record the answer.

• Replace the card.

• Calculate the fraction of those polled supporting Clint.

If the cynic is correct and the election is a toss-up, the actual fraction of the population supporting Clint would equal 1/2 or 0.50. Based on this premise, apply the equations we derived to calculate the mean and variance of the estimated fraction's probability distribution:

$$\text{Sample size} = T = 16, \quad \text{Actual population fraction} = ActFrac = \frac{1}{2} = 0.50$$

$$\text{Mean}[\boldsymbol{EstFrac}] = p = \frac{1}{2} = 0.50, \quad \text{Var}[\boldsymbol{EstFrac}] = \frac{p(1-p)}{T} = \frac{\frac{1}{2} \times \frac{1}{2}}{16} = \frac{\frac{1}{4}}{16} = \frac{1}{64}$$

$$\text{SD}[\boldsymbol{EstFrac}] = \sqrt{\text{Var}[\boldsymbol{EstFrac}]} = \sqrt{\frac{1}{64}} = \frac{1}{8} = 0.125$$

Since the standard deviation is 0.125, the result of Clint's poll, 0.75, is two standard deviations above the mean, 0.50 (figure 4.3).

Next recall the normal distribution's rules of thumb (as listed in table 4.1).

The rules of thumb tell us that the probability of being within two standard deviations of the random variable's mean is approximately 0.95. Recall that the area beneath the normal distribution equals 1.00. Since the normal distribution is symmetric, the probability of being more than two standard deviations above the mean is 0.025 as shown in figure 4.3:

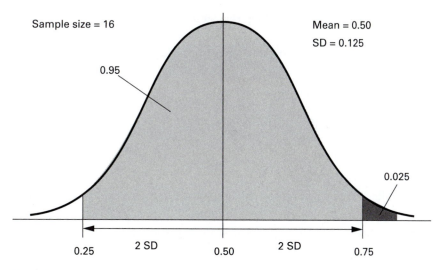

Figure 4.3
Probability distribution of *EstFrac*—Calculating Prob[Results IF cynic correct]

Table 4.1
Normal distribution rules of thumb

Standard deviations from the mean	Probability of being within
1	≈0.68
2	≈0.95
3	>0.99

$$\frac{1.00 - 0.95}{2} = \frac{0.05}{2} = 0.025$$

The answer to the cynic's question is 0.025:

Prob[Results IF cynic correct] = 0.025

If the cynic is actually correct (if the election is actually a toss-up), the probability that the fraction supporting Clint would equal 0.75 or more in one poll of 16 individuals equals 0.025, that is, 1 chance in 40. Clint must now make a decision. He must decide whether or not he is willing to live with the odds of a 1 in 40 chance that the election is actually a toss-up. If he is willing to do so, he will not fund the beer tap rally; otherwise, he will.

4.2.2 Formalizing Hypothesis Testing: Five Steps

The following five steps describe how we can formalize hypothesis testing.

Step 1: Collect evidence; conduct the poll.

Clint polls 16 students selected randomly; 12 of the 16 support him. The estimated fraction of the population supporting Clint is 0.75 or 75 percent:

$$EstFrac = \frac{12}{16} = \frac{3}{4} = 0.75$$

Critical result: 75 percent of those polled support Clint. This evidence, the fact that more than half of those polled, suggests that Clint is ahead.

Step 2: Play the cynic and challenge the results; construct the null and alternative hypotheses.

Cynic's view: Despite the results the election is actually a toss-up; that is, the actual fraction of the population supporting Clint is 0.50.

The null hypothesis adopts the cynical view by challenging the evidence; the cynic always challenges the evidence. By convention, the null hypothesis is denoted as H_0. The alternative hypothesis is consistent with the evidence; the alternative hypothesis is denoted as H_1.

H_0: $ActFrac = 0.50$ $\Rightarrow$ Election is a toss-up; cynic is correct

H_1: $ActFrac > 0.50$ $\Rightarrow$ Clint leads; cynic is incorrect and the evidence is correct

Step 3: Formulate the question to assess the cynic's view and the null hypothesis.

Questions for the cynic:

· **Generic question:** What is the probability that the result would be like the one obtained (or even stronger), if H_0 is true (if the cynic is correct)?

· **Specific question:** The estimated fraction was 0.75 in the poll of 16 individuals: What is the probability that 0.75 or more of the 16 individuals polled would support Clint if H_0 is true (if the cynic is correct and the actual population fraction actually equaled 0.50)?

Answer: Prob[Results IF cynic correct] or Prob[Results IF H_0 true][1]

The magnitude of this probability determines whether we reject or do not reject the null hypothesis; that is, the magnitude of this probability determines the likelihood that the cynic is correct and H_0 is true:

---

1. Traditionally this probability is called the *p*-value. We will use the more descriptive term, however, to emphasize what it actually represents. Nevertheless, you should be aware that this probability is typically called the *p*-value.

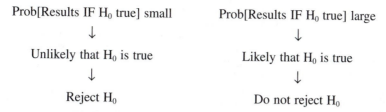

Prob[Results IF H_0 true] small   Prob[Results IF H_0 true] large
↓   ↓
Unlikely that H_0 is true   Likely that H_0 is true
↓   ↓
Reject H_0 Do not reject H_0

Step 4:   Use the general properties of the estimation procedure, the estimated fraction's probability distribution, to calculate Prob[Results IF H_0 true].

Prob[Results IF H_0 true] equals the probability that 0.75 or more of the 16 individuals polled would support Clint if H_0 is true (if the cynic is correct and the actual population fraction actually equaled 0.50); more concisely,

Prob[Results IF H_0 true] = Prob[*EstFrac* is at least 0.75 IF *ActFrac* equals 0.50]

We will use the normal distribution to compute this probability. First calculate the mean and variance of the estimated fraction's probability distribution based on the premise that the null hypothesis is true; that is, calculate the mean and variance based on the premise that the actual fraction of the population supporting Clint is 0.50:

Estimation   Assume H_0 Equation for   Assume H_0
procedure unbiased   true   variance   true

$$\text{Mean}[\textbf{\textit{EstFrac}}] = p = \frac{1}{2} = 0.50$$

$$\text{Var}[\textbf{\textit{EstFrac}}] = \frac{p(1-p)}{T} = \frac{\frac{1}{2} \times \frac{1}{2}}{16} = \frac{\frac{1}{4}}{16} = \frac{1}{64}$$

$$\text{SD}[\textbf{\textit{EstFrac}}] = \sqrt{\text{Var}[\textbf{\textit{EstFrac}}]} = \sqrt{\frac{1}{64}} = \frac{1}{8} = 0.125$$

Recall that z equals the number of standard deviations that the value lies from the mean:

$$z = \frac{\text{Value of random variable} - \text{Distribution mean}}{\text{Distribution standard deviation}}$$

The value of the random variable equals 0.75 (from Clint's poll); the mean equals 0.50, and the standard deviation 0.125:

$$z = \frac{0.75 - 0.50}{0.125} = \frac{0.25}{0.125} = 2.00$$

Next consider the table of right-tail probabilities for the normal distribution. Table 4.2, an abbreviated form of the normal distribution table, provides the probability (see also figure 4.4):

Table 4.2
Selected right-tail probabilities for the normal distribution

z	0.00	0.01
1.9	0.0287	0.0281
2.0	**0.0228**	0.0222
2.1	0.0179	0.0174

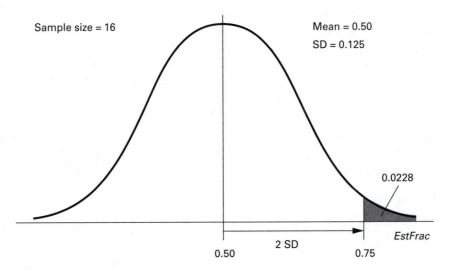

Figure 4.4
Probability distribution of *EstFrac*—Calculating Prob[Results IF H_0 true]

$$\text{Prob[Results IF cynic correct]} = \begin{array}{l} \text{Probability that the result from a single poll would be like} \\ \text{the one actually obtained (or even stronger) IF the cynic is} \\ \text{correct (if the election is a toss-up)} \end{array}$$

$$= 0.0228$$

Step 5: Decide on the standard of proof, a significance level.

Clint must now decide whether he considers a probability of 0.0228 to be small or large. The **significance level** is the dividing line between the probability being small and the probability being large. The significance level Clint chooses implicitly establishes his standard of proof; that is, the significance level establishes what constitutes "proof beyond a reasonable doubt."

If the Prob[Results IF H_0 true] is less than the significance level Clint adopts, he would judge the probability to be "small." Clint would conclude that it is unlikely for the null hypothesis to be true, unlikely that the election is a tossup. He would consider the poll results in which 75 percent of those polled support him to be "proof beyond a reasonable doubt" that he is leading. If instead the probability exceeds Clint's significance level, he would judge the probability to be large. Clint would conclude that it is likely for the null hypothesis to be true, likely that the election is a toss-up. In this case he would consider the poll results as not constituting "proof beyond a reasonable doubt."

<table>
<tr><td align="center">Prob[Results IF H_0 true]
less than significance level</td><td align="center">Prob[Results IF H_0 true]
greater than significance level</td></tr>
<tr><td align="center">↓</td><td align="center">↓</td></tr>
<tr><td align="center">Prob[Results IF H_0 true] small</td><td align="center">Prob[Results IF H_0 true] large</td></tr>
<tr><td align="center">↓</td><td align="center">↓</td></tr>
<tr><td align="center">Unlikely that H_0 is true</td><td align="center">Likely that H_0 is true</td></tr>
<tr><td align="center">↓</td><td align="center">↓</td></tr>
<tr><td align="center">Reject H_0</td><td align="center">Do not reject H_0</td></tr>
<tr><td align="center">↓</td><td align="center">↓</td></tr>
<tr><td align="center">Suggestion: Clint leads</td><td align="center">Suggestion: Election a toss-up</td></tr>
</table>

4.2.3 Significance Levels and the Standard of Proof

Recall our calculation of Prob[Results IF H_0 true]:

$$\text{Prob[Results IF cynic correct]} = \begin{array}{l}\text{Probability that the result from a single poll would be like}\\ \text{the one actually obtained (or even stronger) IF the cynic is}\\ \text{correct (if the election is a toss-up)}\end{array}$$

$$= 0.0228$$

Now consider two different significance levels that are often used in academe: 5 percent and 1 percent:

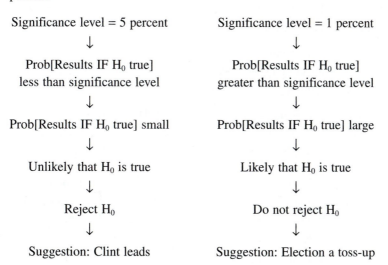

<table>
<tr><td align="center">Significance level = 5 percent</td><td align="center">Significance level = 1 percent</td></tr>
<tr><td align="center">↓</td><td align="center">↓</td></tr>
<tr><td align="center">Prob[Results IF H_0 true]
less than significance level</td><td align="center">Prob[Results IF H_0 true]
greater than significance level</td></tr>
<tr><td align="center">↓</td><td align="center">↓</td></tr>
<tr><td align="center">Prob[Results IF H_0 true] small</td><td align="center">Prob[Results IF H_0 true] large</td></tr>
<tr><td align="center">↓</td><td align="center">↓</td></tr>
<tr><td align="center">Unlikely that H_0 is true</td><td align="center">Likely that H_0 is true</td></tr>
<tr><td align="center">↓</td><td align="center">↓</td></tr>
<tr><td align="center">Reject H_0</td><td align="center">Do not reject H_0</td></tr>
<tr><td align="center">↓</td><td align="center">↓</td></tr>
<tr><td align="center">Suggestion: Clint leads</td><td align="center">Suggestion: Election a toss-up</td></tr>
</table>

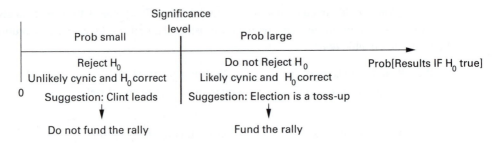

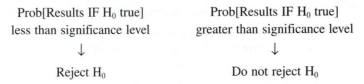

Figure 4.5
Significance levels and Clint's election

If Clint should adopt a 5 percent significance level, he would reject the null hypothesis; Clint would conclude that he leads and would not fund the beer tap rally. If instead he adopts a 1 percent significance level, he will not reject the null hypothesis; Clint would conclude that he is not leading the election and so will fund the beer tap rally. A 1 percent significant level constitutes a higher standard of proof than a 5 percent significance level; a lower significance level makes it more difficult for Clint to conclude that he is leading (figure 4.5).

Now let us generalize. The significance level is the dividing line between what we consider a small and large probability:

Prob[Results IF H_0 true]	Prob[Results IF H_0 true]
less than significance level	greater than significance level
↓	↓
Reject H_0	Do not reject H_0

As we reduce the significance level, we make it more difficult to reject the null hypothesis; we make it more difficult to conclude that Clint is leading. Consequently the significance level and standard of proof are intimately related; as we reduce the significance level, we are implicitly adopting a higher standard of proof:

Lower	More difficult	Higher
significance	→ to reject null →	standard
level	hypothesis	of proof

What is the appropriate standard of proof for Clint? That is, what significance level should he use? There is no definitive answer, only Clint can decide. The significance level Clint's chooses, his standard of proof, depends on a number of factors. In part, it depends on the importance he attaches to winning the election. If he attaches great importance to winning, he would set a very low significance level, making it difficult to reject the null hypothesis. In this case he would be setting a very high standard of proof; much proof would be required for him to reject the notion that the election is a toss-up. Also Clint's choice would depend on how "paranoid" he is. If Clint is a "worrywart" who always focuses on the negative, he would no doubt adopt a low significance level. He would require a very high standard of proof before concluding that he is leading. On the other hand, if Clint is a carefree optimist, he would adopt a higher significance level and thus a lower standard of proof.

4.2.4   Type I and Type II Errors: The Trade-Offs

Traditionally significance levels of 1 percent, 5 percent, and 10 percent are used in academic papers. It is important to note, however, that there is nothing "sacred" about any of these percentages. There is no mechanical way to decide on the appropriate significance level. We can nevertheless address the general factors that should be considered. We will use a legal example to illustrate this point.

Suppose that the police charge a seventeen-year-old male with a serious crime. Strong evidence against him exists. The evidence suggests that he is guilty. But a word of caution is now in order; no evidence can ever prove guilt beyond all doubt. Even confessions do not provide indisputable evidence. There are many examples of an individual confessing to a crime that he/she did not commit.

Again, let us play the cynic. The cynic always challenges the evidence:

Cynic's view: Sure, there is evidence suggesting that the young man is guilty, but the evidence results from the "luck of the draw." The evidence is just coincidental. In fact the young man is innocent.

Let us formulate the null and alternative hypotheses:

H_0: Defendant is innocent; cynic is correct

H_1: Defendant is guilty; cynic is incorrect

The null hypothesis, H_0, reflects the cynic's view. We cannot simply dismiss the null hypothesis as crazy. Many individuals have been convicted on strong evidence when they were actually innocent. Every few weeks we hear about someone who, after being convicted years ago, was released from prison as a consequence of DNA evidence indicating that he/she could not have been guilty of the crime.

Now suppose that you are a juror charged with deciding the fate of the young man. Criminal trials in the United States require the prosecution to prove that the defendant is guilty "beyond a reasonable doubt." The judge instructs you to find the defendant guilty if you believe the evidence meets the "beyond the reasonable doubt" criterion. You and your fellow jurors must now decide what constitutes "proof beyond a reasonable doubt." To help you make this decision, we will make two sets of observations. We will first express each in simple English and then "translate" the English into "hypothesis-testing language"; in doing so, remember the null hypothesis asserts that the defendant is innocent:

	Translating into hypothesis testing language	H_0: Defendant is innocent H_1: Defendant is guilty

Observation one:

The defendant is either		H_0 is either
• actually innocent		• actually true
or	$\rightarrow$	or
• actually guilty		• actually false

Observation two:

The jury must find the defendant either		The jury must either
• guilty		• reject H_0
or	$\rightarrow$	or
• innocent		• not reject H_0

Four possible scenarios exist. Table 4.3 summarizes these scenarios.

It is possible for the jury to make two different types of mistakes:

• **Type I error**: Jury finds the defendant guilty when he is actually innocent; in terms of hypothesis-testing language, the jury rejects the null hypothesis when the null hypothesis is actually true.

Cost of type I error: Type I error means that an innocent young man is incarcerated; this is a cost incurred not only by the young man, but also by society.

• **Type II error**: Jury finds the defendant innocent when he is actually guilty; in terms of hypothesis-testing language, the jury does not reject the null hypothesis when the null hypothesis is actually false.

Cost of type II error: Type II error means that a criminal is set free; this can be costly to society because the criminal is free to continue his life of crime.

Table 4.3
Four possible scenarios

		Jury finds guilty Reject H_0	Jury finds innocent Do not reject H_0
Defendant actually innocent	H_0 **is actually true**	Type I error Imprison innocent man	Correct Free innocent man
Defendant actually guilty	H_0 **is actually false**	Correct Imprison guilty man	Type II error Free guilty man

Table 4.4
Costs of type I and type II errors

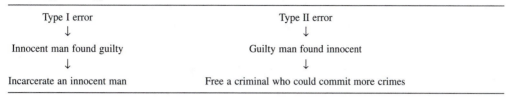

Type I error	Type II error
↓	↓
Innocent man found guilty	Guilty man found innocent
↓	↓
Incarcerate an innocent man	Free a criminal who could commit more crimes

Table 4.4 summarizes the two types of errors.

How much proof should constitute "proof beyond a reasonable doubt?" That is, how much proof should a jury demand before finding the defendant guilty? The answer depends on the relative costs of the two types of errors. As the costs of incarcerating an innocent man (type I error) increase relative to costs of freeing a guilty man (type II error), the jurors should demand a higher standard of proof, thereby making it more difficult to convict an innocent man. To motivate this point, consider the following question:

Question: Suppose that the prosecutor decides to try the seventeen-year-old as an adult rather than a juvenile. How should the jury's standard of proof be affected?

In this case the costs of incarcerating an innocent man (type I error) would increase because the conditions in a prison are more severe than the conditions in a juvenile detention center. Since the costs of incarcerating an innocent man (type I error) are greater, the jury should demand a higher standard of proof, thereby making a conviction more difficult:

Try defendant as adult	→	Cost of incarcerating innocent man becomes greater	→	More difficult to find defendant guilty	→	Higher standard of proof

Translating this into hypothesis testing language:

Try defendant as adult	→	Cost of type I error relative to type II error becomes greater	→	More difficult to reject H_0	→	Higher standard of proof

Now review the relationship between the significance level and the standard of proof; a lower significance level results in a higher standard of proof:

Lower significance level	→	More difficult to reject null hypothesis	→	Higher standard of proof

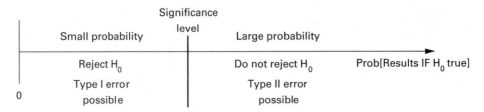

Figure 4.6
Significance levels and the standard of proof

To make it more difficult to reject the null hypothesis, to demand a higher standard of proof, the jury should adopt a lower significance level:

Try defendant as adult	→	Cost of type I error relative to type II error becomes greater	→	More difficult to reject H_0	→	Higher standard of proof

$$\downarrow$$

Lower
significance
level

The choice of the significance level involves trade-offs, a "tightrope act," in which we balance the relative costs of type I and type II error (see figure 4.6). There is no automatic, mechanical way to determine the appropriate significance level. It depends on the circumstances.

Chapter 4 Review Questions

1. Consider an estimation procedure.

    a. What are the general properties of an estimation procedure?

    b. Why are the general properties of an estimation procedure important? Explain.

2. Is there a relationship between the choice of a significance level and the standard of proof? Explain.

3. Focus on type I and type II errors.

    a. What is type I error?

    b. What is type II error?

    c. Does the choice of a significance level affect the likelihood of type I and type II errors? Explain.

Chapter 4 Exercises

1. Evaluate each of the following statements: "When an estimation procedure is unbiased

   a. the estimate will equal the actual value."

   b. the chances of the estimate being less than the actual value equal the chances of the estimate being greater."

   c. the mean of the estimate's probability distribution equals the actual value."

   d. the average of the estimates after many, many repetitions equals the actual value."

2. Thomas Jefferson and Sally Hemings: From *American Sphinx: The Character of Thomas Jefferson* by Joseph J. Ellis, page 21:

   The results, published in the prestigious scientific magazine *Nature* . . . showed a match between Jefferson and Eston Hemings, Sally's last child. The chances of such a match occurring randomly are less than one in a thousand.

   The DNA evidence suggests that a relationship existed between Thomas Jefferson and Sally Hemings.

   a. Play the cynic. What is the cynic's view?

   b. Formulate the null and alternative hypotheses. H_0

   c. What does Prob[Results IF H_0 true] equal? H_1

3. During 2003 the Texas legislature was embroiled in a partisan dispute to redraw the state's US congressional districts. Texas Republicans charged that the districts were drawn unfairly so as to increase the number of Texas Democrats sent to the US House of Representatives. The Republican position was based on a comparison of the statewide popular vote for House candidates in the 2002 election and the number of Democratic and Republican congressmen who were elected:

2002 statewide vote for Congress (total of all votes in the 32 Texas congressional districts)

Democratic votes	1,885,178
Republican votes	2,290,723

2002 Representatives elected

Democratic representatives	17
Republican representatives	15

   a. What is the fraction of voters statewide who cast ballots for a Democratic candidate? Call this fraction *DemVoterFrac*:

   DemVoterFrac = _____

b. What is the fraction of Democrats in the Texas delegation to the House?

c. Unfair districting is called gerrymandering. Do your answers to parts a and b suggest, at least the possibility of gerrymandering as Republicans charged?

d. Play the cynic. What is the cynic's view?

To assess the cynic's view, consider the following experiment: First write the names of each citizen who voted in the Texas election on a card along with the party for whom he/she voted. 1,885,178 of these cards have the name of a Democratic voter and 2,290,723 have the name of a Republican voter. Repeat the following 32 times:

- Thoroughly shuffle the cards.
- Select one card at random.
- Record the party for whom the citizen voted.
- Replace the card.

Then calculate the fraction of the voters drawn who voted for the Democratic candidate; call this fraction *DemCongressFrac*.

There is no "unfair districting" present in this experiment; that is, there is no gerrymandering present. Every Texas voter has an equal chance of being chosen. Consequently any discrepancy between the portion of voters who are Democrats and *DemCongressFrac* is just a random occurrence as the cynic contends.

e. Formulate the null and alternative hypotheses.

H_0: _____

H_1: _____

In words, express Prob[Results IF H_0 true] in terms of *DemCongressFrac* and *DemVoterFrac*.

f. *DemCongressFrac* is a random variable. Using the appropriate equations, calculate

Mean[***DemCongressFrac***]: _____

Var[***DemCongressFrac***]: _____

SD[***DemCongressFrac***]: _____

g. What does Prob[Results IF H_0 true] equal?

4. The Electoral College became especially controversial after the 2000 presidential election when Al Gore won the popular vote but lost the Electoral vote to George W. Bush.

2000 Presidential vote	Gore	Bush
Popular vote	50,999,897	50,456,002
Electoral vote	266	271

a. What fraction of the popular vote was cast for the Democratic candidate? Call this fraction *DemVoterFrac*:

DemVoterFrac = _____

b. What fraction of the Electoral votes was cast for the Democratic candidate?

c. Do your answers to parts a and b suggest, at least the possibility of, Electoral College unfairness? If so, which party, Democratic or Republican, appears to be favored?

d. Play the cynic. What is the cynic's view?

To assess the cynic's view, suppose that the following experiment was used to determine the makeup of the Electoral College: First write the names of each citizen who voted in the 2000 presidential election on a card along with the party for whom he/she voted. Repeat the following 537 times:

· Thoroughly shuffle the cards.

· Select one card at random.

· Record the party for whom the citizen voted.

· Replace the card.

Then calculate the fraction of the voters drawn who voted for the Democratic candidate; call this fraction *DemElectColFrac*.

There is no unfairness present in this experiment; that is, every voter has an equal chance of being chosen for the Electoral College. Consequently any discrepancy between the portion of voters who are Democrats and *DemElectColFrac* is just a random occurrence as the cynic contends.

e. Formulate the null and alternative hypotheses.

H_0: _____

H_1: _____

In words, express Prob[Results IF H_0 true] in terms of *DemElectColFrac* and *DemVoterFrac*.

f. *DemElectColFrac* is a random variable. Using the appropriate equations, calculate

Mean[**DemElectColFrac**]:   _____

Var[**DemElectColFrac**]:   _____

SD[**DemElectColFrac**]:   _____

g. What does Prob[Results IF H_0 true] equal? _____

5. Consider the 2008 presidential election:

2008 Presidential vote	Obama	McCain
Popular vote	69,498,215	59,948,240
Electoral vote	365	173

a. What fraction of the popular vote was cast for the Democratic candidate? Call this fraction *DemVoterFrac*:

DemVoterFrac = _____

b. What fraction of the Electoral votes was cast for the Democratic candidate?

c. Do your answers to parts a and b suggest, at least the possibility of, Electoral College unfairness? If so, which party, Democratic or Republican, appears to be favored?

d. Play the cynic. What is the cynic's view?

To assess the cynic's view, suppose that the following experiment was used to determine the makeup of the Electoral College: First write the names of each citizen who voted in the 2008 Presidential election on a card along with the party for whom he/she voted. Repeat the following 537 times:

· Thoroughly shuffle the cards.

· Select one card at random.

· Record the party for whom the citizen voted.

· Replace the card.

Then calculate the fraction of the voters drawn who voted for the Democratic candidate; call this fraction *DemElectColFrac*.

There is no unfairness present in this experiment; that is, every voter has an equal chance of being chosen for the Electoral College. Consequently any discrepancy between the portion of voters who are Democrats and *DemElectColFrac* is just a random occurrence as the cynic contends.

e. Formulate the null and alternative hypotheses.

H_0: _____

H_1: _____

In words, express Prob[Results IF H_0 true] in terms of *DemElectColFrac* and *DemVoterFrac*.

f. *DemElectColFrac* is a random variable. Using the appropriate equations, calculate

Mean[**DemElectColFrac**]:   _____

Var[**DemElectColFrac**]:   _____

SD[**DemElectColFrac**]:   _____

g. What does Prob[Results IF H_0 true] equal?

6. Recall the game described in the problems for chapters 2 and 3 that you and your roommate played:

• Thoroughly shuffle your roommate's standard deck of fifty-two cards: 13 spades, 13 hearts, 13 diamonds, and 13 clubs.

• Draw one card.

• If the card drawn is red, you win $1 from your roommate; if the card drawn is black, you lose $1.

• Replace the card drawn.

TNW equals your total net winnings after you played the game eighteen times:

$$TNW = v_1 + v_2 + \ldots + v_{18}$$

where v_i = your net winnings from the *i*th repetition of the game. Recall that the mean of *TNW*'s probability distribution equals 0 and the variance equals 18 when the game is played 18 times.

After you finish playing the game eighteen times, you won three times and your roommate won fifteen times; you have lost a total of $12, your *TNW* equals −12.

a. Considering your losses, might you be a little suspicious that your roommate's deck of cards might not be a standard deck containing 26 red cards and 26 black cards? Explain why or why not.

b. Play the cynic. What is the cynic's view?

c. Formulate the null and alternative hypotheses. Express Prob[Results IF H_0 true] in words and in terms of *TNW*.

d. What does Prob[Results IF H_0 true] equal?

7. Recall the game of roulette that we described in the problems of chapters 2 and 3. While playing roulette, you notice that the girlfriend of the casino's manager is also playing roulette. She always bets $1 the first set of twelve numbers. You observe that after she has played fifty times, she has won 35 times and lost 15 times; that is, in net she has won $20, her *TNW* equals 20. Recall that the mean of *TNW*'s probability distribution equals -1.35 and the variance equals 98.60 when someone bets on the first set of twelve numbers for fifty spins of the wheel.

    a. Considering her winnings, might you be a little suspicious that everything was on the "up and up?" Explain why or why not.

    b. Play the cynic. What is the cynic's view?

    c. Formulate the null and alternative hypotheses. Express Prob[Results IF H_0 true] in words and in terms of *TNW*.

    d. What does Prob[Results IF H_0 true] equal?

5 Ordinary Least Squares Estimation Procedure—The Mechanics

Chapter 5 Outline

5.1 Best Fitting Line

5.2 Clint's Assignment

5.3 Simple Regression Model
  5.3.1 Parameters of the Model
  5.3.2 Error Term and Random Influences
  5.3.3 What Is Simple about the Simple Regression Model?
  5.3.4 Best Fitting Line
  5.3.5 Needed: A Systematic Procedure to Determine the Best Fitting Line

5.4 Ordinary Least Squares (OLS) Estimation Procedure
  5.4.1 Sum of Squared Residuals Criterion
  5.4.2 Finding the Best Fitting Line

5.5 Importance of the Error Term
  5.5.1 Absence of Random Influences: A "What If" Question
  5.5.2 Presence of Random Influences: Back to Reality

5.6 Error Terms and Random Influences: A Closer Look

5.7 Standard Ordinary Least Squares (OLS) Premises

5.8 Clint's Assignment: The Two Parts

Chapter 5 Prep Questions

1. The following table reports the (disposable) income earned by Americans and their total savings between 1950 and 1975 in billions of dollars:

Year	Income (billion $)	Savings (billion $)	Year	Income (billion $)	Savings (billion $)	Year	Income (billion $)	Savings (billion $)
1950	210.1	17.9	**1959**	350.5	32.9	**1968**	625.0	67.0
1951	231.0	22.5	**1960**	365.4	33.7	**1969**	674.0	68.8
1952	243.4	23.9	**1961**	381.8	39.7	**1970**	735.7	87.2
1953	258.6	25.5	**1962**	405.1	41.8	**1971**	801.8	99.9
1954	264.3	24.3	**1963**	425.1	42.4	**1972**	869.1	98.5
1955	283.3	24.5	**1964**	462.5	51.1	**1973**	978.3	125.9
1956	303.0	31.3	**1965**	498.1	54.3	**1974**	1071.6	138.2
1957	319.8	32.9	**1966**	537.5	56.6	**1975**	1187.4	153.0
1958	330.5	34.3	**1967**	575.3	67.5			

    a. Construct a scatter diagram for income and savings. Place income on the horizontal axis and savings on the vertical axis.

    b. Economic theory teaches that savings increases with income. Do these data tend to support this theory?

    c. Using a ruler, draw a straight line through these points to estimate the relationship between savings and income. What equation describes this line?

    d. Using the equation, estimate by how much savings will increase if income increases by $1 billion.

2. Three students are enrolled in Professor Jeff Lord's 8:30 am class. Every week, he gives a short quiz. After returning the quiz, Professor Lord asks his students to report the number of minutes they studied; the students always respond honestly. The minutes studied and the quiz scores for the first quiz appear in the table below:[1]

Student	Minutes studied (x)	Quiz score (y)
1	5	66
2	15	87
3	25	90

---

1. NB: These data are not "real." Instead, they were constructed to illustrate important pedagogical points.

a. Construct a scatter diagram for income and savings. Place minutes on the horizontal axis and score on the vertical axis.

b. Ever since first grade, what have your parents and teachers been telling you about the relationship between studying and grades? For the most part, do these data tend to support this theory?

c. Using a ruler, draw a straight line through these points to estimate the relationship between minutes studied and quiz scores. What equation describes this line?

d. Using the equation, estimate by how much a student's quiz score would increase if that student studies one additional minute.

3. Recall that the presence of a random variable brings forth both bad news and good news.

a. What is the bad news?

b. What is the good news?

4. What is the relative frequency interpretation of probability?

5. Calculus problem: Consider the following equation:

$$SSR = (y_1 - b_{Const} - b_x x_1)^2 + (y_2 - b_{Const} - b_x x_2)^2 + (y_3 - b_{Const} - b_x x_3)^2$$

Differentiate SSR with respect to b_{Const} and set the derivative equal to 0:

$$\frac{dSSR}{db_{Const}} = 0$$

Solve for b_{Const}, and show that

$$b_{Const} = \bar{y} - b_x \bar{x}$$

where

$$\bar{y} = \frac{y_1 + y_2 + y_3}{3}$$

$$\bar{x} = \frac{x_1 + x_2 + x_3}{3}$$

6. Again, consider the following equation:

$$SSR = (y_1 - b_{Const} - b_x x_1)^2 + (y_2 - b_{Const} - b_x x_2)^2 + (y_3 - b_{Const} - b_x x_3)^2$$

Let

$$b_{Const} = \bar{y} - b_x \bar{x}$$

Substitute the expression for b_{Const} into the equation for SSR. Show that after the substitution:

$$SSR = [(y_1 - \bar{y}) - b_x(x_1 - \bar{x})]^2 + [(y_2 - \bar{y}) - b_x(x_2 - \bar{x})]^2 + [(y_3 - \bar{y}) - b_x(x_3 - \bar{x})]^2$$

Table 5.1
US annual income and savings data, 1950 to 1975

Year	Income (billion $)	Savings (billion $)	Year	Income (billion $)	Savings (billion $)	Year	Income (billion $)	Savings (billion $)
1950	210.1	17.9	1959	350.5	32.9	1968	625.0	67.0
1951	231.0	22.5	1960	365.4	33.7	1969	674.0	68.8
1952	243.4	23.9	1961	381.8	39.7	1970	735.7	87.2
1953	258.6	25.5	1962	405.1	41.8	1971	801.8	99.9
1954	264.3	24.3	1963	425.1	42.4	1972	869.1	98.5
1955	283.3	24.5	1964	462.5	51.1	1973	978.3	125.9
1956	303.0	31.3	1965	498.1	54.3	1974	1071.6	138.2
1957	319.8	32.9	1966	537.5	56.6	1975	1187.4	153.0
1958	330.5	34.3	1967	575.3	67.5			

5.1   Best Fitting Line

Recall the income and savings data we introduced in the chapter preview questions. Annual time series data of US disposable income and savings from 1950 and 1975 are shown in table 5.1. Economic theory suggests that as American households earn more income, they will save more:

Theory: Additional income increases savings.

Project: Assess the effect of income on savings.

Question: How can we use our data to "test" this theory? That is, how can we assess the effect of income on savings?

Answer: We begin by drawing a scatter diagram of the income–savings data (figure 5.1). Each point represents income and savings of a single year. The lower left point represents income and savings for 1950: (210.1, 17.9). The upper right point represents income and savings for 1975: (1187.4, 153.0). Each other point represents one of the other years.

The data appear to support the theory: as income increases, savings generally increase.

Question: How can we estimate the relationship between income and savings?

Answer: Draw a line through the points that best fits the data; then use the equation for the best fitting line to estimate the relationship (figure 5.2).[2]

---

2. In reality this example exhibits a time series phenomenon requiring the use of sophisticated techniques beyond the scope of an introductory textbook. Nevertheless, it does provide a clear way to motivate the notion of a best fitting line. Consequently this example is a useful pedagogical tool even though more advanced statistical techniques are required to analyze the data properly.

Savings (*y*)

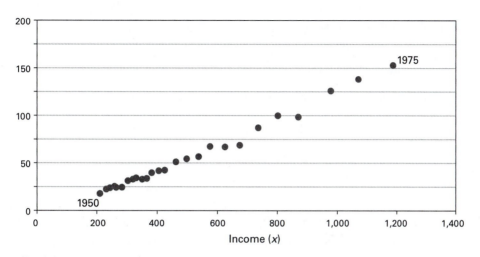

Figure 5.1
Income and savings scatter diagram

Savings (*y*)

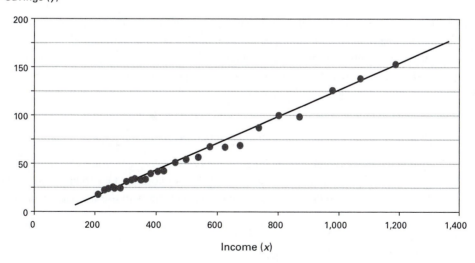

Figure 5.2
Income and savings scatter diagram with best fitting line

By choosing two points on this line, we can solve for the equation of the best fitting line. It looks like the points (200, 15) and (1200, 155) are more or less on the line. Let us use these two points to estimate the slope:

$$\text{Slope} = \frac{\text{Rise}}{\text{Run}} = \frac{155-15}{1200-200} = \frac{140}{1000} = 0.14$$

A little algebra allows us to derive the equation for this line:

$$\frac{y-15}{x-200} = 0.14$$

$$y - 15 = 0.14x - 28$$

$$y = 0.14x - 13$$

This equation suggests that if Americans earn an additional $1 of income, savings will rise by an estimated $0.14; or equivalently, we estimate that a $1,000 increase in income causes a $140 increase in savings. Since the slope is positive, the data appear to support our theory; additional income appears to increase savings.

5.2 Clint's Assignment

Consider a second example. Three students are enrolled in Professor Jeff Lord's 8:30 am class. Every week, he gives a short quiz. After returning the quiz, Professor Lord asks his students to report the number of minutes they studied; the students always respond honestly. The minutes studied and the quiz scores for the first quiz appear in table 5.2.

The theory suggests that a student's score on the quiz depends on the number of minutes he/she studied:

Theory: Additional studying increases quiz scores.

Also it is generally believed that Professor Lord, a very generous soul, awards students some points just for showing up for a quiz so early in the morning. Our friend Clint has been assigned the problem of assessing the theory. Clint's assignment is to use the data from Professor Lord's first quiz to assess the theory:

Table 5.2
First quiz results

Student	Minutes studied (x)	Quiz score (y)
1	5	66
2	15	87
3	25	90

Project: Use data from Professor Lord's first quiz to assess the effect of studying on quiz scores.

5.3 Simple Regression Model

The following equation allows us to use the **simple regression model** to assess the theory:

$$y_t = \beta_{Const} + \beta_x x_t + e_t$$

where

y_t = quiz score received by student t

x_t = number of minutes studied by student t

e_t = error term for student t: random influences

$t = 1, 2,$ and 3, denoting the three students: student 1, student 2, and student 3

y_t, the quiz score, is called the **dependent variable** and x_t, the minutes studied, the **explanatory variable**. The value of the dependent variable depends on the value of the explanatory variable. Or putting it differently, the value of the explanatory variable explains the value of the dependent value.

5.3.1 Parameters of the Model

β_{Const} and β_x, the constant and coefficient of the equation, are called the **parameters of the model**. To interpret the parameters recall the following:

• It is generally believed that Professor Lord gives students some points just for showing up for the quiz.

• The theory postulates that studying more will improve a student's score.

Using these observations, we can interpret the parameters, β_{Const} and β_x:

• β_{Const} represents the number of points Professor Lord gives students just for showing up.

• β_x represents the number of additional points earned for an additional minute of studying.

5.3.2 Error Term and Random Influences

e_t is the **error term**. The error term reflects all the random influences on student t's quiz score, y_t. For example, if, on the one hand, Professor Lord were in an unusually bad humor when he graded one student's quiz, that student's quiz score might be unusually low; this would be reflected by a negative error term. If, on the other hand, Professor Lord were in an unusually good humor, the student's score might be unusually high and a positive error term would result. Professor Lord's disposition is not the only sources of randomness. For example, a particular student could have just "lucked out" by correctly anticipating the questions Professor Lord asked. In this case the student's score would be unusually high, his/her error term would be positive. All such random influences are accounted for by the error term. The error term accounts for all the factors that cannot be determined or anticipated beforehand.

5.3.3   What Is Simple about the Simple Regression Model?

The word simple is used to describe the model because the model includes only a single explanatory variable. Obviously many other factors influence a student's quiz score; the number of minutes studied is only one factor. However, we must start somewhere. We will begin with the simple regression model. Later we will move on and introduce multiple regression models to analyze more realistic scenarios in which two or more explanatory variables are used to explain the dependent variable.

5.3.4   Best Fitting Line

Question: How can Clint use the data to assess the effect of studying on quiz scores?

Answer: He begins by drawing a scatter diagram using the data appearing in table 5.2 (plotted in figure 5.3).

The data appear to confirm the "theory." As minutes studied increase, quiz scores tend to increase.

Question: How can Clint estimate the relationship between minutes studied and the quiz score more precisely?

Answer: Draw a line through the points that best fits the data; then use the best fitting line's equation to estimate the relationship.

Clint's effort to "eyeball" the best fitting line appears in figure 5.4. By choosing two points on this line, Clint can solve for the equation of his best fitting line. It looks like the points (0, 60) and (20, 90) are more or less on the line. He can use these two points to estimate the slope:

$$\text{Slope} = \frac{\text{Rise}}{\text{Run}} = \frac{90 - 60}{20 - 0} = \frac{30}{20} = 1.5$$

Next Clint can use a little algebra to derive the equation for the line:

$$\frac{y - 60}{x - 0} = 1.5$$

$$y - 60 = 1.5x$$

$$y = 60 + 1.5x$$

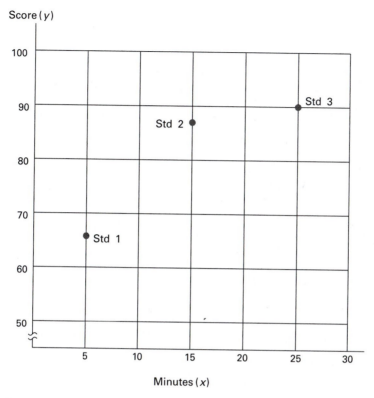

Figure 5.3
Minutes and scores scatter diagram

This equation suggests that an additional minute of studying increases a student's score by 1.5 points.

5.3.5   Needed: A Systematic Procedure to Determine the Best Fitting Line

Let us compare the two examples we introduced. In the income–savings case, the points were clustered tightly around our best fitting line (figure 5.2). Two individuals might not "eyeball" the identical "best fitting line," but the difference would be slight. In the minutes–scores case, however, the points are not clustered nearly so tightly (figure 5.3). Two individuals could "eyeball" the "best fitting line" very differently; therefore two individuals could derive substantially different equations for the best fitting line and would then would report very different estimates of the effect that studying has on quiz scores. Consequently we need a systematic procedure to determine the best fitting line. Furthermore, once we determine the best fitting line, we need to decide how confident we should be in the theory. We will now address two issues:

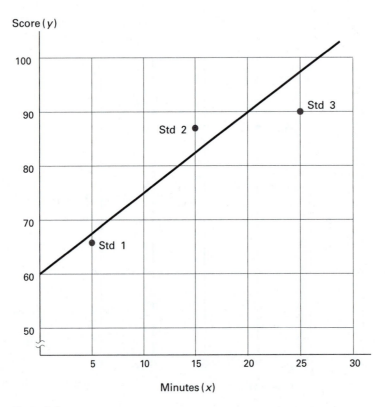

Figure 5.4
Minutes and scores scatter diagram with Clint's eyeballed best fitting line

• What systematic procedure should we use to determine the best fitting line for the data?

• In view of the best fitting line, how much confidence should we have in the theory's validity?

5.4   Ordinary Least Squares (OLS) Estimation Procedure

The **ordinary least squares (OLS) estimation procedure** is the most widely used estimation procedure to determine the equation for the line that "best fits" the data. Its popularity results from two factors:

• The procedure is computationally straightforward; it provides us (and computer software) with a relatively easy way to estimate the regression model's parameters, the constant and slope of the best fitting line.

• The procedure possesses several desirable properties when the error term meets certain conditions.

This chapter focuses on the computational aspects of the ordinary least squares (OLS) estimation procedure. In chapter 6 we turn to the properties of the estimation procedure.

We begin our study of the ordinary least squares (OLS) estimation procedure by introducing a little notation. We must distinguish between the actual values of the parameters and the estimates of the parameters. We have used the Greek letter beta, β, to denote the actual values. Recall the original model:

$$y_t = \beta_{Const} + \beta_x x_t + e_t$$

β_{Const} denotes the actual constant and β_x the actual coefficient.

We will use Roman italicized b's to denote the estimates. b_{Const} denotes the estimate of the constant for the best fitting line and b_x denotes the estimate of the coefficient for the best fitting line. That is, the equation for the best fitting line is

$$y = b_{Const} + b_x x$$

The constant and slope of the best fitting line, b_{Const} and b_x, estimate the values of β_{Const} and β_x.[3]

5.4.1   Sum of Squared Errors Criterion

The ordinary least squares (OLS) estimation procedure chooses b_{Const} and b_x so as to minimize the sum of the squared residuals. We will now use our example to illustrate precisely what this means. We begin by introducing an equation for each student's estimated score: $Esty_1$, $Esty_2$, and $Esty_3$.

$$Esty_1 = b_{Const} + b_x x_1, \quad Esty_2 = b_{Const} + b_x x_2, \quad Esty_3 = b_{Const} + b_x x_3$$

$Esty_1$, $Esty_2$, and $Esty_3$ estimate the score received by students 1, 2, and 3 based on the estimated constant, b_{Const}, the estimated coefficient, b_x, and the number of minutes each student studies, x_1, x_2, and x_3.

The difference between a student's actual score, y_t, and his/her estimated score, $Esty_t$, is called the residual, Res_t:

$$Res_1 = y_1 - Esty_1, \quad Res_2 = y_2 - Esty_2, \quad Res_3 = y_3 - Esty_3$$

Substituting for each student's estimated score:

$$Res_1 = y_1 - b_{Const} - b_x x_1, \quad Res_2 = y_2 - b_{Const} - b_x x_2, \quad Res_3 = y_3 - b_{Const} - b_x x_3$$

---

3. There is another convention that is often used to denote the parameter estimates, the "beta-hat" convention. The estimate of the constant is denoted by $\hat{\beta}_{Const}$ and the coefficient by $\hat{\beta}_x$. While the Roman italicized b's estimation convention will be used throughout this textbook, be aware that you will come across textbooks and articles that use the beta-hat convention. The b's and β's denote the same thing; they are interchangeable.

Next we square each residual and add them together to compute the sum of squared residuals, SSR:

$$SSR = Res_1^2 + Res_2^2 + Res_3^2$$

$$= (y_1 - b_{Const} - b_x x_1)^2 + (y_2 - b_{Const} - b_x x_2)^2 + (y_3 - b_{Const} - b_x x_3)^2$$

We can generalize the sum of squared residuals by considering a sample size of T:

$$SSR = \sum_{t=1}^{T} Res_t^2 = \sum_{t=1}^{T} (y_t - b_{Const} - b_x x_t)^2$$

where T = sample size. b_{Const} and b_x are chosen to minimize the sum of squared residuals. The following equations for b_{Const} and b_x accomplish this:

$$b_{Const} = \bar{y} - b_x \bar{x}, \quad b_x = \frac{\sum_{t=1}^{T} (y_t - \bar{y})(x_t - \bar{x})}{\sum_{t=1}^{T} (x_t - \bar{x})^2}$$

To justify the equations, consider a sample size of 3:

$$SSR = (y_1 - b_{Const} - b_x x_1)^2 + (y_2 - b_{Const} - b_x x_2)^2 + (y_3 - b_{Const} - b_x x_3)^2$$

5.4.2   Finding the Best Fitting Line

First focus on b_{Const}. Differentiate the sum of squared residuals, SSR, with respect to b_{Const} and set the derivative equal to 0:

$$\frac{dSSR}{db_{Const}} = -2(y_1 - b_{Const} - b_x x_1) + -2(y_2 - b_{Const} - b_x x_2) + -2(y_3 - b_{Const} - b_x x_3) = 0$$

Dividing by -2:

$$(y_1 - b_{Const} - b_x x_1) + (y_2 - b_{Const} - b_x x_2) + (y_3 - b_{Const} - b_x x_3) = 0$$

collecting like terms:

$$(y_1 + y_2 + y_3) + (-b_{Const} - b_{Const} - b_{Const}) + (-b_x x_1 - b_x x_2 - b_x x_3) = 0$$

simplifying:

$$(y_1 + y_2 + y_3) - 3b_{Const} - b_x(x_1 + x_2 + x_3) = 0$$

dividing by 3:

$$\frac{y_1 + y_2 + y_3}{3} - b_{Const} - b_x \frac{x_1 + x_2 + x_3}{3} = 0$$

Since $\dfrac{y_1 + y_2 + y_3}{3}$ equals the mean of y, $\bar{y}$, and $\dfrac{x_1 + x_2 + x_3}{3}$ equals the mean of x, $\bar{x}$:

$$\bar{y} - b_{Const} - b_x\bar{x} = 0$$

Our first equation, our equation for b_{Const}, is now justified. To minimize the sum of squared residuals, the following relationship must be met:

$$\bar{y} = b_{Const} + b_x\bar{x} \quad \text{or} \quad b_{Const} = \bar{y} - b_x\bar{x}$$

As illustrated in figure 5.5, this equation simply says that the best fitting line must pass through the point $(\bar{x}, \bar{y})$, the point representing the mean of x, minutes studied, and the mean of y, the quiz scores.

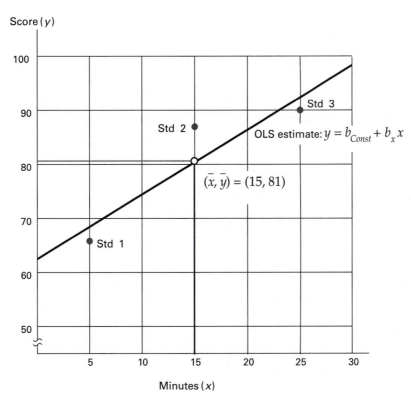

Figure 5.5
Minutes and scores scatter diagram with OLS best fitting line

It is easy to calculate the means:

$$\bar{x} = \frac{x_1 + x_2 + x_3}{3} = \frac{5+15+25}{3} = \frac{45}{3} = 15$$

$$\bar{y} = \frac{y_1 + y_2 + y_3}{3} = \frac{66+87+90}{3} = \frac{243}{3} = 81$$

The best fitting line passes through the point (15, 81).

Next we will justify the equation for b_x. Reconsider the equation for the sum of squared residuals and substitute $\bar{y} - b_x\bar{x}$ for b_{Const}:

$$SSR = (y_1 - b_{Const} - b_x x_1)^2 + (y_2 - b_{Const} - b_x x_2)^2 + (y_3 - b_{Const} - b_x x_3)^2$$

substituting $\bar{y} - b_x\bar{x}$ for b_{Const}:

$$= [y_1 - (\bar{y} - b_x\bar{x}) - b_x x_1]^2 + [y_2 - (\bar{y} - b_x\bar{x}) - b_x x_2]^2 + [y_3 - (\bar{y} - b_x\bar{x}) - b_x x_3]^2$$

simplifying each of the three terms:

$$= [y_1 - \bar{y} + b_x\bar{x} - b_x x_1]^2 + [y_2 - \bar{y} + b_x\bar{x} - b_x x_2]^2 + [y_3 - \bar{y} + b_x\bar{x} - b_x x_3]^2$$

switching of the "b_x terms" within each of the three squared terms:

$$= [y_1 - \bar{y} - b_x x_1 + b_x\bar{x}]^2 + [y_2 - \bar{y} - b_x x_2 + b_x\bar{x}]^2 + [y_3 - \bar{y} - b_x x_3 + b_x\bar{x}]^2$$

factoring out $-b_x$ within each of the three squared terms:

$$= [(y_1 - \bar{y}) - b_x(x_1 - \bar{x})]^2 + [(y_2 - \bar{y}) - b_x(x_2 - \bar{x})]^2 + [(y_3 - \bar{y}) - b_x(x_3 - \bar{x})]^2$$

To minimize the sum of squared residuals, differentiate SSR with respect to b_x and set the derivative equal to 0:

$$\frac{dSSR}{db_x} = -2[(y_1 - \bar{y}) - b_x(x_1 - \bar{x})](x_1 - \bar{x}) - 2[(y_2 - \bar{y}) - b_x(x_2 - \bar{x})](x_2 - \bar{x})$$
$$- 2[(y_3 - \bar{y}) - b_x(x_3 - \bar{x})](x_3 - \bar{x}) = 0$$

dividing by -2:

$$[(y_1 - \bar{y}) - b_x(x_1 - \bar{x})](x_1 - \bar{x}) + [(y_2 - \bar{y}) - b_x(x_2 - \bar{x})](x_2 - \bar{x})$$
$$+ [(y_3 - \bar{y}) - b_x(x_3 - \bar{x})](x_3 - \bar{x}) = 0$$

simplifying the expression:

$$(y_1 - \bar{y})(x_1 - \bar{x}) - b_x(x_1 - \bar{x})^2 + (y_2 - \bar{y})(x_2 - \bar{x}) - b_x(x_2 - \bar{x})^2$$
$$+ (y_3 - \bar{y})(x_3 - \bar{x}) - b_x(x_3 - \bar{x})^2 = 0$$

moving all terms containing b_x to the right side:

$$(y_1 - \bar{y})(x_1 - \bar{x}) + (y_2 - \bar{y})(x_2 - \bar{x}) + (y_3 - \bar{y})(x_3 - \bar{x}) = b_x(x_1 - \bar{x})^2 + b_x(x_2 - \bar{x})^2 + b_x(x_3 - \bar{x})^2$$

factoring out b_x from the right-side terms:

$$(y_1 - \bar{y})(x_1 - \bar{x}) + (y_2 - \bar{y})(x_2 - \bar{x}) + (y_3 - \bar{y})(x_3 - \bar{x}) = b_x[(x_1 - \bar{x})^2 + (x_2 - \bar{x})^2 + (x_3 - \bar{x})^2]$$

solving for b_x:

$$b_x = \frac{(y_1 - \bar{y})(x_1 - \bar{x}) + (y_2 - \bar{y})(x_2 - \bar{x}) + (y_3 - \bar{y})(x_3 - \bar{x})}{(x_1 - \bar{x})^2 + (x_2 - \bar{x})^2 + (x_3 - \bar{x})^2}$$

Now let us generalize this to a sample size of T:

$$b_x = \frac{\sum_{t=1}^{T}(y_t - \bar{y})(x_t - \bar{x})}{\sum_{t=1}^{T}(x_t - \bar{x})^2}$$

Therefore we have justified our second equation.

Let us return to Professor Lord's first quiz to calculate the constant and slope, b_{Const} and b_x, of the ordinary least squares (OLS) best fitting line for the first quiz's data. We have already computed the means for the quiz scores and minutes studied:

$$\bar{x} = \frac{x_1 + x_2 + x_3}{3} = \frac{5 + 15 + 25}{3} = \frac{45}{3} = 15$$

$$\bar{y} = \frac{y_1 + y_2 + y_3}{3} = \frac{66 + 87 + 90}{3} = \frac{243}{3} = 81$$

Now, for each student, calculate the deviation of y from its mean and the deviations of x from its mean:

Student	y_t	$\bar{y}$	$y_t - \bar{y}$	x_t	$\bar{x}$	$x_t - \bar{x}$
1	66	81	−15	5	15	−10
2	87	81	6	15	15	0
3	90	81	9	25	15	10

Next, for each student, calculate the products of the y and x deviations and squared x deviations:

Student	$(y_t - \bar{y})(x_t - \bar{x})$	$(x_t - \bar{x})^2$
1	$(-15)(-10) = 150$	$(-10)^2 = 100$
2	$(6)(0) = 0$	$(0)^2 = 0$
3	$(9)(10) = \underline{90}$	$(10)^2 = \underline{100}$
	Sum = 240	Sum = 200

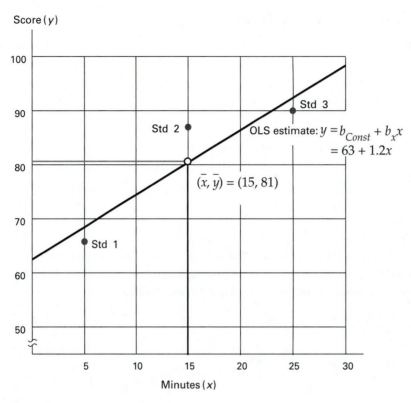

Figure 5.6
Minutes and scores scatter diagram with OLS best fitting line

b_x equals the sum of the products of the y and x deviations divided by the sum of the squared x deviations:

$$b_x = \frac{\sum_{t=1}^{T}(y_t - \bar{y})(x_t - \bar{x})}{\sum_{t=1}^{T}(x_t - \bar{x})^2} = \frac{240}{200} = \frac{6}{5} = 1.2$$

To calculate b_{Const} recall that the best fitting line passes through the point representing the average value of x and y, $(\bar{x}, \bar{y})$ (see figure 5.6):

$$\bar{y} = b_{Const} + b_x\bar{x}$$

Solving for b_{Const} obtains

$$b_{Const} = \bar{y} - b_x\bar{x}$$

We just learned that b_x equals 6/5. The average of the x's, $\bar{x}$, equals 15 and the average of the y's, $\bar{y}$, equals 81. Substituting, we have

$$b_{Const} = 81 - \frac{6}{5}\bar{x}$$
$$= 81 - 18 = 63$$

Using the ordinary least squares (OLS) estimation procedure, we have the best fitting line for Professor Lord's first quiz as

$$y = 63 + \frac{6}{5}x = 63 + 1.2x$$

Consequently the least squares estimates for β_{Const} and β_x are 63 and 1.2. These estimates suggest that Professor Lord gives each student 63 points just for showing up; each minute studied earns the student 1.2 additional points. Based on the regression we estimate that:

- 1 additional minute studied increases the quiz score by 1.2 points.
- 2 additional minutes studied increase the quiz score by 2.4 points.
- And so on.

Let us now quickly calculate the sum of squared residuals for the best fitting line:

Student	x_t	y_t	$Esty_t = 63 + \dfrac{6}{5}x_t = 63 + 1.2x_t$	$Res_t = y_t - Esty_t$	Res_t^2
1	5	66	$63 + \dfrac{6}{5} \times 5 = 63 + 6 = 69$	$66 - 69 = -3$	9
2	15	87	$63 + \dfrac{6}{5} \times 15 = 63 + 6 \times 3 = 63 + 18 = 81$	$87 - 81 = 6$	36
3	25	90	$63 + \dfrac{6}{5} \times 25 = 63 + 6 \times 5 = 63 + 30 = 93$	$90 - 93 = -3$	9
					$SSR = 54$

The sum of squared residuals for the best fitting line is 54.

Econometrics Lab 5.1: Finding the Ordinary Least Squares (OLS) Estimates

We can use our Econometrics Lab to emphasize how the ordinary least squares (OLS) estimation procedure determines the best fitting line by accessing the Best Fitting Line simulation (figure 5.7).

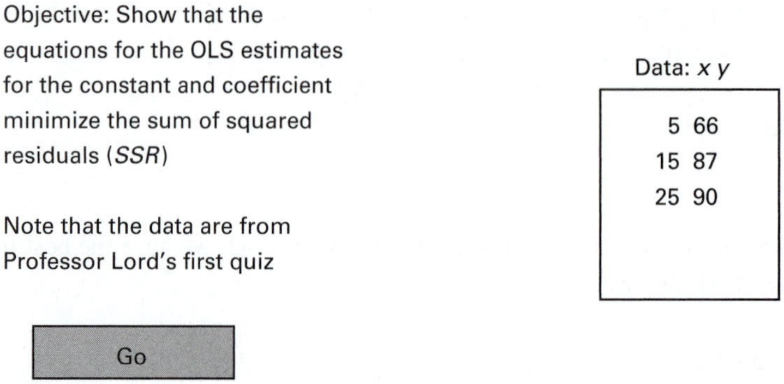

Objective: Show that the
equations for the OLS estimates
for the constant and coefficient
minimize the sum of squared
residuals (*SSR*)

Note that the data are from
Professor Lord's first quiz

Data: *x y*

5	66
15	87
25	90

Go

Figure 5.7
Best Fitting Line simulation—Data

By default the data from Professor Lord's first quiz are specified: the values of *x* and *y* for the first student are 5 and 66, for the second student 15 and 87, and for the third student 25 and 90.

[To access this online material, go to http://mitpress.mit.edu/westhoffeconometrics and select Lab 5.1.]

Click **Go**. A new screen appears as shown in figure 5.8 with two slider bars, one slide bar for the constant and one for the coefficient.

By default the constant and coefficient values are 63 and 1.2, the ordinary least squares (OLS) estimates. Also the arithmetic used to calculate the sum of squared residuals is displayed. When the constant equals 63 and the coefficient equals 1.2, the sum of squared residuals equals 54.00; this is just the value that we calculated.

Next experiment with different values for the constant and coefficient values by moving the two sliders. Convince yourself that the equations we used to calculate the estimate for the constant and coefficient indeed minimize the sum of squared residuals.

Software and the ordinary least squares (OLS) estimation procedure: Fortunately, we do not have to trudge through the laborious arithmetic to compute the ordinary least squares (OLS) estimates. Statistical software can do the work for us.

Professor Lord's first quiz data: Cross-sectional data of minutes studied and quiz scores in the first quiz for the three students enrolled in Professor Lord's class (table 5.3).

[To access this online material, go to http://mitpress.mit.edu/westhoffeconometrics and select Professor Lord's First Quiz.]

Constant   Coefficient

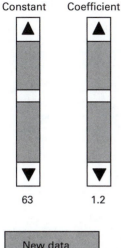

x	Act y	Est y	Res	Res sqr
5.0	66.0	69.0	–3.0	9.00
15.0	87.0	81.0	6.0	36.00
25.0	90.0	93.0	–3.0	9.00
			SSR	= 54.00

63   1.2

New data

Figure 5.8
Best Fitting Line simulation—Parameter estimates

Table 5.3
First quiz results

Student	Minutes studied (x)	Quiz score (y)
1	5	66
2	15	87
3	25	90

Getting Started in EViews

We can use the statistical package EViews to perform the calculations. After opening the workfile in EViews:

• In the Workfile window: Click on the dependent variable, **y**, first; and then, click on the explanatory variable, **x**, while depressing the **<Ctrl>** key.

• In the Workfile window: Double click on a highlighted variable.

• In the Workfile window: Click **Open Equation**.

• In the Equation Specification window: Click **OK**.

This window previews the regression that will be run; note that the dependent variable, "y," is the first variable listed followed by two expressions representing the explanatory variable, "x," and the constant "c."

Do not forget to close the workfile.

Table 5.4
OLS first quiz regression results

Ordinary least squares (OLS)				
Dependent variable: y				
Explanatory variable(s):	Estimate	SE	t-Statistic	Prob
x	1.200000	0.519615	2.309401	0.2601
Const	63.00000	8.874120	7.099296	0.0891
Number of observations	3			
Sum squared residuals	54.00000			
Estimated equation:	$Esty = 63 + 1.2x$			
Interpretation of estimates:				

$b_{Const} = 63$: students receive 63 points for showing up.

$b_x = 1.2$: students receive 1.2 additional points for each additional minute studied.

Critical result: coefficient estimate equals 1.2; positive sign of the coefficient estimate suggests that additional studying increases quiz scores. This evidence lends support to our theory.

Table 5.4 reports the values of the coefficient and constant for the best fitting line. Note that the sum of squared residuals for the best fitting line is also included.

5.5   Importance of the Error Term

Recall the regression model:

$$y_t = \beta_{Const} + \beta_x x_t + e_t$$

where

y_t = quiz score of student t

x_t = minutes studied by student t

e_t = error term for student t

The parameters of the model, the values of the constant, β_{Const}, and the coefficient, β_x, represent the actual number of

• points Professor Lord gives students just for showing up, β_{Const};
• additional points earned for each minute of study, β_x.

Obviously the parameters of the model play an important role, but what about the error term, e_t? To illustrate the importance of the error term, suppose that somehow we know the values of β_{Const} and β_x. For the moment, suppose that β_{Const}, the actual constant, equals 50 and β_x, the actual coefficient, equals 2. In words, this means that Professor Lord gives each student 50 points for showing up; furthermore each minute of study provides the student with two additional points. Consequently the regression model is

$$y_t = 50 + 2x_t + e_t$$

Note: In the real world, we never know the actual values of the constant and coefficient. We are assuming that we do here, just to illustrate the importance of the error term.

The error term reflects all the factors that cannot be anticipated or determined before the quiz is given; that is, the error term represents all random influences. In the absence of random influences, the error terms would equal 0.

5.5.1   Absence of Random Influences: A "What If" Question

Assume, only for the moment, that there are no random influences; consequently each error term would equal 0 (figure 5.9). While this assumption is unrealistic, it allows us to appreciate the important role played by the error term. Focus on the first student taking Professor Lord's first

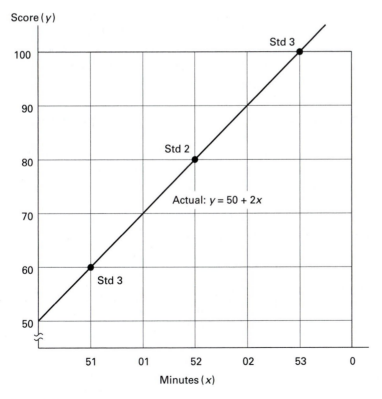

Figure 5.9
Best fitting line with no error term

quiz. The first student studies for 5 minutes. In the absence of random influences (that is, if e_1 equaled 0), what score would the first student receive on the quiz? The answer is 60:

$$y_1 = 50 + 2 \times 5 + 0 = 50 + 10 = 60$$

Next consider the second student. The second student studies for 15 minutes. In the absence of random influences, the second student would receive an 80 on the quiz:

$$y_2 = 50 + 2 \times 15 + 0 = 50 + 30 = 80$$

The third student would receive a 100:

$$y_3 = 50 + 2 \times 25 + 0 = 50 + 50 = 100$$

We summarize this in table 5.5:

In the absence of random influences, the intercept and slope of the best fitting line would equal the actual constant and the actual coefficient, β_{Const} and β_x:

$$y = \beta_{Const} + \beta_x x = 50 + 2x$$

In sum, in the absence of random influences, the error term of each student equals 0 and the best fitting line fits the data perfectly. The slope of this line equals 2, the actual coefficient, and the vertical intercept of the line equals 50, the actual constant. Without random influences, it is easy to determine the actual constant and coefficient by applying a little algebra. We will now use a simulation to emphasize this point (figure 5.10).

Econometrics Lab 5.2: Coefficient Estimates When Random Influences Are Absent

The Coefficient Estimate simulation allows us to do something we cannot do in the real world. It allows us to specify the actual values of the constant and coefficient in the model; that is, we can select β_{Const} and β_x. We can specify the number of values:

- Points Professor Lord gives students just for showing up, β_{Const}; by default, β_{Const} is set at 50.
- Additional points earned for an additional minute of study, β_x; by default, β_x is set at 2.

Table 5.5
Quiz results with no random influences (no error term)

Student	Minutes (x)	Absence of random influences score (y)
1	5	60
2	15	80
3	25	100

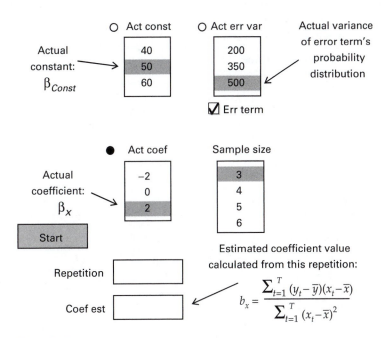

Figure 5.10
Coefficient Estimate simulation

Consequently the regression model is

$$y_t = 50 + 2x_t + e_t$$

Each repetition of the simulation represents a quiz from a single week. In each repetition the simulation does the following:

• Calculates the score for each student based on the actual constant (β_{Const}), the actual coefficient (β_x), and the number of minutes the student studied; then, to be realistic, the simulation can add a random influence in the form of the error term, e_t. An error term is included whenever the Err Term checkbox is checked.

• Applies the ordinary least squares (OLS) estimation procedure to estimate the coefficient.

When the Pause box is checked the simulation stops after each repetition; when it is cleared, quizzes are simulated repeatedly until the "Stop" button is clicked.

 [To access this online material, go to http://mitpress.mit.edu/westhoffeconometrics and select Lab 5.2.]

We can eliminate random influences by clearing the Err Term box. After doing so, click **Start** and then **Continue** a few times. We discover that in the absence of random influences the estimate of the coefficient value always equals the actual value, 2 (see table 5.6).

Table 5.6
Simulation results with no random influences (no error term)

Repetition	Coefficient estimate: No error term
1	2.0
2	2.0
3	2.0
4	2.0

Table 5.7
Quiz results with random influences (with error term)

Student	Minutes (x)	Inclusion of random influences score (y)
1	5	66
2	15	87
3	25	90

This is precisely what we concluded earlier from the scatter diagram. In the absence of random influences, the best fitting line fits the data perfectly. The best fitting line's slope equals the actual value of the coefficient.

5.5.2   Presence of Random Influences: Back to Reality

The real world is not that simple, however; random influences play an important role. In the real world, random influences are inevitably present. In figure 5.11 the actual scores on the first quiz have been added to the scatter diagram. As a consequence of the random influences, students 1 and 2 over perform while student 3 under performs (table 5.7).

As illustrated in figure 5.12, when random influences are present, we cannot expect the intercept and slope of the best fitting line to equal the actual constant and the actual coefficient. The intercept and slope of the best fitting line, b_{Const} and b_x, are affected by the random influences. Consequently the intercept and slope of the best fitting line, b_{Const} and b_x, are themselves random variables. Even if we knew the actual constant and slope, that is, if we knew the actual values of β_{Const} and β_x, we could not predict the values of the constant and slope of the best fitting line, b_{Const} and b_x, with certainty before the quiz was given.

Econometrics Lab 5.3: Coefficient Estimates When Random Influences Are Present

We will now use the Coefficient Estimate simulation to emphasize this point. We will show that in the presence of random influences, the coefficient of the best fitting line is a random variable.

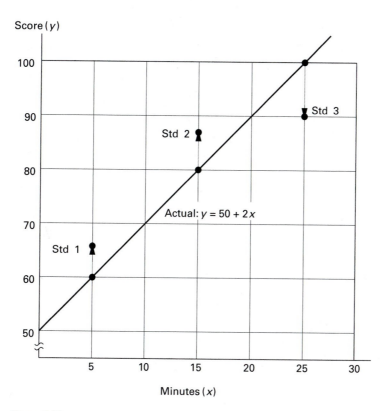

Figure 5.11
Scatter diagram with error term

[To access this online material, go to http://mitpress.mit.edu/westhoffeconometrics and select Lab 5.3.]

Note that the Error Term checkbox is now checked to include the error term. Be certain that the Pause checkbox is checked and then click **Start**. When the simulation computes the best fitting line, the estimated value of the coefficient typically is not 2 despite the fact that the actual value of the coefficient is 2. Click the **Continue** button a few more times to simulate each successive week's quiz. What do you observe? We simply cannot expect the coefficient estimate to equal the actual value of the coefficient. In fact, when random influences are present, the coefficient estimate almost never equals the actual value of the coefficient. Sometimes the estimate is less than the actual value, 2, and sometimes it is greater than the actual value. When random influences are present, the coefficient estimates are random variables.

While your coefficient estimates will no doubt differ from the estimates in table 5.8, one thing is clear. Even if we know the actual value of the coefficient, as we do in the simulation, we cannot predict with certainty the value of the estimate from one repetition. Our last two

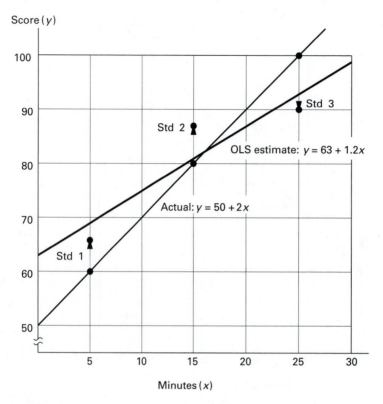

Figure 5.12
OLS best fitting line with error term

Table 5.8
Simulation results with random influences (with error term)

Repetition	Coefficient estimate: With error term
1	1.8
2	1.6
3	3.2
4	1.9

simulations illustrate a critical point: the coefficient estimate is a random variable as a consequence of the random influences introduced by each student's error term.

5.6   Error Terms and Random Influences: A Closer Look

We will now use a simulation to gain insights into random influences and error terms. As we know, random influences are those factors that cannot be anticipated or determined beforehand. Sometimes random influences lead to a higher quiz score, and other times they lead to a lower score. The error terms embody these random influences:

- Sometimes the error term is positive, indicating that the score is higher than "usual."
- Other times the error term is negative indicating that the score is lower than "usual."

If the random influences are indeed random, they should be a "wash" after many, many quizzes. That is, random influences should not systematically lead to higher or lower quiz scores. In other words, if the error terms truly reflect random influences, they should average out to 0 "in the long run."

Econometrics Lab 5.4: Error Terms When Random Influences Are Present

Let us now check to be certain that the simulations are capturing random influences properly by accessing the Error Term simulation (figure 5.13).

[To access this online material, go to http://mitpress.mit.edu/westhoffeconometrics and select Lab 5.4.].

Initially, the Pause checkbox is checked and the error term variance is 500. Now click **Start** and observe that the simulation reports the numerical value error term for each of the three students. Record these three values. Also note that the simulation constructs a histogram for each student's error term and also reports the mean and variance. Click **Continue** again to observe the numerical values of the error terms for the second quiz. Confirm that the simulation is calculating the mean and variance of each student's error terms correctly. Click **Continue** a few more times. Note that the error terms are indeed random variables. Before the quiz is given, we

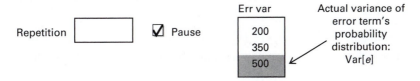

Figure 5.13
Error Term simulation

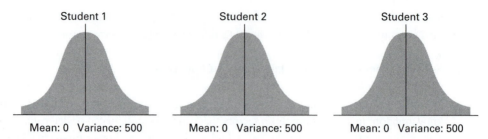

Mean: 0   Variance: 500   Mean: 0   Variance: 500   Mean: 0   Variance: 500

Figure 5.14
Error Term simulation results

cannot predict the numerical value of a student's error term. Each student's histogram shows that sometimes the error term for that student is positive and sometimes it is negative. Next clear the Pause checkbox and click **Continue**. After many, many repetitions click **Stop**.

After many, many repetitions, the mean (average) of each student's error terms equals about 0 (figure 5.14). Consequently each student's error term truly represents a random influence; it does not systematically influence the student's quiz score. It is also instructive to focus on each student's histogram. For each student, the numerical value of the error term is positive about half the time and negative about half the time after many, many repetitions.

In sum, the error terms represent random influences; consequently the error terms have no systematic effect on quiz scores, the dependent variable:

· Sometimes the error term is positive, indicating that the score is higher than "usual."

· Other times the error term is negative indicating that the score is lower than "usual."

What can we say about the student's error terms beforehand, before the next quiz? We can describe their probability distribution. The chances that a student's error term will be positive is the same as the chances it will be negative. For any one quiz, the mean of each student's error term's probability distribution equals 0:

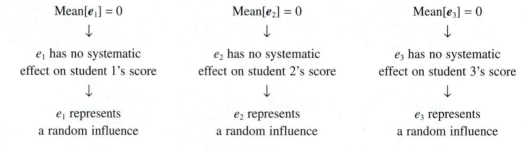

$\text{Mean}[e_1] = 0$	$\text{Mean}[e_2] = 0$	$\text{Mean}[e_3] = 0$
↓	↓	↓
e_1 has no systematic effect on student 1's score	e_2 has no systematic effect on student 2's score	e_3 has no systematic effect on student 3's score
↓	↓	↓
e_1 represents a random influence	e_2 represents a random influence	e_3 represents a random influence

5.7   Standard Ordinary Least Squares (OLS) Premises

Initially, we will make some strong assumptions regarding the explanatory variables and the error terms:

• **Error term equal variance premise:**   The variance of the error term's probability distribution for each observation is the same; all the variances equal Var[e]:

$$\text{Var}[e_1] = \text{Var}[e_2] = \ldots = \text{Var}[e_T] = \text{Var}[e]$$

• **Error term/error term independence premise:**   The error terms are independent: $\text{Cov}[e_i, e_j] = 0$. Knowing the value of the error term from one observation does not help us predict the value of the error term for any other observation.

• **Explanatory variable/error term independence premise:**   The explanatory variables, the x_t's, and the error terms, the e_t's, are not correlated. Knowing the value of an observation's explanatory variable does not help us predict the value of that observation's error term.

We call these premises the standard ordinary least squares (OLS) premises. They make the analysis as straightforward as possible. In part IV of this textbook we relax these premises to study more general cases. Our strategy is to start with the most straightforward case and then move on to more complex ones. While we only briefly cite the premises here, we will return to them in the fourth part of the textbook to study their implications.

5.8   Clint's Assignment: The Two Parts

Recall Clint's assignment. He must assess the effect of studying on quiz scores by using Professor Lord's first quiz as evidence. Clint can apply the ordinary least squares (OLS) estimation procedure; the OLS estimate for the value of the coefficient is 1.2. But we now know that the estimate is a random variable. We cannot expect the coefficient estimate from the one quiz, 1.2, to equal the actual value of the coefficient, the actual impact that studying has on a student's quiz score. We will proceed by dividing Clint's assignment into two related parts:

• **Reliability of the coefficient estimate:**   How reliable is the coefficient estimate calculated from the results of the first quiz? That is, how confident should Clint be that the coefficient estimate, 1.2, will be close to the actual value?

• **Assessment of the theory:**   In view of the fact that Clint's estimate of the coefficient equals 1.2, how confident should Clint be that the theory is correct, that additional studying increases quiz scores?

In the next few chapters we will address these issues.

Chapter 5 Review Questions

1. What criterion does the ordinary least squares (OLS) estimation procedure apply when deriving the best fitting line?

2. How are random influences captured in the simple regression model?

3. When applying the ordinary least squares (OLS) estimation procedure, what type of variables are the parameter estimates as a consequence of random influences?

4. What are the standard ordinary least square (OLS) premises?

Chapter 5 Exercises

1. A colleague of Professor Lord is teaching another course in which three students are enrolled. The number of minutes each student studied and his/her score on the quiz are reported below:

Regression example data: Cross-sectional data of minutes studied and quiz scores from a course taught by Professor Lord's colleague.

x_t = minutes studied by student t

y_t = quiz score received by student t

Student	Minutes studied (x)	Quiz score (y)
1	5	14
2	10	44
3	30	80

a. On a sheet of graph paper, plot a scatter diagram of the data. Then, using a ruler, draw a straight line that, by sight, best fits the data.

b. Using a calculator and the equations we derived in class, apply the least squares estimation procedure to find the best fitting line by filling in the blanks:

First, calculate the means:

Means: $\bar{x} =$ _____ $=$ _____

$\bar{y} =$ _____ $=$ _____

Second, for each student calculate the deviation of x from its mean and the deviation of y from its mean:

Student	y_t	$\bar{y}$	$y_t - \bar{y}$	x_t	$\bar{x}$	$x_t - \bar{x}$
1	14	____	____	5	____	____
2	44	____	____	10	____	____
3	80	____	____	30	____	____

Third, calculate the products of the y and x deviations and squared x deviations for each student; then calculate the sums:

Student	$(y_t - \bar{y})(x_t - \bar{x})$			$(x_t - \bar{x})^2$		
1	_____	=	_____	_____	=	_____
2	_____	=	_____	_____	=	_____
3	_____	=	_____	_____	=	_____
	Sum	=	_____	Sum	=	_____

Now apply the equations:

$$b_x = \frac{\sum_{t=1}^{T}(y_t - \bar{y})(x_t - \bar{x})}{\sum_{t=1}^{T}(x_t - \bar{x})^2} = \frac{}{} = \underline{}$$

$$b_{Const} = \bar{y} = b_x\bar{x} = \underline{} - \underline{} = \underline{} - \underline{} = \underline{}$$

c. Calculate the sum of squared residuals by filling in the following blanks:

Student	x_t	y_t	$Esty_t = b_{Const} + b_x x_t$			$Res_t = y_t - Esty_t$			Res_t^2
1	5	14	_____	=	____	____	– ____	= ____	____
2	10	44	_____	=	____	____	– ____	= ____	____
3	30	80	_____	=	____	____	– ____	= ____	____
								SSR =	____

2. Using statistical software, check your answer to exercise 1.

[To access this online material, go to http://mitpress.mit.edu/westhoffeconometrics and select Regression Example.]

Getting Started in EViews

After opening the file, use the following steps to run the regression:

- In the Workfile window: Click on the dependent variable, **y**, first; and then, click on the explanatory variable, **x**, while depressing the <Ctrl> key.
- In the Workfile window: Double click on a highlighted variable.
- In the Workfile window: Click **Open Equation**.
- In the Equation Specification window: Click **OK**.

Do not forget to close the workfile.

a. Are the calculations you made in problem 1 consistent with those provided by the software?

b. Based on the regression results, what equation estimates the effect of minutes studied on quiz scores?

c. Estimate the effect of minutes studied on quiz scores:

    i. 1 additional minute results in _____ additional points.

    ii. 2 additional minutes result in _____ additional points.

    iii. 5 additional minutes result in _____ additional points.

    iv. 1 fewer minute results in _____ fewer points.

    v. 2 fewer minutes result in _____ fewer points.

3. Consider crude oil production in the United States.

Crude oil production data: Annual time series data of US crude oil production and prices from 1976 to 2004.

OilProdBarrels$_t$ US crude oil productions in year t (thousands of barrels per day)

Price$_t$ Real wellhead price of crude oil in year t (1982–84 dollars per barrel)

Year	Price ($ per barrel)	Crude oil production (1,000s of barrels)	Year	Price ($ per barrel)	Crude oil production (1,000s of barrels)
1976	14.39	8,132	1991	12.14	7,417
1977	14.14	8,245	1992	11.40	7,171
1978	13.80	8,707	1993	9.86	6,847
1979	17.41	8,552	1994	8.90	6,662
1980	26.20	8,597	1995	9.59	6,560
1981	34.95	8,572	1996	11.77	6,465
1982	29.55	8,649	1997	10.74	6,452
1983	26.30	8,688	1998	6.67	6,252
1984	24.91	8,879	1999	9.34	5,881
1985	22.39	8,971	2000	15.52	5,822
1986	11.41	8,680	2001	12.33	5,801
1987	13.56	8,349	2002	12.51	5,746
1988	10.63	8,140	2003	14.98	5,681
1989	12.79	7,613	2004	19.47	5,419
1990	15.33	7,355			

a. What does economic theory teach us about how the real price of crude oil should affect US crude oil production?

b. Using statistical software, estimate the effect that the real price of oil has on US crude oil production.

 [To access this online material, go to http://mitpress.mit.edu/westhoffeconometrics and select Crude Oil Production.]

Getting Started in EViews

After opening the workfile in EViews:

• In the Workfile window: Click on the dependent variable, **oilprodbarrels**, first; and then click on the explanatory variable, **price**, while depressing the <Ctrl> key.

• In the Workfile window: Double click on a highlighted variable.

• In the Workfile window: Click **Open Equation.**

• In Equation Specification window: Click **OK.**

• Do not forget to close the workfile.

c. Do the regression results tend to support the theory? Explain.

d. Estimate the effect of the real price of crude oil on US crude oil production:

   i. How would a $1 increase in the real price affect US crude oil production? _____

   ii. How would a $2 increase in the real price affect US crude oil production? _____

   iii. How would a $5 decrease in the real price affect US crude oil production? _____

4. Consider labor market supply data.

Labor supply data: Cross-sectional data of hours worked and wages for the 92 married workers included in the March 2007 Current Population Survey residing in the Northeast region of the United States who earned bachelor but no advanced degrees.

HoursPerWeek$_t$ Hours worked per week by worker t

Wage$_t$ Wage earned by worker t (dollars per hour)

a. What does economic theory teach us about how the wage rate should affect the number of hours of labor a worker will supply?

b. Using statistical software, estimate the effect that the wage rate has on the number of hours of labor a worker supplies.

 [To access this online material, go to http://mitpress.mit.edu/westhoffeconometrics and select Labor Supply.]

c. Do the regression results tend to support the theory? Explain.

d. Estimate the effect of the wage on labor supply:

i. How would a $1.00 increase in the wage affect the hours of labor supplied? _____

ii. How would a $2.00 increase in the wage affect the hours of labor supplied? _____

iii. How would a $.50 decrease in the wage affect the hours of labor supplied? _____

5. Consider gasoline consumption in the United States.

Gasoline consumption data: Annual time series data US gasoline consumption and prices from 1990 to 1999.

GasCons$_t$ US gasoline consumption in year t (millions of gallons per day)

PriceDollars$_t$ Real price of gasoline in year t (2000 dollars per gallon)

Year	Real price ($ per gal)	Gasoline consumption (millions of gals)	Year	Real price ($ per gal)	Gasoline consumption (millions of gals)
1990	1.43	303.9	1995	1.25	327.1
1991	1.35	301.9	1996	1.31	331.4
1992	1.31	305.3	1997	1.29	336.7
1993	1.25	314.0	1998	1.10	346.7
1994	1.23	319.2	1999	1.19	354.1

a. What does economic theory teach us about how the real price of gasoline should affect US gasoline consumption?

b. Using statistical software, estimate the effect that the real price of gasoline has on US gasoline consumption.

[To access this online material, go to http://mitpress.mit.edu/westhoffeconometrics and select Gasoline Consumption.]

c. Do the regression results tend to support the theory? Explain.

d. Estimate the effect of the real price of gasoline on US gasoline consumption:

i. How would a $1.00 increase in the real price affect US gasoline consumption?

_____

ii. How would a $2.00 increase in the real price affect US gasoline consumption?

_____

iii. How would a $0.50 increase in the real price affect US gasoline consumption?

_____

iv. How would a \$1.00 decrease in the real price affect US gasoline consumption?

———————

v. How would a \$2.00 decrease in the real price affect US gasoline consumption?

———————

6. Consider cigarette smoking data the United States.

Cigarette consumption data: Cross section of per capita cigarette consumption and prices in fiscal year 2008 for the 50 states and the District of Columbia.

$CigConsPC_t$	Cigarette consumption per capita in state t (packs)
$EducCollege_t$	Percentage of population with bachelor degrees in state t
$EducHighSchool_t$	Percentage of population with high school diplomas in state t
$IncPC_t$	Income per capita in state t (1,000s of dollars)
Pop_t	population of state t (persons)
$PriceConsumer_t$	Price of cigarettes in state t paid by consumers (dollars per pack)
$PriceSupplier_t$	Price of cigarettes in state t received by suppliers (dollars per pack)
$RegionMidWest_t$	1 if state t in Midwest census region, 0 otherwise
$RegionNorthEast_t$	1 if state t in Northeast census region, 0 otherwise
$RegionSouth_t$	1 if state t in South census region, 0 otherwise
$RegionWest_t$	1 if state t in West census region, 0 otherwise
$SmokeRateAdult_t$	Percentage of adults who smoke in state t
$SmokeRateYouth_t$	Percentage of youths who smoke in state t
$State_t$	Name of state t
Tax_t	Cigarette tax rate in state t (dollars per pack)
$TobProdPC_t$	Per capita tobacco production in state t (pounds)

Conventional wisdom suggests that high school drop outs are more likely to smoke cigarettes than those who graduate.

a. Using statistical software, estimate the effect that the completion of high school has on per capita cigarette consumption.

[To access this online material, go to http://mitpress.mit.edu/westhoffeconometrics and select Cigarette Consumption.]

b. Do the regression results tend to support the conventional wisdom? Explain.

7. Consider earmark data for the 110th Congress:

House earmark data: Cross-sectional data of proposed earmarks in the 2009 fiscal year for the 451 House members of the 110th Congress.

CongressName$_t$	Name of Congressperson t
CongressParty$_t$	Party of Congressperson t
CongressState$_t$	State of Congressperson t
IncPC$_t$	Income per capita in the Congressperson t's state (dollars)
Number$_t$	Number of earmarks received that were sponsored solely by Congressperson t
PartyDem1$_t$	1 if Congressperson t Democrat; 0 otherwise
PartyRep1$_t$	1 if Congressperson t Republican; 0 otherwise
RegionMidwest$_t$	1 if Congressperson t represents a midwestern state, 0 otherwise
RegionNortheast$_t$	1 if Congressperson t represents a northeastern state; 0 otherwise
RegionSouth$_t$	1 if Congressperson t represents a southern state; 0 otherwise
RegionWest$_t$	1 if Congressperson t represents a western state; 0 otherwise
ScoreLiberal$_t$	Congressperson's t liberal score rating in 2007
Terms$_t$	Number of terms served by Congressperson in the US Congress
UnemRate$_t$	Unemployment rate in Congressperson t's state

a. What is an earmark?

It has been alleged that since the Congress was controlled by Democrats, Democratic members received more solo earmarks than their non-Democratic colleagues.

b. Using statistical software, estimate the effect that the political party of a member of Congress has on the dollars of earmarks received.

 [To access this online material, go to http://mitpress.mit.edu/westhoffeconometrics and select House Earmarks.]

c. Do the regression results tend to support the allegations? Explain.

6 Ordinary Least Squares Estimation Procedure—The Properties

Chapter 6 Outline

6.9   Best Linear Unbiased Estimation Procedure (BLUE)

Chapter 6 Prep Questions

1. Run the Distribution of Coefficient Estimates simulation in the Econometrics Lab by clicking the following link:

[To access this online material, go to http://mitpress.mit.edu/westhoffeconometrics and select Lab 6P.1.]

After completing the lab, fill in the following blanks:

	Numerical value of	Your calculations		Simulation's calculations	
Repetition	coefficient estimate	Mean	Variance	Mean	Variance
1	_____	_____	_____	_____	_____
2	_____	_____	_____	_____	_____
3	_____	_____	_____	_____	_____

Note: You must click the **Next Problem** button to get to the simulation's problem 1.

2. Review the arithmetic of means:

    a. Mean of a constant times a variable: Mean[cx] = _____

    b. Mean of a constant plus a variable: Mean[$c + x$] = _____

    c. Mean of the sum of two variables: Mean[$x + y$] = _____

3. Review the arithmetic of variances:

    a. Variance of a constant times a variable: Var[cx] = _____

    b. Variance of the sum of a variable and a constant: Var[$c + x$] = _____

    c. Variance of the sum of two variables: Var[$x + y$] = _____

    d. Variance of the sum of two independent variables: Var[$x + y$] = _____

4. Consider an estimate's probability distribution:

    a. Why is the mean (center) of the probability distribution important? Explain.

    b. Why is the variance (spread) of the probability distribution important? Explain.

6.1   Clint's Assignment: Assess the Effect of Studying on Quiz Scores

Clint's assignment is to assess the theory that additional studying increases quiz scores. To do so, he must use data from Professor Lord's first quiz, the number of minutes studied, and the quiz score for each of the three students in the course (table 6.1).

Table 6.1
First quiz results

Student	Minutes studied (x)	Quiz score (y)
1	5	66
2	15	87
3	25	90

Project: Use data from Professor Lord's first quiz to assess the effect of studying on quiz scores.

6.2 Review

6.2.1 Regression Model

Clint uses the following regression model to complete his assignment:

$$y_t = \beta_{Const} + \beta_x x_t + e_t$$

where

y_t = quiz score of student t

x_t = minutes studied by student t

e_t = error term for student t

β_{Const} and β_x are the parameters of the model. Let us review their interpretation:

- β_{Const} reflects the number of points Professor Lord gives students just for showing up.
- β_x reflects the number of additional points earned for each additional minute of studying.

6.2.2 The Error Term

The error term, e_t, plays a crucial role in the model. The error term represents random influences. The mean of the error term's probability distribution for each student equals 0:

$$\text{Mean}[e_1] = 0, \quad \text{Mean}[e_2] = 0, \quad \text{Mean}[e_3] = 0$$

Consequently the error terms have no systematic on affect quiz scores. Sometimes the error term will be positive and sometimes it will be negative, but after many, many quizzes each student's error terms will average out to 0. When the probability distribution of the error term is symmetric, the chances that a student will score better than "usual" on one quiz equal the chances that the student will do worse than "usual."

6.2.3 Ordinary Least Squares (OLS) Estimation Procedure

As a consequence of the error terms (random influences) we can never determine the actual values of β_{Const} and β_x; that is, Clint has no choice but to estimate the values. The ordinary least squares (OLS) estimation procedure is the most commonly used procedure for doing this:

$$b_x = \frac{\sum_{t=1}^{T}(y_t - \bar{y})(x_t - \bar{x})}{\sum_{t=1}^{T}(x_t - \bar{x})^2}$$

$$b_{Const} = \bar{y} - b_x\bar{x}$$

Using the results of the first quiz, Clint estimates the values of the coefficient and constant:

First quiz data

Ordinary least squares (OLS) estimates:
$Esty = 63 + 1.2x$

Student	x	y
1	5	66
2	15	87
3	25	90

b_{Const} = estimated points for showing up = 63
b_x = estimated points for each minute studied = 1.2

$$\bar{x} = \frac{x_1 + x_2 + x_3}{3} = \frac{5+15+25}{3} = \frac{45}{3} = 15 \qquad \bar{y} = \frac{y_1 + y_2 + y_3}{3} = \frac{66+87+90}{3} = \frac{243}{3} = 81$$

Student	y_t	$\bar{y}$	$y_t - \bar{y}$	x_t	$\bar{x}$	$x_t - \bar{x}$
1	66	81	−15	5	15	−10
2	87	81	6	15	15	0
3	90	81	9	25	15	10

Student	$(y_t - \bar{y})(x_t - \bar{x})$	$(x_t - \bar{x})^2$
1	(−15)(−10) = 150	$(-10)^2 = 100$
2	(6)(0) = 0	$(0)^2 = 0$
3	(9)(10) = <u>90</u>	$(10)^2 = \underline{100}$
	Sum = 240	Sum = <u>200</u>

$$\sum_{t=1}^{T}(y_t - \bar{y})(x_t - \bar{x}) = 240 \qquad\qquad \sum_{t=1}^{T}(x_t - \bar{x})^2 = 200$$

$$b_x = \frac{\sum_{t=1}^{T}(y_t - \bar{y})(x_t - \bar{x})}{\sum_{t=1}^{T}(x_t - \bar{x})^2} = \frac{240}{200} = \frac{6}{5} = 1.2 \qquad b_{Const} = \bar{y} - b_x\bar{x} = 81 - \frac{6}{5} \times 15 = 63$$

6.2.4   The Estimates, b_{Const} and b_x, Are Random Variables

In the previous chapter we used the Econometrics Lab to show that the estimates for the constant and coefficient, b_{Const} and b_x, are random variables. As a consequence of the error terms (random influences) we could not determine the numerical value of the estimates for the constant and coefficient, b_{Const} and b_x, before we conduct the experiment, even if we knew the actual values of the constant and coefficient, β_{Const} and β_x. Furthermore we can never expect the estimates to equal the actual values. Consequently we must assess the reliability of the estimates. We will focus on the coefficient estimate.

Estimate reliability: How reliable is the coefficient estimate calculated from the results of the first quiz? That is, how confident can Clint be that the coefficient estimate, 1.2, will be close to the actual value of the coefficient?

6.3   Strategy: General Properties and a Specific Application

6.3.1   Review: Assessing Clint's Opinion Poll Results

Clint faced a similar problem when he polled a sample of the student population to estimate the fraction of students supporting him. Twelve of the 16 randomly selected students polled, 75 percent, supported Clint, thereby suggesting that he was leading. But we then observed that it was possible for this result to occur even if the election was actually a toss-up. In view of this, we asked how confident Clint should be in the results of his single poll. To address this issue, we turned to the general properties of polling procedures to assess the reliability of the estimate Clint obtained from his single poll:

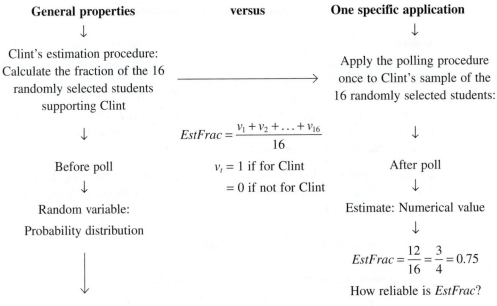

Mean[**EstFrac**] = p = ActFrac = actual fraction of the population supporting Clint

Var[**EstFrac**] $= \dfrac{p(1-p)}{T} = \dfrac{p(1-p)}{16}$, where T = sample size

↓

Mean and variance describe the center and spread of the estimate's probability distribution

While we could not determine the numerical value of the estimated fraction, *EstFrac*, before the poll was conducted, we could describe its probability distribution. Using algebra, we derived the general equations for the mean and variance of the estimated fraction's, *EstFrac*'s, probability distribution. Then we checked our algebra with a simulation by exploiting the relative frequency interpretation of probability: after many, many repetitions, the distribution of the numerical values mirrors the probability distribution for one repetition.

What can we deduce before the poll is
conducted?

General properties of the polling procedure
are described by *EstFrac*'s probability
distribution

Probability distribution is described by its
mean (center) and variance (spread)

↓

Use algebra to derive the equations
for the probability distribution's
mean and variance

$$\text{Mean}[\textbf{\textit{EstFrac}}] = p$$

$$\text{Var}[\textbf{\textit{EstFrac}}] = \frac{p(1-p)}{T}$$ ⟶ Check the algebra with a simulation
by exploiting the relative frequency
interpretation of probability

The estimated fraction's probability distribution allowed us to assess the reliability of Clint's poll.

6.3.2 Preview: Assessing Professor Lord's Quiz Results

Using the ordinary least squares (OLS) estimation procedure we estimated the value of the coefficient to be 1.2. This estimate is based on a single quiz. The fact that the coefficient estimate is positive suggests that additional studying increases quiz scores. But how confident can we be that the coefficient estimate is close to the actual value? To address the reliability issue we will focus on the general properties of the ordinary least squares (OLS) estimation procedure:

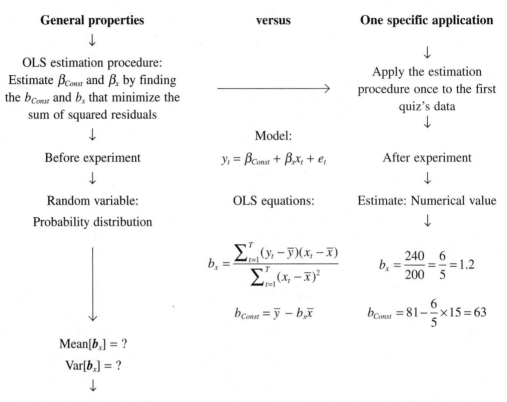

General properties	versus	One specific application

$\downarrow$

OLS estimation procedure:
Estimate β_{Const} and β_x by finding
the b_{Const} and b_x that minimize the
sum of squared residuals

$\longrightarrow$

$\downarrow$

Apply the estimation
procedure once to the first
quiz's data

$\downarrow$

$\downarrow$

Before experiment

Model:

$y_t = \beta_{Const} + \beta_x x_t + e_t$

After experiment

$\downarrow$

$\downarrow$

Random variable:
Probability distribution

OLS equations:

Estimate: Numerical value

$\downarrow$

$$b_x = \frac{\sum_{t=1}^{T}(y_t - \overline{y})(x_t - \overline{x})}{\sum_{t=1}^{T}(x_t - \overline{x})^2}$$

$$b_x = \frac{240}{200} = \frac{6}{5} = 1.2$$

$$b_{Const} = \overline{y} - b_x \overline{x}$$

$$b_{Const} = 81 - \frac{6}{5} \times 15 = 63$$

Mean[b_x] = ?

Var[b_x] = ?

$\downarrow$

Mean and variance describe the center and spread of the estimate's probability distribution

While we cannot determine the numerical value of the coefficient estimate before the quiz is given, we can describe its probability distribution. The probability distribution tells us how likely it is for the coefficient estimate based on a single quiz to equal each of the possible values. Using algebra, we will derive the general equations for the mean and variance of the coefficient estimate's probability distribution. Then we will check our algebra with a simulation by exploiting the relative frequency interpretation of probability: after many, many repetitions the distribution of the numerical values mirrors the probability distribution for one repetition.

What can we deduce before the poll is conducted?

General properties of the OLS estimation
procedure are described by the coefficient
estimate's probability distribution

Probability distribution is described by its mean
(center) and variance (spread)

↓

Use algebra to derive the equations for the   Check the algebra with a simulation
probability distribution's mean and variance → by exploiting the relative frequency
                                                interpretation of probability

The coefficient estimate's probability distribution will allow us to assess the reliability of the coefficient estimate calculated from Professor Lord's quiz.

6.4   Standard Ordinary Least Squares (OLS) Regression Premises

To derive the equations for the mean and variance of the coefficient estimate's probability distribution, we will apply the standard ordinary least squares (OLS) regression premises. As we mentioned chapter 5, these premises make the analysis as straightforward as possible. In later chapters we will relax these premises to study more general cases. In other words, we will start with the most straightforward case and then move on to more complex ones later.

· **Error term equal variance premise:**   The variance of the error term's probability distribution for each observation is the same; all the variances equal $Var[e]$:

$$Var[e_1] = Var[e_2] = \ldots = Var[e_T] = Var[e]$$

· **Error term/error term independence premise:** The error terms are independent: $Cov[e_i, e_j]$ $= 0$. Knowing the value of the error term from one observation does not help us predict the value of the error term for any other observation.

· **Explanatory variable/error term independence premise:** The explanatory variables, the x_t's, and the error terms, the e_t's, are not correlated. Knowing the value of an observation's explanatory variable does not help us predict the value of that observation's error term.

To keep the algebra manageable, we will assume that the explanatory variables are constants in the derivations that follow. This assumption allows us to apply the arithmetic of means and variances easily. While this simplifies our algebraic manipulations, it does not affect the validity of our conclusions.

6.5 New Equation for the Ordinary Least Squares (OLS) Coefficient Estimate

In chapter 5 we derived an equation that expressed the OLS coefficient estimate in terms of the x's and y's:

$$b_x = \frac{\sum_{t=1}^{T}(y_t - \bar{y})(x_t - \bar{x})}{\sum_{t=1}^{T}(x_t - \bar{x})^2}$$

It is advantageous to use a different equation to derive the equations for the mean and variance of the coefficient estimate's probability distribution, however; we will use an equivalent equation that expresses the coefficient estimate in terms of the x's, e's, and β_x rather than in terms of the x's and y's:[1]

$$b_x = \beta_x + \frac{\sum_{t=1}^{T}(x_t - \bar{x})e_t}{\sum_{t=1}^{T}(x_t - \bar{x})^2}$$

To keep the notation as straightforward as possible, we will focus on the 3 observation case. The logic for the general case is identical to the logic for the 3 observation case:

$$b_x = \beta_x + \frac{(x_1 - \bar{x})e_1 + (x_2 - \bar{x})e_2 + (x_3 - \bar{x})e_3}{(x_1 - \bar{x})^2 + (x_2 - \bar{x})^2 + (x_3 - \bar{x})^2}$$

6.6 General Properties: Describing the Coefficient Estimate's Probability Distribution

6.6.1 Mean (Center) of the Coefficient Estimate's Probability Distribution

To calculate the mean of b_x's probability distribution, review the arithmetic of means:

- Mean of a constant times a variable: $\text{Mean}[cx] = c\,\text{Mean}[x]$
- Mean of a constant plus a variable: $\text{Mean}[c + x] = c + \text{Mean}[x]$
- Mean of the sum of two variables: $\text{Mean}[x + y] = \text{Mean}[x] + \text{Mean}[y]$

and recall that the error term represents random influences:

- The mean of each error term's probability distribution is 0:

$$\text{Mean}[e_1] = \text{Mean}[e_2] = \text{Mean}[e_3] = 0$$

---

1. Appendix 6.1 appearing at the end of this chapter shows how we can derive the second equation for the coefficient estimate, b_x, from the first.

Now we apply algebra to the new equation for the coefficient estimate, b_x:

$$\text{Mean}[b_x] = \text{Mean}\left[\beta_x + \frac{(x_1 - \overline{x})e_1 + (x_2 - \overline{x})e_2 + (x_3 - \overline{x})e_3}{(x_1 - \overline{x})^2 + (x_2 - \overline{x})^2 + (x_3 - \overline{x})^2} \right]$$

Applying $\text{Mean}[c + x] = c + \text{Mean}[x]$

$$= \beta_x + \text{Mean}\left[\frac{(x_1 - \overline{x})e_1 + (x_2 - \overline{x})e_2 + (x_3 - \overline{x})e_3}{(x_1 - \overline{x})^2 + (x_2 - \overline{x})^2 + (x_3 - \overline{x})^2} \right]$$

Rewriting the fraction as a product

$$= \beta_x + \text{Mean}\left[\left(\frac{1}{(x_1 - \overline{x})^2 + (x_2 - \overline{x})^2 + (x_3 - \overline{x})^2} \right) \left((x_1 - \overline{x})e_1 + (x_2 - \overline{x})e_2 + (x_3 - \overline{x})e_3 \right) \right]$$

Applying $\text{Mean}[cx] = c\,\text{Mean}[x]$

$$= \beta_x + \frac{1}{(x_1 - \overline{x})^2 + (x_2 - \overline{x})^2 + (x_3 - \overline{x})^2} \text{Mean}\left[\left((x_1 - \overline{x})e_1 + (x_2 - \overline{x})e_2 + (x_3 - \overline{x})e_3 \right) \right]$$

Applying $\text{Mean}[x + y] = \text{Mean}[x] + \text{Mean}[y]$

$$= \beta_x + \frac{1}{(x_1 - \overline{x})^2 + (x_2 - \overline{x})^2 + (x_3 - \overline{x})^2} \left[\text{Mean}[(x_1 - \overline{x})e_1] + \text{Mean}[(x_2 - \overline{x})e_2] + \text{Mean}[(x_3 - \overline{x})e_3] \right]$$

Applying $\text{Mean}[cx] = c\,\text{Mean}[x]$

$$= \beta_x + \frac{1}{(x_1 - \overline{x})^2 + (x_2 - \overline{x})^2 + (x_3 - \overline{x})^2} \left[(x_1 - \overline{x})\text{Mean}[e_1] + (x_2 - \overline{x})\text{Mean}[e_2] + (x_3 - \overline{x})\text{Mean}[e_3] \right]$$

since $\text{Mean}[e_1] = \text{Mean}[e_2] = \text{Mean}[e_3] = 0 = \beta_x$. So, as shown in figure 6.1, we have

$$\text{Mean}[b_x] = \beta_x$$

Consequently the ordinary least squares (OLS) estimation procedure for the value of the coefficient is unbiased. In any one repetition of the experiment, the mean (center) of the probability distribution equals the actual value of the coefficient. The estimation procedure does not systematically overestimate or underestimate the actual coefficient value, β_x. If the probability distribution is symmetric, the chances that the estimate calculated from one quiz will be too high equal the chances that it will be too low.

Econometrics Lab 6.1: Checking the Equation for the Mean

We can use the Distribution of Coefficient Estimates simulation in our Econometrics Lab to replicate the quiz many, many times. But in reality, Clint only has information from one quiz, the first quiz. How then can a simulation be useful? The relative frequency interpretation of

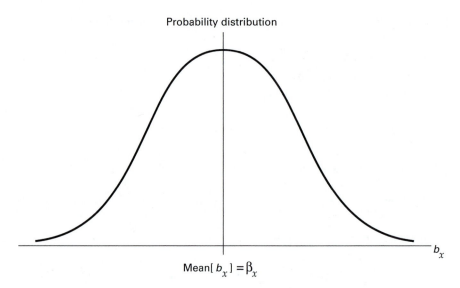

Figure 6.1
Probability distribution of coefficient estimates

probability provides the answer. The relative frequency interpretation of probability tells us that the distribution of the numerical values after many, many repetitions of the experiments mirrors the probability distribution of one repetition. Consequently repeating the experiment many, many times reveals the probability distribution for the one quiz:

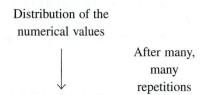

Distribution of the
numerical values

After many,
many
repetitions

Probability distribution

We can use the simulation to check the algebra we used to derive the equation for the mean of the coefficient estimate's probability distribution:

$$\text{Mean}[b_x] = \beta_x$$

If our algebra is correct, the mean (average) of the estimated coefficient values should equal the actual value of the coefficient, β_x, after many, many repetitions (see figure 6.2).

[To access this online material, go to http://mitpress.mit.edu/westhoffeconometrics and select Lab 6.1.]

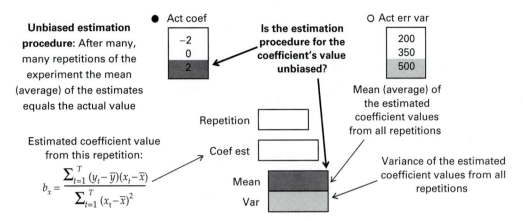

Figure 6.2
Distribution of coefficient estimates simulation

Recall that a simulation allows us to do something that we cannot do in the real world. In the simulation, we can specify the actual values of the constant and coefficient, β_{Const} and β_x. The default setting for the actual coefficient value is 2. Be certain that the Pause checkbox is checked. Click **Start**. Record the numerical value of the coefficient estimate for the first repetition. Click **Continue** to simulate the second quiz. Record the value of the coefficient estimate for the second repetition and calculate the mean and variance of the numerical estimates for the first two repetitions. Note that your calculations agree with those provided by the simulation. Click **Continue** again to simulate the third quiz. Calculate the mean and variance of the numerical estimates for the first three repetitions. Once again, note that your calculations and the simulation's calculations agree. Continue to click **Continue** until you are convinced that the simulation is calculating the mean and variance of the numerical values for the coefficient estimates correctly.

Now clear the Pause checkbox and click **Continue**. The simulation no longer pauses after each repetition. After many, many repetitions click **Stop**.

Question: What does the mean (average) of the coefficient estimates equal?

Answer: It equals about 2.0.

This lends support to the equation for the mean of the coefficient estimate's probability distribution that we just derived (table 6.2). Now change the actual coefficient value from 2 to 4. Click **Start**, and then after many, many repetitions click **Stop**. What does the mean (average) of the estimates equal? Next, change the actual coefficient value to 6 and repeat the process.

Note that in all cases the mean (average) of the estimates for the coefficient value equals the actual value of the coefficient after many, many repetitions (figure 6.3).

The simulations confirm our algebra. The estimation procedure does not systematically underestimate or overestimate the actual value of the coefficient. The ordinary least squares (OLS) estimation procedure for the coefficient value is unbiased.

Table 6.2
Distribution of Coefficient Estimates simulation results

Actual β_x	Equation: Mean of coef estimate prob dist Mean[b_x]	Simulation repetitions	Simulation: Mean (average) of estimated coef values, b_x, from the experiments
2	2	>1,000,000	≈2.0
4	4	>1,000,000	≈4.0
6	6	>1,000,000	≈6.0

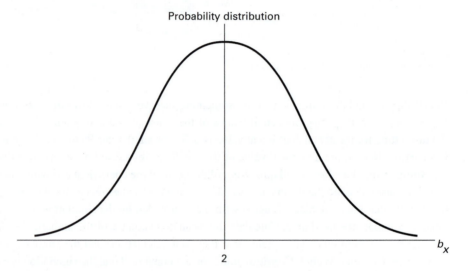

Figure 6.3
Histogram of coefficient value estimates

6.6.2   Variance (Spread) of the Coefficient Estimate's Probability Distribution

Next we turn our attention to the variance of the coefficient estimate's probability distribution. To derive the equation for the variance, begin by reviewing the arithmetic of variances:

· Variance of a constant times a variable: $\text{Var}[cx] = c^2 \, \text{Var}[x]$

· Variance of the sum of a variable and a constant: $\text{Var}[c + x] = \text{Var}[x]$

· Variance of the sum of two independent variables: $\text{Var}[x + y] = \text{Var}[x] + \text{Var}[y]$

Focus on the first two standard ordinary least squares (OLS) premises:

· Error term/equal variance premise: $\text{Var}[e_1] = \text{Var}[e_2] = \text{Var}[e_3] = \text{Var}[e]$.

· Error term/error term independence premise: The error terms are independent; that is, $\text{Cov}[e_i, e_j] = 0$.

Recall the new equation for b_x:

$$b_x = \beta_x + \frac{(x_1 - \overline{x})e_1 + (x_2 - \overline{x})e_2 + (x_3 - \overline{x})e_3}{(x_1 - \overline{x})^2 + (x_2 - \overline{x})^2 + (x_3 - \overline{x})^2}$$

Therefore

$$\text{Var}[b_x] = \text{Var}\left[\beta_x + \frac{(x_1 - \overline{x})e_1 + (x_2 - \overline{x})e_2 + (x_3 - \overline{x})e_3}{(x_1 - \overline{x})^2 + (x_2 - \overline{x})^2 + (x_3 - \overline{x})^2}\right]$$

Applying $\text{Var}[c + x] = \text{Var}[x]$

$$= \text{Var}\left[\frac{(x_1 - \overline{x})e_1 + (x_2 - \overline{x})e_2 + (x_3 - \overline{x})e_3}{(x_1 - \overline{x})^2 + (x_2 - \overline{x})^2 + (x_3 - \overline{x})^2}\right]$$

Rewriting the fraction as a product

$$= \text{Var}\left[\left(\frac{1}{(x_1 - \overline{x})^2 + (x_2 - \overline{x})^2 + (x_3 - \overline{x})^2}\right)\left((x_1 - \overline{x})e_1 + (x_2 - \overline{x})e_2 + (x_3 - \overline{x})e_3\right)\right]$$

Applying $\text{Var}[cx] = c^2\text{Var}[x]$

$$= \frac{1}{[(x_1 - \overline{x})^2 + (x_2 - \overline{x})^2 + (x_3 - \overline{x})^2]^2}\,\text{Var}\left[\left((x_1 - \overline{x})e_1 + (x_2 - \overline{x})e_2 + (x_3 - \overline{x})e_3\right)\right]$$

Error term/error term independence premise:

$$\text{Var}[x + y] = \text{Var}[x] + \text{Var}[y]$$

$$= \frac{1}{\left[(x_1 - \overline{x})^2 + (x_2 - \overline{x})^2 + (x_3 - \overline{x})^2\right]^2}\left[\text{Var}[(x_1 - \overline{x})e_1] + \text{Var}[(x_2 - \overline{x})e_2] + \text{Var}[(x_3 - \overline{x})e_3]\right]$$

Applying $\text{Var}[cx] = c^2\,\text{Var}[x]$

$$= \frac{1}{\left[(x_1 - \overline{x})^2 + (x_2 - \overline{x})^2 + (x_3 - \overline{x})^2\right]^2}\left[(x_1 - \overline{x})^2\,\text{Var}[e_1] + (x_2 - \overline{x})^2\,\text{Var}[e_2] + (x_3 - \overline{x})^2\,\text{Var}[e_3]\right]$$

Error term/equal variance premise:

$$\text{Var}[e_1] = \text{Var}[e_2] = \text{Var}[e_3] = \text{Var}[e]$$

$$= \frac{1}{\left[(x_1 - \overline{x})^2 + (x_2 - \overline{x})^2 + (x_3 - \overline{x})^2\right]^2}\left[(x_1 - \overline{x})^2\,\text{Var}[e] + (x_2 - \overline{x})^2\,\text{Var}[e] + (x_3 - \overline{x})^2\,\text{Var}[e]\right]$$

Factoring out the $\text{Var}[e]$

$$= \frac{1}{\left[(x_1 - \overline{x})^2 + (x_2 - \overline{x})^2 + (x_3 - \overline{x})^2\right]^2}\left[(x_1 - \overline{x})^2 + (x_2 - \overline{x})^2 + (x_3 - \overline{x})^2\right]\text{Var}[e]$$

Simplifying

$$= \frac{\text{Var}[e]}{(x_1 - \overline{x})^2 + (x_2 - \overline{x})^2 + (x_3 - \overline{x})^2}$$

We can generalize this:

$$\text{Var}[b_x] = \frac{\text{Var}[e]}{\sum_{t=1}^{T}(x_t - \overline{x})^2}$$

The variance of the coefficient estimate's probability distribution equals the variance of the error term's probability distribution divided by the sum of squared x deviations.

Econometrics Lab 6.2: Checking the Equation for the Variance

We will now use the Distribution of Coefficient Estimates simulation to check the equation that we just derived for the variance of the coefficient estimate's probability distribution (figure 6.4).

[To access this online material, go to http://mitpress.mit.edu/westhoffeconometrics and select Lab 6.2.]

The simulation automatically spreads the x values uniformly between 0 and 30. We will continue to consider three observations; accordingly, the x values are 5, 15, and 25. To convince yourself of this, be certain that the Pause checkbox is checked. Click **Start** and then **Continue** a few times to observe that the values of x are always 5, 15, and 25.

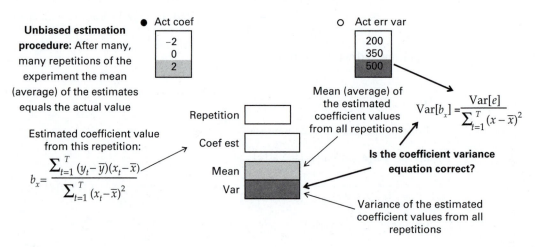

Figure 6.4
Distribution of Coefficient Estimates simulation

Next recall the equation we just derived for the variance of the coefficient estimate's probability distribution:

$$Var[b_x] = \frac{Var[e]}{\sum_{t=1}^{T}(x_t - \overline{x})^2} = \frac{Var[e]}{(x_1 - \overline{x})^2 + (x_2 - \overline{x})^2 + (x_3 - \overline{x})^2}$$

By default, the variance of the error term probability distribution is 500; therefore the numerator equals 500. Let us turn our attention to the denominator, the sum of squared x deviations. We have just observed that the x values are 5, 15, and 25. Their mean is 15 and their sum of squared deviations from the mean is 200:

$$\overline{x} = \frac{x_1 + x_2 + x_3}{3} = \frac{5+15+25}{3} = \frac{45}{3} = 15$$

Student	x_t	$\overline{x}$	$x_t - \overline{x}$	$(x_t - \overline{x})^2$
1	5	15	−10	$(-10)^2 = 100$
2	15	15	0	$(0)^2 = 0$
3	25	15	10	$(10)^2 = \underline{100}$
				Sum = 200

$$\sum_{t=1}^{T}(x_t - \overline{x})^2 = 200$$

That is,

$$(x_1 - \overline{x})^2 + (x_2 - \overline{x})^2 + (x_3 - \overline{x})^2 = 200$$

When the variance of the error term's probability distribution equals 500 and the sum of squared x deviations equals 200, the variance of the coefficient estimate's probability distribution equals 2.50:

$$Var[b_x] = \frac{Var[e]}{\sum_{t=1}^{T}(x_t - \overline{x})^2} = \frac{Var[e]}{(x_1 - \overline{x})^2 + (x_2 - \overline{x})^2 + (x_3 - \overline{x})^2} = \frac{500}{200} = 2.50$$

To show that the simulation confirms this, be certain that the Pause checkbox is cleared and click **Continue**. After many, many repetitions click **Stop**. Indeed, after many, many repetitions of the experiment the variance of the numerical values is about 2.50. The simulation confirms the equation we derived for the variance of the coefficient estimate's probability distribution.

6.7   Estimation Procedures and the Estimate's Probability Distribution: Importance of the Mean (Center) and Variance (Spread)

Let us review what we learned about estimation procedures when we studied Clint's opinion poll in chapter 3:

• **Importance of the probability distribution's mean:**   Formally, an estimation procedure is unbiased whenever the mean (center) of the estimate's probability distribution equals the actual value. The relative frequency interpretation of probability provides intuition: If the experiment were repeated many, many times the average of the numerical values of the estimates will equal the actual value. An unbiased estimation procedure does not systematically underestimate or overestimate the actual value. If the probability distribution is symmetric, the chances that the estimate calculated from one repetition of the experiment will be too high equal the chances the estimate will be too low (figure 6.5).

• **Importance of the probability distribution's variance:**   When the estimation procedure is unbiased, the variance of the estimate's probability distribution's variance (spread) reveals the estimate's reliability; the variance tells us how likely it is that the numerical value of the estimate calculated from one repetition of the experiment will be close to the actual value (figure 6.6).

   When the estimation procedure is unbiased, the variance of the estimate's probability distribution determines reliability.

• On the one hand, as the variance decreases, the probability distribution becomes more tightly cropped around the actual value making it more likely for the estimate to be close to the actual value.

• On the other hand, as the variance increases, the probability distribution becomes less tightly cropped around the actual value making it less likely for the estimate to be close to the actual value.

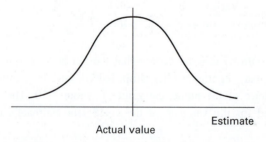

Figure 6.5
Probability distribution of estimates—Importance of the mean

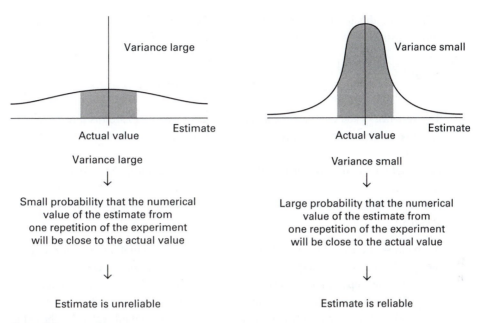

Figure 6.6
Probability distribution of estimates—Importance of the variance

6.8   Reliability of the Coefficient Estimate

We will focus on the variance of the coefficient estimate's probability distribution to explain what influences its reliability. We will consider three factors:

- Variance of the error term's probability distribution
- Sample size
- Range of the x's

6.8.1   Estimate Reliability and the Variance of the Error Term's Probability Distribution

What is our intuition here? The error term represents the random influences. It is the error term that introduces uncertainty into the mix. On the one hand, as the variance of the error term's probability distribution increases, uncertainty increases; consequently the available information becomes less reliable, and we would expect the coefficient estimate to become less reliable. On the other hand, as the variance of the error term's probability distribution decreases, the available information becomes more reliable, and we would expect the coefficient estimate to become more reliable.

To justify this intuition, recall the equation for the variance of the coefficient estimate's probability distribution:

$$\text{Var}[b_x] = \frac{\text{Var}[e]}{\sum_{t=1}^{T}(x_t - \bar{x})^2} = \frac{\text{Var}[e]}{(x_1 - \bar{x})^2 + (x_2 - \bar{x})^2 + (x_3 - \bar{x})^2}$$

The variance of the coefficient estimate's probability distribution is directly proportional to the variance of the error term's probability distribution.

Econometrics Lab 6.3: Variance of the Error Term's Probability Distribution

[To access this online material, go to http://mitpress.mit.edu/westhoffeconometrics and select Lab 6.3.]

We will use the Distribution of Coefficient Estimates simulation to confirm the role played by the variance of the error term's probability distribution. To do so, check the From–To checkbox. Two lists now appear: a From list and a To list. Initially, 1.0 is selected in the From list and 3.0 in the To list. Consequently the simulation will report the percent of repetitions in which the coefficient estimate falls between 1.0 and 3.0. Since the default value for the actual coefficient, β_x, equals 2.0, the simulation reports on the percent of repetitions in which the coefficient estimate falls within 1.0 of the actual value. The simulation reports the percent of repetitions in which the coefficient estimate is "close to" the actual value where "close to" is considered to be within 1.0.

By default, the variance of the error term's probability distribution equals 500 and the sample size equals 3. Recall that the sum of the squared x deviations equals 200 and therefore the variance of the coefficient estimate's probability distribution equals 2.50:

$$\text{Var}[b_x] = \frac{\text{Var}[e]}{\sum_{t=1}^{T}(x_t - \bar{x})^2} = \frac{\text{Var}[e]}{(x_1 - \bar{x})^2 + (x_2 - \bar{x})^2 + (x_3 - \bar{x})^2} = \frac{500}{200} = 2.50$$

Be certain that the Pause checkbox is cleared. Click **Start,** and then after many, many repetitions, click **Stop**. As table 6.3 reports, the coefficient estimate lies within 1.0 of the actual coefficient value in 47.3 percent of the repetitions.

Now reduce the variance of the error term's probability distribution from 500 to 50. The variance of the coefficient estimate's probability distribution now equals 0.25:

$$\text{Var}[b_x] = \frac{\text{Var}[e]}{\sum_{t=1}^{T}(x_t - \bar{x})^2} = \frac{\text{Var}[e]}{(x_1 - \bar{x})^2 + (x_2 - \bar{x})^2 + (x_3 - \bar{x})^2} = \frac{50}{200} = \frac{1}{4} = 0.25$$

Click **Start,** and then after many, many repetitions click **Stop**. The histogram of the coefficient estimates is now more closely cropped around the actual value, 2.0. The percent of repetitions

Table 6.3
Distribution of Coefficient Estimates simulation reliability results

Actual values					Probability distribution Equations		Simulations: Estimated coefficient values, b_x		
β_x	Var[e]	Sample Size	x Min	x Max	Mean[b_x]	Var[b_x]	Mean (average)	Variance	Percent between 1.0 and 3.0
2	500	3	0	30	2.0	2.50	≈2.0	≈2.50	≈47.3%
2	50	3	0	30	2.0	0.25	≈2.0	≈0.25	≈95.5%

in which the coefficient estimate lies within 1.0 of the actual coefficient value rises from 47.3 percent to 95.5 percent.

Why is this increase important? The variance measures the spread of the probability distribution. This is important when the estimation procedure is unbiased. As the variance decreases, the probability distribution becomes more closely cropped around the actual coefficient value and the chances that the coefficient estimate obtained from one quiz will lie close to the actual value increases. The simulation confirms this; after many, many repetitions the percent of repetitions in which the coefficient estimate lies between 1.0 and 3.0 increases from 47.3 percent to 95.5 percent. Consequently, as the error term's variance decreases, we can expect the estimate from one quiz to be more reliable. As the variance of the error term's probability distribution decreases, the estimate is more likely to be close to the actual value. This is consistent with our intuition, is it not?

6.8.2 Estimate Reliability and the Sample Size

Next we will investigate the effect of the sample size, the number of observations, used to calculate the estimate. Increase the sample size from 3 to 5. What does our intuition suggest? As we increase the number of observations, we will have more information. With more information the estimate should become more reliable; that is, with more information the variance of the coefficient estimate's probability distribution should decrease. Using the equation, let us now calculate the variance of the coefficient estimate's probability distribution when there are 5 observations. With 5 observations the x values are spread uniformly at 3, 9, 15, 21, and 27; the mean (average) of the x's, $\bar{x}$, equals 15 and the sum of the squared x deviations equals 360:

$$\bar{x} = \frac{x_1 + x_2 + x_3 + x_4 + x_5}{5} = \frac{3 + 9 + 15 + 21 + 27}{3} = \frac{75}{5} = 15$$

Student	x_t	$\bar{x}$	$x_t - \bar{x}$	$(x_t - \bar{x})^2$
1	3	15	−12	$(-12)^2 = 144$
2	9	15	−6	$(-6)^2 = 36$
3	15	15	0	$(0)^2 = 0$
4	21	15	6	$(6)^2 = 36$
5	27	15	12	$(12)^2 = \underline{144}$
				Sum = 360

$$\sum_{t=1}^{T} (x_t - \bar{x})^2 = 360$$

Applying the equation for the value of the coefficient estimate's probability distribution obtains

$$\text{Var}[b_x] = \frac{\text{Var}[e]}{\sum_{t=1}^{T}(x_t - \bar{x})^2} = \frac{\text{Var}[e]}{(x_1 - \bar{x})^2 + (x_2 - \bar{x})^2 + (x_3 - \bar{x})^2 + (x_4 - \bar{x})^2 + (x_5 - \bar{x})^2}$$

$$= \frac{50}{(3-15)^2 + (9-15)^2 + (15-15)^2 + (21-15)^2 + (27-15)^2}$$

$$= \frac{50}{(-12)^2 + (6)^2 + (0)^2 + (6)^2 + (12)^2} = \frac{50}{144 + 36 + 0 + 36 + 144} = \frac{50}{360} = 0.1388\ldots \approx 0.14$$

The variance of the coefficient estimate's probability distribution falls from 0.25 to 0.14. The smaller variance suggests that the coefficient estimate will be more reliable.

Econometrics Lab 6.4: Sample Size

Are our intuition and calculations supported by the simulation? The answer is in fact yes.

[To access this online material, go to http://mitpress.mit.edu/westhoffeconometrics and select Lab 6.4.]

Note that the sample size has increased from 3 to 5. Click **Start**, and then after many, many repetitions click **Stop** (table 6.4).

After many, many repetitions the percent of repetitions in which the coefficient estimate lies between 1.0 and 3.0 increases from 95.5 percent to 99.3 percent. As the sample size increases, we can expect the estimate from one quiz to be more reliable. As the sample size increases, the estimate is more likely to be close to the actual value.

6.8.3   Estimate Reliability and the Range of x's

Let us again begin by appealing to our intuition. As the range of x's becomes smaller, we are basing our estimates on less variation in the x's, less diversity; accordingly we are basing our

Table 6.4
Distribution of Coefficient Estimates simulation reliability results

Actual values					Probability distribution Equations		Simulations: Estimated coefficient values, b_x		
β_x	Var[e]	Sample size	x Min	x Max	Mean[b_x]	Var[b_x]	Mean (average)	Variance	Percent between 1.0 and 3.0
2	500	3	0	30	2.0	2.50	≈2.0	≈2.50	≈47.3%
2	50	3	0	30	2.0	0.25	≈2.0	≈0.25	≈95.5%
2	50	5	0	30	2.0	0.14	≈2.0	≈0.14	≈99.3%

estimates on less information. As the range becomes smaller, the estimate should become less reliable, and consequently the variance of the coefficient estimate's probability distribution should increase. To confirm this, increase the minimum value of x from 0 to 10 and decrease the maximum value from 30 to 20. The five x values are now spread uniformly between 10 and 20 at 11, 13, 15, 17, and 19; the mean (average) of the x's, $\bar{x}$, equals 15 and the sum of the squared x deviations equals 40:

$$\bar{x} = \frac{x_1 + x_2 + x_3 + x_4 + x_5}{5} = \frac{11+13+15+17+19}{3} = \frac{75}{5} = 15$$

Student	x_t	$\bar{x}$	$x_t - \bar{x}$	$(x_t - \bar{x})^2$
1	11	15	−4	$(-4)^2 = 16$
2	13	15	−2	$(-2)^2 = 4$
3	15	15	0	$(0)^2 = 0$
4	17	15	2	$(2)^2 = 4$
5	19	15	4	$(6)^2 = \underline{16}$
				Sum = 40

$$\sum_{t=1}^{T} (x_t - \bar{x})^2 = 40$$

Applying the equation for the value of the coefficient estimate's probability distribution:

$$Var[b_x] = \frac{Var[e]}{\sum_{t=1}^{T}(x_t - \bar{x})^2} = \frac{Var[e]}{(x_1 - \bar{x})^2 + (x_2 - \bar{x})^2 + (x_3 - \bar{x})^2 + (x_4 - \bar{x})^2 + (x_5 - \bar{x})^2}$$

$$= \frac{50}{(11-15)^2 + (13-15)^2 + (15-15)^2 + (17-15)^2 + (19-15)^2}$$

$$= \frac{50}{(-4)^2 + (2)^2 + (0)^2 + (2)^2 + (4)^2} = \frac{50}{16+4+0+4+16} = \frac{50}{40} = \frac{5}{4} = 1.25$$

Table 6.5
Distribution of Coefficient Estimates simulation reliability results

Actual values					Probability distribution Equations		Simulations: Estimated coefficient values, b_x		
β_x	Var[e]	Sample size	x Min	x Max	Mean[b_x]	Var[b_x]	Mean (average)	Variance	Percent between 1.0 and 3.0
2	500	3	0	30	2.0	2.50	≈2.0	≈2.50	≈47.3%
2	50	3	0	30	2.0	0.25	≈2.0	≈0.25	≈95.5%
2	50	5	0	30	2.0	0.14	≈2.0	≈0.14	≈99.3%
2	50	5	10	20	2.0	1.25	≈2.0	≈1.25	≈62.8%

The variance of the coefficient estimate's probability distribution increases from about 0.14 to 1.25.

Econometrics Lab 6.5: Range of x's

Our next lab confirms our intuition.

[To access this online material, go to http://mitpress.mit.edu/westhoffeconometrics and select Lab 6.5.]

After changing the minimum value of x to 10 and the maximum value to 20, click the **Start**, and then after many, many repetitions click **Stop**.

After many, many repetitions the percent of repetitions in which the coefficient estimate lies between 1.0 and 3.0 decreases from 99.3 percent to 62.8 percent (table 6.5). An estimate from one repetition will be less reliable. As the range of the x's decreases, the estimate is less likely to be close to the actual value.

6.8.4   Reliability Summary

Our simulation results illustrate relationships between information, the variance of the coefficient estimate's probability distribution, and the reliability of an estimate:

More and/or more reliable information	Less and/or less reliable information
↓	↓
Variance of coefficient estimate's probability distribution smaller	Variance of coefficient estimate's probability distribution larger
↓	↓
Estimate more reliable; more likely the estimate is "close to" the actual value	Estimate less reliable; less likely the estimate is "close to" the actual value

6.9   Best Linear Unbiased Estimation Procedure (BLUE)

In chapter 5 we introduced the mechanics of the ordinary least squares (OLS) estimation procedure and in this chapter we analyzed the procedure's properties. Why have we devoted so much attention to this particular estimation procedure? The reason is straightforward. When the standard ordinary least squares (OLS) premises are satisfied, no other linear estimation procedure produces more reliable estimates. In other words, the ordinary least squares (OLS) estimation procedure is the **best linear unbiased estimation procedure (BLUE)**. Let us now explain this more carefully.

If an estimation procedure is the best linear unbiased estimation procedure (BLUE), it must exhibit three properties:

· The estimate must be a linear function of the dependent variable, the y_i's.

· The estimation procedure must be unbiased; that is, the mean of the estimate's probability distribution must equal the actual value.

· No other linear unbiased estimation procedure can be more reliable; that is, the variance of the estimate's probability distribution when using any other linear unbiased estimation procedure cannot be less than the variance when the best linear unbiased estimation procedure is used.

The Gauss–Markov theorem proves that the ordinary least squares (OLS) estimation procedure is the best linear unbiased estimation procedure.[2] We will illustrate the theorem by describing two other linear unbiased estimation procedures that while unbiased, are not as reliable as the ordinary least squares (OLS) estimation procedure. Note that while we would never use either of these estimation procedures to do serious analysis, they are useful pedagogical tools. They allow us to illustrate what we mean by the best linear unbiased estimation procedure.

6.9.1   Two New Estimation Procedures

We will now consider the Any Two and the Min–Max estimation procedures:

· **Any Two estimation procedure:**   Choose any two points on the scatter diagram (figure 6.7); draw a straight line through the points. The coefficient estimate equals the slope of this line.

· **Min–Max estimation procedure:**   Choose two specific points on the scatter diagram (figure 6.8); the point with the smallest value of x and the point with the largest value of x; draw a straight line through the two points. The coefficient estimate equals the slope of this line.

---

2. The proof appears at the end of this chapter in appendix 6.2.

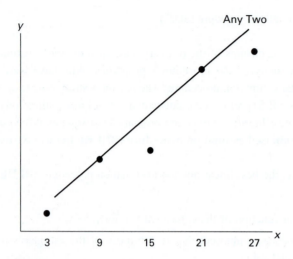

Figure 6.7
Any Two estimation procedure

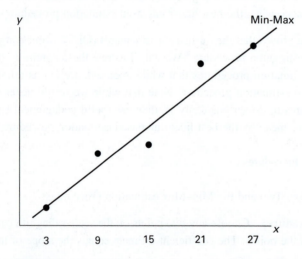

Figure 6.8
Min–Max estimation procedure

Table 6.6
BLUE simulation results

| Estimation procedure | Sample size = 5 | | Simulations: Estimated coefficient values, b_x | | |
| | Actual Values | | | | |
	β_x	Var[e]	Mean (average)	Variance	Percent between 1.0 and 3.0
OLS	2.0	500	≈2.0	≈1.4	≈60.4%
Any Two	2.0	50	≈2.0	≈14.0	≈29.0%
Min–Max	2.0	50	≈2.0	≈1.7	≈55.2%

Econometrics Lab 6.6: Comparing the Ordinary Least Squares (OLS), Any Two, and Min–Max Estimation Procedures

We will now use the BLUE simulation in our Econometrics Lab to justify our emphasis on the ordinary least squares (OLS) estimation procedure.

[To access this online material, go to http://mitpress.mit.edu/westhoffeconometrics and select Lab 6.6.]

By default, the sample size equals 5 and the variance of the error term's probability distribution equals 500. The From–To values are specified as 1.0 and 3.0 (table 6.6).

Initially the ordinary least squares (OLS) estimation procedure is specified. Be certain that the Pause checkbox is cleared. Click **Start**, and then after many, many repetitions click **Stop**. For the OLS estimation procedure, the average of the estimated coefficient values equals about 2.0 and the variance 1.4. 60.4 percent of the estimates lie with 1.0 of the actual value. Next select the Any Two estimation procedure instead of OLS. Click **Start**, and then after many, many repetitions click **Stop**. For the Any Two estimation procedure, the average of the estimated coefficient values equals about 2.0 and the variance 14.0; 29.0 percent of the estimates lie within 1.0 of the actual value. Repeat the process one last time after selecting the Min–Max estimation procedure; the average equals about 2.0 and the variance 1.7; 55.2 percent of the estimates lie with 1.0 of the actual value.

Let us summarize:

• In all three cases the average of the coefficient estimates equal 2.0, the actual value; after many, many repetitions the mean (average) of the estimates equals the actual value. Consequently all three estimation procedures for the coefficient value appear to be unbiased.

• The variance of the coefficient estimate's probability distribution is smallest when the ordinary least squares (OLS) estimation procedure is used. Consequently the ordinary least squares (OLS) estimation procedure produces the most reliable estimates.

What we have just observed can be generalized. When the standard ordinary least squares (OLS) regression premises are met, the ordinary least squares (OLS) estimation procedure is the best linear unbiased estimation procedure because no other linear unbiased estimation procedure produces estimates that are more reliable.

Chapter 6 Review Questions

1. Consider the ordinary least squares (OLS) estimation procedure.

   a. Why is the mean of the estimate's probability distribution important? Explain.

   b. Why is the variance of the estimate's probability distribution important? Explain.

2. Consider the ordinary least squares (OLS) estimation procedure. When the variance of the error term's probability distribution increases:

   a. How, if at all, is the mean of the coefficient estimate's probability distribution affected?

   b. How, if at all, is the variance of the coefficient estimate's probability distribution affected?

   c. How is the reliability of the coefficient estimate affected? Explain intuitively why this occurs.

3. Consider the ordinary least squares (OLS) estimation procedure. When the sample size increases:

   a. How, if at all, is the mean of the coefficient estimate's probability distribution affected?

   b. How, if at all, is the variance of the coefficient estimate's probability distribution affected?

   c. How is the reliability of the coefficient estimate affected? Explain intuitively why this occurs.

4. Consider the ordinary least squares (OLS) estimation procedure. When the range of the explanatory variable decreases:

   a. How, if at all, is the mean of the coefficient estimate's probability distribution affected?

   b. How, if at all, is the variance of the coefficient estimate's probability distribution affected?

   c. How is the reliability of the coefficient estimate affected? Explain intuitively why this occurs.

5. Why have we placed so much emphasis on the ordinary least squares (OLS) estimation procedure?

Chapter 6 Exercises

1. Assume that the standard ordinary least square (OLS) premises are met. Let (x_i, y_i) and (x_j, y_j) be the values of the explanatory and dependent variables from two different observations.

Also let

b_{Slope} = slope of the straight line connecting the two points representing these two observations

a. Express b_{Slope} in terms of x_i, y_i, x_j, and y_j.

Consider the simple regression model and two different observations, i and j:

$$y_i = \beta_{Const} + \beta_x x_i + e_i$$

$$y_j = \beta_{Const} + \beta_x x_j + e_j$$

b. Using the simple regression model, substitute for y_i and y_j in the expression for b_{Slope}. (Assume that x_i does not equal x_j.)

c. What does the mean of b_{Slope}'s probability distribution, Mean[b_{Slope}], equal?

d. What does the variance of b_{Slope}'s probability distribution, Var[b_{Slope}], equal?

2. Assume that the standard ordinary least square (OLS) premises are met. Consider the Min–Max estimation procedure that we simulated in Econometrics Lab 6.6. Let

- The actual coefficient equals 2 ($\beta_x = 2$).
- The variance of the error term's probability distribution equals 500 (Var[e] = 500).
- The sample size equals 5, and the values of the x's equal: 3, 9, 15, 21, and 27.

Using your answers to exercise 1:

a. What does the mean of the Min–Max estimate's probability distribution equal?

b. What does the variance of the Min–Max estimate's probability distribution equal?

c. Are your answers consistent with the simulations of the Min–Max estimation procedure that we reported at the end of this chapter?

3. Assume that the standard ordinary least square (OLS) premises are met. Consider the Any Two estimation procedure that we simulate in this chapter's Econometrics Lab 6.6. Let

- The actual coefficient equals 2 ($\beta_x = 2$).
- The variance of the error term's probability distribution equals 500 (Var[e] = 500).
- The sample size is 5, and the values of the x's are: 3, 9, 15, 21, and 27.

Using your answers to exercise 1:

a. What does the mean of the Any Two estimate's probability distribution equal?

b. What does the variance of the Any Two estimate's probability distribution equal?

c. Are your answers consistent with the simulations of the Any Two estimation procedure that we reported at the end of this chapter?

Revisit the US crude oil production data.

Crude oil production data: Annual time series data of US crude oil production and prices from 1976 to 2004.

OilProdBarrels$_t$ US crude oil productions in year *t* (thousands of barrels per day)

Price$_t$ Real price of crude oil in year *t* (dollars per barrel—1982–84 = 100)

4. Using statistical software, generate a new variable that expresses crude oil production in thousands of gallons per day rather than thousands of barrels per day. Call the new variable *OilProdGallons*. Note that there are 42 gallons in 1 barrel.

[To access this online material, go to http://mitpress.mit.edu/westhoffeconometrics and select Crude Oil Production.]

Getting Started in EViews

After opening the file:

- In the Workfile window: click **Genr**.

- In the Generate Series by Equation window enter the formula for the new series:

*OilProdGallons = OilProdBarrels*42*

Note that the asterisk, *, is EViews' multiplication symbol.

- Click **OK**.

    a. Run the following ordinary least squares (OLS) regressions:

Dependent variable: *OilProdBarrels* (crude oil production expressed in barrels)
Explanatory variable: *Price*

        i. Based on this *OilProdBarrels* regression, estimate the effect of a $1 increase in price on the barrels of oil produced.

        ii. Based on your answer to part i, estimate the effect of a $1 increase in price on the gallons of oil produced. (Remember, there are 42 gallons in 1 barrel.)

    b. Run the following ordinary least squares (OLS) regressions:

Dependent variable: *OilProdGallons* (crude oil production expressed in gallons)
Explanatory variable: *Price*

Based on this *OilProdGallons* regression, estimate the effect of a $1 increase in price on the gallons of oil produced.

c. Do the units in which the dependent variable is measured influence the estimate of how the explanatory variable affects the dependent variable?

5. Using statistical software, generate a new variable that adds the constant 1,000 to *OilProdBarrels* in every year. Call the new variable *OilProdBarrels1000*.

[To access this online material, go to http://mitpress.mit.edu/westhoffeconometrics and select Crude Oil Production.]

Getting Started in EViews

After opening the file:

• In the Workfile window: click **Genr.**

• In the Generate Series by Equation window enter the formula for the new series:

OilProdBarrelsPlus1000 = OilProdBarrels + 1000

Note that the asterick, *, is EViews multiplication symbol.

• Click **OK.**

a. Run two ordinary least squares (OLS) regressions:

i. Dependent variable: *OilProdBarrels*

Explanatory variable: *Price*

What equation estimates the dependent variable, *OilProdBarrels*; that is, what is the equation for the best fitting line?

ii. Dependent variable: *OilProdBarrelsPlus1000*

Explanatory variable: *Price*

What equation estimates the dependent variable, *OilProdBarrelsPlus1000*; that is, what is the equation for the best fitting line?

b. Compare the equations for the best fitting lines.

c. Explain the shift in the best fitting line?

Revisit the US gasoline consumption data.

Gasoline consumption data: Annual time series data US gasoline consumption and prices from 1990 to 1999.

GasCons$_t$ US gasoline consumption in year t (millions of gallons per day)

PriceDollars$_t$ Real price of gasoline in year t (dollars per gallon –2000 dollars)

6. Using statistical software, generate a new variable that expresses the price of gasoline in cents rather than dollars. Call this new variable *PriceCents*.

[To access this online material, go to http://mitpress.mit.edu/westhoffeconometrics and select Gasoline Consumption.]

  a. Run the following ordinary least squares (OLS) regressions:

Dependent variable: *GasCons*

Explanatory variable: *PriceDollars*

  i. Based on this *PriceDollars* regression, estimate the effect of a $1 increase in price on the gallons of gasoline demanded.

  ii. Based on your answer to part i, estimate the effect a 1 cent increase in price would have on the gallons of gasoline demanded.

  b. Run the following ordinary least squares (OLS) regressions:

Dependent variable: *GasCons*

Explanatory variable: *PriceCents*

  Based on this *PriceCents* regression, estimate the effect that a 1 cent increase in price has on the gallons of gasoline demanded.

  c. Do the units in which the explanatory variable is measured influence the estimate of how the explanatory variable affects the dependent variable?

7. Generate a new variable that equals the dollar price of gasoline, *PriceDollars*, plus 2. Call this new variable *PriceDollarsPlus2*.

[To access this online material, go to http://mitpress.mit.edu/westhoffeconometrics and select Gasoline Consumption.]

  a. Run two ordinary least squares (OLS) regressions:

  i. Dependent variable: *GasCon*

  Explanatory variable: *PriceDollars*

  What equation estimates the dependent variable, *GasCons*; that is, what is the equation for the best fitting line?

  ii. Dependent variable: *GasCon*

  Explanatory variable: *PriceDollarsPlus2*

  What equation estimates the dependent variable, *GasCons*; that is, what is the equation for the best fitting line?

b. Compare the estimated constants in the two regressions.

c. Compare the estimated coefficients in the two regressions.

d. What happens to the ordinary least squares (OLS) best fitting line when a constant is added to the explanatory variable?

Appendix 6.1: New Equation for the OLS Coefficient Estimate

Begin by recalling the expression for b_x that we derived previously in chapter 5:

$$b_x = \frac{\sum_{t=1}^{T}(y_t - \bar{y})(x_t - \bar{x})}{\sum_{t=1}^{T}(x_t - \bar{x})^2}$$

b_x is expressed in terms of the x's and y's. We wish to express b_x in terms of the x's, e's, and β_x.

Strategy: Focus on the numerator of the expression for b_x and substitute for the y's to express the numerator in terms of the x's, e's, and β_x. As we will shortly show, once we do this, our goal will be achieved.

We begin with the numerator, $\sum_{t=1}^{T}(y_t - \bar{y})(x_t - \bar{x})$, and substitute $\beta_{Const} + \beta_x x_t + e_t$ for y_t:

$$\sum_{t=1}^{T}(y_t - \bar{y})(x_t - \bar{x}) = \sum_{t=1}^{T}(\beta_{Const} + \beta_x x_t + e_t - \bar{y})(x_t - \bar{x})$$

Rearranging terms

$$= \sum_{t=1}^{T}(\beta_{Const} - \bar{y} + \beta_x x_t + e_t)(x_t - \bar{x})$$

Adding and subtracting $\beta_x \bar{x}$

$$= \sum_{t=1}^{T}(\beta_{Const} + \beta_x \bar{x} - \bar{y} + \beta_x x_t - \beta_x \bar{x} + e_t)(x_t - \bar{x})$$

Simplifying

$$= \sum_{t=1}^{T}[(\beta_{Const} + \beta_x \bar{x} - \bar{y}) + \beta_x (x_t - \bar{x}) + e_t)](x_t - \bar{x})$$

Splitting the summation into three parts

$$= \sum_{t=1}^{T}(\beta_{Const} + \beta_x \bar{x} - \bar{y})(x_t - \bar{x}) + \sum_{t=1}^{T}\beta_x (x_t - \bar{x})^2 + \sum_{t=1}^{T}(x_t - \bar{x})e_t$$

Simplifying the first and second terms

$$= (\beta_{Const} + \beta_x \bar{x} - \bar{y}) \sum_{t=1}^{T} (x_t - \bar{x}) + \beta_x \sum_{t=1}^{T} (x_t - \bar{x})^2 + \sum_{t=1}^{T} (x_t - \bar{x}) e_t$$

Now focus on the first term, $(\beta_{Const} + \beta_x \bar{x} - \bar{y}) \sum_{t=1}^{T} (x_t - \bar{x})$. What does $\sum_{t=1}^{T} (x_t - \bar{x})$ equal?

$$\sum_{t=1}^{T} (x_t - \bar{x}) = \sum_{t=1}^{T} x_t - \sum_{t=1}^{T} \bar{x}$$

Replacing $\sum_{t=1}^{T} \bar{x}$ with $T\bar{x}$,

$$= \sum_{t=1}^{T} x_t - T\bar{x}$$

since $\bar{x} = \sum_{t=1}^{T} x_t / T$

$$= \sum_{t=1}^{T} x_t - T \frac{\sum_{t=1}^{T} x_t}{T}$$

Simplifying

$$= \sum_{t=1}^{T} x_t - \sum_{t=1}^{T} x_t$$

$$= 0$$

Next return to the expression for the numerator, $\sum_{t=1}^{T} (y_t - \bar{y})(x_t - \bar{x})$:

$$\sum_{t=1}^{T} (y_t - \bar{y})(x_t - \bar{x}) = (\beta_{Const} + \beta_x \bar{x} - \bar{y}) \sum_{t=1}^{T} (x_t - \bar{x}) + \beta_x \sum_{t=1}^{T} (x_t - \bar{x})^2 + \sum_{t=1}^{T} (x_t - \bar{x}) e_t$$

$$\downarrow \sum_{t=1}^{T} (x_t - \bar{x}) = 0$$

$$= 0 + \beta_x \sum_{t=1}^{T} (x_t - \bar{x})^2 + \sum_{t=1}^{T} (x_t - \bar{x}) e_t$$

Therefore

$$\sum_{t=1}^{T} (y_t - \bar{y})(x_t - \bar{x}) = \beta_x \sum_{t=1}^{T} (x_t - \bar{x})^2 + \sum_{t=1}^{T} (x_t - \bar{x}) e_t$$

Last, apply this to the equation we derived for b_x in chapter 5:

$$b_x = \frac{\sum_{t=1}^{T} (y_t - \bar{y})(x_t - \bar{x})}{\sum_{t=1}^{T} (x_t - \bar{x})^2}$$

Substituting for the numerator

$$= \frac{\beta_x \sum_{t=1}^{T}(x_t - \bar{x})^2 + \sum_{t=1}^{T}(x_t - \bar{x})e_t}{\sum_{t=1}^{T}(x_t - \bar{x})^2}$$

Splitting the single fraction into two

$$= \frac{\beta_x \sum_{t=1}^{T}(x_t - \bar{x})^2}{\sum_{t=1}^{T}(x_t - \bar{x})^2} + \frac{\sum_{t=1}^{T}(x_t - \bar{x})e_t}{\sum_{t=1}^{T}(x_t - \bar{x})^2}$$

Simplifying the first term

$$= \beta_x + \frac{\sum_{t=1}^{T}(x_t - \bar{x})e_t}{\sum_{t=1}^{T}(x_t - \bar{x})^2}$$

We have now expressed b_x in terms of the x's, e's, and β_x.

Appendix 6.2: Gauss–Markov Theorem

Gauss–Markov theorem: When the standard ordinary least squares (OLS) premises are satisfied, the ordinary least squared (OLS) estimation procedure is the best linear unbiased estimation procedure.

Proof   Let

b_x^{OLS} = ordinary least squares (OLS) estimate

First, note that b_x^{OLS} is a linear function of the y's:[3]

$$b_x^{OLS} = \frac{\sum_{t=1}^{T}(y_t - \bar{y})(x_t - \bar{x})}{\sum_{t=1}^{T}(x_i - \bar{x})^2}$$

where

$$w_t^{OLS} = \frac{(x_t - \bar{x})}{\sum_{i=1}^{T}(x_i - \bar{x})^2}$$

---

3. To reduce potential confusion, the summation index in the denominator has been changed from t to i.

Let w_t^{OLS} equal the ordinary least squares (OLS) "linear weights"; more specifically,

$$b_x^{OLS} = \sum_{t=1}^{T} w_t^{OLS}(y_t - \bar{y})$$

Now let us derive two properties of w_t^{OLS}:

- $\sum_{t=1}^{T} w_t^{OLS} = 0$

- $\sum_{t=1}^{T} w_t^{OLS}(x_t - \bar{x}) = 1$

First, $\sum_{t=1}^{T} w_t^{OLS} = 0$:

$$\sum_{t=1}^{T} w_t^{OLS} = \sum_{t=1}^{T} \frac{(x_t - \bar{x})}{\sum_{i=1}^{T}(x_i - \bar{x})^2}$$

Placing the summation in the numerator

$$= \frac{\sum_{t=1}^{T}(x_t - \bar{x})}{\sum_{t=1}^{T}(x_i - \bar{x})^2}$$

Splitting the summations in the numerator

$$= \frac{\sum_{t=1}^{T} x_t - \sum_{t=1}^{T} \bar{x}}{\sum_{t=1}^{T}(x_i - \bar{x})^2}$$

since there are $T\bar{x}$ terms

$$= \frac{\sum_{t=1}^{T} x_t - T\bar{x}}{\sum_{t=1}^{T}(x_i - \bar{x})^2}$$

and since $\bar{x} = \sum_{t=1}^{T} x_t / T$

$$= \frac{\sum_{t=1}^{T} x_t - T\left(\sum_{t=1}^{T} x_t / T\right)}{\sum_{t=1}^{T}(x_i - \bar{x})^2}$$

Simplifying

$$= \frac{\sum_{t=1}^{T} x_t - \sum_{t=1}^{T} x_t}{\sum_{t=1}^{T} (x_i - \overline{x})^2}$$

and since the numerator equals 0,

$$= 0$$

Second, $\sum_{t=1}^{T} w_t^{OLS} = 0$:

$$\sum_{t=1}^{T} w_t^{OLS}(x_t - \overline{x}) = \sum_{t=1}^{T} \frac{(x_t - \overline{x})}{\sum_{i=1}^{T}(x_i - \overline{x})^2}(x_t - \overline{x})$$

Simplifying

$$= \sum_{t=1}^{T} \frac{(x_t - \overline{x})^2}{\sum_{i=1}^{T}(x_i - \overline{x})^2}$$

Placing the summation in the numerator

$$= \frac{\sum_{t=1}^{T}(x_t - \overline{x})^2}{\sum_{t=1}^{T}(x_i - \overline{x})^2}$$

and since the numerator and denominator are equal,

$$= 1$$

Next consider a new linear estimation procedure whose weights are $w_t^{OLS} + w_t'$. Only when each w_t' equals 0 will this procedure to identical to the ordinary least squares (OLS) estimation procedure. Let b_x' equal the coefficient estimate calculated using this new linear estimation procedure:

$$b_x' = \sum_{t=1}^{T}(w_t^{OLS} + w_t')y_t$$

Now let us perform a little algebra:

$$b_x' = \sum_{t=1}^{T}(w_t^{OLS} + w_t')y_t$$

Substituting $\beta_{Const} + \beta_x x_t + e_t$ for y_t

$$= \sum_{t=1}^{T}(w_t^{OLS} + w_t')(\beta_{Const} + \beta_x x_t + e_t)$$

Multiplying through

$$= \sum_{t=1}^{T} (w_t^{OLS} + w_t')\beta_{Const} + \sum_{t=1}^{T} (w_t^{OLS} + w_t')\beta_x x_t + \sum_{t=1}^{T} (w_t^{OLS} + w_t')e_t$$

Factoring out β_{Const} from the first term and β_x from the second

$$= \beta_{Const} \sum_{t=1}^{T} (w_t^{OLS} + w_t') + \beta_x \sum_{t=1}^{T} (w_t^{OLS} + w_t')x_t + \sum_{t=1}^{T} (w_t^{OLS} + w_t')e_t$$

Again, simplifying the first two terms

$$= \beta_{Const} \sum_{t=1}^{T} w_t^{OLS} + \beta_{Const} \sum_{t=1}^{T} w_t' + \beta_x \sum_{t=1}^{T} w_t^{OLS} x_t + \beta_x \sum_{t=1}^{T} w_t' x_t + \sum_{t=1}^{T} (w_t^{OLS} + w_t')e_t$$

since $\sum_{t=1}^{T} w_t^{OLS} x_t = 0$ and $\sum_{t=1}^{T} w_t^{OLS} x_t = 1$

$$= 0 + \beta_{Const} \sum_{t=1}^{T} w_t' + \beta_x + \beta_x \sum_{t=1}^{T} w_t' x_t + \sum_{t=1}^{T} (w_t^{OLS} + w_t')e_t$$

Therefore

$$b_x' = \beta_{Const} \sum_{t=1}^{T} w_t' + \beta_x + \beta_x \sum_{t=1}^{T} w_t' x_t + \sum_{t=1}^{T} (w_t^{OLS} + w_t')e_t$$

Now calculate the mean of the new estimate's probability distribution, Mean[b_x']:

$$\text{Mean}[b_x'] = \text{Mean}\left[\beta_{Const} \sum_{t=1}^{T} w_t' + \beta_x + \beta_x \sum_{t=1}^{T} w_t' x_t + \sum_{t=1}^{T} (w_t^{OLS} + w_t')e_t \right]$$

since $\text{Mean}[c + x] = c + \text{Mean}[x]$

$$= \beta_{Const} \sum_{t=1}^{T} w_t' + \beta_x + \beta_x \sum_{t=1}^{T} w_t' x_t + \text{Mean}\left[\sum_{t=1}^{T} (w_t^{OLS} + w_t')e_t \right]$$

Focusing on the last term, $\text{Mean}[cx] = c \, \text{Mean}[x]$,

$$= \beta_{Const} \sum_{t=1}^{T} w_t' + \beta_x + \beta_x \sum_{t=1}^{T} w_t' x_t + \sum_{t=1}^{T} (w_t^{OLS} + w_t')\text{Mean}[e_t]$$

Focusing on the last term, since the error terms represents random influences, $\text{Mean}[e_t] = 0$,

$$= \beta_{Const} \sum_{t=1}^{T} w_t' + \beta_x + \beta_x \sum_{t=1}^{T} w_t' x_t$$

The new linear estimation procedure must be unbiased:

$$\text{Mean}[b_x'] = \beta_x$$

Therefore

$$\sum\nolimits_{t=1}^{T} w_t' = 0 \quad \text{and} \quad \sum\nolimits_{t=1}^{T} w_t' x_t = 0$$

Next calculate the variance of b_x':

$$\text{Var}[b_x'] = \text{Var}\left[\beta_{Const} \sum\nolimits_{t=1}^{T} w_t' + \beta_x + \beta_x \sum\nolimits_{t=1}^{T} w_t' x_t + \sum\nolimits_{t=1}^{T} (w_t^{OLS} + w_t') e_t \right]$$

since $\text{Var}[c + x] = \text{Var}[x]$

$$= \text{Var}\left[\sum\nolimits_{t=1}^{T} (w_t^{OLS} + w_t') e_t \right]$$

Since the error terms are independent, covariances equal 0: $\text{Var}[x + y] = \text{Var}[x] + \text{Var}[y]$

$$= \sum\nolimits_{t=1}^{T} \text{Var}[(w_t^{OLS} + w_t') e_t]$$

and since $\text{Var}[cx] = c^2 \, \text{Var}[x]$

$$= \sum\nolimits_{t=1}^{T} (w_t^{OLS} + w_t')^2 \, \text{Var}[e_t]$$

The variance of each error term's probability distribution is identical, so $\text{Var}[e]$

$$= \sum\nolimits_{t=1}^{T} (w_t^{OLS} + w_t')^2 \, \text{Var}[e]$$

Factoring out $\text{Var}[e]$

$$= \text{Var}[e] \sum\nolimits_{t=1}^{T} (w_t^{OLS} + w_t')^2$$

Expanding the squared terms

$$= \text{Var}[e] \sum\nolimits_{t=1}^{T} (w_t^{OLS})^2 + 2 w_t^{OLS} w_t' + (w_t')^2$$

Splitting up the summation

$$= \text{Var}[e] \left[\sum\nolimits_{t=1}^{T} (w_t^{OLS})^2 + 2 \sum\nolimits_{t=1}^{T} w_t^{OLS} w_t' + \sum\nolimits_{t=1}^{T} (w_t')^2 \right]$$

Now focus on the cross product terms, $\sum\nolimits_{t=1}^{T} w_t^{OLS} w_t'$:

$$\sum\nolimits_{t=1}^{T} w_t^{OLS} w_t' = \sum\nolimits_{t=1}^{T} \frac{(x_t - \overline{x})}{\sum\nolimits_{i=1}^{T} (x_i - \overline{x})^2} w_t'$$

Placing the summation in the numerator

$$= \frac{\sum_{t=1}^{T}(x_t - \bar{x})w_t'}{\sum_{i=1}^{T}(x_i - \bar{x})^2}$$

Splitting the summations in the numerator

$$= \frac{\sum_{t=1}^{T}\left(x_t w_t' - \sum_{t=1}^{T} \bar{x}w_t'\right)}{\sum_{i=1}^{T}(x_i - \bar{x})^2}$$

Factoring out $\bar{x}$ from the second term in the numerator

$$= \frac{\sum_{t=1}^{T} x_t w_t' - \bar{x}\sum_{t=1}^{T} w_t'}{\sum_{i=1}^{T}(x_i - \bar{x})^2}$$

since $\sum_{t=1}^{T} x_t w_t' = 0$ and $\sum_{t=1}^{T} w_t' = 0$

$$= \frac{0 - 0}{\sum_{i=1}^{T}(x_i - \bar{x})^2}$$

and since the numerator equals 0,

$$= 0$$

Therefore

$$\mathrm{Var}[b_x'] = \mathrm{Var}[e]\left[\sum_{t=1}^{T}(w_t^{OLS})^2 + 2\sum_{t=1}^{T} w_t^{OLS} w_t' + \sum_{t=1}^{T}(w_t')^2\right]$$

since $\sum_{t=1}^{T} w_t^{OLS} w_t' = 0$

$$= \mathrm{Var}[e]\left[\sum_{t=1}^{T}(w_t^{OLS})^2 + \sum_{t=1}^{T}(w_t')^2\right]$$

The variance of the estimate's probability distribution is minimized whenever each w_t' equals 0, whenever the estimation procedure is the ordinary least squares (OLS) estimation procedure.

7 Estimating the Variance of an Estimate's Probability Distribution

Chapter 7 Prep Questions

1. Consider an estimate's probability distribution:

   a. Why is the mean of the probability distribution important?

   b. Why is the variance of the probability distribution important?

2. Consider Professor Lord's first quiz.

   a. Suppose that we know the actual value of the constant and coefficient. More specifically, suppose that the actual value of the constant is 50 and the actual value of the coefficient is 2. Fill in the blanks below to calculate each student's error term and the error term squared. Then compute the sum of the squared error terms.

$$\beta_{Const} = 50 \quad \beta_x = 2 \quad e_t = y_t - (\beta_{Const} + \beta_x x_t)$$

Student	x_t	y_t	$50 + 2x$	e_t 1st quiz	e_t^2 1st quiz
1	5	66	$50 + 2 \times \underline{\quad} = \underline{\quad}$	_____	_____
2	15	87	$50 + 2 \times \underline{\quad} = \underline{\quad}$	_____	_____
3	25	90	$50 + 2 \times \underline{\quad} = \underline{\quad}$	_____	_____

Sum = _____

   b. In reality, we do not know the actual value of the constant and coefficient. We used the ordinary least squares (OLS) estimation procedure to estimate their values. The estimated constant was 63 and the estimated value of the coefficient was 6/5. Fill in the blanks below to calculate each student's residual and the residual squared. Then, compute the sum of the squared residuals.

$$b_{Const} = 63$$

$$b_x = \frac{6}{5} = 1.2 \qquad Res_t = y_t - (b_{Const} + b_x x_t)$$

Student	x_t	y_t	$Esty_t = 63 + \dfrac{6}{5} x_t$	Res_t 1st quiz	Res_t^2 1st quiz
1	5	66	$63 + \dfrac{6}{5} \times 69 = \underline{\quad}$	_____	_____
2	15	87	$63 + \dfrac{6}{5} \times 81 = \underline{\quad}$	_____	_____
3	25	90	$63 + \dfrac{6}{5} \times 93 = \underline{\quad}$	_____	_____

Sum = _____

c. Compare the sum of squared errors with the sum of squared residuals.

d. In general, when applying the ordinary least squares (OLS) estimation procedure could the sum of squared residuals ever exceed the sum of squared errors? Explain.

3. Suppose that student 2 had missed Professor Lord's quiz.

Student	x_t	y_t	
1	5	66	x_t = minutes studied
3	25	90	y_t = quiz score

a. Plot a scatter diagram of the data.

b. What is the equation for the best fitting line?

c. What are the residuals for each observation?

d. Suppose that the quiz scores were different. For example, suppose that student 1 received a 70 instead of 66.

   i. What is the equation for the best fitting line now?

   ii. What are the residuals for each observation?

e. Again, suppose that the quiz scores were different. For example, suppose that student 1 received an 86 instead of 66 of 70.

   i. What is the equation for the best fitting line now?

   ii. What are the residuals for each observation?

f. In general, when there are only two observations what will the residuals for the best fitting line equal? Explain.

7.1 Review

7.1.1 Clint's Assignment: Assess the Effect of Studying on Quiz Scores

Clint's assignment is to assess the effect of studying on quiz scores:

Project: Use data from Professor Lord's first quiz to assess the effect of studying on quiz scores.

7.1.2 General Properties of the Ordinary Least Squares (OLS) Estimation Procedure

An estimate's probability distribution describes the general properties of the estimation procedure. In the last chapter we showed that when the standard ordinary least squares (OLS) premises are met, the mean of the coefficient estimate's probability distribution equals the actual value, β_x, and the variance equals the variance of the error term's probability distribution divided by the sum of the squared x deviations, $\text{Var}[e]/\sum_{t=1}^{T}(x_t - \bar{x})^2$:

$$\text{Mean}[b_x] = \beta_x, \quad \text{Var}[b_x] = \frac{\text{Var}[e]}{\sum_{t=1}^{T}(x_t - \overline{x})^2}$$

7.1.3   Importance of the Coefficient Estimate's Probability Distribution

Let us now review the importance of the mean and variance. In general, the mean and variance of the coefficient estimate's probability distribution play important roles:

· **Mean:**   When the mean of the estimate's probability distribution equals the actual value the estimation procedure is unbiased. An unbiased estimation procedure does not systematically underestimate or overestimate the actual value.

· **Variance:**   When the estimation procedure is unbiased, the variance of the estimate's probability distribution determines the reliability of the estimate. As the variance decreases, the probability distribution becomes more tightly cropped around the actual value making it more likely for the coefficient estimate to be close to the actual value:

Mean of estimate's probability distribution equals actual value		Variance of estimate's probability distribution	
↓		↓	
Estimation procedure is unbiased	→	Determines the reliability of the estimate	→ As variance decreases reliability increases

We can apply these general concepts to the ordinary least squares (OLS) estimation procedure. The mean of the coefficient estimate's probability distribution, Mean[b_x], equals the actual value of the coefficient, β_x; consequently the ordinary least squares (OLS) estimation procedure is unbiased. The variance of the coefficient estimate's probability distribution is now important; the variance determines the reliability of the estimate. What does the variance equal? We derived the equation for the variance:

$$\text{Var}[b_x] = \frac{\text{Var}[e]}{\sum_{t=1}^{T}(x_t - \overline{x})^2}$$

But neither Clint nor we know the variance of the error term's probability distribution, Var[e]. How then can the variance of the variance of the coefficient estimate's probability distribution be calculated? How can of Clint proceed? When Clint was faced with a similar problem before, what did he do? Clint used the econometrician's philosophy:

Econometrician's philosophy: If you lack the information to determine the value directly, estimate the value to the best of your ability using the information you do have.

What information does Clint have? Clint has the data from Professor Lord's first quiz (table 7.1).

Table 7.1
First quiz results

Student	Minutes studied (x)	Quiz score (y)
1	5	66
2	15	87
3	25	90

How can Clint use this information to estimate the variance of the coefficient estimate's probability distribution?

7.2   Strategy to Estimate the Variance of the Coefficient Estimate's Probability Distribution

Clint needs a procedure to estimate the variance of the coefficient estimate's probability distribution. Ideally this procedure should be unbiased. That is, it should not systematically underestimate or overestimate the actual variance. His approach will be based on the relationship between the variance of the coefficient estimate's probability distribution and the variance of the error term's probability distribution that we derived in chapter 6:

$$\text{Var}[b_x] = \frac{\text{Var}[e]}{\sum_{t=1}^{T}(x_t - \overline{x})^2}$$

Clint's strategy is to replace the actual variances in this equation with estimated variances:

$$\text{EstVar}[b_x] = \frac{\text{EstVar}[e]}{\sum_{t=1}^{T}(x_t - \overline{x})^2}$$

where

$\text{EstVar}[b_x]$ = estimated variance of the coefficient estimate's probability distribution

$\text{EstVar}[e]$ = estimated variance of the error term's probability distribution

Clint adopts a two-step strategy:

Step 1:   Clint estimates the variance of the error term's probability distribution.

Step 2:   Clint uses the estimate for the variance of the error term's probability distribution to estimate the variance for the coefficient estimate's probability distribution.

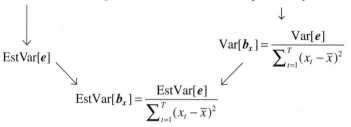

Step 1: Estimate the variance of the error term's probability distribution from the available information—data from the first quiz

$$\mathrm{EstVar}[e]$$

Step 2: Apply the relationship between the variances of coefficient estimate's and error term's probability distributions

$$\mathrm{Var}[b_x] = \frac{\mathrm{Var}[e]}{\sum_{t=1}^{T}(x_t - \overline{x})^2}$$

$$\mathrm{EstVar}[b_x] = \frac{\mathrm{EstVar}[e]}{\sum_{t=1}^{T}(x_t - \overline{x})^2}$$

7.3   Step 1: Estimating the Variance of the Error Term's Probability Distribution

The data from Professor Lord's first quiz is the only available information that Clint can use to estimate the variance of the error term's probability distribution, Var[e].

We will now describe three attempts to estimate the variance using the results of Professor Lord's first quiz by calculating the following:

1. Variance of the error term's numerical values from the first quiz.

2. Variance of the residual's numerical values from the first quiz.

3. "Adjusted" variance of the residual's numerical values from the first quiz.

In each case we will use simulations to assess these attempts by exploiting the relative frequency interpretation of probability:

Relative frequency interpretation of probability: After many, many repetitions of the experiment, the distribution of the numerical values from the experiments mirrors the random variable's probability distribution; the two distributions are identical:

Distribution of the
 numerical values

After many,
many
repetitions

Probability distribution

The first two attempts fail. Nevertheless, they provide the motivation for the third attempt which succeeds. Even though the first two attempts fail, it is instructive to explore them.

7.3.1 First Attempt to Estimate the Variance of the Error Term's Probability Distribution: Variance of the Error Term's Numerical Values from the First Quiz

In reality Clint cannot observe the actual parameters, β_{Const} and β_x, but for the moment, assume that we know them. If we were privy to the actual parameters, we would be able to calculate the actual numerical values of the error terms for each of our three students from the first quiz:

Student 1's error term   Student 2's error term   Student 3's error term

$\downarrow$ $\downarrow$ $\downarrow$

$e_1 = y_1 - (\beta_{Const} + \beta_x x_1)$ $e_2 = y_2 - (\beta_{Const} + \beta_x x_2)$ $e_3 = y_3 - (\beta_{Const} + \beta_x x_3)$

How could we use these three numerical values for the error terms from the first quiz to estimate the variance of the error term's probability distribution? Why not calculate the variance of the numerical values of the three error terms and then use that variance to estimate the variance of the error term's probability distribution? That is,

EstVar[e] = Var[e_1, e_2, and e_3 for 1st quiz]

Recall that the variance is the average of the squared deviations from the mean:

EstVar[e] = Var[e_1, e_2, and e_3 for 1st quiz]

$$= \frac{(e_1 - \text{Mean}[e])^2 + (e_2 - \text{Mean}[e])^2 + (e_3 - \text{Mean}[e])^2}{3}$$

Since the error terms represent random influences, the mean of the error term's probability distribution must equal 0. Therefore the deviations from the mean are just e_1, e_2, and e_3. The variance is the sum of the squared errors divided by 3:

EstVar[e] = Var[e_1, e_2, and e_3 for 1st quiz]

$$= \frac{e_1^2 + e_2^2 + e_3^2 \text{ for 1st quiz}}{3} = \frac{SSE \text{ for 1st quiz}}{3}$$

In our simulation we can specify the value of the actual parameters; by default, β_{Const} equals 50 and β_x equals 2. Using these values, calculate the numerical values of the error terms:

First quiz: $\beta_{Const} = 50$ $\beta_x = 2$ $e_t = y_t - (\beta_{Const} + \beta_x x_t)$

Student	x_t	y_t	$\beta_{Const} + \beta_x x_t = 50 + 2x_t$	$e_t = y_t - (50 + 2x_t)$	e_t^2
1	5	66	$50 + 2 \times 5 = 60$	$66 - 60 = 6$	$6^2 = 36$
2	15	87	$50 + 2 \times 15 = 80$	$87 - 80 = 7$	$7^2 = 49$
3	25	90	$50 + 2 \times 25 = 100$	$90 - 100 = -10$	$-10^2 = \underline{100}$
					Sum = 185

$\text{EstVar}[e] = \text{Var}[e_1, e_2, \text{and } e_3 \text{ for 1st quiz}]$

$$= \frac{e_1^2 + e_2^2 + e_3^2 \text{ for 1st quiz}}{3} = \frac{SSE \text{ for 1st quiz}}{3} = \frac{185}{3} = 61\frac{2}{3}$$

Can we expect variance of the numerical values, 61 2/3, to equal the actual variance of the coefficient estimate's probability distribution? Absolutely not, random influences are present. In fact we can be all but certain that the actual variance of the coefficient estimate's probability distribution will not equal 61 2/3. What then can we hope for? We can hope that this procedure is unbiased. We can hope that the procedure does not systematically overestimate or underestimate the actual value. But is the estimation procedure really unbiased?

Econometrics Lab 7.1: Is the First Attempt Estimation Procedure Unbiased?

We address this question by using the Estimating Variances simulation in our Econometrics Lab figure 7.1):

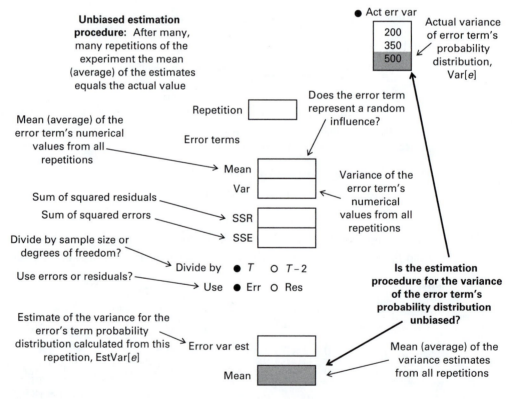

Figure 7.1
Variance of the error term's probability distribution simulation

[To access this online material, go to http://mitpress.mit.edu/westhoffeconometrics and select Lab 7.1.]

Some new boxes now appear:

• In the "Use" line, "Err" is selected, indicating that the simulation will calculate the numerical value of each student's error term and then square the error terms to estimate the variance of the error term's probability distribution.

• In the "Divide by" line, "T" is selected. T equals the sample size, 3 in this case. The simulation will divide the sum of the squared errors by 3 to estimate the variance of the error term's probability distribution.

By selecting "Err" in the "Use" line and "T" in the "Divide by" line, the simulation mimics the procedure that we just described to estimate the variance of the error term's probability distribution. Also note that the actual variance of the error term's probability distribution equals 500 by default.

Be certain that the Pause checkbox is checked and click **Start**. The simulation reports the sum of squared errors (SSE) and the estimate for variance of the error term's probability distribution (Error Var Est) based on the data for the first repetition:

$$\text{EstVar}[e] = \text{Var}[e_1, e_2, \text{and } e_3 \text{ for 1st repetition}]$$
$$= \frac{\text{Sum of squared errors for 1st repetition}}{T}$$

Convince yourself that the simulation is calculating EstVar[e] correctly by applying the procedure we just outlined. Then click **Continue** to simulate a second quiz. The simulation now reports on the estimate for variance of the error term's probability distribution (Error Var Est) based on the data for the second repetition:

$$\text{EstVar}[e] = \text{Var}[e_1, e_2, \text{and } e_3 \text{ for 2nd repetition}]$$
$$= \frac{\text{Sum of squared errors for 2nd repetition}}{T}$$

Again, convince yourself that the simulation is calculating EstVar[e] by applying the procedure we outlined. Also the simulation calculates the mean (average) of the two variance estimates; the mean of the variance estimates is reported in the Mean line directly below Error Var Est. Convince yourself that the simulation is calculating the mean of the variance estimates correctly.

Click **Continue** a few more times. Note that for some repetitions the estimated variance is less than the actual variance and sometimes the estimate is greater than the actual. Does this estimation procedure for the variance systematically underestimate or overestimate the actual variance or is the estimation procedure unbiased? We can apply the relative frequency interpretation of probability to address this question by comparing the mean (average) of the variance estimates with the actual variance after many, many repetitions. If the estimation procedure is unbiased, the mean of the variance estimates will equal the actual variance of the error term's probability distribution, 500 in this case, after many, many repetitions:

After many, many repetitions

↓

Mean (average) of the estimates   =   Actual value

↓

Estimation procedure is unbiased

Clear the Pause checkbox and click **Continue**; after many, many repetitions click **Stop**. The mean of the estimates for the error term's variance equals about 500, the actual variance. Next change the actual variance to 200; click **Start**, and then after many, many repetitions click **Stop**. Again, the mean of the estimates approximately equals the actual value. Finally, change the actual variance to 50 and repeat the procedure (table 7.2).

The simulation illustrates that this estimation procedure does not systematically underestimate or overestimate the actual variance; that is, this estimation procedure for the variance of the error term's probability distribution is unbiased. But does this help Clint? Unfortunately, it does not. To calculate the error terms we must know that actual value of the constant, β_{Const}, and the actual value of the coefficient, β_x. In a simulation we can specify the actual values of the parameters, β_{Const} and β_x, but neither Clint nor we know the actual values for Professor Lord's quiz. After all, if Clint knew the actual value of the coefficient, he would not need to go through the trouble of estimating it, would he? The whole problem is that Clint will never know what the actual value equals, that is why he must estimate it. Consequently this estimation procedure does not help Clint; he lacks the information to perform the calculations. So, what should he do?

Table 7.2
Error Term Variance simulation results—First attempt

Actual value Var[e]	Simulation repetitions	Mean (average) of the estimates for the variance of the error term's probability distribution SSE divided by T
500	>1,000,000	≈500
200	>1,000,000	≈200
50	>1,000,000	≈50

7.3.2   Second Attempt to Estimate the Variance of the Error Term's Probability Distribution: Variance of the Residual's Numerical Values from the First Quiz

Clint cannot calculate the actual values of the error terms because he does not know the actual values of the parameters, β_{Const} and β_x. So he decides to do the next best thing. He has already used the data from the first quiz to estimate the values of β_{Const} and β_x.

First quiz	Student	Minutes studied (x)	Quiz score (y)
	1	5	66
	2	15	87
	3	25	90

$$b_x = \frac{\sum_{t=1}^{T}(y_t - \bar{y})(x_t - \bar{x})}{\sum_{t=1}^{T}(x_t - \bar{x})^2} = \frac{240}{200} = \frac{6}{5} = 1.2 \qquad b_{Const} = \bar{y} - b_x\bar{x} = 81 - \frac{6}{5} \times 15 = 81 - 18 = 63$$

Clint's estimate of β_{Const} is 63 and β_x is 1.2. Consequently, why not use these estimated values for the constant and coefficient to estimate the numerical values of error terms for the three students? In other words, just use the residuals to estimate the error terms:

$$Res_1 = y_1 - (b_{Const} + b_x\, x_1), \quad Res_2 = y_2 - (b_{Const} + b_x\, x_2), \quad Res_3 = y_3 - (b_{Const} + b_x\, x_3)$$

Then use the variance of the three numerical values of the residuals to estimate the variance of the error term's probability distribution:

$$EstVar[e] = Var[Res_1, Res_2, \text{ and } Res_3 \text{ for 1st quiz}]$$

Recall that the variance equals the average of the squared deviations from the mean:

$$EstVar[e] = Var[Res_1, Res_2, \text{ and } Res_3 \text{ for 1st quiz}]$$
$$= \frac{(Res_1 - \text{Mean}[Res])^2 + (Res_2 - \text{Mean}[Res])^2 + (Res_3 - \text{Mean}[Res])^2}{3}$$

Clint has all the information needed to perform these calculations:

First quiz: $\qquad b_{Const} = 63 \quad B_x = \dfrac{6}{5} = 1.2$

Student	x_t	y_t	$Est_t = b_{Const} + b_x x_t = 63 + \dfrac{6}{5}x_t$	$Res_t = y_t - Esty_t$	Res_t^2
1	5	66	$63 + \dfrac{6}{5} \times 5 = 69$	$66 - 69 = -3$	$-3^2 = 9$
2	15	87	$63 + \dfrac{6}{5} \times 15 = 81$	$87 - 81 = 6$	$6^2 = 36$
3	25	90	$63 + \dfrac{6}{5} \times 25 = 93$	$90 - 93 = \underline{-3}$	$-3^2 = \underline{9}$
				Sum = 0	Sum = 54

What is the mean of the residuals? Clearly, the mean is 0:[1]

$$Mean[\textbf{Res}] = Mean[Res_1, Res_2, \text{ and } Res_3 \text{ for 1st quiz}]$$
$$= \frac{Res_1 + Res_2 + Res_3}{3} + \frac{-3 + 6 - 3}{3} = 0$$

Clint can easily calculate the variance of the estimated errors when using the residuals to do so:

$$EstVar[e] = Var[Res_1, Res_2, \text{ and } Res_3 \text{ for 1st quiz}]$$
$$= \frac{(Res_1 - Mean[\textbf{Res}])^2 + (Res_2 - Mean[\textbf{Res}])^2 + (Res_3 - Mean[\textbf{Res}])^2}{3}$$
$$= \frac{Res_1^2 + Res_2^2 + Res_3^2}{3}$$
$$= \frac{\text{Sum of squared residuals for 1st quiz}}{3} = \frac{\text{SSR for 1st quiz}}{3} = \frac{54}{3} = 18$$

The good news is that Clint can indeed perform these calculations. He can calculate the residuals and therefore can estimate the variance of the error term's probability distribution using this procedure. Unfortunately, there is also some bad news. This estimation procedure is biased; it systematically underestimates the variance of the error term's probability distribution.

---

1. Using a little algebra, we can in fact show that the mean of the residuals must always equal 0 when we use the ordinary least squares (OLS) estimation procedure.

Econometrics Lab 7.2: Is the Second Attempt Estimation Procedure Unbiased?

To illustrate this, return to the Estimating Variances simulation.

[To access this online material, go to http://mitpress.mit.edu/westhoffeconometrics and select Lab 7.2.]

Note that the "Res" is selected in the "Use" line, indicating that the variance of the residuals rather than the error terms will be used to estimate the variance of the error term's probability distribution. As before, the actual variance of the error term's probability distribution is specified as 500 by default. Be certain that the Pause checkbox is cleared; click **Start** and after many, many repetitions click **Stop**. The mean (average) of the estimates for the variance equals about 167 while the actual variance of the error term is 500. Next select a variance of 200 and then 50 and repeat the process. Convince yourself that this procedure consistently underestimates the variance.

The mean of the estimates is less than the actual values; this estimation procedure is biased downward (table 7.3). This estimation procedure systematically underestimates the variance of the error term's probability distribution.

Econometrics Lab 7.3: Comparing the Sum of Squared Residuals and the Sum of Squared Errors

To understand why this estimation procedure is biased downward, we will return to the Estimating Variances simulation.

[To access this online material, go to http://mitpress.mit.edu/westhoffeconometrics and select Lab 7.3.]

This time, be certain that the Pause checkbox is checked and then click **Start**. Note that both the sum of squared errors and the sum of squared residuals are reported. Which is less in the first repetition? Click the **Continue** button to run the second repetition. Which sum is less in the second repetition? Continue to do this until you recognize the pattern that is emerging. The sum of squared residuals is always less than the sum of squared errors. Why?

Table 7.3
Error Term Variance simulation results—Second attempt

Actual value Var[e]	Simulation repetitions	Mean (average) of the estimates for the variance of the error term's probability distribution SSR divided by T
500	>1,000,000	≈167
200	>1,000,000	≈67
50	>1,000,000	≈17

Recall how b_{Const} and b_x were chosen. They were chosen so as to minimize the sum of squared residuals:

$$SSR = Res_1^2 + Res_2^2 + Res_3^2 = (y_1 - b_{Const} - b_x x_1)^2 + (y_2 - b_{Const} - b_x x_2)^2 + (y_3 - b_{Const} - b_x x_3)^2$$

and compare it to the sum of squared errors:

$$SSE = e_1^2 + e_2^2 + e_3^2 = (y_1 - \beta_{Const} - \beta_x x_1)^2 + (y_2 - \beta_{Const} - \beta_x x_2)^2 + (y_3 - \beta_{Const} - \beta_x x_3)^2$$

The sum of squared residuals, $Res_1^2 + Res_2^2 + Res_3^2$, would equal the actual sum of squared errors, $e_1^2 + e_2^2 + e_3^2$, only if b_{Const} equaled β_{Const} and b_x equaled β_x:

Only if
$$b_{Const} = \beta_{Const} \text{ and } b_x = \beta_x$$
$$\downarrow$$
$$Res_1^2 + Res_2^2 + Res_3^2 = e_1^2 + e_2^2 + e_3^2$$

As a consequence of random influences we can never expect the estimates to equal the actual values, however. That is, we must expect the sum of squared residuals to be less than the sum of squared errors:

Typically
$$b_{Const} \neq \beta_{Const} \text{ and } b_x \neq \beta_x$$
$$\downarrow$$
$$Res_1^2 + Res_2^2 + Res_3^2 < e_1^2 + e_2^2 + e_3^2$$

Divide both sides of the inequality by 3 to compare the variance of the Res's and e's:

$$\frac{Res_1^2 + Res_2^2 + Res_3^2}{3} < \frac{e_1^2 + e_2^2 + e_3^2}{3}$$
$$\downarrow$$
$$\text{Var}[Res_1, Res_2, \text{ and } Res_3] < \text{Var}[e_1, e_2, \text{ and } e^3]$$

The variance of the residuals will be less than the variance of the actual errors. Recall our first attempt to estimate the variance of the error term's probability distribution. When we used the variance of the actual errors, the procedure was unbiased:

$$\frac{Res_1^2 + Res_2^2 + Res_3^2}{3} < \frac{e_1^2 + e_2^2 + e_3^2}{3}$$
$$\downarrow$$
$$\text{Var}[Res_1, Res_2, \text{ and } Res_3] < \text{Var}[e_1, e_2, \text{ and } e_3]$$
$$\downarrow \qquad\qquad\qquad \downarrow$$

Systematically   Unbiased estimation
underestimates variance   procedure

Using the variance of the residuals leads to bias because it systematically underestimates the variance of the error term's numerical values. So now, what can Clint do?

7.3.3 Third Attempt to Estimate the Variance of the Error Term's Probability Distribution: "Adjusted" Variance of the Residual's Numerical Values from the First Quiz

While we will not provide a mathematical proof, Clint can correct for this bias by calculating what we will call the "adjusted" variance of the residuals. Instead of dividing the sum of squared residuals by the sample size, Clint can calculate the adjusted variance by dividing by what are called the **degrees of freedom**:

$$\text{EstVar}[e] = \text{AdjVar}[Res_1, Res_2, \text{ and } Res_3 \text{ for 1st quiz}]$$
$$= \frac{\text{Sum of squared residuals for 1st quiz}}{\text{Degrees of freedom}}$$

where

Degrees of freedom = Sample size − Number of estimated parameters

The degrees of freedom equal the sample size less the number of estimated parameters. For the time being, do not worry about precisely what the degrees of freedom represent and why they solve the problem of bias. We will motivate the rationale later in this chapter. We do not wish to be distracted from Clint's efforts to estimate the variance of the error term's probability distribution at this time. So let us postpone the rationalization for now. For the moment we will accept that fact that the degrees of freedom equal 1 in this case:

Degrees of freedom = Sample size − Number of estimated parameters = 3 − 2 = 1

We subtract 2 because we are estimating the values of 2 parameters: the constant, β_{Const}, and the coefficient, β_x.

Clint has the information necessary to perform the calculations for the adjusted variance of the residuals. Recall that we have already calculated the sum of squared residuals:

First quiz: $b_{Const} = 63$ $b_x = \dfrac{6}{5} = 1.2$

Student	x_t	y_t	$Est_t = b_{Const} + b_x x_t = 63 + \dfrac{6}{5} x_t$	$Res_t = y_t - Esty_t$	Res_t^2
1	5	66	$63 + \dfrac{6}{5} \times 5 = 69$	$66 - 69 = -3$	$-3^2 = 9$
2	15	87	$63 + \dfrac{6}{5} \times 15 = 81$	$87 - 81 = 6$	$6^2 = 36$
3	25	90	$63 + \dfrac{6}{5} \times 25 = 93$	$90 - 93 = \underline{-3}$	$-3^2 = \underline{9}$
				Sum = 0	Sum = 54

So we need only divide the sum, 54, by the degrees of freedom to use the adjusted variance to estimate the variance of the error term's probability distribution:

$$EstVar[e] = AdjVar[Res_1, Res_2, \text{ and } Res_3 \text{ for 1st quiz}]$$

$$= \frac{\text{Sum of squared residuals for 1st quiz}}{\text{Degrees of freedom}} = \frac{54}{1} = 54$$

Econometrics Lab 7.4: Is the Third Attempt Estimation Procedure Unbiased?

We will use the Estimating Variances simulation to illustrate that this third estimation procedure is unbiased.

[To access this online material, go to http://mitpress.mit.edu/westhoffeconometrics and select Lab 7.4.]

In the "Divide by" line, select "T−2" instead of "T." Since we are estimating two parameters, the simulation will be dividing by the degrees of freedom instead of the sample size. Initially the variance of the error term's probability distribution is specified as 500. Be certain that the Pause checkbox is cleared; click **Start**, and then after many, many repetitions click **Stop**. The mean (average) of the variance estimates equals about 500, the actual variance. Next repeat the process by selecting a variance of 200 and then 50. Table 7.4 gives the results. In each case the mean of the estimates equals the actual value after many, many repetitions. This estimation procedure proves to be unbiased.

Table 7.4
Error Term Variance simulation results—Third attempt

Actual value Var[e]	Simulation repetitions	Mean (average) of the estimates for the variance of the error term's probability distribution SSR divided by $T-2$
500	>1,000,000	≈ 500
200	>1,000,000	≈ 200
50	>1,000,000	≈ 50

7.4   Step 2: Use the Estimate for the Variance of the Error Term's Probability Distribution to Estimate the Variance of the Coefficient Estimate's Probability Distribution

At last Clint has found an unbiased estimation procedure for the variance of the error term's probability distribution:

EstVar[e] = AdjVar[Res_1, Res_2, and Res_3 for 1st quiz] = 54

But why did he need this estimate in the first place? He needs it to estimate the variance of the coefficient estimate's probability distribution in order to assess the reliability of the coefficient estimate. Recall his two-step strategy:

Step 1:   Estimate the variance of the error term's probability distribution from the available information—data from the first quiz

Step 2: Apply the relationship between the variances of coefficient estimate's and error term's probability distributions

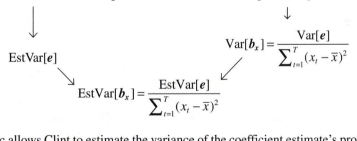

A little arithmetic allows Clint to estimate the variance of the coefficient estimate's probability distribution:

$$\text{EstVar}[b_x] = \frac{\text{EstVar}[e]}{(x_1 - \bar{x}) + (x_2 - \bar{x}) + (x_3 - \bar{x})}$$

$$= \frac{54}{(5-15)^2 + (15-15)^2 + (25-15)^2}$$

$$= \frac{54}{(-10)^2 + (0)^2 + (10)^2} = \frac{54}{100 + 100} = \frac{54}{200} = .27$$

Recall that the standard deviation is the square root of the variance; hence we can calculate the estimated standard deviation by computing the square root of estimated variance:

$$\text{EstSD}[b_x] = \sqrt{\text{EstVar}[b_x]} = \sqrt{0.27} = 0.5196$$

The estimated standard deviation is called the **standard error**:

$$\text{SE}[b_x] = \text{EstSD}[b_x]$$
$$= \text{Estimated standard deviation of } b_x \text{ s probability distribution}$$
$$= \sqrt{\text{EstVar}[b_x]} = \sqrt{0.27} = 0.5196$$

The standard error equals the square root of the estimated variance.

Let us summarize Clint's two-step strategy:

Step 1:   Clint estimates the variance of the error term's probability distribution.

Step 2:   Clint uses the estimate for the variance of the error term's probability distribution to estimate the variance for the coefficient estimate's probability distribution.

Step 1: Estimate the variance of the error term's probability distribution from the available information—data from the first quiz

$$\downarrow$$

$$\text{EstVar}[e] = \text{AdjVar}[Res\text{'s}]$$
$$= \frac{SSR}{\text{Degrees of freedom}} = \frac{54}{1} = 54$$

Step 2: Apply the relationship between the variances of coefficient estimate's and error term's probability distributions

$$\downarrow$$

$$\text{Var}[b_x] = \frac{\text{Var}[e]}{\sum_{t=1}^{T}(x_t - \bar{x})^2}$$

$$\text{EstVar}[b_x] = \frac{\text{EstVar}[e]}{\sum_{t=1}^{T}(x_t - \bar{x})^2} = \frac{54}{200} = 0.27$$

$$\text{EstSD}[b_x] = \sqrt{\text{EstVar}[b_x]} = \sqrt{0.27} = 0.5196$$

We have already used a simulation to show that step 1 is justified; that is, we have shown that the estimation procedure for the variance of the error term's probability distribution is unbiased. Now we will justify the step 2 by showing that the estimation procedure for the variance of the coefficient estimate's probability distribution is also unbiased. To do so, we will once again exploit the relative frequency interpretation of probability:

Distribution of the
numerical values

$$\downarrow$$

After many,
many
repetitions

Probability distribution

An estimation procedure is unbiased whenever the mean (average) of the estimated numerical values equals the actual value after many, many repetitions:

After many, many repetitions

$\downarrow$

Mean (average) of the estimates   =   Actual value

$\downarrow$

Estimation procedure is unbiased

Econometrics Lab 7.5: Is Estimation Procedure for the Variance of the Coefficient Estimate's Probability Distribution Unbiased?

We will use our Estimating Variance simulation in the Econometrics Lab to show that this two-step estimation procedure for the variance of the coefficient estimate's probability distribution is unbiased (figure 7.2).

[To access this online material, go to http://mitpress.mit.edu/westhoffeconometrics and select Lab 7.5.]

By default, the actual variance of the error term's probability distribution is 500 and the sample size is 3. We can now calculate the variance of the coefficient estimate's probability distribution:

$$\text{Var}[b_x] = \frac{\text{Var}[e]}{\sum_{t=1}^{T}(x_t - \overline{x})^2}$$

From before recall that the sum of x squared deviations equals 200:

$$\sum_{t=1}^{T}(x_t - \overline{x})^2 = 200$$

and that when the variance of the error term's probability distribution is specified as 500 and the sum of the squared x deviations equals 200, the variance of the coefficient estimates probability distribution equals 2.50:

$$\text{Var}[b_x] = \frac{\text{Var}[e]}{\sum_{t=1}^{T}(x_t - \overline{x})^2} = \frac{500}{200} = 2.50$$

Let us begin by confirming that the simulation is performing the calculations correctly. Be certain that the Pause button is checked, and then click **Start**. The sum of squared residuals and the sum of squared x deviations are reported for the first repetition. Use this information along with a pocket calculator to compute the estimate for the variance of the coefficient estimate's probability distribution, EstVar[b_x]:

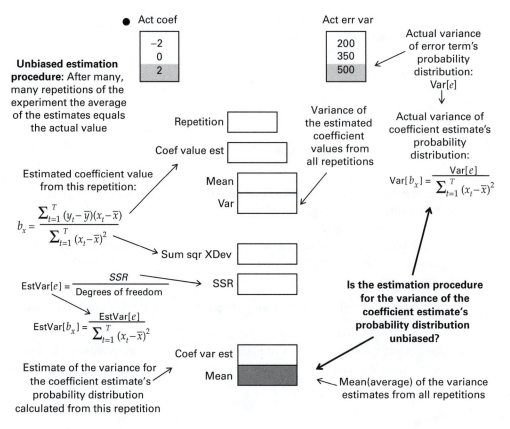

Figure 7.2
Variance of the coefficient estimate's probability distribution simulation

$$EstVar[\boldsymbol{b_x}] = \frac{EstVar[\boldsymbol{e}]}{\sum_{t=1}^{T}(x_t - \overline{x})^2}$$

where

$$EstVar[\boldsymbol{e}] = \frac{SSR}{\text{Degrees of freedom}}$$

Compare your calculation with the simulation's estimate. You will discover that they are identical. Next click **Continue** and perform the same calculation for the second repetition. Again, you will discover that the simulation has calculated the estimate for the variance of the coefficient estimate's probability distribution correctly. Also confirm that the simulation is computing the mean of the variance estimates correctly by taking the average of the coefficient variance estimates from the first two repetitions.

Is the estimation procedure for the variance of the
coefficient estimate's probability distribution unbiased?

Actual Var[e_t]	Variance of the coefficient estimate's probability distribution	Mean (average) of the estimates for the variance of the coefficient estimate's probability distribution
500	2.50	≈2.50
200	1.00	≈1.00
50	0.25	≈0.25

Click **Continue** a few more times. The variance estimate should be less than the actual value, 2.50, in some of the repetitions and greater than the actual value in others. Now the critical question:

Critical question: After many, many repetitions, will the mean (average) of the variance estimates equal the actual variance of the coefficient estimate's probability distribution?

If the answer is yes, the variance estimation procedure is unbiased; the procedure is not systematically overestimating or underestimating the actual variance. If instead the answer is no, the variance estimation procedure is biased. To answer this question, clear the Pause checkbox and click **Continue**. After many, many repetitions click **Stop**. What do you observe? After many, many repetitions the average of the coefficient's variance estimates indeed equals about 2.50.

Repeat this process after you change the error term variance to 200 and then to 50. As reported above, the answer to the critical question is yes in all cases. The estimation procedure for the variance of the coefficient estimate's probability distribution is unbiased.

7.5 Tying up a Loose End: Degrees of Freedom

7.5.1 Reviewing Our Second and Third Attempts to Estimate the Variance of the Error Term's Probability Distribution

Earlier in this chapter we postponed our explanation of degrees of freedom because it would have interrupted the flow of our discussion. We will now return to the topic by reviewing Clint's efforts to estimate the variance of the error term's probability distribution. Since Clint can never observe the actual constant, β_{Const}, and the actual coefficient, β_x, he cannot calculate the actual values of the error terms. He can, however, use his estimates for the constant, b_{Const}, and coefficient, b_x, to estimate the errors by calculating the residuals:

Error terms   Residuals
$$\downarrow \qquad\qquad\qquad \downarrow$$

$$e_t = y_t - (\beta_{Const} + \beta_x x_t) \quad Res_t = y_t - (b_{Const} + b_x x_t)$$

We can think of the residuals as the estimated "error terms." Now let us briefly review our second and third attempts to estimate the variance of the error term's probability distribution.

In our second attempt we used the variance of the residuals ("estimated errors") to estimate the variance of the error term's probability distribution. The variance is the average of the squared deviations from the mean:

$Var[Res_1, Res_2,$ and Res_3 for 1st quiz]

$$= \frac{(Res_1 - \text{Mean}[\textbf{Res}])^2 + (Res_2 - \text{Mean}[\textbf{Res}])^2 + (Res_3 - \text{Mean}[\textbf{Res}])^2}{\text{Sample size}}$$

Since the residuals are the "estimated errors," it seemed natural to divide the sum of squared residuals by the sample size, 3 in Clint's case. Furthermore, since the Mean[Res] = 0,

$$\text{EstVar}[Res_1, Res_2, \text{and } Res_3 \text{ for 1st quiz}] = \frac{Res_1^2 + Res_2^2 + Res_3^2}{\text{Sample size}} = \frac{SSR}{\text{Sample size}} = \frac{SSR}{3}$$

But we showed that this procedure was biased; the Estimating Variance simulation revealed that it systematically underestimated the error term's variance.

We then modified the procedure; instead of dividing by the sample size, we divided by the degrees of freedom, the sample size less the number of estimated parameters:

$\text{AdjVar}[Res_1, Res_2,$ and Res_3 for 1st quiz]

$$= \frac{Res_1^2 + Res_2^2 + Res_3^2}{\text{Degrees of freedom}} = \frac{SSR}{\text{Degrees of freedom}} = \frac{SSR}{1}$$

Degrees of freedom = Sample size − Number of estimated parameters
$$= 3 - 2 = 1$$

The Estimating Variances simulation illustrated that this modified procedure was unbiased.

7.5.2   How Do We Calculate an Average?

Why does dividing by 1 rather than 3 "work?" That is, why do we subtract 2 from the sample size when calculating the average of the squared residuals ("estimated errors")? To provide some intuition, we will briefly revisit Amherst precipitation in the twentieth century (table 7.5).

Calculating the mean for June obtains

$$\text{Mean (average) for June} = \frac{0.75 + 4.54 + \ldots + 7.99}{100} = \frac{377.76}{100} = 3.78$$

Table 7.5
Monthly precipitation in Amherst, MA, during the twentieth century

Year	Jan	Feb	Mar	Apr	May	Jun	Jul	Aug	Sep	Oct	Nov	Dec
1901	2.09	0.56	5.66	5.80	5.12	0.75	3.77	5.75	3.67	4.17	1.30	8.51
1902	2.13	3.32	5.47	2.92	2.42	4.54	4.66	4.65	5.83	5.59	1.27	4.27
⋮	⋮	⋮	⋮	⋮	⋮	⋮	⋮	⋮	⋮	⋮	⋮	⋮
2000	3.00	3.40	3.82	4.14	4.26	7.99	6.88	5.40	5.36	2.29	2.83	4.24

Each of the 100 Junes in the twentieth century provides one piece of information that we use to calculate the average. To calculate an average, we divide the sum by the number of pieces of information.

Key principle: To calculate a mean (an average), we divide the sum by the number of pieces of information:

$$\text{Mean (average)} = \frac{\text{Sum}}{\text{Number of pieces of information}}$$

Hence, to calculate the average of the squared deviations, the variance, we must divide by the number of pieces of information.

Now let us return to our efforts to estimate the variance of the error term's probability distribution:

Claim: The degrees of freedom equal the number of pieces of information that are available to estimate the variance of the error term's probability distribution.

To justify this claim, suppose that the sample size were 2. Plot the scatter diagram (figure 7.3):

• With only two observations, we only have two points.

• The best fitting line passes directly through each of the two points on the scatter diagram.

• Consequently the two residuals, "the two estimated errors," for each observation must always equal 0 when the sample size is 2 regardless of what the actual variance of the error term's probability distribution equals:

$Res_1 = 0$ and $Res_2 = 0$ regardless of what the variance actually equals.

The first two residuals, "the first two estimated errors," provide no information about the actual variance of the error term's probability distribution because the line fits the data perfectly—both residuals equal 0. Only with the introduction of a third observation do we get some sense of the error term's variance (figure 7.4).

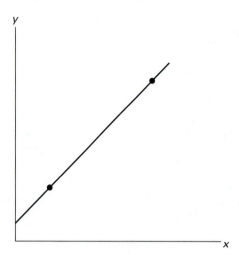

Figure 7.3
Degrees of freedom—Two observations

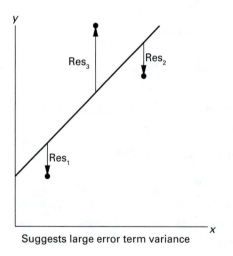

Suggests large error term variance

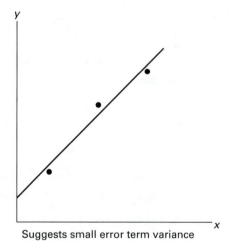

Suggests small error term variance

Figure 7.4
Degrees of freedom—Three observations

To summarize:

· The first two observations provide no information about the error term; stated differently, the first two observations provide "zero" information about the error term's variance.

· The third observation provides the first piece of information about the error term's variance.

This explains why Clint should divide by 1 to calculate the "average" of the squared deviations. In general, the degrees of freedom equal the number of pieces of information that we have to estimate the variance of the error term's probability distribution:

Degrees of freedom = Sample size − Number of estimated parameters

To calculate the average of the sum of squared residuals, we should divide the sum of squared residuals by the degrees of freedom, the number of pieces of information.

7.6 Summary: The Ordinary Least Squares (OLS) Estimation

7.6.1 Three Important Parts

The ordinary least squares (OLS) estimation procedure actually includes three procedures; a procedure to estimate the following:

· Regression parameters
· Variance of the error term's probability distribution
· Variance of the coefficient estimate's probability distribution

All three estimation procedures are unbiased. (Recall that we are assuming that the standard ordinary least squares (OLS) premises are met. We will address the importance of these premises in part IV of the textbook.) We will now review the calculations and then show that statistical software performs all these calculations for us.

Estimating the Value of the Regression Parameters
We calculated the ordinary least squares (OLS) estimates, b_x and b_{Const}, by using the appropriate equations; these estimates minimize the sum of squared residuals:

$$b_x = \frac{\sum_{t=1}^{T}(y_t - \bar{y})(x_t - \bar{x})}{\sum_{t=1}^{T}(x_t - \bar{x})^2} = \frac{240}{200} = \frac{6}{5} = 1.2, \quad b_{Const} = \bar{y} - b_x\bar{x} = 81 - \frac{6}{5} \times 15 = 81 - 18 = 63$$

Estimating the Variance of the Error Term's Probability Distribution
Once we calculate the estimates, it is easy to calculate the sum of squared residuals, *SSR*:

$$SSR = \sum_{t=1}^{T} Res_t^2 = \sum_{t=1}^{T}(y_t - Esty_t)^2 = \sum_{t=1}^{T}(y_t - b_{Const} - b_x x_t)^2 = 54$$

We estimated the variance of the error term's probability distribution, EstVar[e], by dividing the sum of squared residuals by the degrees of freedom:

$$\text{EstVar}[e] = \text{AdjVar}[Res_1 + Res_2 + Res_3] = \frac{SSR}{\text{Degrees of freedom}} = \frac{54}{1} = 54$$

The square root of this estimated variance is typically called the **standard error of the regression**:

$$\text{SE of regression} = \sqrt{\text{EstVar}[e]} = \sqrt{54} = 7.348$$

Note that the term standard error always refers to the square root of an estimated variance.

Estimating the Variance of the Coefficient Estimate's Probability Distribution

The estimated value of the error term's probability distribution allowed us to estimate the variance of the coefficient estimate's probability distribution, EstVar[b_x]:

$$\text{EstVar}[b_x] = \frac{\text{EstVar}[e]}{\sum_{t=1}^{T}(x_t - \bar{x})^2} = \frac{54}{200} = 0.27$$

The square root of this estimated variance of the coefficient estimate's probability distribution is called the standard error of the coefficient estimate, SE[b_x]:

$$\text{SE}[b_x] = \sqrt{\text{EstVar}[b_x]} = \sqrt{0.27} = 0.5196$$

We illustrated that these estimation procedure have nice properties. When the standard ordinary least squares (OLS) premises are satisfied:

• Each of these procedures is unbiased.

• The procedure to estimate the value of the parameters is the best linear unbiased estimation procedure (BLUE).

7.6.2 Regression Results

In reality, we did not have to make all these laborious calculations. Statistical software performs these calculations for us thereby saving us the task of performing the arithmetic (table 7.6):

Professor Lord's first quiz data: Cross-sectional data of minutes studied and quiz scores in the first quiz for the three students enrolled in Professor Lord's class.

x_t = minutes studied by student t

y_t = quiz score received by student t

[To access this online material, go to http://mitpress.mit.edu/westhoffeconometrics and select Professor Lord's First Quiz.]

Table 7.6
Quiz scores' regression results

Ordinary least squares (OLS)				
Dependent variable: y				
Explanatory variable(s):	Estimate	SE	t-Statistic	Prob
x	1.200000	0.519615	2.309401	0.2601
Const	63.00000	8.874120	7.099296	0.0891
Number of observations	3			
Sum squared residuals	54.00000			
SE of Regression	7.348469			
Estimated equation: $Esty = 63 + 1.2x$				

We previously noted the regression results report the parameter estimates and the sum of squared residuals. While statistical software typically does not report the estimated variance of the error term's probability distribution, it does report the standard error of the regression, SE of regression, which is just the square root of the estimated variance of the error term's probability distribution. We can easily calculate the estimated variance of the error term's probability distribution from the regression results by squaring the standard error of the regression:

$EstVar[e] = 7.328469^2 = 54$

Similarly, while the statistical software does not report the estimated variance of the coefficient estimate's probability distribution, it does report its standard error. We can easily calculate the estimated variance of the coefficient estimates probability distribution from the regression results by squaring the standard error of the coefficient estimate:

$EstVar[b_x] = 0.519615^2 = 0.27$

Chapter 7   Review Questions

1. Consider the ordinary least squares (OLS) estimation procedure. How is the variance of the coefficient estimate's probability distribution related to the variance of the error term's probability distribution?

2. What strategy have we used to estimate the variance of the coefficient estimate's probability distribution?

3. Consider our first attempt to estimate the variance of the error term's probability distribution:

$$EstVar[e] = Var[e_1, e_2, \ldots, e_T] = \frac{e_1^2 + e_2^2 + \ldots + e_T^2}{\text{Sample size}} = \frac{SSE}{\text{Sample size}}$$

Why did this attempt fail?

4. Consider our second attempt to estimate the variance of the error term's probability distribution:

$$\text{EstVar}[e] = \text{Var}[Res_1, Res_2, \ldots, Res_T] = \frac{Res_1^2 + Res_2^2 + \ldots + Res_T^2}{\text{Sample size}} = \frac{SSR}{\text{Sample size}}$$

Why did this attempt fail?

5. Consider our third attempt to estimate the variance of the error term's probability distribution:

$$\text{EstVar}[e] = \text{Var}[Res_1, Res_2, \ldots, Res_T] = \frac{Res_1^2 + Res_2^2 + \ldots + Res_T^2}{\text{Degrees of freedom}} = \frac{SSR}{\text{Degrees of freedom}}$$

This attempt succeeded. Explain why it is appropriate to divide by the degrees of freedom rather than the sample size.

Chapter 7 Exercises

Recall Professor Lord's colleague who is teaching another course in which three students are enrolled.

Regression example data: Cross-sectional data of minutes studied and quiz scores from a course taught by Professor Lord's colleague.

x_t = minutes studied by student t

y_t = quiz score received by student t

Student	Minutes studied (x)	Quiz score (y)
1	5	14
2	10	44
3	30	80

1. The simple regression model for the quiz is

$$y_t = \beta_{Const} + \beta_x x_t + e_t$$

Using a calculator and the equations we derived in class, apply the least squares estimation procedure to find the best fitting line by filling in the blanks:

First, calculate the means:

Means: $\bar{x} =$ _____ =

$\bar{y} =$ _____ =

Second, for each student calculate the deviation of x from its mean and the deviation of y from its mean:

Student	y_t	$\bar{y}$	$y_t - \bar{y}$	x_t	$\bar{x}$	$x_t - \bar{x}$
1	14	___	___	5	___	___
2	44	___	___	10	___	___
3	80	___	___	30	___	___

Third, calculate the products of the y and x deviations and squared x deviations for *each* student; then calculate the sums:

Student	$(y_t - \bar{y})(x_t - \bar{x})$		$(x_t - \bar{x})^2$	
1	_____	= ____	_____	= ____
2	_____	= ____	_____	= ____
3	_____	= ____	_____	= ____
	Sum = ____		Sum = ____	

Now, apply the formulas:

$$b_x = \frac{\sum_{t=1}^{T}(y_t - \bar{y})(x_t - \bar{x})}{\sum_{t=1}^{T}(x_t - \bar{x})^2} = \frac{\quad\quad\quad}{\quad\quad\quad} = \underline{\quad\quad}$$

$$b_{Const} = \bar{y} - b_x\bar{x} = \underline{\quad} - \underline{\quad\quad} = \underline{\quad} - \underline{\quad} = \underline{\quad}$$

2. Calculate the sum of squared residuals by filling in the following blanks:

Student	x_t	y_t	$Esty_t = b_{Const} + b_x x_t$		$Res_t = y_t - Esty_t$		Res_t^2
1	5	14	_____	= ___	___ − ___	= ___	___
2	10	44	_____	= ___	___ − ___	= ___	___
3	30	80	_____	= ___	___ − ___	= ___	___
						SSR =	___

(handwritten above formula: 10   2.4)

3. Finally, use the quiz data to estimate the variance and standard deviation of the coefficient estimate's probability distribution.

4. Check your answers to exercises 1, 2, and 3 using statistical software.

[To access this online material, go to http://mitpress.mit.edu/westhoffeconometrics and select Regression Example.]

5. Consider the following regression results:

Ordinary least squares (OLS)

Dependent variable: y

Explanatory variable(s):	Estimate	SE
x	15.26071	4.492548
Const	−27.32826	86.78952
Number of observations	10	
SE of regression	78.09296	

Based on the results:

a. Can you estimate the variance of the error term's probability distribution, EstVar[e]?

If so, what does it equal?

Yes _____   No _____   _____

b. Can you estimate the variance of the coefficient estimate's probability distribution, EstVar[b_x]?

If so, what does it equal?

Yes _____   No _____   _____

c. Can you calculate $\sum_{t=1}^{T}(x_t - \bar{x})^2$?

If so, what does it equal?

Yes _____   No _____   _____

d. Can you calculate $\sum_{t=1}^{T}(y_t - \bar{y})(x_t - \bar{x})$?

If so, what does it equal?

Yes _____   No _____   _____

e. Can you calculate the sum of squared residuals, *SSR*?

If so, what does it equal?

Yes _____   No _____   _____

f. Can you calculate sum of squared errors, *SSE*?

If so, what does it equal?

Yes _____   No _____   _____

8 Interval Estimates and Hypothesis Testing

Chapter 8 Prep Questions

1. Run the following simulation and answer the questions posed. Summarize your answers by filling in the following blanks:

[To access this online material, go to http://mitpress.mit.edu/westhoffeconometrics and select Lab 8P.1.]

Actual values β_x	Var[e]	From value	To value	Repetitions between From and To values
2	50	1.5	2.5	≈_____%
2	50	1.0	3.0	≈_____%
2	50	0.5	3.5	≈_____%

2. In the simulation you just ran (question 1):

.25

a. Using the appropriate equation, compute the variance of the coefficient estimate's probability distribution? _____

b. What is the standard deviation of the coefficient estimate's probability distribution? _____

√.25

c. Using the normal distribution's "rules of thumb," what is the probability that the coefficient estimate in one repetition would lie between:

i. 1.5 and 2.5? _____

ii. 1.0 and 3.0? _____

iii. 0.5 and 3.5? _____

d. Are your answers to part c consistent with your simulation results?

3. Recall the normal distribution. What is the definition of the normal distribution's z?

4. Recall the regression results from Professor Lord's first quiz:

Ordinary least squares (OLS)

Dependent variable: y

Explanatory variable(s):	Estimate	SE	t-Statistic	Prob
x	1.200000	0.519615	2.309401	0.2601
Const	63.00000	8.874120	7.099296	0.0891
Number of observations	3			
Sum squared residuals	54.00000			
SE of regression	7.348469			

a. Does the positive coefficient estimate suggest that studying more will improve a student's quiz score? Explain.

Consider the views of a cynic:

Cynic's view: Studying has no impact on a student's quiz score; the positive coefficient estimate obtained from the first quiz was just "the luck of the draw." In fact, studying does not affect quiz scores.

b. If the cynic were correct and studying has no impact on quiz scores, what would the actual coefficient, β_x, equal?

c. Is it possible that the cynic is correct? To help you answer this question, run the following simulation:

[To access this online material, go to http://mitpress.mit.edu/westhoffeconometrics and select Lab 8.P4.]

8.1 Clint's Assignment: Taking Stock

We will begin by taking stock of where Clint stands. Recall the theory he must assess:

Theory: Additional studying increases quiz scores.

Clint's assignment is to assess the effect of studying on quiz scores:

Project: Use data from Professor Lord's first quiz to assess the effect of studying on quiz scores.

Clint uses a simple regression model to assess the theory. Quiz score is the dependent variable and number of minutes studied is the explanatory variable:

$$y_t = \beta_{Const} + \beta_x x_t + e_t$$

where

y_t = quiz score of student t

x_t = minutes studied by student t

e_t = error term for student t

β_{Const} and β_x are the model's parameters. They incorporate the view that Professor Lord awards each student some points just for showing up; subsequently, the number of additional points each student earns depends on how much he/she studied:

• β_{Const} represents the number of points Professor Lord gives a student just for showing up.

• β_x represents the number of additional points earned for each additional minute of study.

Since the values of β_{Const} and β_x are not observable, Clint adopted the econometrician's philosophy:

Econometrician's philosophy: If you lack the information to determine the value directly, estimate the value to the best of your ability using the information you do have.

Clint used the results of the first quiz to estimate the values of β_{Const} and β_x by applying the ordinary least squares (OLS) estimation procedure to find the best fitting line:

First quiz data

Student	x	y

$$b_x = \frac{\sum_{t=1}^{T}(y_t - \bar{y})(x_t - \bar{x})}{\sum_{t=1}^{T}(x_t - \bar{x})^2} = \frac{240}{200} = \frac{6}{5} = 1.2$$

Student	x	y	
1	5	66	$\rightarrow \quad b_{Const} = \bar{y} - b_x\bar{x} = 81 - \dfrac{6}{5} \times 15 = 81 - 18 = 63$
2	15	87	
3	25	90	

Clint's estimates suggest that Professor Lord gives each student 63 points for showing up; subsequently, each student earns 1.2 additional points for each additional minute studied.

Clint realizes that he cannot expect the coefficient estimate to equal the actual value; in fact, he is all but certain that it will not. So now Clint must address two related issues:

· **Estimate reliability:**   How reliable is the coefficient estimate, 1.2, calculated from the first quiz? That is, how confident should Clint be that the coefficient estimate, 1.2, will be close to the actual value?

· **Theory assessment:**   How confident should Clint be that the theory is correct, that studying improves quiz scores?

We will address both of these issues in this chapter. First, we consider estimate reliability.

8.2   Estimate Reliability: Interval Estimate Question

The interval estimate question quantifies the notion of reliability:

Interval estimate question: What is the probability that the estimate, 1.20, lies within _____ of the actual value? _____

The general properties of the ordinary least squares (OLS) estimation procedure allow us to address this question. It is important to distinguish between the general properties and one specific application. Recall that the general properties refer to what we know about the estimation procedure before the quiz is given; the specific application refers to the numerical values of the estimates calculated from the results of the first quiz:

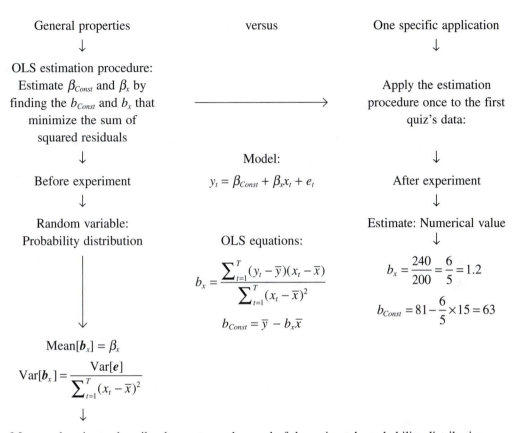

General properties   versus   One specific application
↓   ↓

OLS estimation procedure:
Estimate β_{Const} and β_x by   Apply the estimation
finding the b_{Const} and b_x that   ⟶   procedure once to the first
minimize the sum of   quiz's data:
squared residuals
↓   ↓

Before experiment   Model: After experiment
↓ $y_t = \beta_{Const} + \beta_x x_t + e_t$ ↓

Random variable: Estimate: Numerical value
Probability distribution   OLS equations: ↓

$$b_x = \frac{\sum_{t=1}^{T}(y_t - \overline{y})(x_t - \overline{x})}{\sum_{t=1}^{T}(x_t - \overline{x})^2}$$ $$b_x = \frac{240}{200} = \frac{6}{5} = 1.2$$

$$b_{Const} = \overline{y} - b_x\overline{x}$$ $$b_{Const} = 81 - \frac{6}{5} \times 15 = 63$$

$$\text{Mean}[b_x] = \beta_x$$

$$\text{Var}[b_x] = \frac{\text{Var}[e]}{\sum_{t=1}^{T}(x_t - \overline{x})^2}$$

↓

Mean and variance describe the center and spread of the estimate's probability distribution

The estimates are random variables and a quiz can be viewed as an experiment. We cannot determine the numerical value of an estimate with certainty before the experiment (quiz) is conducted. What then do we know beforehand? We can describe the probability distribution of the estimate. We know that the mean of the coefficient estimate's probability distribution equals the actual value of the coefficient and its variance equals the variance of the error term's probability distribution divided by the sum of squared x deviations:

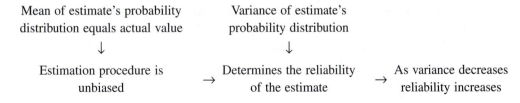

Mean of estimate's probability   Variance of estimate's
distribution equals actual value   probability distribution
↓   ↓

Estimation procedure is   Determines the reliability   As variance decreases
unbiased   →   of the estimate   →   reliability increases

Both the mean and variance of the coefficient estimate's probability distribution play a crucial role:

• Since the mean of the coefficient estimate's probability distribution, Mean[b_x], equals the actual value of the coefficient, β_x, the estimation procedure is unbiased; the estimation procedure does not systematically underestimate or overestimate the actual coefficient value.

• When the estimation procedure for the coefficient value is unbiased, the variance of the estimate's probability distribution, Var[b_x], determines the reliability of the estimate; as the variance decreases, the probability distribution becomes more tightly cropped around the actual value; consequently it becomes more likely for the coefficient estimate to be close to the actual coefficient value.

To assess his estimate's reliability, Clint must consider the variance of the coefficient estimate's probability distribution. But we learned that Clint can never determine the actual variance of the error term's probability distribution, Var[e]. Instead, Clint employs a two step strategy for estimating the variance of the coefficient estimate's probability distribution:

Step 1: Estimate the variance of the error term's probability distribution from the available information – data from the first quiz

Step 2: Apply the relationship between the variances of coefficient estimate's and error term's probability distributions

$$\downarrow \qquad\qquad\qquad\qquad \downarrow$$

$$\text{EstVar}[e] = \text{AdjVar}[\boldsymbol{Res's}]$$

$$= \frac{SSR}{\text{Degrees of freedom}} = \frac{54}{1} = 54 \qquad\qquad \text{Var}[b_x] = \frac{\text{Var}[e]}{\sum_{t=1}^{T}(x_t - \bar{x})^2}$$

$$\text{EstVar}[b_x] = \frac{\text{EstVar}[e]}{\sum_{t=1}^{T}(x_t - \bar{x})^2} = \frac{54}{200} = 0.27$$

$$\text{EstSD}[b_x] = \sqrt{\text{EstVar}[b_x]} = \sqrt{0.27} = 0.5196$$

Unfortunately, there is one last complication before we can address the interval estimate question.

8.2.1 Normal Distribution versus the Student t-Distribution: One Last Complication

We begin by reviewing the normal distribution. Recall that the variable z played a critical role in using the normal distribution:

$$z = \frac{\text{Value of random variable} - \text{Distribution mean}}{\text{Distribution standard deviation}}$$

$$= \text{Number of standard deviations from the mean}$$

In words, z equals the number of standard deviations the value lies from the mean. But Clint does not know what the variance and standard deviation of the coefficient estimate's probability distribution equal. That is why he must estimate them. Consequently he cannot use the normal distribution to calculate probabilities.

When the standard deviation is not known and must be estimated, the Student t-distribution must be used. The variable t is similar to the variable z; instead of equaling the number of standard deviations the value lies from the mean, t equals the number of estimated standard deviations the value lies from the mean:

$$t = \frac{\text{Value of random variable} - \text{Distribution mean}}{\text{Estimated distribution standard deviation}}$$

$$= \text{Number of estimated standard deviations from the mean}$$

Recall that the estimated standard deviation is called the standard error; hence

$$t = \frac{\text{Value of random variable} - \text{Distribution mean}}{\text{Standard error}}$$

$$= \text{Number of standard errors from the distribution mean}$$

Like the normal distribution, the t-distribution is symmetric about its mean. Since estimating the standard deviation introduces an additional element of uncertainty, the Student t-distribution is more "spread out" than the normal distribution as illustrated in figure 8.1. The Student

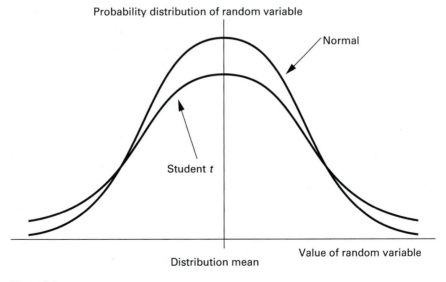

Figure 8.1
Normal and Student t-distributions

t-distribution's "spread" depends on the degrees of freedom. As the number of degrees of freedom increase, we have more information; consequently the *t*-distribution's spread decreases, moving it closer and closer to the normal distribution. Since the "spread" of the Student *t*-distribution depends on the degrees of freedom, the table describing the Student *t*-distribution is more cumbersome than the normal distribution table. Fortunately, our Econometrics Lab allows us to avoid the cumbersome Student *t*-distribution table.

8.2.2   Assessing the Reliability of a Coefficient Estimate

How reliable is the coefficient estimate, 1.2, calculated from the first quiz? That is, how confident should Clint be that the coefficient estimate, 1.2, will be close to the actual value? The interval estimate question to address this question:

Interval estimate question: What is the probability that the coefficient estimate, 1.2, lies within _____ of the actual coefficient value? _____

We begin by filling in the first blank, choosing our "close to" value. The value we choose depends on how demanding we are; that is, our "close to" value depends on the range that we consider to be "close to" the actual value. For purposes of illustration, we will choose 1.5; so we write 1.5 in the first blank.

Interval estimate question: What is the probability that the coefficient estimate, 1.2, lies within **1.5** of the actual coefficient value? _____

Figure 8.2 illustrates the probability distribution of the coefficient estimate and the probability that we wish to calculate. The estimation procedure we used to calculate the coefficient estimate, the ordinary least squares (OLS) estimation procedure is unbiased:

$$\text{Mean}[b_x] = \beta_x$$

Consequently we place the actual coefficient value, β_x, at the center of the probability distribution.

As discussed above, we must use the Student *t*-distribution rather than the normal distribution since we must estimate the standard deviation of the probability distribution. The regression results from Professor Lord's first quiz provide the estimate (table 8.1).

The standard error equals the estimated standard deviation. *t* equals the number of standard errors (estimated standard deviations) that the value lies from the distribution mean:

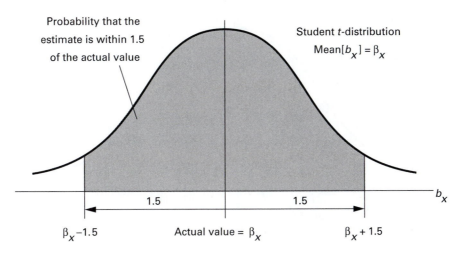

Figure 8.2
Probability distribution of coefficient estimate—"Close to" value equals 1.5

Table 8.1
Quiz scores regression results

	Ordinary least squares (OLS)			
Dependent variable: y				
Explanatory variable(s):	Estimate	SE	t-Statistic	Prob
x	1.200000	0.519615	2.309401	0.2601
Const	63.00000	8.874120	7.099296	0.0891
Number of observations	3			
Sum squared residuals	54.00000			
SE of regression	7.348469			

Estimated equation: $Esty = 63 + 1.2x$

Interpretation of estimates:

$b_{Const} = 63$: Students receive 63 points for showing up

$b_x = 1.2$: Students receive 1.2 additional points for each additional minute studied

Critical result: The coefficient estimate equals 1.2. The positive sign of the coefficient estimate, suggests that additional studying increases quiz scores. This evidence lends support to our theory.

$$t = \frac{\text{Value of random variable} - \text{Distribution mean}}{\text{Standard error}}$$

$$= \text{Number of standard errors from the distribution mean}$$

Since the distribution mean equals the actual value, we can "translate" 1.5 below and above the actual value into t's. Since the standard error equals 0.5196, 1.5 below and above the actual value translates into 2.89 standard errors below and above the actual value:

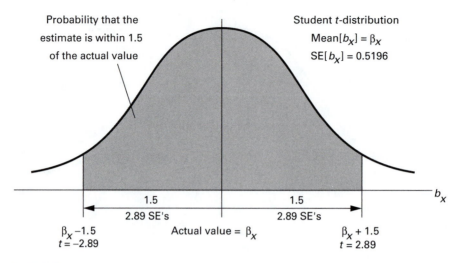

Probability that the
estimate is within 1.5
of the actual value

Student t-distribution
Mean$[b_X] = \beta_X$
SE$[b_X] = 0.5196$

1.5   1.5
2.89 SE's   2.89 SE's

$\beta_X - 1.5$ Actual value $= \beta_X$ $\beta_X + 1.5$
$t = -2.89$ $t = 2.89$

b_X

Figure 8.3
Probability distribution of coefficient estimate—"Close to" value equals 1.5

1.5 below actual value   1.5 above actual value
↓   ↓

$\dfrac{1.5}{0.5196} = 2.89$ SE's below actual value $\dfrac{1.5}{0.5196} = 2.89$ SE's above actual value

To summarize:

| The probability that the estimate lies within 1.5 of the actual value | = | The probability that the estimate lies within 2.89 SE's of the actual value |

↓

That is, between t's of
−2.89 and 2.89

Figure 8.3 adds this information to the probability distribution graph.

Econometrics Lab 8.1: Calculating the Tail Probabilities

We can now use the Econometrics Lab to calculate the probability that the estimate is within 1.5 of the actual value by computing probabilities the left and right tails probabilities.[1]

---

1. Appendix 8.2 shows how we can use the Student t-distribution table to address the interval estimate question. Since the table is cumbersome, we will use the Econometrics Lab to do so.

[To access this online material, go to http://mitpress.mit.edu/westhoffeconometrics and select Lab 8.1a.]

· **Left tail:**   The following information has been entered:

Degrees of freedom: 1

t: −2.89

Click **Calculate**. The left tail probability is approximately 0.11.

[To access this online material, go to http://mitpress.mit.edu/westhoffeconometrics and select Lab 8.1b.]

· **Right tail:**   The following information has been entered:

Degrees of freedom: 1

t: 2.89

Click **Calculate**. The right tail probability is approximately 0.11.

Since the Student t-distribution is symmetric, both the left and right tail probabilities equal 0.11 (figure 8.4). Hence, the probability that the estimate is within 1.5 of the actual value equals 0.78:

$$1.00 - (0.11 + 0.11) = 0.78.$$

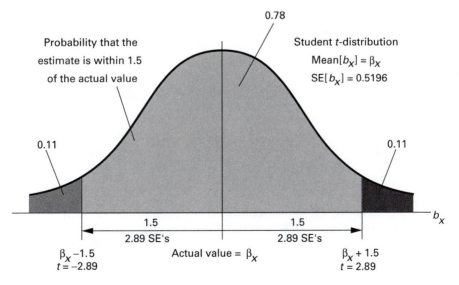

Figure 8.4
Probability distribution of coefficient estimate—Applying Student t-distribution

We can now fill in the second blank in the interval estimate question:

Interval estimate question: What is the probability that the coefficient estimate, 1.2, lies within **1.5** of the actual coefficient value? **0.78**

We will turn our attention to assessing the theory.

8.3   Theory Assessment: Hypothesis Testing

Hypothesis testing allows Clint to assess how much confidence he should have in the theory. We begin by motivating hypothesis testing using the same approach as we took with Clint's opinion poll. We will play the role of the cynic. Then we will formalize the process.

8.3.1   Motivating Hypothesis Testing: The Cynic

Recall that the "theory" suggests that a student's score on the quiz depends on the number of minutes he/she studies:

Theory: Additional studying increases scores.

Review the regression model:

$$y_t = \beta_{Const} + \beta_x x_t + e_t$$

The theory suggests that β_x is positive. Review the regression results for the first quiz (table 8.2).

Table 8.2
Quiz scores regression results

Ordinary least squares (OLS)				
Dependent variable: y				
Explanatory variable(s):	Estimate	SE	t-Statistic	Prob
x	1.200000	0.519615	2.309401	0.2601
Const	63.00000	8.874120	7.099296	0.0891
Number of observations	3			
Sum squared residuals	54.00000			
SE of regression	7.348469			

Estimated equation: $Esty = 63 + 1.2x$

Interpretation of estimates:

  $b_{Const} = 63$: Students receive 63 points for showing up

  $b_x = 1.2$: Students receive 1.2 additional points for each additional minute studied

Critical result: The coefficient estimate equals 1.2. The positive sign of the coefficient estimate, suggests that additional studying increases quiz scores. This evidence lends support to our theory.

The estimate for β_x, 1.2, is positive. We estimate that an additional minute of studying increases a student's quiz score by 1.2 points. This lends support to Clint's theory. But, how much confidence should Clint have in the theory? Does this provide definitive evidence that Clint's theory is correct, or should we be skeptical? To answer this question, recall our earlier hypothesis-testing discussion and play the cynic. What would a cynic's view of our theory and the regression results be?

Cynic's view: Studying has no impact on a student's quiz score; the positive coefficient estimate obtained from the first quiz was just "the luck of the draw." In fact, studying has no effect on quiz scores; the actual coefficient, β_x, equals 0.

Is it possible that our cynic is correct?

Econometrics Lab 8.2: Assessing the Cynic's View

We will use a simulation to show that it is.
A positive coefficient estimate can arise in one repetition of the experiment even when the actual coefficient is 0.

[To access this online material, go to http://mitpress.mit.edu/westhoffeconometrics and select Lab 8.2.]

In the simulation, the default actual coefficient value is 0. Check the From–To checkbox. Also 0 is specified in the From list. In the To list, no value is specified; consequently there is no upper From–To bound. The From–To Percent box will report the percent of repetitions in which the coefficient estimate equals 0 or more. Be certain that the "Pause" checkbox is cleared. Click **Start**, and then after many, many repetitions click **Stop**. In about half of the repetitions the coefficient estimate is positive; that is, when the actual coefficient, β_x, equals 0, the estimate is positive about half the time. The histogram illustrates this. Now, we can apply the relative frequency interpretation of probability. If the actual coefficient were 0, the probability of obtaining a positive coefficient from one quiz would be about one-half as illustrated in figure 8.5.

Consequently we cannot dismiss the cynic's view as absurd.

To assess the cynic's view, we pose the following question:

Question for the cynic: What is the probability that the result would be like the one obtained (or even stronger), if studying actually has no impact on quiz scores? That is, what is the probability that the coefficient estimate from the first quiz would be 1.2 or more, if studying had no impact on quiz scores (if the actual coefficient, β_x, equals 0)?

Answer: Prob[Results IF cynic correct].

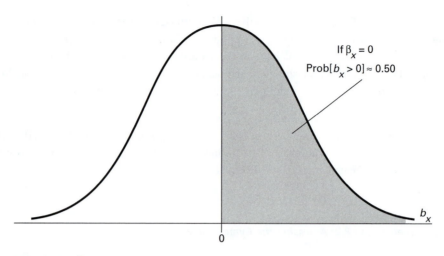

$$\text{If } \beta_x = 0$$
$$\text{Prob}[b_x > 0] \approx 0.50$$

0

b_x

Figure 8.5
Probability distribution of coefficient estimate—Could the cynic be correct?

The magnitude of the probability determines the likelihood that the cynic is correct, the likelihood that studying has no impact on quiz scores:

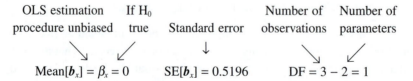

Prob[Results IF cynic correct] small   Prob[Results IF cynic correct] large

↓   ↓

Unlikely that the   Likely that the
cynic is correct   cynic is correct

↓   ↓

Unlikely that the   Likely that the
studying has no impact   studying has no impact

To compute this probability, let us review what we know about the probability distribution of the coefficient estimate:

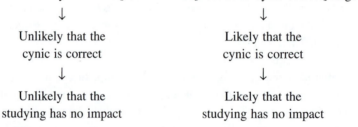

OLS estimation   If H_0 Number of   Number of
procedure unbiased   true   Standard error   observations   parameters

↘   ↙   ↓   ↘   ↙

$\text{Mean}[b_x] = \beta_x = 0$ $\text{SE}[b_x] = 0.5196$ $\text{DF} = 3 - 2 = 1$

Question for the cynic: What is the probability that the coefficient estimate from the first quiz would be 1.2 or more, if studying had no impact on quiz scores (if the actual coefficient, β_x, equaled 0)?

How can we answer this question? We turn to the Econometrics Lab.

Econometrics Lab 8.3: Using the Econometrics Lab to Calculate Prob[Results IF cynic correct]

[To access this online material, go to http://mitpress.mit.edu/westhoffeconometrics and select Lab 8.3.]

The appropriate information has been entered:

Mean: 0

Standard error: 0.5196

Value: 1.2

Degrees of freedom: 1

Click **Calculate**. The probability that the estimate lies in the right tail equals 0.13. The answer to the question for the cynic is 0.13 (figure 8.6):

In fact there is an even easier way to compute the probability. We do not even need to use the Econometrics Lab to because the statistical software calculates this probability automatically. To illustrate this, we will first calculate the *t*-statistic based on the premise that the cynic is correct, based on the premise that the actual value of the coefficient equals 0:

$$t = \frac{\text{Value of random variable} - \text{Distribution mean}}{\text{Standard Error}} = \frac{1.2 - 0}{0.5196} = 2.309$$

= Number of standard errors from the distribution mean

1.2 lies 2.309 standard errors from 0. Next return to the regression results (table 8.3) and focus attention on the row corresponding to the coefficient and on the "*t*-Statistic" and "Prob" columns.

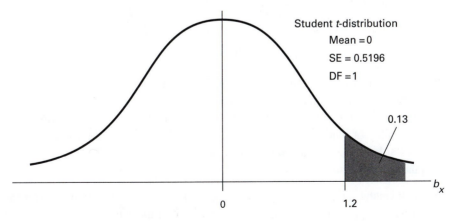

Figure 8.6
Probability distribution of coefficient estimate—Prob[Results IF cynic correct]

Table 8.3
Quiz scores regression results

Ordinary least squares (OLS)				
Dependent variable: y				
Explanatory variable(s):	Estimate	SE	t-Statistic	Prob
x	1.200000	0.519615	2.309401	0.2601
Const	63.00000	8.874120	7.099296	0.0891
Number of observations	3			
Sum squared residuals	54.00000			
SE of regression	7.348469			

Estimated equation: $Esty = 63 + 1.2x$

Interpretation of estimates:

$b_{Const} = 63$: Students receive 63 points for showing up

$b_x = 1.2$: Students receive 1.2 additional points for each additional minute studied

Critical result: The coefficient estimate equals 1.2. The positive sign of the coefficient estimate, suggests that additional studying increases quiz scores. This evidence lends support to our theory.

Two interesting observations emerge:

• First, the t-Statistic column equals 2.309, the value of the t-statistic we just calculated; the t-statistic based on the premise that the cynic is correct and the actual coefficient equals 0. The t-Statistic column reports the number of standard errors the coefficient estimate based on the premise that the actual coefficient equals 0.

• Second, the Prob column equals 0.2601. This is just twice the probability we just calculated using the Econometrics Lab:

$2 \times$ Prob[Results IF cynic correct] = Prob column

$$2 \times 0.13 = 0.26$$

The Prob column is based on the premise that the actual coefficient equals 0 and then focuses on the two tails of the probability distribution where each tail begins 1.2 (the numerical value of the coefficient estimate) from 0. As figure 8.7 illustrates, the value in the Prob column equals the probability of lying in the tails; the probability that the estimate resulting from one week's quiz lies at least 1.2 from 0 assuming that the actual coefficient, β_x, equals 0. That is, the Prob column reports the tails probability:

Tails probability: The probability that the coefficient estimate, b_x, resulting from one regression would lie at least 1.2 from 0 based on the premise that the actual coefficient, β_x, equals 0.

Consequently we do not need to use the Econometrics Lab to answer the question that we pose for the cynic:

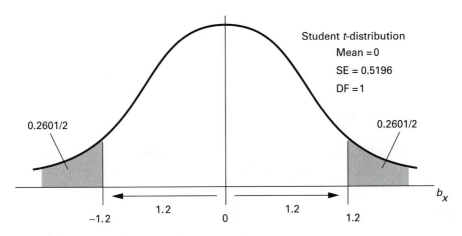

Figure 8.7
Probability distribution of coefficient estimate—Tails probability

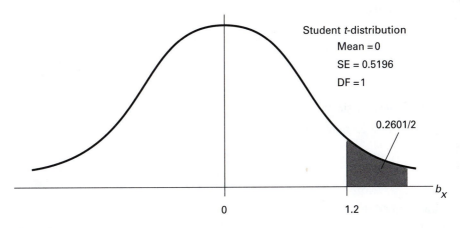

Figure 8.8
Probability distribution of coefficient estimate—Prob[Results IF cynic correct]

Question for the cynic: What is the probability that the coefficient estimate from the first quiz is 1.2 or more, if studying had no impact on quiz scores (if the actual coefficient, β_x, equals 0)?

Answer: Prob[Results IF cynic correct]

We can use the regression results to answer this question. From the Prob column we know that the tails probability equals 0.2601. As shown in Figure 8.8, we are only interested in the right tail, however, the probability that the coefficient estimate will equal 1.2 or more, if the actual coefficient equals 0.

Since the Student t-distribution is symmetric, the probability of lying in one of the tails is 0.2601/2. The answer to the question we posed to assess the cynic's view is 0.13:

$$\text{Prob[Results IF cynic correct]} = \frac{\text{Tails probability}}{2} = \frac{0.2601}{2} \approx 0.13$$

8.3.2   Formalizing Hypothesis Testing: The Steps

We formalized hypothesis testing in chapter 4 when we considered Clint's public opinion poll. We will follow the same steps here, with one exception. We add a step 0 to construct an appropriate model to assess the theory.

Theory: Additional studying increases quiz scores.

Step 0:   Formulate a model reflecting the theory to be tested.

We have already constructed this model:

$$y_t = \beta_{Const} + \beta_x x_t + e_t$$

where

y_t = quiz score

x_t = minutes studied

β_{Const} = points for showing up

β_x = points for each minute studied

The theory suggests that β_x is positive.

PS

Book title / need / lesh, Then

Need Book online

→ Name or legionten

Step 1:   Collect data, run the regression, and interpret the estimates (table 8.4).

First quiz data

Student	x	y
1	5	66
2	15	87
3	25	90

$\rightarrow$ b_{Const} = estimated points for showing up = 63

b_x = estimated points for each minute studied = 1.2

Step 2: Play the cynic and challenge the results; construct the null and alternative hypotheses.

Cynic's view: Despite the results, studying has no impact on quiz scores. The results were just "the luck of the draw."

Table 8.4
Quiz scores regression results

Ordinary least squares (OLS)				
Dependent variable: y				
Explanatory variable(s):	Estimate	SE	t-Statistic	Prob
x	1.200000	0.519615	2.309401	0.2601
Const	63.00000	8.874120	7.099296	0.0891
Number of observations	3			
Sum squared residuals	54.00000			
SE of regression	7.348469			

Estimated equation: $Esty = 63 + 1.2x$

Interpretation of estimates:

$b_{Const} = 63$: Students receive 63 points for showing up

$b_x = 1.2$: Students receive 1.2 additional points for each additional minute studied

Critical result: The coefficient estimate equals 1.2. The positive sign of the coefficient estimate, suggests that additional studying increases quiz scores. This evidence lends support to our theory.

Now we construct the null and alternative hypotheses. Like the cynic, the null hypothesis challenges the evidence; the alternative hypothesis is consistent with the evidence:

H_0: $\beta_x = 0$ Cynic is correct: studying has no impact on a student's quiz score.

H_1: $\beta_x > 0$ Cynic is incorrect: additional studying increases quiz scores.

Step 3:   Formulate the question to assess the cynic's view and the null hypothesis.

Questions for the cynic:

• **Generic question:**   What is the probability that the results would be like those we actually obtained (or even stronger), if the cynic is correct and studying actually has no impact?

• **Specific question:**   The regression's coefficient estimate was 1.2: What is the probability that the coefficient estimate in one regression would be 1.2 or more if H_0 were actually true (if the actual coefficient, β_x, equals 0)?

Answer: Prob[Results IF cynic correct] or Prob[Results IF H_0 true]

The magnitude of this probability determines whether we reject the null hypothesis:

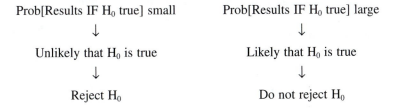

Step 4: Use the general properties of the estimation procedure, the probability distribution of the estimate, to calculate Prob[Results IF H_0 true].

OLS estimation If H_0 Number of   Number of
procedure unbiased   true   Standard error   observations   parameters

$$\text{Mean}[b_x] = \beta_x = 0 \qquad \text{SE}[b_x] = 0.5196 \qquad \text{DF} = 3 - 2 = 1$$

We have already calculated this probability. First, we did so using the Econometrics Lab. Then, we noted that the statistical software had done so automatically. We need only divide the tails probability, as reported in the Prob column of the regression results, by 2:

$$\text{Prob}[\text{Results IF } H_0 \text{ true}] = \frac{0.2601}{2} \approx 0.13$$

The probability that the coefficient estimate in one regression would be 1.2 or more if H_0 were actually true (if the actual coefficient, β_x, equals 0) is 0.13.

Step 5: Decide on the standard of proof, a significance level.

The significance level is the dividing line between the probability being small and the probability being large.

Prob[Results IF H_0 true]   Prob[Results IF H_0 true]
less than significance level   greater than significance level
↓   ↓
Prob[Results IF H_0 true] small   Prob[Results IF H_0 true] large
↓   ↓
Unlikely that H_0 is true   Likely that H_0 is true
↓   ↓
Reject H_0 Do not reject H_0

Recall that the traditional significant levels used in academia are 1, 5, and 10 percent. Obviously 0.13 is greater than 0.10. Consequently Clint would not reject the null hypothesis that studying has no impact on quiz scores even with a 10 percent significance level.

8.4   Summary: The Ordinary Least Squares (OLS) Estimation Procedure

8.4.1   Regression Model and the Role of the Error Term

Let us sum up what we have learned about the ordinary least squares (OLS) estimation procedure:

$$y_t = \beta_{Const} + \beta_x x_t + e_t$$

where

y_t = dependent variable

e_t = error term

x_t = explanatory variable

$t = 1, 2, \ldots, T$

T = sample size

The error term is a random variable; it represents random influences. The mean of the each error term's probability distribution equals 0:

$Mean[e_t] = 0$ for each $t = 1, 2, \ldots, T$

8.4.2   Standard Ordinary Least Squares (OLS) Premises

· **Error term equal variance premise:**   The variance of the error term's probability distribution for each observation is the same; all the variances equal Var[e]:

$$Var[e_1] = Var[e_2] = \ldots = Var[e_T] = Var[e]$$

· **Error term/error term independence premise:**   The error terms are independent: $Cov[e_i, e_j] = 0$. Knowing the value of the error term from one observation does not help us predict the value of the error term for any other observation.

· **Explanatory variable/error term independence premise:**   The explanatory variables, the x_t's, and the error terms, the e_t's, are not correlated. Knowing the value of an observation's explanatory variable does not help us predict the value of that observation's error term.

8.4.3   Ordinary Least Squares (OLS) Estimation Procedure: Three Important Estimation Procedure

There are three important estimation procedures embedded within the ordinary least squares (OLS) estimation procedures:

· A procedure to estimate the values of the regression parameters, β_x and β_{Const}:

$$b_x = \frac{\sum_{t=1}^{T}(y_t - \bar{y})(x_t - \bar{x})}{\sum_{t=1}^{T}(x_t - \bar{x})^2} \quad \text{and} \quad b_{Const} = \bar{y} - b_x \bar{x}$$

• A procedure to estimate the variance of the error term's probability distribution, Var[e]:

$$\text{EstVar}[e] = \frac{SSR}{\text{Degrees of freedom}}$$

• A procedure to estimate the variance of the coefficient estimate's probability distribution, Var[b_x]:

$$\text{EstVar}[b_x] = \frac{\text{EstVar}[e]}{\sum_{t=1}^{T}(x_t - \bar{x})^2}$$

8.4.4 Properties of the Ordinary Least Squares (OLS) Estimation Procedure and the Standard Ordinary Least Squares (OLS) Premises

When the standard ordinary least square (OLS) premises are met:

• Each estimation procedure is unbiased; each estimation procedure does not systematically underestimate or overestimate the actual value.

• The ordinary least squares (OLS) estimation procedure for the coefficient value is the best linear unbiased estimation procedure (BLUE).

Causation versus Correlation

Our theory and step 0 illustrate the important distinction between causation and correlation:

Theory: Additional studying increases quiz scores.

Step 0:   Formulate a model reflecting the theory to be tested.

$$y_t = \beta_{Const} + \beta_x x_t + e_t$$

where

y_t = quiz score

x_t = minutes studied

e_t = error term

β_{Const} = points for showing up

β_x = points for each minute studied

The theory suggests that β_x is positive.

Our model is a causal model. An increase in studying causes a student's quiz score to increase:

Increase in studying (x_t)

↓   Causes

Quiz score to increase (y_t)

Correlation results whenever a causal relationship describes the reality accurately. That is, when additional studying indeed increases quiz scores, studying and quiz scores will be (positively) correlated:

· Knowing the number of minutes a student studies allows us to predict his/her quiz score.

· Knowing a student's quiz score helps us predict the number of minutes he/she has studied.

More generally, a causal model that describes reality accurately implies correlation:

Causation   implies   Correlation

   Beware that correlation need not imply causation, however. For example, consider precipitation in the Twin Cities, precipitation in Minneapolis and precipitation in St Paul. Since the cities are near each other precipitation in the two cities are highly correlated. When it rains in Minneapolis, it also always rains in St Paul, and vice versa. But there is no causation involved here. Rain in Minneapolis does not cause rain in St. Paul, nor does rain in St. Paul cause rain in Minneapolis. The rain is caused by the weather system moving over the cities. In general, the correlation of two variables need not imply that a causal relationship exists between the variables:

Correlation   need not imply   Causation

Chapter 8 Review Questions

1. What is the "template" for the interval estimation question?

2. To compute interval estimates, when is it appropriate to use the

   a. normal distribution?

   b. Student t-distribution?

3. What are the formal hypothesis-testing steps?

4. We have focused on three estimation procedures embedded within the ordinary least squares (OLS) estimation procedures. What are they?

5. When the standard ordinary least squares (OLS) premises are met, what can we conclude about the estimation procedures embedded within the ordinary least squares (OLS) estimation procedures?

Chapter 8 Exercises

Consider petroleum consumption in Nebraska:

Petroleum consumption data for Nebraska: Annual time series data of petroleum consumption and prices for Nebraska from 1990 to 1999

PetroCons_t   Consumption of petroleum in year t (1,000's of gallons)

Cpi_t   Midwest Consumer Price Index in year t (1982–84 100)

Pop_t   Nebraska population in year t

PriceNom_t   Nominal price of petroleum in year t (dollars per gallon)

Year	Midwest CPI	Petroleum consumption (1,000s of gallons)	Nebraska population	Petroleum price (dollars per gallon)
1990	127.4	1,604,232	1,578,417	1.07
1991	132.4	1,562,862	1,595,919	1.04
1992	136.1	1,587,474	1,611,687	1.01
1993	140.0	1,578,612	1,625,590	1.01
1994	144.0	1,626,828	1,639,041	1.01
1995	148.4	1,657,950	1,656,992	1.02
1996	153.0	1,822,212	1,673,740	1.12
1997	156.7	1,804,572	1,686,418	1.08
1998	159.3	1,905,330	1,695,816	0.92
1999	162.7	1,929,060	1,704,764	0.98

1. Focus on the following simple regression model of demand:

Model: $PetroConsPC_t = \beta_{Const} + \beta_P PriceReal_t + e_t$

where

$t = 1970, 1971, \ldots, 2004$

$PetroConsPC_t$ = per capita consumption of petroleum (gallons) in year t

$PriceReal_t$ = real price of petroleum (dollars per gallon, adjusted by the CPI) in year t

    a. Generate the variables $PetroConsPC_t$ and *PriceReal*. In doing so, be certain that the units are correct; that is, express the variable $PetroConsPC_t$ in terms of gallons and $PriceReal_t$ in terms real dollars per gallon. Note that the variable $PetroCons_t$ is reported in units of 1,000s of gallons; account for this when you generate $PetroConsPC_t$. Note: Check to be certain that your new variables have been generated correctly.

[To access this online material, go to http://mitpress.mit.edu/westhoffeconometrics and select Petroleum Consumption - Neb.]

    b. Estimate the parameters of the model. Interpret b_P, the estimate for β_P.

Consider the reliability of the coefficient estimate.

c. Should we use the normal distribution or the Student t-distribution? Explain.

d. What is the probability that the coefficient estimate falls within:

   i. 400 of the actual coefficient value? _____

   ii. 300 of the actual coefficient value? _____

   iii. 200 of the actual coefficient value? _____

Use the Econometrics Lab to compute the probabilities:

[To access this online material, go to http://mitpress.mit.edu/westhoffeconometrics and select t-Distribution.]

2. Again, consider Nebraska's petroleum consumption data in the 1990's and the model cited in question 1.

   a. What does economic theory teach us about how the real price of petroleum should affect Nebraska petroleum consumption?

   b. Apply the hypothesis-testing approach that we developed to assess the theory.

[To access this online material, go to http://mitpress.mit.edu/westhoffeconometrics and select Petroleum Consumption - Neb.]

   c. What is your assessment of the theory? Explain.

3. Revisit the gasoline consumption data:

Gasoline consumption data: Annual time series data US gasoline consumption and prices from 1990 to 1999

$GasCons_t$ US gasoline consumption in year t (millions of gallons per day)

$PriceDollars_t$ Real price of gasoline in year t (dollars per gallon –2000 dollars)

   a. What does economic theory teach us about how the real price of gasoline should affect US gasoline consumption?

   b. Apply the hypothesis-testing approach that we developed to assess the theory.

[To access this online material, go to http://mitpress.mit.edu/westhoffeconometrics and select Gasoline Consumption.]

   c. What is your assessment of the theory? Explain.

4. Revisit the cigarette consumption data.

Cigarette consumption data: Cross section of per capita cigarette consumption and prices in fiscal year 2008 for the 50 states and the District of Columbia

CigConsPC$_t$	Cigarette consumption per capita in state t (packs)
EducCollege$_t$	Percent of population with bachelor degrees in state t
EducHighSchool$_t$	Percent of population with high school diplomas in state t
IncPC$_t$	Income per capita in state t (1,000's of dollars)
Pop$_t$	Population of state t (persons)
PriceConsumer$_t$	Price of cigarettes in state t paid by consumers (dollars per pack)
PriceSupplier$_t$	Price of cigarettes in state t received by suppliers (dollars per pack)
RegionMidWest$_t$	1 if state t in Midwest census region, 0 otherwise
RegionNorthEast$_t$	1 if state t in Northeast census region, 0 otherwise
RegionSouth$_t$	1 if state t in South census region, 0 otherwise
RegionWest$_t$	1 if state t in West census region, 0 otherwise
SmokeRateAdult$_t$	Percent of adults who smoke in state t
SmokeRateYouth$_t$	Percent of youths who smoke in state t
State$_t$	Name of state t
Tax$_t$	Cigarette tax rate in state t (dollars per pack)
TobProdPC$_t$	Per capita tobacco production in state t (pounds)

Conventional wisdom suggests that high school dropouts are more likely to smoke cigarettes than those who graduate.

a. Apply the hypothesis-testing approach that we developed to assess the conventional wisdom.

[To access this online material, go to http://mitpress.mit.edu/westhoffeconometrics and select Cigarette Consumption.]

b. What is your assessment of the conventional wisdom? Explain.

5. Revisit the congressional earmarks data.

House earmark data: Cross-sectional data of proposed earmarks in the 2009 fiscal year for the 451 House members of the 110th Congress.

CongressName$_t$	Name of Congressperson t
CongressParty$_t$	Party of Congressperson t
CongressState$_t$	State of Congressperson t
IncPC$_t$	Income per capita in the Congressperson t's state (dollars)
Number$_t$	Number of earmarks received that were sponsored solely by Congressperson t
PartyDem1$_t$	1 if Congressperson t Democrat; 0 otherwise
PartyRep1$_t$	1 if Congressperson t Republican; 0 otherwise
RegionMidwest$_t$	1 if Congressperson t represents a midwestern state, 0 otherwise
RegionNortheast$_t$	1 if Congressperson t represents a northeastern state; 0 otherwise
RegionSouth$_t$	1 if Congressperson t represents a southern state; 0 otherwise
RegionWest$_t$	1 if Congressperson t represents a western state; 0 otherwise
ScoreLiberal$_t$	Congressperson's t liberal score rating in 2007
Terms$_t$	Number of terms served by Congressperson in the US Congress
UnemRate$_t$	Unemployment rate in Congressperson t's state

It has been alleged that since the Congress was controlled by Democrats, Democratic members received more solo earmarks than their non-Democratic colleagues.

   a. Apply the hypothesis-testing approach that we developed to assess the allegation.

[To access this online material, go to http://mitpress.mit.edu/westhoffeconometrics and select House Earmarks.]

   b. What is your assessment of the allegations? Explain.

6. Consider wage and age data.

Wage and age data: Cross-sectional data of wages and ages for 190 union members included in the March 2007 Current Population Survey who have earned high school degrees, but have not had any additional education.

Age$_t$ Age of worker t (years)

Wage$_t$ Wage rate of worker t (dollars)

Many believe that unions strongly support the seniority system. Some union contracts require employers to pay workers who have been on the job for many years more than newly hired workers. Consequently older workers should typically be paid more than younger workers:

Seniority theory: Additional years of age increases wage rate.

Use data from the March 2007 Current Population Survey to investigate the seniority theory.

   a. Apply the hypothesis-testing approach that we developed to assess the seniority theory.

[To access this online material, go to http://mitpress.mit.edu/westhoffeconometrics and select Wage and Age.]

   b. What is your assessment of the theory? Explain.

7. Revisit the effect that the price of crude oil has on crude oil production:

Crude oil production data: Annual time series data of US crude oil production and prices from 1976 to 2004.

OilProdBarrels_t   US crude oil productions in year t (thousands of barrels per day)

Price_t   Real wellhead price of crude oil in year t (1982–84 dollars per barrel)

   a. What does economic theory teach us about how the real price of crude oil should affect US crude oil production?

   b. Apply the hypothesis-testing approach that we developed to assess the theory.

[To access this online material, go to http://mitpress.mit.edu/westhoffeconometrics and select Crude Oil Production.]

   c. What is your assessment of the theory? Explain.

Appendix 8.1 Student *t*-Distribution Table—Right-Tail Critical Values

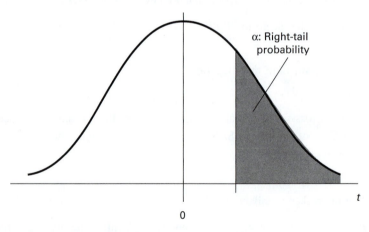

Figure 8.9
Student *t*-distribution—Right-tail probabilities

Table 8.5
Right-tail critical values for the Student *t*-distribution

Degrees of freedom	$\alpha = 0.10$	$\alpha = 0.05$	$\alpha = 0.025$	$\alpha = 0.01$	$\alpha = 0.005$
1	3.078	6.314	12.706	31.821	63.657
2	1.886	2.920	4.303	6.965	9.925
3	1.638	2.353	3.182	4.541	5.841
4	1.533	2.132	2.776	3.747	4.604
5	1.476	2.015	2.571	3.365	4.032
6	1.440	1.943	2.447	3.143	3.707
7	1.415	1.895	2.365	2.998	3.499
8	1.397	1.860	2.306	2.896	3.355
9	1.383	1.833	2.262	2.821	3.250
10	1.372	1.812	2.228	2.764	3.169
11	1.363	1.796	2.201	2.718	3.106
12	1.356	1.782	2.179	2.681	3.055
13	1.350	1.771	2.160	2.650	3.012
14	1.345	1.761	2.145	2.624	2.977
15	1.341	1.753	2.131	2.602	2.947
16	1.337	1.746	2.120	2.583	2.921
17	1.333	1.740	2.110	2.567	2.898
18	1.330	1.734	2.101	2.552	2.878
19	1.328	1.729	2.093	2.539	2.861
20	1.325	1.725	2.086	2.528	2.845
21	1.323	1.721	2.080	2.518	2.831
22	1.321	1.717	2.074	2.508	2.819
23	1.319	1.714	2.069	2.500	2.807
24	1.318	1.711	2.064	2.492	2.797
25	1.316	1.708	2.060	2.485	2.787
26	1.315	1.706	2.056	2.479	2.779
27	1.314	1.703	2.052	2.473	2.771
28	1.313	1.701	2.048	2.467	2.763
29	1.311	1.699	2.045	2.462	2.756
30	1.310	1.697	2.042	2.457	2.750
31	1.309	1.696	2.040	2.453	2.744
32	1.309	1.694	2.037	2.449	2.738
33	1.308	1.692	2.035	2.445	2.733
34	1.307	1.691	2.032	2.441	2.728
35	1.306	1.690	2.030	2.438	2.724
36	1.306	1.688	2.028	2.434	2.719
37	1.305	1.687	2.026	2.431	2.715
38	1.304	1.686	2.024	2.429	2.712
39	1.304	1.685	2.023	2.426	2.708

Table 8.5
(continued)

Degrees of freedom	$\alpha = 0.10$	$\alpha = 0.05$	$\alpha = 0.025$	$\alpha = 0.01$	$\alpha = 0.005$
40	1.303	1.684	2.021	2.423	2.704
50	1.299	1.676	2.009	2.403	2.678
60	1.296	1.671	2.000	2.390	2.660
70	1.294	1.667	1.994	2.381	2.648
80	1.292	1.664	1.990	2.374	2.639
90	1.291	1.662	1.987	2.368	2.632
100	1.290	1.660	1.984	2.364	2.626
110	1.289	1.659	1.982	2.361	2.621
120	1.289	1.658	1.980	2.358	2.617

Table 8.6
Right-tail critical values for the Student t-distribution

Degrees of freedom	$\alpha = 0.10$	$\alpha = 0.05$	$\alpha = 0.025$	$\alpha = 0.01$	$\alpha = 0.005$
1	**3.078**	6.314	12.706	31.821	63.657
2	1.886	2.920	4.303	6.965	9.925
3	1.638	2.353	3.182	4.541	5.841

Appendix 8.2 Assessing the Reliability of a Coefficient Estimate Using the Student t-Distribution Table

We begin by describing the Student t-distribution table; a portion of it appears in table 8.6.

The first column represents the degrees of freedom. The numbers in the body of the table are called the "critical values." A critical value equals the number of standard errors a value lies from the mean. The top row specifies α's value of, the "right-tail probability." Figure 8.10 helps us understand the table.

Since the t-distribution is symmetric, the "left tail probability" also equals α. The probability of lying within the tails, in the center of the distribution, is $1 - 2\alpha$. This no doubt sounds confusing, but everything should become clear after we show how Clint can use this table to answer the interval estimate question.

Interval estimate question: What is the probability that the estimate, 1.2, lies within _____ of the actual value? _____

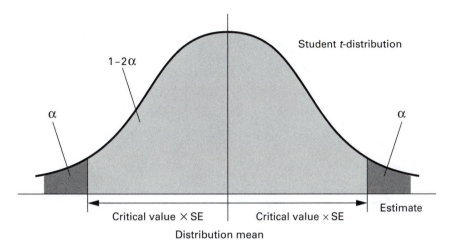

Figure 8.10
Student *t*-distribution—Illustrating the probabilities

Let us review the regression results from Professor Lord's first quiz:

Coefficient estimate = b_x = 1.2

Standard error of coefficient estimate = SE[b_x] = 0.5196

Next we will modify figure 8.10 to reflect our specific example. Focus on figure 8.11:

• We are interested in the coefficient estimate; consequently we replace the horizontal axis label by substituting b_x for *estimate*.

• Also we know that the estimation procedure Clint uses, the ordinary least squares (OLS) estimation procedure, is unbiased; hence the distribution mean equals the actual value. We can replace the *distribution mean* with the actual coefficient value, β_x.

Now let us help Clint fill in the blanks. When using the table we begin by filling in the second blank rather than the first.

Second blank: Choose α to specify the tail probability.

Clint must choose a value for α. As we will see, the value he chooses depends on how demanding he is. For example, suppose that Clint believes that a 0.80 probability of the estimate lying in the center of the distribution, close to the mean, is good enough. He would then choose an α equal to 0.10. To understand why, note that when α equals 0.10, the probability of the estimate lying in the right tail would be 0.10. Since the *t*-distribution is symmetric, the probability of the estimate lying in the left tail would be 0.10 also. Therefore the probability that the estimate lies in the center of the distribution would be 0.80; accordingly we write 0.80 in the second blank.

What is the probability that the estimate, 1.2, lies within _____ of the actual value? 0.80

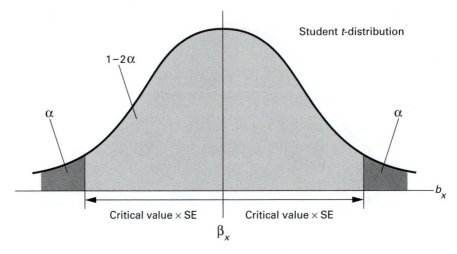

Figure 8.11
Student *t*-distribution—Illustrating the probabilities for coefficient estimate

Table 8.7
Right-tail critical values for the Student *t*-distribution—α equals 0.10 and degrees of freedom equals 1

Degrees of freedom	α = 0.10	α = 0.05	α = 0.025	α = 0.01	α = 0.005
1	**3.078**	6.314	12.706	31.821	63.657
2	1.886	2.920	4.303	6.965	9.925
3	1.638	2.353	3.182	4.541	5.841

First blank: Calculate tail boundaries.

The first blank quantifies what "close to" means. The standard error and the Student *t*-distribution table allow us to fill in the first blank. To do so, we begin by calculating the degrees of freedom. Recall that the degrees of freedom equal 1:

Degrees of freedom = Sample size − Number of estimated parameters

$$= 3 - 2$$

$$= 1$$

Clint chose a value of α equal to 0.10 (figure 8.12). Table 8.7 indicates that the critical value for α = 0.10 with one degree of freedom is 3.078. The probability that the estimate falls within 3.078 standard errors of the mean is 0.80. Next the regression results report that the standard error equals 0.5196:

$$SE[b_x] = 0.5196$$

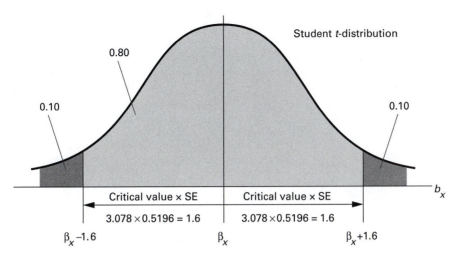

Figure 8.12
Student t-distribution—Calculations for an α equal to 0.10

After multiplying the critical value given in the table, 3.078, by the standard error, 0.5196, we can fill in the first blank:

$3.078 \times 0.5196 = 1.6$

What is the probability that the estimate, **1.2**, lies within **1.6** of the actual value? **0.80**

9   One-Tailed Tests, Two-Tailed Tests, and Logarithms

Chapter 9 Outline

Chapter 9 Prep Questions

1. Suppose that the following equation describes how Q and P are related: $Q = \beta_{Const}P^{\beta_P}$.

   a. What does dQ/dP equal?

   b. Focus on the ratio of P to Q; that is, focus on P/Q. Substitute $\beta_{Const}P^{\beta_P}$ for Q and show that P/Q equals $1/\beta_{Const}P^{\beta_P-1}$.

   c. Show that $(dQ/dP)(P/Q)$ equals β_P.

2. We would like to express the percent changes algebraically. To do so, we begin with an example. Suppose that X increases from 200 to 220.

   a. In percentage terms by how much has X increased?

   b. Argue that you have implicitly used the following equation to calculate the percent change:

$$\text{Percent change in } X = \frac{\Delta X}{X} \times 100$$

3. Suppose that a household spends \$1,000 of its income on a particular good every month.

   a. What does the product of the good's price, P, and the quantity of the good purchased by the household each month, Q, equal?

   b. Solve for Q.

   c. Consider the function $Q = \beta_{Const}P^{\beta_P}$. What would

      i. β_{Const} equal?

      ii. β_P equal?

4. Let y be a function of x: $y = f(x)$. What is the differential approximation? That is, $\Delta y \approx$ _____

5. What is the expression for a derivative of a natural logarithm? That is, what does $d\log(z)/dz$ equal?[1]

9.1 A One-Tailed Hypothesis Test: The Downward Sloping Demand Curve

Microeconomic theory tells us that the demand curve is typically downward sloping. In introductory economics and again in intermediate microeconomics we present sound logical arguments justifying the shape of the demand curve. History has taught us many times, however, that just because a theory sounds sensible does not necessary mean that it is true. We must test this theory to determine if it is supported by real world evidence. We will focus on gasoline consumption in the United States during the 1990s to test the downward sloping demand theory.

---

1. Be aware that sometimes natural logarithms are denoted as $\ln(z)$ rather than $\log(z)$. We will use the $\log(z)$ notation for natural logarithms throughout this textbook.

Gasoline consumption data: Annual time series data US gasoline consumption and prices from 1990 to 1999.

GasCons$_t$ US gasoline consumption in year t (millions of gallons per day)

PriceDollars$_t$ Real price of gasoline in year t (dollars per gallon—2000 dollars)

Year	Real price ($ per gallon)	Gasoline consumption (millions of gals)	Year	Real price ($ per gallon)	Gasoline consumption (millions of gals)
1990	1.43	303.9	**1995**	1.25	327.1
1991	1.35	301.9	**1996**	1.31	331.4
1992	1.31	305.3	**1997**	1.29	336.7
1993	1.25	314.0	**1998**	1.10	346.7
1994	1.23	319.2	**1999**	1.19	354.1

Theory: A higher price decreases the quantity demanded; the demand curve is downward sloping.

Project: Assess the effect of gasoline prices on gasoline consumption.

Step 0:   Formulate a model reflecting the theory to be tested.

   Our model will be a simple linear equation:

$$GasCons_t = \beta_{Const} + \beta_P PriceDollars_t + e_t$$

where

GasCons$_t$ = quantity of gasoline demanded in year t (millions of gallons)

PriceDollars$_t$ = price in year t (1990 dollars)

   The theory suggests that β_P should be negative. A higher price decreases the quantity demanded; the demand curve is upward sloping.

Step 1:   Collect data, run the regression, and interpret the estimates.

   The gasoline consumption data can be accessed by clicking within the box below.

[To access this online material, go to http://mitpress.mit.edu/westhoffeconometrics and select Gasoline Consumption.]

   While the regression results (table 9.1) indeed support the theory, remember that we can never expect an estimate to equal the actual value; sometimes the estimate will be greater than the actual value and sometimes less. The fact that the estimate of the price coefficient is negative, −151.7, is comforting, but it does not prove that the actual price coefficient, β_P, is negative. In fact we do not have and can never have indisputable evidence that the theory is correct. How do we proceed?

Table 9.1
Gasoline demand regression results

Ordinary least squares (OLS)				
Dependent variable: *GasCons*				
Explanatory variable(s):	Estimate	SE	*t*-Statistic	Prob
PriceDollars	−151.6556	47.57295	−3.187853	0.0128
Const	516.7801	60.60223	8.527410	0.0000
Number of observations	10			

Estimated equation: *EstGasCons* = 516.8 − 151.7*PriceDollars*

Interpretation of estimates:

$b_P = -151.7$: A \$1 increase in the real price of gasoline decreases the quantity of gasoline demanded by 151.7 million gallons.

Critical result: The coefficient estimate equals −151.7. The negative sign of the coefficient estimate suggests that a higher price reduces the quantity demanded. This evidence supports the downward sloping demand theory.

Step 2:   Play the cynic and challenge the results; construct the null and alternative hypotheses.

Cynic's view: The price actually has no effect on the quantity of gasoline demanded; the negative coefficient estimate obtained from the data was just "the luck of the draw." The actual coefficient, β_P, equals 0.

Now, we construct the null and alternative hypotheses:

$H_0: \beta_P = 0$ Cynic's view is correct: Price has no effect on quantity demanded

$H_1: \beta_P < 0$ Cynic's view is incorrect: A higher price decreases quantity demanded

The null hypothesis, like the cynic, challenges the evidence. The alternative hypothesis is consistent with the evidence.

Step 3:   Formulate the question to assess the cynic's view and the null hypothesis.

Question for the cynic:

• **Generic question:**   What is the probability that the results would be like those we actually obtained (or even stronger), if the cynic is correct and the price actually has no impact?

• **Specific question:**   The regression's coefficient estimate was −151.7: What is the probability that the coefficient estimate in one regression would be −151.7 or less, if H_0 were actually true (if the actual coefficient, β_P, equals 0)?

Answer: Prob[Results IF cynic correct] or Prob[Results IF H_0 true]

The magnitude of this probability determines whether we reject the null hypothesis:

Prob[Results IF H_0 true] small   Prob[Results IF H_0 true] large

↓   ↓

Unlikely that H_0 is true   Likely that H_0 is true

↓   ↓

Reject H_0 Do not reject H_0

Step 4:   Use the general properties of the estimation procedure, the probability distribution of the estimate, to calculate Prob[Results IF H_0 true].

If the null hypothesis were true, the actual price coefficient would equal 0. Since ordinary least squares (OLS) estimation procedure for the coefficient value is unbiased, the mean of the probability distribution for the coefficient estimates would be 0. The regression results provide us with the standard error of the coefficient estimate. The degrees of freedom equal 8: the number of observations, 10, less the number of parameters we are estimating, 2 (the constant and the coefficient).

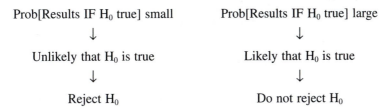

OLS estimation   Number of   Number of
procedure unbiased   If H_0 true   Standard error   observations   parameters

Mean[b_P] = β_P = 0   SE[b_P] = 47.6   DF = 10 − 2 = 8

We now have the information needed to calculate Prob[Results IF H_0 true], the probability of result like the one obtained (or even stronger) if the null hypothesis, H_0, were true. We could use the Econometrics Lab to compute this probability, but in fact the statistical software has already done this for us (table 9.2).

Recall that the Prob column reports the tails probability:

Tails probability: The probability that the coefficient estimate, b_P, resulting from one regression would lie at least 151.7 from 0, if the actual coefficient, β_P, equals 0.

The tails probability reports the probability of lying in the two tails (figure 9.1). We are only interested in the probability that the coefficient estimate will be −151.7 or less; that is, we are only interested in the left tail. Since the Student t-distribution is symmetric, we divide the tails probability by 2 to calculated Prob[Results IF H_0 true]:

$$\text{Prob[Results IF } H_0 \text{ true]} = \frac{0.0128}{2} = 0.0064$$

Table 9.2
Gasoline demand regression results

Ordinary least squares (OLS)				
Dependent variable: *GasCons*				
Explanatory variable(s):	Estimate	SE	*t*-Statistic	Prob
PriceDollars	−151.6556	47.57295	−3.187853	0.0128
Const	516.7801	60.60223	8.527410	0.0000
Number of observations	10			

Estimated equation: *EstGasCons* = 516.8 − 151.7*PriceDollars*

Interpretation of estimates:

$b_P = -151.7$: A $1 increase in the real price of gasoline decreases the quantity of gasoline demanded by 151.7 million gallons.

Critical result: The coefficient estimate equals −151.7. The negative sign of the coefficient estimate suggests that a higher price reduces the quantity demanded. This evidence supports the downward sloping demand theory.

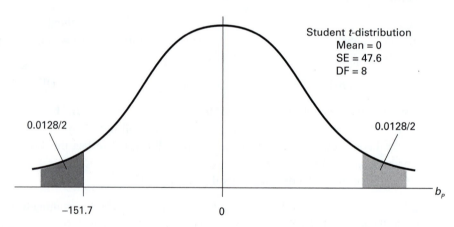

Figure 9.1
Probability distribution of linear model's coefficient estimate

Step 5: Decide on the standard of proof, a significance level.

The significance level is the dividing line between the probability being small and the probability being large.

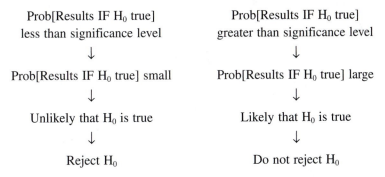

Prob[Results IF H_0 true]
less than significance level

$\downarrow$

Prob[Results IF H_0 true] small

$\downarrow$

Unlikely that H_0 is true

$\downarrow$

Reject H_0

Prob[Results IF H_0 true]
greater than significance level

$\downarrow$

Prob[Results IF H_0 true] large

$\downarrow$

Likely that H_0 is true

$\downarrow$

Do not reject H_0

The traditional significance levels in academe are 1, 5, and 10 percent. In this case, the Prob[Results IF H_0 true] equals 0.0064, less than 0.01. So, even with a 1 percent significance level, we would reject the null hypothesis that price has no impact on the quantity. This result supports the theory that the demand curve is downward sloping.

9.2 One-Tailed versus Two-Tailed Tests

Thus far we have considered only one-tailed tests because the theories we have investigated suggest that the coefficient was greater than a specific value or less than a specific value:

• **Quiz score theory:** The theory suggested that studying increases quiz scores, that the coefficient of minutes studied was greater than 0.

• **Demand curve theory:** The theory suggested that a higher price decreases the quantity supplied, that the coefficient of price was less than 0.

In these cases, we were only concerned with one side or one tail of the distribution, either the right tail or the left tail. Some theories, however, suggest that the coefficient equals a specific value. In these cases, both sides (both tails) of the distribution are relevant and two-tailed tests are appropriate. We will now investigate one such theory, the budget theory of demand.

9.3 A Two-Tailed Hypothesis Test: The Budget Theory of Demand

The budget theory of demand postulates that households first decide on the total number of dollars to spend on a good. Then, as the price of the good fluctuates, households adjust the quantity they purchase to stay within their budgets. We will focus on gasoline consumption to assess this theory:

Budget theory of demand: Expenditures for gasoline are constant. That is, when gasoline prices change, households adjust the quantity demanded so as to keep their gasoline expenditures constant. Expressing this mathematically, the budget theory of demand postulates that the price, P, times the quantity, Q, of the good demanded equals a constant:

$P \times Q = BudAmt$

where

$BudAmt$ = budget amount

Project: Assess the budget theory of demand.

As we will learn, the price elasticity of demand is critical in assessing the budget theory of demand. Consequently we will now review the verbal definition of the price elasticity of demand and show how we can make it mathematically rigorous.

Verbal definition: The price elasticity demand equals the percent change in the quantity demanded resulting from a 1 percent change in price.

To convert the verbal definition into a mathematical one, we start with the verbal definition:

Price elasticity of demand = Percent change in quantity demanded resulting from a 1 percent change in price

Convert this verbal definition into a ratio:

$$= \frac{\text{Percent change in the quantity}}{\text{Percent change in the price}}$$

Next let us express the percent changes algebraically. To do so, consider an example. Suppose that the variable X increases from 200 to 220; this constitutes a 10 percent increase. How did we calculate that?

X: 200 → 220

Percent change in $X = (220 - 200)/200 \times 100 = (20/200) \times 100 = 0.1 \times 100 = 10$ percent. We can generalize this:

$$\text{Percent change in } X = \frac{\Delta X}{X} \times 100$$

Substituting for the percent changes

$$= \frac{(\Delta Q/Q) \times 100}{(\Delta P/P) \times 100}$$

Simplifying

$$= \frac{\Delta Q}{\Delta P} \frac{P}{Q}$$

Taking limits as ΔP approaches 0,

$$= \frac{dQ}{dP} \frac{P}{Q}$$

There always exists a potential confusion surrounding the numerical value for the price elasticity of demand. Since the demand curve is downward sloping, dQ/dP is negative. Consequently the price elasticity of demand will be negative. Some textbooks, in an effort to avoid negative numbers, refer to price elasticity of demand as an absolute value. This can lead to confusion, however. Accordingly we will adopt the more straightforward approach: our elasticity of demand will be defined so that it is negative.

Now we are prepared to embark on the hypothesis-testing process.

Step 0:   Formulate a model reflecting the theory to be tested.

The appropriate model is the constant price elasticity model:

$$Q = \beta_{Const} P^{\beta_P}$$

Before doing anything else, however, let us now explain why this model indeed exhibits constant price elasticity. We start with the mathematical definition of the price elasticity of demand:

$$\text{Price elasticity of demand} = \frac{dQ}{dP} \frac{P}{Q}$$

Now compute the price elasticity of demand when $Q = \beta_{Const} P^{\beta_P}$:

$$\text{Price elasticity of demand} = \frac{dQ}{dP} \frac{P}{Q}$$

Recall the rules of differentiation:

$$\frac{dQ}{dP} = \beta_{Const} \beta_P P^{\beta_P - 1}$$

Substituting for dQ/dP

$$= \beta_{Const} \beta_P P^{\beta_P - 1} \frac{P}{Q}$$

Substituting $\beta_{Const}P^{\beta_P}$ for Q

$$= \beta_{Const}\beta_P P^{\beta_P - 1} \frac{P}{\beta_{Const} P^{\beta_P}}$$

Simplifying

$$= \beta_P$$

The price elasticity of demand just equals the value of β_P, the exponent of the price, P.

A little algebra allows us to show that the budget theory of demand postulates that the price elasticity of demand, β_P, equals -1. First start with the budget theory of demand:

$$P \times Q = BudAmt$$

Multiply through by P^{-1}

$$Q = BudAmt \times P^{-1}$$

Compare this to the constant price elasticity demand model:

$$Q = \beta_{Const}P^{\beta_P}$$

Clearly,

$$\beta_{Const} = BudAmt \quad \text{and} \quad \beta_P = -1$$

This allows us to reframe the budget theory of demand in terms of the price elasticity of demand, β_P:

Budget theory of demand: $\beta_P = -1.0$

Natural logarithms allow us to convert the constant price elasticity model into its linear form:

$$Q = \beta_{Const} P^{\beta_P}$$

Taking natural logarithms of both sides:

$\log(Q) = \log(\beta_{Const}) + \beta_P \log(P)$
$Log\ Q = \qquad c \quad + \beta_P\ Log\ P$

where

$Log\ Q = \log(Q)$
$\qquad c = \log(\beta_{Const})$
$Log\ P = \log(P)$

Step 1:   Collect data, run the regression, and interpret the estimates.

Recall that we are using US gasoline consumption data to assess the theory.

Gasoline consumption data: Annual time series data for US gasoline consumption and prices from 1990 to 1999.

GasCons_t   US gasoline consumption in year *t* (millions of gallons per day)

PriceDollars_t   Real price of gasoline in year *t* (dollars per gallon—chained 2000 dollars)

We must generate the two variables: the logarithm of quantity and the logarithm of price:

- $LogQ_t = \log(GasCons_t)$
- $LogP_t = \log(PriceDollars_t)$

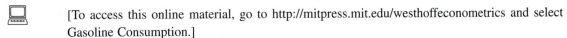 [To access this online material, go to http://mitpress.mit.edu/westhoffeconometrics and select Gasoline Consumption.]

Getting Started in EViews

To generate the new variables, open the workfile.

- In the Workfile window: click **Genr**.
- In the Generate Series by Equation window: enter the formula for the new series:

logq = log(gascons)

- Click **OK**.

Repeat the process to generate the logarithm of price.

- In the Workfile window: click **Genr**.
- In the Generate Series by Equation window: enter the formula for the new series:

logp = log(pricedollars)

- Click **OK**.

Now we can use EViews to run a regression with logq, the logarithm of quantity, as the dependent variable and logp, the logarithm of price, as the explanatory variable.

- In the Workfile window: Click on the dependent variable, **logq**, first, and then click on the explanatory variable, **logp**, while depressing the **<Ctrl> key**.
- In the Workfile window: Double click on a highlighted variable.
- In the Workfile window: Click **Open Equation**.
- In the Equation Specification window: Click **OK**.
- Do not forget to close the workfile.

Note that estimate for the price elasticity of demand equals −0.586 (table 9.3). Since the budget theory of demand postulates that the price elasticity of demand equals −1.0, the critical result is not whether the estimate is above or below −1.0. Instead, the critical result is that the estimate does not equal −1.0; more specifically, the estimate is 0.414 from −1.0. Had the estimate been −1.414 rather than −0.586, the results would have been just as troubling as far as the budget theory of demand is concerned (see figure 9.2).

Step 2: Play the cynic and challenge the results; construct the null and alternative hypotheses.

The cynic always challenges the evidence. The regression results suggest that the price elasticity of demand does not equal −1.0 since the coefficient estimate equals −0.586. Accordingly, the cynic challenges the evidence by asserting that it does equal −1.0.

Table 9.3
Budget theory of demand regression results

Ordinary least squares (OLS)				
Dependent variable: $LogQ$				
Explanatory variable(s):	Estimate	SE	t-Statistic	Prob
$LogP$	−0.585623	0.183409	−3.192988	0.0127
$Const$	5.918487	0.045315	130.6065	0.0000
Number of observations	10			

Estimated equation: $EstLogQ = 5.92 - 0.586 LogP$

Interpretation of estimates:

$b_P = -0.586$: A 1 percent increase in the price decreases the quantity demand by 0.586 percent. That is, the estimate for the price elasticity of demand equals −0.586.

Critical result: The coefficient estimate equals −0.586. The coefficient estimate does not equal −1.0; the estimate is 0.414 from −1. This evidence suggests that the budget theory of demand is incorrect.

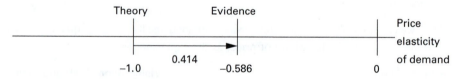

Figure 9.2
Number line illustration of critical result

Cynic's view: Sure the coefficient estimate from regression suggests that the price elasticity of demand does not equal −1.0, but this is just "the luck of the draw." The actual price elasticity of demand equals −1.0.

Question: Can we dismiss the cynic's view as absurd?

Answer: No, as a consequence of random influences. Even if the actual price elasticity equals −1.0, we could never expect the estimate to equal precisely −1.0. The effect of random influences is captured formally by the "statistical significance question:"

Statistical significance question: Is the estimate of −0.586 statistically different from −1.0? More precisely, if the actual value equals −1.0, how likely would it be for random influences to cause the estimate to be 0.414 or more from −1.0?

We will now construct the null and alternative hypotheses to address this question:

H_0: $\beta_P = -1.0$ Cynic's view is correct; actual price elasticity of demand equals −1.0.

H_1: $\beta_P \neq -1.0$ Cynic's view is incorrect; actual price elasticity of demand does not equal −1.0.

Step 3:   Formulate the question to assess the cynic's view and the null hypothesis.

Question for the cynic:

· **Generic question:**   What is the probability that the results would be like those we actually obtained (or even stronger), if the cynic is correct and the actual price elasticity of demand equals −1.0?

· **Specific question:**   The regression's coefficient estimate was −0.586: What is the probability that the coefficient estimate, b_P, in one regression would be at least 0.414 from −1.0, if H_0 were actually true (if the actual coefficient, β_P, equals −1.0)?

Answer: Prob[Results IF cynic correct] or Prob[Results IF H_0 true]

The magnitude of this probability determines whether we reject the null hypothesis:

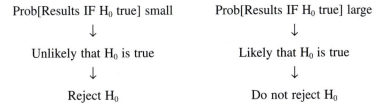

Step 4:   Use the general properties of the estimation procedure, the probability distribution of the estimate, to calculate Prob[Results IF H_0 true].

If the null hypothesis were true, the actual coefficient would equal −1.0. Since ordinary least squares (OLS) estimation procedure for the coefficient value is unbiased, the mean of the probability distribution of coefficient estimates would be −1.0. The regression results provide us with the standard error of the coefficient estimate. The degrees of freedom equal 8: the number of observations, 10, less the number of parameters we are estimating, 2 (the constant and the coefficient).

OLS estimation procedure unbiased	If H_0 true	Standard error	Number of observations	Number of parameters
$\searrow$	$\swarrow$	$\downarrow$	$\searrow$	$\swarrow$

$$\text{Mean}[b_P] = \beta_P = -1.0 \qquad \text{SE}[b_P] = 0.183 \qquad \text{DF} = 10 - 2 = 8$$

Can we use the "tails probability" as reported in the regression results to compute Prob[Results IF H_0 true]? Unfortunately, we cannot. The tails probability appearing in the Prob column of the regression results is based on the premise that the actual value of the coefficient equals 0. Our null hypothesis claims that the actual coefficient equals −1.0, not 0. Accordingly the regression results appearing in table 9.3 do not report the probability we need.

We can, however, use the Econometrics Lab to compute the probability.

Econometrics Lab 9.1: Using the Econometrics Lab to Calculate Prob[Results IF H_0 True]

We will calculate this probability in two steps:
• First, calculate the right-tail probability. Calculate the probability that the estimate lies 0.414 or more above −1.0; that is, the probability that the estimate lies at or above −0.586.

[To access this online material, go to http://mitpress.mit.edu/westhoffeconometrics and select Lab 9.1a.]

The following information has been entered:

Mean: −1.0   Value: −0.586

Standard error: 0.183   Degrees of freedom: 8

Click **Calculate**. The right-tail probability equals 0.027.

• Second, calculate the left-tail probability. Calculate the probability that the estimate lies 0.414 or more below −1.0; that is, the probability that the estimate lies at or below −1.414.

[To access this online material, go to http://mitpress.mit.edu/westhoffeconometrics and select Lab 9.1b.]

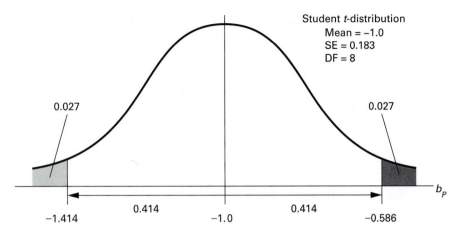

Figure 9.3
Probability distribution of constant elasticity model's coefficient estimate

The following information has been entered:

Mean: −1.0   Value: −1.414

Standard error: 0.183   Degrees of freedom: 8

Click **Calculate**. The left-tail probability equals 0.027.
As shown in figure 9.3 the probability that the estimate lies at least 0.414 from −1.0 equals
0.054, the sum of the right- and left-tail probabilities:

$$
\begin{array}{ccc}
\text{Left tail} & & \text{Right tail} \\
\downarrow & & \downarrow
\end{array}
$$

$$\text{Prob[Results IF } H_0 \text{ true]} \approx 0.027 + 0.027 = 0.054.$$

Recall why we could not use the tails probability appearing in the regression results to calculate the probability? The regression's tail's probability is based on the premise that the value
of the actual coefficient equals 0. Our null hypothesis, however, is based on the premise that the
value of the actual coefficient equals −1.0. So the regression results do not report the probability
we need.

9.4 Hypothesis Testing Using Clever Algebraic Manipulations

It is very convenient to use the regression results to calculate the probabilities, however. In fact
we can do so by being clever. Since the results report the tails probability based on the premise

that the actual coefficient equals 0, we can cleverly define a new coefficient that equals 0 whenever the price elasticity of demand equals -1.0. The following definition accomplishes this:

$\beta_{Clever} = \beta_P + 1.0$

The critical property of β_{Clever}'s definition is that the price elasticity of demand, β_P, equals -1.0 if and only if β_{Clever} equals 0:

$\beta_P = -1.0 \Leftrightarrow \beta_{Clever} = 0$

Next recall the log form of the constant price elasticity model:

$LogQ_t = c + \beta_P LogP_t$

where

$LogQ_t = \log(GasCons_t)$
$LogP_t = \log(Price_t)$

Let us now perform a little algebra. Since $\beta_{Clever} = \beta_P + 1.0$, $\beta_P = \beta_{Clever} - 1.0$. Let us substitute for β_P:

$LogQ_t = c + \beta_P LogP_t$

Substituting for β_P obtains

$LogQ = c + (\beta_{Clever} - 1.0) LogP_t$

Multiplying through by $LogP_t$ obtains

$LogQ = c + \beta_{Clever} LogP_t - LogP_t$

Moving $LogP_t$ to the left-hand side obtains

$LogQ_t + LogP_t = c + \beta_{Clever} LogP_t$
$LogQPlusLogP_t = c + \beta_{Clever} LogP$

where

$LogQPlusLogP_t = LogQ_t + LogP_t$

We can now express the hypotheses in terms of β_{Clever}. Recall that $\beta_P = -1.0$ if and only if $\beta_{Clever} = 0$:

H_0: $\beta_P = -1.0 \Leftrightarrow H_0$: $\beta_{Clever} = 0$ Actual price elasticity of demand equals -1.0.
H_1: $\beta_P \neq -1.0 \Leftrightarrow H_1$: $\beta_{Clever} \neq 0$ Actual price elasticity of demand does not equal -1.0.

[To access this online material, go to http://mitpress.mit.edu/westhoffeconometrics and select Gasoline Consumption.]

Getting Started in EViews

To generate the new variables, open the workfile.

· In the Workfile window: click **Genr**.

· In the Generate Series by Equation window: enter the formula for the new series; for example,

   logqpluslogp = logq + logp

· Click **OK**.

Now we can use EViews to run a regression with yclever as the dependent variable and logp as the explanatory variable.

· In the Workfile window: Click on the dependent variable, **logqpluslogp**, first; and then click on the explanatory variable, **logp**, while depressing the **<Ctrl> key**.

· In the Workfile window: Double click on a highlighted variable.

· In the Workfile window: Click **Open Equation**.

· In the Equation Specification window: Click **OK**.

· Do not forget to close the workfile.

Table 9.4
Budget theory of demand regression results with clever algebra

Ordinary least squares (OLS)				
Dependent variable: *LogQPlusLogP*				
Explanatory variable(s):	Estimate	SE	*t*-Statistic	Prob
LogP	0.414377	0.183409	2.259308	0.0538
Const	5.918487	0.045315	130.6065	0.0000
Number of observations	10			

Estimated equation: $EstLogQ = 5.92 + 0.414LogP$

Critical result: The coefficient estimate, b_{Clever}, equals 0.414. The coefficient estimate does not equal 0; the estimate is 0.414 from 0. This evidence suggests that the budget theory of demand is incorrect.

First let us compare the estimates for β_P in table 9.3 and β_{Clever} in table 9.4
• Estimate for β_P, b_P, equals −0.586;
• Estimate for β_{Clever}, b_{Clever}, equals 0.414.

This is consistent with the definition of β_{Clever}. By definition, β_{Clever} equals β_P plus 1.0:

$$\beta_{Clever} = \beta_P + 1.0$$

The estimate of β_{Clever} equals the estimate of β_P plus 1:

$$b_{Clever} = b_P + 1.0$$
$$= -0.586 + 1.0$$
$$= 0.414$$

Next calculate Prob[Results IF H_0 true] focusing on β_{Clever}:

• **Generic question:**   What is the probability that the results would be like those we actually obtained (or even stronger), if the cynic is correct?

• **Specific question:**   The regression's coefficient estimate was 0.414. What is the probability that the coefficient estimate, b_{Clever}, in one regression would be at least 0.414 from 0, if H_0 were actually true (if the actual coefficient, β_{Clever}, equals 0)?

The tails probability appearing in the regression results is based on the premise that the actual value of the coefficient equals 0. Consequently the tails probability answers the question (figure 9.4).

Answer: Prob[Results IF H_0 true] = 0.0538 ≈ 0.054

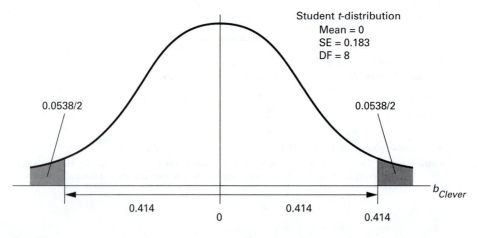

Figure 9.4
Probability distribution of constant elasticity model's coefficient estimate = clever approach

This is the same value for the probability that we computed when we used the Econometrics Lab. By a clever algebraic manipulation, we can get the statistical software to perform the probability calculations. Now we turn to the final hypothesis-testing step.

Step 5:   Decide on the standard of proof, a significance level.

The significance level is the dividing line between the probability being small and the probability being large.

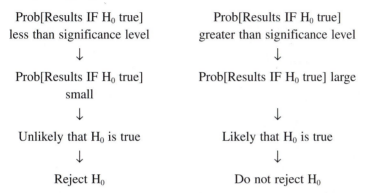

Prob[Results IF H_0 true]   Prob[Results IF H_0 true]
less than significance level   greater than significance level
↓   ↓
Prob[Results IF H_0 true]   Prob[Results IF H_0 true] large
small
↓   ↓
Unlikely that H_0 is true   Likely that H_0 is true
↓   ↓
Reject H_0 Do not reject H_0

At a 1 or 5 percent significance level, we do not reject the null hypothesis that the elasticity of demand equals −1.0, thereby supporting the budget theory of demand. That is, at a 1 or 5 percent significance level, the estimate of −0.586 is not statistically different from −1.0.

9.5   Summary: One-Tailed and Two-Tailed Tests

The theory that we are testing determines whether we should use of a one-tailed or two-tailed test. When the theory suggests that the actual value of a coefficient is greater than or less than a specific constant, a one-tailed test is appropriate. Most economic theories fall into this category. In fact most economic theories suggest that the actual value of the coefficient is either greater than 0 or less than 0 (see figure 9.5). For example, economic theory teaches that the price should have a negative influence on the quantity demanded; similarly theory teaches that the price should have a positive influence on the quantity supplied. In most cases economists use one-tailed tests. However, some theories suggest that the coefficient equals a specific value; in these cases a two-tailed test is required.

9.6   Logarithms: A Useful Econometric Tool to Fine Tune Hypotheses—The Math

The constant price elasticity model is just one example of how logarithms can be a useful econometric tool. Generally, logarithms provide a very convenient way to test hypotheses that

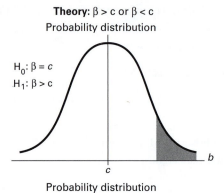

Theory: $\beta > c$ or $\beta < c$
Probability distribution

$H_0: \beta = c$
$H_1: \beta > c$

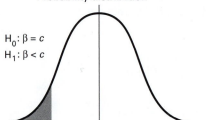

Probability distribution

$H_0: \beta = c$
$H_1: \beta < c$

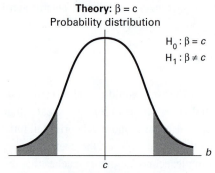

Theory: $\beta = c$
Probability distribution

$H_0: \beta = c$
$H_1: \beta \neq c$

Prob[Results IF H_0 true] =
Probability of obtaining results like those
we actually got (or even stronger), if H_0 is true

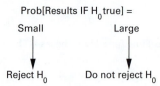

Prob[Results IF H_0 true] =

Small   Large

Reject H_0 Do not reject H_0

Figure 9.5
One-tailed and two-tailed tests—A comparison

are expressed in terms of percentages rather than "natural" units. To see how, we will first review three concepts:

· The interpretation of the coefficient estimate
· The differential approximation
· The derivative of a logarithm

9.6.1   Interpretation of the Coefficient Estimate: $Esty = b_{Const} + b_x x$

Let x increase by Δx: $x \to x + \Delta x$. Consequently the estimated value of y will increase by Δy: $Esty \to Esty + \Delta y$:

$$Esty + \Delta y = b_{Const} + b_x (x + \Delta x)$$

Multiply through by b_x,

$$Esty + \Delta y = b_{Const} + b_x x + b_x \Delta x$$

Reconsider the original equation

$$Esty = b_{Const} + b_x x$$

Subtracting the original equation obtains

$$\Delta y = b_x \Delta x$$

In words, b_x estimates the unit change in the dependent variable y resulting from a one unit change in explanatory variable x.

9.6.2   Differential Approximation: $\Delta y \approx (dy/dx)\Delta x$

In words, the derivative tells us by approximately how much y changes when x changes by a small amount; that is, the derivative equals the change in y caused by a one (small) unit change in x.

9.6.3 Derivative of a Natural Logarithm: $d \log(z)/dx = 1/z$

The derivative of the natural logarithm of z with respect to z equals 1 divided by z.[2] We have already considered the case in which both the dependent variable and explanatory variable are logarithms. Now we will consider two cases in which only one of the two variables is a logarithm:

- Dependent variable is a logarithm.
- Explanatory variable is a logarithm.

9.6.4 Dependent Variable Logarithm: $y = \log(z)$

Regression: $\quad Esty = b_{Const} + b_x x \qquad$ where $y = \log(z)$

Interpreting $b_x \qquad \downarrow \qquad\qquad\qquad \downarrow \qquad\qquad$ Differential approximation

$$\Delta y = b_x \, \Delta x \qquad \Delta y \approx \frac{d \log(z)}{dz} \Delta z$$

$\qquad\qquad\qquad\qquad\qquad\qquad \downarrow \qquad\qquad$ Derivative of logarithm

$$\Delta y \approx \frac{1}{z}\Delta z = \frac{\Delta z}{z}$$

Substituting $\Delta z/z$ for Δy,

$$\frac{\Delta z}{z} \approx b_x \, \Delta x$$

$$\frac{\Delta z}{z} \times 100 \approx (b_x \times 100)\Delta x \qquad\qquad$$ Multiply both sides of the equation by 100,

Interpretation of $\Delta z/z \times 100$: percent change in z

Percent change in $z \approx (b_x \times 100) \, \Delta x$

In words, when the dependent variable is a logarithm, $b_x \times 100$ estimates the percent change in the dependent variable resulting from a one unit change in the explanatory variable, which is the percent change in y resulting from a one (natural) unit change in x.

---

2. The log notation refers to the natural logarithm (logarithm base e), not the logarithm base 10.

9.6.5 Explanatory Variable Logarithm of z: x = log(z)

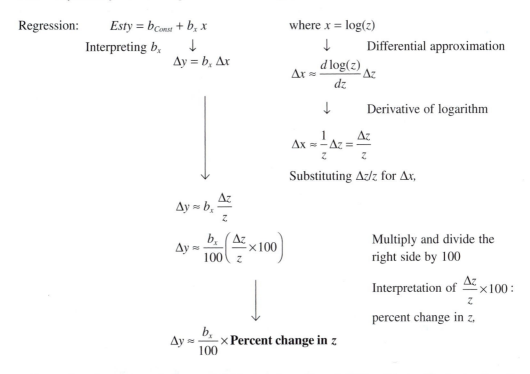

Regression: $Esty = b_{Const} + b_x \, x$ where $x = \log(z)$

Interpreting b_x ↓   ↓   Differential approximation

$$\Delta y = b_x \, \Delta x$$

$$\Delta x \approx \frac{d \log(z)}{dz} \Delta z$$

↓   Derivative of logarithm

$$\Delta x \approx \frac{1}{z} \Delta z = \frac{\Delta z}{z}$$

Substituting $\Delta z / z$ for Δx,

$$\Delta y \approx b_x \frac{\Delta z}{z}$$

$$\Delta y \approx \frac{b_x}{100} \left(\frac{\Delta z}{z} \times 100 \right)$$ Multiply and divide the right side by 100

Interpretation of $\dfrac{\Delta z}{z} \times 100$:

percent change in z,

$$\Delta y \approx \frac{b_x}{100} \times \textbf{Percent change in } z$$

In words, when the explanatory variable is a logarithm, $b_x/100$ estimates the (natural) unit change in the dependent variable resulting from a 1 percent change in the explanatory variable, which is the unit change in z resulting from a 1 percent change in z.

9.7 Using Logarithms—An Illustration: Wages and Education

To illustrate the usefulness of logarithms, consider the effect of a worker's high education on his/her wage. Economic theory (and common sense) suggests that a worker's wage is influenced by the number of years of education he/she completes:

Theory: Additional years of education increases a workers wage rate.

Project: Assess the effect of education on salary.

To assess this theory we will focus on the effect of high school education; we consider workers who have completed the ninth, tenth, eleventh, or twelfth grades and have not continued on to college or junior college. We will use data from the March 2007 Current Population Survey. In the process we can illustrate the usefulness of logarithms. Logarithms allow us to fine-tune our hypotheses by expressing them in terms of percentages.

Wage and education data: Cross-sectional data of wages and education for 212 workers included in the March 2007 Current Population Survey residing in the Northeast region of the United States who have completed the ninth, tenth, eleventh, or twelfth grades, but have not continued on to college or junior college.

$Wage_t$ Wage rate earned by worker t (dollars per hour)

$HSEduc_t$ Highest high school grade completed by worker t (9, 10, 11, or 12 years)

We can consider four models that capture the theory in somewhat different ways:

• Linear model

• Log dependent variable model

• Log explanatory variable model

• Log-log (constant elasticity) model

9.7.1   Linear Model: $Wage_t = \beta_{Const} + \beta_E HSEduc_t + e_t$

The linear model includes no logarithms. Wage is expressed in dollars and education in years.

[To access this online material, go to http://mitpress.mit.edu/westhoffeconometrics and select Wage and High School Education.]

As table 9.5 reports we estimate that an additional year of high school increases the wat by about $1.65 per hour. It is very common to express wage increases in this way. All the time we hear people say that they received a $1.00 per hour raise or a $2.00 per hour raise. It is also very

Table 9.5
Wage regression results with linear model

Ordinary least squares (OLS)				
Dependent variable: Wage				
Explanatory variable(s):	Estimate	SE	*t*-Statistic	Prob
HSEduc	1.645899	0.555890	2.960834	0.0034
Const	−3.828617	6.511902	−0.587941	0.5572
Number of observations	212			

Estimated equation: $EstWage = -3.83 + 1.65HSEduc$

Interpretation of estimates:

  $b_E = 1.65$: 1 additional year of high school education increases the wage by about $1.65 per hour.

common to hear raises expressed in percentage terms. When the results of labor new contracts are announced the wage increases are typically expressed in percentage terms; management agreed to give workers a 2 percent increase or a 3 percent increase. This observation leads us to our next model: the log dependent variable model.

9.7.2   Log Dependent Variable Model: $LogWage_t = \beta_{Const} + \beta_E HSEduc_t + e_t$

[To access this online material, go to http://mitpress.mit.edu/westhoffeconometrics and select Wage and High School Education.]

First we must generate a new dependent variable, the log of wage:

$LogWage = \log(Wage)$

The dependent variable ($LogWage$) is expressed in terms of the logarithm of dollars; the explanatory variable ($HSEduc$) is expressed in years (table 9.6).

Let us compare the estimates derived by our two models:

• The linear model implicitly assumes that the impact of one additional year of high school education is the same for each worker in terms of dollars. We estimate that a worker's wage increases by $1.65 per hour for each additional year of high school (table 9.5).

• The log dependent variable model implicitly assumes that the impact of one additional year of high school education is the same for each worker in terms of percentages. We estimate that a worker's wage increases by 11.4 percent for each additional year of high school (table 9.6).

The estimates each model provides differ somewhat. For example, consider two workers, the first earning $10.00 per hour and a second earning $20.00. On the one hand, the linear model estimates that an additional year of high school would increase the wage of each worker by

Table 9.6
Wage regression results with log dependent variable model

Ordinary Least Squares (OLS)				
Dependent variable: *LogWage*				
Explanatory variable(s):	Estimate	SE	*t*-Statistic	Prob
HSEduc	0.113824	0.033231	3.425227	0.0007
Const	1.329791	0.389280	3.416030	0.0008
Number of Observations	212			

Estimated equation: *EstLogWage* = 1.33 + 0.114*HSEduc*

Interpretation of estimates:

$b_E = 0.114$: 1 additional year of high school education increases the wage by about 11.4 percent.

$1.65 per hour. On the other hand, the log dependent variable model estimates that an additional hear of high school would increase the wage of the first worker by 11.4 percent of $10.00, $1.14 and the second worker by 11 percent of $20.00, $2.28.

As we will see, the last two models (the log explanatory variable and log-log models) are not particularly natural in this context of this example. We seldom express differentials in education as percentage differences. Nevertheless, the log explanatory variable and log-log models are appropriate in many other contexts. Therefore we will apply them to our wage and education data even thought the interpretations will sound unusual.

9.7.3 Log Explanatory Variable Model: $Wage_t = \beta_{Const} + \beta_E LogHSEduc_t + e_t$

[To access this online material, go to http://mitpress.mit.edu/westhoffeconometrics and select Wage and High School Education.]

Generate a new dependent variable, the log of experience:

$LogHSEduc = \log(HSEduc)$

The dependent variable (*Wage*) is expressed in terms of dollars; the explanatory variable (*LogHSEduc*) is expressed in terms of the log of years. As mentioned above, this model is not particularly appropriate for this example because we do not usually express education differences in percentage terms. Nevertheless, the example does illustrate how we interpret the coefficient in a log explanatory variable model. The regression results estimate that a 1 percent increase in high school education increases the way by about $.17 per hour (table 9.7).

Table 9.7
Wage regression results with log explanatory variable model

Ordinary least squares (OLS)				
Dependent variable: *Wage*				
Explanatory variable(s):	Estimate	SE	*t*-Statistic	Prob
LogHSEduc	17.30943	5.923282	2.922270	0.0039
Const	−27.10445	14.55474	−1.862242	0.0640
Number of observations	212			

Estimated equation: $EstWage = -27.1 + 17.31 LogHSEduc$
Interpretation of estimates:
  $b_E = 17.31$: A 1 percent increase in high school education increases the wage by about $.17 per hour.

Table 9.8
Wage regression results with constant elasticity model

Ordinary least squares (OLS)				
Dependent variable: *LogWage*				
Explanatory variable(s):	Estimate	SE	*t*-Statistic	Prob
LogHSEduc	1.195654	0.354177	3.375868	0.0009
Const	−0.276444	0.870286	−0.317647	0.7511
Number of observations	212			

Estimated equation: *EstLogWage* = −0.28 + 1.20*LogHSEduc*

Interpretation of estimates:

b_E = 1.20: A 1 percent increase in high school education increases the wage by about 1.2 percent.

9.7.4 Log-Log (Constant Elasticity) Model: $LogWage_t = \beta_{Const} + \beta_E LogHSEduc_t + e_t$

[To access this online material, go to http://mitpress.mit.edu/westhoffeconometrics and select Wage and High School Education.]

Both the dependent and explanatory variables are expressed in terms of logs. This is just the constant elasticity model that we discussed earlier. The regression results estimate that a 1 percent increase in high school education increases the wage by 1.2 percent (table 9.8).

While the log-log model is not particularly appropriate in this case, we have already seen that it can be appropriate in other contexts. For example, this was the model we used to assess the budget theory of demand earlier in this chapter.

9.8 Summary: Logarithms and the Interpretation of Coefficient Estimates

Dependent variable: y — Explanatory variable: x

Coefficient estimate: Estimates the (natural) **unit** change in y resulting from a one (natural) **unit** change in x

Dependent variable: $\log(y)$ — Explanatory variable: x

Coefficient estimate multiplied by 100: Estimates the **percent** change in y resulting from a one (natural) **unit** change in x

Dependent variable: y — Explanatory variable: $\log(x)$

Coefficient estimate divided by 100: Estimates the (natural) **unit** change in y resulting from a 1 **percent** change in x

Dependent variable: $\log(y)$ — Explanatory variable: $\log(x)$

Coefficient estimate: Estimates the **percent** change in y resulting from a 1 **percent** change in x

Chapter 9 Review Questions

1. Consider the general structure of the theory, the null hypothesis, and alternative hypothesis. When is a

    a. One-tailed hypothesis appropriate?

Theory: _____

H_0: _____

H_1: _____

    b. Two-tailed hypothesis appropriate?

Theory: _____

H_0: _____

H_1: _____

2. How should the coefficient estimate be interpreted when the dependent and explanatory variables are specified as:

    a. Dependent variable: y and explanatory variable: x

    b. Dependent variable: $\log(y)$ and explanatory variable: x

    c. Dependent variable: y and explanatory variable: $\log(x)$

    d. Dependent variable: $\log(y)$ and explanatory variable: $\log(x)$

Chapter 9 Exercises

Revisit Nebraska petroleum consumption.

Petroleum consumption data for Nebraska: Annual time series data of petroleum consumption and prices for Nebraska from 1990 to 1999.

PetroCons$_t$ Consumption of petroleum in year t (1,000s of gallons)

Cpi$_t$ Midwest Consumer Price Index in year t (1982–84 100)

Pop$_t$ Nebraska population in year t

PriceNom$_t$ Nominal price of petroleum in year t (dollars per gallon)

1. Generate two new variables from the Nebraska data:

PetroConsPC$_t$ Per capita consumption of petroleum in year t (gallons)

PriceReal$_t$ Real price of petroleum in year t (dollars per gallon)

[To access this online material, go to http://mitpress.mit.edu/westhoffeconometrics and select Petroleum Consumption - Neb.]

    a. Petroleum consumption includes the consumption of all petroleum products: gasoline, fuel oil, and so on. Consequently, would you expect petroleum to be a necessity or a luxury?

    b. In view of your answer to part a, would expect the per capita demand for petroleum to be inelastic? Explain.

    c. Consequently, why would the numerical value of the real price elasticity of demand be greater than −1.0? (Remember the "number line." Note that −0.8, −0.6, etc., are all greater than −1.0.)

    d. Apply the hypothesis-testing approach that we developed to assess the theory. Calculate Prob[Results IF H_0 true] in two ways:

        i. Using the Econometrics Lab.

[To access this online material, go to http://mitpress.mit.edu/westhoffeconometrics and select *t*-Distribution.]

        ii. Using the "clever definition" approach.

    e. What is your assessment of the theory? Explain.

2. Consider the budget theory of demand in the context of per capita petroleum consumption:

PriceReal × *PetroConsPC* = *RealBudAmt*

where

RealBudAmt = real budgeted amount

    a. Apply the hypothesis-testing approach that we developed to assess budget theory of demand.

[To access this online material, go to http://mitpress.mit.edu/westhoffeconometrics and select Petroleum Consumption - Neb.]

    Calculate Prob[Results IF H_0 true] in two ways:

        i. Using the Econometrics Lab.

[To access this online material, go to http://mitpress.mit.edu/westhoffeconometrics and select *t*-Distribution.]

        ii. Using the "clever definition" approach.

    b. What is your assessment of the theory? Explain.

3. Revisit the US crude oil supply data.

Crude oil production data: Annual time series data of US crude oil production and prices from 1976 to 2004.

OilProdBarrels$_t$ US crude oil productions in year t (thousands of barrels per day)

Price$_t$ Real wellhead price of crude oil in year t (1982–84 dollars per barrel)

Consider the following rather bizarre theory of supply:

Theory of supply: The price elasticity of supply equals 0.10.

   a. Apply the hypothesis-testing approach that we developed to assess the theory.

[To access this online material, go to http://mitpress.mit.edu/westhoffeconometrics and select Crude Oil Production.]

Calculate Prob[Results IF H$_0$ true] in two ways:

    i. Using the Econometrics Lab.

[To access this online material, go to http://mitpress.mit.edu/westhoffeconometrics and select *t*-Distribution.]

    ii. Using the "clever definition" approach.

   b. What is your assessment of the theory? Explain.

4. Revisit the gasoline consumption data.

Gasoline consumption data: Annual time series data for US gasoline consumption and prices from 1990 to 1999.

GasCons$_t$ US gasoline consumption in year t (millions of gallons per day)

PriceDollars$_t$ Real price of gasoline in year t (chained 2000 dollars per gallon)

   a. Would you theorize the price elasticity of demand for gasoline to be elastic or inelastic? Explain.

   b. Apply the hypothesis-testing approach that we developed to assess the theory.

[To access this online material, go to http://mitpress.mit.edu/westhoffeconometrics and select Gasoline Consumption.]

   c. What is your assessment of the theory? Explain.

5. Revisit the cigarette consumption data.

Cigarette consumption data: Cross section of per capita cigarette consumption and prices in fiscal year 2008 for the 50 states and the District of Columbia.

CigConsPC$_t$ Cigarette consumption per capita in state t (packs)

PriceConsumer$_t$ Price of cigarettes in state t paid by consumers (dollars per pack)

    a. Would you theorize that the price elasticity of demand for cigarettes would be elastic or inelastic? Explain.

    b. Use the ordinary least squares (OLS) estimation procedure to estimate the price elasticity of demand.

[To access this online material, go to http://mitpress.mit.edu/westhoffeconometrics and select Cigarette Consumption.]

    c. Does your estimate for the price elasticity of demand support your theory? Explain.

6. Reconsider the Current Population Survey wage data.

Wage and age data: Cross section data of wages and ages for 190 union members included in the March 2007 Current Population Survey who have earned high school degrees, but have not had any additional education.

Age$_t$ Age of worker t (years)

Wage$_t$ Wage rate of worker t (dollars per hour)

And recall the seniority theory:

Seniority theory: Additional years of age increases wage rate.

We often describe wage increases in terms of percent changes. Apply the hypothesis-testing approach that we developed to assess this "percent increase version" of the seniority theory.

    a. Apply the hypothesis-testing approach that we developed to assess the seniority theory.

[To access this online material, go to http://mitpress.mit.edu/westhoffeconometrics and select Wage and Age.]

    b. What is your assessment of the theory? Explain.

7. Revisit the effect that the Current Population Survey labor supply data.

Labor supply data: Cross-sectional data of hours worked and wages for the 92 married workers included in the March 2007 Current Population Survey residing in the Northeast region of the United States who earned bachelor, but no advanced, degrees.

HoursPerWeek$_t$ Hours worked per week by worker t

Wage$_t$ Wage earned by worker t (dollars per hour)

   Consider the theory that the supply elasticity is inelastic; that is, that the wage elasticity is less than 1.

   a. Apply the hypothesis-testing approach that we developed to assess the inelastic labor supply theory.

[To access this online material, go to http://mitpress.mit.edu/westhoffeconometrics and select Labor Supply.]

   b. What is your assessment of the theory? Explain.

10 Multiple Regression Analysis—Introduction

Chapter 10 Prep Questions

1. Consider the following constant elasticity model:

$$Q = \beta_{Const} P^{\beta_P} I^{\beta_I} ChickP^{\beta_{CP}}$$

where

Q = quantity of beef demanded

P = price of beef (the good's own price)

I = household Income

$ChickP$ = price of chicken

    a. Show that if $\beta_{CP} = -\beta_P - \beta_I$, then

$$Q = \beta_{Const} \left(\frac{P}{ChickP} \right)^{\beta_P} \left(\frac{I}{ChickP} \right)^{\beta_I}$$

b. If $\beta_{CP} = -\beta_P - \beta_I$, what happens to the quantity of beef demanded when the price of beef (the good's own price, P), income (I), and the price of chicken ($ChickP$) all double?

c. If $\beta_P + \beta_I + \beta_{CP} = 0$, what happens to the quantity of beef demanded when the price of beef (the good's own price, P), income (I), and the price of chicken ($ChickP$) all double?

2. Again, consider the following constant elasticity model:

$$Q = \beta_{Const} P^{\beta_P} I^{\beta_I} ChickP^{\beta_{CP}}$$

What does $\log(Q)$ equal, where log is the natural logarithm?

3. Consider the following model:

$$\log(Q) = \log(\beta_{Const}) + \beta_P \log(P) + \beta_I \log(I) + \beta_{CP} \log(ChickP)$$

Let $\beta_{Clever} = \beta_P + \beta_I + \beta_{CP}$. Show that

$$\log(Q) = \log(\beta_{Const}) + \beta_P[\log(P) - \log(ChickP)] + \beta_I[\log(I) - \log(ChickP)] + \beta_{Clever} \log(ChickP)$$

10.1   Simple versus Multiple Regression Analysis

Thus far we have focused our attention on **simple regression analysis** where the model assumes that only a single explanatory variable affects the dependent variable. In the real world, however, a dependent variable typically depends on many explanatory variables. For example, while economic theory teaches that the quantity of a good demanded depends on the good's own price, theory also tells us that the quantity depends on other factors also: income, the price of other goods, and so on. **Multiple regression analysis** allows us to assess such theories.

10.2   Goal of Multiple Regression Analysis

• Multiple regression analysis attempts to sort out the individual effect of each explanatory variable.

• An explanatory variable's coefficient estimate allows us to estimate the change in the dependent variable resulting from a change in that particular explanatory variable while all other explanatory variables remain constant.

10.3   A One-Tailed Test: Downward Sloping Demand Theory

We begin by explicitly stating the theory:

Downward sloping demand theory: The quantity of a good demanded by a household depends on its price and other relevant factors. When the good's own price increases while all other relevant factors remain constant, the quantity demanded decreases.

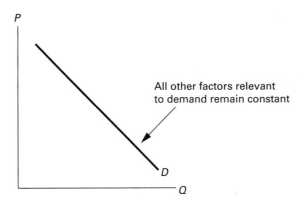

P

All other factors relevant
to demand remain constant

D

Q

Figure 10.1
Downward sloping demand curve

Project: Assess the downward sloping demand theory.

Graphically, the theory is illustrated by a downward sloping demand curve (figure 10.1). When we draw a demand curve for a good, we implicitly assume that all factors relevant to demand other than that good's own price remain the constant.

    We will focus on the demand for a particular good, beef, to illustrate the importance of multiple regression analysis. We now apply the hypothesis-testing steps.

Step 0:   Formulate a model reflecting the theory to be tested.

We will use a linear demand model to test the theory. Naturally the quantity of beef demanded depends on its own price, the price of beef. Furthermore we postulate that the quantity of beef demanded also depends on income and the price of chicken. In other words, our model proposes that the factors relevant to the demand for beef, other than beef's own price, are income and the price of chicken.

$$Q = \beta_{Const} + \beta_P P_t + \beta_I I_t + \beta_{ChickP} ChickP_t + e_t$$

where

Q_t = quantity of beef demanded

P_t = price of beef (the good's own price)

I_t = household Income

$ChickP_t$ = price of chicken

    The theory suggests that when income and the price of chicken remain constant, an increase in the price of beef (the good's own price) decreases the quantity of beef demanded (figure 10.2); similarly, when income and the price chicken remain constant, a decrease in the price of beef (the good's own price) increases the quantity of beef demanded:

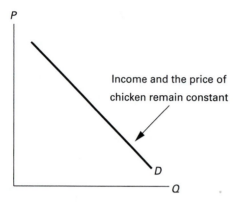

Figure 10.2
Downward sloping demand curve for beef

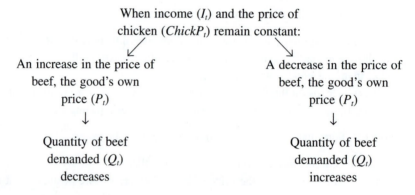

The theory suggests that the model's price coefficient, β_P, is negative:

$$
\begin{array}{ccccccc}
 & P_t \text{ Increases} & & I_t \text{ Constant} & & Chick_t \text{ Constant} & \\
 & \downarrow & & \downarrow & & \downarrow & \\
Q = \beta_{Const} + & \beta_P P_t & + & \beta_I I_t & + & \beta_{ChickP} ChickP_t & + e_t \\
 & \downarrow & & \downarrow & & \downarrow & \\
 & \text{Decreases} & & \text{Constant} & & \text{Constant} & \\
 & \downarrow & & & & & \\
 & \beta_P < 0 & & & & &
\end{array}
$$

Economic theory teaches that the sign of coefficients for the explanatory variables other than the good's own price may be positive or negative. Their signs depend on the particular good in question:

• The sign of β_I depends on whether beef is a normal or inferior good. Beef is generally regarded as a normal good; consequently we would expect β_I to be positive: an increase in income results in an increase in the quantity of beef demanded.

Beef a normal good

$$\downarrow$$

$$\beta_I > 0$$

• The sign of β_{CP} depends on whether beef and chicken are substitutes or complements. Beef and chicken are generally believed to be substitutes; consequently, we would expect β_{CP} to be positive. An increase in the price of chicken would cause consumers to substitute beef for the now more expensive chicken; that is, an increase in the price of chicken results in an increase in the quantity of beef demanded.

Beef and chicken substitutes

$$\downarrow$$

$$\beta_{CP} > 0$$

Step 1:   Collect data, run the regression, and interpret the estimates.

Beef consumption data: Monthly time series data of beef consumption, beef prices, income, and chicken prices from 1985 and 1986 (table 10.1).

Q_t Quantity of beef demanded in month t (millions of pounds)

P_t Price of beef in month t (cents per pound)

I_t Disposable income in month t (billions of 1985 dollars)

$ChickP_t$ Price of chicken in month t (cents per pound)

These data can be accessed at the following link:

[To access this online material, go to http://mitpress.mit.edu/westhoffeconometrics and select Beef Demand.]

We now use the ordinary least squares (OLS) estimation procedure to estimate the model's parameters (table 10.2).

   To interpret these estimates, let us for the moment replace the numerical value of each estimate with the italicized lower case Roman letter b, *b*, that we use to denote the estimate. That is, replace the estimated:

• Constant, 159,032, with b_{Const}

• Price coefficient, −549.5, with b_P

• Income coefficient, 24.25, with b_I

• Chicken price coefficient, 287.4, with b_{CP}

$$EstQ = 159{,}032 - 549.5P + 24.25I + 287.4ChickP$$
$$\downarrow \qquad \downarrow \qquad \downarrow \qquad \downarrow$$
$$EstQ = b_{Const} + b_P P + b_I I + b_{CP} ChickP$$

Table 10.1
Monthly beef demand data from 1985 and 1986

Year	Month	Q	P	I	ChickP
1985	1	211,865	168.2	5,118	75.0
1985	2	216,183	168.2	5,073	75.9
1985	3	216,481	161.8	5,026	74.8
1985	4	219,891	157.2	5,131	73.7
1985	5	221,934	155.9	5,250	73.6
1985	6	217,428	157.2	5,137	74.6
1985	7	219,486	152.9	5,138	71.4
1985	8	218,972	151.9	5,133	69.3
1985	9	218,742	147.4	5,152	70.9
1985	10	212,243	160.4	5,180	72.3
1985	11	209,344	168.4	5,189	76.2
1985	12	215,232	172.1	5,213	75.7
1986	1	222,379	159.7	5,219	75.0
1986	2	219,337	152.9	5,247	73.7
1986	3	224,257	149.9	5,301	74.2
1986	4	235,454	144.6	5,313	75.1
1986	5	230,326	151.9	5,319	74.6
1986	6	228,821	150.1	5,315	77.1
1986	7	229,108	156.5	5,339	85.6
1986	8	225,543	164.3	5,343	93.3
1986	9	220,516	160.6	5,348	81.9
1986	10	221,239	163.2	5,344	92.5
1986	11	223,737	162.9	5,351	82.7
1986	12	226,660	160.4	5,345	81.8

Table 10.2
Beef demand regression results—Linear model

Ordinary least squares (OLS)				
Dependent variable: Q				
Explanatory variable(s):	Estimate	SE	t-Statistic	Prob
P	−549.4847	130.2611	−4.218333	0.0004
I	24.24854	11.27214	2.151192	0.0439
$ChickP$	287.3737	193.3540	1.486257	0.1528
$Const$	159,032.4	61,472.68	2.587041	0.0176
Number of observations	24			

Estimated equation: $EstQ = 159{,}032 - 549.5P + 24.25I + 287.4ChickP$

The coefficient estimates attempt to separate out the individual effect that each explanatory variable has on the dependent variable. To justify this, focus on the estimate of the beef price coefficient, b_P. It estimates by how much the quantity of beef changes when the price of beef (the good's own price) changes while income and the price of chicken (all other explanatory variables) remain constant. More formally, when all other explanatory variables remain constant:

$$\Delta Q = b_P \Delta P \quad \text{or} \quad b_P = \frac{\Delta Q}{\Delta P}$$

where

ΔQ = change in the quantity of beef demanded

ΔP = change in the price of beef, the good's own price

A little algebra explains why. We begin with the equation estimating our model:

$$EstQ = b_{Const} + b_P P + b_I I + b_{CP} ChickP$$

Now increase the price of beef (the good's own price) by ΔP while keeping all other explanatory variables constant. ΔQ estimates the resulting change in quantity of beef demanded.

	From	To
Price:	P	$\rightarrow P + \Delta P$
Quantity:	$EstQ$	$\rightarrow EstQ + \Delta Q$

while all other explanatory variables remain constant; that is, while I and $ChickP$ remain constant.

In the equation estimating our model, substitute $EstQ + \Delta Q$ for $EstQ$ and $P + \Delta P$ for P:

$$
\begin{array}{lcllll}
EstQ & = & b_{Const} + & b_P P & + b_I I & + b_{CP} ChickP \\
\downarrow & & & \downarrow & & \text{Substituting} \\
EstQ + \Delta Q & = & b_{Const} + & b_P(P + \Delta P) & + b_I I & + b_{CP} ChickP \\
& & & \downarrow & & \text{Multiplying through by } b_P \\
EstQ + \Delta Q & = & b_{Const} + & b_P P + b_P \Delta P & + b_I I & + b_{CP} ChickP \\
\\
EstQ & = & b_{Const} + & b_P P & + b_I I & + b_{CP} ChickP \quad \text{Original equation} \\
& & & & & \text{Subtracting the equations} \\
\\
\Delta Q & = & 0 + & b_P \Delta P & + 0 + & 0 \\
& & & & & \text{Simplifying}
\end{array}
$$

$$\Delta Q \qquad = \; b_P \Delta P$$

Dividing through by ΔP

$$\frac{\Delta Q}{\Delta P} \qquad = \; b_P \qquad \text{while all other explanatory variables remain constant}$$

To summarize,

$$\Delta Q = b_P \Delta P \quad \text{or} \quad b_P = \frac{\Delta Q}{\Delta P}$$

while all other explanatory variables (*I* and *ChickP*) remain constant.

Note that the sign of b_P determines whether or not the data support the downward sloping demand theory. A demand curve illustrates what happens to the quantity demanded when the price of the good changes while all other factors that affect demand (in the case income and the price of chicken) remain constant. b_P is the estimated "slope" of the demand curve.

The word slope has been placed in quotes. Why is this? Slope is defined as rise divided by run. As figure 10.3 illustrates, b_P equals run over rise, however. This occurred largely by an historical accident. When economists, Alfred Marshall in particular, first developed demand and supply curves, they placed the price on the vertical axis and the quantity on the horizontal axis. Consequently b_P actually equals the reciprocal of the estimated slope. To avoid using the awkward phrase "the reciprocal of the estimated slope" repeatedly, we place the word slope within double quotes to denote this.

Now let us interpret the other coefficients. Using similar logic, we have

$$\Delta Q = b_I \Delta I \quad \text{or} \quad b_I = \frac{\Delta Q}{\Delta I}$$

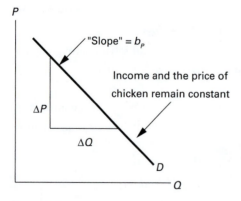

Figure 10.3
Demand curve "slope"

while all other explanatory variables (P and $ChickP$) remain constant. b_I estimates the change in quantity when income changes while all other explanatory variables (the price of beef and the price of chicken) remain constant.

$$\Delta Q = b_{CP}\Delta ChickP \quad \text{or} \quad b_{CP} = \frac{\Delta Q}{\Delta PChick}$$

while all other explanatory variables (P and I) remain constant. b_{CP} estimates the change in quantity when the price of chicken changes while all other explanatory variables (the price of beef and income) remain constant.

What happens when the price of beef (the good's own price), income, and the price of chicken change simultaneously? The total estimated change in the quantity of beef demanded just equals the sum of the individual changes; that is, the total estimated change in the quantity of beef demanded equals the change resulting from the change in

- the price of beef (the good's own price)

plus
- income

plus
- the price of chicken

The following equation expresses this succinctly:

Total change	Change in the price of beef (the good's own price)	Change in income	Change in the price of chicken
↓	↓	↓	↓
$\Delta Q \quad =$	$b_P \Delta P$	$+ \quad b_I \Delta I$	$+ \quad b_{CP}\, \Delta ChickP$

Each term estimates the change in the dependent variable, quantity of beef demanded, resulting from a change in each individual explanatory variable.

The estimates achieve the goal:

Goal of multiple regression analysis: Multiple regression analysis attempts to sort out the individual effect of each explanatory variable. An explanatory variable's coefficient estimate allows us to estimate the change in the dependent variable resulting from a change in that particular explanatory variable while all other explanatory variables remain constant.

Now let us interpret the numerical values of the coefficient estimates,

Estimated effect of a change in the price of beef (the good's own price):

$$\Delta Q = b_P \Delta P = -549.5\Delta P$$

while all other explanatory variables remain constant.

Interpretation: The ordinary least squares (OLS) estimate of the price coefficient equals −549.5; that is, we estimate that if the price of beef increases by 1 cent while income and the price of chicken remain unchanged, the quantity of beef demanded decreases by about 549.5 million pounds.

Estimated effect of a change in income:

$$\Delta Q = b_I \Delta I = 24.25 \Delta I$$

while all other explanatory variables remain constant.

Interpretation: The ordinary least squares (OLS) estimate of the income coefficient equals 24.25; that is, we estimate that if disposable income increases by 1 billion dollars while the price of beef and the price of chicken remain unchanged, the quantity of beef demanded increases by about 24.25 million pounds.

Estimated effect of a change in the price of chicken:

$$\Delta Q = b_{CP} \Delta ChickP = 287.4 \Delta ChickP$$

while all other explanatory variables remain constant.

Interpretation: The ordinary least squares (OLS) estimate of the chicken price coefficient equals 287.4; that is, we estimate that if the price of chicken increases by 1 cent while the price of beef and income remain unchanged, the quantity of beef demanded increases by about 287.4 million pounds.

Putting the three estimates together obtains

$$\Delta Q = b_p \Delta P + b_I \Delta I + b_{CP} \Delta ChickP$$

or

$$\Delta Q = -549.5 \Delta P + 24.25 \Delta I + 287.4 \Delta ChickP$$

We estimate that the total change in the quantity of beef demanded equals −549.5 times the change in the price of beef (the good's own price) plus 24.25 times the change in disposable income plus 287.4 times the change in the price of chicken.

Recall that the sign of the estimate for the good's own price coefficient, b_P, determines whether or not the data support the downward sloping demand theory. b_P estimates the change in the quantity of beef demanded when the price of beef (the good's own price) changes while the other explanatory variables, income and the price of chicken, remain constant. The theory postulates that an increase in the good's own price decreases the quantity of beef demanded. The negative price coefficient estimate lends support to the theory.

Critical result: The own price coefficient estimate is −549.5. The negative sign of the coefficient estimate suggests that an increase in the price decreases the quantity of beef demanded. This evidence supports the downward sloping theory.

Now let us continue with the hypothesis testing steps.

Step 2:   Play the cynic and challenge the results; construct the null and alternative hypotheses.

The cynic is skeptical of the evidence supporting the view that the actual price coefficient, β_P, is negative; that is, the cynic challenges the evidence and hence the downward sloping demand theory:

Cynic's view: Sure, the price coefficient estimate from the regression suggests that the demand curve is downward sloping, but this is just "the luck of the draw." The actual price coefficient, β_P, equals 0.

H_0: $\beta_P = 0$ Cynic is correct: The price of beef (the good's own price) has no effect on quantity of beef demanded.

H_1: $\beta_P < 0$ Cynic is incorrect: An increase in the price decreases quantity of beef demanded.

The null hypothesis, like the cynic, challenges the evidence: an increase in the price of beef has no effect on the quantity of beef demanded. The alternative hypothesis is consistent with the evidence: an increase in the price decreases the quantity of beef demanded.

Step 3:   Formulate the question to assess the cynic's view and the null hypothesis.

· **Generic question:**   What is the probability that the results would be like those we obtained (or even stronger), if the cynic is correct and the price of beef actually has no impact?

· **Specific question:**   What is the probability that the coefficient estimate, b_P, in one regression would be −549.5 or less, if H_0 were true (if the actual price coefficient, β_P, equals 0)?

Answer: Prob[Results IF cynic correct] or Prob[Results IF H_0 true].

Figure 10.4 illustrates the Prob[Results IF H_0 true].

Step 4:   Use the general properties of the estimation procedure, the probability distribution of the estimate, to calculate Prob[Results IF H_0 true] (figure 10.5).

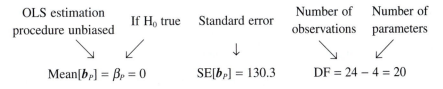

OLS estimation procedure unbiased	If H_0 true	Standard error	Number of observations	Number of parameters
$\searrow$	$\swarrow$	$\downarrow$	$\searrow$	$\swarrow$
$\text{Mean}[b_P] = \beta_P = 0$		$\text{SE}[b_P] = 130.3$	$\text{DF} = 24 - 4 = 20$	

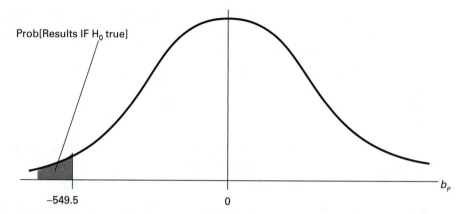

Figure 10.4
Probability distribution of coefficient estimate for the beef price

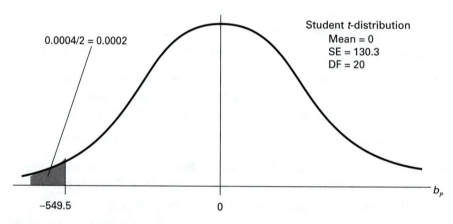

Figure 10.5
Calculating Prob[Results IF H_0 true]

We can now calculate Prob[Results IF H_0 true]. The easiest way is to use the regression results. Recall that the tails probability is reported in the Prob column. The tails probability is .0004; therefore, to calculate Prob[Results IF H_0 true] we need only divide 0.0004 by 2 (table 10.3).

$$\text{Prob[Results IF } H_0 \text{ true]} = \frac{0.0004}{2} \approx 0.0002$$

Step 5: Decide on the standard of proof, a significance level.

The significance level is the dividing line between the probability being small and the probability being large.

Table 10.3
Beef demand regression results—Linear model

Ordinary least squares (OLS)				
Dependent variable: Q				
Explanatory variable(s):	Estimate	SE	t-Statistic	Prob
P	−549.4847	130.2611	−4.218333	0.0004
I	24.24854	11.27214	2.151192	0.0439
$ChickP$	287.3737	193.3540	1.486257	0.1528
$Const$	159,032.4	61,472.68	2.587041	0.0176
Number of observations	24			

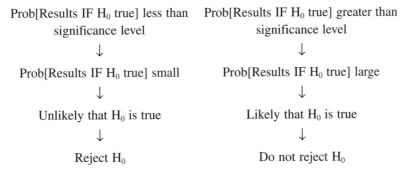

We can reject the null hypothesis at the traditional significance levels of 1, 5, and 10 percent. Consequently the data support the downward sloping demand theory.

10.4 A Two-Tailed Test: No Money Illusion Theory

We will now consider a second theory regarding demand. Microeconomic theory teaches that there is no money illusion; that is, if all prices and income change by the same proportion, the quantity of a good demanded will not change. The basic rationale of this theory is clear. Suppose that all prices double. Every good would be twice as expensive. If income also doubles, however, consumers would have twice as much to spend. When all prices and income double, there is no reason for a consumer to change his/her spending patterns; that is, there is no reason for a consumer to change the quantity of any good he/she demands.

We can use indifference curve analysis to motivate this more formally.[1] Recall the household's utility maximizing problem:

max   Utility $= U(X, Y)$

s.t. $P_X X + P_Y Y = I$

---

1. If you are not familiar with indifference curve analysis, please skip to the Linear Demand Model and Money Illusion Theory section and accept the fact that the no money illusion theory is well grounded in economic theory.

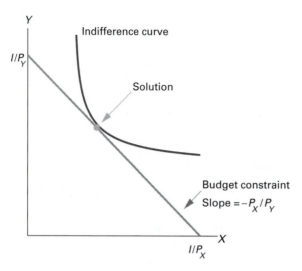

Figure 10.6
Utility maximization

A household chooses the bundle of goods that maximizes its utility subject to its budget constraint. How can we illustrate the solution to the household's problem? First, we draw the budget constraint. To do so, let us calculate its intercepts.

$$P_X X + P_Y Y = I$$

X-intercept: $Y = 0$ Y-intercept: $X = 0$

↓   ↓

$P_X X = I$ $P_Y Y = I$

↓   ↓

$X = \dfrac{I}{P_X}$ $Y = \dfrac{I}{P_Y}$

Next, to maximize utility, we find the highest indifference curve that still touches the budget constraint as illustrated in figure 10.6.

Now suppose that all prices and income double:

	Before				**After**	
max	Utility = U(X, Y)	$P_X \rightarrow 2P_X$		max	Utility = U(X, Y)	
s.t.	$P_X X + P_Y Y = I$	$P_Y \rightarrow 2P_Y$		s.t.	$2P_X X + 2P_Y Y = 2I$	
		$I \rightarrow 2I$				

How is the budget constraint affected? To answer this question, calculate the intercepts after all prices and income have doubled and then compare them to the original ones:

$$2P_XX + 2P_YY = 2I$$

X-intercept: $Y = 0$ Y-intercept: $X = 0$

$$\downarrow \qquad\qquad\qquad\qquad \downarrow$$

$$2P_XX = 2I \qquad\qquad\qquad 2P_YY = 2I$$

$$\downarrow \qquad\qquad\qquad\qquad \downarrow$$

$$X = \frac{2I}{2P_X} = \frac{I}{P_X} \qquad\qquad Y = \frac{2I}{2P_Y} = \frac{I}{P_Y}$$

Since the intercepts have not changed, the budget constraint line has not changed; hence, the solution to the household's constrained utility maximizing problem will not change.

In sum, the no money illusion theory is based on sound logic. But remember, many theories that appear to be sensible turn out to be incorrect. That is why we must test our theories.

Project: Use the beef demand data to assess the no money illusion theory.

Can we use our linear demand model to do so? Unfortunately, the answer is no. The linear demand model is inconsistent with the proposition of no money illusion. We will now explain why.

10.4.1 Linear Demand Model and Money Illusion Theory

The linear demand model is inconsistent with the no money illusion proposition because it implicitly assumes that "slope" of the demand curve equals a constant value, β_P, and unaffected by income or the price chicken.[2] To understand why, consider the linear model:

$$Q = \beta_{Const} + \beta_P P + \beta_I I + \beta_{CP} ChickP$$

and recall that when we draw a demand curve income and the price of chicken remain constant. Consequently for a demand curve:

$$Q = Q_{Intercept} + \beta_P P$$

where

$$Q_{Intercept} = \beta_{Const} + \beta_I I + \beta_{CP} ChickP$$

---

2. Again, recall that quantity is plotted on the horizontal and price is plotted on the vertical axis, the slope of the demand curve is actually the reciprocal of β_P, $1/\beta_P$. That is why we place the word "slope" within quotes. This does not affect the validity of our argument, however. The important point is that the linear model implicitly assumes that the "slope" of the demand curve is constant, unaffected by changes in other factors relevant to demand.

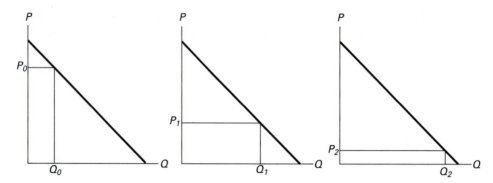

Figure 10.7
Demand curve for beef

This is just an equation for a straight line; β_P equals the "slope" of the demand curve.

Now consider three different beef prices and the quantity of beef demanded at each of the prices while income and chicken prices remain constant:

	Income and the price of chicken constant		
Price of beef	P_0	P_1	P_2
	↓	↓	↓
Quantity of beef demanded	Q_0	Q_1	Q_2

When the price of beef is P_0, Q_0 units of beef are demanded; when the price of beef is P_1, Q_1 units of beef are demanded; and when the price of beef is P_2, Q_2 units of beef are demanded (figure 10.7).

Now, suppose that income and the price of chicken doubles. When there is no money illusion:

- Q_0 units of beef would still be demanded if the price of beef rises from P_0 to $2P_0$.
- Q_1 units of beef would still be demanded if the price of beef rises from P_1 to $2P_1$.
- Q_2 units of beef would still be demanded if the price of beef rises from P_2 to $2P_2$.

	After income and the price of chicken double		
Price of beef	$2P_0$	$2P_1$	$2P_2$
	↓	↓	↓
Quantity of beef demanded	Q_0	Q_1	Q_2

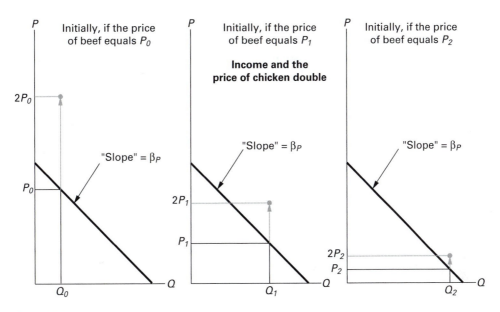

Figure 10.8
Demand curve for beef and no money illusion

Figure 10.8 illustrates this.

We can now sketch in the new demand curve that emerges when income and the price of chicken double. Just connect the points $(Q_0, 2P_0)$, $(Q_1, 2P_1)$, and $(Q_2, 2P_2)$. As figure 10.9 illustrates, the slope of the demand curve has changed.

But now recall that the linear demand model implicitly assumes that "slope" of the demand curve equals a constant value, β_P, and unaffected by income or the price chicken. Consequently a linear demand model is intrinsically inconsistent with the existence of no money illusion. We cannot use a model that is inconsistent with the theory to assess the theory. So, we must find a different model.

10.4.2 Constant Elasticity Demand Model and Money Illusion Theory

To test the theory of no money illusion, we need a model of demand that can be consistent with it. The constant elasticity demand model is such a model:

$$Q = \beta_{Const} P^{\beta_P} I^{\beta_I} ChickP^{\beta_{CP}}$$

The three exponents equal the elasticities. The beef price exponent equals the own price elasticity of demand, the income exponent equals the income elasticity of demand, and the exponent of the price of chicken equals the cross price elasticity of demand:

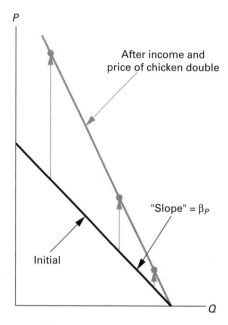

Figure 10.9
Two demand curves for beef—Before and after income and the price of chicken doubling

β_P = (Own) price elasticity of demand

   = Percent change in the quantity of beef demanded resulting from a 1 percent change in the price of beef (the good's own price)

$$= \frac{dQ}{dP} \frac{P}{Q}$$

β_I = Income elasticity of demand

   = Percent change in the quantity of beef demanded resulting from a 1 percent change in income

$$= \frac{dQ}{dI} \frac{I}{Q}$$

β_{CP} = Cross price elasticity of demand

   = Percent change in the quantity of beef demanded resulting from a 1 percent change in the price of chicken

$$= \frac{dQ}{dChickP} \frac{ChickP}{Q}$$

A little algebra allows us to show that the constant elasticity demand model is consistent with the money illusion theory whenever the exponents sum to 0. Let $\beta_P + \beta_I + \beta_{CP} = 0$ and solve for β_{CP}:

$$\beta_P + \beta_I + \beta_{CP} = 0$$
$$\downarrow$$
$$\beta_{CP} = -\beta_P - \beta_I$$

Now apply this result to the constant elasticity model:

$$Q = \beta_{Const}P^{\beta_P}I^{\beta_I}ChickP^{\beta_{CP}}$$

Substituting for β_{CP}

$$\beta_{Const}P^{\beta_P}I^{\beta_I}ChickP^{(-\beta_P-\beta_I)}$$

Splitting the exponent

$$\beta_{Const}P^{\beta_P}I^{\beta_I}ChickP^{-\beta_P}ChickP^{-\beta_I}$$

Moving negative exponents to denominator

$$= \beta_{Const}\left(\frac{P^{\beta_P}}{ChickP^{\beta_P}}\right)\left(\frac{I^{\beta_I}}{ChickP^{\beta_I}}\right)$$

Simplifying

$$= \beta_{Const}\left(\frac{P}{ChickP}\right)^{\beta_P}\left(\frac{I}{ChickP}\right)^{\beta_I}$$

What happens to the two fractions whenever the price of beef (the good's own price), income, and the price of chicken change by the same proportion? Both the numerators and denominators increase by the same proportion; hence the fractions remain the same. Therefore the quantity of beef demanded remains the same. This model of demand is consistent with our theory whenever the exponents sum to 0.

Let us begin the hypothesis testing process. We have already completed step 0.

Step 0: Formulate a model reflecting the theory to be tested.

$$Q = \beta_{Const}P^{\beta_P}I^{\beta_I}ChickP^{\beta_{CP}}$$

No money illusion theory: The elasticities sum to 0: $\beta_P + \beta_I + \beta_{CP} = 0$.

Step 1: Collect data, run the regression, and interpret the estimates.

Natural logarithms convert the original equation for the constant elasticity demand model into its "linear" form:

$$\log(Q_t) = \log(\beta_{Const}) + \beta_P\log(P_t) + \beta_I\log(I_t) + \beta_{CP}\log(ChickP_t) + e_t$$

Table 10.4
Beef demand regression results—Constant elasticity model

	Ordinary least squares (OLS)			
Dependent variable: $LogQ$				
Explanatory variable(s):	Estimate	SE	t-Statistic	Prob
$LogP$	−0.411812	0.093532	−4.402905	0.0003
$LogI$	0.508061	0.266583	1.905829	0.0711
$LogChickP$	0.124724	0.071415	1.746465	0.0961
$Const$	9.499258	2.348619	4.044615	0.0006
Number of observations	24			
Estimated equation: $EstLogQ = 9.50 − 0.41LogP + 0.51LogI + 0.12LogChick$				

To apply the ordinary least squares (OLS) estimation procedure we must first generate the logarithms:

$$\log(Q_t) = \log(\beta_{Const}) + \beta_P\log(P_t) + \beta_I\log(I_t) + \beta_{CP}\log(ChickP_t) + e_t$$
$$\downarrow \qquad \downarrow \qquad \downarrow \qquad \downarrow \qquad \downarrow \qquad \downarrow$$
$$LogQ_t = \log(\beta_{Const}) + \beta_P LogP_t + \beta_I LogI_t + \beta_{CP} LogChickP_t + e_t$$

where

$LogQ_t = \log(Q_t)$
$LogP_t = \log(P_t)$
$LogI_t = \log(I_t)$
$LogChickP_t = \log(ChickP_t)$

Next we run a regression with the log of the quantity of beef demanded as the dependent variable; the log of the price of beef (the good's own price), log of income, and the log of the price of the price of chicken are the explanatory variables (table 10.4).

[To access this online material, go to http://mitpress.mit.edu/westhoffeconometrics and select Beef Demand.]

Interpreting the Estimates

b_P = Estimate for the (own) price elasticity of demand = −0.41

We estimate that a 1 percent increase in the price of beef (the good's own price) decreases the quantity of beef demanded by 0.41 percent when income and the price of chicken remain constant.

b_I = Estimate for the income elasticity of demand = 0.51

We estimate that a 1 percent increase in income increases the quantity of beef demanded by 0.51 percent when the price of beef and the price of chicken remain constant.

b_{CP} = Estimate for the cross price elasticity of demand = 0.12

We estimate that a 1 percent increase in the price of chicken increases the quantity of beef demanded by 0.12 percent when the price of beef and income remain constant.

What happens when the price of beef (the good's own price), income, and the price of chicken increase by 1 percent simultaneously? The total estimated percent change in the quantity of beef demanded equals sum of the individual changes. That is, the total estimated percent change in the quantity of beef demanded equals the estimated percent change in the quantity demanded resulting from

• a 1 percent change in the price of beef (the good's own price)

plus

• a 1 percent change in income

plus

• a 1 percent change in the price of chicken.

The estimated percent change in the quantity demanded equals the sum of the elasticity estimates. We can express this succinctly:

$$
\begin{array}{rcccccc}
 & & \text{Price of beef} & & \text{Income} & & \text{Price of chicken} \\
\text{Estimated} & & \downarrow & & \downarrow & & \downarrow \\
\text{percent change} = & & b_P & + & b_I & + & b_{CP} \\
\text{in } Q \quad = & & -0.41 & + & 0.51 & + & 0.12 \\
 = & & 0.22 & & & &
\end{array}
$$

(above: "1 Percent increase in" with arrows pointing to Price of beef, Income, Price of chicken)

A 1 percent increase in all prices and income results in a 0.22 percent increase in quantity of beef demanded, suggesting that money illusion is present. As far as the no money illusion theory is concerned, the sign of the elasticity estimate sum is not critical. The fact that the estimated sum is +0.22 is not crucial; a sum of −0.22 would be just as damning. What is critical is that the sum does not equal 0 as claimed by the money illusion theory.

Critical result: The sum of the elasticity estimates equals 0.22. The sum does not equal 0; the sum is 0.22 from 0. This evidence suggests that money illusion is present and the no money illusion theory is incorrect.

Since the critical result is that the sum lies 0.22 from 0, a two-tailed test, rather than a one-tailed test is appropriate.

Step 2: Play the cynic and challenge the results; construct the null and alternative hypotheses.

Cynic's view: Sure, the elasticity estimates do not sum to 0 suggesting that money illusion exists, but this is just "the luck of the draw." In fact money illusion is not present; the sum of the actual elasticities equals 0.

The cynic claims that the 0.22 elasticity estimate sum results simply from random influences. A more formal way of expressing the cynic's view is to say that the 0.22 estimate for the elasticity sum is not statistically different from 0. An estimate is not statistically different from 0 whenever the nonzero results from random influences.

Let us now construct the null and alternative hypotheses:

H_0: $\beta_P + \beta_I + \beta_{CP} = 0$ Cynic's is correct: Money illusion not present

H_1: $\beta_P + \beta_I + \beta_{CP} \neq 0$ Cynic's is incorrect: Money illusion present

The null hypothesis, like the cynic, challenges the evidence. The alternative hypothesis is consistent with the evidence. Can we dismiss the cynic's view as nonsense?

Econometrics Lab 10.1: Could the Cynic Be Correct?

[To access this online material, go to http://mitpress.mit.edu/westhoffeconometrics and select Lab 10.1.]

We will use a simulation to show that the cynic could indeed be correct. In this simulation, Coef1, Coef2, and Coef3 denote the coefficients for the three explanatory variables. By default, the actual values of the coefficients are $-0.5, 0.4$, and 0.1. The actual values sum to 0 (figure 10.10).

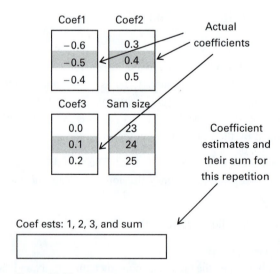

Figure 10.10
Sum of the elasticity estimates and random influences

Be certain that the Pause checkbox is checked. Click **Start**. The coefficient estimates for each of the three coefficients and their sum are reported:

• The coefficient estimates do not equal their actual values.

• The sum of the coefficient estimates does not equal 0 even though the sum of the actual coefficient values equals 0.

Click **Continue** a few more times. As a consequence of random influences we could never expect the estimate for an individual coefficient to equal its actual value. Therefore we could never expect a sum of coefficient estimates to equal the sum of their actual values. Even if the actual elasticities sum to 0, we could never expect the sum of their estimates to equal precisely 0. Consequently we cannot dismiss the cynic's view as nonsense.

Step 3:   Formulate the question to assess the cynic's view and the null hypothesis.

• **Generic question:**   What is the probability that the results would be like those we actually obtained (or even stronger), if the cynic is correct and money illusion was not present?

• **Specific question:**   The sum of the coefficient estimates is 0.22 from 0. What is the probability that the sum of the coefficient estimates in one regression would be 0.22 or more from 0, if H_0 were true (if the sum of the actual elasticities equaled 0)?

Answer: Prob[Results IF H_0 true]

Prob[Results IF H_0 true] small	Prob[Results IF H_0 true] large
↓	↓
Unlikely that H_0 is true	Likely that H_0 is true
↓	↓
Reject H_0	Do not reject H_0
↓	↓
Estimate sum is statistically different from 0	Estimate sum is not statistically different from 0

Step 4:   Use the general properties of the estimation procedure, the probability distribution of the estimate, to calculate Prob[Results IF H_0 true].

How can we calculate this probability? We will explore three approaches that can be used:

• Clever algebraic manipulation

• Wald (*F*-distribution) test

• Letting statistical software do the work

10.4.3   Calculating Prob[Results IF H$_0$ true]: Clever Algebraic Manipulation

We begin with the clever algebraic manipulation approach. This approach exploits the tails probability reported in the regression printout. Recall that the tails probability is based on the premise that the actual value of the coefficient equals 0. Our strategy takes advantage of this:

· First, cleverly define a new coefficient that equals 0 when the null hypothesis is true.

· Second, reformulate the model to incorporate the new coefficient.

· Third, use the ordinary least squares (OLS) estimation procedure to estimate the parameters of the new model.

· Last, focus on the estimate of the new coefficient. Use the new coefficient estimate's tails probability to calculate Prob[Results IF H$_0$ true].

Step 0:   Formulate a model reflecting the theory to be tested.

Begin with the null and alternative hypotheses:

H$_0$: $\beta_P + \beta_I + \beta_{CP} = 0$ Cynic is correct: Money illusion not present

H$_1$: $\beta_P + \beta_I + \beta_{CP} \neq 0$ Cynic is incorrect: Money illusion present

Now cleverly define a new coefficient so that the null hypothesis is true when the new coefficient equals 0:

$$\beta_{Clever} = \beta_P + \beta_I + \beta_{CP}$$

Clearly, β_{Clever} equals 0 if and only if the elasticities sum to 0 and no money illusion exists; that is, β_{Clever} equals 0 if and only if the null hypothesis is true.

Now we will use algebra to reformulate the constant elasticity of demand model to incorporate β_{Clever}:

$$\log(Q_t) = \log(\beta_{Const}) + \beta_P \log(P_t) + \beta_I \log(I_t) + \beta_{CP} \log(ChickP_t) + e_t$$

$$\beta_{Clever} = \beta_P + \beta_I + \beta_{CP}$$

Solving for β_{CP}

$$= \beta_{Clever} - \beta_P - \beta_I$$

Substitute for β_{CP}:

$$= \log(\beta_{Const}) + \beta_P \log(P_t) + \beta_I \log(I_t) + (\beta_{Clever} - \beta_P - \beta_I)\log(ChickP_t) + e_t$$

Multiply $\log(ChickP_t)$ term:

$$= \log(\beta_{Const}) + \beta_P \log(P_t) + \beta_I \log(I_t)$$

$$+ \beta_{Clever} \log(ChickP_t) - \beta_P \log(ChickP_t) - \beta_I \log(ChickP_t) + e_t$$

Rearrange terms:

$$= \log(\beta_{Const}) + \beta_P \log(P_t) - \beta_P \log(ChickP_t)$$

$$+ \beta_I \log(I_t) - \beta_I \log(ChickP_t) + \beta_{Clever} \log(ChickP_t) + e_t$$

Factor the β_P and β_I terms:

$$= \log(\beta_{Const}) + \beta_P[\log(P_t) - \log(ChickP_t)]$$

$$+ \beta_I[\log(I_t) - \log(ChickP_t)] + \beta_{Clever} \log(ChickP_t) + e_t$$

Define new variables:

$$LogQ_t = \log(\beta_{Const}) + \beta_P LogPLessLogChickP_t$$

$$+ \beta_I logILessLogChickP_t + \beta_{Clever} LogChickP_t + e_t$$

where

$LogQ_t = \log(Q_t)$

$LogPLessLogChickP_t = \log(P_t) - \log(ChickP_t)$

$LogILessLogChickP_t = \log(I_t) - \log(ChickP_t)$

$LogChickP_t = \log(ChickP_t)$

Step 1:   Collect data, run the regression, and interpret the estimates.

[To access this online material, go to http://mitpress.mit.edu/westhoffeconometrics and select Beef Demand.]

Now, use the ordinary least squares (OLS) estimation procedure to estimate the parameters of this model (table 10.5).

It is important to note that the estimates of the reformulated model are consistent with the estimates of the original model (table 10.4):

· The estimate of the price coefficient is the same in both cases, −0.41.

· The estimate of the income coefficient is the same in both cases, 0.51.

· In the reformulated model, the estimate of β_{Clever} equals 0.22, which equals the sum of the elasticity estimates in the original model.

Step 2:   Play the cynic and challenge the results; reconstruct the null and alternative hypotheses.

Cynic's view: Sure, b_{Clever}, the estimate for the sum of the actual elasticities, does not equal 0, suggesting that money illusion exists, but this is just "the luck of the draw." In fact money illusion is not present; the sum of the actual elasticities equals 0.

Table 10.5
Beef demand regression results—Constant elasticity model

Ordinary least squares (OLS)				
Dependent variable: $LogQ$				
Explanatory variable(s):	Estimate	SE	t-Statistic	Prob
$LogPLessLogChickP$	−0.411812	0.093532	−4.402905	0.0003
$LogILessLogChickP$	0.508061	0.266583	1.905829	0.0711
$LogChickP$	0.220974	0.275863	0.801027	0.4325
$Const$	9.499258	2.348619	4.044615	0.0006
Number of observations	24			

Estimated equation: $EstLogQ = 9.50 - 0.41 LogPLessLogChickP + 0.51 LogILessLogChickP + 0.22 LogChick$

Critical result: b_{Clever}, the estimate for the sum of the actual elasticities, equals 0.22. The estimate does not equal 0; the estimate is 0.22 from 0. This evidence suggests that money illusion is present and the no money illusion theory is incorrect.

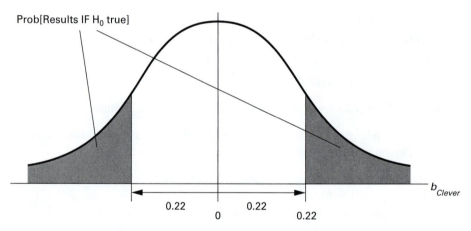

Figure 10.11
Probability distribution of the clever coefficient estimate

We now reformulate the null and alternative hypotheses in terms of β_{Clever}:

H_0: $\beta_P + \beta_I + \beta_{CP} = 0$ $\Rightarrow$ $\beta_{Clever} = 0$ Cynic is correct: Money illusion not present
H_1: $\beta_P + \beta_I + \beta_{CP} \neq 0$ $\Rightarrow$ $\beta_{Clever} \neq 0$ Cynic is incorrect: Money illusion present

We have already shown that we cannot dismiss the cynic's view as nonsense. As a consequence of random influences we could never expect the estimate for β_{Clever} to equal precisely 0, even if the actual elasticities sum to 0.

Step 3: Formulate the question to assess the cynic's view and the null hypothesis (figure 10.11).

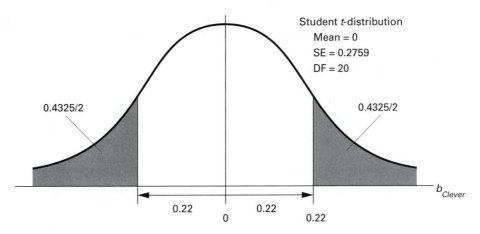

Figure 10.12
Calculating Prob[Results IF H$_0$ true]

· **Generic question:**   What is the probability that the results would be like those we obtained (or even stronger), if the cynic is correct and no money illusion was present?

· **Specific question:**   What is the probability that the coefficient estimate in one regression, b_{Clever}, would be at least 0.22 from 0, if H$_0$ were true (if the actual coefficient, β_{Clever}, equals 0)?

Answer: Prob[Results IF H$_0$ true]

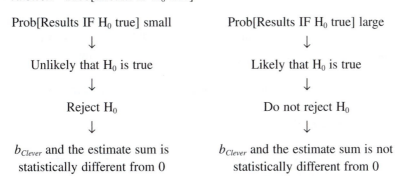

Prob[Results IF H$_0$ true] small	Prob[Results IF H$_0$ true] large
↓	↓
Unlikely that H$_0$ is true	Likely that H$_0$ is true
↓	↓
Reject H$_0$	Do not reject H$_0$
↓	↓
b_{Clever} and the estimate sum is statistically different from 0	b_{Clever} and the estimate sum is not statistically different from 0

Step 4:   Use the general properties of the estimation procedure, the probability distribution of the estimate, to calculate Prob[Results IF H$_0$ true] (figure 10.12).

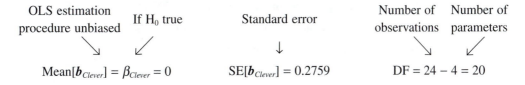

OLS estimation procedure unbiased	If H$_0$ true	Standard error	Number of observations	Number of parameters

$$\text{Mean}[b_{Clever}] = \beta_{Clever} = 0 \qquad \text{SE}[b_{Clever}] = 0.2759 \qquad \text{DF} = 24 - 4 = 20$$

The software automatically computes the tails probability based on the premise that the actual value of the coefficient equals 0. This is precisely what we need, is it not? The regression printout reports that the tails probability equals 0.4325. Consequently

Prob[Results IF H_0 true] = 0.4325.

Step 5: Decide on the standard of proof, a significance level.

The significance level is the dividing line between the probability being small and the probability being large.

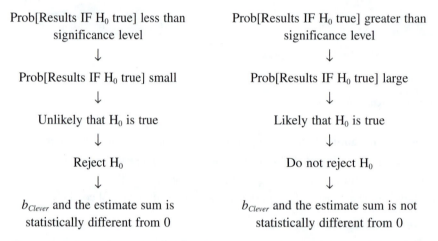

Prob[Results IF H_0 true] less than significance level	Prob[Results IF H_0 true] greater than significance level
↓	↓
Prob[Results IF H_0 true] small	Prob[Results IF H_0 true] large
↓	↓
Unlikely that H_0 is true	Likely that H_0 is true
↓	↓
Reject H_0	Do not reject H_0
↓	↓
b_{Clever} and the estimate sum is statistically different from 0	b_{Clever} and the estimate sum is not statistically different from 0

The probability exceeds the traditional significance levels of 1, 5, and 10 percent. Based on the traditional significance levels, we would not reject the null hypothesis. We would conclude that β_{Clever} and the estimate sum is not statistically different from 0, thereby supporting the no money illusion theory.

In the next chapter we will explore two other ways to calculate Prob[Results IF H_0 true].

Chapter 10 Review Questions

1. How does multiple regression analysis differ from simple regression analysis?

2. Consider the following linear demand model:

$$Q_t = \beta_{Const} + \beta_P P_t + \beta_I I_t + \beta_{CP} ChickP_t + e_t$$

    a. What is the interpretation of the own price coefficient estimate, b_P?

    b. What is the interpretation of the income coefficient estimate, b_I?

    c. What is the interpretation of the chicken price coefficient estimate, b_{CP}?

3. Is the linear demand model consistent with the no money illusion theory?

4. Consider the following constant elasticity demand model:

$$Q = \beta_{Const}\, P^{\beta_P} I^{\beta_I} ChickP^{\beta_{CP}}$$

    a. What is the interpretation of the own price exponent estimate, b_P?

    b. What is the interpretation of the income exponent estimate, b_I?

    c. What is the interpretation of the chicken price exponent estimate, b_{CP}?

5. Is the constant elasticity demand model consistent with the no money illusion theory?

Chapter 10 Exercises

Agricultural production data: Cross-sectional agricultural data for 140 nations in 2000 that cultivated more than 10,000 square kilometers of land.

$Labor_t$	Number of agricultural workers in country t (persons)
$Land_t$	Land under cultivation in country t (sq km)
$Machinery_t$	Number of agricultural machines in country t (tractors)
$ValueAdded_t$	Agricultural valued added in country t (2000 US dollars)

1. Focus on the following linear model for value added:

Model: $ValueAdded_t = \beta_{Const} + \beta_{Labor}Labor_t + \beta_{Land}Land_t + \beta_{Machinery}Machinery_t + e_t$

    a. What is your theory regarding how the quantity of labor, land, and machinery affects agricultural value added?

    b. What does your theory imply about the signs of the model's coefficients?

    c. What are the appropriate hypotheses?

    d. Use the ordinary least squares (OLS) estimation procedure to estimate the coefficients. Interpret the coefficient estimates.

 [To access this online material, go to http://mitpress.mit.edu/westhoffeconometrics and select Agricultural Production.]

    e. What can you conclude about your theory?

2. Instead of focusing on a linear value-added model, consider the constant elasticity model for value added:

Model: $ValueAdded = \beta_{Const} Labor^{\beta_{Labor}} Land^{\beta_{Land}} Machinery^{\beta_{Machinery}}$

Definition: The value-added function exhibits constant returns to scale if and only if increasing each input by the same factor will increase *ValueAdded* by that same factor.

For example, suppose that the value-added function exhibits constant returns to scale. If twice as much labor, land, and machinery are used, then value added will double also.

a. Begin with the equation for the constant elasticity model for value added.

$$ValueAdded = \beta_{Const}Labor^{\beta_{Labor}}Land^{\beta_{Land}}Machinery^{\beta_{Machinery}}$$

Then double labor, land, and machinery; that is, in the equation replace

- *Labor* with 2*Labor*
- *Land* with 2*Land*
- *Machinery* with 2*Machinery*

Derive the expression for *NewValueAdded* in terms of *ValueAdded*:
NewValueAdded = _____

b. If the value-added function exhibits constant returns to scale, how must the new expression for value added, *NewValueAdded* , be related to the original expression for value added, *ValueAdded*?

c. If the value-added function exhibits constant returns to scale, what must the sum of the exponents, $\beta_{Labor} + \beta_{Land} + \beta_{Machinery}$, equal?

3. Consider the constant elasticity model for value added

Model: $ValueAdded = \beta_{Const}Labor^{\beta_{Labor}}Land^{\beta_{Land}}Machinery^{\beta_{Machinery}}$

and the following theory:

Theory: The value added function exhibits constant returns to scale.

a. Take natural logarithms to derive the log form of the constant elasticity model for value added.

b. Estimate the parameters of the model.

[To access this online material, go to http://mitpress.mit.edu/westhoffeconometrics and select Agricultural Production.]

c. Formulate the null and alternative hypotheses.

4. Assess the constant returns to scale theory.

a. Focus on the following "clever" coefficient definitions:

   i. $\beta_{Clever} = \beta_{Labor} + \beta_{Land} + \beta_{Machinery}$

   ii. $\beta_{Clever} = \beta_{Labor} + \beta_{Land} + \beta_{Machinery} - 1$

   iii. $\beta_{Clever} = \beta_{Labor} + \beta_{Land} + \beta_{Machinery} + 1$

Which of these is an appropriate "clever" definition to assess the constant returns to scale theory?

b. Incorporate the "clever" coefficient into the log form of the constant elasticity model for value added.

c. Estimate the parameters of the equation that incorporates the new coefficient.

[To access this online material, go to http://mitpress.mit.edu/westhoffeconometrics and select Agricultural Production.]

d. Express the constant returns to scale hypotheses in terms of the "clever" coefficient definition.

e. Is a one-tail or a two-tail test appropriate to assess the constant returns to scale theory? Use your estimate of the clever coefficient to assess the theory.

Cigarette consumption data: Cross section of per capita cigarette consumption and prices in fiscal year 2008 for the 50 states and the District of Columbia.

$CigConsPC_t$	Cigarette consumption per capita in state t (packs)
$IncPC_t$	Income per capita in state t (1,000's of dollars)
$PriceConsumer_t$	Price of cigarettes in state t paid by consumers (dollars per pack)
$SmokeRateYouth_t$	Percent of youths who smoke in state t

5. Revisit the cigarette consumption data.

a. What is your theory regarding how:

i. The price of cigarettes affects per capita cigarette consumption?

ii. Per capita income affects per capita cigarette consumption?

b. Based on your theory, construct a linear regression model. What equation depicts your model?

c. What does your theory imply about the sign of the coefficients?

d. What are the appropriate hypotheses?

e. Use the ordinary least squares (OLS) estimation procedure to estimate the coefficients. Interpret the coefficient estimates.

[To access this online material, go to http://mitpress.mit.edu/westhoffeconometrics and select Cigarette Consumption.]

f. Is a one-tail or a two-tail test appropriate to assess your theories? Explain. What can you conclude about your theories?

6. Again, revisit the cigarette consumption data.

a. Instead of a linear model, consider a constant elasticity model to capture the impact that the price of cigarettes and income per capita have on cigarette consumption. What equation depicts your model?

b. What does your theory imply about the sign of the coefficients?

c. What are the appropriate hypotheses?

d. Use the ordinary least squares (OLS) estimation procedure to estimate the coefficients. Interpret the coefficient estimates.

 [To access this online material, go to http://mitpress.mit.edu/westhoffeconometrics and select Cigarette Consumption.]

e. Is a one-tail or a two-tail test appropriate to assess your theories? Explain. What can you conclude about your theories?

7. Again, revisit the cigarette consumption data.

a. What is your theory regarding how

i. The price of cigarettes affects the youth smoking rate?

ii. Per capita income affects the youth smoking rate?

b. Based on your theory, construct a linear regression model. What equation depicts your model?

c. What does your theory imply about the signs of the model's coefficients?

d. What are the appropriate hypotheses?

e. Use the ordinary least squares (OLS) estimation procedure to estimate the coefficients. Interpret the coefficient estimates.

 [To access this online material, go to http://mitpress.mit.edu/westhoffeconometrics and select Cigarette Consumption.]

f. Is a one-tail or a two-tail test appropriate to assess your theories? Explain. What can you conclude about your theories?

11 Hypothesis Testing and the Wald Test

Chapter 11 Prep Questions

1. Consider the log form of the constant elasticity demand model:

$$\log(Q_t) = \log(\beta_{Const}) + \beta_P \log(P_t) + \beta_I \log(I_t) + \beta_{CP} \log(ChickP_t) + e_t$$

Show that if $\beta_P + \beta_I + \beta_{CP} = 0$, then

$$\log(Q_t) = \log(\beta_{Const}) + \beta_P[\log(P_t) - \log(ChickP_t)] + \beta_I[\log(I_t) - \log(ChickP_t)] + e_t$$

Hint: Assume that the coefficients sum to 0 and solve for β_{CP} in terms β_P and β_I; then substitute this expression for β_{CP} into the log form of the constant elasticity demand model.

2. Review how the ordinary least squares (OLS) estimation procedure determines the value of the parameter estimates. What criterion does this procedure use to determine the value of the parameter estimates?

3. Recall that the presence of a random variable brings forth both bad news and good news.

   a. What is the bad news?

   b. What is the good news?

4. Focus on our beef consumption data:

Beef consumption data: Monthly time series data of beef consumption, beef prices, income, and chicken prices from 1985 and 1986.

Q_t	Quantity of beef demanded in month t (millions of pounds)
P_t	Price of beef in month t (cents per pound)
I_t	Disposable income in month t (billions of chained 1985 dollars)
$ChickP_t$	Price of chicken in month t (cents per pound)

Consider the log form of the constant elasticity demand model:

Model: $\log(Q_t) = \log(\beta_{Const}) + \beta_P \log(P_t) + \beta_I \log(I_t) + \beta_{CP} \log(ChickP_t) + e_t$

   a. Use the ordinary least squares (OLS) estimation procedure to estimate the parameters of the constant elasticity demand model.

   [To access this online material, go to http://mitpress.mit.edu/westhoffeconometrics and select Beef Demand.]

   i. What does the sum of squared residuals equal?

   ii. What is the ordinary least squares (OLS) estimate for

   - β_P?
   - β_I?
   - β_{CP}?
   - $\log(\beta_{Const})$?

   What criterion do these estimates satisfy?

   b. Now, consider a different restriction. Restrict the value of β_{CP} to 0.

   i. Incorporate this restriction into the constant elasticity demand model. What is the equation describing the restricted model?

   ii. We wish to use the ordinary least squares (OLS) estimation procedure to estimate the remaining parameters.

- What dependent variable should we use?
- What explanatory variables should we use?
- Run the regression.
- What does the sum of squared residuals equal?

iii. Compared to unrestricted regression, part a, has the sum of squared residuals risen or fallen? Explain why.

c. Now restrict the value of β_{CP} to 1.

i. Incorporate this restriction into the constant elasticity demand model. What is the equation describing the restricted model?

ii. We wish to use the ordinary least squares (OLS) estimation procedure to estimate the remaining parameters.

- What dependent variable should we use?
- What explanatory variables should we use?
- Run the regression.
- What does the sum of squared residuals equal?

iii. Compared to unrestricted regression, part a, has the sum of squared residuals risen or fallen? Explain why.

11.1   No Money Illusion Theory: Taking Stock

The money illusion theory contends that whenever all prices and income change by the same proportion the quantity demanded is unaffected. In terms of elasticities, this means that a good's elasticities (own price, income, and cross price) sum to 0. Let us briefly review the steps that we undertook in the last chapter to assess this theory.

Project: Assess the no money illusion theory.

Since the linear demand model is intrinsically inconsistent with the no money illusion theory, we cannot use it to assess the theory. The constant elasticity demand model can be used, however:

Constant elasticity demand model: $Q = \beta_{Const} P^{\beta_P} I^{\beta_I} ChickP^{\beta_{CP}}$

where

β_P = (own) price elasticity of demand

β_I = income elasticity of demand

β_{CP} = cross price elasticity of demand

When the elasticities sum to 0, no money illusion exists:

No money illusion theory: The elasticities sum to 0: $\beta_P + \beta_I + \beta_{CP} = 0$.

Next we converted the constant elasticity demand model into a linear relationship by taking natural logarithms:

$$\log(Q_t) = \log(\beta_{Const}) + \beta_P \log(P_t) + \beta_I \log(I_t) + \beta_{CP} \log(ChickP_t) + e_t$$

We then used the ordinary least squares (OLS) estimation procedure to estimate the elasticities:

[To access this online material, go to http://mitpress.mit.edu/westhoffeconometrics and select Beef Demand.]

If all prices and income increase by 1 percent, the quantity of beef demanded would increase by 0.22 percent. The sum of the elasticity estimates does not equal 0; more specifically, the sum lies 0.22 from 0. The nonzero sum suggests that money illusion exists (table 11.1).

However, as a consequence of random influences, we could never expect the sum of the elasticity estimates to equal exactly precisely 0, even if the sum of the actual elasticities did equal 0. Consequently we followed the hypothesis testing procedure. We played the cynic in order to construct the null and alternative hypotheses. Finally, we needed to calculate the probability that the results would be like those we obtained (or even stronger), if the cynic is correct and null hypothesis is actually true; that is, we needed to calculate Prob[Results IF H_0 true].

Table 11.1
Beef demand regression results—Constant elasticity model

Ordinary least squares (OLS)				
Dependent variable: *LogQ*				
Explanatory variable(s):	Estimate	SE	*t*-Statistic	Prob
LogP	−0.411812	0.093532	−4.402905	0.0003
LogI	0.508061	0.266583	1.905829	0.0711
LogChickP	0.124724	0.071415	1.746465	0.0961
Const	9.499258	2.348619	4.044615	0.0006
Number of observations	24	Degrees of freedom		20

Estimated equation: *EstLogQ* = 9.50 − 0.41*LogP* + 0.51*LogI* + 0.12*LogChick*

Interpretation of estimates:

$b_P = -0.41$: (Own) price elasticity of demand = −0.41

$b_I = 0.51$: Income elasticity of demand = 0.51

$b_{ChickP} = 0.12$: Cross price elasticity of demand = 0.12

Critical result: Sum of the elasticity estimates ($b_P + b_I + b_{CP} = -0.41 + 0.51 + 0.12 = 0.22$) does not equal 0; the estimate is 0.22 from 0. This evidence suggests that money illusion is present and the no money illusion theory is incorrect.

11.2 No Money Illusion Theory: Calculating Prob[Results IF H$_0$ true]

11.2.1 Clever Algebraic Manipulation

In the last chapter we explored one way to calculate this probability, the clever algebraic manipulation approach. First we cleverly defined a new coefficient that equals 0 if and only if the null hypothesis is true:

$$\beta_{Clever} = \beta_P + \beta_I + \beta_{CP}$$

We then reformulated the null and alternative hypotheses in terms of the new coefficient, β_{Clever}:

H$_0$: $\beta_P + \beta_I + \beta_{CP} = 0 \Rightarrow \beta_{Clever} = 0 \Rightarrow$ Money illusion not present

H$_1$: $\beta_P + \beta_I + \beta_{CP} \neq 0 \Rightarrow \beta_{Clever} \neq 0 \Rightarrow$ Money illusion present

After incorporating the new coefficient into the model, we used the ordinary least squares (OLS) estimation procedure to estimate the value of the new coefficient. Since the null hypothesis is now expressed as the new, clever coefficient equaling 0, the new coefficient's tails probability reported in the regression printout is the probability that we need:

Step 4

Prob[Results IF H$_0$ true] = 0.4325

 read tails prob.

We will now explore two other ways to calculate this probability:

- Wald (*F*-distribution) test
- Letting statistical software do the work

11.2.2 Wald (*F*-Distribution) Test

$\overline{x}$
DOF

The Wald test involves two different regressions:

- Restricted regression reflects H$_0$; the restricted regression "enforces" the theory. *restricted model*
- Unrestricted regression reflects H$_1$; the unrestricted regression does not "enforce" the theory.

unrestricted

We will now discuss each regression.

Restricted Regression Reflects H$_0$
The restricted regression enforces the theory; that is, the restricted regression imposes the restriction specified by the null hypothesis. In this case the null hypothesis requires the elasticities sum to equal 0:

$$\beta_P + \beta_I + \beta_{CP} = 0$$ *=> the restriction*

unrestricted   log Q = log P$_{CH}$ ...

We now incorporate this restriction into the constant elasticity demand model:

$$\log(Q_t) = \log(\beta_{Const}) + \beta_P \log(P_t) + \beta_I \log(I_t) + \beta_{CP} \log(ChickP_t) + e_t$$

$\beta_P + \beta_I + \beta_{CP} = 0$. Solving for β_{CP}

 $\beta_{CP} = -(\beta_P + \beta_I)$. Substituting for β_{CP}

$$= \log(\beta_{Const}) + \beta_P \log(P_t) + \beta_I \log(I_t) + (\beta_P + \beta_I)\log(ChickP_t) + e_t$$

Multiplying $\log(ChickP_t)$ term

$$= \log(\beta_{Const}) + \beta_P \log(P_t) + \beta_I \log(I_t) - \beta_P \log(ChickP_t) - \beta_I \log(ChickP_t) + e_t$$

Rearranging terms

$$= \log(\beta_{Const}) + \beta_P \log(P_t) - \beta_P \log(ChickP_t) + \beta_I \log(I_t) - \beta_I \log(ChickP_t) + e_t$$

Factoring the β_P and β_I terms

$$= \log(\beta_{Const}) + \beta_P[\log(P_t) - \log(ChickP_t)] + \beta_I[\log(I_t) - \log(ChickP_t)] + e_t$$

Now define new variables:

$$LogQ_t = \log(\beta_{Const}) + \beta_P LogPLessLogChickP_t + \beta_I logILessLogChickP_t + e_t$$

where

$LogQ_t = \log(Q_t)$
$LogPLessLogChickP_t = \log(P_t) - \log(ChickP_t)$
$LogILessLogChickP_t = \log(I_t) - \log(ChickP_t)$
$LogChickP_t = \log(ChickP_t)$

Next estimate the parameters of the restricted equation (table 11.2).

[To access this online material, go to http://mitpress.mit.edu/westhoffeconometrics and select Beef Demand.]

To compute the cross price elasticity estimate, we must remember that the restricted regression is based on the premise that the sum of the elasticities equals 0. Hence

$$b_P + b_I + b_{CP} = 0$$

and

$$b_{CP} = -(b_P + b_I) = -(-0.47 + 0.30) = 0.17$$

For future reference, note in the restricted regression the sum of squared residuals equals 0.004825 and the degrees of freedom equal 21:

$$SSR_R = 0.004825, \quad DF_R = 24 - 3 = 21$$

Table 11.2
Beef demand regression results—Restricted model

Ordinary least squares (OLS)				
Dependent variable: $LogQ$				
Explanatory variable(s):	Estimate	SE	t-Statistic	Prob
$LogPLessLogChickP$	−0.467358	0.062229	−7.510284	0.0000
$LogILessLogChickP$	0.301906	0.068903	4.381606	0.0003
$Const$	11.36876	0.260482	43.64516	0.0000
Number of observations	24	Degrees of freedom		21
Sum of squared residuals	0.004825			

Estimated equation: $EstLogQ = 11.4 - 0.47LogPLessLogChickP + 0.30LogILessLogChickP$

Interpretation of estimates:

$b_P = -0.47$: (Own) price elasticity of demand $= -0.47$

$b_I = 0.30$: Income elasticity of demand $= 0.30$

Unrestricted Regression Reflects H₁

The unrestricted regression does not force the model to enforce the theory; that is, the unrestricted regression considers the model that reflects the alternative hypothesis allowing the parameter estimates to take on any values. We have already run the unrestricted regression to estimate the coefficients of this model. The log of the quantity of beef demanded is the dependent variable; the logs of the price of beef (the good's own price), income, and the price of chicken are the explanatory variables:

$$\log(Q_t) = \log(\beta_{Const}) + \beta_P \log(P_t) + \beta_I \log(I_t) + \beta_{CP} \log(ChickP_t) + e_t$$

Let us review the regression printout (table 11.3). Record the sum of squared residuals and the degrees of freedom in the unrestricted regression:

$$SSR_U = 0.004675, \quad DF_U = 24 - 4 = 20$$

Comparing the Restricted Sum of Squared Residuals and the Unrestricted Sum of Squared Residuals: The F-Statistic

Next we compare the sum of squared residuals for the restricted and unrestricted regressions:

$$SSR_R = 0.004825, \quad SSR_U = 0.004675$$

The sum of squared residuals from the restricted equation is larger.

Question: Is this a coincidence?

Answer: No. Let us now explain why.

$$F = \frac{(SSR_R - SSR_U)/(DF_R - DF_R)}{SSR_U / DF_U}$$

Table 11.3
Beef demand regression results—Unrestricted model

	Ordinary least squares (OLS)			
Dependent variable: $LogQ$				
Explanatory variable(s):	Estimate	SE	t-Statistic	Prob
$LogP$	−0.411812	0.093532	−4.402905	0.0003
$LogI$	0.508061	0.266583	1.905829	0.0711
$LogChickP$	0.124724	0.071415	1.746465	0.0961
$Const$	9.499258	2.348619	4.044615	0.0006
Number of observations	24	Degrees of freedom		20
Sum of squared residuals	.004675			

Estimated equation: $EstLogQ = 9.50 - 0.41LogP + 0.51LogI + 0.12LogChick$

Table 11.4
Comparison of parameter estimates

	Restricted regression	Unrestricted regression
b_P	−0.47	−0.41
b_I	0.30	0.51
b_{ChickP}	0.17	0.12
b_{Const}	9.50	11.37
SSR	0.004825	0.004675

The parameter estimates of the restricted and unrestricted regressions differ (table 11.4). Recall that the estimates of the constant and coefficients are chosen so as to minimize the sum of squared residuals. In the unrestricted regression no restrictions are placed on the coefficient estimates; when b_P equals −0.41, b_I equals 0.51, and b_{ChickP} equals 0.12, the sum of squared residuals is minimized. The estimates of the unrestricted regression minimize the sum of squared residuals. The estimates of the restricted regression do not equal the estimates of the unrestricted regression. Hence the restricted sum of square residuals is greater than the unrestricted sum. More generally:

• The unrestricted equation places no restrictions on the estimates.

• Enforcing a restriction impedes our ability to make the sum of squared residuals as small as possible.

• A restriction can only increase the sum of squared residuals; a restriction cannot reduce the sum:

$SSR_R \geq SSR_U$

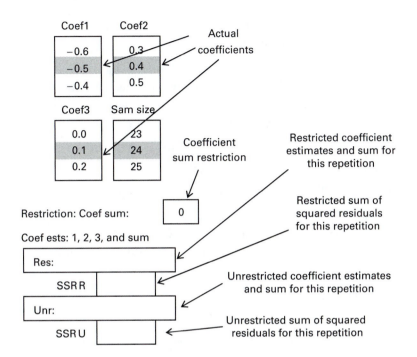

Figure 11.1
Restricted and unrestricted sum of square residuals simulation

Econometrics Lab 11.1: The Restricted and Unrestricted Sums of Squared Residuals

[To access this online material, go to http://mitpress.mit.edu/westhoffeconometrics and select Lab 11.1.]

This simulation emphasizes the point. It mimics the problem at hand by including three explanatory variables whose coefficients are denoted as Coef1, Coef2, and Coef3. By default the actual values of the three coefficients are −0.5, 0.4, and 0.1, respectively. The simulation allows us to specify a restriction on the coefficient sum. By default a coefficient sum of 0 is imposed (figure 11.1).

Be certain the Pause checkbox is checked and click **Start**. The first repetition is now performed. The simulation calculates the parameter estimates for both the restricted and unrestricted equations. The sum of the restricted coefficient estimates equals 0; the sum of the unrestricted coefficient does not equal 0. If our logic is correct the restricted sum will be greater than the unrestricted sum. Check the two sums. Indeed, the restricted sum is greater. Click **Continue** a few times. Each time the restricted sum is always greater than the unrestricted sum confirming our logic.

Now let us consider a question:

Question: Since the imposition of a restriction can only make the sum of squared residuals larger, how much larger should we expect it be?

The answer to this question depends on whether or not the restriction is actually true. On the one hand, if in reality the restriction is not true, we would expect the sum of squared residuals to increase by a large amount. On the other hand, if the restriction is actually true, we would expect the sum of squared residuals to increase only modestly.

Restriction not true	Restriction true
↓	↓

SSR_R much larger than SSR_U SSR_R only a little larger than SSR_U

How do we decide if the restricted sum of squared residuals is much larger or just a little larger than the unrestricted sum? For reasons that we will not delve into, we compare the magnitudes of the restricted and unrestricted sum of squared residuals by calculating what statisticians call the F-statistic:

$$F = \frac{(SSR_R - SSR_U)/(DF_R - DF_U)}{SSR_U / DF_U}$$

On the one hand, when the restricted sum is much larger than the unrestricted sum,

- $SSR_R - SSR_U$ is large

and

- the F-statistic is large.

On the other hand, when the restricted sum is only a little larger than the unrestricted sum,

- $SSR_R - SSR_U$ is small

and

- the F-statistic is small.

Note that since the restricted sum of squared residuals (SSR_R) cannot be less than the unrestricted sum (SSR_U), F-statistic can never be negative (figure 11.2):

$F \geq 0$

Furthermore the F-statistic is a random variable. The claim is based on the fact that:

- Since the parameter estimates for both the restricted and unrestricted equations are random variables both the restricted and unrestricted sums of squared residuals are random variables.
- Since both the restricted and unrestricted sums of squared residuals are random variables, the F-statistic is a random variable.

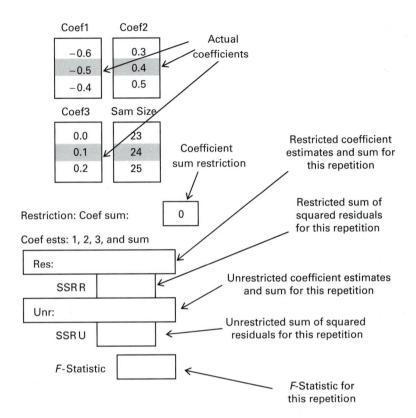

Figure 11.2
Sums of square residuals and the F-statistic simulation

Econometrics Lab 11.2: The F-Statistic Is a Random Variable

[To access this online material, go to http://mitpress.mit.edu/westhoffeconometrics and select Lab 11.2.]

Again, let us use a simulation to illustrate that the F-statistic is a random variable. Be certain the Pause checkbox is checked and click **Start**. Then click **Continue** a few times. We cannot predict the sums of squared residuals or the F-statistic beforehand. Clearly, the sums of squared residuals and the F-statistic are random variables.

Let us now put this all together:

H_0: $\beta_P + \beta_I + \beta_{CP} = 0 \Rightarrow$ Money illusion not present $\Rightarrow$ Restriction true

H_1: $\beta_P + \beta_I + \beta_{CP} \neq 0 \Rightarrow$ Money illusion present $\Rightarrow$ Restriction not true

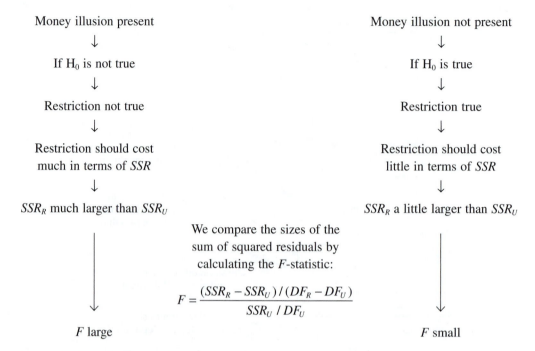

Now calculate the numerical value of our F-statistic:

$$SSR_R = 0.004825 \quad DF_R = 24 - 3 = 21$$
$$SSR_U = 0.\underline{004675} \quad DF_U = 24 - 4 = \underline{20}$$
$$SSR_R - SSR_U = 0.000150 \quad DF_R - DF_U = 1$$

$$F = \frac{(SSR_R - SSR_U)/(DF_R - DF_U)}{SSR_U / DF_U} = \frac{0.000150/1}{0.004675/20} = \frac{0.000150}{0.000234} = 0.64$$

Next consider the views of our cynic.

Cynic's view: Sure, the F-statistic is 0.64, but the F-statistic will always be positive because the restricted sum of squared residuals (SSR_R) will always be greater than the unrestricted sum (SSR_U). An F-statistic of 0.64 results from "the luck of the draw."

We can characterize the cynic's view as follows:

· An F-statistic of 0.64 is small; it is not statistically different from 0.

· The restricted sum of squared errors is larger than the unrestricted sum only as a consequence of the luck of the draw.

· The restriction is true.

· The null hypothesis, H_0, is actually true and money illusion is not present.

Question assess the cynic's view:

· **Generic question:**   What is the probability that the results would be like those we obtained (or even stronger), if the cynic is correct and H_0 is actually true?

· **Specific question:**   What is the probability that the F-statistic from one pair of regressions would be 0.64 or more, if H_0 were true, if the restriction is true and money illusion is not present?

Answer: Prob[Results IF H_0 true]

Prob[Results IF H_0 true] small	Prob[Results IF H_0 true] large
↓	↓
Unlikely that H_0 is true	Likely that H_0 is true
↓	↓
Reject H_0	Do not reject H_0
↓	↓
Reject the no money illusion theory	Do not reject the no money illusion theory

We must calculate Prob[Results IF H_0 true]. Before doing so, however, recall that the F-statistic is a random variable. Recall what we have learned about random variables:

· The bad news is that we cannot predict the value of a random variable beforehand.

· The good news is that in this case we can describe its probability distribution.

The F-distribution describes the probability distribution of the F-statistic. As figure 11.3 shows, the F-distribution looks very different than the normal and Student t-distribution. The normal and Student t-distributions were symmetric bell shaped curves. The F-distribution is neither

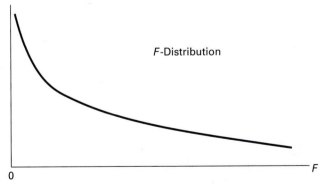

F-Distribution

Figure 11.3
F-Distribution

symmetric nor bell shaped. Since the F-statistic can never be negative, the F-distribution begins at F equals 0. Its precise shape depends on the numerator's and the denominator's degrees of freedom, the degrees of freedom of the restricted and unrestricted regressions.

Econometrics Lab 11.3: The Restricted and Unrestricted Sums of Squared Residuals and the F-Distribution

[To access this online material, go to http://mitpress.mit.edu/westhoffeconometrics and select Lab 11.3.]

Now we will use the simulation to calculate Prob[Results IF H_0 true] (figure 11.4):

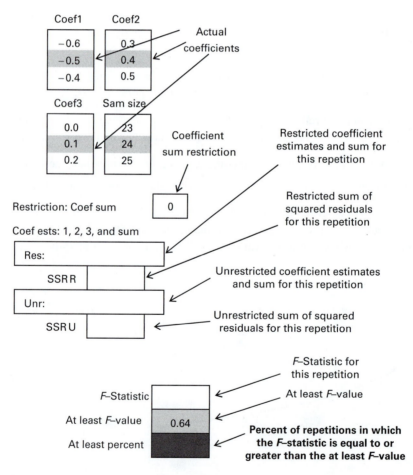

Figure 11.4
F-Distribution simulation

- By default, the actual values of the three coefficients (Coef1, Coef2, and Coef3) are −0.5, 0.4, and 0.1, respectively. The actual values of the coefficients sum to 0. Hence the premise of the null hypothesis is met; that is, H_0 is true.

- Also the At Least F-Value is set at 0.64; this is the value of the F-statistic that we just calculated for the restricted and unrestricted beef demand regressions. Click **Continue** a few more times. Sometimes the F-statistic is less than 0.64; other times it is greater than 0.64. Note the At Least Percent line; the simulation is calculating the percent of repetitions in which the F-statistics is equal to or greater than 0.64.

- Clear the Pause checkbox, click **Start**, and then after many, many repetitions click **Stop**. The F-statistic equals 0.64 or more in about 43 percent of the repetitions.

We can now apply the relative frequency interpretation of probability; in one repetition of the experiment, the probability that the F-statistic would be 0.64 or more when the null hypothesis is true equals 0.43:

Prob[Results IF H_0 true] = 0.43

There is another way to calculate this probability that does not involve a simulation. Just as there are tables that describe the normal and Student t-distributions, there are tables describing the F-distribution. Unfortunately, F-distribution tables are even more cumbersome than Student t-tables. Fortunately, we can use our Econometrics Lab to perform the calculation instead.

Econometrics Lab 11.4: F-Distribution Calculations

We wish to calculate the probability that the F-statistic from one pair of regressions would be 0.64 or more, if H_0 were true (if there is no money illusion, if actual elasticities sum to 0), Prob[Results IF H_0 true] (figure 11.5).

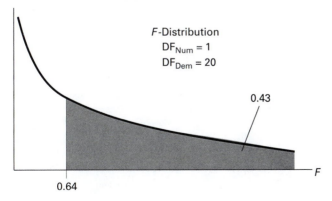

Figure 11.5
Calculating Prob[Results IF H_0 true]—Using a simulation

Access the following link:

[To access this online material, go to http://mitpress.mit.edu/westhoffeconometrics and select Lab 11.4.]

Recall our F-statistic calculation:

$$F = \frac{(SSR_R - SSR_U)/(DF_R - DF_U)}{SSR_U / DF_U} = \frac{0.000150/1}{0.004675/20} = \frac{0.000150}{0.000234} = 0.64$$

The following information has been entered:

Sum of squares numerator = 0.000150

Sum of squares denominator = 0.004675

Degrees of freedom numerator = 1

Degrees of freedom denominator = 20

Click **Calculate**:

Prob[Results IF H_0 true] = 0.43

11.2.3 Calculating Prob[Results IF H_0 true]: Let the Software Do the Work

Many statistical software packages can be used to conduct a Wald test automatically.

[To access this online material, go to http://mitpress.mit.edu/westhoffeconometrics and select Beef Demand.]

First estimate the unrestricted regression (table 11.5). Then choose the Wald test option and impose the appropriate restriction that the coefficients sum to 0.

Table 11.5
Beef demand regression results—Unrestricted model

Ordinary least squares (OLS)				
Dependent variable: $LogQ$				
Explanatory variable(s):	Estimate	SE	t-Statistic	Prob
$LogP$	−0.411812	0.093532	−4.402905	0.0003
$LogI$	0.508061	0.266583	1.905829	0.0711
$LogChickP$	0.124724	0.071415	1.746465	0.0961
$Const$	9.499258	2.348619	4.044615	0.0006
Number of observations	24	Degrees of freedom		20
Sum of squared residuals	0.004675			
Estimated equation: $EstLogQ = 9.50 - 0.41LogP + 0.51LogI + 0.12LogChick$				

Getting Started in EViews

After running the unrestricted regression:

· In the Equation window: Click **View**, **Coefficient Diagnostics**, and **Wald Test—Coefficient Restrictions**.

· In the Wald Test window: Enter the restriction; in this case,

C(1) + C(2) + C(3) = 0

· Click OK.

Prob[Results IF H_0 true]: The F-statistic equals 0.64 (table 11.6). The probability that the F-statistic from one pair of regressions would be 0.64 or more, if H_0 were true (if there is no money illusion, if actual elasticities sum to 0) equals 0.43.

We have now described three ways to calculate Prob[Results IF H_0 true]. Let us compare the results (table 11.7).

While the methods use different approaches, they produce identical conclusions. In fact it can be shown rigorously that the methods are equivalent.

Table 11.6
Beef demand regression results—Wald test of No Money Illusion theory

| | **Wald test** | | | |
| | | Degrees of freedom | | |
	Value	Num	Dem	Prob
F-statistic	0.641644	1	20	0.4325

Table 11.7
Comparison of the methods to calculate Prob[Results IF H_0 true]

Method	Prob[Results IF H_0 true]
t-Test using clever definition	0.43
Wald test using restricted and unrestricted regressions	0.43
Wald test using statistical software	0.43

11.3   Testing the Significance of the "Entire" Model

Next we will consider a set of null and alternative hypotheses that assess the entire model:

H_0: $\beta_P = 0$, $\beta_I = 0$, and $\beta_{CP} = 0$ No explanatory variables has an effect on the dependent variable

H_1: $\beta_P \neq 0$ and/or $\beta_I \neq 0$ and/or $\beta_{CP} \neq 0$ At least one explanatory variable has an effect on (at least one coefficient does not equal 0)   the dependent variable

On the one hand, if the null hypothesis were true, none of the explanatory variables would affect the dependent variable, and consequently the model would be seriously deficient. On the other hand, if the alternative hypothesis were true, at least one of the explanatory variables would be influencing the dependent variable.

We will use the restricted and unrestricted regressions approach to calculate Prob[Results IF H_0 true]. We begin with estimating the restricted and unrestricted regressions.

[To access this online material, go to http://mitpress.mit.edu/westhoffeconometrics and select Beef Demand.]

Restricted equation—reflects H_0: $\beta_P = 0$, $\beta_I = 0$, and $\beta_{CP} = 0$ (table 11.8):

Model: $LogQ_t = \log(\beta_{Const}) + e_t$

Unrestricted equation—reflects H_1: $\beta_P \neq 0$ and/or $\beta_I \neq 0$ and/or $\beta_{CP} \neq 0$:

Model: $LogQ_t = \log(\beta_{Const}) + \beta_P LogP + \beta_I LogI_t + \beta_{CP} LogChickP_t + e_t$

We have estimated the unrestricted regression before (table 11.9).

Table 11.8
Beef demand regression results—No explanatory variables

Ordinary least squares (OLS)				
Dependent variable: *LogQ*				
Explanatory variable(s):	Estimate	SE	*t*-Statistic	Prob
Const	12.30576	0.005752	2139.539	0.0000
Number of observations	24	Degrees of freedom		23
Sum of squared residuals	0.018261			

Table 11.9
Beef demand regression results—Unrestricted model

Ordinary least squares (OLS)				
Dependent variable: $LogQ$				
Explanatory variable(s):	Estimate	SE	t-Statistic	Prob
$LogP$	−0.411812	0.093532	−4.402905	0.0003
$LogI$	0.508061	0.266583	1.905829	0.0711
$LogChickP$	0.124724	0.071415	1.746465	0.0961
$Const$	9.499258	2.348619	4.044615	0.0006
Number of observations	24	Degrees of freedom		20
Sum of squared residuals	0.004675			
Estimated equation: $EstLogQ = 9.50 - 0.41LogP + 0.51LogI + 0.12LogChick$				

Next we compute the F-statistic and calculate Prob[Results IF H_0 true]:

$$SSR_R = 0.018261 \qquad\qquad DF_R = 24 - 1 = 23$$
$$SSR_U = 0.\underline{004675} \qquad\qquad DF_U = 24 - 4 = \underline{20}$$
$$SSR_R - SSR_U = 0.013586 \qquad\qquad DF_R - DF_U = 3$$

$$F = \frac{(SSR_R - SSR_U)/(DF_R - DF_U)}{SSR_U / DF_U} = \frac{0.013586/3}{0.004675/20} = \frac{0.004529}{0.000234} = 19.4$$

Prob[Results IF H_0 true]:   What is the probability that the F-statistic from one pair of regressions would be 19.4 or more, if the H_0 were true (i.e., if both prices and income have no effect on quantity of beef demanded, if each of the actual coefficients, β_P, β_I, and β_{CP}, equals 0)?

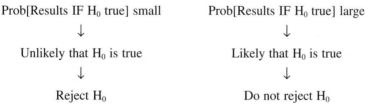

Prob[Results IF H_0 true] small   Prob[Results IF H_0 true] large
↓   ↓
Unlikely that H_0 is true   Likely that H_0 is true
↓   ↓
Reject H_0 Do not reject H_0

Econometrics Lab 11.5: Calculating Prob[Results IF H_0 true]

[To access this online material, go to http://mitpress.mit.edu/westhoffeconometrics and select Lab 11.5.]

Using the Econometrics Lab, we conclude that the probability of obtaining the results like we did if null hypothesis were true is less than 0.0001:

Prob[Results IF H_0 true] < 0.0001

Also we could let a statistical package do the work by using it to run the Wald test.

[To access this online material, go to http://mitpress.mit.edu/westhoffeconometrics and select Beef Demand.]

After running the unrestricted regression, choose the Wald test option and impose the restriction that all the coefficients equal 0.

Getting Started in EViews

After running the unrestricted regression:

· Click **View**, **Coefficient Diagnostics**, and **Wald Test—Coefficient Restrictions**.

· Enter the restriction; in this case,

$$C(1) = C(2) = C(3) = 0$$

· Click **OK**.

Prob[Results IF H_0 true] < 0.0001

Note that even though the Wald test printout reports the probability to be 0.0000 (table 11.10), it is not precisely 0 because the printout reports the probability only to four decimals. To emphasize this fact, we report that Prob[Results IF H_0 true] is less than 0.0001.

In fact most statistical packages automatically report this F-statistic and the probability when we estimate the unrestricted model (table 11.11).

The values appear in the F-statistic and Prob[F-statistic] rows:

F-statistic = 19.4

Prob[Results IF H_0 True] = 0.000004

Using a significance level of 1 percent, we would conclude that Prob[Results IF H_0 true] is small. Consequently we would reject the null hypothesis that none of the explanatory variables included in the model has an effect on the dependent variable.

Table 11.10
Demand regression results—Wald test of entire model

		Wald test		
		Degrees of freedom		
	Value	Num	Dem	Prob
F-statistic	19.37223	3	20	0.0000

Table 11.11
Beef demand regression results—Unrestricted model

Ordinary least squares (OLS)				
Dependent variable: $LogQ$				
Explanatory variable(s):	Estimate	SE	t-Statistic	Prob
$LogP$	−0.411812	0.093532	−4.402905	0.0003
$LogI$	0.508061	0.266583	1.905829	0.0711
$LogChickP$	0.124724	0.071415	1.746465	0.0961
$Const$	9.499258	2.348619	4.044615	0.0006
Number of observations	24	Degrees of freedom		20
Sum of squared residuals	0.004675			
F-Statistic	19.3722	Prob[F-statistic]		0.000004

Estimated equation: $EstLogQ = 9.50 - 0.41LogP + 0.51LogI + 0.12LogChick$

11.4 Equivalence of Two-Tailed t-Tests and Wald Tests (F-tests)

A two-tailed t-test is equivalent to a Wald test. We will use the constant elasticity demand model to illustrate this:

$$\log(Q) = \log(\beta_{Const}) + \beta_P \log(P) + \beta_I \log(I) + \beta_{CP} \log(ChickP)$$

Focus on the coefficient of the price of chicken, β_{CP}. Consider the following two-tailed hypotheses:

H_0: $\beta_{CP} = 0 \Rightarrow$ Price of chicken has no effect on the quantity of beef demanded

H_1: $\beta_{CP} \neq 0 \Rightarrow$ Price of chicken has an effect on the quantity of beef demanded

We will first calculate Prob[Results IF H_0 true] using a two-tailed t-test and then using a Wald test.

11.4.1 Two-Tailed t-Test

We begin by estimating the parameters of the model (table 11.12):

Model: $LogQ_t = c + \beta_P LogP_t + \beta_I LogI_t + \beta_{CP} LogChickP_t + e_t$

[To access this online material, go to http://mitpress.mit.edu/westhoffeconometrics and select Beef Demand.]

Table 11.12
Beef demand regression results—Unrestricted model

Ordinary least squares (OLS)				
Dependent variable: $LogQ$				
Explanatory variable(s):	Estimate	SE	t-Statistic	Prob
$LogP$	−0.411812	0.093532	−4.402905	0.0003
$LogI$	0.508061	0.266583	1.905829	0.0711
$LogChickP$	0.124724	0.071415	1.746465	0.0961
$Const$	9.499258	2.348619	4.044615	0.0006
Number of observations	24	Degrees of freedom		20
Sum of squared residuals	0.004675			

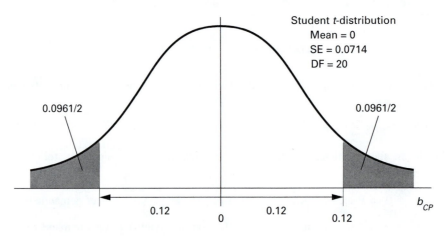

Figure 11.6
Calculating Prob[Results IF H_0 true]—Using a t-test

Next calculate Prob[Results IF H_0 true].

Prob[Results IF H_0 true]:   What is the probability that the coefficient estimate in one regression, b_{CP}, would be at least 0.12 from 0, if H_0 were true (if the actual coefficient, β_{CP}, equals 0)?

OLS estimation   If H_0 Number of   Number of
procedure unbiased   true   Standard error   observations   parameters

↘   ↙   ↓   ↘   ↙

Mean$[b_{CP}] = \beta_{CP} = 0$ SE$[b_{CP}] = 0.0714$ DF $= 24 - 4 = 20$

Since the tails probability is based on the premise that the actual coefficient value equals 0, the tails probability reported in the regression printout is just what we are looking for (figure 11.6):

Prob[Results IF H_0 true] = 0.0961

11.4.2   Wald Test

Next we turn to a Wald test. Let us review the rationale behind the Wald test:

• The null hypothesis enforces the restriction and the alternative hypothesis does not:

H_0: Restriction true H_1: Restriction not true

• We run two regressions: restricted and unrestricted. The restricted regression reflects the null hypothesis and the unrestricted regression the alternative hypothesis:

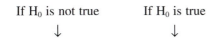

If H_0 is not true   If H_0 is true

↓   ↓

Restriction is not true   Restriction is true

• SSR_R cannot be less than SSR_U: Since the least squares estimation procedure chooses the estimates so as to minimize the sum of squared residuals, any restriction can only increase, not decrease, the sum of squared residuals.

• So the question becomes: By how much does the SSR_R exceed SSR_U? The answer depends on whether or not the null hypothesis is actual true:

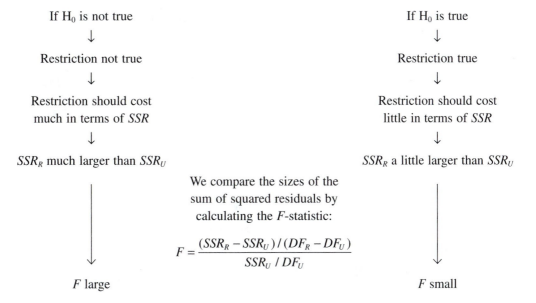

If H_0 is not true   If H_0 is true

↓   ↓

Restriction not true   Restriction true

↓   ↓

Restriction should cost   Restriction should cost
much in terms of SSR little in terms of SSR

↓   ↓

SSR_R much larger than SSR_U SSR_R a little larger than SSR_U

We compare the sizes of the
sum of squared residuals by
calculating the F-statistic:

$$F = \frac{(SSR_R - SSR_U)/(DF_R - DF_U)}{SSR_U/DF_U}$$

F large F small

Now let us apply this to the problem at hand:

Model: $LogQ_t = \log(\beta_{Const}) + \beta_P LogP_t + \beta_I LogI_t + \beta_{CP} LogChickP_t + e_t$

Recall the hypotheses:

H_0: $\beta_{CP} = 0 \Rightarrow$ Price of chicken has no effect on the quantity of beef demanded

H_1: $\beta_{CP} \neq 0 \Rightarrow$ Price of chicken has an effect on the quantity of beef demanded

Next estimate the restricted and unrestricted regressions:

• Restricted regression—reflects the null hypothesis, $\beta_{CP} = 0$. For the restricted regression, we just drop the price of chicken, *PChick*, as an explanatory variable because its coefficient is specified as 0 (table 11.13):

Model: $LogQ = \log(\beta_{Const}) + \beta_P LogP + \beta_I LogI + e_t$

• Unrestricted regression—consistent with the alternative hypothesis, $\beta_{CP} \neq 0$. For the unrestricted regression, we include the price of chicken, *PChick*, as an explanatory variable. This is just the regression we have run many times before (table 11.14):

Model: $LogQ_t = c + \beta_P LogP_t + \beta_I LogI_t + \beta_{CP} LogChickP_t + e_t$

Table 11.13
Beef demand regression results—Restricted model

Ordinary least squares (OLS)				
Dependent variable: *LogQ*				
Explanatory variable(s):	Estimate	SE	*t*-Statistic	Prob
LogP	−0.305725	0.074513	−4.102963	0.0005
LogI	0.869706	0.175895	4.944466	0.0001
Const	6.407302	1.616841	3.962852	0.0007
Number of observations	24	Degrees of freedom		21
Sum of squared residuals	0.005388			

Table 11.14
Beef demand regression results—Unrestricted model

Ordinary least squares (OLS)				
Dependent variable: *LogQ*				
Explanatory variable(s):	Estimate	SE	*t*-Statistic	Prob
LogP	−0.411812	0.093532	−4.402905	0.0003
LogI	0.508061	0.266583	1.905829	0.0711
LogChickP	0.124724	0.071415	1.746465	0.0961
Const	9.499258	2.348619	4.044615	0.0006
Number of observations	24	Degrees of freedom		20
Sum of squared residuals	0.004675			

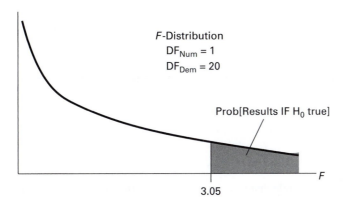

Figure 11.7
Calculating Prob[Results IF H_0 true]—Using an F-test

Using these two regressions, we can now calculate the F-statistic (figure 11.7):

$$SSR_R = 0.005388 \qquad\qquad DF_R = 24 - 3 = 21$$
$$SSR_U = 0.\underline{004675} \qquad\qquad DF_U = 24 - 4 = \underline{20}$$
$$SSR_R - SSR_U = 0.000713 \qquad\qquad DF_R - DF_U = 1$$

$$F = \frac{(SSR_R - SSR_U)/(DF_R - DF_U)}{SSR_U / DF_U} = \frac{0.000713/1}{0.004675/20} = \frac{0.000713}{0.000234} = 3.05$$

Prob[Results IF H_0 true]:   What is the probability that the F-statistic from one pair of regressions would be 3.05 or more, if the H_0 were true (if the actual coefficient, β_{CP}, equals 0; that is, if the price of chicken has no effect on the quantity of beef demanded)?

We can use either the Econometrics Lab to calculate this probability.

Econometrics Lab 11.6: Calculating Prob[Results IF H_0 true]

[To access this online material, go to http://mitpress.mit.edu/westhoffeconometrics and select Lab 11.6.]

Prob[Results IF H_0 true] = 0.0961

Alternatively we could use statistical software to calculate the probability. After running the unrestricted regression, choose the Wald test option and impose the restriction that all the coefficients equal 0.

After running the unrestricted regression:

· Click **View**, **Coefficient Diagnostics**, and **Wald Test—Coefficient Restrictions**.
· Enter the restriction; in this case

C(3) = 0

· Click **OK**.

Using either method, we conclude that based on a Wald test, the Prob[Results IF H_0 true] equals 0.0961(table 11.15).

Now compare Prob[Results IF H_0 true]'s calculated for the two-tailed t-test and the Wald test:

t-Test: Prob[Results IF H_0 true] = 0.0961

Wald test: Prob[Results IF H_0 true] = 0.0961

The probabilities are identical. This is not a coincidence. It can be shown rigorously that a two-tailed t-test is a special case of the Wald test.

11.5   Three Important Distributions

We have introduced three distributions that are used to assess theories: Normal, Student-t, and F (figure 11.8).

· **Theories involving a single variable:** Normal distribution and Student t-distribution. The normal distribution is used whenever we know the standard deviation of the distribution; the normal distribution is described by its mean and standard deviation.

Often we do not know the standard deviation of the distribution, however. In these cases we turn to the Student t-distribution; it is described by its mean, estimated standard deviation (standard error), and the degrees of freedom. The Student t-distribution is more "spread out" than the

Table 11.15
Beef demand regression results—Wald test of *LogChickP* coefficient

		Wald test		
			Degrees of freedom	
	Value	Num	Dem	Prob
F-Statistic	3.050139	1	20	0.0961

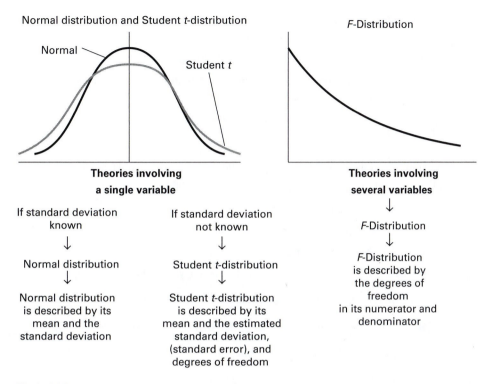

Figure 11.8
Normal distribution, Student t-distribution, and F-distribution

normal distribution because an additional element of uncertainty is added when the standard deviation is not known and must be estimated.

· **Theories involving several variables:** F-Distribution. The F-distribution can be used to assess relationships among two or more estimates. We compute the F-statistic by using the sum of squared residuals and the degrees of freedom in the restricted and unrestricted regressions:

$$F = \frac{(SSR_R - SSR_U)/(DF_R - DF_U)}{SSR_U / DF_U}$$

The F-distribution is described by the degrees of freedom in the numerator and denominator, $DF_R - DF_U$ and DF_U.

Chapter 11 Review Questions

1. Consider a Wald test. Can the restricted sum of squared residuals be less than the unrestricted sum of squared residuals? Explain.

2. How is a Wald test F-statistic related to the restricted and unrestricted sum of squared residuals?

3. How is a two-tailed t-test related to the Wald test?

4. What are the three important probability distributions we have introduced? When is it appropriate to use each of them?

Chapter 11 Exercises

Agricultural production data: Cross-sectional agricultural data for 140 nations in 2000 that cultivated more than 10,000 square kilometers of land.

Labor$_t$ Number of agricultural workers in country t (persons)

Land$_t$ Land under cultivation in country t (sq km)

Machinery$_t$ Number of agricultural machines in country t (tractors)

ValueAdded$_t$ Agricultural valued added in country t (2000 US dollars)

1. Focus on the log form of the constant elasticity value added model:

$$\log(ValueAdded_t) = \log(\beta_{Const}) + \beta_{Labor}\log(Labor_t) + \beta_{Land}\log(Land_t)$$

$$+ \beta_{Machinery}\log(Machinery_t) + e_t$$

and consider the constant returns to scale theory.

    a. Express the null and alternative hypotheses for the constant returns to scale theory in terms of β_{Labor}, β_{Land}, and $\beta_{Machinery}$.

    b. Assess the constant returns to scale theory using the "clever" definition approach.

[To access this online material, go to http://mitpress.mit.edu/westhoffeconometrics and select Agricultural Production.]

2. Focus on the log form of the constant elasticity value added model:

$$\log(ValueAdded_t) = \log(\beta_{Const}) + \beta_{Labor}\log(Labor_t) + \beta_{Land}\log(Land_t)$$

$$+ \beta_{Machinery}\log(Machinery_t) + e_t$$

Assess the constant returns to scale theory using the Wald approach.

    a. Consider the unrestricted regression.

        i. Estimate the parameters of the unrestricted regression.

[To access this online material, go to http://mitpress.mit.edu/westhoffeconometrics and select Agricultural Production.]

    ii. What does the unrestricted sum of squared residuals equal?

    iii. What do the unrestricted degrees of freedom equal?

  b. Consider the restricted regression.

    i. If constant returns to scale are present, what condition would β_{Labor}, β_{Land}, and $\beta_{Machinery}$ satisfy?

    ii. Derive the equation that describes the restricted regression.

    iii. Estimate the parameters of the restricted regression.

[To access this online material, go to http://mitpress.mit.edu/westhoffeconometrics and select Agricultural Production.]

    iv. What does the restricted sum of squared residuals equal?

    v. What do the restricted degrees of freedom equal?

  c. Using your answers to the previous parts, compute the F-statistic for the Wald test.

  d. Using the Econometrics Lab, compute Prob[Results IF H_0 true].

[To access this online material, go to http://mitpress.mit.edu/westhoffeconometrics and select F-Distribution.]

3. Assess the constant returns to scale theory using the Wald approach the "easy way" with statistical software.

[To access this online material, go to http://mitpress.mit.edu/westhoffeconometrics and select Agricultural Production.]

4. Compare the Prob[Results IF H_0 true] that has been calculated in three ways: clever algebra, Wald test using the Econometrics Lab, and Wald test using statistical software.

Cigarette consumption data: Cross section of per capita cigarette consumption and prices in fiscal year 2008 for the 50 states and the District of Columbia.

CigConsPC$_t$	Cigarette consumption per capita in state t (packs)
PriceConsumer$_t$	Price of cigarettes in state t paid by consumers (dollars per pack)
PriceSupplier$_t$	Price of cigarettes in state t received by suppliers (dollars per pack)
Tax$_t$	Cigarette tax rate in state t (dollars per pack)

5. Reconsider state cigarette consumption data.

[To access this online material, go to http://mitpress.mit.edu/westhoffeconometrics and select Cigarette Consumption.]

We, as consumers, naturally think of the price of cigarettes as what we must pay to purchase a pack of cigarettes:

$PriceConsumer_t$ = price from the standpoint of the consumer in state t

The seller of cigarettes, however, must pass the cigarette tax on to the government. From the standpoint of the supplier, the price from the supplier's standpoint equals the price from the producer's standpoint less the tax:

$PriceSupplier_t = PriceConsumer_t - Tax_t$

or

$PriceConsumer_t = PriceSupplier_t + Tax_t$

Convince yourself that the values of *PriceConsumer*, *PriceSupplier*, and *Tax* for our cigarette consumption data are actually related in this way.

Consider the following model:

$CigConsPC_t = \beta_{Const} + \beta_{PriceSupplier}PriceSupplier_t + \beta_{Tax}Tax_t + e_t$

This model raises the possibility that consumers of cigarettes react differently to the price received by the supplier and the tax received by the government even though they both affect the price paid by consumers in the same way.

a. Use the ordinary least squares (OLS) estimation procedure to estimate the coefficients of *PriceSupplier_t* and *Tax_t*.

b. Interpret the coefficient estimates.

6. Continue using cigarette consumption data and focus on the following null and alternative hypothesis:

$H_0: \beta_{PriceSupplier} = \beta_{Tax}$

$H_1: \beta_{PriceSupplier} \neq \beta_{Tax}$

[To access this online material, go to http://mitpress.mit.edu/westhoffeconometrics and select Cigarette Consumption.]

a. In words, what does the null hypothesis suggest? What does the alternative hypothesis suggest?

b. Use the cigarette consumption data and a clever algebraic manipulation to calculate Prob[Results IF H_0 true].

7. Continue using the cigarette consumption data in order to use the Wald test to calculate Prob[Results IF H_0 true].

[To access this online material, go to http://mitpress.mit.edu/westhoffeconometrics and select Cigarette Consumption.]

a. Use the ordinary least squares (OLS) estimation procedure to estimate the parameters of the unrestricted regression. What do the unrestricted sum of square residuals and degrees of freedom equal?

b. Derive the equation that describes the restricted regression.

c. Use the ordinary least squares (OLS) estimation procedure to estimate the parameters of the restricted regression. What do the restricted sum of square residuals and degrees of freedom equal?

d. Compute the F-statistic for the Wald test.

e. Using the Econometrics Lab, compute Prob[Results IF H_0 true].

[To access this online material, go to http://mitpress.mit.edu/westhoffeconometrics and select F-Distribution.]

8. Continue using the cigarette consumption data in order to calculate Prob[Results IF H_0 true] the "easy way."

[To access this online material, go to http://mitpress.mit.edu/westhoffeconometrics and select Cigarette Consumption.]

a. Use statistical software to compute Prob[Results IF H_0 true].

b. Compare the Prob[Results IF H_0 true] that has been calculated in three ways: clever algebra, Wald test using the Econometrics Lab, and statistical software.

12 Model Specification and Development

Chapter 12 Prep Questions

1. Consider a multiple regression model. When a particular explanatory variable has no effect on the dependent variable, what does the actual value of its coefficient equal?

2. The 1992 Clinton presidential campaign focused on the economy and made the phrase "It's the economy stupid" famous. Bill Clinton and his political advisors relied on the theory that voters hold the President and his party responsible for the state of the economy. When the economy performs well, the President's party gets credit; when the economy performs poorly, the President's party takes the blame.

"It's the economy stupid" theory: The American electorate is sensitive to economic conditions. Good economic conditions increase the vote for the President's party; bad economic conditions decrease the vote for the President's party.

Consider the following model:

$$VotePresParty_t = \beta_{Const} + \beta_{UnemPriorAvg}UnemPriorAvg_t + e_t$$

where

$VotePresParty_t$ = percent of the popular vote received by the incumbent President's party in year t

$UnemPriorAvg_t$ = average unemployment rate in the three years prior to election, that is, three years prior to year t

a. Assuming that the "It's the economy stupid" theory is correct, would $\beta_{UnemPriorAvg}$ be positive, negative or zero?

b. For the moment assume that when you run the appropriate regression, the sign of the coefficient estimate agrees with your answer to part a. Formulate the null and alternative hypotheses for this model.

3. Again focus on the on the "It's the economy stupid" theory. Consider a second model:

$$VotePresParty_t = \beta_{Const} + \beta_{UnemCurrent}UnemCurrent_t + e_t$$

where

$UnemCurrent_t$ = unemployment rate in the current year, year t

a. Assuming that the theory is correct, would $\beta_{UnemCurrent}$ be positive, negative or zero?

b. For the moment assume that when you run the appropriate regression, the sign of the coefficient estimate agrees with your answer to part a. Formulate the null and alternative hypotheses for this model.

4. Again focus on the on the "It's the economy stupid" theory. Consider a third model:

$$VotePresParty_t = \beta_{Const} + \beta_{UnemTrend}UnemTrend_t + e_t$$

where

$UnemCurrent_t$ = unemployment rate change from previous year; that is, the unemployment rate trend in year t (Note: If the unemployment rate is rising, the trend will be a positive number; if the unemployment rate is falling, the trend will be a negative number.)

a. Assuming that the theory is correct, would $\beta_{UnemTrend}$ be positive, negative or zero?

b. For the moment assume that when you run the appropriate regression, the sign of the coefficient estimate agrees with your answer to part a. Formulate the null and alternative hypotheses for this model.

5. The following table reports the percent of the popular vote received by the Democrats, Republicans, and third parties for every presidential election since 1892.

Year	VotePartyDem	VotePartyRep	VotePartyThird
1892	46.1	43.0	10.9
1896	46.7	51.0	2.3
1900	45.5	51.7	2.8
1904	37.6	56.4	6.0
1908	43.0	51.7	5.3
1912	41.8	23.2	35.0
1916	49.2	46.1	4.7
1920	34.1	60.3	5.6
1924	28.5	54.0	17.5
1928	40.8	58.3	0.9
1932	57.4	39.6	3.0
1936	60.8	36.5	2.7
1940	54.7	44.8	0.5
1944	53.4	45.9	0.7
1948	49.6	45.1	5.3
1952	44.4	55.1	0.5
1956	42.0	57.4	0.6
1960	49.7	49.5	0.8
1964	61.1	38.5	0.4
1968	42.7	43.4	13.9
1972	37.5	60.7	1.8
1976	50.1	48.0	1.9
1980	41.0	50.7	8.3
1984	40.6	58.8	0.6
1988	46.6	53.4	0.0
1992	43.3	37.7	19.0
1996	50.0	42.0	8.0
2000	48.4	47.9	3.7
2004	48.3	50.7	1.0
2008	52.9	45.6	1.5

Focus your attention on the vote received by third party candidates.

a. Which election stands out as especially unusual?

b. What were the special political circumstances that explain why this particular election is so unusual?

12.1   Model Specification: Ramsey REgression Specification Error Test (RESET)

We have introduced two different models of demand:

• The linear demand model:

$$Q_t = \beta_{Const} + \beta_P P_t + \beta_I I_t + \beta_{CP} ChickP_t + e_t$$

• The constant elasticity demand model:

$$LogQ_t = c + \beta_P LogP_t + \beta_I LogI_t + \beta_{CP} LogChickP_t + e_t$$

Project: Assess the specification of the demand models.

12.1.1   RESET Logic

Both models use the same information to explain the quantity of beef demanded: the price of beef (the good's own price), income, and the price of chicken. The models use this information differently, however. That is, the two models specify two different ways in which the quantity of beef demanded is related to the price of beef (the good's own price), income, and the price of chicken. We will now explore how we might decide whether or not a particular specification of the model can be improved. The **RESET** test is designed to do just this. In the test we modify the original model to construct an **artificial model**. An artificial model is not designed to test a theory, but rather it is designed to assess the original model.

  To explain the RESET test, we begin with the general form of the simple linear regression model: y is the dependent variable and x is the explanatory variable:

$$y_t = \beta_{Const} + \beta_x x_t + e_t$$

We use the ordinary least squares (OLS) estimation procedure to estimate the model's parameters:

• b_{Const} estimates β_{Const}

• b_x estimates β_x

The parameter estimates can be used to estimate the value of y:

$$Esty = b_{Const} + b_x x$$

The estimated value of y is sometimes called the fitted value of y.

Now we come to the RESET test. We specify an artificial model which adds an explanatory variable to the original model. The new explanatory variable is the estimated value of y squared:

$$y_t = \gamma_{Const} + \gamma_x x_t + \gamma_{Esty2} Esty_t^2 + \varepsilon_t$$

The artificial model looks just like the original model with one addition: the square of the estimated value for the original model's dependent variable, $Esty^2$.

$Esty$ is calculated from the information used to estimate the original model. Consequently the artificial model adds no new information. The artificial model uses the same information as the original model, but uses it in a different way. This is the rationale behind the RESET test:

Critical point: The artificial model adds no new information. It is just using the same information in a different form.

Question: Can this new form of the information in the artificial model help us explain the dependent variable significantly better? The coefficient of $Esty^2$ provides the answer to this question. If γ_{Esty2}, the coefficient of $Esty^2$, equals 0, the new form of the information is adding no explanatory power; if γ_{Esty2} does not equal 0, the new form adds power. We now construct the appropriate null and alternative hypotheses:

H_0: $\gamma_{Esty2} = 0 \Rightarrow$ New form of the information adds NO explanatory power

H_1: $\gamma_{Esty2} \neq 0 \Rightarrow$ New form of the information adds explanatory power

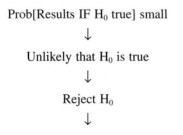

Prob[Results IF H_0 true] small
↓
Unlikely that H_0 is true
↓
Reject H_0
↓
Unlikely that the new form of the information adds no explanatory power
↓
Likely that the new form of the information adds explanatory power
↓
There is reason to consider a new model that uses the information in a different form

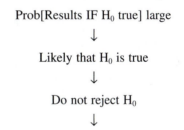

Prob[Results IF H_0 true] large
↓
Likely that H_0 is true
↓
Do not reject H_0
↓
Likely that the new form of the information adds no explanatory power

There is no compelling reason to consider a new model that uses the information in a different form

12.1.2   Linear Demand Model

We will now consider the linear model of beef demand to illustrate the RESET test:

Original model: $Q_t = \beta_{Const} + \beta_P P_t + \beta_I I_t + \beta_{CP} ChickP_t + e_t$

[To access this online material, go to http://mitpress.mit.edu/westhoffeconometrics and select Beef Demand.]

First run the regression to estimate the parameters of the original model (table 12.1):
Next construct the artificial model:

Artificial model: $Q_t = \gamma_{Const} + \gamma_P P_t + \gamma_I I_t + \gamma_{CP} ChickP_t + \gamma_{EstQ2} EstQ_t^2 + \varepsilon_t$

$EstQ$ is the estimated value of Q based on the original model:

$EstQ = 159{,}032 - 549.5P + 24.25I + 287.4ChickP$

Step 1:   Collect data, run the regression, and interpret the estimates.

After generating $EstQ$, we square it to generate $EstQSquared$:

$EstQSquared = EstQ^2$

Then we use the ordinary least squares (OLS) estimation procedure to estimate the model's parameters (table 12.2):

Step 2:   Play the cynic and challenge the results; construct the null and alternative hypotheses.

Cynic's view: Despite the results, the new form of the information adds no explanatory power. The coefficient $EstQ^2$, γ_{EstQ2}, actually equals 0.

Table 12.1
Beef demand regression results—Linear model

Ordinary least squares (OLS)				
Dependent variable: Q				
Explanatory variable(s):	Estimate	SE	t-Statistic	Prob
P	−549.4847	130.2611	−4.218333	0.0004
I	24.24854	11.27214	2.151192	0.0439
$ChickP$	287.3737	193.3540	1.486257	0.1528
$Const$	159,032.4	61,472.68	2.587041	0.0176
Number of observations	24			

Estimated equation: $EstQ = 159{,}032 - 549.5P + 24.25I + 287.4ChickP$

Table 12.2
Beef demand regression results—Artificial model

Ordinary least squares (OLS)				
Dependent variable: Q				
Explanatory variable(s):	Estimate	SE	t-Statistic	Prob
P	13,431.05	5,861.208	2.291515	0.0335
I	−593.4581	259.1146	−2.290330	0.0336
ChickP	−7,054.644	3,082.373	−2.288706	0.0337
EstQSquared	5.79E-05	2.42E-05	2.385742	0.0276
Const	−1,085,301.0	524,497.0	−2.069223	0.0524
Number of observations	24			

Critical result: The *EstQSquared* coefficient estimate is 0.0000579. The estimate does not equal 0; the estimate is 0.0000579 from 0. This evidence suggests that the new form of the information adds explanatory power.

H_0: $\gamma_{EstQ2} = 0$ Cynic is correct: New form of the information adds NO explanatory power; there is no compelling reason to consider a new specification of the original model.

H_1: $\gamma_{EstQ2} \neq 0$ Cynic is incorrect: New form of the information adds explanatory power; there is reason to consider a new specification of the original model.

Step 3:   Formulate the question to assess the cynic's view and the null hypothesis.

• **Generic question:**   What is the probability that the results would be like those we actually obtained (or even stronger), if the cynic is correct the new form of the information adds NO explanatory power?

• **Specific question:**   The regression's estimate of γ_{EstQ2} was 0.0000579. What is the probability that the estimate of γ_{EstQ2} from one regression would be at least 0.0000579 from 0, if H_0 were true (i.e., if γ_{EstQ2} actually equaled 0, if the different form of the information did not improve the regression)?

Answer: Prob[Results IF H_0 true]

The size of this probability determines whether we reject the null hypothesis:

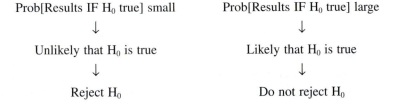

Table 12.3
Beef demand regression results—Linear model RESET test

Ramsey RESET test				
Dependent variable: Q				
Explanatory variable(s):	Estimate	SE	*t*-Statistic	Prob
P	13,431.11	5,861.274	2.291499	0.0335
I	−593.4412	259.1094	−2.290311	0.0336
ChickP	−7,054.195	3,082.207	−2.288683	0.0337
C	−1,085,437.0	524,557.3	−2.069244	0.0524
Fitted^2	5.79E-05	2.43E-05	2.385725	0.0276
Number of observations	24			

Critical result: The *Fitted^2* coefficient estimate is 0.0000579. The estimate does not equal 0; the estimate is 0.0000579 from 0. This evidence suggests that the new form of the information adds explanatory power.

Steps 4 and 5:   The tails probability reported in the regression results is the probability that we need:

Prob[Results IF H_0 true] = 0.0276

We would reject the null hypothesis at the 5 percent significance level although not at the 1 percent significance level. This suggests that it may be prudent to investigate an alternative specification of the original model.

Fortunately, statistical software provides a very easy way to run a RESET test by generating the new variable automatically (table 12.3).

[To access this online material, go to http://mitpress.mit.edu/westhoffeconometrics and select Beef Demand.]

Getting Started in EViews

After running the unrestricted regression:

• Click **View, Stability Diagnostics, Ramsey RESET Test**.

• Enter the number of fitted terms to include, **1** in this case (we want one "fitted" term, $EstQ^2$).

• Click **OK**.

Our calculations and those provided by the statistical software are essentially the same. The slight differences that do emerge result from the fact that we rounded off some decimal places from the parameter estimates of the original model when we generated the estimated value of Q, $EstQ$.

Summarizing the RESET logic:

- $EstQ^2$ adds no additional information; it is just using the same information in a different form.
- In the case of our linear demand model, including $EstQ^2$ in the artificial regression improves the results "significantly" at the 5 percent significance level suggesting it may be prudent to investigate an alternative specification of the original model.

12.1.3   Constant Elasticity Demand Model

Next consider a different specification of the model, a constant elasticity demand model:

Original model: $LogQ_t = c + \beta_P LogP_t + \beta_I LogI_t + \beta_{CP} LogChickP_t + e_t$

We then estimate its parameters using the ordinary least squares (OLS) estimation procedure (table 12.4).

[To access this online material, go to http://mitpress.mit.edu/westhoffeconometrics and select Beef Demand.]

Now let us construct the artificial model:

$LogQ_t = \gamma_{Const} + \gamma_P LogP_t + \gamma_I LogI_t + \gamma_{CP} LogChickP_t + \gamma_{EstQ2} EstLongQ_t^2 + \varepsilon_t$

Step 1:   Collect data, run the regression, and interpret the estimates.

We will estimate the artificial model using statistical software (table 12.5).

Step 2:   Play the cynic and challenge the results; construct the null and alternative hypotheses.

Cynic's view: Despite the results, the new form of the information adds no explanatory power.

Table 12.4
Beef demand regression results—Constant elasticity model

Ordinary least squares (OLS)				
Dependent variable: $LogQ$				
Explanatory variable(s):	Estimate	SE	t-Statistic	Prob
$LogP$	−0.411812	0.093532	−4.402905	0.0003
$LogI$	0.508061	0.266583	1.905829	0.0711
$LogChickP$	0.124724	0.071415	1.746465	0.0961
$Const$	9.499258	2.348619	4.044615	0.0006
Number of observations	24			

Estimated equation: $EstLogQ = 9.50 - 0.41LogP + 0.51LogI + 0.12LogChick$

Table 12.5
Beef demand regression results—Constant elasticity Model RESET test

Ramsey RESET test				
Dependent variable: Q				
Explanatory variable(s):	Estimate	SE	t-Statistic	Prob
LogP	108.0339	54.18066	1.993956	0.0607
LogI	−133.2683	66.83651	−1.993944	0.0607
LogChickP	−32.73312	16.41626	−1.993946	0.0607
Const	−872.3276	440.5753	−1.979974	0.0624
Fitted^2	10.70320	5.347430	2.001560	0.0598
Number of observations	24			

Critical result: The *Fitted^2* coefficient is 10.7. The estimate does not equal 0; the estimate is 10.7 from 0. This evidence suggests that the new form of the information adds explanatory power.

The coefficient *EstLogQ²*, γ_{EstQ2}, actually equals 0.

H_0: $\gamma_{EstQ2} = 0$ Cynic is correct: New form of the information adds NO explanatory power; there is no compelling reason to consider a new specification of the original model.

H_1: $\gamma_{EstQ2} \neq 0$ Cynic is incorrect: New form of the information adds explanatory power; there is reason to consider a new specification of the original model.

Step 3:   Formulate the question to assess the cynic's view and the null hypothesis.

· **Generic question:**   What is the probability that the results would be like those we actually obtained (or even stronger), if the cynic is correct the new form of the information adds NO explanatory power?

· **Specific question:**   The regression's estimate of γ_{EstQ2} was 10.7. What is the probability that the estimate of γ_{EstQ2} from one regression would be at least 10.7 from 0, if H_0 were true (that is, if γ_{EstQ2} actually equaled 0, if the different form of the information did not improve the regression)?

Answer: Prob[Results IF H_0 true]

The size of this probability determines whether we reject the null hypothesis:

Prob[Results IF H_0 true] small   Prob[Results IF H_0 true] large

↓   ↓

Unlikely that H_0 is true   Likely that H_0 is true

↓   ↓

Reject H_0 Do not reject H_0

Steps 4 and 5:   The tails probability reported in the regression results is the probability that we need:

Prob[Results IF H_0 true] = 0.0598

Using the traditional significance levels of 1 or 5 percent, we do not reject the null hypothesis and conclude that there is no compelling reason to specify a new model.

12.2   Model Development: The Effect of Economic Conditions on Presidential Elections

12.2.1   General Theory: "It's the economy stupid"

The 1992 Clinton presidential campaign focused on the economy and made the phrase "It's the economy stupid" famous. Bill Clinton, the Democratic challenger, and his political advisors relied of the theory that voters hold the Republican President, George H. W. Bush, and his party responsible for the state of the economy. When the economy performs well, the President's party gets credit; when the economy performs poorly, the President's party takes the blame:

"It's the economy stupid" theory: The American electorate is sensitive to economic conditions. Good economic conditions increase the vote for the President's party; bad economic conditions decrease the vote for the President's party.

Project: Assess the effect of economic conditions on presidential elections.

Clearly, we need data to test this theory. Fortunately, we have already collected some data. Data from 1890 to 2008 can be easily accessed:

Presidential election data: Annual time series data of US presidential election and economic statistics from 1890 to 2008.

$VotePartyDem_t$	Percent of popular vote received by the Democratic candidate in year t
$VotePartyRep_t$	Percent of popular vote received by the Republican candidate in year t
$VotePartyThird_t$	Percent of the popular vote received by third (minor) party candidates in year t
$PresPartyR1_t$	1 if incumbent President is Republican in year t; 0 if Democrat in year t
$PresIncum_t$	1 if incumbent President is a candidate in year t, 0 otherwise
$PresPartyTerms_t$	Number of consecutive terms the incumbent President's party has held the presidency in year t
$UnemCurrent_t$	Unemployment rate in year t (percent)
$RealGdpCurrent_t$	Real GDP in year t
$RealGdpGrowth_t$	Real GDP growth rate in year t (percent)
$PriceCpiCurrent_t$	Price level in year t (CPI)
$InflCpiCurrent_t$	Inflation rate in year t based on the CPI (percent)
$PriceGdpCurrent_t$	GDP price deflator in year t
$InflGdpCurrent_t$	Inflation rate in year t based on the GDP price deflator (percent)

[To access this online material, go to http://mitpress.mit.edu/westhoffeconometrics and select Presidential Election – 1892–2008.]

12.2.2   Generate Relevant Variables

First note that the data does not include the variable that we are trying to explain: the vote received by the incumbent President's party:

$VotePresParty_t$ Percent of popular vote received by the President's party in year t

Fortunately, we can generate it from the variables that we have. We have data reporting the percent of the popular vote received by the Democratic and Republican candidates, $VotePartyDem_t$ and $VotePartyRep_t$. Also another variable indicates the incumbent President's party, $PresPartyR1_t$. Focus attention on these three variables:

$VotePartyDem_t$ Percent of popular vote received by the Democratic candidate in year t

$VotePartyRep_t$ Percent of popular vote received by the Republican candidate in year t

$PresPartyR1_t$ 1 if the President is a Republican in year t, 0 if Democrat in year t

We can use the following equation to generate the variable $VotePresParty$:

$$VotePresParty_t = PresPartyR1_t \times VotePartyRep_t + (1 - PresPartyR1_t) \times VotePartyDem_t$$

To show that this new variable indeed equals the vote receive by the President's party consider the two possibilities:

• When the Republicans are occupying the White House,

$$PresPartyR1_t = 1 \quad \text{and} \quad 1 - PresPartyR1_t = 0$$

The new variable $VotePresParty_t$ will equal the vote received by the Republican candidate:

$$VotePresParty_t = PresPartyR1_t \times VotePartyRep_t + (1 - PresPartyR1_t) \times VotePartyDem_t$$

$$= 1 \times VotePartyRep_t + 0 \times VotePartyDem_t$$

$$= VotePartyRep_t$$

• When the Democrats are occupying the White House,

$$PresPartyR1_t = 0 \quad \text{and} \quad 1 - PresPartyR1_t = 1$$

The new variable $VotePresParty_t$ will equal the vote received by the Democratic candidate:

$$VotePresParty_t = PresPartyR1_t \times VotePartyRep_t + (1 - PresPartyR1_t) \times VotePartyDem_t$$

$$= 0 \times VotePartyRep_t + 1 \times VotePartyDem_t$$

$$= VotePartyDem_t$$

Table 12.6
Checking generated variables

Year	VotePartyDem	VotePartyRep	PresPartyR1	VotePresParty
1892	46.1	43.0	1	43.0
1896	46.7	51.0	0	46.7
1900	45.5	51.7	1	51.7
1904	37.6	56.4	1	56.4
1908	43.0	51.7	1	51.7

After generating any new variable, it is important to check to be certain that it is generated correctly. The first few elections are reported in table 12.6. Everything looks fine. When Republicans hold the White House (when $PresPartyRI_t$ equals 1), the new variable, $VotePresParty_t$, equals the vote received by the Republican candidate ($VotePartyRep_t$). Alternatively, when Democrats hold the White House (when $PresPartyR1_t$ equals 0), $VotePresParty_t$ equals the vote received by the Democratic candidate ($VotePartyDem_t$).

12.2.3   Data Oddities

Next let us look at our voting data to investigate the possibility of data oddities (table 12.7). In all but a handful of elections, third (minor) parties captured only a small percent of the total vote. In some years third parties received a substantial fraction, however. The election of 1912 is the most notable example.

In the 1912 election more than a third of votes are siphoned off from the Republicans and Democrats. How should deal with this? One approach is just to focus on those elections that were legitimate two-party elections. In this approach, we might ignore all elections in which third (minor) parties receive at least 10 percent or perhaps 15 percent of the votes cast. If we were to pursue this approach, however, we would be discarding information. Econometricians never like to throw away information. Another approach would be to focus just on the two major parties by expressing the percent of votes just in terms of those votes casted just for the Republican and Democratic candidates. Let us call this variable $VotePresPartyTwo_t$:

$VotePresPartyTwo_t$ Percent of popular vote received by the incumbent President's party
based on the two major parties (ignoring third parties) in year t

We can generate this variable by using the following equation:

$$VotePresPartyTwo = 100 \times VotePresParty/(VotePartyRep + VotePartyDem)$$

As always, it is important to be certain that the new variable has been generated correctly (table 12.8). Undoubtedly there are other ways to account for third parties. In this chapter, however, we will do so by focusing on the variable $VotePresPartyTwo$.

Table 12.7
Checking for data oddities

Year	VotePartyDem	VotePartyRep	VotePartyThird
1892	46.1	43.0	10.9
1896	46.7	51.0	2.3
1900	45.5	51.7	2.8
1904	37.6	56.4	6.0
1908	43.0	51.7	5.3
1912	41.8	23.2	35.0
1916	49.2	46.1	4.7
1920	34.1	60.3	5.6
1924	28.5	54.0	17.5
1928	40.8	58.3	0.9
1932	57.4	39.6	3.0
1936	60.8	36.5	2.7
1940	54.7	44.8	0.5
1944	53.4	45.9	0.7
1948	49.6	45.1	5.3
1952	44.4	55.1	0.5
1956	42.0	57.4	0.6
1960	49.7	49.5	0.8
1964	61.1	38.5	0.4
1968	42.7	43.4	13.9
1972	37.5	60.7	1.8
1976	50.1	48.0	1.9
1980	41.0	50.7	8.3
1984	40.6	58.8	0.6
1988	46.6	53.4	0.0
1992	43.3	37.7	19.0
1996	50.0	42.0	8.0
2000	48.4	47.9	3.7
2004	48.3	50.7	1.0
2008	52.9	45.6	1.5

Table 12.8
Checking generated variables

Year	VotePres	VotePartyDem	VotePartyRep	VotePresPartyTwo
1892	43.00000	46.10000	43.00000	48.26038
1896	46.70000	46.70000	51.00000	47.79939
1900	51.70000	45.50000	51.70000	53.18930
1904	56.40000	37.60000	56.40000	60.00000

12.2.4   Model Formulation and Assessment: An Iterative Process

Now we will illustrate the iterative process that that econometricians use to develop their models. There is no "cookbook" procedure we can follow. Common sense and inventiveness play critical roles in model development:

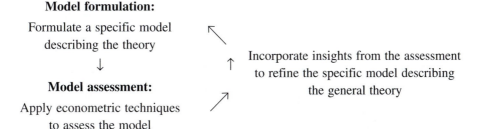

Model formulation:

Formulate a specific model
describing the theory

↓

Incorporate insights from the assessment
to refine the specific model describing
the general theory

Model assessment:

Apply econometric techniques
to assess the model

Gradually we refine the specific details of the model using an iterative process: model formulation and model assessment. In a real sense this is as much of an art as a science.

12.2.4   Specific Voting Models

We will describe specific models that attempt to explain the percent of the vote received by the President's party. In doing so, we will illustrate how the iterative process of model formulation and model assessment leads us from one model to the next. We begin by observing that the unemployment rate is most frequently cited economic statistic. Every month the Bureau of Labor Statistics announces the previous month's unemployment rate. The announcement receives headline attention in the newspapers and on the evening news broadcasts. Consequently it seems natural to begin with models that focus on the unemployment rate. We will eventually refine our model by extending our focus to another important economic variable, inflation.

Model 1:   Past performance—Electorate is sensitive to how well the economy has performed in the three years prior to the election.

The first model implicitly assumes that voters conscientiously assess economic conditions over the three previous years of the President's administration. If conditions have been good, the President and his party are rewarded with more votes. If conditions have been bad, fewer votes would be received. More specifically, we use the average unemployment rate in the three years prior to the election to quantify economic conditions over the three previous years of the President's administration.

Step 0:   Formulate a model reflecting the theory to be tested.

$$VotePresPartyTwo_t = \beta_{Const} + \beta_{UnemPriorAvg} UnemPriorAvg_t + e_t$$

where

$UnemPriorAvg_t$ = average unemployment rate in the three years prior to election; that is, three years prior to year t

Theory: A high the average unemployment rate during the three years prior to the election will decrease the votes for the incumbent President's party; a low average unemployment rate will increase the votes. The actual value of the coefficient, $\beta_{UnemPriorAvg}$, is negative:

$$\beta_{UnemPriorAvg} < 0$$

Step 1:   Collect data, run the regression, and interpret the estimates.

After generating the variable *UnemPriorAvg* we use the ordinary least squares (OLS) estimation procedure to estimate the model's parameters (table 12.9).

The coefficient estimate is 0.33. The coefficient estimate directly contradicts our theory. Accordingly we will abandon this model and go "back to the drawing board." We will consider another model.

Model 2:   Present performance—Electorate is sensitive to how well the economy is performing during the election year itself.

Our analysis of the first model suggests that voters may not have a long memory; accordingly, the second model suggests that voters are myopic; voters judge the President's party only on the current economic climate; they do not care what has occurred in the past. More specifically, we use the current unemployment rate to assess economic conditions.

Table 12.9
Election regression results—Past performance model

Ordinary least squares (OLS)				
Dependent variable: *VotePresPartyTwo*				
Explanatory variable(s):	Estimate	SE	*t*-Statistic	Prob
UnemPriorAvg	0.331914	0.319360	1.039310	0.3079
Const	49.70180	2.595936	19.14600	0.0000
Number of observations	29			

Estimated equation: *EstVotePresPartyTwo* = 49.7 + 0.33*UnemPriorAvg*

Interpretation of estimates:

$b_{UnemPriorAvg}$ = 0.33: A 1 percentage point increase in the average unemployment rate during the three years prior to the election increases the vote the President's party receives by 0.33 percentage points.

Critical result: The coefficient estimate for *UnemPriorAvg* equals 0.33. The positive sign of the coefficient estimate suggests that a higher average unemployment rate in the three years prior to the election increases the votes received by the President's party. This evidence tends to refute the "It's the economy stupid" theory.

Step 0: Formulate a model reflecting the theory to be tested.

$$VotePresPartyTwo_t = \beta_{Const} + \beta_{UnemCurrent}UnemCurrent_t + e_t$$

where

$UnemCurrent_t$ = unemployment rate in the current year, year t

Theory: A high unemployment rate in the election year itself will decrease the votes for incumbent President's party; a low unemployment rate will increase the votes. The actual value of the coefficient, $\beta_{UnemCurrent}$, is negative:

$$\beta_{UnemCurrent} < 0$$

Step 1: Collect data, run the regression, and interpret the estimates.

We use the ordinary least squares (OLS) estimation procedure to estimate the second model's parameters (table 12.10).

The coefficient estimate is -0.12. This is good news. The evidence supports our theory. Now we will continue on to determine how confident we should be in our theory.

Step 2: Play the cynic and challenge the results; construct the null and alternative hypotheses.

Cynic's view: Despite the results, the current unemployment rate does not affect the votes received by the incumbent President's party.

H_0: $\beta_{UnemCurrent} = 0$ Cynic is correct: Current unemployment rate has no effect on votes

H_1: $\beta_{UnemCurrent} < 0$ Cynic is incorrect: High unemployment rate reduces votes for the incumbent President's party

Table 12.10
Election regression results—Present performance model

Ordinary least squares (OLS)				
Dependent variable: *VotePresPartyTwo*				
Explanatory variable(s):	Estimate	SE	*t*-Statistic	Prob
UnemCurrent	−0.124858	0.294305	−0.424247	0.6746
Const	52.70895	2.414476	21.83039	0.0000
Number of observations	30			

Estimated equation: $EstVotePresPartyTwo = 52.7 - 0.12UnemCurrent$

Interpretation of estimates:

$b_{UnemCurrent} = 0.12$: A 1 percentage point increase in the election year unemployment rate decreases the vote the President's party receives by 0.12 percentage points.

Critical result: The coefficient estimate for *UnemCurrent* equals −0.12. The negative sign of the coefficient estimate suggests that a higher unemployment rate in the election year reduces the votes received by the President's party. This evidence lends support to the "It's the economy stupid" theory.

Step 3: Formulate the question to assess the cynic's view and the null hypothesis.

· **Generic question:** What is the probability that the results would be like those we actually obtained (or even stronger), if the cynic is correct and the current unemployment rate actually has no impact?

· **Specific question:** The regression's coefficient estimate was −0.12. What is the probability that the coefficient estimate in one regression would be −0.12 or less, if H_0 were actually true (if the actual coefficient, $\beta_{UnemCurrent}$, equals 0)?

Answer: Prob[Results IF H_0 true] (figure 12.1)

The size of this probability determines whether we reject the null hypothesis:

Prob[Results IF H_0 true] small   Prob[Results IF H_0 true] large

$\downarrow$ $\downarrow$

Unlikely that H_0 is true   Likely that H_0 is true

$\downarrow$ $\downarrow$

Reject H_0 Do not reject H_0

Steps 4 and 5:   Use the EViews regression printout to calculate Prob[Results IF H_0 true] (figure 12.2).

The tails probability answers the following question:

Question: If actual value of the coefficient were 0, what is the probability that the estimate would be at least 0.12 from 0?

Answer: 0.6746

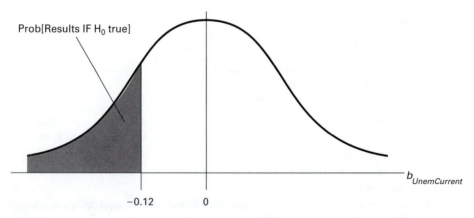

Figure 12.1
Probability distribution of coefficient estimate

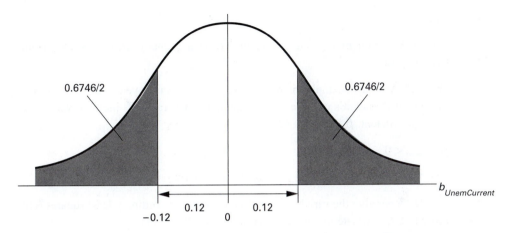

Figure 12.2
Probability distribution of coefficient estimate

The probability of being in the left-hand tail equals the tails probability divided by 2:

$$\text{Prob[Results IF } H_0 \text{ true]} = \frac{0.6746}{2} \approx 0.34$$

This is not good news. By the traditional standards, a significance level of 1, 5, or 10 percent, this probability is large; we cannot reject the null hypothesis which asserts that the current unemployment rate has not effect on votes.

Model 2 provides both good and bad news. The coefficient sign supports the theory suggesting that we are on the right track. Voters appear to have a short memory; they appear to be more concerned with present economic conditions than the past. The bad news is that the coefficient for the current unemployment rate does not meet the traditional standards of significance.

Model 3:   Present trend—Electorate is sensitive to the current trend, whether economic conditions are improving or deteriorating during the election year.

The second model suggests that we may be on the right track by just focusing on the election year. The third model speculates that voters are concerned with the trend in economic conditions during the election year. If economic conditions are improving, the incumbent President's party is rewarded with more votes. On the other hand, if conditions are deteriorating, fewer votes would be received. We use the trend in the unemployment rate to assess the trend in economic conditions.

Step 0:   Formulate a model reflecting the theory to be tested.

$$VotePresPartyTwo_t = \beta_{Const} + \beta_{UnemTrend}UnemTrend_t + e_t$$

where

UnemTrend$_t$ = unemployment rate change from previous year; that is, the unemployment rate trend in year *t*

Theory: A rising unemployment rate during the election year will decrease the votes of the incumbent President's party; a falling unemployment rate will increase votes. The actual value of the coefficient, $\beta_{UnemTrend}$, is negative:

$$\beta_{UnemTrend} < 0$$

Step 1:   Collect data, run the regression, and interpret the estimates.

After generating the variable *UnemTrend,* we use the ordinary least squares (OLS) estimation procedure to estimate the model's parameters (table 12.11).

The coefficient estimate is −0.75. This is good news. The evidence supports our theory. Now we will continue on to determine how confident we should be in our theory.

Step 2:   Play the cynic and challenge the results; construct the null and alternative hypotheses.

Cynic's view: Despite the results, the unemployment rate trend does not affect the votes received by the incumbent President's party.

Table 12.11
Election regression results—Present trend model

Ordinary least squares (OLS)				
Dependent variable: *VotePresPartyTwo*				
Explanatory variable(s):	Estimate	SE	*t*-Statistic	Prob
UnemTrend	−0.752486	0.568784	−1.322973	0.1965
Const	51.95260	1.325732	39.18785	0.0000
Number of observations	30			

Estimated equation: *EstVotePresPartyTwo* = 52.0 − 0.75*UnemTrend*

Interpretation of estimates:

$b_{UnemTrend} = -0.75$: A 1 percentage point rise in the unemployment from the previous year decreases the vote the President's party receives by 0.75 percentage points. On the contrary, a 1 percentage point fall in the unemployment rate increases the vote by 0.75 percentage points.

Critical result: The *UnemTrend* coefficient estimate equals −0.75. The negative sign of the coefficient estimate suggests that deteriorating economic conditions as evidenced by a rising unemployment will decrease the vote received by the President's party. On the contrary, improving economic conditions as evidenced by a falling unemployment rate will increase the votes received by the President's party. This evidence lends support to the "It's the economy stupid" theory.

H_0: $\beta_{UnemTrend} = 0$ Cynic is correct: Unemployment rate trend has no effect on votes

H_1: $\beta_{UnemTrend} < 0$ Cynic is incorrect: A rising unemployment rate (a positive value for *UnemTrend*) decreases the vote for the incumbent President's party; a falling unemployment rate trend (a negative value for *UnemTrend*) increases the vote.

Steps 3, 4, and 5:   We will now calculate Prob[Results IF H_0 true]. We have done this several times now, we know that since we are conducting a one-tailed test, the Prob[Results IF H_0 true] equals half the tails probability:

$$\text{Prob[Results IF } H_0 \text{ true]} = \frac{0.1965}{2} \approx 0.10$$

While this probability is still considered large at the 5 percent significance level, we appear to be on the right track. We will shortly consider a fourth model; it postulates that when judging economic conditions, the electorate considers not only the unemployment rate trend but also the trend in prices, the inflation rate.

Before moving on to model 4, however, let us illustrate the subtle difference between models 2 and 3 by using each to estimate the vote received by the President's party in 2008. For model 2 we only need the unemployment rate for 2008 to calculate the estimate; for model 3 we not only need the unemployment rate in 2008 but also the unemployment rate in the previous year, 2007:

Unemployment rate in 2008 = 5.81%   Unemployment rate in 2007 = 4.64%

Model 2:   In 2008,

$$UnemCurrent = 5.81$$

$$
\begin{aligned}
EstVotePresPartyTwo &= 52.7 - 0.12 UnemCurrent \\
&= 52.7 - 0.12 \times 5.81 \\
&= 52.7 - 0.7 \\
&= 52.0
\end{aligned}
$$

Model 2's estimate depends only on the unemployment rate in the current year, 2008 in this case. The unemployment rate for 2007 is irrelevant. The estimate for 2008 would be the same regardless of what the unemployment rate for 2007 equaled.

Model 3:   In 2008,

$$UnemTrend = 5.81 - 4.64 = 1.17$$

$$EstVotePresPartyTwo = 52.0 - 0.75UnemTrend$$

$$= 52.0 - 0.75 \times 1.17$$

$$= 52.0 - 0.9$$

$$= 51.1$$

Model 3's estimate depends on the change in the unemployment rate; consequently the unemployment rates in both years are important.

Model 4:   Present trend II—Electorate is sensitive not only to the unemployment rate trend, but also the trend in prices, the inflation rate.

The fourth model, like the third, theorizes that voters are concerned with the trend. If economic conditions are improving, the incumbent President's party is rewarded with more votes. If conditions were deteriorating, fewer votes would be received. The fourth model postulates that voters are not only concerned with the trend in the unemployment rate but also the trend in prices. The inflation rate measures the trend in prices. A 2 percent inflation rate means that prices are on average rising by 2 percent, a 3 percent inflation rate means that prices are rising by 3 percent, and so on.

Step 0:   Formulate a model reflecting the theory to be tested.

$$VotePresPartyTwo_t = \beta_{Const} + \beta_{UnemTrend}UnemTrend_t + \beta_{InflCpiCurrent}InflCpiCurrent_t + e_t$$

where

$UnemTrend_t$ = change in the unemployment rate in the current year, in year t

$InflCpiCurrent_t$ = inflation rate based on the CPI in the current year, in year t

Theory:

• A rising unemployment rate during the election year will decrease the votes of the incumbent President's party; a falling unemployment rate will increase votes. The actual value of the *Unem-Trend* coefficient, $\beta_{UnemTrend}$, is negative:

$\beta_{UnemTrend} < 0$

• An increase in the inflation rate during the election year will decrease the votes of the incumbent President's party; a decrease in the inflation rate will increase votes. The actual value of the *InflCpiCurrent* coefficient, $\beta_{InflCpiCurrent}$, is negative:

$\beta_{InflCpiCurrent} < 0$

Table 12.12
Election regression results—Present trend model

Ordinary least squares (OLS)				
Dependent variable: *VotePresPartyTwo*				
Explanatory variable(s):	Estimate	SE	*t*-Statistic	Prob
UnemTrend	−1.068160	0.560702	−1.905040	0.0675
InflCpiCurrent	−0.585465	0.286421	−2.044071	0.0508
Const	53.57059	1.484912	36.07662	0.0000
Number of observations	30			

Estimated equation: $EstVotePresPartyTwo = 53.6 - 1.07UnemTrend - 0.59InflCpiCurrent$

$b_{UnemTrend} = -1.07$: A 1 percentage point rise in the unemployment rate from the previous year decreases the vote the President's party receives by 1.07 percent age points.

$b_{InflCpiCurrent} = -0.59$: A 1 percent rise in prices decreases the vote the President's party receives by 0.59 percent.

Critical result: The *UnemTrend* coefficient estimate equals −1.07. The negative sign of the coefficient estimate suggests that deteriorating economic conditions as evidenced by a rising unemployment will decrease the vote received by the President's party. This evidence lends support to the "It's the economy stupid" theory.

The *InflCpiCurrent* coefficient estimate equals −0.59. The negative sign of the coefficient estimate suggests that a rising prices decrease the votes received by the President's party. This evidence lends support to the "It's the economy stupid" theory.

Step 1:   Collect data, run the regression, and interpret the estimates (table 12.12).

On the one hand, both coefficients suggest that deteriorating economic conditions decrease the votes received by the President's party. On the other hand, improving economic conditions increase the vote.

Step 2: Play the cynic and challenge the results; construct the null and alternative hypotheses.

Cynic's view of unemployment rate trend: Despite the results, the unemployment trend has no effect.

Cynic's view of inflation rate: Despite the results, the trend in prices has no effect.

Unemployment trend hypotheses   Inflation hypotheses

$H_0: \beta_{UnemTrend} = 0$ $H_0: \beta_{InflCpiCurrent} = 0$

$H_1: \beta_{UnemTrend} < 0$ $H_1: \beta_{InflCpiCurrent} < 0$

Steps 3, 4, and 5:   Using the tails probabilities reported in the regression printout, we can easily compute Prob[Results IF H_0 True] for each of our theories:

Unemployment Trend   Inflation

$\text{Prob[Results IF } H_0 \text{ true]} = \dfrac{0.0675}{2} \approx 0.034$ $\text{Prob[Results IF } H_0 \text{ true]} = \dfrac{0.0508}{2} \approx 0.025$

At the 5 percent significance level both of these probabilities are small. Hence, at the 5 percent significance level, we can reject the null hypotheses that the unemployment trend and inflation have no effect on the vote for the incumbent President's party. This supports the notion that "it's the economy stupid."

This example illustrates the model formulation and assessment process. As mentioned before, the process is as much of an art as a science. There is no routine "cookbook" recipe that we can apply. It cannot be emphasized enough that we must use our common sense and inventiveness.

Chapter 12 Review Questions

1. What is an artificial model?

2. Consider a multiple regression model. When a particular explanatory variable has no effect on the dependent variable, what does its coefficient equal?

3. Consider the "artificial explanatory variable" in the context of a RESET test:

    a. What does the "artificial explanatory variable" not add to the regression?

    b. What does the "artificial explanatory variable" add to the regression?

4. Consider the "artificial explanatory variable" in the context of a RESET test.

    a. If the coefficient estimate of the artificial explanatory variable does not significantly differ from 0:

       i. Does the new form of the information add significant explanatory power in explaining the dependent variable?

       ii. Is there a compelling reason to consider a new specification of the model?

    2. If the coefficient estimate of the artificial explanatory variable does significantly differ from 0:

       i. Does the new form of the information add significant explanatory power in explaining the dependent variable?

       ii. Would it prudent to consider a new specification of the model?

Chapter 12 Exercises

1. Revisit the presidential election data.

Presidential election data: Annual time series data of US presidential election and economic statistics from 1890 to 2008.

$VotePartyDem_t$ Percent of popular vote received by the Democratic candidate in year t

$VotePartyRep_t$ Percent of popular vote received by the Republican candidate in year t

$VotePartyThird_t$ Percent of the popular vote received by third (minor) party candidates in year t (percent)

$PresPartyR1_t$ 1 if incumbent President is Republican in year t; 0 if Democrat

$PresIncum_t$ 1 if incumbent President is a candidate in year t, 0 otherwise

$PresPartyTerms_t$ Number of consecutive terms the incumbent President's party has held the presidency in year t

$RealGdpGrowth_t$ Real GDP growth rate in year t (percent)

$InflGdpCurrent_t$ Inflation rate in year t based on the GDP price deflator (percent)

[To access this online material, go to http://mitpress.mit.edu/westhoffeconometrics and select Presidential Election – 1892–2008.]

Consider the following factors that may or may not influence the vote for the incumbent President's party:

· Real GDP growth rate

· Inflation rate

· Number of consecutive terms the incumbent President's party has held the presidency

a. Formulate a theory explaining how each of these factors should affect the presidential vote.

b. Present a model incorporating these factors. What do your theories imply about the sign of each coefficient?

c. Use the ordinary least squares (OLS) estimation procedure to estimate the coefficients. Interpret the coefficient estimates.

d. Formulate the null and alternative hypotheses.

e. Calculate Prob[Results IF H_0 true] and assess your theories.

Cigarette consumption data: Cross section of per capita cigarette consumption and prices in fiscal year 2008 for the 50 states and the District of Columbia.

CigConsPC$_t$	Cigarette consumption per capita in state t (packs)
EducCollege$_t$	Percent of population with bachelor degrees in state t
EducHighSchool$_t$	Percent of population with high school diplomas in state t
IncPC$_t$	Income per capita in state t (1,000s of dollars)
Pop$_t$	Population of state t (persons)
PriceConsumer$_t$	Price of cigarettes in state t paid by consumers (dollars per pack)
PriceSupplier$_t$	Price of cigarettes in state t received by suppliers (dollars per pack)
RegionMidWest$_t$	1 if state t in Midwest census region, 0 otherwise
RegionNorthEast$_t$	1 if state t in Northeast census region, 0 otherwise
RegionSouth$_t$	1 if state t in South census region, 0 otherwise
RegionWest$_t$	1 if state t in West census region, 0 otherwise
SmokeRateAdult$_t$	Percent of adults who smoke in state t
SmokeRateYouth$_t$	Percent of youths who smoke in state t
State$_t$	Name of state t
Tax$_t$	Cigarette tax rate in state t (dollars per pack)
TobProdPC$_t$	Per capita tobacco production in state t (pounds)

2. Revisit the cigarette consumption data.

[To access this online material, go to http://mitpress.mit.edu/westhoffeconometrics and select Cigarette Consumption.]

a. Focus on the cigarette tax rate, *Tax*. Which state has the highest tax rate and which state has the lowest tax rate?

b. Consider the following linear model that attempts to explain the cigarette tax rate:

$$Tax_t = \beta_{Const} + \beta_{TobProdPC}TobProdPC_t + e_t$$

What rationale might justify this model? That is, devise a theory explaining why a state's tobacco production should affect the state's tax on cigarettes. What does your theory suggest about the sign of the coefficient, $\beta_{TobProd}$?

c. Use the ordinary least squares (OLS) estimation procedure to estimate the model's parameters. Interpret the coefficient estimate.

d. Formulate the null and alternative hypotheses.

e. Calculate Prob[Results IF H_0 true] and assess your theory.

3. Revisit the cigarette consumption data.

[To access this online material, go to http://mitpress.mit.edu/westhoffeconometrics and select Cigarette Consumption.]

a. Perform a RESET test on the linear model explaining the cigarette tax rate. What do you conclude?

Getting Started in EViews

After running the original regression:

- Click **View, Stability Diagnostics, Ramsey RESET Test**.
- Be certain that **1** is selected as the number of fitted terms.
- Click **OK**.

Consider the following nonlinear model:

$$Tax_t = \beta_{Const} + \beta_{TobProd}\sqrt{TobProdPC_t} + e_t$$

b. Apply the hypothesis testing approach that we developed to assess this model.

Getting Started in EViews

Generate a square root with one of the following commands:

SqrtTobProdPC = sqr(TobProdPC)

or

SqrtTobProdPC = TobProdPC^.5

In EViews, the term sqr is the square root function and the character ^ represents an exponent.

c. Perform a RESET test for the nonlinear model. What do you conclude?

4. Revisit the cigarette consumption data.

[To access this online material, go to http://mitpress.mit.edu/westhoffeconometrics and select Cigarette Consumption.]

Consider how the price of cigarettes paid by consumers and per capita income affect the adult smoking rate.

a. Formulate a theory explaining how each of these factors should affect the adult smoking rate.

b. Present a linear model incorporating these factors. What do your theories imply about the sign of each coefficient?

c. Use the ordinary least squares (OLS) estimation procedure to estimate the coefficients. Interpret the coefficient estimates.

d. Formulate the null and alternative hypotheses.

e. Calculate Prob[Results IF H_0 true] and assess your theory.

f. Perform a RESET test for your model. What do you conclude?

5. Revisit the cigarette consumption data.

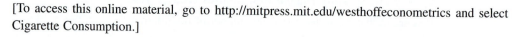

[To access this online material, go to http://mitpress.mit.edu/westhoffeconometrics and select Cigarette Consumption.]

Focus your attention on explaining the youth smoking rate. Choose the variables that you believe should affect the youth smoking rate.

a. Formulate a theory explaining how each of these factors should affect the youth smoking rate.

b. Present a linear model incorporating these factors. What do your theories imply about the sign of each coefficient?

c. Use the ordinary least squares (OLS) estimation procedure to estimate the coefficients. Interpret the coefficient estimates.

d. Formulate the null and alternative hypotheses.

e. Calculate Prob[Results IF H_0 true] and assess your theory.

f. Perform a RESET test for your model. What do you conclude?

13 Dummy and Interaction Variables

Chapter 13 Prep Questions

1. Recall our first regression example, Professor Lord's quiz:

Student	Minutes Studied (x)	Quiz Score (y)
1	5	66
2	15	87
3	25	90

Consider the most simple of all possible models, one that does not include even a single explanatory variable:

Model: $y_t = \beta_{Const} + e_t$

b_{Const} denotes the estimate of β_{Const}:

Estimates: $Esty_t = b_{Const}$

Residuals: $Res_t = y_t - Esty_t$

The sum of squared residuals equals:

$$SSR = Res_1^2 + Res_2^2 + Res_3^2 = (y_1 - b_{Const})^2 + (y_2 - b_{Const})^2 + (y_3 - b_{Const})^2$$

Using calculus derive the equation for b_{Const} that minimizes the sum of squared residuals by expressing b_{Const} in terms of y_1, y_2, and y_3.

2. Consider the following faculty salary data:[1]

Faculty salary data: Artificially generated cross section salary data and characteristics for 200 faculty members.

$Salary_t$	Salary of faculty member t (dollars)
$Experience_t$	Teaching experience for faculty member t (years)
$Articles_t$	Number of articles published by faculty member t
$SexM1_t$	1 if faculty member t is male; 0 if female

You can access these data by clicking on the following link:

[To access this online material, go to http://mitpress.mit.edu/westhoffeconometrics and select Faculty Salaries.]

   a. What is the average salary for all 200 faculty members?

   b. What is the average salary for the men?

   c. What is the average salary for the women?

---

1. As a consequence of privacy concerns, these data were artificially generated.

Getting Started in EViews

For all faculty members:

- In the Workfile window: double click **Salary**.
- In the Workfile window: click **View**, then click **Descriptive Statistics,** then click **Histogram and Stats**.

For men only:

- In the Workfile window: click **Sample**.
- To include only men, enter **SexM1 = 1** in the If condition window.
- Click **OK**.

For women only:

- In the Workfile window: click **Sample**.
- To include only women, enter **SexM1 = 0** in the If condition window.
- Click **OK**.

Note: Do not forget to "turn off" the sample.

- In the Workfile window: click **Sample**.
- lear the If condition window.
- Click **OK**.

    d. Consider the following model:

$$Salary = \beta_{Const} + e_t$$

What is the value of the estimated constant?

Getting Started in EViews

To estimate the model, you must "trick" EViews into running the appropriate regression:

- In the Workfile window: highlight **Salary** and then while depressing <Ctrl> highlight one other variable, say **SexM1**.
- In the Workfile window: double click a highlighted variable.
- Click **Open Equation**.
- In the Equation Specification window delete **SexM1** so that the line specifying the equation looks like this:

salary c

- Click **OK**.

e. Now consider a second model:

$$Salary_t = \beta_{Const} + \beta_{SexM1}SexM1_t + e_t$$

Run the appropriate regression to estimate the values of the constant and coefficient. What is the estimated salary for men? What is the estimated salary for women?

f. Compare your answers to d and e with your answers to a, b, and c. What conclusions can you draw concerning averages and the regression estimates?

3. Consider the following model explaining Internet use in various countries:

$$LogUsersInternet_t = \beta^{Int}_{Const} + \beta^{Int}_{Year}Year_t + \beta^{Int}_{CapHum}CapitalHuman_t$$
$$+ \beta^{Int}_{CapPhy}CapitalPhysical_t + \beta^{Int}_{GDP}Gdp_t + \beta^{Int}_{Auth}Auth_t + e^{Int}_t$$

where

$LogUsersInternet_t$ = logarithm of Internet users per 1,000 people for observation t

$Year_t$ = year for observation t

$CapitalHuman_t$ = literacy rate for observation t (percent of population 15 and over)

$CapitalPhysical_t$ = telephone mainlines per 10,000 people for observation t

$GdpPC_t$ = per capita real GDP in nation t (1,000s of "international" dollars)

$Auth_t$ = the Freedom House measures of political authoritarianism for observation t normalized to a 0 to 10 scale. 0 represents the most democratic rating and 10 the most authoritarian. During the 1995 to 2002 period, Canada and the United States had a 0 rating; Iraq and the Democratic Republic of Korea (North Korea) rated 10.

a. Note that the dependent variable is the logarithm of Internet users. Interpret the coefficient of $Year$, β^{Int}_{Year}.

b. Develop a theory that explains how each explanatory variable affects Internet use. What do your theories suggest about the sign of each coefficient?

4. Consider a similar model explaining television use in various countries:

$$LogUsersTV_t = \beta^{TV}_{Const} + \beta^{TV}_{Year}Year_t + \beta^{TV}_{CapHum}CapitalHuman_t + \beta^{TV}_{CapPhy}CapitalPhysical_t$$
$$+ \beta^{TV}_{GDP}Gdp_t + \beta^{TV}_{Auth}Auth_t + e^{TV}_t$$

where

$LogUsersTV_t$ = logarithm of television users per 1,000 people for observation t

a. Develop a theory that explains how each explanatory variable affects television use.

b. Based on your theories, which coefficients should be qualitatively similar (have the same sign) as those in the Internet use model and which may be qualitatively different?

13.1   Preliminary Mathematics: Averages and Regressions Including Only a Constant

Before investigating the possibility of discrimination in academia, we will consider a technical issue that will prove useful. While a regression that includes only a constant (i.e., a regression with no explanatory variables) is not interesting in itself, it teaches us an important lesson. When a regression includes only a constant, the ordinary least squares (OLS) estimate of the constant equals the average of the dependent variable's values. A little calculus allows us to prove this:

Model $y_t = \beta_{Const} + e_t$

Estimates $Esty_t = b_{Const}$

Residuals $Res_t = y_t - Esty_t$

Now compute the sum of the squared residuals:

$$SSR = Res_1^2 + Res_2^2 + Res_3^2$$
$$= (y_1 - Esty_1)^2 + (y_2 - Esty_2)^2 + (y_3 - Esty_3)^2$$
$$= (y_1 - b_{Const})^2 + (y_2 - b_{Const})^2 + (y_3 - b_{Const})^2$$

To minimize the sum of squared residuals, differentiate with respect to b_{Const} and set the derivative equal to 0:

$$\frac{dSSR}{db_{Const}} = -2(y_1 - b_{Const}) - 2(y_2 - b_{Const}) - 2(y_3 - b_{Const}) = 0$$

Divide by −2:

$$y_1 - b_{Const} + y_2 - b_{Const} + y_3 - b_{Const} = 0$$

Rearrange terms:

$$y_1 + y_2 + y_3 = 3b_{Const}$$

Divide by 3:

$$\frac{y_1 + y_2 + y_3}{3} = b_{Const}$$

where $\dfrac{y_1 + y_2 + y_3}{3}$ equals the mean of y, $\bar{y}$,

$$\bar{y} = b_{Const}$$

We have just shown that when a regression includes only a constant the ordinary least squares (OLS) estimate of the constant equals the average value of the dependent variable, y.

13.2 An Example: Discrimination in Academe

Now we consider faculty salary data. It is important to keep in mind that these data were artificially generated; the data are not "real." Artificially generated, rather than real, data are used as a consequence of privacy concerns.

Faculty salary data: Artificially generated cross-sectional salary data and characteristics for 200 faculty members.

[To access this online material, go to http://mitpress.mit.edu/westhoffeconometrics and select Faculty Salaries.]

$Salary_t$ Salary of faculty member t (dollars)

$Experience_t$ Teaching experience for faculty member t (years)

$Articles_t$ Number of articles published by faculty member t

$SexM1_t$ 1 if faculty member t is male; 0 if female

Project: Assess the possibility of discrimination in academe.

We begin by examining the average salaries of men and women.

13.2.1 Average Salaries

First let us report the average salaries:

Both males and females	$82,802
Males only	91,841
Females only	63,148
Difference	28,693

On average, males earn nearly $30,000 more than females. This certainly raises the possibility that gender discrimination exists, does it not?

13.2.2 Dummy Variables

A **dummy variable** separates the observations into two disjoint groups; a dummy variable equals 1 for one group and 0 for the other group. The variable *SexM1* is a dummy variable; *SexM1* denotes whether a faculty member is a male of female; *SexM1* equals 1 if the faculty member is a male and 0 if female. We will now show that dummy variables prove very useful in exploring the possibility of discrimination by considering three types of models:

· **Type 1 models:** No explanatory variables; only a constant.

· **Type 2 models:** A constant and a single dummy explanatory variable denoting sex.

· **Type 3 models:** A constant, a dummy explanatory variable denoting sex, and other explanatory variable(s).

13.2.3   Models

Type 1 Models: No Explanatory Variables; Only a Constant

We begin with a model that includes no explanatory variables; that is, a model that includes only a constant. We are doing this to confirm our conclusion that a regression with only a constant is equivalent to computing an average of the dependent variable.

Step 0:   Formulate a model reflecting the theory to be tested.

Model: $Salary_t = \beta_{Const} + e_t$

Since this model includes only a constant, we are theorizing that except for random influences each faculty member earns the same salary. That is, this model attributes all variations in income to random influences.

Step 1:   Collect data, run the regression, and interpret the estimates.

Getting Started in EViews

To estimate the model, you must "trick" EViews into running the appropriate regression:

· In the Workfile window: highlight **Salary** and then while depressing <Ctrl> highlight one other variable, say **SexM1**.

· In the Workfile window: double click a highlighted variable.

· Click **Open Equation**.

· In the Equation Specification window delete **SexM1** so that the window looks like this:

salary c

· Click **OK**.

Table 13.1 confirms the fact that when a regression only includes a constant, the ordinary least squares (OLS) estimate of the constant is just the average of the dependent variable. To emphasize this fact, we will now run two more regressions with only a constant: one regression including only men (table 13.2) and one including only women (table 13.3).

Table 13.1
Discrimination regression results—All observations

Ordinary least squares (OLS)				
Dependent variable: *Salary*				
Explanatory variable(s):	Estimate	SE	*t*-Statistic	Prob
Const	82,802.40	1,929.422	42.91565	0.0000
Number of observations	200			

Table 13.2
Discrimination regression results—Males only

Dependent variable: *Salary*
Explanatory variables: None
Sample: *SexM1* = 1

Ordinary least squares (OLS)				
Dependent variable: *Salary*				
Explanatory variable(s):	Estimate	SE	*t*-Statistic	Prob
Const	91,840.58	2,259.201	40.65180	0.0000
Number of observations	137	Sample	*SexM1* = 1	

Table 13.3
Discrimination regression results—Females only

Ordinary least squares (OLS)				
Dependent variable: *Salary*				
Explanatory variable(s):	Estimate	SE	*t*-Statistic	Prob
Const	63,147.94	2,118.879	29.80252	0.0000
Number of observations	63	Sample	*SexM1* = 0	

Compare the regression results to the salary averages:

Both males and females $82,802
Males only   91,841
Females only   63,148

Tables 13.1, 13.2, and 13.3 illustrate the important lesson that type 1 models teach us. In a regression that includes only a constant, the ordinary least squares (OLS) estimate of the constant is the average of the dependent variable. Next let us consider a slightly more complicated model.

Type 2 Models: A Constant and a Single Dummy Explanatory Variable Denoting Sex

Step 0:   Formulate a model reflecting the theory to be tested.

$$Salary_t = \beta_{Const} + \beta_{SexM1}SexM1_t + e_t$$

where *SexM1* equals 1 for males and 0 for females

Discrimination theory: Women are discriminated against in the job market; hence, men earn higher salaries than women. Since *SexM1* equals 1 for males and 0 for females, β_{SexM1} should be positive indicating that men will earn more than women: $\beta_{SexM1} > 0$.

Step 1:   Collect data, run the regression, and interpret the estimates.

Using the ordinary least squares (OLS) estimation procedure, we estimate the parameters (table 13.4):

For emphasis, let us apply the estimated equation to men and then to women by plugging in their values for *SexM1*:

Estimated equation: $EstSalary = 63,148 + 28,693SexM1$

We can now compute the estimated salary for men and women:

For men	For women
$SexM1 = 1$	$SexM1 = 0$
$EstSalary_{Men} = 63,148 + 28,693 = 91,841$	$EstSalary_{Women} = 63,148 + 0 = 63,148$

Next note something very interesting by comparing the regression results to the salary averages:

Table 13.4
Discrimination regression results—Male sex dummy

Ordinary least squares (OLS)				
Dependent variable: *Salary*				
Explanatory variable(s):	Estimate	SE	*t*-Statistic	Prob
SexM1	28,692.65	3,630.670	7.902852	0.0000
Const	63,147.94	3,004.914	21.01489	0.0000
Number of observations	200			

Estimated equation: $EstSalary = 63,148 + 28,693SexM1$

Interpretation of estimates:

$b_{SexM1} = 28,693$: Men earn \$28,693 more than women

Critical result: The *SexM1* coefficient estimate equals 28,693. This evidence, the positive sign of the coefficient estimate, suggests that men earn more than women thereby supporting the discrimination theory.

Males only   91,841

Females only   63,148

Difference   28,693

An ordinary least squares (OLS) regression that includes only a constant and a dummy variable is equivalent to comparing averages. The conclusions are precisely the same: men earn \$28,693 more than women. The dummy variable's coefficient estimate equals the difference of the averages.

Step 2: Play the cynic and challenge the results; construct the null and alternative hypotheses.

Cynic's view: Despite the results, there is no discrimination.

H_0: $\beta_{SexM1} = 0$ Cynic is correct: No discrimination

H_1: $\beta_{SexM1} > 0$ Cynic is incorrect: Discrimination in favor of men, against women

Step 3:   Formulate the question to assess the cynic's view and the null hypothesis.

· **Generic question for discrimination hypothesis:**   What is the probability that the results would be like those we obtained (or even stronger), if the cynic is correct and no discrimination were present?

· **Specific question for discrimination hypothesis:** What is the probability that the coefficient estimate, b_{SexM1}, in one regression would be 2,240 or more, if H_0 were true (if the actual coefficient, β_{SexM1}, equals 0)?

Steps 4 and 5:   To calculate the Prob[Results IF H_0 true], use the tails probability reported in the regression printout. This is easy to do. Since this is a one-tailed test, we divide the tails probability by 2:[2]

$$\text{Prob[Results IF } H_0 \text{ true]} = \frac{<0.0001}{2} = <0.0001$$

Clearly, the Prob[Results IF H_0 true] is very small. We can reject the null hypothesis which asserts that no discrimination exists.

Before we continue, let us point out that our dummy variable, *SexM1*, assigned 1 to males and 0 to females. This was an arbitrary choice. We could just as easily assigned 0 to males and 1 to females, could we not? To see what happens when we switch the assignments, generate a new variable, *SexF1*:

---

2. Note that even though the tails probability is reported as 0.0000, the probability can never precisely equal 0. It will always exceed 0. Consequently, instead of writing 0.0000, we write < 0.0001 to emphasize the fact that the probability can never equal precisely 0.

$SexF1 = 1 - SexM1$

For men	For women
$SexM1 = 1$	$SexM1 = 0$
$SexF1 = 1 - 1 = 0$	$SexF1 = 1 - 0 = 1$

Step 0: Formulate a model reflecting the theory to be tested.

$Salary_t = \beta_{Const} + \beta_{SexF1}SexF1_t + e_t$

where $SexF1_t = 1$ if faculty member t is female; 0 if male.

Discrimination theory: Women are discriminated against in the job market; hence women earn lower salaries than men. Since $SexF1$ equals 1 for females and 0 for males, β_{SexF1} should be negative indicating that women will earn less than men: $\beta_{SexF1} < 0$.

Step 1: Collect data, run the regression, and interpret the estimates.

After we generate the new dummy variable, $SexF1$, we can easily run the regression (table 13.5).

 Let us apply this estimated equation to men and then to women by plugging in their values for $SexF1$:

For men	For women
$SexF1 = 0$	$SexF1 = 1$
$EstSalary_{Men} = 91{,}841 - 0 = 91{,}841$	$EstSalary_{Women} = 91{,}841 - 28{,}693 = 63{,}148$

The results are precisely the same as before. This is reassuring. The decision to assign 1 to one group and 0 to the other group is completely arbitrary. It would be very discomforting if this

Table 13.5
Discrimination regression results—Female sex dummy

Ordinary least squares (OLS)				
Dependent variable: *Salary*				
Explanatory variable(s):	Estimate	SE	*t*-Statistic	Prob
SexF1	−28,692.65	3,630.670	−7.902852	0.0000
Const	91,840.58	2,037.708	45.07052	0.0000
Number of observations	200			

Estimated equation: $EstSalary = 91{,}841 - 28{,}693 SexF1$

Interpretation of estimates:

 $bSexF1 = -28{,}693$: Women earn \$28,693 less than men

Critical result: The *SexF1* coefficient estimate equals −28,683. This evidence, the negative sign of the coefficient estimate, suggests that women earn less than men thereby supporting the discrimination theory.

arbitrary decision affected our conclusions. The fact that the arbitrary decision does not affect the results is crucial.

Step 2: Play the cynic and challenge the results; construct the null and alternative hypotheses.

Cynic's view: Despite the results, there is no discrimination.

H_0: $\beta_{SexF1} = 0$ Cynic is correct: No discrimination

H_1: $\beta_{SexF1} < 0$ Cynic is incorrect: Discrimination in favor of men, against women

The null hypothesis, like the cynic, challenges the evidence. The alternative hypothesis is consistent with the evidence.

Steps 3, 4, and 5: It is easy to calculate the Prob[Results IF H_0 true] by using the tails probability reported in the regression printout. Since this is a one-tailed test, we divide the tails probability by 2:

$$\text{Prob[Results IF } H_0 \text{ true]} = \frac{<0.0001}{2} = <0.0001$$

Since the probability is so small, we reject the null hypothesis that no discrimination exists.

Bottom line:

· Our choice of the base group for the dummy variable (i.e., the group that is assigned a value of 0 for the dummy variable) does not influence the results.

· Type 2 models, models that include only a constant and a dummy variable, are equivalent to comparing averages.

Question: Do type 2 models provide convincing evidence of gender discrimination?

On the one hand, yes:

· The dummy variable coefficients suggest that women earn less than men.

· The dummy variable coefficients are very significant—the probability of obtaining results like we obtained if no discrimination exists is less than 0.0001.

On the other hand, what implicit assumption is this discrimination model making? The model implicitly assumes that the only relevant factor in determining faculty salaries is gender. Is this reasonable? Well, very few individuals contend that gender is the only factor. Many individuals believe that gender is one factor, perhaps an important factor, affecting salaries, but they believe that other factors such as education and experience also play a role.

Type 3 Models: A Constant, a Dummy Explanatory Variable Denoting Sex, and Other Explanatory Variable(s)

While these models allow the possibility of gender discrimination, they also permit us to explore the possibility that other factors affect salaries too. To explore such models, let us include both a dummy variable and the number of years of experience as explanatory variables.

Step 0:   Formulate a model reflecting the theory to be tested.

$$Salary_t = \beta_{Const} + \beta_{SexF1}SexF1_t + \beta_{Exper}Experience_t + e_t$$

Theories:

- **Discrimination:**   As before, we theorize that women are discriminated against: $\beta_{SexF1} < 0$.

- **Experience:**   It is generally believed that in most occupations, employees with more experience earn more than employees with less experience. Consequently we theorize that the experience coefficient should be positive: $\beta_{Exper} > 0$.

Step 1:   Collect data, run the regression, and interpret the estimates.

We can now compute the estimated salary for men and women (table 13.6):

$$EstSalary = 42{,}238 - 2{,}240SexF1 + 2{,}447Experience$$

Table 13.6
Discrimination regression results—Female sex dummy and experience

	Ordinary least squares (OLS)			
Dependent variable: *Salary*				
Explanatory variable(s):	Estimate	SE	*t*-Statistic	Prob
SexF1	−2,240.053	3,051.835	−0.734002	0.4638
Experience	2,447.104	163.3812	14.97787	0.0000
Const	42,237.61	3,594.297	11.75129	0.0000
Number of observations	200			

Estimated equation: $EstSalary = 42{,}238 - 2{,}240SexF1 + 2{,}447Experience$

Interpretation of estimates:

$b_{SexF1} = -2{,}240$: Women earn about \$2,240 less than men after accounting for experience

$b_{Exper} = 2{,}447$: Each additional year of experience results in a \$2,447 increase in salary for both men and women

Critical result: The *SexF1* coefficient estimate equals −2,240. The negative sign of the coefficient estimate suggests that women earn less than men. This evidence supports the discrimination theory.

The *Experience* coefficient estimate equals 2,447. The positive sign of the coefficient estimate suggests that additional experience increases salaries. This evidence supports the experience theory.

For men, $SexF1 = 0$:

$$EstSalary_{Men} = 42{,}238 - 0 + 2{,}447Experience$$

$$= 42{,}238 + 2{,}447Experience$$

For women, $SexF1 = 1$:

$$EstSalary_{Women} = 42{,}238 - 2{,}240 + 2{,}447Experience$$

$$39{,}998 + 2{,}447Experience$$

We can illustrate the estimated salaries of men and women graphically (figure 13.1).

Step 2: Play the cynic and challenge the results; construct the null and alternative hypotheses.

- **Cynic's view on discrimination:** Despite the results, there is no discrimination.
- **Cynic's view on experience:** Despite the results, experience does not increase salary.

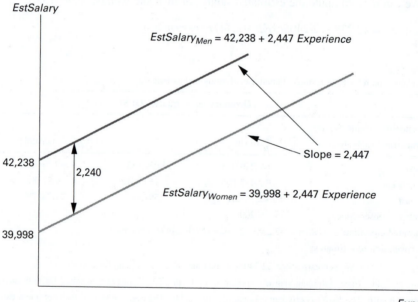

Figure 13.1
Salary discrimination

Discrimination hypotheses   Experience hypotheses

$H_0: \beta_{SexF1} = 0$ No discrimination $H_0: \beta_{Exper} = 0$ Experience has no effect on salary

$H_1: \beta_{SexF1} < 0$ Discrimination $H_1: \beta_{Exper} > 0$ Experience increases salary

The null hypothesis, like the cynic, challenges the evidence. The alternative hypothesis is consistent with the evidence. We will proceed by focusing on discrimination.

Step 3:   Formulate the question to assess the cynic's view and the null hypothesis.

· **Generic question for discrimination hypothesis:**   What is the probability that the results would be like those we obtained (or even stronger), if the cynic is correct and no discrimination were present?

· **Specific question for discrimination hypothesis:**   The regression's coefficient estimate was −2,240. What is the probability that the coefficient estimate in one regression would be −2,240 or less, if H_0 were true (if the actual coefficient, β_{SexF1}, equals 0; i.e., if no discrimination existed)?

Answer: Prob[Results IF H_0 true]

Step 4 and 5:   Use the general properties of the estimation procedure, the probability distribution of the estimate (figure 13.2), to calculate Prob[Results IF H_0 true].

$$\text{Prob[Results IF } H_0 \text{ true]} = \frac{0.4638}{2} = 0.23$$

At the traditional significance levels of 1, 5, and 10 percent, we cannot reject the null hypothesis that no discrimination exists. What should we make of this dramatic change?

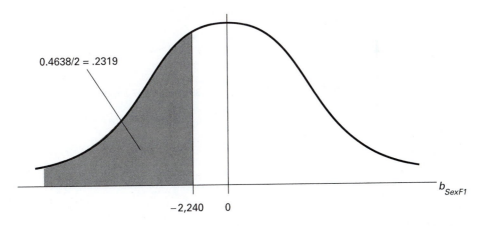

Figure 13.2
Probability distribution of coefficient estimate

13.2.4   Beware of Implicit Assumptions

Focus on our last model: $Salary_t = \beta_{Const} + \beta_{SexF1}SexF1_t + \beta_{Exper}Experience_t + e_t$.

Implicit assumption: One year of added experience increases the salary of men and women by equal amounts.

In other words, this model implicitly assumes that women start behind men by a certain amount and then remain behind men by that same amount for each level of experience. We will call this "lump sum" discrimination. Figure 13.3 illustrates this well; the slopes of the lines representing the estimated salaries for men and women are equal.

Might gender discrimination take another form? Yes. Experience could affect the salaries of men and women differently. It is possible for a man to receive more for an additional year of experience than a woman. In other words, could men be more highly rewarded for experience than women? Our last model excludes this possibility because it implicitly assumes that a year of added experience increases the salary of men and women by equal amounts. To explore the possibility of this second type of discrimination, we will introduce interaction variables. We will refer to this type of discrimination as "raise" discrimination.

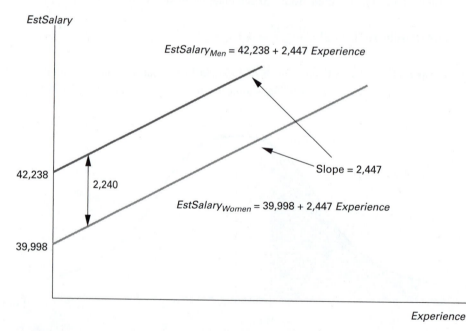

Figure 13.3
Estimated discrimination equations with "lump sum" discrimination

13.2.5 Interaction Variables

An **interaction variable** allows us to explore the possibility that one explanatory variable influences the effect that a second explanatory variable has on the dependent variable. We generate an interaction variable by multiplying the two variables together. We will focus on the interaction of *Experience* and *SexF1* by generating the variable *Exper_SexF1*:

$$Exper\_SexF1 = Experience \times SexF1$$

We will now add the interaction variable, *Exper_SexF1*, to our last model.

Step 0: Formulate a model reflecting the theory to be tested.

$$Salary_t = \beta_{Const} + \beta_{SexF1}SexF1_t + \beta_{Exper}Experience_t + \beta_{Exper\_SexF1}Exper\_SexF1_t + e_t$$

Theories:

· **"Lump sum" discrimination:** As before, we theorize that women are discriminated against: $\beta_{SexF1} < 0$.

· **Experience:** As before, we theorize that the experience coefficient should be positive: $\beta_{Exper} > 0$.

· **"Raise" discrimination:** One year of additional experience should increase the salary of women by less than their male counterparts. Hence we theorize that the coefficient of the interaction variable is negative: $\beta_{Exper\_SexF1} < 0$. (If it is not clear why you should expect this coefficient to be negative, be patient. It should become clear shortly.)

Step 1: Collect data, run the regression, and interpret the estimates (table 13.7).

Table 13.7
Discrimination regression results—Female sex dummy, experience, and Female sex dummy–Experience interaction variable

Ordinary least squares (OLS)				
Dependent variable: *Salary* **Explanatory variable(s):**	Estimate	SE	*t*-Statistic	Prob
SexF1	10,970.26	5,538.331	1.980787	0.0490
Experience	2,676.158	179.6929	14.89295	0.0000
Exper_SexF1	−1,134.665	399.9411	−2.837081	0.0050
Const	37,594.67	3,892.412	9.658451	0.0000
Number of observations	200			

Estimated equation: *EstSalary* = 37,595 + 10,970*SexF1* + 2,676*Experience* − 1,135*Exper_SexF1*

Now let us apply the estimated equation to men and women:

For men   For women

$SexF1 = 0$ $SexF1 = 1$

$Exper\_SexF1 = 0$ $Exper\_SexF1 = Experience$

For men,

$EstSalary_{Men} = 37{,}595 + 10{,}970SexF1 + 2{,}676Experience - 1{,}135Exper\_SexF1$

$$= 37{,}595 + 0 + 2{,}676Experience - 0$$

$$= 37{,}595 + 2{,}676Experience$$

For women,

$EstSalary_{Women} = 37{,}595 + 10{,}970SexF1 + 2{,}676Experience - 1{,}135Exper\_SexF1$

$$= 37{,}595 + 10{,}970 + 2{,}676Experience - 1{,}135Experience$$

$$= 48{,}565 + 1{,}541Experience$$

Plot the estimated salary for men and women (figure 13.4). We can use this regression to assess the possibility of two different types of discrimination. One of the estimates is a little surprising:

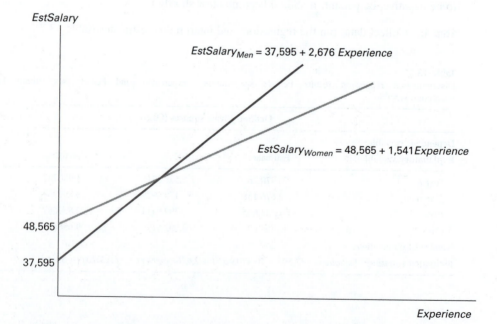

Figure 13.4
Estimated discrimination equations with "lump sum" and "raise" discrimination

- **"Lump sum" discrimination:** As before, the coefficient of the sex dummy variable, *SexF1*, assesses the possibility of "lump sum" discrimination. The coefficient estimate is positive. This is unexpected. It suggests that when faculty members are hired from graduate school with no experience, women receive about $10,970 more than men. The positive coefficient estimate suggests that reverse discrimination exists at the entry level.

- **"Raise" discrimination:** The coefficient of the interaction variable, *Exper_SexF1*, assesses the possibility of this more subtle type of discrimination, "raise" discrimination. The coefficient estimate is negative. It suggests that a woman is receives $1,135 less than a man for an additional year of experience. The negative coefficient estimate suggests that women receive smaller annual raises than their male counterparts.

These regression results paint a more complex picture of possible discrimination than is often contemplated. Again, recall that as a consequence of privacy concerns these data were artificially generated. Consequently, do not conclude that the conclusions we have suggested here necessarily reflect the "real world." This example was used because it illustrates how multiple regression analysis can exploit dummy variables and interaction variables to investigate important issues, such as the presence of discrimination.

13.2.6 Conclusions

- **Beware of averages:** We should not consider differences in averages, by themselves, as evidence of discrimination. When we just consider average salaries, we are implicitly adopting a model of salary determination that few, if anyone, consider realistic. We implicitly assume that the only factor that determines an individual's salary is his/her sex. While many would argue that gender is one factor, very few would argue that gender is the only factor.

- **Power of multiple regression analysis:** Since is it naïve to consider just averages, what quantitative tools should we use to assess the presence of discrimination? Multiple regression analysis is an appropriate tool. It allows us to consider the roles played by several factors in the determination of salary and separates out the individual influence of each. Multiple regression analysis allows us to consider not only the role of gender, but also the role that the other factors may play. Multiple regression analysis sorts out the impact that each individual explanatory variable has on the dependent variable.

- **Flexibility of multiple regression analysis:** Not only does multiple regression analysis allow us to consider the roles played by various factors in salary determination, but also it allows us to consider various types of potential discrimination. The preceding example illustrates how we can assess the possible presence "lump sum" discrimination and/or "raise" discrimination.

13.3   An Example: Internet and Television Use

Next we consider Internet and television use:

Project: Assess the determinants of Internet and television use internationally.

Internet and TV data: Panel data of Internet, TV, economic, and political statistics for 208 countries from 1995 to 2002.

[To access this online material, go to http://mitpress.mit.edu/westhoffeconometrics and select Internet and TV Use – 1995–2002.]

$LogUsersInternet_t$ Logarithm of Internet users per 1,000 people for observation t

$LogUsersTV_t$ Logarithm of television users per 1,000 people for observation t

$Year_t$ Year for observation t

$CapitalHuman_t$ Literacy rate for observation t (percent of literate population 15 and over)

$CapitalPhysical_t$ Telephone mainlines per 10,000 people for observation t

$GdpPC_t$ Per capita real GDP in nation t (1,000s of "international" dollars)

$Auth_t$ The Freedom House measures of political authoritarianism for observation t normalized to a 0 to 10 scale. 0 represents the most democratic rating and 10 the most authoritarian. During the 1995–2002 period, Canada and the United States had a 0 rating; Iraq and the Democratic Republic of Korea (North Korea) rated 10.

Step 0:   Formulate a model reflecting the theory to be tested.

Internet model: $LogHsersInternet_t = \beta_{Const}^{Int} + \beta_{Year}^{Int} Year_t + \beta_{CapHum}^{Int} CapitalHuman_t$

$$+ \beta_{CopPhy}^{Int} CapitalPhysical_t + \beta_{GDP}^{Int} GdpPC_t + \beta_{Auth}^{Int} Auth_t$$

$$+ e_t^{Int}$$

Television model: $LogUsersTV_t = \beta_{Const}^{TV} + \beta_{Year}^{TV} Year_t + \beta_{CapHum}^{TV} CapitalHuman_t$

$$+ \beta_{CapPhy}^{TV} CapitalPhysical_t + \beta_{GDP}^{TV} GdpPC_t + \beta_{Auth}^{TV} Auth_t + e_t^{TV}$$

The dependent variable in both the Internet and television models is the logarithm of users. This is done so that the coefficients can be interpreted as percentages.

13.3.1   Similarities and Differences

The theory behind the effect of human capital, physical capital, and per capita GDP on both Internet and television use is straightforward: Additional human capital, physical capital, and per capita GDP should stimulate both Internet and television use.

We postulate that the impact of time and political factors should be different for the two media, however:

• As an emerging technology, we theorize that there should be, on the one hand, substantial growth of Internet use over time—even after accounting for all the other factors that may affect Internet use. Television, on the other hand, is a mature technology. After accounting for all the other factors, time should play little or no role in explaining television use.

• We postulate that the political factors should affect Internet and television use differently. On the one hand, since authoritarian nations control the content of television, we would expect authoritarian nations to promote television; television provides the authoritarian nation the means to get the government's message out. On the other hand, since it is difficult to control Internet content, we would expect authoritarian nations to suppress Internet use.

Table 13.8 summarizes our theories and presents the appropriate null and alternative hypotheses. As table 13.8 reports, all the hypothesis tests are one-tailed tests with the exception of the *Year* coefficient in the television use model.

Let us begin by focusing on Internet use.

Step 1: Collect data, run the regression, and interpret the estimates.

Since the dependent variables are logarithms, we interpret the coefficient estimates in terms of percentages (table 13.9). The signs of all the coefficient estimates support our theories.

Table 13.8
Theories and hypotheses for Internet and television use

Variable	*LogUsersInternet*		*LogUsersTV*	
	Theory	**Hypotheses**	**Theory**	**Hypotheses**
Year Emerging versus mature technology	$\beta_{Year}^{Int} > 0$	$H_0: \beta_{Year}^{Int} = 0$ $H_1: \beta_{Year}^{Int} > 0$	$\beta_{Year}^{TV} = 0$	$H_0: \beta_{Year}^{TV} = 0$ $H_1: \beta_{Year}^{TV} \neq 0$
CapitalHuman Literacy rate	$\beta_{CapHum}^{Int} > 0$	$H_0: \beta_{CapHum}^{Int} = 0$ $H_1: \beta_{CapHum}^{Int} > 0$	$\beta_{CapHum}^{TV} > 0$	$H_0: \beta_{CapHum}^{TV} = 0$ $H_1: \beta_{CapHum}^{TV} > 0$
CapitalPhysical Telephone (main) lines per 1,000 people	$\beta_{CapPhy}^{Int} > 0$	$H_0: \beta_{CapPhy}^{Int} = 0$ $H_1: \beta_{CapPhy}^{Int} > 0$	$\beta_{CapPhy}^{TV} > 0$	$H_0: \beta_{CapPhy}^{TV} = 0$ $H_1: \beta_{CapPhy}^{TV} > 0$
GdpPC Per capita real GDP	$\beta_{GDP}^{Int} > 0$	$H_0: \beta_{GDP}^{Int} = 0$ $H_1: \beta_{GDP}^{Int} > 0$	$\beta_{GDP}^{TV} > 0$	$H_0: \beta_{GDP}^{TV} = 0$ $H_1: \beta_{GDP}^{TV} > 0$
Auth 0-Democratic 10-Authoritarian	$\beta_{Auth}^{Int} < 0$	$H_0: \beta_{Auth}^{Int} = 0$ $H_1: \beta_{Auth}^{Int} < 0$	$\beta_{Auth}^{TV} > 0$	$H_0: \beta_{Auth}^{TV} = 0$ $H_1: \beta_{Auth}^{TV} > 0$

Table 13.9
Internet regression results

Ordinary least squares (OLS)				
Dependent variable: *LogUsersInternet*				
Explanatory variable(s):	Estimate	SE	*t*-Statistic	Prob
Year	0.449654	0.017078	26.32965	0.0000
CapitalHuman	0.023725	0.002470	9.606597	0.0000
CapitalPhysical	0.002056	0.000480	4.286193	0.0000
GdpPC	0.118177	0.011461	10.31146	0.0000
Auth	−0.095836	0.013999	−6.845761	0.0000
Const	−899.3201	34.17432	−26.31567	0.0000
Number of observations	566			

Estimated equation: $EstLogUsersInternet = -899.3 + 0.450Year + 0.024CapitalHuman + 0.002CapitalPhysical + 0.118GdpPC - 0.096Auth$

Interpretation of estimates: After accounting for all other explanatory variables

$\beta_{Year}^{Int} = 0.450$: A one unit increase in *Year* increases Internet use by 45 percent. That is, after accounting for all other explanatory variables, the estimated annual rate of Internet use is 45 percent per year. This is just the type of rapid growth we would expect for an emerging technology.

$b_{CapHum}^{Int} = 0.024$: A one percentage point increase in the literacy rate, *CapitalHuman*, increases Internet use by 2.4 percent

$b_{CapPhy}^{Int} = 0.002$: A one unit increase in telephone mainlines per 10,000 persons, *CapitalPhysical*, increases Internet use by 0.2 percent

$b_{GFP}^{Int} = 0.118$: A 1,000 international dollar increase in gross domestic product, *GdpPC*, increases Internet use by 11.8 percent

$b_{Auth}^{Int} = 0.096$: A 1 unit increase in the authoritarian index, *Auth*, decreases Internet use by 9.6 percent

Next estimate the television use model (table 13.10).

Steps 2, 3, 4, and 5:   Table 13.11 summarizes the remaining steps.

Note that all the results support the theories and all the coefficients except for the *Year* coefficient in the television regression are significant at the 1 percent level. It is noteworthy that the regression results suggest that the impact of *Year* and *Auth* differ for the two media just as we postulated. Our results suggest that after accounting for all other explanatory variables:

• Internet use grows by an estimated 45 percent per year whereas the annual growth rate of television use does not differ significantly from 0.

• Increases in the authoritarian index results to a significant decrease Internet use, but a significant increase television use.

Table 13.10
Television regression results

Ordinary least squares (OLS)				
Dependent variable: *LogUsersTV*				
Explanatory variable(s):	Estimate	SE	*t*-Statistic	Prob
Year	0.022989	0.015903	1.445595	0.1487
CapitalHuman	0.036302	0.001915	18.95567	0.0000
CapitalPhysical	0.001931	0.000510	3.789394	0.0002
GdpPC	0.058877	0.012338	4.772051	0.0000
Auth	0.063345	0.012825	4.939278	0.0000
Const	−44.95755	31.77155	−1.415025	0.1575
Number of observations	742			

Estimated equation: $EstLogUsersTV = -45.0 + 0.023Year + 0.036CapitalHuman + 0.002CapitalPhysical + 0.059GdpPC + 0.063Auth$

Interpretation of estimates: After accounting for all other explanatory variables

$b_{Year}^{TV} = 0.023$: A one unit increase in *Year* increases television use by 2.3 percent. The tails probability indicates that after accounting for all other explanatory variables, we cannot reject the null hypothesis that there is no growth in television use at the traditional significance levels. This is what we would expect for a mature technology.

$b_{CapHum}^{TV} = 0.036$: A one percentage point increase in the literacy rate, *CapitalHuman*, increases television use by 3.6 percent

$b_{CapPhy}^{TV} = 0.002$: A one unit increase in telephone mainlines per 10,000 persons, *CapitalPhysical*, increases television use by 0.2 percent

$b_{CDP}^{TV} = 0.058$: A 1,000 international dollar increase in gross domestic product, *GdpPC*, increases television use by 5.9 percent

$b_{Auth}^{TVt} = 0.063$: A 1 unit increase in the authoritarian index, *Auth*, increases television use by 6.3 percent

Table 13.11
Coefficient estimates and Prob[Results IF H_0 true]

	LogUsersInternet	*LogUsersTV*
Year	0.450* (<0.0001)	0.023 (0.1487)
CapitalHuman	0.024* (<0.0001)	0.036* (<0.0001)
CapitalPhysical	0.002* (<0.0001)	0.002* (0.0001)
GdpPC	0.118* (<0.0001)	0.059* (<0.0001)
Auth	−0.096 (<0.0001)	0.064* (<0.0001)

Prob[Results IF H_0 true] in parentheses. * indicates significance at the 1 percent level.

13.3.2 Interaction Variable: Economic and Political Interaction

Next let us investigate the following question:

Question: Does per capita GDP have a greater impact on Internet use in authoritarian nations than nonauthoritarian ones?

Some argue that the answer to this question is yes; that is, that per capita GDP has a greater impact on Internet use in authoritarian nations. Their rationale is based on the following logic:

• In authoritarian nations, citizens have few sources of uncensored information. There are few, if any, uncensored newspapers, news magazines, etc. available. The only source of uncensored information is the Internet. Consequently the effect of per capita GDP on Internet use will be large.

• In nonauthoritarian nations, citizens have many sources of uncensored information. Higher per capita GDP will no doubt stimulate Internet use, but it will also stimulate the purchase of uncensored newspapers, news magazines, etc. Consequently the effect on Internet use will be modest.

An authoritarian index–GDP interaction variable can be used to explore this issue. To do so, generate the interaction variable *Auth_GdpPC*, the product of the authoritarian index and per capita GDP:

$$Auth\_GdpPC = Auth \times GdpPC$$

Step 0: Formulate a model reflecting the theory to be tested.

Add this interaction variable to the Internet model:

$$LogUsersInternet_t = \beta_{Const}^{Int} + \beta_{Year}^{Int} Year_t + \beta_{CapHum}^{Int} CapitalHuman_t$$
$$+ \beta_{CapPhy}^{Int} CapitalPhysical_t + \beta_{GDP}^{Int} GdpPC_t + \beta_{Auth}^{Int} Auth_t$$
$$+ \beta_{Auth\_GDP}^{Int} Auth\_GdpPC_t + e_t^{Int}$$

If the theory regarding the interaction of authoritarianism and per capita GDP is correct, the coefficient of the interaction variable, *Auth_GdpPC*, should positive: $\beta_{Auth\_GDP}^{Int} > 0$. (If you are not certain why, it should become clear shortly.) The null and alternative hypotheses are

H_0: $\beta_{Auth\_GDP}^{Int} = 0$

H_1: $\beta_{Auth\_GDP}^{Int} > 0$

Step 1: Collect data, run the regression, and interpret the estimates.

Focus attention on the estimated effect of GDP. To do so, consider both the *GDP* and *Auth_GDP* terms in the estimated equation (table 13.12):

Table 13.12
Internet regression results—With interaction variable

Ordinary least squares (OLS)				
Dependent variable: *LogUsersInternet*				
Explanatory variable(s):	Estimate	SE	*t*-Statistic	Prob
Year	0.472826	0.016320	28.97241	0.0000
CapitalHuman	0.021560	0.002341	9.211160	0.0000
CapitalPhysical	0.003246	0.000473	6.859161	0.0000
GdpPC	0.033394	0.014715	2.269342	0.0236
Auth	−0.229875	0.020586	−11.16651	0.0000
Auth_GdpPC	0.017505	0.002064	8.480178	0.0000
Const	−944.9202	32.64247	−28.94757	0.0000
Number of observations	566			

Estimated equation: $EstLogUsersInternet = -944.9 + 0.473Year$
$$+ 0.022CapitalHuman + 0.003CapitalPhysical$$
$$+ 0.033GdpPC - 0.230Auth$$
$$+ 0.0175Auth\_GdpPC$$

Table 13.13
Interaction variable estimate calculations

Authoritarian index	Estimated effect of per capita GDP	
0	$0.033GdpPC + 0.0175 \times 0 \times GdpPC$ $0.033GdpPC + 0$	$= 0.033GdpPC$
2	$0.033GdpPC + 0.0175 \times 2 \times GdpPC$ $0.033GdpPC + 0.035GdpPC$	$= 0.068GdpPC$
4	$0.033GdpPC + 0.0175 \times 4 \times GdpPC$ $0.033GdpPC + 0.070GdpPC$	$= 0.103GdpPC$
6	$0.033GdpPC + 0.0175 \times 6 \times GdpPC$ $0.033GdpPC + 0.105GdpPC$	$= 0.138GdpPC$
8	$0.033GdpPC + 0.0175 \times 8 \times GdpPC$ $0.033GdpPC + 0.140GdpPC$	$= 0.173GdpPC$

$0.033GdpPC + 0.0175\ Auth\_GdpPC$

$0.033GdpPC + 0.0175\ Auth \times GdpPC$

We will now estimate the impact of GDP for several values of the authoritarian index (table 13.13).

Recall that as the authoritarian index increases, the level of authoritarianism rises. Therefore the estimates suggest that as a nation becomes more authoritarian, a $1,000 increase in per capita GDP increases Internet use by larger amounts. This supports the position of those who believe that citizens of all nations seek out uncensored information. In authoritarian nations, citizens have few sources of uncensored information; therefore, as per capita GDP rises, they embrace the uncensored information the Internet provides more enthusiastically than do citizens of non-authoritarian nation in which other sources of uncensored information are available.

Chapter 13 Review Questions

1. What is a dummy variable?

2. When is a regression equivalent to calculating an average?

3. What implicit assumption do we make when we use averages to draw conclusions?

4. What is an interaction variable?

Chapter 13 Exercises

Faculty salary data: Artificially constructed cross section salary data and characteristics for 200 faculty members.

$Salary_t$ Salary of faculty member t (dollars)

$Experience_t$ Teaching experience for faculty member t (years)

$Articles_t$ Number of articles published by faculty member t

$SexM1_t$ 1 if faculty member t is male; 0 if female

1. Reconsider the faculty salary data and add the number of articles each faculty member has published to the model:

$$Salary_t = \beta_{Const} + \beta_{SexF1}SexF1_t + \beta_{Exper}Experience_t + \beta_{Exper\_SexF1Exper}SexF1_t + \beta_{Art}Articles_t + e_t$$

   a. What is your theory regarding how the number of published articles should affect salary? What does your theory suggest about the sign of the *Articles* coefficient?

   b. Use the ordinary least squares (OLS) estimation procedure to estimate the parameters of the model. Interpret the published articles coefficient estimate.

[To access this online material, go to http://mitpress.mit.edu/westhoffeconometrics and select Faculty Salaries.]

   c. Formulate the null and alternative hypotheses regarding the effect of published articles.

   d. Assess the effect of published articles.

2. Again, reconsider the faculty salary data and add an article–sex interaction variable to the faculty salary model:

$$Salary_t = \beta_{Const} + \beta_{SexF1}SexF1_t + \beta_{Exper}Experience_t + \beta_{Exper\_SexF1}Exper\_SexF1_t + \beta_{Art}Articles_t$$

$$+ \beta_{Art\_SexF1}Articles\_Sex_t + e_t$$

where *Articles_Sex = Articles × SexF1.*

a. Focus on the following allegation:

Allegation: Women receive less credit for their publications than do their male colleagues.

What does the allegation suggest about the sign of the *Articles_Sex* coefficient?

b. Use the ordinary least squares (OLS) estimation procedure to estimate the parameters of the model. Interpret the published articles–sex interaction coefficient estimate.

[To access this online material, go to http://mitpress.mit.edu/westhoffeconometrics and select Faculty Salaries.]

c. Formulate the null and alternative hypotheses regarding the allegation.

d. Calculate Prob[Results IF H_0 true] and assess the allegation.

House earmark data: Cross-sectional data of proposed earmarks in the 2009 fiscal year for the 451 House members of the 110th Congress.

[To access this online material, go to http://mitpress.mit.edu/westhoffeconometrics and select House Earmarks.]

This file includes the following data variables:

CongressName$_t$	Name of Congressperson *t*
CongressParty$_t$	Party of Congressperson *t*
CongressState$_t$	State of Congressperson *t*
IncPC$_t$	Income per capita in the Congressperson *t*'s state (dollars)
Number$_t$	Number of earmarks received that were sponsored solely by Congressperson *t*
PartyDem1$_t$	1 if Congressperson *t* Democrat; 0 otherwise
PartyRep1$_t$	1 if Congressperson *t* Republican; 0 otherwise
RegionMidwest$_t$	1 if Congressperson *t* represents a midwestern state, 0 otherwise
RegionNortheast$_t$	1 if Congressperson *t* represents a northeastern state; 0 otherwise
RegionSouth$_t$	1 if Congressperson *t* represents a southern state; 0 otherwise
RegionWest$_t$	1 if Congressperson *t* represents a western state; 0 otherwise
ScoreLiberal$_t$	Congressperson's *t* liberal score rating in 2007
Terms$_t$	Number of terms served by Congressperson in the US Congress
UnemRate$_t$	Unemployment rate in Congressperson *t*'s state

3. Revisit the House earmark data and consider the following model:

$$Number_t = \beta_{Const} + \beta_{Terms}Terms_t + \beta_{Liberal}ScoreLiberal_t + \beta_{Income}IncomePC_t + e_t$$

a. Develop a theory that explains how each explanatory variable affects the number of solo earmarks. What do your theories suggest about the sign of each coefficient?

b. Use the ordinary least squares (OLS) estimation procedure to estimate the coefficients. Interpret the coefficient estimates.

[To access this online material, go to http://mitpress.mit.edu/westhoffeconometrics and select House Earmarks.]

c. Formulate the null and alternative hypotheses.

d. Calculate Prob[Results IF H_0 true] and assess your theory.

4. Again consider the House earmark data and add a liberal–Democrat interaction variable to the number of solo earmarks model:

$$Number_t = \beta_{Const} + \beta_{Terms}Terms_t + \beta_{Liberal}ScoreLiberal_t + \beta_{Income}IncomePC_t$$

$$+ \beta_{Lib\_Dem} \, Lib\_Dem_t + e_t$$

where $Lib\_Dem_t = ScoreLiberal_t \times PartyDemocrat_t$

a. Focus on the following allegation:

Allegation: Liberal Democrats receive more earmarks than their non-Democratic liberal colleagues.

What does the allegation suggest about the sign of the *Lib_Dem* coefficient?

b. Use the ordinary least squares (OLS) estimation procedure to estimate the parameters of the model. Interpret the *Lib_Dem* interaction coefficient estimate. What do you conclude about the allegation?

[To access this online material, go to http://mitpress.mit.edu/westhoffeconometrics and select House Earmarks.]

5. Revisit the House earmark data:

[To access this online material, go to http://mitpress.mit.edu/westhoffeconometrics and select House Earmarks.]

Consider the following model:

$$Number_t = \beta_{Const} + \beta_{Terms}Terms_t + \beta_{Liberal}ScoreLiberal_t + \beta_{Income}IncomePC_t$$

$$+ \beta_{NE}RegionNortheast_t + e_t$$

a. Focus on the following allegation:

Allegation: Members of Congress from the Northeast receive more earmarks than their colleagues from other parts of the country.

What does the allegation suggest about the sign of the *RegionNortheast* coefficient?

b. Use the ordinary least squares (OLS) estimation procedure to estimate the parameters of the model. Interpret the Northeast region coefficient estimate.

c. Formulate the null and alternative hypotheses regarding the allegation.

d. Calculate Prob[Results IF H_0 true] and assess the allegation.

14 Omitted Explanatory Variables, Multicollinearity, and Irrelevant Explanatory Variables

Chapter 14 Prep Questions

1. Review the goal of multiple regression analysis. In words, explain what multiple regression analysis attempts to do?

2. Recall that the presence of a random variable brings forth both bad news and good news.

    a. What is the bad news?

    b. What is the good news?

3. Consider an estimate's probability distribution. Review the importance of its mean and variance:

a. Why is the mean of the probability distribution important? Explain.

b. Why is the variance of the probability distribution important? Explain.

4. Suppose that two variables are positively correlated.

a. In words, what does this mean?

b. What type of graph do we use to illustrate their correlation? What does the graph look like?

c. What can we say about their correlation coefficient?

d. When two variables are perfectly positively correlated, what will their correlation coefficient equal?

5. Suppose that two variables are independent (uncorrelated).

a. In words, what does this mean?

b. What type of graph do we use to illustrate their correlation? What does the graph look like?

c. What can we say about their correlation coefficient?

Baseball data: Panel data of baseball statistics for the 588 American League games played during the summer of 1996.

Attendance$_t$	Paid attendance for game t
DateDay$_t$	Day of game t
DateMonth$_t$	Month of game t
DateYear$_t$	Year of game t
DayOfWeek$_t$	Day of the week for game t (Sunday = 0, Monday = 1, etc.)
DH$_t$	Designator hitter for game t (1 if DH permitted; 0 otherwise)
HomeGamesBehind$_t$	Games behind of the home team for before game t
HomeIncome$_t$	Per capita income in home team's city for game t
HomeLosses$_t$	Season losses of the home team before game t
HomeNetWins$_t$	Net wins (wins less losses) of the home team before game t
HomeSalary$_t$	Player salaries of the home team for game t (millions of dollars)
HomeWins$_t$	Season wins of the home team before the game before game t
PriceTicket$_t$	Average price of tickets sold for game t's home team (dollars)
VisitGamesBehind$_t$	Games behind of the visiting team before game t
VisitLosses$_t$	Season losses of the visiting team before the game t
VisitNetWins$_t$	Net wins (wins less losses) of the visiting team before game t
VisitSalary$_t$	Player salaries of the visiting team for game t (millions of dollars)
VisitWins$_t$	Season wins of the visiting team before the game

6. Focus on the baseball data.

   a. Consider the following simple model:

$$Attendance_t = \beta_{Const} + \beta_{Price}PriceTicket_t + e_t$$

   Attendance depends only on the ticket price.

   i. What does the economist's downward sloping demand curve theory suggest about the sign of the *PriceTicket* coefficient, β_{Price}?

   ii. Use the ordinary least squares (OLS) estimation procedure to estimate the model's parameters. Interpret the regression results.

[To access this online material, go to http://mitpress.mit.edu/westhoffeconometrics and select 1996 American League Summer.]

   b. Consider a second model:

$$Attendance_t = \beta_{Const} + \beta_{Price}PriceTicket_t + \beta_{HomeSalary}HomeSalary_t + e_t$$

   Attendance depends not only on the ticket price but also on the salary of the home team.

   i. Devise a theory explaining the effect that home team salary should have on attendance. What does your theory suggest about the sign of the *HomeSalary* coefficient, $\beta_{HomeSalary}$?

   ii. Use the ordinary least squares (OLS) estimation procedure to estimate both of the model's coefficients. Interpret the regression results.

   c. What do you observe about the estimates for the *PriceTicket* coefficients in the two models?

7. Again, focus on the baseball data and consider the following two variables:

Attendance$_t$ Paid attendance at the game *t*

PriceTicket$_t$ Average ticket price in terms of dollars for game *t*

You can access these data by clicking the following link:

[To access this online material, go to http://mitpress.mit.edu/westhoffeconometrics and select 1996 American League Summer.]

Generate a new variable, *PriceCents*, to express the price in terms of cents rather than dollars:

$$PriceCents = 100 \times PriceTicket$$

   a. What is the correlation coefficient for *PriceTicket* and *PriceCents*?

   b. Consider the following model:

$$Attendance_t = \beta_{Const} + \beta_{PriceTicket}PriceTicket_t + \beta_{PriceCents}PriceCents_t + e_t$$

Run the regression to estimate the parameters of this model. You will get an "unusual" result. Explain this by considering what multiple regression analysis attempts to do.

8. The following are excerpts from an article appearing in the *New York Times* on September 1, 2008:

Doubts Grow over Flu Vaccine in Elderly by Brenda Goodman

The influenza vaccine, which has been strongly recommended for people over 65 for more than four decades, is losing its reputation as an effective way to ward off the virus in the elderly.

A growing number of immunologists and epidemiologists say the vaccine probably does not work very well for people over 70 . . .

The latest blow was a study in *The Lancet* last month that called into question much of the statistical evidence for the vaccine's effectiveness. . . .

The study found that people who were healthy and conscientious about staying well were the most likely to get an annual flu shot. . . . [others] are less likely to get to their doctor's office or a clinic to receive the vaccine.

Dr. David K. Shay of the Centers for Disease Control and Prevention, a co-author of a commentary that accompanied Dr. Jackson's study, agreed that these measures of health . . . "were not incorporated into early estimations of the vaccine's effectiveness" and could well have skewed the findings.

    a. Does being healthy and conscientious about staying well increase or decrease the chances of getting flu?

    b. According to the article, are those who are healthy and conscientious about staying well more or less likely to get a flu shot?

    c. The article alleges that previous studies did not incorporate health and conscientious in judging the effectiveness of flu shots. If the allegation is true, have previous studies overestimated or underestimated the effectiveness of flu shots?

    d. Suppose that you were the director of your community's health department. You are considering whether or not to subsidize flu vaccines for the elderly. Would you find the previous studies useful? That is, would a study that did not incorporate health and conscientious in judging the effectiveness of flu shots help you decide if your department should spend your limited budget to subsidize flu vaccines? Explain.

14.1 Review

14.1.1 Unbiased Estimation Procedures

Estimates are random variables. Consequently there is both good news and bad news. Before the data are collected and the parameters are estimated:

• **Bad news:**   On the one hand, we cannot determine the numerical values of the estimates with certainty (even if we knew the actual values).

• **Good news:**   On the other hand, we can often describe the probability distribution of the estimate telling us how likely it is for the estimate to equal its possible numerical values.

Mean (Center) of the Estimate's Probability Distribution

An unbiased estimation procedure does not systematically underestimate or overestimate the actual value (figure 14.1). The mean (center) of the estimate's probability distribution equals the actual value. Applying the relative frequency interpretation of probability, when the experiment is repeated many, many times, the average of the numerical values of the estimates equals the actual value.

If the distribution is symmetric, we can provide an interpretation that is perhaps even more intuitive. When the experiment were repeated many, many times,

• half the time the estimate is greater than the actual value;

• half the time the estimate is less than the actual value.

Accordingly we can apply the relative frequency interpretation of probability. In one repetition, the chances that the estimate will be greater than the actual value equal the chances that the estimate will be less.

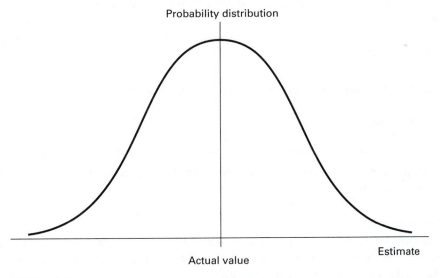

Figure 14.1
Probability distribution of an estimate—Unbiased estimation procedure

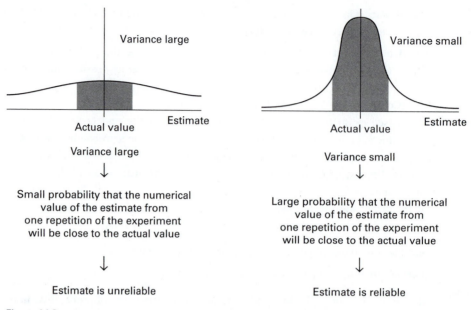

Figure 14.2
Probability distribution of an estimate—Importance of variance

Variance (Spread) of the Estimate's Probability Distribution Variance

When the estimation procedure is unbiased, the distribution variance (spread) indicates the estimate's reliability, the likelihood that the numerical value of the estimate will be close to the actual value (figure 14.2).

14.1.2   Correlated and Independent (Uncorrelated) Variables

Two variables are

• correlated whenever the value of one variable does help us predict the value of the other;

• independent (uncorrelated) whenever the value of one variable does not help us predict the value of the other.

Scatter Diagrams

The Dow Jones and Nasdaq growth rates are positively correlated. Most of the scatter diagram points lie in the first and third quadrants (figure 14.3). When the Dow Jones growth rate is high, the Nasdaq growth rate is usually high also. Similarly, when the Dow Jones growth rate is low, the Nasdaq growth rate is usually low also. Knowing one growth rate helps us predict the other. Amherst precipitation and the Nasdaq growth rate are independent, uncorrelated. The scatter diagram points are spread rather evenly across the graph. Knowing the Nasdaq growth rate does not help us predict Amherst precipitation, and vice versa.

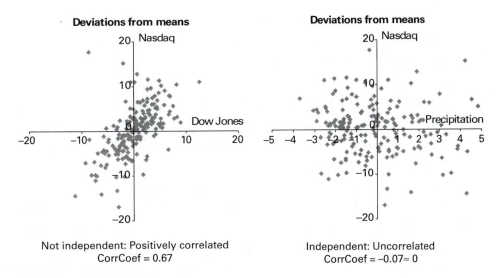

Figure 14.3
Scatter diagrams, correlation, and independence

Correlation Coefficient

The correlation coefficient indicates the degree to which two variables are correlated; the correlation coefficient ranges from -1 to $+1$:

· $= 0 =$ **Independent (uncorrelated):**   Knowing the value of one variable does not help us predict the value of the other.

· $> 0 =$ **Positive correlation:**   Typically, when the value of one variable is high, the value of the other variable will be high.

· $< 0 =$ **Negative correlation:**   Typically, when the value of one variable is high, the value of the other variable will be low.

14.2   Omitted Explanatory Variables

We will consider baseball attendance data to study the omitted variable phenomena.

Project: Assess the determinants of baseball attendance.

Baseball data: Panel data of baseball statistics for the 588 American League games played during the summer of 1996.

$Attendance_t$	Paid attendance for game t
$DateDay_t$	Day of game t
$DateMonth_t$	Month of game t
$DateYear_t$	Year of game t
$DayOfWeek_t$	Day of the week for game t (Sunday = 0, Monday = 1, etc.)
DH_t	Designator hitter for game t (1 if DH permitted; 0 otherwise)
$HomeGamesBehind_t$	Games behind of the home team before game t
$HomeIncome_t$	Per capita income in home team's city for game t
$HomeLosses_t$	Season losses of the home team before game t
$HomeNetWins_t$	Net wins (wins less losses) of the home team before game t
$HomeSalary_t$	Player salaries of the home team for game t (millions of dollars)
$HomeWins_t$	Season wins of the home team before game t
$PriceTicket_t$	Average price of tickets sold for game t's home team (dollars)
$VisitGamesBehind_t$	Games behind of the visiting team before game t
$VisitLosses_t$	Season losses of the visiting team before game t
$VisitNetWins_t$	Net wins (wins less losses) of the visiting team before game t
$VisitSalary_t$	Player salaries of the visiting team for game t (millions of dollars)
$VisitWins_t$	Season wins of the visiting team before the game

14.2.1   A Puzzle: Baseball Attendance

Let us begin our analysis by focusing on the price of tickets. Consider the following two models that attempt to explain game attendance:

Model 1:   Attendance depends on ticket price only.

The first model has a single explanatory variable, ticket price, *PriceTicket*:

$$Attendance_t = \beta_{Const} + \beta_{Price}PriceTicket_t + e_t$$

Downward sloping demand theory: This model is based on the economist's downward sloping demand theory. An increase in the price of a good decreases the quantity demand. Higher ticket prices should reduce attendance; hence the *PriceTicket* coefficient should be negative:

$$\beta_{Price} < 0$$

We will use the ordinary least squares (OLS) estimation procedure to estimate the model's parameters (table 14.1):

Table 14.1
Baseball attendance regression results—Ticket price only

Ordinary least squares (OLS)				
Dependent variable: *Attendance*				
Explanatory variable(s):	Estimate	SE	*t*-Statistic	Prob
PriceTicket	1,896.611	142.7238	13.28868	0.0000
Const	3,688.911	1,839.117	2.005805	0.0453
Number of observations	585			

Estimated equation: *EstAttendance* = 3,688 + 1,897*PriceTicket*

Interpretation of estimates:

$b_{PriceTicket}$ = 1,897. We estimate that a \$1.00 increase in the price of tickets increases attendance by 1,897 per game.

[To access this online material, go to http://mitpress.mit.edu/westhoffeconometrics and select 1996 American League Summer.]

The estimated coefficient for the ticket price is positive suggesting that higher prices lead to an increase in quantity demanded. This contradicts the downward sloping demand theory, does it not?

Model 2:   Attendance depends on ticket price and salary of home team.

In the second model, we include not only the price of tickets, *PriceTicket*, as an explanatory variable, but also the salary of the home team, *HomeSalary*:

$$Attendance_t = \beta_{Const} + \beta_{Price}PriceTicket_t + \beta_{HomeSalary}HomeSalary_t + e_t$$

We can justify the salary explanatory variable in the grounds that fans like to watch good players. We will call this the star theory. Presumably a high salary team has better players, more stars, on its roster and accordingly will draw more fans.

Star theory: Teams with higher salaries will have better players, which will increase attendance. The *HomeSalary* coefficient should be positive:

$$\beta_{HomeSalary} > 0$$

Now use the ordinary least squares (OLS) estimation procedure to estimate the parameters (table 14.2). These coefficient estimates lend support to our theories.

The two models produce very different results concerning the effect of the ticket price on attendance. More specifically, the coefficient estimate for ticket price changes drastically from 1,897 to −591 when we add home team salary as an explanatory variable. This is a disquieting puzzle. We will solve this puzzle by reviewing the goal of multiple regression analysis and then explaining when omitting an explanatory variable will prevent us from achieving the goal.

Table 14.2
Baseball attendance regression results—Ticket price and home team salary

	Ordinary least squares (OLS)			
Dependent variable: *Attendance*				
Explanatory variable(s):	Estimate	SE	*t*-Statistic	Prob
PriceTicket	−590.7836	184.7231	−3.198211	0.0015
HomeSalary	783.0394	45.23955	17.30874	0.0000
Const	9,246.429	1,529.658	6.044767	0.0000
Number of observations	585			

Estimated equation: *EstAttendance* = 9,246 − 591*PriceTicket* + 783*HomeSalary*

Interpretation of estimates:

$b_{PriceTicket}$ = −591. We estimate that a $1.00 increase in the price of tickets decreases attendance by 591 per game.

$b_{HomeSalary}$ = 783. We estimate that a $1 million increase in the home team salary increases attendance by 783 per game.

14.2.2   Goal of Multiple Regression Analysis

Multiple regression analysis attempts to sort out the individual effect of each explanatory variable. The estimate of an explanatory variable's coefficient allows us to assess the effect that an individual explanatory variable has on the dependent variable. An explanatory variable's coefficient estimate estimates the change in the dependent variable resulting from a change in that particular explanatory variable while all other explanatory variables remain constant.

In model 1 we estimate that a $1.00 increase in the ticket price increase attendance by nearly 2,000 per game, whereas in model 2, we estimate that a $1.00 increase decreases attendance by about 600 per game. The two models suggest that the individual effect of the ticket price is very different. The omitted variable phenomenon allows us to resolve this puzzle.

14.2.3   Omitted Explanatory Variables and Bias

Claim: Omitting an explanatory variable from a regression will bias the estimation procedure whenever two conditions are met. Bias results if the omitted explanatory variable

· influences the dependent variable;

· is correlated with an included explanatory variable.

When these two conditions are met, the coefficient estimate of the included explanatory variable is a composite of two effects, the influence that the

· included explanatory variable itself has on the dependent variable (direct effect);

· omitted explanatory variable has on the dependent variable because the included explanatory variable also acts as a proxy for the omitted explanatory variable (proxy effect).

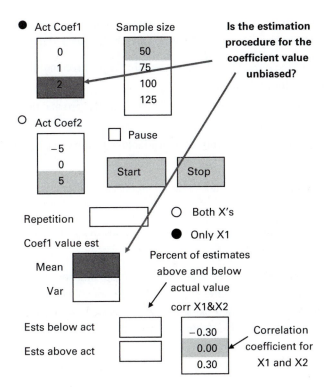

Figure 14.4
Omitted variable simulation

Since the goal of multiple regression analysis is to sort out the individual effect of each explanatory variable we want to capture only the direct effect.

Econometrics Lab 14.1: Omitted Variable Proxy Effect

We can now use the Econometrics Lab to justify our claims concerning omitted explanatory variables. The following regression model including two explanatory variables is used (figure 14.4):

Model: $y_t = \beta_{Const} + \beta_{x1}x1_t + \beta_{x2}x2_t + e_t$

[To access this online material, go to http://mitpress.mit.edu/westhoffeconometrics and select Lab 14.1.]

The simulation provides us with two options; we can either include both explanatory variables in the regression, "Both Xs" or just one, "Only X1." By default the "Only X1" option is selected, consequently the second explanatory variable is omitted. That is, $x1_t$ is the included explanatory variable and $x2_t$ is the omitted explanatory variable. For simplicity, assume that $x1$'s coefficient, β_{x1}, is positive. We will consider three cases to illustrate when bias does and does not result:

· **Case 1:** The coefficient of the omitted explanatory variable is positive and the two explanatory variables are independent (uncorrelated).

· **Case 2:** The coefficient of the omitted explanatory variable equals zero and the two explanatory variables are positively correlated.

· **Case 3:** The coefficient of the omitted explanatory variable is positive and the two explanatory variables are positively correlated.

We will now show that only in the last case does bias result because only in the last case is the proxy effect is present.

Case 1: The coefficient of the omitted explanatory variable is positive and the two explanatory variables are independent (uncorrelated).

Will bias result in this case? Since the two explanatory variables are independent (uncorrelated), an increase in the included explanatory variable, $x1_t$, typically will not affect the omitted explanatory variable, $x2_t$. Consequently the included explanatory variable, $x1_t$, will not act as a proxy for the omitted explanatory variable, $x2_t$. Bias should not result.

We will use our lab to confirm this logic. By default, the actual coefficient for the included explanatory variable, $x1_t$, equals 2 and the actual coefficient for the omitted explanatory variable, $x2_t$, is nonzero, it equals 5. Their correlation coefficient, Corr X1&X2, equals 0.00; hence the two explanatory variables are independent (uncorrelated). Be certain that the Pause checkbox is cleared. Click **Start** and after many, many repetitions, click **Stop**. Table 14.3 reports that the average value of the coefficient estimates for the included explanatory variable equals its actual value. Both equal 2.0. The ordinary least squares (OLS) estimation procedure is unbiased.

The ordinary least squares (OLS) estimation procedure captures the individual influence that the included explanatory variable itself has on the dependent variable. This is precisely the effect that we wish to capture. The ordinary least squares (OLS) estimation procedure is unbiased; it is doing what we want it to do.

Table 14.3
Omitted variables simulation results

Actual coef 1	Actual coef 2	Corr coef	Mean (average) of coef1 estimates	Percent of coef1 estimates	
				Below actual value	Above actual value
2	5	0.00	≈2.0	≈50	≈50

Table 14.4
Omitted variables simulation results

Actual coef 1	Actual coef 2	Corr coef	Mean (average) of coef1 estimates	Percent of coef1 estimates	
				Below actual value	Above actual value
2	5	0.00	≈2.0	≈50	≈50
2	0	0.30	≈2.0	≈50	≈50

Case 2:   The coefficient of the omitted explanatory variable equals zero and the two explanatory variables are positively correlated.

In the second case the two explanatory variables are positively correlated; when the included explanatory variable, $x1_t$, increases, the omitted explanatory variable, $x2_t$, will typically increase also. But the actual coefficient of the omitted explanatory variable, β_{x2}, equals 0; hence, the dependent variable, y_t, is unaffected by the increase in $x2_t$. There is no proxy effect because the omitted variable, $x2_t$, does not affect the dependent variable; hence bias should not result.

		Typically
Included	Positive	omitted
variable	correlation	variable
$x1_t$ up	$\longrightarrow$	$x2_t$ up
$\downarrow$ $\beta_{x1} > 0$		$\downarrow$ $\beta_{x2} = 0$
y_t up		y_t unaffected
$\downarrow$		$\downarrow$
Direct effect		No proxy effect

To confirm our logic with the simulation, be certain that the actual coefficient for the omitted explanatory variable equals 0 and the correlation coefficient equals 0.30. Click **Start** and then after many, many repetitions, click **Stop**. Table 14.4 reports that the average value of the coefficient estimates for the included explanatory variable equals its actual value. Both equal 2.0. The ordinary least squares (OLS) estimation procedure is unbiased.

Again, the ordinary least squares (OLS) estimation procedure captures the influence that the included explanatory variable itself has on the dependent variable. Again, there is no proxy effect and all is well.

Case 3: The coefficient of the omitted explanatory variable is positive and the two explanatory variables are positively correlated.

As with case 2 the two explanatory variables are positively correlated; when the included explanatory variable, $x1_t$, increases the omitted explanatory variable, $x2_t$, will typically increase also. But now the actual coefficient of the omitted explanatory variable, β_{x2}, is no longer 0, it is positive; hence an increase in the omitted explanatory variable, $x2_t$, increases the dependent variable. In additional to having a direct effect on the dependent variable, the included explanatory variable, $x1_t$, also acts as a proxy for the omitted explanatory variable, $x2_t$. There is a proxy effect.

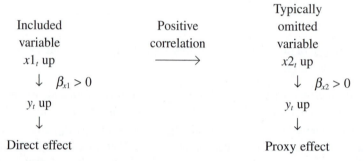

In the simulation, the actual coefficient of omitted explanatory variable, β_{x2}, once again equals 5. The two explanatory variables are positively correlated, the correlation coefficient equals 0.30. Click **Start** and then after many, many repetitions click **Stop**. Table 14.5 reports that the average value of the coefficient estimates for the included explanatory variable, 3.5, exceeds its actual value, 2.0. The ordinary least squares (OLS) estimation procedure is biased upward.

Now we have a problem. The ordinary least squares (OLS) estimation procedure overstates the influence of the included explanatory variable, the effect that the included explanatory variable itself has on the dependent variable.

Table 14.5
Omitted variables simulation results

Actual coef 1	Actual coef 2	Corr coef	Mean (average) of coef1 estimates	Percent of coef1 estimates	
				Below actual value	Above actual value
2	5	0.00	≈2.0	≈50	≈50
2	0	0.30	≈2.0	≈50	≈50
2	5	0.30	≈3.5	≈28	≈72

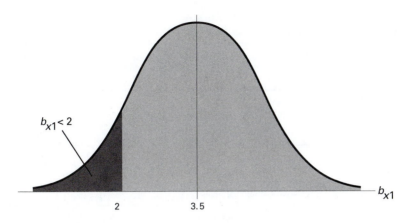

Figure 14.5
Probability distribution of an estimate—Upward bias

Let us now take a brief aside. Case 3 provides us with the opportunity to illustrate what bias does and does not mean.

· **What bias does mean:**   Bias means that the estimation procedure systematically overestimates or underestimates the actual value. In this case, upward bias is present. The average of the estimates is greater than the actual value after many, many repetitions.

· **What bias does not mean:**   Bias does not mean that the value of the estimate in a single repetition must be less than the actual value in the case of downward bias or greater than the actual value in the case of upward bias. Focus on the last simulation. The ordinary least squares (OLS) estimation procedure is biased upward as a consequence of the proxy effect. Despite the upward bias, however, the estimate of the included explanatory variable is less than the actual value in many of the repetitions as shown in figure 14.5.

Upward bias does not guarantee that in any one repetition the estimate will be greater than the actual value. It just means that it will be greater "on average." If the probability distribution is symmetric, the chances of the estimate being greater than the actual value exceed the chances of being less.

Now we return to our three omitted variable cases by summarizing them (table 14.6).

Econometrics Lab 14.2: Avoiding Omitted Variable Bias

Question: Is the estimation procedure biased or unbiased when both explanatory variables are included in the regression?

Table 14.6
Omitted variables simulation summary

Case	Does the omitted variable influence the dependent variable?	Is the omitted variable correlated with an included variable?	Estimation procedure for the included variable is
1	Yes	No	Unbiased
2	No	Yes	Unbiased
3	Yes	Yes	Biased

Table 14.7
Omitted variables simulation results—No omitted variables

Actual coef 1	Actual coef 2	Correlation parameter	Mean of coef 1 estimates
2	5	0.3	≈ 2.0

[To access this online material, go to http://mitpress.mit.edu/westhoffeconometrics and select Lab 14.2.]

To address this question, "Both Xs" is now selected. This means that both explanatory variables, $x1_t$ and $x2_t$, will be included in the regression. Both explanatory variables affect the dependent variable and they are correlated. As we saw in case 3, if one of the explanatory variables is omitted, bias will result. To see what occurs when both explanatory variables are included, click **Start** and after many, many repetitions, click **Stop**. When both variables are included the ordinary least squares (OLS) estimation procedure is unbiased (table 14.7).

Conclusion: To avoid omitted variable bias, all relevant explanatory variables should be included in a regression.

14.2.4   Resolving the Baseball Attendance Puzzle

We begin by reviewing the baseball attendance models:

• Model 1: Attendance depends on ticket price only.

$Attendance_t = \beta_{Const} + \beta_{Price}PriceTicket_t + e_t$

Estimated equation: $EstAttendance = 3,688 + 1,897PriceTicket$

Interpretation: We estimate that $1.00 increase in the price of tickets increases by 1,897 per game.

• Model 2:   Attendance depends on ticket price and salary of home team.

$$Attendance_t = \beta_{Const} + \beta_{Price}PriceTicket_t + \beta_{HomeSalary}HomeSalary_t + e_t$$

Estimated equation: $EstAttendance = 9{,}246 - 591PriceTicket + 783HomeSalary$

Interpretation: We estimate the following:

- \$1.00 increase in the price of tickets decreases attendance by 591 per game.
- \$1 million increase in the home team salary increases attendance by 783 per game.

The ticket price coefficient estimate is affected dramatically by the presence of home team salary; in model 1 the estimate is much higher 1,897 versus −591. Why?

   We will now argue that when ticket price is included in the regression and home team salary is omitted, as in model 1, there reason to believe that the estimation procedure for the ticket price coefficient will be biased. We just learned that the omitted variable bias results when the following two conditions are met; when an omitted explanatory variable:

- influences the dependent variable

and

- is correlated with an included explanatory variable.

Now focus on model 1:

$$Attendance_t = \beta_{Const} + \beta_{Price}PriceTicket_t + e_t$$

Model 1 omits home team salary, $HomeSalary_t$. Are the two omitted variable bias conditions met?

- It certainly appears reasonable to believe that the omitted explanatory variable, $HomeSalary_t$, affects the dependent variable, $Attendance_t$. The club owner who is paying the high salaries certainly believes so. The owner certainly hopes that by hiring better players more fans will attend the games. Consequently it appears that the first condition required for omitted variable bias is met.

- We can confirm the correlation by using statistical software to calculate the correlation matrix (table 14.8).

Table 14.8
Ticket price and home team salary correlation matrix

	Correlation matrix	
	PriceTicket	*HomeSalary*
PriceTicket	1.000000	0.777728
HomeSalary	0.777728	1.000000

The correlation coefficient between $PriceTicket_t$ and $HomeSalary_t$ is 0.78; the variables are positively correlated. The second condition required for omitted variable bias is met.

We have reason to suspect bias in model 1. When the included variable, $PriceTicket_t$, increases the omitted variable, $HomeSalary_t$, typically increases also. An increase in the omitted variable, $HomeSalary_t$, increases the dependent variable, $Attendance_t$:

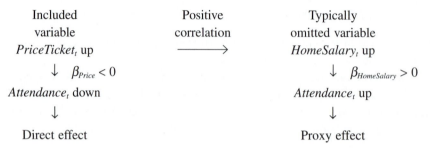

In additional to having a direct effect on the dependent variable, the included explanatory variable, $PriceTicket_t$, also acts as a proxy for the omitted explanatory variable, $HomeSalary_t$. There is a proxy effect and upward bias results. This provides us with an explanation of why the ticket price coefficient estimate in model 1 is greater than the estimate in model 2.

14.2.5   Omitted Variable Summary

Omitting an explanatory variable from a regression biases the estimation procedure whenever two conditions are met. Bias results if the omitted explanatory variable:

• influences the dependent variable;
• is correlated with an included explanatory variable.

When these two conditions are met, the coefficient estimate of the included explanatory variable is a composite of two effects; the coefficient estimate of the included explanatory reflects two influences:

• The included explanatory variable, which has an effect on the dependent variable (direct effect).

• The omitted explanatory variable, which has an effect on the dependent variable because the included explanatory variable also acts as a proxy for the omitted explanatory variable (proxy effect).

The bad news is that the proxy effect leads to bias. The good news is that we can eliminate the proxy effect and its accompanying bias by including the omitted explanatory variable. But now, we will learn that if two explanatory variables are highly correlated a different problem can emerge.

14.3   Multicollinearity

The phenomenon of **multicollinearity** occurs when two explanatory variables are highly correlated. Recall that multiple regression analysis attempts to sort out the influence of each individual explanatory variable. But what happens when we include two explanatory variables in a single regression that are perfectly correlated? Let us see.

14.3.1   Perfectly Correlated Explanatory Variables

In our baseball attendance workfile, ticket prices, $PriceTicket_t$, are reported in terms of dollars. Generate a new variable, $PriceCents_t$, reporting ticket prices in terms of cents rather than dollars:

$$PriceCents_t = 100 \times PriceTicket_t$$

Note that the variables $PriceTicket_t$ and $PriceCents_t$ are perfectly correlated. If we know one, we can predict the value of the other with complete accuracy. Just to confirm this, use statistical software to calculate the correlation matrix (table 14.9).

The correlation coefficient of $PriceTicket_t$ and $PriceCents_t$ equals 1.00. The variables are indeed perfectly correlated. Now run a regression with *Attendance* as the dependent variable and both *PriceTicket* and *PriceCents* as explanatory variables.

Dependent variable: *Attendance*

Explanatory variables: *PriceTicket* and *PriceCents*

Your statistical software will report a diagnostic. Different software packages provide different messages, but basically the software is telling us that it cannot run the regression.

Why does this occur? The reason is that the two variables are perfectly correlated. Knowing the value of one allows us to predict perfectly the value of the other with complete accuracy. Both explanatory variables contain precisely the same information. Multiple regression analysis attempts to sort out the influence of each individual explanatory variable. But if both variables contain precisely the same information, it is impossible to do this. How can we possibly separate out each variable's individual effect when the two variables contain the identical information? We are asking statistical software to do the impossible.

Table 14.9
EViews dollar and cent ticket price correlation matrix

	Correlation matrix	
	PriceTicket	*PriceCents*
PriceTicket	1.000000	1.000000
PriceCents	1.000000	1.000000

Explanatory variables
perfectly correlated

$\downarrow$

Knowing the value of one
explanatory value allows
us to predict perfectly the
value of the other

$\downarrow$

Both variables contain
precisely the same information

$\downarrow$

Impossible to separate out the
individual effect of each variable

Next we consider a case in which the explanatory variables are highly, although not perfectly, correlated.

14.3.2   Highly Correlated Explanatory Variables

To investigate the problems created by highly correlated explanatory variable, we will use our baseball data to investigate a model that includes four explanatory variables:

$$Attendance_t = \beta_{Const} + \beta_{Price}PriceTicket_t + \beta_{HomeSalary}HomeSalary_t$$

$$+ \beta_{HomeNW}HomeNetWins_t + \beta_{HomeGB}HomeGamesBehind_t + e_t$$

where

$Attendance_t$ = paid attendance for game t

$PriceTicket_t$ = average price of tickets sold for game t's home team (dollars)

$HomeSalary_t$ = player salaries of the home team for game t (millions of dollars)

$HomeNetWins_t$ = the difference between the number of wins and losses of the home team before game t

$HomeGamesBehind_t$ = games behind of the home team before game t

The variable $HomeNetWins_t$ equals the difference between the number of wins and losses of the home team. It attempts to capture the quality of the team. On the one hand, $HomeNetWins_t$ will be positive and large for a high-quality team, a team that wins many more games than it losses. On the other hand, $HomeNetWins_t$ will be a negative number for a low-quality team. Since baseball fans enjoy watching high-quality teams, we would expect high-quality teams to be rewarded with greater attendance:

Table 14.10
2009 final season standings—AL East

Team	Wins	Losses	Home net wins	Games behind
New York Yankees	103	59	44	0
Boston Red Sox	95	67	28	8
Tampa Bay Rays	84	78	6	19
Toronto Blue Jays	75	87	−12	28
Baltimore Orioles	64	98	−34	39

The variable *HomeGamesBehind$_t$* captures the home team's standing in its divisional race. For those who are not baseball fans, note that all teams that win their division automatically qualify for the baseball playoffs. Ultimately the two teams what win the American and National League playoffs meet in the World Series. Since it is the goal of every team to win the World Series, each team strives to win its division. Games behind indicates how close a team is to winning its division. To explain how games behind are calculated, consider the final standings of the American League Eastern Division in 2009 (table 14.10).

The Yankees had the best record; the games behind value for the Yankees equals 0. The Red Sox won eight fewer games than the Yankees; hence the Red Sox were 8 games behind. The Rays won 19 fewer games than the Yankees; hence the Rays were 19 games behind. Similarly the Blue Jays were 28 games behind and the Orioles 39 games behind.[1] During the season if a team's games behind becomes larger, it becomes less likely the team will win its division, less likely for that team to qualify for the playoffs, and less likely for that team to eventually win the World Series. Consequently, if a team's games behind becomes larger, we would expect home team fans to become discourage resulting in less attendance.

We use the terms team quality and division race to summarize our theories regarding home net wins and home team games behind:

· **Team quality theory:**   More net wins increase attendance. $\beta_{HomeNW} > 0$.
· **Division race theory:**   More games behind decreases attendance. $\beta_{HomeGB} < 0$.

We would expect *HomeNetWins$_t$* and *HomeGamesBehind$_t$* to be negatively correlated. As *HomeNetWins* decreases, a team moves farther from the top of its division and consequently *HomeGamesBehind$_t$* increases. We would expect the correlation coefficient for *HomeNetWins$_t$* and *HomeGamesBehind$_t$* to be negative. Let us check by computing their correlation matrix:

[To access this online material, go to http://mitpress.mit.edu/westhoffeconometrics and select 1996 American League Summer.]

---

1. In this example all teams have played the same number of games. When a different number of games have been played, the calculation becomes a little more complicated. Games behind for a non–first place team equals

(Wins of first − Wins of trailing) + (Losses of trailing − Losses of first)

2

Table 14.11
HomeNetWins and *HomeGamesBehind* correlation matrix

	Correlation matrix	
	HomeNetWins	*HomeGamesBehind*
HomeNetWins	1.000000	−0.962037
HomeGamesBehind	−0.962037	1.000000

Table 14.12
Attendance regression results

Ordinary least squares (OLS)				
Dependent variable: *Attendance*				
Explanatory variable(s):	Estimate	SE	*t*-Statistic	Prob
PriceTicket	−437.1603	190.4236	−2.295725	0.0220
HomeSalary	667.5796	57.89922	11.53003	0.0000
HomeNetWins	60.53364	85.21918	0.710329	0.4778
HomeGamesBehind	−84.38767	167.1067	−0.504993	0.6138
Const	11,868.58	2,220.425	5.345184	0.0000
Number of observations	585			

Estimated equation: *EstAttendance* = 11,869 − 437*PriceTicket* + 668*HomeSalary* + 61*HomeNetWins* − 84*HomeGamesBehind*

Interpretation of estimates:

$b_{PriceTicket} = -437$. We estimate that a \$1.00 increase in the price of tickets decreases attendance by 437 per game.

$b_{HomeSalary} = 668$. We estimate that a \$1 million increase in the home team salary increases attendance by 668 per game.

$b_{HomeGamesBehind} = -84$. We estimate that 1 additional game behind decreases attendance by 84 per game.

Table 14.11 reports that the correlation coefficient for *HomeGamesBehind$_t$* and *HomeNetWins$_t$* equals −0.962. Recall that the correlation coefficient must lie between −1 and +1. When two variables are perfectly negatively correlated their correlation coefficient equals −1. While *HomeGamesBehind$_t$* and *HomeNetWins$_t$* are not perfectly negatively correlated, they come close; they are highly negatively correlated.

We use the ordinary least squares (OLS) estimation procedure to estimate the model's parameters (table 14.12).

The sign of each estimate supports the theories. Focus on the two new variables included in the model: *HomeNetWins$_t$* and *HomeGamesBehind$_t$*. Construct the null and alternative hypotheses.

Team quality theory		Division race theory	
H_0: $\beta_{HomeNW} = 0$	Team quality has no effect on attendance	H_0: $\beta_{HomeGB} = 0$	Games behind has no effect on attendance
H_1: $\beta_{HomeNW} > 0$	Team quality increases attendance	H_1: $\beta_{HomeGB} < 0$	Games behind decreases attendance

While the signs coefficient estimates are encouraging, some of results are disappointing:

• The coefficient estimate for *HomeNetWins*$_t$ is positive supporting our theory, but what about the Prob[Results IF H_0 true]? What is the probability that the estimate from one regression would equal 60.53 or more, if the H_0 were true (i.e., if the actual coefficient, β_{HomeNW}, equals 0, if home team quality has no effect on attendance)? Using the tails probability, we can easily calculate the probability

$$\text{Prob[Results IF } H_0 \text{ true]} = \frac{0.4778}{2} \approx 0.24$$

We cannot reject the null hypothesis at the traditional significance levels of 1, 5, or 10 percent, suggesting that it is quite possible for the null hypothesis to be true, quite possible that home team quality has no effect on attendance.

• Similarly the coefficient estimate for *HomeGamesBehind*$_t$ is negative supporting our theory, but what about the Prob[Results IF H_0 true]? What is the probability that the estimate from one regression would equal −84.39 or less, if the H_0 were true (i.e., if the actual coefficient, β_{HomeGB}, equals 0, if games behind has no effect on attendance)? Using the tails probability, we can easily calculate the probability

$$\text{Prob[Results IF } H_0 \text{ true]} = \frac{0.6138}{2} \approx 0.31$$

Again, we cannot reject the null hypothesis at the traditional significance levels of 1, 5, or 10 percent, suggesting that it is quite possible for the null hypothesis to be true, quite possible that games behind has no effect on attendance.

Should we abandon our "theory" as a consequence of these regression results?

Let us perform a Wald test (table 14.13) to access the proposition that both coefficients equal 0:

H_0: $\beta_{HomeNW} = 0$ and $\beta_{HomeGB} = 0$ Neither team quality nor games behind have an effect on attendance

H_1: $\beta_{HomeNW} \neq 0$ and/or $\beta_{HomeGB} \neq 0$ Either team quality and/or games behind have an effect on attendance

Table 14.13
EViews Wald test results

| | | **Wald test** | | |
| | | Degrees of freedom | | |
	Value	Num	Dem	Prob
F-Statistic	5.046779	2	580	0.0067

Prob[Results IF H_0 true]: What is the probability that the *F*-statistic would be 111.4 or more, if the H_0 were true (i.e., if both β_{HomeNW} and β_{HomeGB} equal 0, if both team quality and games behind have no effect on attendance)?

Prob[Results IF H_0 true] = 0.0067

We can reject the null hypothesis at a 1 percent significance level; it is unlikely that both team quality and games behind have no effect on attendance.

There appears to be a paradox when we compare the *t*-tests and the Wald test:

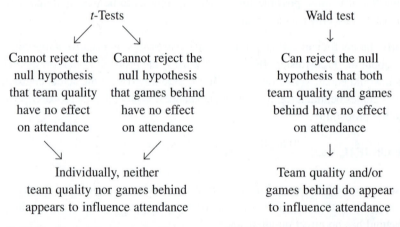

Individually, neither team quality nor games behind appears to influence attendance significantly, but taken together by asking if team quality and/or games behind influence attendance, we conclude that they do.

Next let us run two regressions each of which includes only one of the two troublesome explanatory variables (tables 14.14 and 14.15). When only a single explanatory variable is included the coefficient is significant.

Table 14.14
EViews attendance regression results—*HomeGamesBehind* omitted

Ordinary least squares (OLS)				
Dependent variable: *Attendance*				
Explanatory variable(s):	Estimate	SE	*t*-Statistic	Prob
PriceTicket	−449.2097	188.8016	−2.379268	0.0177
HomeSalary	672.2967	57.10413	11.77317	0.0000
HomeNetWins	100.4166	31.99348	3.138658	0.0018
Const	11,107.66	1,629.863	6.815087	0.0000
Number of observations	585			

Estimated equation: $EstAttendance = 11{,}108 - 449 PriceTicket + 672 HomeSalary + 100 HomeNetWins$

Interpretation of estimates:

$b_{PriceTicket} = -449$. We estimate that a \$1.00 increase in the price of tickets decreases attendance by 449 per game.

$b_{HomeSalary} = 672$. We estimate that a \$1 million increase in the home team salary increases attendance by 672 per game.

$b_{HomeNetWins} = 100$. We estimate that 1 additional home net win increases attendance by 100 per game.

Table 14.15
EViews attendance regression results—*HomeNetWins* omitted

Ordinary least squares (OLS)				
Dependent variable: *Attendance*				
Explanatory variable(s):	Estimate	SE	*t*-Statistic	Prob
PriceTicket	−433.4971	190.2726	−2.278295	0.0231
HomeSalary	670.8518	57.69106	11.62835	0.0000
HomeGamesBehind	−194.3941	62.74967	−3.097931	0.0020
Const	12,702.16	1,884.178	6.741486	0.0000
Number of observations	585			

Estimated equation: $EstAttendance = 12{,}702 - 433 PriceTicket + 671 HomeSalary - 194 HomeGamesBehind$

Interpretation of estimates:

$b_{PriceTicket} = -433$. We estimate that a \$1.00 increase in the price of tickets decreases attendance by 433 per game.

$b_{HomeSalary} = 671$. We estimate that a \$1 million increase in the home team salary increases attendance by 671 per game.

$b_{HomeGamesBehind} = -194$. We estimate that 1 additional game behind decreases attendance by 194 per game.

14.3.3   "Earmarks" of Multicollinearity

We are observing what we will call the earmarks of multicollinearity:

• Explanatory variables are highly correlated.
• A regression including both explanatory variables: On the one hand, t-tests do not allow us to reject the null hypothesis that the coefficient of each individual variable equals 0; when considering each explanatory variable individually, we cannot reject the hypothesis that each individually has no influence. On the other hand, a Wald test allows us to reject the null hypothesis that the coefficients of both explanatory variables equal 0; when considering both explanatory variables together, we can reject the hypothesis that they have no influence.
• Regressions with only one explanatory variable appear to produce "good" results.

How can we explain this? Recall that multiple regression analysis attempts to sort out the influence of each individual explanatory variable. When two explanatory variables are perfectly correlated, it is impossible for the ordinary least squares (OLS) estimation procedure to separate out the individual influences of each variable. Consequently, if two variables are highly correlated, as team quality and games behind are, it may be very difficult for the ordinary least squares (OLS) estimation procedure to separate out the individual influence of each explanatory variable. This difficulty evidences itself in the variance of the coefficient estimates' probability distributions. When two highly correlated variables are included in the same regression, the variances of each estimate's probability distribution is large. This explains our t-test results.

<table>
<tr><td align="center">Explanatory variables
perfectly correlated</td><td align="center">Explanatory variables
highly correlated</td></tr>
<tr><td align="center">↓</td><td align="center">↓</td></tr>
<tr><td align="center">Knowing the value of one
variable allows us to predict
the other perfectly</td><td align="center">Knowing the value of one
variable allows us to
predict the other very accurately</td></tr>
<tr><td align="center">↓</td><td align="center">↓</td></tr>
<tr><td align="center">Both variables contain
the same information</td><td align="center">In some sense, both variables
contain nearly the same information</td></tr>
<tr><td align="center">↓</td><td align="center">↓</td></tr>
<tr><td align="center">Impossible to separate out
their individual effects</td><td align="center">Difficult to separate out
their individual effects</td></tr>
<tr><td align="center"></td><td align="center">↓</td></tr>
<tr><td align="center"></td><td align="center">Large variance of each coefficient
estimate's probability distribution</td></tr>
</table>

We use a simulation to justify our explanation (figure 14.6).

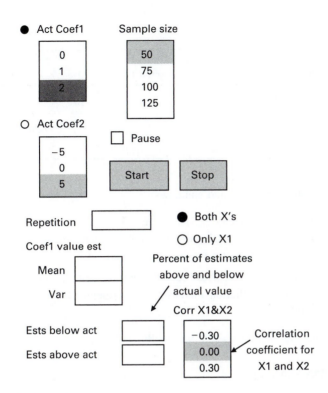

Figure 14.6
Multicollinearity simulation

Econometrics Lab 14.3: Multicollinearity

Our model includes two explanatory variables, $x1_t$ and $x2_t$:

Model: $y = \beta_{Const} + \beta_{x1}x1_t + \beta_{x2}x2_t + e_t$

[To access this online material, go to http://mitpress.mit.edu/westhoffeconometrics and select Lab 14.3.]

By default the actual value of the coefficient for the first explanatory variable equals 2 and actual value for the second equals 5. Note that the "Both Xs" is selected; both explanatory variables are included in the regression. Initially, the correlation coefficient is specified as 0.00; that is, initially the explanatory variables are independent. Be certain that the Pause checkbox is cleared and click **Start**. After many, many repetitions click **Stop**. Next repeat this process for a correlation coefficient of 0.30, a correlation coefficient of 0.60, and a correlation coefficient of 0.90 (table 14.16).

Table 14.16
Multicollinearity simulation results

Actual coef 1	Correlation parameter	Mean of coef 1 estimates	Variance of coef 1 estimates
2	0.00	≈ 2.0	≈ 6.5
2	0.30	≈ 2.0	≈ 7.2
2	0.60	≈ 2.0	≈ 10.1
2	0.90	≈ 2.0	≈ 34.2

The simulation reveals both good news and bad news:

· **Good news**:   The ordinary least squares (OLS) estimation procedure is unbiased. The mean of the estimate's probability distribution equals the actual value. The estimation procedure does not systematically underestimate or overestimate the actual value.

· **Bad news**:   As the two explanatory variables become more correlated, the variance of the coefficient estimate's probability distribution increases. Consequently the estimate from one repetition becomes less reliable.

The simulation illustrates the phenomenon of multicollinearity.

14.4   Irrelevant Explanatory Variables

An **irrelevant explanatory variable** is a variable that does not influence the dependent variable. Including an irrelevant explanatory variable can be viewed as adding "noise," an additional element of uncertainty, into the mix. An irrelevant explanatory variable adds a new random influence to the model. If our logic is correct, irrelevant explanatory variables should lead to both good news and bad news:

· **Good news:**   Random influences do not cause the ordinary least squares (OLS) estimation procedure to be biased. Consequently the inclusion of an irrelevant explanatory variable should not lead to bias.

· **Bad news:**   The additional uncertainty added by the new random influence means that the coefficient estimate is less reliable; the variance of the coefficient estimate's probability distribution should rise when an irrelevant explanatory variable is present.

We will use our Econometrics Lab to justify our intuition.

Econometrics Lab 14.4: Irrelevant Explanatory Variables

[To access this online material, go to http://mitpress.mit.edu/westhoffeconometrics and select Lab 14.4.]

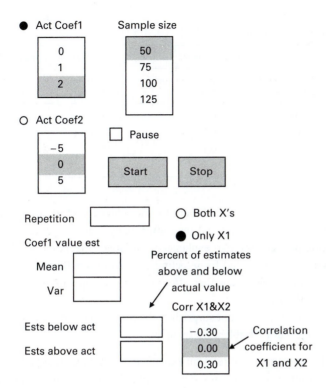

Figure 14.7
Irrelevant explanatory variable simulation

Once again, we use a two explanatory variable model:

Model: $y = \beta_{Const} + \beta_{x1}x1_t + \beta_{x2}x2_t + e_t$

By default the first explanatory variable, $x1_t$, is the relevant explanatory variable; the default value of its coefficient is 2. The second explanatory variable, $x2_t$, is the irrelevant one (figure 14.7). An irrelevant explanatory variable has no effect on the dependent variable; consequently the actual value of its coefficient, β_{x2}, equals 0.

Initially the "Only X1" option is selected indicating that only the relevant explanatory variable, $x1_t$, is included in the regression; the irrelevant explanatory variable, $x2_t$, is not included. Click **Start** and then after many, many repetitions click **Stop**. Since the irrelevant explanatory variable is not included in the regression, correlation between the two explanatory variables will have no impact on the results. Confirm this by changing correlation coefficients from 0.00 to 0.30 in the "Corr X1&X2" list. Click **Start** and then after many, many repetitions click **Stop**. Similarly show that the results are unaffected when the correlation coefficient is 0.60 and 0.90.

Subsequently investigate what happens when the irrelevant explanatory variable is included by selecting the "Both Xs" option; the irrelevant explanatory, $x2_t$, will now be included in the

Table 14.17
Irrelevant explanatory variable simulation results

Actual coef 1	Corr coef for variables 1 and 2	Only variable 1 included		Variables 1 and 2 included	
		Mean of coef 1 estimates	Variance of coef 1 estimates	Mean of coef 1 estimates	Variance of coef 1 estimates
2.0	0.00	≈2.0	≈6.4	≈2.0	≈6.5
2.0	0.30	≈2.0	≈6.4	≈2.0	≈7.2
2.0	0.60	≈2.0	≈6.4	≈2.0	≈10.1
2.0	0.90	≈2.0	≈6.4	≈2.0	≈34.2

regression. Be certain that the correlation coefficient for the relevant and irrelevant explanatory variables initially equals 0.00. Click **Start** and then after many, many repetitions click **Stop**. Investigate how correlation between the two explanatory variables affects the results when the irrelevant explanatory variable is included by selecting correlation coefficient values of 0.30, 0.60, and 0.90. For each case click **Start** and then after many, many repetitions click **Stop**. Table 14.17 reports the results of the lab.

The results reported in table 14.17 are not surprising; the results support our intuition. On the one hand, when only the relevant (variable 1) is included:

• The mean of the coefficient estimate for relevant explanatory variable, $x1_t$, equals 2, the actual value; consequently the ordinary least squares (OLS) estimation procedure for the coefficient estimate is unbiased.

• Naturally, the variance of the coefficient estimate is not affected by correlation between the relevant and irrelevant explanatory variables because the irrelevant explanatory variable is not included in the regression.

On the other hand, when both relevant and irrelevant variables (variables 1 and 2) are included:

• The mean of the coefficient estimates for relevant explanatory variable, $x1_t$, still equals 2, the actual value; consequently, the ordinary least squares (OLS) estimation procedure for the coefficient estimate is unbiased.

• The variance of the coefficient estimate is greater whenever the irrelevant explanatory variable is included even when the two explanatory variables are independent (when the correlation coefficient equals 0.00). This occurs because the irrelevant explanatory variable is adding a new random influence to the model.

• As the correlation between the relevant and irrelevant explanatory variables increases it becomes more difficult for the ordinary least squares (OLS) estimation procedure to separate out the individual influence of each explanatory variable. As we saw with multicollinearity, this difficulty evidences itself in the variance of the coefficient estimate's probability distributions. As the two explanatory variables become more correlated the variance of the coefficient estimate's probability distribution increases.

The simulation illustrates the effect of including an irrelevant explanatory variable in a model. While it does not cause bias, it does make the coefficient estimate of the relevant explanatory variable less reliable by increasing the variance of its probability distribution.

Chapter 14 Review Questions

1. Consider an omitted explanatory variable:

    a. What problem can arise?

    b. Under what circumstances will the problem arise?

2. Suppose that multicollinearity is present in a regression.

    a. What is the "good news?"

    b. What is the "bad news?"

3. Suppose that an irrelevant explanatory variable is included in a regression.

    a. What is the "good news?"

    b. What is the "bad news?"

Chapter 14 Exercises

Cigarette consumption data: Cross section of per capita cigarette consumption and prices in fiscal year 2008 for the 50 states and the District of Columbia.

$CigConsPC_t$	Cigarette consumption per capita in state t (packs)
$EducCollege_t$	Percent of population with bachelor degrees in state t
$EducHighSchool_t$	Percent of population with high school diplomas in state t
$IncPC_t$	Income per capita in state t (1,000's of dollars)
Pop_t	Population of state t (persons)
$PriceConsumer_t$	Price of cigarettes in state t paid by consumers (dollars per pack)
$PriceSupplier_t$	Price of cigarettes in state t received by suppliers (dollars per pack)
$RegionMidWest_t$	1 if state t in Midwest census region, 0 otherwise
$RegionNorthEast_t$	1 if state t in Northeast census region, 0 otherwise
$RegionSouth_t$	1 if state t in South census region, 0 otherwise
$RegionWest_t$	1 if state t in West census region, 0 otherwise
$SmokeRateAdult_t$	Percent of adults who smoke in state t
$SmokeRateYouth_t$	Percent of youths who smoke in state t
$State_t$	Name of state t
Tax_t	Cigarette tax rate in state t (dollars per pack)
$TobProdPC_t$	Per capita tobacco production in state t (pounds)

1. Consider the following model:

$$CigConsPC_t = \beta_{Const} + \beta_{Price}PriceConsumer_t + \beta_{EduColl}EducCollege_t$$

$$+ \beta_{TobProd}TobProdPC_t + e_t$$

a. Develop a theory that explains how each explanatory variable affects per capita cigarette consumption. What do your theories suggest about the sign of each coefficient?

b. Use the ordinary least squares (OLS) estimation procedure to estimate the parameters of the model.

[To access this online material, go to http://mitpress.mit.edu/westhoffeconometrics and select Cigarette Consumption.]

c. Formulate the null and alternative hypotheses.

d. Calculate Prob[Results IF H_0 true] and assess your theories.

2. Consider a second model explaining cigarette consumption:

$$CigConsPC_t = \beta_{Const} + \beta_{Price}PriceConsumer_t + \beta_I IncPC_t$$

$$+ \beta_{TobProd}TobProdPC_t + e_t$$

a. Develop a theory that explains how each explanatory variable affects per capita cigarette consumption. What do your theories suggest about the sign of each coefficient?

b. Use the ordinary least squares (OLS) estimation procedure to estimate the parameters of the model.

[To access this online material, go to http://mitpress.mit.edu/westhoffeconometrics and select Cigarette Consumption.]

c. Formulate the null and alternative hypotheses.

d. Calculate Prob[Results IF H_0 true] and assess your theories.

3. Consider a third model explaining cigarette consumption:

$$CigConsPC_t = \beta_{Const} + \beta_{Price}PriceConsumer_t + \beta_{EduColl}EducCollege_t$$

$$+ \beta_I IncPC_t + \beta_{TobProd}TobProdPC_t + e_t$$

a. Develop a theory that explains how each explanatory variable affects per capita cigarette consumption. What do your theories suggest about the sign of each coefficient?

b. Use the ordinary least squares (OLS) estimation procedure to estimate the parameters of the model.

[To access this online material, go to http://mitpress.mit.edu/westhoffeconometrics and select Cigarette Consumption.]

    c. Formulate the null and alternative hypotheses.

    d. Calculate Prob[Results IF H_0 true] and assess your theories.

4. Focus on the coefficient estimates of *EducCollege* and *IncomePC* in exercises 1, 2, and 3.

    a. Compare the estimates.

    b. Provide a scenario to explain why the estimates may have changed as they did.

House earmark data: Cross-sectional data of proposed earmarks in the 2009 fiscal year for the 451 House members of the 110th Congress.

CongressName$_t$	Name of Congressperson t
CongressParty$_t$	Party of Congressperson t
CongressState$_t$	State of Congressperson t
IncPC$_t$	Income per capita in the Congressperson t's state (dollars)
Number$_t$	Number of earmarks received that were sponsored solely by Congressperson t
PartyDem1$_t$	1 if Congressperson t Democrat; 0 otherwise
PartyRep1$_t$	1 if Congressperson t Republican; 0 otherwise
RegionMidwest$_t$	1 if Congressperson t represents a midwestern state, 0 otherwise
RegionNortheast$_t$	1 if Congressperson t represents a northeastern state; 0 otherwise
RegionSouth$_t$	1 if Congressperson t represents a southern state; 0 otherwise
RegionWest$_t$	1 if Congressperson t represents a western state; 0 otherwise
ScoreLiberal$_t$	Congressperson's t liberal score rating in 2007
Terms$_t$	Number of terms served by Congressperson in the US Congress
UnemRate$_t$	Unemployment rate in Congressperson t's state

5. Consider the following model explaining the number of solo earmarks:

$$Number_t = \beta_{Const} + \beta_{Terms}Terms_t + \beta_{Liberal}ScoreLiberal_t + e_t$$

    a. Develop a theory that explains how each explanatory variable affects the number of solo earmarks. What do your theories suggest about the sign of each coefficient?

    b. Use the ordinary least squares (OLS) estimation procedure to estimate the parameters of the model.

[To access this online material, go to http://mitpress.mit.edu/westhoffeconometrics and select House Earmarks.]

    c. Formulate the null and alternative hypotheses.

    d. Calculate Prob[Results IF H_0 true] and assess your theories.

6. Consider a second model explaining the number of solo earmarks:

$$Number_t = \beta_{Const} + \beta_{Terms}Terms_t + \beta_{Dem}PartyDemocrat_t + e_t$$

    a. Develop a theory that explains how each explanatory variable affects the number of solo earmarks. What do your theories suggest about the sign of each coefficient?

    b. Use the ordinary least squares (OLS) estimation procedure to estimate the parameters of the model.

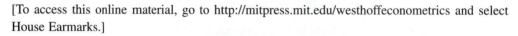

[To access this online material, go to http://mitpress.mit.edu/westhoffeconometrics and select House Earmarks.]

    c. Formulate the null and alternative hypotheses.

    d. Calculate Prob[Results IF H_0 true] and assess your theories.

7. Consider a third model explaining the number of solo earmarks:

$$Number_t = \beta_{Const} + \beta_{Terms}Terms_t + \beta_{Liberal}ScoreLiberal_t$$
$$+ \beta_{Dem}PartyDemocrat_t + e_t$$

    a. Develop a theory that explains how each explanatory variable affects the number of solo earmarks. What do your theories suggest about the sign of each coefficient?

    b. Use the ordinary least squares (OLS) estimation procedure to estimate the parameters of the model.

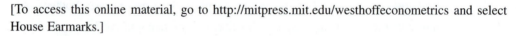

[To access this online material, go to http://mitpress.mit.edu/westhoffeconometrics and select House Earmarks.]

    c. Formulate the null and alternative hypotheses.

    d. Calculate Prob[Results IF H_0 true] and assess your theories.

8. Focus on the coefficient estimates of *ScoreLiberal* and *PartyDemocrat* in exercises 5, 6, and 7.

    a. Compare the standard errors.

    b. Provide a scenario to explain why the standard errors may have changed as they did.

15 Other Regression Statistics and Pitfalls

Chapter 15 Prep Questions

1. A friend believes that the internet is displacing the television as a source of news and entertainment. The friend theorizes that after accounting for other factors, television usage is falling by 1 percent annually:

−1.0 Percent growth rate theory: After accounting for all other factors, the annual growth rate of television users is negative, −1.0 percent.

Recall the model we used previously to explain television use:

$$LogUsersTV_t = \beta_{Const}^{TV} + \beta_{Year}^{TV}Year_t + \beta_{CapHum}^{TV}CapitalHuman_t$$
$$+ \beta_{CapPhy}^{TV}CapitalPhysical_t + \beta_{GDP}^{TV}GdpPC_t + \beta_{Auth}^{TV}Auth_t + e_t^{TV}$$

and the data we used:

Internet and TV data: Panel data of Internet, TV, economic, and political statistics for 208 countries from 1995 to 2002.

[To access this online material, go to http://mitpress.mit.edu/westhoffeconometrics and select Internet and TV Use – 1995–2002.]

$LogUsersInternet_t$	Logarithm of Internet users per 1,000 people for observation t
$LogUsersTV_t$	Logarithm of television users per 1,000 people for observation t
$Year_t$	Year for observation t
$CapitalHuman_t$	Literacy rate for observation t (percent of population 15 and over)
$CapitalPhysical_t$	Telephone mainlines per 10,000 people for observation t
$GdpPC_t$	Per capita real GDP in nation t (1,000's of "international" dollars)
$Auth_t$	Freedom House measures of political authoritarianism for observation t normalized to a 0 to 10 scale. 0 represents the most democratic rating and 10 the most authoritarian. During the 1995 to 2002 period, Canada and the United States had a 0 rating; Iraq and the Democratic Republic of Korea (North Korea) rated 10.

Now assess your friend's theory.

a. Use the ordinary least squares (OLS) estimation procedure to estimate the model's parameters.

[To access this online material, go to http://mitpress.mit.edu/westhoffeconometrics and select Internet and TV Use – 1995–2002.]

b. Formulate the appropriate null and alternative hypotheses. Is a one-tailed or a two-tailed test appropriate?

c. Use the Econometrics Lab to calculate the Prob[Results IF H_0 true].

[To access this online material, go to http://mitpress.mit.edu/westhoffeconometrics and select t-Distribution.]

2. A regression's coefficient of determination, called the R-squared, is referred to as the goodness of fit. It equals the portion of the dependent variable's squared deviations from its mean that is explained by the parameter estimates:

$$R^2 = \frac{\text{Explained squared deviations from the mean}}{\text{Actual squared deviations from the mean}} = \frac{\sum_{t=1}^{T}(Esty_t - \bar{y})^2}{\sum_{t=1}^{T}(y_t - \bar{y})^2}$$

Calculate the R-squared for Professor Lord's first quiz by filling in the following blanks:

			Actual y deviation from mean	Actual squared deviation	Esty equals	Explained y deviation from mean	Explained squared deviation
Student	x_t	y_t	$y_t - \bar{y}$	$(y_t - \bar{y})^2$	$63 + 1.2x$	$Esty_t - \bar{y}$	$(Esty_t - \bar{y})^2$
1	5	66	_____	_____	_____	_____	_____
2	15	87	_____	_____	_____	_____	_____
3	25	<u>90</u>	_____	_____	_____	_____	_____

$$\sum_{t=1}^{T}(y_t - \bar{y})^2 = \_\_\_\_\_$$

$$\sum_{t=1}^{T} y_t = \_\_\_\_ \qquad\qquad\qquad \sum_{t=1}^{T}(Esty_t - \bar{y})^2 = \_\_\_\_\_$$

$$\bar{y} = \frac{}{3} = \_\_\_\_ \qquad\qquad R\text{-Squared} = \frac{}{} = _____$$

3. Students frequently experience difficulties when analyzing data. To illustrate some of these pitfalls, we first review the goal of multiple regression analysis:

Goal of multiple regression analysis: Multiple regression analysis attempts to sort out the individual effect of each explanatory variable. An explanatory variable's coefficient estimate allows us to estimate the change in the dependent variable resulting from a change in that particular explanatory variable while all other explanatory variables remain constant.

Reconsider our baseball data for 1996.

Baseball data: Panel data of baseball statistics for the 588 American League games played during the summer of 1996.

Attendance$_t$	Paid attendance for game t
DH$_t$	Designator hitter for game t (1 if DH permitted; 0 otherwise)
HomeSalary$_t$	Player salaries of the home team for game t (millions of dollars)
PriceTicket$_t$	Average price of tickets sold for game t's home team (dollars)
VisitSalary$_t$	Player salaries of the visiting team for game t (millions of dollars)

Now consider several pitfalls that students often encounter:

a. Explanatory variable has the same value for all observations. Run the following regression:

[To access this online material, go to http://mitpress.mit.edu/westhoffeconometrics and select 1996 American League Summer.]

Dependent variable: *Attendance*

Explanatory variables: *PriceTicket*, *HomeSalary*, and *DH*

    i. What happens?

    ii. What is the value of DH_t for each of the observations?

    iii. Why is it impossible to determine the effect of an explanatory variable if the explanatory variable has the same value for each observation? Explain.

b. One explanatory variable is a linear combination of other explanatory variables. Generate a new variable, the ticket price in terms of cents:

$$PriceCents = 100 \times PriceTicket$$

Run the following regression:

[To access this online material, go to http://mitpress.mit.edu/westhoffeconometrics and select 1996 Amercian League Summer.]

Dependent variable: *Attendance*

Explanatory variables: *PriceTicket*, *PriceCents*, and *HomeSalary*

    i. What happens?

    ii. Is it possible to sort out the effect of two explanatory variables when they contain redundant information?

c. One explanatory variable is a linear combination of other explanatory variables—another example. Generate a new variable, the total salaries of the two teams playing:

$$TotalSalary = HomeSalary + VisitSalary$$

Run the following regression:

[To access this online material, go to http://mitpress.mit.edu/westhoffeconometrics and select 1996 American League Summer.]

Dependent variable: *Attendance*

Explanatory variables: *PriceTicket*, *HomeSalary*, *VisitSalary*, and *TotalSalary*

    i. What happens?

    ii. Is it possible to sort out the effect of explanatory variables when they are linear combinations of each other and therefore contain redundant information?

d. Dependent variable is a linear combination of explanatory variables. Run the following regression:

[To access this online material, go to http://mitpress.mit.edu/westhoffeconometrics and select 1996 American League Summer.]

Dependent variable: *TotalSalary*

Explanatory variables: *HomeSalary* and *VisitSalary*

What happens?

e. Outlier observations. First, run the following regression:

[To access this online material, go to http://mitpress.mit.edu/westhoffeconometrics and select 1996 American League Summer.]

Dependent variable: *Attendance*

Explanatory variables: *PriceTicket* and *HomeSalary*

> **i.** What is the coefficient estimate for the ticket price?
>
> **ii.** Look at the first observation. What is the value of *HomeSalary* for the first observation?

Now access a second workfile in which a single value was entered incorrectly:

[To access this online material, go to http://mitpress.mit.edu/westhoffeconometrics and select 1996 American League Summer Outlier.]

> **iii.** Look at the first observation. What is the value of *HomeSalary* for the first observation? Is the value that was entered correctly?

Run the following regression:

Dependent variable: *Attendance*

Explanatory variables: *PriceTicket* and *HomeSalary*

> **iv.** Compare the coefficient estimates in the two regressions.

4. Return to our faculty salary data.

Faculty salary data: Artificially constructed cross section salary data and characteristics for 200 faculty members.

Salary_t   Salary of faculty member t (dollars)

Experience_t   Teaching experience for faculty member t (years)

Articles_t   Number of articles published by faculty member t

SexM1_t   1 if faculty member t is male; 0 if female

As we did in chapter 13, generate the dummy variable *SexF1,* which equals 1 for a woman and 0 for a man. Run the following three regressions specifying *Salary* as the dependent variable:

[To access this online material, go to http://mitpress.mit.edu/westhoffeconometrics and select Faculty Salaries.]

> **a.** Explanatory variables: *SexF1* and *Experience*
>
> **b.** Explanatory variables: *SexM1* and *Experience*
>
> **c.** Explanatory variables: *SexF1*, *SexM1*, and *Experience*—but without a constant

Getting Started in EViews

To estimate the third model (part c) using EViews, you must "fool" EViews into running the appropriate regression:

• In the Workfile window: highlight **Salary** and then while depressing <Ctrl> highlight *SexF1*, *SexM1*, and *Experience*.

• In the Workfile window: double click on a highlighted variable.

• Click **Open Equation**.

• In the Equation Specification window delete **c** so that the window looks like this:

salary sexf1 sexm1 experience.

• Click **OK**.

For each regression, what is the equation that estimates the salary for

    i. men?

    ii. women?

Last, run one more regression specifying *Salary* as the dependent variable:

    d. Explanatory variables: *SexF1*, *SexM1*, and *Experience*—but with a constant. What happens?

5. Consider a system of linear equations of 2 equations and 3 unknowns. Can you solve for all three unknowns?

15.1 Two-Tailed Confidence Intervals

15.1.1 Confidence Interval Approach: Which Theories Are Consistent with the Data?

Our approach thus far has been to present a theory first and then use data to assess the theory:

• First, we presented a theory.

• Second, we analyzed the data to determine whether or not the data were consistent with the theory.

In other words, we have started with a theory and then decided whether or not the data were consistent with the theory.

    The **confidence interval** approach reverses this process. Confidence intervals indicate the range of theories that are consistent with the data.

• First, we analyze the data.

• Second, we consider various theories and determine which theories are consistent with the data and which are not.

In other words, the confidence interval approach starts with the data and then decides what theories are compatible.

   Hypothesis testing plays a key role in both approaches. Consequently we must choose a significance level. A confidence interval's "size" and the significance level are intrictly related:

   Two-tailed confidence interval + Significance level = 100%

Since the traditional significance levels are 10, 5, and 1 percent, the three most commonly used confidence intervals are 90, 95, and 99 percent:

• For a 90 percent confidence interval, the significance level is 10 percent.

• For a 95 percent confidence interval, the significance level is 5 percent.

• For a 99 percent confidence interval, the significance level is 1 percent.

A theory is consistent with the data if we cannot reject the null hypothesis at the confidence interval's significance level. No doubt this sounds confusing, so let us work through an example using our international television data:

15.1.2 A Confidence Interval Example: Television Growth Rates

Project: Which growth theories are consistent with the international television data?

Internet and TV data: Panel data of Internet, TV, economic, and political statistics for 208 countries from 1995 to 2002.

[To access this online material, go to http://mitpress.mit.edu/westhoffeconometrics and select Internet and TV Use – 1995–2002.]

$LogUsersInternet_t$	Logarithm of Internet users per 1,000 people for observation t
$LogUsersTV_t$	Logarithm of television users per 1,000 people for observation t
$Year_t$	Year for observation t
$CapitalHuman_t$	Literacy rate for observation t (percent of population 15 and over)
$CapitalPhysical_t$	Telephone mainlines per 10,000 people for observation t
$GdpPC_t$	Per capita real GDP in nation t (1,000's of "international" dollars)
$Auth_t$	Freedom House measures of political authoritarianism for observation t normalized to a 0 to 10 scale. 0 represents the most democratic rating and 10 the most authoritarian. During the 1995 to 2002 period, Canada and the United States had a 0 rating; Iraq and the Democratic Republic of Korea (North Korea) rated 10.

We begin by specifying the "size" of the confidence interval. Let us use a 95 percent confidence interval which means that we are implicitly choosing a significance level of 5 percent. The following two steps formalize the procedure to decide whether a theory lies within the two-tailed 95 percent confidence interval:

Step 1:   Analyze the data. Use the ordinary least squares (OLS) estimation procedure to estimate the model's parameters.

Step 2:   Consider a specific theory. Is the theory consistent with the data? Does the theory lie within the confidence interval?

• **Step 2a:**   Based on the theory, construct the null and alternative hypotheses. The null hypothesis reflects the theory.

• **Step 2b:**   Compute Prob[Results IF H_0 true].

• **Step 2c:**   Do we reject the null hypothesis?

Yes: Reject the theory. The data are not consistent with the theory. The theory does not lie within the confidence interval.

No: The data are consistent with the theory. The theory does lie within the confidence interval.

Recall that we decided to use a 95 percent confidence interval and consequently a 5 percent significance level:

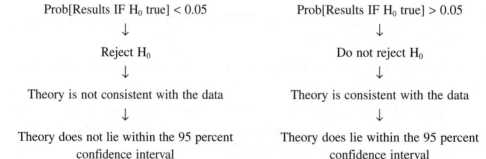

We will illustrate the steps by focusing on four growth rate theories postulating what the growth rate of television use equals after accounting for other relevant factors:

• 0.0 percent growth rate theory

• −1.0 percent growth rate theory

• 4.0 percent growth rate theory

• 6.0 percent growth rate theory

0.0   Percent Growth Rate Theory

Since television is a mature technology we begin with a theory postulating that time will have no impact on television use after accounting for other factors; that is, after accounting for other factors the growth rate of television use will equal 0.0. We will now apply our two steps to determine if the 0.0 percent growth rate theory lies within the 95 percent confidence interval:

Step 1:   Analyze the data. Use the ordinary least squares (OLS) estimation procedure to estimate the model's parameters.

We will apply the same model to explain television use that we used previously:

Model:

$$LogUsersTV_t = \beta_{Const}^{TV} + \beta_{Year}^{TV} Year_t + \beta_{CapHum}^{TV} CapitalHuman_t$$
$$+ \beta_{CapPhy}^{TV} CapitalPhysical_t + \beta_{GDP}^{TV} GdpPC_t + \beta_{Auth}^{TV} Auth_t + e_t^{TV}$$

We already estimated the parameters of this model in chapter 13 (table 15.1).

Step 2:   0.0 Percent growth rate theory. Focus on the effect of time. Is a 0.0 percent growth theory consistent with the data? Does the theory lie within the confidence interval?

0.0 Percent growth rate theory: After accounting for all other explanatory variables, time has no effect on television use; that is, after accounting for all other explanatory variables, the annual growth rate of television use equals 0.0 percent. Accordingly the actual coefficient of *Year*, β_{Year}^{TV}, equals 0.000.

Table 15.1
Television regression results

Ordinary least squares (OLS)				
Dependent variable: *LogUsersTV*				
Explanatory variable(s):	Estimate	SE	*t*-Statistic	Prob
Year	0.022989	0.015903	1.445595	0.1487
CapitalHuman	0.036302	0.001915	18.95567	0.0000
CapitalPhysical	0.001931	0.000510	3.789394	0.0002
GdpPC	0.058877	0.012338	4.772051	0.0000
Auth	0.063345	0.012825	4.939278	0.0000
Const	−44.95755	31.77155	−1.415025	0.1575
Number of observations	742			

Estimated equation: *EstLogUsersTV* = −45.0 + 0.023*Year* + 0.036*CapitalHuman* + 0.002*CapitalPhysical*
+ 0.058*GdpPC* + 0.064*Auth*

- **Step 2a:**   Based on the theory, construct the null and alternative hypotheses.

H_0: $\beta_{Year}^{TV} = 0.000$

H_1: $\beta_{Year}^{TV} \neq 0.000$

- **Step 2b:**   Compute Prob[Results IF H_0 true].

Prob[Results IF H_0 true] = Probability that the coefficient estimate would be at least 0.023 from 0.000, if H_0 were true (if the actual coefficient equals, β_{Year}^{TV}, 0.000).

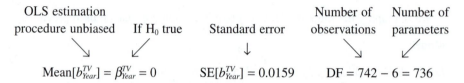

We can use the Econometrics Lab to calculate the probability of obtaining the results if the null hypothesis is true. Remember that we are conducting a two-tailed test.

Econometrics Lab 15.1: Calculate Prob[Results IF H_0 true].

First, calculate the right-hand tail probability.

[To access this online material, go to http://mitpress.mit.edu/westhoffeconometrics and select Lab 15.1a.]

Question: What is the probability that the estimate lies at or above 0.023?

Answer: 0.0742 (figure 15.1)

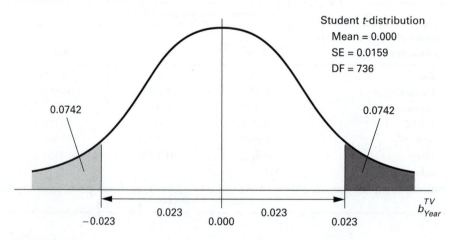

Figure 15.1
Probability distribution of coefficient estimate—0.0 Percent growth rate theory

Second, calculate the left hand tail probability.

[To access this online material, go to http://mitpress.mit.edu/westhoffeconometrics and select Lab 15.1b.]

Question: What is the probability that the estimate lies at or below −0.023?

Answer: 0.0742

The Prob[Results IF H_0 true] equals the sum of the right and the left tail two probabilities:

$$\text{Left tail} \qquad \text{Right tail}$$
$$\downarrow \qquad\qquad \downarrow$$
$$\text{Prob[Results IF } H_0 \text{ true]} \ = \ 0.074 \ + \ 0.074 \ \approx \ 0.148$$

• **Step 2c:** Do we reject the null hypothesis? No, we do not reject the null hypothesis at a 5 percent significance level; Prob[Results IF H_0 true] equals 0.148, which is greater than 0.05. The theory is consistent with the data; hence 0.000 does lie within the 95 percent confidence interval.

Let us now apply the procedure to three other theories:

• **−1.0 Percent growth rate theory:** After accounting for all other factors, the annual growth rate of television users is −1.0 percent; that is, β_{Year}^{TV} equals −0.010.

• **4.0 Percent growth rate theory:** After accounting for all other factors, the annual growth rate of television users is 4.0 percent; that is, β_{Year}^{TV} equals 0.040.

• **6.0 Percent growth rate theory:** After accounting for all other factors, the annual growth rate of television users is 6.0 percent; that is, β_{Year}^{TV} equals 0.060.

We will not provide justification for any of these theories. The confidence interval approach does not worry about justifying the theory. The approach is pragmatic; the approach simply asks whether or not the data support the theory.

−1.0 Percent Growth Rate Theory

Step 1: Analyze the data. Use the ordinary least squares (OLS) estimation procedure to estimate the model's parameters.

We have already done this.

Step 2: −1.0 Percent growth rate theory. Is the theory consistent with the data? Does the theory lie within the confidence interval?

• **Step 2a:** Based on the theory, construct the null and alternative hypotheses.

H_0: $\beta_{Year}^{TV} = -0.010$

H_1: $\beta_{Year}^{TV} \neq -0.010$

· **Step 2b:** Compute Prob[Results IF H_0 true].

To compute Prob[Results IF H_0 true], we first pose a question:

Question: How far is the coefficient estimate, 0.023, from the value of the coefficient specified by the null hypothesis, −0.010?

Answer: 0.033

Accordingly

Prob[Results IF H_0 true] = Probability that the coefficient estimate would be at least 0.033 from −0.010, if H_0 were true (if the actual coefficient equals, β_{Year}^{TV}, −0.010)

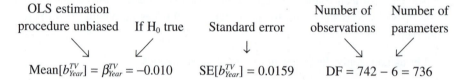

We can use the Econometrics Lab to calculate the probability of obtaining the results if the null hypothesis is true. Once again, remember that we are conducting a two-tailed test:

Econometrics Lab 15.2: Calculate Prob[Results IF H_0 true]

First, calculate the right-hand tail probability (figure 15.2).

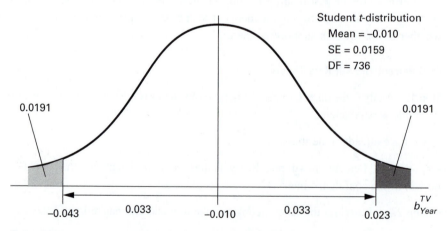

Figure 15.2
Probability distribution of coefficient estimate——1.0 Percent growth rate theory

[To access this online material, go to http://mitpress.mit.edu/westhoffeconometrics and select Lab 15.2a.]

Question: What is the probability that the estimate lies 0.033 or more above −0.010, at or above 0.023?

Answer: 0.0191

Second, calculate the left-hand tail probability.

[To access this online material, go to http://mitpress.mit.edu/westhoffeconometrics and select Lab 15.2b.]

Question: What is the probability that the estimate lies 0.033 or more below −0.010, at or below −0.043?

Answer: 0.0191

The Prob[Results IF H_0 true] equals the sum of the of the two probabilities:

	Left tail	Right tail		
	↓	↓		
Prob[Results IF H_0 true] =	0.019	+	0.019	≈ 0.038

• **Step 2c:** Do we reject the null hypothesis?

Yes, we do reject the null hypothesis at a 5 percent significance level; Prob[Results IF H_0 true] equals 0.038, which is less than 0.05. The theory is not consistent with the data; hence −0.010 does not lie within the 95 percent confidence interval.

4.0 Percent Growth Rate Theory
Following the same procedure for the 4.0 percent growth rate theory:

Prob[Results IF H_0 true] ≈ 0.285

We do not reject the null hypothesis at a 5 percent significance level. The theory is consistent with the data; hence 0.040 does lie within the 95 percent confidence interval.

6.0 Percent Growth Rate Theory
Again, following the same procedure for the 6.0 percent growth rate theory:

Prob[Results IF H_0 true] ≈ 0.020

We do reject the null hypothesis at a 5 percent significance level. The theory is not consistent with the data; hence 0.060 does not lie within the 95 percent confidence interval.

We summarize the four theories in figure 15.3 and table 15.2.

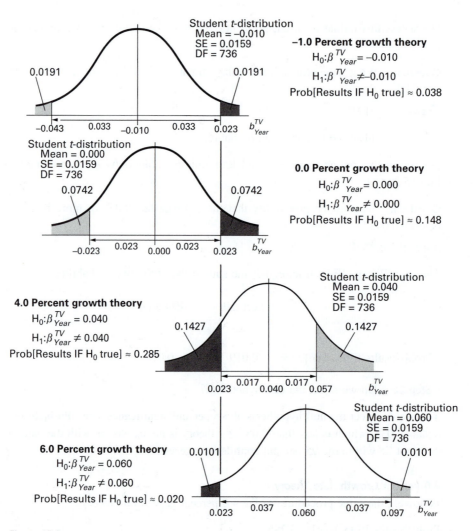

Figure 15.3
Probability distribution of coefficient estimate—Comparison of growth rate Theories

Table 15.2
Growth rate theories and the 95 percent confidence interval

Growth rate theory	Null and alternative hypotheses		Prob[Results IF H_0 true]	Confidence interval
−1%	H_0: $\beta_{Year}^{TV} = -0.010$	H_1: $\beta_{Year}^{TV} \neq -0.010$	≈0.038	No
0%	H_0: $\beta_{Year}^{TV} = 0.000$	H_1: $\beta_{Year}^{TV} \neq 0.000$	≈0.148	Yes
4%	H_0: $\beta_{Year}^{TV} = 0.040$	H_1: $\beta_{Year}^{TV} \neq 0.040$	≈0.285	Yes
6%	H_0: $\beta_{Year}^{TV} = 0.060$	H_1: $\beta_{Year}^{TV} \neq 0.060$	≈0.020	No

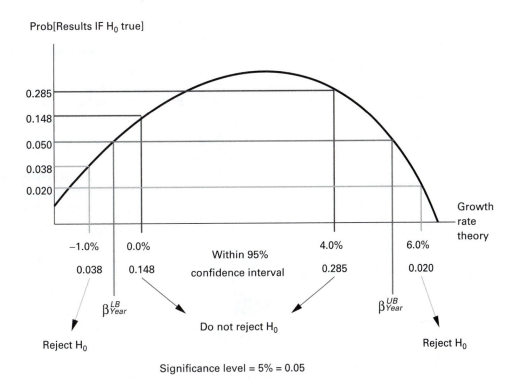

Figure 15.4
Lower and Upper Confidence Interval Bounds

Now we will make two observations and pose two questions:

• The 0.0 percent growth rate theory lies within the confidence interval, but the −1.0 percent theory does not (figure 15.4).

Question: What is the lowest growth rate theory that is consistent with the data; that is, what is the lower bound of the confidence interval, β_{Year}^{LB}?

• The 4.0 percent growth rate theory lies within the confidence interval, but the 6.0 percent theory does not (figure 15.4).

Question: What is the highest growth rate theory that is consistent with the data; that is, what is the upper bound of the confidence interval, β_{Year}^{UB}?

Figure 15.5 answers these questions visually by illustrating the lower and upper bounds. The Prob[Results IF H_0 true] equals 0.05 for both lower and upper bound growth theories because our calculations are based on a 95 percent confidence interval:

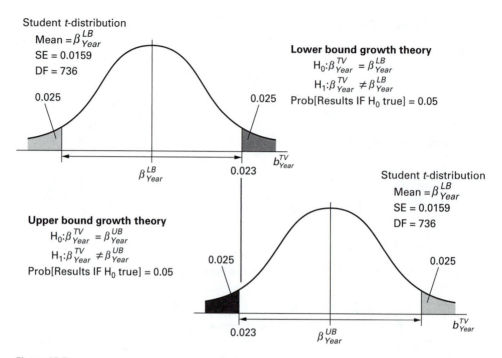

Figure 15.5
Probability distribution of coefficient estimate—Lower and upper confidence intervals

· The lower bound growth theory postulates a growth rate that is less than that estimated. Hence the coefficient estimate, 0.023, marks the right-tail border of the lower bound.

· The upper bound growth theory postulates a growth rate that is greater than that estimated. Hence the coefficient estimate, 0.023, marks the left-tail border of the upper bound.

Econometrics Lab 15.3: Calculating the 95 Percent Confidence Interval

We can use the Econometrics Lab to calculate the lower and upper bounds:

· **Calculating the lower bound, β_{Year}^{LB}:**   For the lower bound, the right-tail probability equals 0.025.

[To access this online material, go to http://mitpress.mit.edu/westhoffeconometrics and select Lab 15.3a.]

The appropriate information is already entered for us:

Standard error: 0.0159

Value: 0.023

Degrees of freedom: 736

Area to right: 0.025

Click **Calculate.** The reported mean is the lower bound.

Mean: −0.0082

$\beta_{Year}^{LB} = -0.0082$

· **Calculating the Upper Bound, β_{Year}^{UB}:**   For the upper bound, the left-tail probability equals 0.025. Accordingly the right-tail probability will equal 0.975.

[To access this online material, go to http://mitpress.mit.edu/westhoffeconometrics and select Lab 15.3b.]

The appropriate information is already entered for us:

Standard error: 0.0159

Value: 0.023

Degrees of freedom: 736

Area to right: 0.975

Click **Calculate**. The reported mean is the upper bound.

Mean: 0.0542

$\beta_{Year}^{UB} = 0.0542$

In this case −0.0082 and 0.0542 mark the bounds of the two-tailed 95 percent confidence interval:

· For any growth rate theory between −0.82 percent and 5.42 percent:

Prob[Results IF H_0 true] > 0.05 → Do not reject H_0 at the 5 percent significance level.

· For any growth rate theory below −0.82 percent or above 5.42 percent:

Prob[Results IF H_0 true] < 0.05 → Reject H_0 at the 5 percent significance level.

15.1.3   Calculating Confidence Intervals with Statistical Software

Fortunately, statistic software provides us with an easy and convenient way to compute confidence intervals. The software does all the work for us.

Table 15.3
95 Percent confidence interval calculations

	95 Percent interval estimates		
Dependent variable: *LogUsersTV*			
Explanatory variable(s):	Estimate	Lower	Upper
Year	0.022989	−0.008231	0.054209
CapitalHuman	0.036302	0.034656	0.083099
CapitalPhysical	0.001931	0.000931	0.002932
GdpPC	0.058877	0.032542	0.040061
Auth	0.063345	0.038167	0.088522
Const	−44.95755	−107.3312	17.41612
Number of observations	742		

Getting Started in EViews

After running the appropriate regression:

· In the Equation window: Click **View**, **Coefficient Diagnostics**, and **Confidence Intervals**.

· In the Confidence Intervals window: Enter the confidence levels you wish to compute. (By default the values of .90, .95, and .99 are entered.)

· Click **OK**.

Table 15.3 reports that the lower and upper bounds for the 95 percent confidence interval are −0.0082 and 0.0542. These are the same values that we calculated using the Econometrics Lab.

15.2   Coefficient of Determination (Goodness of Fit), R-Squared (R^2)

All statistical packages report the coefficient of determination, the R-squared, in their regression printouts. The R-squared seeks to capture the "goodness of fit." It equals the portion of the dependent variable's squared deviations from its mean that is explained by the parameter estimates:

$$R^2 = \frac{\text{Explained squared deviations from the mean}}{\text{Actual squared deviations from the mean}} = \frac{\sum_{t=1}^{T}(Esty_t - \overline{y})^2}{\sum_{t=1}^{T}(y_t - \overline{y})^2}$$

To explain how the coefficient of determination is calculated, we will revisit Professor Lord's first quiz (table 15.4). Recall the theory, the model, and our analysis:

Theory: An increase in the number of minutes studied results in an increased quiz score.

Model: $y_t = \beta_{Const} + \beta_x x_t + e_t$

Table 15.4
First quiz data

Student	Minutes studied (x)	Quiz score (y)
1	5	66
2	15	87
3	25	90

Table 15.5
First quiz regression results

	Ordinary least squares (OLS)			
Dependent variable: y				
Explanatory variable(s):	Estimate	SE	t-Statistic	Prob
x	1.200000	0.519615	2.309401	0.2601
Const	63.00000	8.874120	7.099296	0.0891
Number of observations	3			
R-squared	0.842105			

Estimated equation: $Esty = 63 + 1.2x$

Interpretation of estimates:

$b_{Const} = 63$: Students receive 63 points for showing up.

$b_x = 1.2$: Students receive 1.2 additional points for each additional minute studied.

Critical result: The coefficient estimate equals 1.2. The positive sign of the coefficient estimate, suggests that additional studying increases quiz scores. This evidence lends support to our theory.

where

x_t = minutes studied by student t

y_t = quiz score earned by student t

Theory: $\beta_x > 0$

We used the ordinary least squares (OLS) estimation procedure to estimate the model's parameters (table 15.5).

[To access this online material, go to http://mitpress.mit.edu/westhoffeconometrics and select Professor Lord's First Quiz.]

Next we formulated the null and alternative hypotheses to determine how much confidence we should have in the theory:

H_0: $\beta_x = 0$ Studying has no impact on a student's quiz score

H_1: $\beta_x > 0$ Additional studying increases a student's quiz score

Table 15.6
R-squared calculations for first quiz

Student	x_t	y_t	Actual y deviation from mean $y_t - \bar{y}$	Actual squared deviation $(y_t - \bar{y})^2$	Esty equals $63 + 1.2x$	Explained y deviation from mean $Esty_t - \bar{y}$	Explained squared deviation $(Esty_t - \bar{y})^2$
1	5	66	−15	225	69	−12	144
2	15	87	6	36	81	0	0
3	25	90	9	81	93	12	144

$$\sum_{t=1}^{T} y_t = 243 \qquad \sum_{t=1}^{T}(y_t - \bar{y})^2 = 342 \qquad\qquad \sum_{t=1}^{T}(Esty_t - \bar{y})^2 = 288$$

$$\bar{y} = \frac{243}{3} = 81 \qquad\qquad R\text{-squared} = \frac{288}{342} = 0.84$$

We then calculated Prob[Results IF H_0 true], the probability of the results like we obtained (or even stronger) if studying in fact had no impact on quiz scores. The tails probability reported in the regression printout allows us to calculate this easily. Since a one-tailed test is appropriate, we divide the tails probability by 2:

$$\text{Prob[Results IF } H_0 \text{ true]} = \frac{0.2601}{2} \approx 0.13$$

We cannot reject the null hypothesis that studying has no impact even at the 10 percent significance level.

The regression printout reports that the R-squared equals about .84; this means that 84 percent of the dependent variable's squared deviations from its mean are explained by the parameter estimates. Table 15.6 shows the calculations required to compute the R-squared:
The R-squared equals $\sum_{t=1}^{T}(Esty_t - \bar{y})^2$ divided $\sum_{t=1}^{T}(y_t - \bar{y})^2$:

$$R^2 = \frac{\text{Explained squared deviations from the mean}}{\text{Actual squared deviations from the mean}} = \frac{\sum_{t=1}^{T}(Esty_t - \bar{y})^2}{\sum_{t=1}^{T}(y_t - \bar{y})^2} = \frac{288}{342} = 0.84$$

Note that 84 percent of the y's squared deviations are explained by the estimated constant and coefficient. Our calculation of the R-squared agrees with the regression printout.

While the R-squared is always calculated and reported by all statistical software, it is not useful in assessing theories. We will justify this claim by considering a second quiz that Professor Lord administered. Each student studies the same number of minutes and earns the same score in the second quiz as he/she did in the first quiz (table 15.7).

Before we run another regression that includes the data from both quizzes, let us apply our intuition:

Table 15.7
Second quiz data

Student	Minutes studied (x)	Quiz score (y)
1	5	66
2	15	87
3	25	90

Table 15.8
First and second quiz regression results

	Ordinary least squares (OLS)			
Dependent variable: y				
Explanatory variable(s):	Estimate	SE	t-Statistic	Prob
x	1.200000	0.259808	4.618802	0.0099
Const	63.00000	4.437060	14.19859	0.0001
Number of observations	6			
R-squared	0.842105			

• Begin by focusing on only the first quiz. Taken in isolation, first quiz suggests that studying improves quiz scores. We cannot be very confident of this, however, since we cannot reject the null hypothesis even at a 10 percent significance level.

• Next consider only the second quiz. Since the data from the second quiz is identical to the data from the first quiz, the regression results would be identical. Hence, taken in isolation, the second quiz suggests that studying improves quiz scores.

Each quiz in isolation suggests that studying improves quiz scores. Now consider both quizzes together. The two quizzes taken together reinforce each other; this should make us more confident in concluding that studying improves quiz scores, should it not?

If our intuition is correct, how should the Prob[Results IF H_0 true] be affected when we consider both quizzes together? Since we are more confident in concluding that studying improves quiz scores, the probability should be less. Let us run a regression using data from both the first and second quizzes to determine whether or not this is true (table 15.8).

[To access this online material, go to http://mitpress.mit.edu/westhoffeconometrics and select Professor Lord's First and Second Quizzes.]

Using data from both quizzes:

$$\text{Prob[Results IF } H_0 \text{ true]} = \frac{0.0099}{2} \approx 0.005$$

Table 15.9
R-squared calculations for first and second quizzes

Quiz/ student	x_t	y_t	Actual y deviation from mean $y_t - \bar{y}$	Actual squared deviation $(y_t - \bar{y})^2$	Esty equals $63 + 1.2x$	Explained y deviation from mean $Esty_t - \bar{y}$	Explained squared deviation $(Esty_t - \bar{y})^2$
1/1	5	66	−15	225	69	−12	144
1/2	15	87	6	36	81	0	0
1/3	25	90	9	81	93	12	144
2/1	5	66	−15	225	69	−12	144
2/2	15	87	6	36	81	0	0
2/3	25	90	9	81	93	12	144

$$\sum_{t=1}^{T} y_t = 486 \qquad \sum_{t=1}^{T}(y_t - \bar{y})^2 = 684 \qquad \sum_{t=1}^{T}(Esty_t - \bar{y})^2 = 576$$

$$\bar{y} = \frac{486}{6} = 81 \qquad\qquad R\text{-squared} = \frac{576}{684} = 0.84$$

As a consequence of the second quiz, the probability has fallen from 0.13 to 0.005; clearly, our confidence in the theory rises. We can now reject the null hypothesis that studying has no impact at the traditional significance levels of 1, 5, and 10 percent. Our calculations confirm our intuition.

Next consider the R-squared for the last regression that includes both quizzes. The regression printout reports that the R-squared has not changed; the R-squared is still 0.84. Table 15.9 explains why:

$$R^2 = \frac{\text{Explained squared deviations from the mean}}{\text{Actual squared deviations from the mean}} = \frac{\sum_{t=1}^{T}(Esty_t - \bar{y})^2}{\sum_{t=1}^{T}(y_t - \bar{y})^2} = \frac{586}{684} = 0.84$$

The R-squared still equals 0.84. Both the actual and explained squared deviations have doubled; consequently their ratio, the R-squared, remains unchanged. Clearly, the R-squared does not help us assess our theory. We are now more confident in the theory, but the value of the R-squared has not changed. The bottom line is that if we are interested in assessing our theories we should focus on hypothesis testing, not on the R-squared.

15.3   Pitfalls

Frequently econometrics students using statistical software encounter pitfalls that are frustrating. We will now discuss several of these pitfalls and describe the warning signs that accompany them. We begin by reviewing the "goal" of multiple regression analysis:

Goal of multiple regression analysis: Multiple regression analysis attempts to sort out the individual effect of each explanatory variable. An explanatory variable's coefficient estimate allows us to estimate the change in the dependent variable resulting from a change in that particular explanatory variable while all other explanatory variables remain constant.

We will consider five common pitfalls that often befell students:

- Explanatory variable has the same value for all observations.
- One explanatory variable is a linear combination of other explanatory variables.
- Dependent variable is a linear combination of explanatory variables.
- Outlier observations.
- Dummy variable trap.

We will illustrate the first four pitfalls by revisiting our baseball attendance data that reports on every game played in the American League during the summer of 1996 season.

Project: Assess the determinants of baseball attendance.

Baseball data: Panel data of baseball statistics for the 588 American League games played during the summer of 1996.

$Attendance_t$ Paid attendance for game t

DH_t Designator hitter for game t (1 if DH permitted; 0 otherwise)

$HomeSalary_t$ Player salaries of the home team for game t (millions of dollars)

$PriceTicket_t$ Average price of tickets sold for game t's home team (dollars)

$VisitSalary_t$ Player salaries of the visiting team for game t (millions of dollars)

[To access this online material, go to http://mitpress.mit.edu/westhoffeconometrics and select 1996 American League Summer.]

We begin with a model that we have studied before in which attendance, $Attendance$, depends on two explanatory variables, ticket price, $PriceTicket$, and home team salary, $HomeSalary$:

$$Attendance_t = \beta_{Const} + \beta_{Price}PriceTicket_t + \beta_{HomeSalary}HomeSalary_t + e_t$$

Recall the regression results from chapter 14 (table 15.10).

15.3.1   Explanatory Variable Has the Same Value for All Observations

One common pitfall is to include an explanatory variable in a regression that has the same value for each observation. To illustrate this, consider the variable DH:

DH_t Designator hitter for game t (1 if DH permitted; 0 otherwise)

Table 15.10
Baseball attendance regression results

Ordinary least squares (OLS)				
Dependent variable: *Attendance*				
Explanatory variable(s):	Estimate	SE	*t*-Statistic	Prob
PriceTicket	−590.7836	184.7231	−3.198211	0.0015
HomeSalary	783.0394	45.23955	17.30874	0.0000
Const	9,246.429	1,529.658	6.044767	0.0000
Number of observations	585			

Estimated equation: *EstAttendance* = 9,246 − 591*PriceTicket* + 783*HomeSalary*

Interpretation:

$b_{PriceTicket}$ = −591. We estimate that a $1.00 increase in the price of tickets decreases attendance by 591 per game.

$b_{HomeSalary}$ = 783. We estimate that a $1 million increase in the home team salary increases attendance by 783 per game.

Our baseball data includes only American League games in 1996. Since interleague play did not begin until 1997 and all American League games allowed designated hitters, the variable DH_t equals 1 for each observation. Let us try to use the ticket price, *PriceTicket*, home team salary, *HomeSalary*, and the designated hitter dummy variable, *DH*, to explain attendance, *Attendance*:

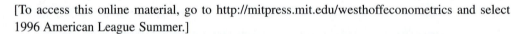

[To access this online material, go to http://mitpress.mit.edu/westhoffeconometrics and select 1996 American League Summer.]

The statistical software issues a diagnostic. While the verbiage differs from software package to software package, the message is the same: the software cannot perform the calculations that we requested. That is, the statistical software is telling us that it is being asked to do the impossible.

What is the intuition behind this? To determine how a dependent variable is affected by an explanatory variable, we must observe how the dependent variable changes when the explanatory variable changes. The intuition is straightforward:

• On the one hand, if the dependent variable tends to rise when the explanatory variable rises, the explanatory variable affects the dependent variable positively suggesting a positive coefficient.

• On the other hand, if the dependent variable tends to fall when the explanatory variable rises, the explanatory variable affects the dependent variable negatively suggesting a negative coefficient.

The evidence of how the dependent variable changes when the explanatory variable changes is essential. In the case of our baseball example, there is no variation in the designated hitter explanatory variable, however; the DH_t equals 1 for each observation. We have no way to assess the effect that the designated hitter has on attendance. We are asking our statistical software to do the impossible. While we have attendance information when the designated hitter was used, we have no attendance information when the designated hitter was not used. How then can we expect the software to assess the impact of the designed hitter on attendance?

15.3.2 One Explanatory Variable Is a Linear Combination of Other Explanatory Variables

We have already seen one example of this when we discussed multicollinearity in the previous chapter. We included both the ticket price in terms of dollars and the ticket price in terms of cents as explanatory variables. The ticket price in terms of cents was a linear combination of the ticket price in terms of dollars:

$$PriceCents = 100 \times PriceTicket$$

Let us try to use the ticket price, *PriceTicket*, home team salary, *HomeSalary*, and the ticket price in terms of cents, *PriceCents*, to explain attendance, *Attendance*:

[To access this online material, go to http://mitpress.mit.edu/westhoffeconometrics and select 1996 American League Summer.]

When both measures of the price were included in the regression our statistical software will issue a diagnostic indicating that it is being asked to do the impossible. Statistical software cannot separate out the individual influence of the two explanatory variables, *PriceTicket* and *PriceCents*, because they contain precisely the same information; the two explanatory variables are redundant. We are asking the software to do the impossible.

In fact any linear combination of explanatory variables produces this problem. To illustrate this, we consider two regressions. The first specifies three explanatory variables: ticket price, home team salary, and visiting team salary (table 15.11).

Table 15.11
Baseball attendance

Ordinary least squares (OLS)				
Dependent variable: *Attendance*				
Explanatory variable(s):	Estimate	SE	*t*-Statistic	Prob
PriceTicket	−586.5197	179.5938	−3.265813	0.0012
HomeSalary	791.1983	44.00477	17.97983	0.0000
VisitSalary	163.4448	27.73455	5.893181	0.0000
Const	3,528.987	1,775.648	1.987437	0.0473
Number of observations	585			

Estimated equation: *EstAttendance* = 3,529 − 587*PriceTicket* + 791*HomeSalary* + 163*VisitSalary*

[To access this online material, go to http://mitpress.mit.edu/westhoffeconometrics and select 1996 American League Summer.]

Now generate a new variable, *TotalSalary*:

TotalSalary = *HomeSalary* + *VisitSalary*

TotalSalary is a linear combination of *HomeSalary* and *VisitSalary*. Let us try to use the ticket price, *PriceTicket*, home team salary, *HomeSalary*, and visiting team salary, *VisitSalary*, and total salary, *TotalSalary*, to explain attendance, *Attendance*:

[To access this online material, go to http://mitpress.mit.edu/westhoffeconometrics and select 1996 American League Summer.]

Our statistical software will issue a diagnostic indicating that it is being asked to do the impossible.

The information contained in *TotalSalary* is already included in *HomeSalary* and *VisitSalary*. Statistical software cannot separate out the individual influence of the three explanatory variables because they contain redundant information. We are asking the software to do the impossible.

15.3.3   Dependent Variable Is a Linear Combination of Explanatory Variables

Suppose that the dependent variable is a linear combination of the explanatory variables. The following regression illustrates this scenario. *TotalSalary* is by definition the sum of *HomeSalary* and *VisitSalary*. Total salary, *TotalSalary*, is the dependent variable; home team salary, *HomeSalary*, and visiting team salary, *VisitSalary*, are the explanatory variables (table 15.12).

[To access this online material, go to http://mitpress.mit.edu/westhoffeconometrics and select 1996 American League Summer.]

The estimates of the constant and coefficients reveal the definition of *TotalSalary*:

TotalSalary = *HomeSalary* + *VisitSalary*

Table 15.12
Total salary

Ordinary least squares (OLS)				
Dependent variable: *TotalSalary*				
Explanatory variable(s):	Estimate	SE	*t*-Statistic	Prob
HomeSalary	1.000000	8.58E − 17	1.17E + 16	0.0000
VisitSalary	1.000000	8.61E − 17	1.16E + 16	0.0000
Const	0.000000	4.24E − 15	0.000000	1.0000
Number of observations	588			

Estimated Equation: *EstTotalSalary* = 1.000*HomeSalary* + 1.000*VisitSalary*

Furthermore the standard errors are very small, approximately 0. In fact they are precisely equal to 0, but they are not reported as 0's as a consequence of how digital computers process numbers. We can think of these very small standard errors as telling us that we are dealing with an "identity" here, something that is true by definition.

15.3.4   Outlier Observations

We should be aware of the possibility of "outliers" because the ordinary least squares (OLS) estimation procedure is very sensitive to them. An outlier can occur for many reasons. One observation could have a unique characteristic or one observation could include a mundane typo. To illustrate the effect that an outlier may have, once again consider the games played in the summer of the 1996 American League season.

[To access this online material, go to http://mitpress.mit.edu/westhoffeconometrics and select 1996 American League Summer.]

The first observation reports the game played in Milwaukee on June 1, 1996: the Cleveland Indians visited the Milwaukee Brewers. The salary for the home team, the Brewers, totaled 20.232 million dollars in 1996:

Observation	Month	Day	Home team	Visiting team	Home team salary
1	6	1	Milwaukee	Cleveland	20.23200
2	6	1	Oakland	New York	19.40450
3	6	1	Seattle	Boston	38.35453
4	6	1	Toronto	Kansas City	28.48671
5	6	1	Texas	Minnesota	35.86999

Review the regression in table 15.13.

Suppose that a mistake was made in entering the Milwaukee's player salary for the first observation; suppose that the decimal point was misplaced and that 20232.00 was entered instead of

Table 15.13
Baseball attendance regression with correct data

Ordinary least squares (OLS)				
Dependent variable: *Attendance*				
Explanatory variable(s):	Estimate	SE	*t*-Statistic	Prob
PriceTicket	−590.7836	184.7231	−3.198211	0.0015
HomeSalary	783.0394	45.23955	17.30874	0.0000
Const	9,246.429	1,529.658	6.044767	0.0000
Number of observations	585			

Estimated equation: *EstAttendance* = 9,246 − 591*PriceTicket* + 783*HomeSalary*

Table 15.14
Baseball attendance regression with an outlier

Ordinary least squares (OLS)				
Dependent variable: *Attendance*				
Explanatory variable(s):	Estimate	SE	*t*-Statistic	Prob
PriceTicket	1,896.379	142.8479	13.27552	0.0000
HomeSalary	−0.088467	0.484536	−0.182580	0.8552
Const	3,697.786	1,841.286	2.008263	0.0451
Number of observations	585			
Estimated equation: *EstAttendance* = 3,698 + 1,896*PriceTicket* − .0885*HomeSalary*				

20.23200. All the other values were entered correctly. You can access the data including this "outlier" in table 15.14.

[To access this online material, go to http://mitpress.mit.edu/westhoffeconometrics and select 1996 American League Summer Outlier.]

Observation	Month	Day	Home team	Visiting team	Home team salary
1	6	1	Milwaukee	Cleveland	20232.00
2	6	1	Oakland	New York	19.40450
3	6	1	Seattle	Boston	38.35453
4	6	1	Toronto	Kansas City	28.48671
5	6	1	Texas	Minnesota	35.86999

Even though only a single value has been altered, the estimates of both coefficients changes dramatically. The estimate of the ticket price coefficient changes from about −591 to 1,896 and the estimate of the home salary coefficient changes from 783.0 to −0.088. This illustrates how sensitive the ordinary least squares (OLS) estimation procedure can be to an outlier. Consequently we must take care to enter data properly and to check to be certain that we have generated any new variables correctly.

15.3.5   Dummy Variable Trap

To illustrate the dummy variable trap, we will revisit our faculty salary data:

Project: Assess the possibility of discrimination in academe.

Faculty salary data: Artificially constructed cross-sectional salary data and characteristics for 200 faculty members.

Salary_t	Salary of faculty member t (dollars)
Experience_t	Years of teaching experience for faculty member t
Articles_t	Number of articles published by faculty member t
SexM1_t	1 if faculty member t is male; 0 if female

We will investigate models that include only dummy variables and years of teaching experience. More specifically, we will consider four cases:

Model	Dependent variable	Explanatory variables	Constant
1	*Salary*	*SexF1* and *Experience*	Yes
2	*Salary*	*SexM1* and *Experience*	Yes
3	*Salary*	*SexF1*, *SexM1*, and *Experience*	No
4	*Salary*	*SexF1*, *SexM1*, and *Experience*	Yes

We begin by generating the variable *SexF1* as we did in chapter 13:

$$SexF1 = 1 - SexM1$$

Now we will estimate the parameters of the four models (table 15.15). First, model 1.

Model 1:

$$Salary_t = \beta_{Const} + \beta_{SexF1}SexF1_t + \beta_E Experience_t + e_t$$

[To access this online material, go to http://mitpress.mit.edu/westhoffeconometrics and select Faculty Salaries.]

Table 15.15
Faculty salary regression

Ordinary least squares (OLS)				
Dependent variable: *Salary*				
Explanatory variable(s):	Estimate	SE	*t*-Statistic	Prob
SexF1	−2,240.053	3,051.835	−0.734002	0.4638
Experience	2,447.104	163.3812	14.97787	0.0000
Const	42,237.61	3,594.297	11.75129	0.0000
Number of observations	200			
Estimated equation: *EstSalary* = 42,238 − 2,240*SexF1* + 2,447*Experience*				

We calculate the estimated salary equation for men and women. For men, $SexF1 = 0$:

$$EstSalary = 42{,}238 - 2{,}240 SexF1 + 2{,}447 Experience$$

$$EstSalary_{Men} = 42{,}238 - 0 + 2{,}447 Experience$$
$$= 42{,}238 + 2{,}447 Experience$$

The intercept for men equals \$42,238; the slope equals 2,447.
   For women, $SexF1 = 1$:

$$EstSalary = 42{,}238 - 2{,}240 SexF1 + 2{,}447 Experience$$

$$EstSalary_{Women} = 42{,}238 - 2{,}240 + 2{,}447 Experience$$
$$= 39{,}998 + 2{,}447 Experience$$

The intercept for women equals \$39,998; the slope equals 2,447.
   It is easy to plot the estimated salary equations for men and women (figure 15.6). Both plotted lines have the same slope, 2,447. The intercepts differ, however. The intercept for men is 42,238 while the intercept for women is 39,998:

Model 2:

$$Salary_t = \beta_{Const} + \beta_{SexM1} SexM1_t + \beta_E Experience_t + e_t$$

$$EstSalary = b_{Const} + b_{SexM1} SexM1 + b_E Experience$$

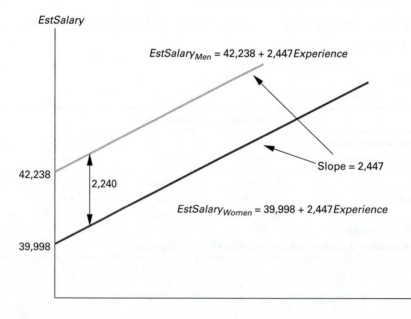

Figure 15.6
Estimated salaries equations for men and women

Let us attempt to calculate the second model's estimated constant and the estimated male sex dummy coefficient, b_{Const} and b_{SexM1}, using the intercepts from model 1.

For men

$SexM1 = 1$

$EstSalary_{Men} = b_{Const} + b_{SexM1} + b_E Experience$

$Intercept_{Men} = b_{Const} + b_{SexM1}$

$42,238 = b_{Const} + b_{SexM1}$

For women

$SexM1 = 0$

$EstSalary_{Women} = b_{Const} + b_E Experience$

$Intercept_{Women} = b_{Const}$

$39,998 = b_{Const}$

We now have two equations:

$42,238 = b_{Const} + b_{SexM1}$

$39,998 = b_{Const}$

and two unknowns, b_{Const} and b_{SexM1}. It is easy to solve for the unknowns. The second equation tells us that b_{Const} equals 39,998:

$b_{Const} = 39,998$

We focus on the first equation:

$$42,238 \;=\; b_{Const} \;+\; b_{SexM1}$$
$$\downarrow \qquad\qquad \text{substituting for } b_{Const}$$
$$42,238 \;=\; 39,998 \;+\; b_{SexM1}$$

We solve for b_{SexM1}:

$b_{SexM1} = 42,238 - 39,998 = 2,240$

Using the estimates from model 1, we compute that the estimate for model 2's estimate for the constant, which should be 39,998 and the estimate for the male sex dummy coefficient, which should be 2,240.

Let us now run the regression. The regression confirms our calculations (table 15.16).

Model 3:

$Salary_t = \beta_{SexF1} SexF1_t + \beta_{SexM1} SexM1_t + \beta_E Experience_t + e_t$

$EstSalary = b_{SexF1} SexF1 + b_{SexM1} SexM1 + b_E Experience$

Again, let us attempt to calculate the third model's estimated female sex dummy coefficient and its male sex dummy coefficient, b_{SexF1} and b_{SexM1}, using the intercepts from model 1.

Table 15.16
Faculty salary regression

Ordinary least squares (OLS)				
Dependent variable: *Salary*				
Explanatory variable(s):	Estimate	SE	*t*-Statistic	Prob
SexM1	2,240.053	3,051.835	0.734002	0.4638
Experience	2,447.104	163.3812	14.97787	0.0000
Const	39,997.56	2,575.318	15.53112	0.0000
Number of observations	200			

Estimated equation: *EstSalary* = 39,998 + 2,240*SexM1* + 2,447*Experience*

For men	For women
$SexF1 = 0$ and $SexM1 = 1$	$SexF1 = 1$ and $SexM1 = 0$
$EstSalary_{Men} = b_{SexM1} + b_E Experience$	$EstSalary_{Women} = b_{SexF1} + b_E Experience$
$Intercept_{Men} = b_{SexM1}$	$Intercept_{Women} = b_{SexF1}$
$42{,}238 = b_{SexM1}$	$39{,}998 = b_{SexF1}$

We now have two equations:

$$42{,}238 = b_{SexM1}$$

$$39{,}998 = b_{SexF1}$$

and two unknowns, b_{SexF1} and b_{SexM1}. Using the estimates from model 1, we compute that the estimate for model 3's estimate for the male sex dummy coefficient should be 42,238 and the estimate for the female sex dummy coefficient should be 39,998.

Let us now run the regression:

Getting Started in EViews

To estimate the third model (part c) using EViews, you must "fool" EViews into running the appropriate regression:

• In the Workfile window: highlight **Salary** and then while depressing <Ctrl>, highlight *SexF1*, *SexM1*, and *Experience*.

• In the Workfile window: double click on a highlighted variable.

• Click **Open Equation**.

• In the Equation Specification window delete **c** so that the window looks like this:
salary sexf1 sexm1 experience.

• Click **OK**.

Table 15.17
Faculty salary regression

	Ordinary least squares (OLS)			
Dependent variable: *Salary*				
Explanatory variable(s):	Estimate	SE	*t*-Statistic	Prob
SexF1	39,997.56	2,575.318	15.53112	0.0000
SexM1	42,237.61	3,594.297	11.75129	0.0000
Experience	2,447.104	163.3812	14.97787	0.0000
Number of observations	200			
Estimated equation: *EstSalary* = 39,998 *SexM1* + 42,238*SexM1* + 2,447*Experience*				

Again, the regression results (table 15.17) confirm our calculations.

Model 4:

$$Salary_t = \beta_{Const} + \beta_{SexF1}SexF1_t + \beta_{SexM1}SexM1_t + \beta_E Experience + e_t$$

$$EstSalary = b_{Const} + b_{SexF1}SexF1 + b_{SexM1}SexM1 + b_E Experience$$

Question: Can we calculate the fourth model's b_{Const}, b_{SexF1}, and b_{SexM1} using model 1's intercepts?

For men	For women
$SexF1 = 0$ and $SexM1 = 1$	$SexF1 = 1$ and $SexM1 = 0$
$EstSalary_{Men} = b_{Const} + b_{SexM1} + b_E Experience$	$EstSalary_{Women} = b_{Const} + b_{SexF1} + b_E Experience$
$Intercept_{Men} = b_{Const} + b_{SexM1}$	$Intercept_{Women} = b_{Const} + b_{SexF1}$
$42,238 = b_{Const} + b_{SexM1}$	$39,998 = b_{Const} + b_{SexF1}$

We now have two equations:

$$42,238 = b_{Const} + b_{SexM1}$$

$$39,998 = b_{Const} + b_{SexF1}$$

and three unknowns, b_{Const}, b_{SexF1}, and b_{SexM1}. We have more unknowns than equations. We cannot solve for the three unknowns. It is impossible. This is called a dummy variable trap:

Dummy variable trap: A model in which there are more parameters representing the intercepts than there are intercepts.

There are three parameters, b_{Const}, b_{SexF1}, and b_{SexM1}, estimating the two intercepts.
   Let us try to run the regression:

[To access this online material, go to http://mitpress.mit.edu/westhoffeconometrics and select Faculty Salaries.]

Our statistical software will issue a diagnostic telling us that it is being asked to do the impossible. In some sense, the software is being asked to solve for three unknowns with only two equations.

Chapter 15 Review Questions

1. Explain in words how the confidence interval approach differs from the approach we have taken thus far.

2. If you wish to assess a theory should you be concerned with the coefficient of determination, the R-squared?

3. What is the goal of multiple regression analysis?

4. In each case, what issue arises for multiple regression analysis and in words explain why it arises:

  a. Explanatory variable has the same value for all observations.

  b. One explanatory variable is a linear combination of other explanatory variables.

  c. Dependent variable is a linear combination of explanatory variables.

  d. Outlier observations.

  e. Dummy variable trap.

Chapter 15 Exercises

Internet and TV data: Panel data of Internet, TV, economic, and political statistics for 208 countries from 1995 to 2002.

$LogUsersInternet_t$	Logarithm of Internet users per 1,000 people for observation t
$LogUsersTV_t$	Logarithm of television users per 1,000 people for observation t
$Year_t$	Year for observation t
$CapitalHuman_t$	Literacy rate for observation t (percent of population 15 and over)
$CapitalPhysical_t$	Telephone mainlines per 10,000 people for observation t
$GdpPC_t$	Per capita real GDP in nation t (1,000's of "international" dollars)
$Auth_t$	The Freedom House measures of political authoritarianism for observation t normalized to a 0 to 10 scale. 0 represents the most democratic rating and 10 the most authoritarian. During the 1995 to 2002 period, Canada and the United States had a 0 rating; Iraq and the Democratic Republic of Korea (North Korea) rated 10.

1. Consider the following model of Internet use:

$$LogUsersInternet_t = \beta_{Const}^{Int} + \beta_{Year}^{Int} Year_t + \beta_{CapHum}^{Int} CapitalHuman_t$$
$$+ \beta_{CapPhy}^{Int} CapitalPhysical_t + \beta_{GDP}^{Int} GdpPC_t + \beta_{Auth}^{Int} Auth_t + e_t^{Int}$$

a. Use the ordinary least squares (OLS) estimation procedure to estimate the model's parameters.

[To access this online material, go to http://mitpress.mit.edu/westhoffeconometrics and select Internet and TV Use.]

b. Compute the two-tailed 95 percent confidence interval for the coefficient estimate of *Year*.

[To access this online material, go to http://mitpress.mit.edu/westhoffeconometrics and select *t*-Distribution.]

2. Consider the following model of television use:

$$\text{Log}UsersTV_t = \beta_{Const} + \beta_{Year}Year_t + e_t$$

a. Use the ordinary least squares (OLS) estimation procedure to estimate the model's parameters.

[To access this online material, go to http://mitpress.mit.edu/westhoffeconometrics and select Internet and TV Use.]

b. Compute the two-tailed the 95 percent confidence interval for the coefficient estimate *Year*.

[To access this online material, go to http://mitpress.mit.edu/westhoffeconometrics and select *t*-Distribution.]

Petroleum data consumption for Massachusetts and Nebraska: Panel data of petroleum consumption and prices for two states, Massachusetts and Nebraska, from 1990 to 1999.

Cpi_t	Northeast CPI for Massachusetts; Midwest CPI for Nebraska
$PetroCons_t$	Consumption of petroleum for observation t (1,000s of gallons)
$PetroConsPC_t$	Per capita consumption of petroleum for observation t (gallons)
Pop_t	Population for observation t (persons)
$PriceNom_t$	Nominal price of petroleum for observation t (dollars per gallon)
$Mass_t$	1 if observation t is Massachusetts; 0 if Nebraska
$Year_t$	Year

Consider the following model:

$$PetroConsPC_t = \beta_{Const} + \beta_P PriceReal_t + e_t$$

where $t = 1990, 1991, \ldots, 1999$.

Generate the variable *PriceReal*.

3. Estimate this model for Massachusetts by restricting your sample to Massachusetts observations only. Use the ordinary least squares (OLS) estimation procedure to estimate the parameters of the model.

a. What equation describes estimated per capita petroleum consumption in Massachusetts, $EstPetroConsPC_{Mass}$?

[To access this online material, go to http://mitpress.mit.edu/westhoffeconometrics and select Petroleum Consumption – Mass and Neb.]

Getting Started in EViews

In the Workfile window:
- Click **Sample**.
- To include only the Massachusetts data, enter $Mass1 = 1$ in the If condition window.
- Click **OK**.

b. What is the estimated intercept of the best fitting line?

c. What is the estimated slope of the best fitting line?

Getting Started in EViews

NB: Do not forget that the Sample option behaves like a toggle switch. It remains on until you turn it off.
Therefore, before proceeding, in the Workfile window:
- Click **Sample**.
- Clear the If condition window.
- Click **OK**.

4. Estimate the model for Nebraska by restricting your sample to Nebraska observations only. Use the ordinary least squares (OLS) estimation procedure to estimate the parameters of the model.

a. What equation describes estimated per capita petroleum consumption in Nebraska, $EstPetroConsPC_{Neb}$?

[To access this online material, go to http://mitpress.mit.edu/westhoffeconometrics and select Petroleum Consumption – Mass and Neb.]

Getting Started in EViews

In the Workfile window:

· Click **Sample**.

· To include only the Nebraska data, enter $Mass1 = 0$ in the If condition window.

· Click **OK**.

b. What is the estimated intercept of the best fitting line?

c. What is the estimated slope of the best fitting line?

Getting Started in EViews

NB: Do not forget that the Sample option behaves like a toggle switch. It remains on until you turn it off.

Therefore, before proceeding, in the Workfile window:

· Click **Sample**.

· Clear the If condition window.

· Click **OK**.

5.

a. Consider the following new model:

$$PetroConsPC_t = \beta_{Mass}Mass1_t + \beta_{Neb}Neb1_t + \beta_{PMass}PriceReal\_Mass_t$$
$$+ \beta_{PNeb}PriceReal\_Neb_t + e_t$$

where

$Neb1_t = 1 - Mass1_t$

$PriceReal\_Mass_t = PriceReal_t \times Mass1_t$

$PriceReal\_Neb_t = PriceReal_t \times Neb1_t$

Let b_{Mass}, b_{Neb}, b_{PMass}, and b_{PNeb} equal the ordinary least squares (OLS) estimates of the parameters:

$$EstPetroConsPC =$$
$$b_{Mass}Mass1 + b_{Neb}Neb1 + b_{PMass}PriceReal\_Mass + b_{PNeb}PriceReal\_Neb$$

i. What equation estimates per capita petroleum consumption in Massachusetts?

ii. What is the intercept of this equation?

iii. What is the slope of this equation?

b. Focus on Nebraska. Based on this model:

   i. What equation estimates per capita petroleum consumption in Nebraska?

   ii. What is the intercept of this equation?

   iii. What is the slope of this equation?

c. Recall your answers to exercises 3 and 4. Can you solve for the numerical values of b_{Mass}, b_{Neb}, b_{PMass}, and b_{PNeb} using these answers? If so, do so; if not, explain why not.

d. Next use the ordinary least squares (OLS) estimation procedure to estimate the parameters of this model.

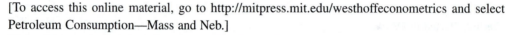

[To access this online material, go to http://mitpress.mit.edu/westhoffeconometrics and select Petroleum Consumption—Mass and Neb.]

e. Are your results for parts c and d consistent?

6. Consider the following new model explaining petroleum consumption:

$PetroConsPC_t =$
$$\beta_{Const} + \beta_{Mass}Mass1_t + \beta_{PNeb}Neb1_t + \beta_{PMass}PriceReal\_Mass_t + \beta_{PNeb}PriceReal\_Neb_t + e_t$$

Let b_{Const}, b_{Mass}, b_{Neb}, b_{PMass}, and b_{PNeb} equal the ordinary least squares (OLS) estimates of the parameters:

$EstPetroConsPC =$
$$b_{Const} + b_{Mass}Mass1 + b_{Neb}Neb + b_{PMass}PriceReal\_Mass + b_{PNeb}PriceReal\_Neb$$

a. Focus on Massachusetts. Based on this model:

   i. What equation estimates per capita petroleum consumption in Massachusetts?

   ii. What is the intercept of this equation?

   iii. What is the slope of this equation?

b. Focus on Nebraska. Based on this model:

   i. What equation estimates per capita petroleum consumption in Nebraska?

   ii. What is the intercept of this equation?

   iii. What is the slope of this equation?

c. Recall your answers to exercises 3 and 4. Can you solve for the numerical values of b_{Const}, b_{Mass}, b_{Neb}, b_{PMass}, and b_{PNeb} using these answers? If so, do so; if not, explain why not.

d. Next use the ordinary least squares (OLS) estimation procedure to estimate the parameters of this model.

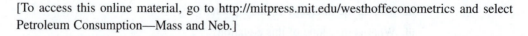

[To access this online material, go to http://mitpress.mit.edu/westhoffeconometrics and select Petroleum Consumption—Mass and Neb.]

e. Are your results for parts c and d consistent?

7. Consider the following new model:

$$PetroConsPC_t =$$
$$\beta_{Mass}Mass1_t + \beta_{PNeb}Neb1_t + \beta_P PriceReal_t + \beta_{PMass}PriceReal\_Mass_t + \beta_{PNeb}PriceReal\_Neb_t + e_t$$

Let b_{Mass}, b_{Neb}, b_{Const}, b_P, and b_{PNeb} equal the ordinary least squares (OLS) estimates of the parameters:

$$EstPetroConsPC =$$
$$b_{Mass}Mass1 + b_{Neb}Neb1_t + b_P PriceReal + b_{PMass}PriceReal\_Mass + b_{PNeb}PriceReal\_Neb$$

a. Focus on Massachusetts. Based on this model:

i. What equation estimates per capita petroleum consumption in Massachusetts?

ii. What is the intercept of this equation?

iii. What is the slope of this equation?

b. Focus on Nebraska. Based on this model:

i. What equation estimates per capita petroleum consumption in Nebraska?

ii. What is the intercept of this equation?

iii. What is the slope of this equation?

c. Recall your answers to exercises 3 and 4. Can you solve for the numerical values of b_{Mass}, b_{Neb}, b_P, b_{PMass}, and b_{PNeb} using these answers? If so, do so; if not, explain why not.

d. Next use the ordinary least squares (OLS) estimation procedure to estimate the parameters of this model.

[To access this online material, go to http://mitpress.mit.edu/westhoffeconometrics and select Petroleum Consumption—Mass and Neb.]

e. Are your results for parts c and d consistent?

16 Heteroskedasticity

Chapter 16 Prep Questions

1. What are the standard ordinary least squares (OLS) premises?

2. In chapter 6 we showed that the ordinary least squares (OLS) estimation procedure for the coefficient value was unbiased; that is, we showed that

$\text{Mean}[b_x] = \beta_x$

Review the algebra. What role, if any, did the first standard ordinary least squares (OLS) premise, the error term equal variance premise, play?

3. In chapter 6 we showed that the variance of the coefficient estimate's probability distribution equals the variance of the error term's probability distribution divided by the sum of the squared x deviations; that is, we showed that

$$\text{Var}[b_x] = \frac{\text{Var}[e]}{\sum_{t=1}^{T}(x_t - \bar{x})^2}$$

Review the algebra. What role, if any, did the first standard ordinary least squares (OLS) premise, the error term equal variance premise, play?

4. Consider the following data describing Internet use in 1992:

1992 Internet data: Cross-sectional data of Internet use and gross domestic product for 29 countries in 1992.

Country$_t$ Name of country t

GdpPC$_t$ Per capita GDP (1,000's of real "international" dollars) in nation t

LogUsersInternet$_t$ Log of Internet users per 1,000 people in nation t

Focus on the following model:

$LogUsersInternet_t = \beta_{Const} + \beta_{GDP}GdpPC_t + e_t$

   a. What is your theory concerning how per capita GDP should affect Internet use? What does your theory suggest about the sign of the *GdpPC* coefficient, β_{GDP}?

   b. Run the appropriate regression. Do the data support your theory?

[To access this online material, go to http://mitpress.mit.edu/westhoffeconometrics and select Internet Use—1992.]

   c. What are the appropriate null and alternative hypotheses?

   d. After running the regression, plot a scatter diagram of those residuals and per capita GDP.

Getting Started in EViews

- Run the ordinary least squares (OLS) regression.
- The residuals from the regression we just ran are automatically stored by EViews as the variable **resid**.
- In the Workfile window: First Click **gdppc**; then hold down the <Ctrl> key and click **resid**.
- In the Workfile window: Double click on a highlighted variable
- In the Workfile window: Click **Open Group**.
- In the Group window: Click **View** and then **Graph**.
- In the Graph Options window: Click **Scatter**.

   e. Based on the scatter diagram, what do you conclude about the variance of the residuals as per capita GDP increases?

5. Again, consider the following model:

$$LogUsersInternet_t = \beta_{Const} + \beta_{GDP}GdpPC_t + e_t$$

Assume that the variance of the error term's probability distribution is proportional to each nation's per capita GDP:

$$Var[e_t] = V \times GdpPC_t$$

where V is a constant.

Now divide both sides of the equation that specifies the model by the square root of per capita GDP, $\sqrt{GdpPC_t}$. Let

$$\varepsilon_t = \frac{e_t}{\sqrt{GdpPC_t}}$$

What is the variance of ε_t's probability distribution?

16.1   Review

16.1.1   Regression Model

We begin by reviewing the basic regression model:

$$y_t = \beta_{Const} + \beta_x x_t + e_t, \qquad t = 1, 2, \ldots, T$$

where

y_t = dependent variable

e_t = error term

x_t = explanatory variable

T = sample size

The error term is a random variable that represents random influences: $\text{Mean}[e_t] = 0$

16.1.2   The Standard Ordinary Least Squares (OLS) Premises

We will now focus our attention on the standard ordinary least squares (OLS) regression premises:

· **Error term equal variance premise:** The variance of the error term's probability distribution for each observation is the same; all the variances equal $\text{Var}[e]$:

$$\text{Var}[e_1] = \text{Var}[e_2] = \ldots = \text{Var}[e_T] = \text{Var}[e]$$

· **Error term/error term independence premise:** The error terms are independent: $\text{Cov}[e_i, e_j] = 0$.

Knowing the value of the error term from one observation does not help us predict the value of the error term for any other observation.

· **Explanatory variable/error term independence premise:** The explanatory variables, the x_t's, and the error terms, the e_t's, are not correlated.

Knowing the value of an observation's explanatory variable does not help us predict the value of that observation's error term.

16.1.3   Estimation Procedures Embedded within the Ordinary Least Squares (OLS) Estimation Procedure

The ordinary least squares (OLS) estimation procedure includes three important estimation procedures:

· Values of the regression parameters, β_x and β_{Const}:

$$b_x = \frac{\sum_{t=1}^{T}(y_t - \overline{y})(x_t - \overline{x})}{\sum_{t=1}^{T}(x_t - \overline{x})^2} \quad \text{and} \quad b_{Const} = \overline{y} - b_x\overline{x}$$

· Variance of the error term's probability distribution, $\text{Var}[e]$:

$$\text{EstVar}[e] = \frac{SSR}{\text{Degrees of freedom}}$$

• Variance of the coefficient estimate's probability distribution, $\text{Var}[b_x]$:

$$\text{EstVar}[b_x] = \frac{\text{EstVar}[e]}{\sum_{t=1}^{T}(x_t - \bar{x})^2}$$

When the standard ordinary least squares (OLS) regression premises are met:

• Each estimation procedure is unbiased; that is, each estimation procedure does not systematically underestimate or overestimate the actual value.

• The ordinary least squares (OLS) estimation procedure for the coefficient value is the best linear unbiased estimation procedure (BLUE).

Crucial point: When the ordinary least squares (OLS) estimation procedure performs its calculations, it implicitly assumes that the standard ordinary least squares (OLS) regression premises are satisfied.

In this chapter we will focus on the first standard ordinary least squares (OLS) premise, the error term equal variance premise. We begin by examining precisely what the premise means. Subsequently we investigate what problems do and do not emerge when the premise is violated and finally what can be done to address the problems that do arise.

16.2   What Is Heteroskedasticity?

Heteroskedasticity refers to the variances of the error terms' probability distributions. The syllable "hetero" means different; the syllable "skedasticity" refers to the spread of the distribution. Heteroskedasticity means that the spread of the error term's probability distribution differs from observation to observation. Recall the error term equal variance premise:

• **Error term equal variance premise:** The variance of the error term's probability distribution for each observation is the same; all the variances equal $\text{Var}[e]$:

$$\text{Var}[e_1] = \text{Var}[e_2] = \ldots = \text{Var}[e_T] = \text{Var}[e]$$

The presence of heteroskedasticity violates the error term equal variance premise.

We begin by illustrating the effect of heteroskedasticity on the error terms. Consider the three students in Professor Lord's class who must take a quiz every Tuesday morning:

Student 1	Student 2	Student 3
$y_1 = \beta_{Const} + \beta_x x_1 + e_1$	$y_2 = \beta_{Const} + \beta_x x_2 + e_2$	$y_3 = \beta_{Const} + \beta_x x_3 + e_3$
y_1 = Student 1's score	y_2 = Student 2's score	y_3 = Student 3's score
x_1 = Student 1's studying	x_2 = Student 2's studying	x_3 = Student 3's studying
e_1 = Student 1's error term	e_2 = Student 2's error term	e_3 = Student 3's error term

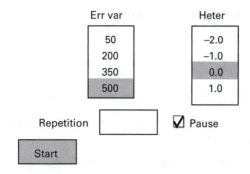

Figure 16.1
Heteroskedasticity simulation

The error terms, the e_t's, represent random influences; that is, the error terms have no systematic effort on the dependent variable y_t. Consequently the mean of each error term's probability distribution, Mean[e_t], equals 0. In other words, if the experiment were repeated many, many times, the error term would average out to be 0. When the distribution is symmetric, half the time the error term would be positive leading to a higher than normal value of y_t and half the time it would be negative leading to a lower than normal value of y_t. We will use a simulation to illustrate this (figure 16.1).

Econometrics Lab 16.1: The Error Terms and Heteroskedasticity

[To access this online material, go to http://mitpress.mit.edu/westhoffeconometrics and select Lab 16.1.]

The list labeled Heter is the "heteroskedasticity factor." Initially, Heter is specified as 0, meaning that no heteroskedasticity is present. Click **Start** and then **Continue** a few times to note that the distribution of each student's error terms is illustrated in the three histograms at the top of the window. Also the mean and variance of each student's error terms are computed. Next uncheck the Pause checkbox and click **Continue**; after many, many repetitions of the experiment click **Stop**. The mean of each student's error term is approximately 0, indicating that the error terms truly represent random influences; the error terms have no systematic affect on a student's quiz score. Furthermore the spreads of each student's error term distribution appear to be nearly identical; the variance of each student's error term is approximately the same. Hence the error term equal variance premise is satisfied (figure 16.2).

Next change the value of the Heter. When a positive value is specified, the distribution spread increases as we move from student 1 to student 2 to student 3; when a negative value is specified, the spread decreases. Specify 1 instead of 0. Note that when you do this, the title of the variance list changes to Mid Err Var. This occurs because heteroskedasticity is now present and the variances differ from student to student. The list specifies the variance of the middle student's, student 2's, error term probability distribution. By default student 2's variance is 500. Now, click **Start** and then after many, many repetitions of the experiment click **Stop**. The distribution spreads of each student's error terms are not identical (figure 16.3).

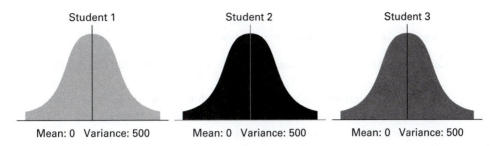

Figure 16.2
Error term probability distributions—Error term equal variance premise satisfied

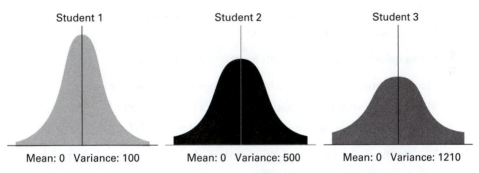

Figure 16.3
Error term probability distributions—Error term equal variance premise violated

The error term equal variance premise is now violated. What might cause this discrepancy? Suppose that student 1 tries to get a broad understanding of the material and hence reads all the assignment albeit quickly. However, student 3 guesses on what material will be covered on the quiz and spends his/her time thoroughly studying only that material. When student 3 guesses right, he/she will do very well on the quiz, but when he/she guesses wrong, he/she will do very poorly. Hence we would expect student 3's quiz scores to be more volatile than student 1's. This volatility is reflected by the variance of the error terms. The variance of student 3's error term distribution would be greater than student 1's.

16.3 Heteroskedasticity and the Ordinary Least Squares (OLS) Estimation Procedure: The Consequences

16.3.1 The Mathematics

Now let us explore the consequences of heteroskedasticity. We will focus on two of the three estimation procedures embedded within the ordinary least squares (OLS) estimation procedure:

• Value of the coefficient.

• Variance of the coefficient estimate's probability distribution.

Question: Are these estimation procedures still unbiased when heteroskedasticity is present?

Ordinary Least Squares (OLS) Estimation Procedure for the Coefficient Value

Begin by focusing on the coefficient value. Previously we showed that the estimation procedure for the coefficient value was unbiased by

• applying the arithmetic of means;

and

• recognizing that the means of the error terms' probability distributions equal 0 (since the error terms represent random influences).

Let us quickly review. First recall the arithmetic of means:

Mean of a constant plus a variable: $\text{Mean}[c + x] = c + \text{Mean}[x]$

Mean of a constant times a variable: $\text{Mean}[cx] = c\,\text{Mean}[x]$

Mean of the sum of two variables: $\text{Mean}[x + y] = \text{Mean}[x] + \text{Mean}[y]$

To keep the mathematics straightforward, we focused on a sample size of 3:
　Equation for coefficient estimate:

$$b_x = \beta_x + \frac{\sum_{t=1}^{T}(x_t - \bar{x})e_t}{\sum_{t=1}^{T}(x_t - \bar{x})^2} = \beta_x + \frac{(x_1 - \bar{x})e_1 + (x_2 - \bar{x})e_2 + (x_3 - \bar{x})e_3}{(x_1 - \bar{x})^2 + (x_2 - \bar{x})^2 + (x_3 - \bar{x})^2}$$

Now some algebra:[1]

$$\text{Mean}[b_x] = \text{Mean}\left[\beta_x + \frac{(x_1 - \bar{x})e_1 + (x_2 - \bar{x})e_2 + (x_3 - \bar{x})e_3}{(x_1 - \bar{x})^2 + (x_2 - \bar{x})^2 + (x_3 - \bar{x})^2}\right]$$

Applying $\text{Mean}[c + x] = c + \text{Mean}[x]$

$$= \beta_x + \text{Mean}\left[\frac{(x_1 - \bar{x})e_1 + (x_2 - \bar{x})e_2 + (x_3 - \bar{x})e_3}{(x_1 - \bar{x})^2 + (x_2 - \bar{x})^2 + (x_3 - \bar{x})^2}\right]$$

Rewriting the fraction as a product

$$= \beta_x + \text{Mean}\left[\left(\frac{1}{(x_1 - \bar{x})^2 + (x_2 - \bar{x})^2 + (x_3 - \bar{x})^2}\right)((x_1 - \bar{x})e_1 + (x_2 - \bar{x})e_2 + (x_3 - \bar{x})e_3)\right]$$

---

1. Recall that to keep the algebra straightforward, we assume that the explanatory variables are constants. By doing so, we can apply the arithmetic of means easily. Our results are unaffected by this assumption.

Applying $\text{Mean}[cx] = c\,\text{Mean}[x]$

$$= \beta_x + \frac{1}{(x_1 - \bar{x})^2 + (x_2 - \bar{x})^2 + (x_3 - \bar{x})^2}\,\text{Mean}\big[((x_1 - \bar{x})e_1 + (x_2 - \bar{x})e_2 + (x_3 - \bar{x})e_3)\big]$$

Applying $\text{Mean}[x + y] = \text{Mean}[x] + \text{Mean}[y]$

$$= \beta_x + \frac{1}{(x_1 - \bar{x})^2 + (x_2 - \bar{x})^2 + (x_3 - \bar{x})^2}\big[\text{Mean}[(x_1 - \bar{x})e_1] + \text{Mean}[(x_2 - \bar{x})e_2] + \text{Mean}[(x_3 - \bar{x})e_3]\big]$$

Applying $\text{Mean}[cx] = c\,\text{Mean}[x]$

$$= \beta_x + \frac{1}{(x_1 - \bar{x})^2 + (x_2 - \bar{x})^2 + (x_3 - \bar{x})^2}\big[(x_1 - \bar{x})\text{Mean}[e_1] + (x_2 - \bar{x})\text{Mean}[e_2] + (x_3 - \bar{x})\text{Mean}[e_3]\big]$$

Since $\text{Mean}[e_1] = \text{Mean}[e_2] = \text{Mean}[e_3] = 0$
$$= \beta_x$$

What is the critical point here? We have not relied on the error term equal variance premise to show that the estimation procedure for the coefficient value is unbiased. Consequently we suspect that the estimation procedure for the coefficient value should still be unbiased in the presence of heteroskedasticity.

Ordinary Least Squares (OLS) Estimation Procedure for the Variance of the Coefficient Estimate's Probability Distribution

Next consider the estimation procedure for the variance of the coefficient estimate's probability distribution used by the ordinary least squares (OLS) estimation procedure. The strategy involves two steps:

• First, we used the adjusted variance to estimate the variance of the error term's probability distribution: $\text{EstVar}[e] = SSR/\text{Degrees of freedom}$.

• Second, we applied the equation relating the variance of the coefficient estimates probability distribution and the variance of the error term's probability distribution: $\text{Var}[b_x] = \text{Var}[e]\big/ \sum_{t=1}^{T}(x_t - \bar{x})^2$

Step 1: Estimate the variance of the error term's probability distribution from the available information—data from the first quiz

$\downarrow$

$$\text{EstVar}[e] = \frac{SSR}{\text{Degrees of freedom}}$$

Step 2: Apply the relationship between the variances of coefficient estimate's and error term's probability distributions

$\downarrow$

$$\text{Var}[b_x] = \frac{\text{Var}[e]}{\sum_{t=1}^{T}(x_t - \bar{x})^2}$$

$$\text{EstVar}[b_x] = \frac{\text{EstVar}[e]}{\sum_{t=1}^{T}(x_t - \bar{x})^2}$$

This strategy is grounded on the premise that the variance of each error term's probability distribution is the same, the error term equal variance premise:

$$\text{Var}[e_1] = \text{Var}[e_2] = \ldots = \text{Var}[e_T] = \text{Var}[e]$$

Unfortunately, when heteroskedasticity is present, the error term equal variance premise is violated because there is not a single $\text{Var}[e]$. The variance differs from observation to observation. When heteroskedasticity is present the strategy used by the ordinary least squares (OLS) estimation procedure to estimate the coefficient estimate's probability distribution is based on a faulty premise. The ordinary least squares (OLS) estimation procedure is trying to estimate something that does not exist, a single $\text{Var}[e]$. Consequently we should be suspicious of the procedure.

16.4.2   Our Suspicions

So, where do we stand? We suspect that when heteroskedasticity is present, the ordinary least squares (OLS) estimation procedure for the

• coefficient value will still be unbiased;
• variance of the coefficient estimate's probability distribution may be biased.

16.4.3   Confirming Our Suspicions

We will use the Econometrics Lab to address the two suspicions.

Econometrics Lab 16.2: Heteroskedasticity and the Ordinary Least Squares (OLS) Estimation Procedure

[To access this online material, go to http://mitpress.mit.edu/westhoffeconometrics and select Lab 16.2.]

The simulation (figure 16.4) allows us to address the two critical questions:

• **Question 1:**   Is the estimation procedure for the coefficient's value unbiased; that is, does the mean of the coefficient estimate's probability distribution equal the actual coefficient value? The relative frequency interpretation of probability allows us to address this question by using the simulation. After many, many repetitions the distribution of the estimated values mirrors the probability distribution. Therefore we need only compare the mean of the estimated coefficient values with the actual coefficient values. If the two are equal after many, many repetitions, the estimation procedure is unbiased.

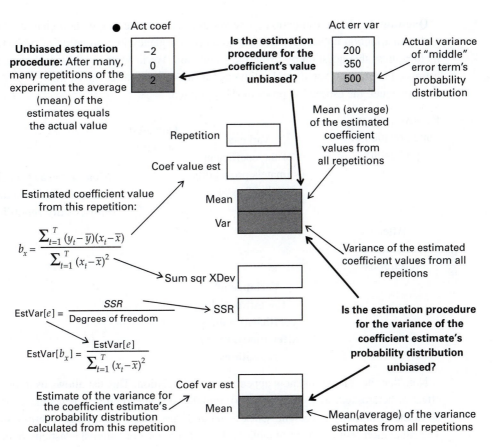

Figure 16.4
Heteroskedasticity simulation

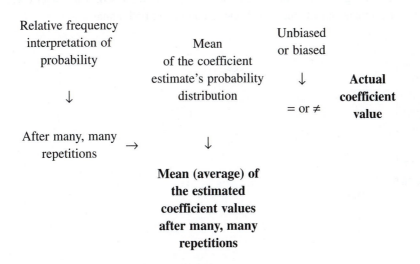

• **Question 2:**   Is the estimation procedure for the variance of the coefficient estimate's probability distribution unbiased? Again, the relative frequency interpretation of probability allows us to address this question by using the simulation. We need only compare the variance of the estimated coefficient values and estimates for the variance after many, many repetitions. If the two are equal, the estimation procedure is unbiased.

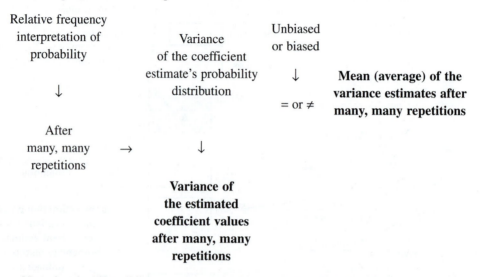

Note that the "Heter" list now appears in this simulation. This list allows us to investigate the effect of heteroskedasticity (figure 16.5). Initially, 0 is specified as a benchmark, meaning that no heteroskedasticity is present. Click **Start** and then after many, many repetitions click **Stop**. The simulation results appear in table 16.1. In the absence of heteroskedasticity both estimation procedures are unbiased:

• The estimation procedure for the coefficient value is unbiased. The mean (average) of the coefficient estimates equals the actual coefficient value; both equal 2.

Heter

−2.0
−1.0
0.0
1.0
2.0

Figure 16.5
Heteroskedasticity factor list

Table 16.1
Heteroskedasticity simulation results

	Is OLS estimation procedure for the coefficient's value unbiased?		Is OLS estimation procedure for the variance of the of the coefficient estimate's robability distribution unbiased?	
	Actual coefficient value	Estimate of coefficient value	Variance of the estimated coefficient values	Estimate of the variance for coefficient estimate's probability distribution
	↓	↓	↓	↓
Heter factor	**Actual value of β_x**	**Mean (average) of the estimated values, b_x, from all repetitions**	**Variance of the estimated coefficient values, b_x, from all repetitions**	**Average of estimated variances, EstVar[b_x], from all repetitions**
0	2.0	≈2.0	≈2.5	≈2.5
1	2.0	≈2.0	≈3.6	≈2.9

• The estimation procedure for the variance of the coefficient estimates probability distribution is unbiased. The mean (average) of the variance estimates equals the actual variance of the coefficient estimates; both equal 2.5.

When the standard ordinary least squares (OLS) premises are satisfied, both estimation procedures are unbiased.

Next we will investigate the effect of heteroskedasticity by selecting 1.0 from the "Heter" list. Heteroskedasticity is now present. Click **Start** and then after many, many repetitions click **Stop**.

• The estimation procedure for the coefficient value is unbiased. The mean (average) of the coefficient estimates equals the actual coefficient value; both equal 2.

• The estimation procedure for the variance of the coefficient estimates probability distribution is biased. The mean (average) of the estimated variances equals 2.9, while the actual variance equals 3.6.

The simulation results confirm our suspicions. When heteroskedasticity is present there is some good news, but also some bad news:

• **Good news:** The ordinary least squares (OLS) estimation procedure for the coefficient value is still unbiased.

• **Bad news:** The ordinary least squares (OLS) estimation procedure for the variance of the coefficient estimate's probability distribution is biased.

When the estimation procedure for the variance of the coefficient estimate's probability distribution is biased, all calculations based on the estimate of the variance will be flawed also; that is, the standard errors, t-statistics, and tail probabilities appearing on the ordinary least squares (OLS) regression printout are unreliable. Consequently we will use an example to explore how we can account for the presence of heteroskedasticity.

16.5   Accounting for Heteroskedasticity: An Example

We can account for heteroskedasticity by applying the following steps:

Step 1:   Apply the ordinary least squares (OLS) estimation procedure.

Estimate the model's parameters with the ordinary least squares (OLS) estimation procedure.

Step 2:   Consider the possibility of heteroskedasticity.

· Ask whether there is reason to suspect that heteroskedasticity may be present.

· Use the ordinary least squares (OLS) regression results to "get a sense" of whether hetereoskedasticity is a problem by examining the residuals.

· If the presence of hetereoskedasticity is suspected, formulate a model to explain it.

· Use the Breusch–Pagan–Godfrey approach by estimating an artificial regression to test for the presence of heteroskedasticity.

Step 3:   Apply the generalized least squares (GLS) estimation procedure.

· Apply the model of heteroskedasticity and algebraically manipulate the original model to derive a new, tweaked model in which the error terms do not suffer from heteroskedasticity.

· Use the ordinary least squares (OLS) estimation procedure to estimate the parameters of the tweaked model.

We will illustrate this approach by considering the effect of per capita GDP on Internet use.

Theory: Higher per capita GDP increases Internet use.

Project: Assess the effect of GDP on Internet use.

To assess the theory we construct a simplified model with a single explanatory variable, per capita GDP. Previously we showed that several other factors proved important in explaining Internet use. We include only per capita GDP here for pedagogical reasons: to provide a simple illustration of how we can account for the presence of heteroskedasticity.

$$LogUsersInternet_t = \beta_{Const} + \beta_{GDP}GdpPC_t + e_t$$

where

$LogUsersInternet_t$ = log of Internet users per 1,000 people in nation t

$GdpPC_t$ = per capita GDP (1,000s of real "international" dollars) in nation t

The theory suggests that the model's coefficient, β_{GDP}, is positive. To keep the exposition clear, we will use data from a single year, 1992, to test this theory:

Table 16.2
Internet regression results

Ordinary least squares (OLS)				
Dependent variable: *LogUsersInternet*				
Explanatory variable(s):	Estimate	SE	*t*-Statistic	Prob
GdpPC	0.100772	0.032612	3.090019	0.0046
Const	−0.486907	0.631615	−0.770891	0.4475
Number of observations	29			

Estimated equation: $EstLogUsersInternet = -0.487 + 0.101 GdpPC$

Interpretation of estimates:

  $b_{GDP} = 10.1$: a \$1,000 increase in real per capita GDP results in a 10.1 percent increase in Internet users.

Critical result: The *GdpPC* coefficient estimate equals 0.101. The positive sign of the coefficient estimate suggests that higher per capita GDP increases Internet use. This evidence supports the theory.

1992 Internet data: Cross-sectional data of Internet use and gross domestic product for 29 countries in 1992.

Country$_t$	Name of country t
GdpPC$_t$	Per capita GDP (1,000s of real "international" dollars) in nation t
LogUsersInternet$_t$	Log of Internet users per 1,000 people in country t
Year$_t$	Year

We now follow the steps outlined above.

Step 1:   Apply the ordinary least squares (OLS) estimation procedure.

Using statistical software, we run a regression with the log of Internet use as the dependent variable and the per capita GDP as the explanatory variable (table 16.2).

 [To access this online material, go to http://mitpress.mit.edu/westhoffeconometrics and select Internet Use—1992.]

Since the evidence appears to support the theory, we construct the null and alternative hypotheses:

H$_0$: $\beta_{GDP} = 0$ Per capita GDP does not affect Internet use

H$_1$: $\beta_{GDP} > 0$ Higher per capita GDP increases Internet use

As always, the null hypothesis challenges the evidence; the alternative hypothesis is consistent with the evidence. Next we calculate Prob[Results IF H$_0$ true].

Prob[Results IF H$_0$ true]: What is the probability that the *GdpPC* estimate from one repetition of the experiment will be 0.101 or more, if H$_0$ were true (i.e., if the per capita GDP has no effect on the Internet use, if β_{GDP} actually equals 0)?

We now apply the properties of the coefficient estimate's probability distribution:

OLS estimation procedure unbiased	If H$_0$ true	Standard error	Number of observations	Number of parameters
↘	↙	↓	↘	↙

$$\text{Mean}[b_{GDP}] = \beta_{GDP} = 0 \quad \text{SE}[b_{GDP}] = 0.0326 \quad \text{DF} = 29 - 2 = 27$$

Econometrics Lab 16.3: Calculating Prob[Results IF H$_0$ true]

[To access this online material, go to http://mitpress.mit.edu/westhoffeconometrics and select Lab 16.3.]

To emphasize that the Prob[Results IF H$_0$ true] depends on the standard error we will use the Econometrics Lab to calculate the probability. The following information has been entered in the lab:

Mean = 0   Value = 0.101

Standard error = 0.0326   Degrees of freedom = 27

Click **Calculate**.

Prob[Results IF H$_0$ true] = 0.0023.

We use the standard error provided by the ordinary least squares (OLS) regression results to compute the Prob[Results IF H$_0$ true].

We can also calculate Prob[Results IF H$_0$ true] using the tails probability reported in the regression printout. Since this is a one-tailed test, we divide the tails probability by 2:

$$\text{Prob[Results IF H}_0 \text{ true]} = \frac{0.0046}{2} \approx 0.0023$$

Based on the 1 percent significance level, we would reject that null hypothesis. We would reject the hypothesis that per capita GDP has no effect on Internet use.

There may a problem with this, however. The equation used by the ordinary least squares (OLS) estimation procedure to estimate the variance of the coefficient estimate's probability distribution assumes that the error term equal variance premise is satisfied. Our simulation revealed that when heteroskedasticity is present and the error term equal variance premise is violated, the ordinary least squares (OLS) estimation procedure estimating the variance of the coefficient estimate's probability distribution was flawed. Recall that the standard error equals the square root of the estimated variance. Consequently, if heteroskedasticity is present, we may have entered the wrong value for the standard error into the Econometrics Lab when we calculated Prob[Results IF H_0 true]. When heteroskedasticity is present the ordinary least squares (OLS) estimation procedure bases it computations on a faulty premise, resulting in flawed standard errors, t-Statistics, and tails probabilities. Consequently we should move on to the next step.

Step 2:   Consider the possibility of heteroskedasticity.

We must pose the following question:

Question: Is there reason to believe that heteroskedasticity could possibly be present?

Intuition leads us to suspect that the answer is yes. When the per capita GDP is low, individuals have little to spend on any goods other than the basic necessities. In particular, individuals have little to spend on Internet use and consequently Internet use will be low. This will be true for all countries in which per capita GDP is low. On the contrary, when per capita GDP is high, individuals can afford to purchase more goods. Naturally, consumer tastes vary from nation to nation. In some high per capita GDP nations, individuals will opt to spend much on Internet use while in other nations individuals will spend little. A scatter diagram of per capita GDP and Internet use appears to confirm our intuition (figure 16.6).

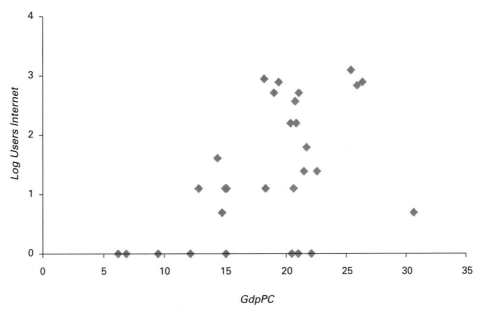

Figure 16.6
Scatter diagram: *GdpPC* versus *LogUsersInternet*

As per capita GDP rises we observe a greater variance for the log of Internet use per 1,000 persons. In nations with low levels of per capita GDP (less than $15,000), the log varies between about 0 and 1.6. Whereas in nations with high level of per capita GDP (more than $15,000), the log varies between about 0 and 3.20. What does this suggest about the error term in our model:

$$LogUsersInternet_t = \beta_{Const} + \beta_{GDP}GdpPC_t + e_t$$

Two nations with virtually the same level of per capita GDP have quite different rates of Internet use. The error term in the model would capture these differences. Consequently, as per capita GDP increases, we would expect the variance of the error term's probability distribution to increase.

Of course, we can never observe the error terms themselves. We can, however, think of the residuals as the estimated error terms:

Error term	Residual
↓	↓
$y_t = \beta_{Const} + \beta_x x_t + e_t$	$Res_t = y_t - Est_t$
↓	↓
$e_t = y_t - (\beta_{Const} + \beta_x x_t)$	$Res_t = y_t - (b_{Const} + b_x x_t)$

Since the residuals are observable we can plot a scatter diagram of the residuals, the estimated errors, and per capita GDP to illustrate how they are related (figure 16.7).

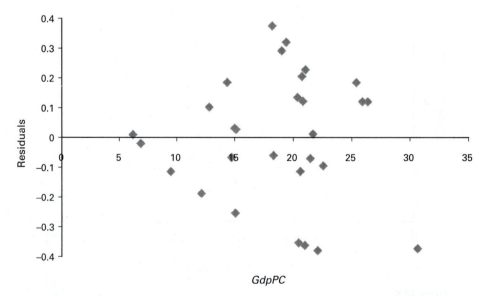

Figure 16.7
Scatter Diagram: *GdpPC* versus *Residuals*

Getting Started in EViews

· Run the ordinary least squares (OLS) regression.

· The residuals from the regression we just ran are automatically stored by EViews as the variable **resid**.

· In the Workfile window: First Click **gdppc**; then hold down the <Ctrl> key and click **resid**.

· In the Workfile window: Double click on a highlighted variable.

· In the Workfile window: Click **Open Group**.

· In the Group window: Click **View** and then **Graph**.

· In the Graph Options window: Click **Scatter**.

Our suspicions appear to be borne out. The residuals in nations with high per capita GDP are more spread out than in nations with low per capita GDP. It appears that heteroskedasticity could be present. The error term equal variance premise may be violated. Consequently we must be suspicious of the standard errors and probabilities appearing in the regression printout; the ordinary least squares (OLS) estimation procedure is calculating these values based on what could be an invalid premise, the error term equal variance premise.

Since the scatter diagram suggests that our fears may be warranted, we now test the heteroskedasticity more formally. While there are several different approaches, we will focus on the Breusch–Pagan–Godfrey test, which utilizes an artificial regression based on the following model:

Heteroskedasticity model:

$$(e_t - \text{Mean}[e_t])^2 = \alpha_{Const} + \alpha_{GDP}GdpPC_t + v_t$$

The model suggests that as $GdpPC_t$ increases, the squared deviation of the error term from its mean increases. Based on the scatter diagram appearing in figure 16.7, we suspect that α_{GDP} is positive:

Theory:

$$\alpha_{GDP} > 0$$

We can simplify this model by recognizing that the error term represents random influences; hence the mean of its probability distribution equals 0; hence,

$$(e_t - \text{Mean}[e_t])^2 = e_t^2$$

So our model becomes

Heteroskedasticity model:

$$e_t^2 = \alpha_{Const} + \alpha_{GDP}GdpPC_t + v_t$$

Table 16.3
Breusch–Pagan–Godfrey results

	Ordinary least squares (OLS)			
Dependent variable: *ResSqr*				
Explanatory variable(s):	Estimate	SE	*t*-Statistic	Prob
GdpPC	0.086100	0.031863	2.702189	0.0118
Const	−0.702317	0.617108	−1.138078	0.2651
Number of observations	29			

Critical result: The *GdpPC* coefficient estimate equals .086. The positive sign of the coefficient estimate suggests that higher per capita GDP increases the squared deviation of the error term from its mean. This evidence supports the theory that heteroskedasticity is present.

Of course, we can never observe the error terms themselves. We can, however, think of the residuals as the estimates of the error terms. We substitute the residual squared for the error term squared:

Heteroskedasticity model:

$$ResSqr_t = \alpha_{Const} + \alpha_{GDP}GdpPC_t + v_t$$

where $ResSqr_t$ = square of the residual for nation t.

We must generate the new variable *ResSqr*. To do so, run the original regression so that the statistical software calculates the residuals. After gaining access to the residuals, square them to generate the new residuals squared variable, *ResSqr*. Then estimate the model's parameters (table 16.3).

[To access this online material, go to http://mitpress.mit.edu/westhoffeconometrics and select Internet Use—1992.]

Next formulate the null and alternative hypotheses for the artificial regression model:

H_0: $\alpha_{GDP} = 0$ Per capita GDP does not affect the squared deviation of the residual

H_1: $\alpha_{GDP} > 0$ Higher per capita GDP increases the squared deviation of the residual

and compute Prob[Results IF H_0 true] from the tails probability reported in the regression printout:

$$\text{Prob[Results IF } H_0 \text{ true]} = \frac{0.0118}{2} \approx 0.0059$$

Statistical software can perform the Breusch–Pagan–Godfrey test automatically:

Getting Started in EViews

- Run the ordinary least squares (OLS) regression.
- In the equation window, click **View**, **Residual Diagnostics**, and **Heteroskedasticity Tests**
- The Breusch–Pagan–Godfrey test is the default
- After checking the explanatory variables (the regressors), click **OK**.

We reject the null hypothesis at the traditional significance levels of 1, 5, and 10 percent. Our formal test reinforces our suspicion that heteroskedasticity is present. Furthermore note that the estimate of the constant is not statistically significantly different from 0 even at the 10 percent significance level. We will exploit this to simplify the mathematics that follow. We assume that the variance of the error term's probability distribution is directly proportional to per capita GDP:

$$\text{Var}[e_t] = V \times GdpPC_t$$

where V equals a constant.

As per capita GDP increases the variance of the error term's probability increases just as the scatter diagram suggests. We will now use this specification of error term variance to tweak the original model to "eliminate" heteroskedasticity. This approach is called the generalized least square (GLS) estimation procedure.

Step 3: Apply the generalized least squares (GLS) estimation procedure.

Strategy: Algebraically manipulate the original model so that the problem of heteroskedasticity is eliminated in the new model. That is, tweak the original model so that variance of each nation's error term's probability distribution is the same. We can accomplish this with just a little algebra.

Based on our scatter diagram and the Breusch–Pagan–Godfrey test, we assume that the variance of the error term's probability distribution is proportional to per capita GDP:

$$\text{Var}[e_t] = V \times GdpPC_t$$

where V equals a constant.

We begin with our original model:

Original model:

$$LogUsersInternet_t = \beta_{Const} + \beta_{GDP}GdpPC_t + e_t$$

Now divide both sides of the equation by $\sqrt{GdpPC_t}$. (For the moment, do not worry about why we divide by $\sqrt{GdpPC_t}$; we will justify that shortly.)

Tweaked model:

$$\frac{LogUsersInternet_t}{\sqrt{GdpPC_t}} = \frac{\beta_{Const}}{\sqrt{GdpPC_t}} + \beta_{GDP}\frac{GdpPC_t}{\sqrt{GdpPC_t}} + \frac{e_t}{\sqrt{GdpPC_t}}$$

$$= \frac{\beta_{Const}}{\sqrt{GdpPC_t}} + \beta_{GDP}\sqrt{GdpPC_t} + \varepsilon_t$$

where $\varepsilon_t = e_t / \sqrt{GdpPC_t}$.

To understand why we divided by $\sqrt{GdpPC_t}$, focus on the error term, ε_t, in the tweaked model. What does the variance of this error term's probability distribution equal?

$$Var[\varepsilon_t] = Var\left[\frac{e_t}{\sqrt{GdpPC_t}}\right]$$

$\downarrow$ Arithmetic of variances: $Van[cx] = c^2 Var[x]$

$$= \frac{1}{GdpPC_t}Var[e_t]$$

$\downarrow$ $Var[e_t] = V \times GpcPC_t$, where V equals a constant

$$= \frac{1}{GdpPC_t}V \times GpcPC_t$$

$$= V$$

We divided the original model by $\sqrt{GdpPC_t}$ so that the variance of the error term's probability distribution in the tweaked model equals V for each observation. Consequently the error term equal variance premise is satisfied in the tweaked model. Therefore the ordinary least squares (OLS) estimation procedure computations of the estimates for the variance of the error term's probability distribution will not be flawed in the tweaked model.

The dependent and explanatory variables in the new tweaked model are:

Tweaked dependent variable: $AdjLogUsersInternet_t = \dfrac{LogUsersInternet_t}{\sqrt{GdpPC_t}}$

Tweaked explanatory variables: $AdjConst_t = \dfrac{1}{\sqrt{GdpPC_t}}$

$$AdjGdpPC_t = \sqrt{GdpPC_t}$$

NB: The tweaked model does not include a constant.

When we run a regression with the new dependent and new explanatory variables, we should now have an unbiased procedure to estimate the variance of the coefficient estimate's probability distribution. Be careful to eliminate the constant when running the tweaked regression (table 16.4).

[To access this online material, go to http://mitpress.mit.edu/westhoffeconometrics and select Internet Use—1992.]

Table 16.4
Tweaked Internet regression results

Ordinary least squares (OLS)				
Dependent variable: *AdjLogUsersInternet*				
Explanatory variable(s):	Estimate	SE	*t*-Statistic	Prob
AdjGdpPC	0.113716	0.026012	4.371628	0.0002
AdjConst	−0.726980	0.450615	−1.613306	0.1183
Number of observations	29			

Estimated equation: *EstAdjLogUsersInternet* = −0.727*AdjConst* + 0.114*GdpPC*

Interpretation of estimates:

$b_{GDP} = 11.4$: a \$1,000 increase in real per capita GDP results in a 11.4 percent increase in Internet users

Table 16.5
Comparison of Internet regression results

	β_{GDP} coefficient estimate	Standard error	*t*-Statistic	Tails probability
Ordinary least squares (OLS)	0.101	0.033	3.09	0.0046
Generalized least squares (GLS)	0.114	0.026	4.37	0.0002

Now let us compare the tweaked regression for β_{GDP} and the original one (table 16.5).

The most striking differences are the calculations that are based on the estimated variance of the coefficient probability distribution: the standard error, the *t*-Statistic, and Prob values. This is hardly surprising. The ordinary least squares (OLS) regression calculations are based on the error term equal variance premise. Our analysis suggests that this premise is violated ordinary least squares (OLS) regression, however. Consequently the standard Error, *t*-Statistic, and Prob. calculations, will be flawed when we use the ordinary least squares (OLS) estimation procedure. The general least squares (GLS) regression corrects for this.

Recall the purpose of our analysis in the first place: Assess the effect of per capita GDP on Internet use. Recall our theory and associated hypotheses:

Theory: Higher per capita GDP increases Internet use.

H_0: $\beta_{GDP} = 0$ Per capita GDP does not affect Internet use

H_1: $\beta_{GDP} > 0$ Higher per capita GDP increases Internet use

We see that the value of the tails probability decreases from 0.0046 to 0.0002. Since a one-tailed test is appropriate, the Prob[Results IF H_0 true] declines from 0.0023 to 0.0001. Accounting for heteroskedasticity has an impact on the analysis.

16.6   Justifying the Generalized Least Squares (GLS) Estimation Procedure

We will now use a simulation to illustrate that the generalized least squares (GLS) estimation procedure for the following cases:

• Value of the coefficient estimate is unbiased.

• Variance of the coefficient estimate's probability distribution is unbiased.

• Value of the coefficient estimate is the best linear unbiased estimation procedure (BLUE).

Econometrics Lab 16.4: Generalized Least Squares (GLS) Estimation Procedure

[To access this online material, go to http://mitpress.mit.edu/westhoffeconometrics and select Lab 16.4.].]

A new drop down box now appears in figure 16.8. We can specify the estimation procedure: either ordinary least squares (OLS) or generalized least squares (GLS). Initially, OLS is specified indicating that the ordinary least squares (OLS) estimation procedure is being used. Also note that by default 0.0 is specified in the Heter list, which means that no heteroskedasticity is present. Recall our previous simulations illustrating that the ordinary least squares (OLS) estimation procedure to estimate the coefficient value and the ordinary least squares (OLS) procedure to estimate the variance of the coefficient estimate's probability distribution were both unbiased when no heteroskedasticity is present. To review this, click **Start** and then after many, many repetitions click **Stop**.

Next introduce heteroskedasticity by selecting 1.0 from the "Heter" list. Recall that while the ordinary least squares (OLS) estimation procedure for the coefficient's value was still unbiased, the ordinary least squares (OLS) estimation procedure for the variance of the coefficient estimate's probability distribution was biased. To review this, click **Start** and then after many, many repetitions click **Stop**.

Finally, select the generalized least squares (GLS) estimation procedure instead of the ordinary least squares (OLS) estimation procedure. Click **Start** and then after many, many repetitions click **Stop**. The generalized least squares (GLS) results are reported in the last row of table 16.6. When heteroskedasticity is present and the generalized least squares (GLS) estimation procedure is used, the variance of the estimated coefficient values from each repetition of the experiment equals the average of the estimated variances. This suggests that the generalized least squares (GLS) procedure indeed provides an unbiased estimation procedure for the variance. Also note that when heteroskedasticity is present, the variance of the estimated values resulting from generalized least squares (GLS) is less than ordinary least squares (OLS), 2.3 versus 2.9. What does this suggest? The lower variance suggests that the generalized least squares (GLS) procedure provides more reliable estimates when heteroskedasticity is present. In fact it can be shown that the generalized least squares (GLS) procedure is indeed the best linear unbiased estimation (BLUE) procedure when heteroskedasticity is present.

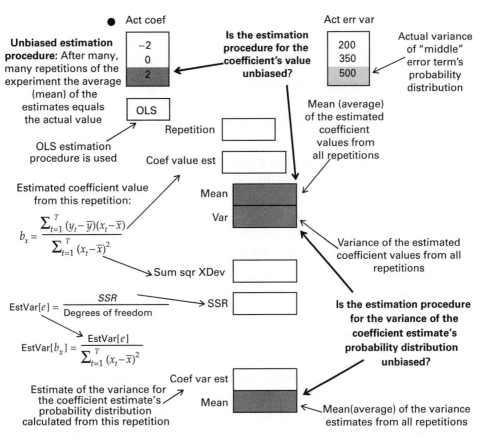

Figure 16.8
Heteroskedasticity simulation

Table 16.6
Heteroskedasticity simulation results

		Is OLS estimation procedure for the coefficient's value unbiased?		Is OLS estimation procedure for the variance of the of the coefficient estimate's probability distribution unbiased?	
		Actual coefficient value ↓	Estimate of coefficient value ↓	Variance of the estimated coefficient values ↓	Estimate of the variance for coefficient estimate's probability distribution ↓
Heter factor	Estim proc	**Actual value of β_x**	**Mean (average) of the estimated values, b_x, from all repetitions**	**Variance of the estimated coefficient values, b_x, from all repetitions**	**Average of estimated variances, EstVar[b_x], from all repetitions**
0	OLS	2.0	≈2.0	≈2.5	≈2.5
1	OLS	2.0	≈2.0	≈3.6	≈2.9
1	GLS	2.0	≈2.0	≈2.3	≈2.3

Let us summarize:

Is the estimation procedure:	Standard premises	Heteroskedasticity	
	OLS	OLS	GLS
an unbiased estimation procedure for the coefficient's value?	Yes	Yes	Yes
variance of the coefficient estimate's probability distribution?	Yes	No	Yes
for the coefficient value the best linear unbiased estimation procedure (BLUE)?	Yes	No	Yes

16.7 Robust Standard Errors

We have seen that two issues emerge when heteroskedasticity is present:

· The standard error calculations made by the ordinary least squares (OLS) estimation procedure are flawed.

· While the ordinary least squares (OLS) for the coefficient value is unbiased, it is not the best linear unbiased estimation procedure (BLUE).

Robust standard errors address the first issue and are particularly appropriate when the sample size is large. White standard errors constitute one such approach. We will not provide a rigorous justification of this approach, the mathematics is too complex. We will, however, provide the motivation by taking a few liberties. Begin by reviewing our derivation of the variance of the coefficient estimate's probability distribution, $\text{Var}[b_x]$, presented in chapter 6:

$$b_x = \beta_x + \frac{\sum_{t=1}^{T}(x_t - \bar{x})e_t}{\sum_{t=1}^{T}(x_t - \bar{x})^2} = \beta_x + \frac{(x_1 - \bar{x})e_1 + (x_2 - \bar{x})e_2 + (x_3 - \bar{x})e_3}{(x_1 - \bar{x})^2 + (x_2 - \bar{x})^2 + (x_3 - \bar{x})^2}$$

Next a little algebra obtains

$$\text{Var}[b_x] = \text{Var}\left[\beta_x + \frac{(x_1 - \bar{x})e_1 + (x_2 - \bar{x})e_2 + (x_3 - \bar{x})e_3}{(x_1 - \bar{x})^2 + (x_2 - \bar{x})^2 + (x_3 - \bar{x})^2}\right]$$

Applying $\text{Var}[c + x] = \text{Var}[x]$

$$= \text{Var}\left[\frac{(x_1 - \bar{x})e_1 + (x_2 - \bar{x})e_2 + (x_3 - \bar{x})e_3}{(x_1 - \bar{x})^2 + (x_2 - \bar{x})^2 + (x_3 - \bar{x})^2}\right]$$

Rewriting the fraction as a product

$$= \text{Var}\left[\left(\frac{1}{(x_1 - \bar{x})^2 + (x_2 - \bar{x})^2 + (x_3 - \bar{x})^2}\right)\left((x_1 - \bar{x})e_1 + (x_2 - \bar{x})e_2 + (x_3 - \bar{x})e_3\right)\right]$$

Applying $\text{Var}[cx] = c^2\,\text{Var}[x]$

$$= \frac{1}{\left[(x_1 - \bar{x})^2 + (x_2 - \bar{x})^2 + (x_3 - \bar{x})^2\right]^2}\,\text{Var}\left[((x_1 - \bar{x})e_1 + (x_2 - \bar{x})e_2 + (x_3 - \bar{x})e_3)\right]$$

Error term/error term independence premise: The error terms are independent, $\text{Var}[x + y] = \text{Var}[x] + \text{Var}[y]$

$$= \frac{1}{\left[(x_1 - \bar{x})^2 + (x_2 - \bar{x})^2 + (x_3 - \bar{x})^2\right]^2}\left[\text{Var}[(x_1 - \bar{x})e_1] + \text{Var}[(x_2 - \bar{x})e_2] + \text{Var}[(x_3 - \bar{x})e_3]\right]$$

Applying $\text{Var}[cx] = c^2\text{Var}[x]$

$$= \frac{1}{\left[(x_1 - \bar{x})^2 + (x_2 - \bar{x})^2 + (x_3 - \bar{x})^2\right]^2}$$
$$\left[(x_1 - \bar{x})^2\,\text{Var}[e_1] + (x_2 - \bar{x})^2\,\text{Var}[e_2] + (x_3 - \bar{x})^2\,\text{Var}[e_3]\right]$$

Generalizing

$$= \frac{\sum_{t=1}^{T}(x_t - \bar{x})^2\,\text{Var}[e_t]}{\left[\sum_{t=1}^{T}(x_t - \bar{x})^2\right]^2}$$

Focus on $\text{Var}[e_t]$ and recall that the variance equals the average of the squared deviations from the mean:

$\text{Var}[e_t] = \text{Average of } (e_t - \text{Mean}[e_t])^2$

Since error terms represent random influences, the mean equals 0 and since we are considering a single error term, the average is e_t^2:

$\text{Var}[e_t] = e_t^2$

While the error terms are not observable, we can think of the residuals as the estimated error term. Consequently we will use Res_t^2 to estimate e_t^2:

$e_t^2 \rightarrow Res_t^2$

Table 16.7
Internet regression results—Robust standard errors

Ordinary least squares (OLS)				
Dependent variable: *LogUsersInternet*				
Explanatory variable(s):	Estimate	SE	*t*-Statistic	Prob
GdpPC	0.100772	0.032428	3.107552	0.0044
Const	−0.486907	0.525871	−0.925906	0.3627
		White heteroskedasticity-consistent SEs		
Number of observations	29			

Estimated equation: *EstLogUsersInternet* = −0.487 + 0.101*GdpPC*

Applying this to the equation for the variance of the coefficient estimate's probability distribution obtains

$$\text{Var}[b_x] = \frac{\sum_{t=1}^{T}(x_t - \bar{x})^2 \text{Var}[e_t]}{\left[\sum_{t=1}^{T}(x_t - \bar{x})^2\right]^2}$$

$$\downarrow \qquad \text{Substituting } e_t^2 \text{ for } \text{Var}[e_t]$$

$$= \frac{\sum_{t=1}^{T}(x_t - \bar{x})^2 e_t^2}{\left[\sum_{t=1}^{T}(x_t - \bar{x})^2\right]^2}$$

$$\downarrow \qquad \text{Residuals as estimated error terms: } e_t^2 \rightarrow Res_t^2$$

$$\text{EstVar}[b_x] = \frac{\sum_{t=1}^{T}(x_t - \bar{x})^2 Res_t^2}{\left[\sum_{t=1}^{T}(x_t - \bar{x})^2\right]^2}$$

The White robust standard error is the square root of the estimated variance.[2] Statistical software makes it easy to compute robust standard errors (table 16.7).

[To access this online material, go to http://mitpress.mit.edu/westhoffeconometrics and select Internet Use—1992.]

Getting Started in EViews

- Run the ordinary least squares (OLS) regression.
- In the equation window, click **Estimate** and **Options**.
- In the Coefficient covariance matrix box select White from the drop down list.
- Click OK.

---

2. While it is beyond the scope of this textbook, it can be shown that although this estimation procedure is biased, the magnitude of the bias diminishes and approaches zero as the sample size approaches infinity.

Chapter 16 Review Questions

1. In words, what is heteroskedasticity?

2. When heteroskedasticity is present, are all the standard ordinary least (OLS) premises satisfied? If not, which one(s) is violated?

3. Suppose that we are using the ordinary least squares (OLS) estimation procedure and that heteroskedasticity is present.

    a. What is the "good news?"

    b. What is the "bad news?"

4. When heteroskedasticity is present, how do we account for it?

Chapter 16 Exercises

Judicial data: Cross-sectional data of judicial and economic statistics for the fifty states in 2000.

$JudExp_t$	State and local expenditures for the judicial system per 100,000 persons in state t
$CrimesAll_t$	Crimes per 100,000 persons in state t
$GdpPC_t$	Real per capita GDP in state t (2000 dollars)
Pop_t	Population in state t (persons)
$UnemRate_t$	Unemployment rate in state t (percent)
$State_t$	Name of state t
$Year_t$	Year

1. We wish to explain state and local judicial expenditures. To do so, consider the following linear model:

$$JudExp_t = \beta_{Const} + \beta_{Crimes}CrimesAll_t + \beta_{GDP}GdpPC_t + e_t$$

    a. Develop a theory regarding how each explanatory variable influences the dependent variable. What does your theory imply about the sign of each coefficient?

    b. Using the ordinary least squares (OLS) estimation procedure, estimate the value of each coefficient using the Judicial Data. Interpret the coefficient estimates. What are the critical results?

[To access this online material, go to http://mitpress.mit.edu/westhoffeconometrics and select Judicial Expenses.]

   c. Formulate the null and alternative hypotheses.

   d. Calculate Prob[Results IF H_0 true]'s and assess your theories.

2. Consider the possibility of heteroskedasticity in the judicial expenditure model.

   a. Intuitively, is there reason to suspect that heteroskedasticity might exist? More specifically, is there reason to suspect that the variance of the error term's probability distribution may be correlated with per capita real GDP?

   b. Consider the ordinary least squares (OLS) estimates of the parameters that you computed in the previous question. Plot the residuals versus per capita real GDP. Does your graph appear to confirm your suspicions concerning the presence of heteroskedasticity?

[To access this online material, go to http://mitpress.mit.edu/westhoffeconometrics and select Judicial Expenses.]

   c. Based on your suspicions, formulate a linear model of heteroskedasticity.

   d. Use the Breusch–Pagan–Godfrey approach to test for the presence of heteroskedasticity.

3. Apply the generalized least squares (GLS) estimation procedure to the judicial expenditure model. To simplify the mathematics, use the following equation to model the variance of the error term's probability distribution:

$$\text{Var}[e_t] = V \times GdpPC_t$$

where V equals a constant.

   a. Apply this heteroskedasticity model to manipulate algebraically the original model to derive a new, tweaked model in which the error terms do not suffer from heteroskedasticity.

   b. Use the ordinary least squares (OLS) estimation procedure to estimate the parameters of the tweaked model.

[To access this online material, go to http://mitpress.mit.edu/westhoffeconometrics and select Judicial Expenses.]

4. How, if at all, does accounting for heteroskedasticity affect the assessment of your theories?

Burglary and poverty data: Cross section of burglary and economic statistics for the fifty states in 2002.

$PovRate_t$ Individuals below the poverty level in state t (percent)

$Burglaries_t$ Burglaries per 100,000 persons in state t

Pop_t Population in state t (persons)

$UnemRate_t$ Unemployment rate in state t (percent)

$State_t$ Name of state t

5. We wish to explain poverty. To do so, consider the following linear model:

$$PovRate_t = \beta_{Const} + \beta_{Unem}UnemRate_t + \beta_{Burg}Burglaries_t + e_t$$

a. Develop a theory regarding how each explanatory variable influences the dependent variable. What does your theory imply about the sign of each coefficient?

b. Using the ordinary least squares (OLS) estimation procedure, estimate the value of each coefficient using the burglary and poverty data. Interpret the coefficient estimates. What are the critical results?

[To access this online material, go to http://mitpress.mit.edu/westhoffeconometrics and select Poverty.]

c. Formulate the null and alternative hypotheses.

d. Calculate Prob[Results IF H_0 true]'s and assess your theories.

6. Consider the possibility of heteroskedasticity in the poverty model.

a. Intuitively, is there reason to suspect that heteroskedasticity might exist? More specifically, is there reason to suspect that the variance of the error term's probability distribution may be correlated with the state's population?

Hint: Before answering, consider the following:

• The unemployment rate is calculated from a sample of the population. The sample size in each state is approximately proportional to the state's population.

• Is the reported unemployment rate is a state with a large population more or less reliable that a state with a small population?

• Would you expect the variance of the error term's probability distribution in a large state to be more or less than the variance in a small state?

b. Consider the ordinary least squares (OLS) estimates of the parameters that you computed in the previous question. Plot the residuals versus population.

[To access this online material, go to http://mitpress.mit.edu/westhoffeconometrics and select Porvety.]

    i. Does your graph appear to confirm your suspicions concerning the presence of heteroskedasticity?

    ii. If so, does the variance appear to be directly or inversely proportion to population?

  c. Based on your suspicions, formulate a model of heteroskedasticity.

  d. Use the Breusch–Pagan–Godfrey approach to test for the presence of heteroskedasticity.

7. Apply the generalized least squares (GLS) estimation procedure to the judicial expenditure model. To simplify the mathematics use the following equation to model the variance of the error term's probability distribution:

$$\text{Var}[e_t] = \frac{V}{Pop_t}$$

where *V* equals a constant.

  a. Apply this heteroskedasticity model to manipulate algebraically the original model to derive a new, tweaked model in which the error terms do not suffer from heteroskedasticity.

  b. Use the ordinary least squares (OLS) estimation procedure to estimate the parameters of the tweaked model.

[To access this online material, go to http://mitpress.mit.edu/westhoffeconometrics and select Poverty.]

8. How, if at all, does accounting for heteroskedasticity affect the assessment of your theories.

17 Autocorrelation (Serial Correlation)

Chapter 17 Prep Questions

1. What are the standard ordinary least squares (OLS) premises?

2. In chapter 6 we showed that the ordinary least squares (OLS) estimation procedure for the coefficient value was unbiased; that is, we showed that

$\text{Mean}[b_x] = \beta_x$

Review the algebra. What role, if any, did the second premise ordinary least squares (OLS) premise, the error term/error term independence premise, play?

3. In chapter 6 we showed that the variance of the coefficient estimate's probability distribution equals the variance of the error term's probability distribution divided by the sum of the squared x deviations; that is, we showed that

$$\text{Var}[b_x] = \frac{\text{Var}[e]}{\sum_{t=1}^{T}(x_t - \bar{x})^2}$$

Review the algebra. What role, if any, did the second premise ordinary least squares (OLS) premise, the error term/error term independence premise, play?

4. Suppose that two variables are positively correlated.

a. In words, what does this mean?

b. What type of graph do we use to illustrate their correlation? What does the graph look like?

c. What can we say about their covariance and correlation coefficient?

5. Suppose that two variables are independent.

a. In words, what does this mean?

b. What type of graph do we use to illustrate their correlation? What does the graph look like?

c. What can we say about their covariance and correlation coefficient?

6. Consider the following model and data:

$ConsDur_t = \beta_{Const} + \beta_I Inc_t + e_t$

Consumer durable data: Monthly time series data of consumer durable production and income statistics 2004 to 2009.

$ConsDur_t$ Consumption of durables in month t (billions of 2005 chained dollars)

$Cons_t$ Consumption in month t (billions of 2005 chained dollars)

Inc_t Disposable income in month t (billions of 2005 chained dollars)

a. What is your theory concerning how disposable income should affect the consumption of consumer durables? What does your theory suggest about the sign of the income coefficient, β_I?

b. Run the appropriate regression. Do the data support your theory?

[To access this online material, go to http://mitpress.mit.edu/westhoffeconometrics and select Consumption and Disposable Income.]

    c. Graph the residuals.

Getting Started in EViews

- Run the regression and close the Equation window.
- Click **View**.
- Click **Actual, Fitted, Residual**.
- Click **Residual Graph**.

    d. If the residual is positive in one month, is it usually positive in the next month?

    e. If the residual is negative in one month, is it usually negative in the next month?

7. Consider the following equations:

$$y_t = \beta_{Const} + \beta_x x_t + e_t$$

$$e_t = \rho e_{t-1} + v_t$$

$$Esty_t = b_{Const} + b_x x_t$$

$$Res_t = y_t - Esty_t$$

Start with the last equation, the equation for Res_t. Using algebra and the other equations, show that

$$Res_t = (\beta_{Const} - b_{Const}) + (\beta_x - b_x)x_t + \rho e_{t-1} + v_t$$

8. Consider the following equations:

$$y_t = \beta_{Const} + \beta_x x_t + e_t$$

$$y_{t-1} = \beta_{Const} + \beta_x x_{t-1} + e_{t-1}$$

$$e_t = \rho e_{t-1} + v_t$$

Multiply the y_{t-1} equation by ρ. Then subtract it from the y_t equation. Using algebra and the e_t equation show that

$$(y_t - \rho y_{t-1}) = (\beta_{Const} - \rho\beta_{Const}) + \beta_x(x_t - \rho x_{t-1}) + v_t$$

17.1   Review

17.1.1   Regression Model

We begin by reviewing the basic regression model:

$$y_t = \beta_{Const} + \beta_x x_t + e_t, \qquad t = 1, 2, \ldots, T$$

where
y_t = dependent variable

e_t = error term

x_t = explanatory variable

T = sample size

The error term is a random variable that represents random influences: $\text{Mean}[e_t] = 0$

17.1.2   The Standard Ordinary Least Squares (OLS) Premises

Again, we begin by focusing our attention on the standard ordinary least squares (OLS) regression premises:

· **Error term equal variance premise:**   The variance of the error term's probability distribution for each observation is the same; all the variances equal Var[e]:

$$\text{Var}[e_1] = \text{Var}[e_2] = \ldots = \text{Var}[e_T] = \text{Var}[e]$$

· **Error term/error term independence premise:**   The error terms are independent: $\text{Cov}[e_i, e_j] = 0$.

Knowing the value of the error term from one observation does not help us predict the value of the error term for any other observation.

· **Explanatory variable/error term independence premise:**   The explanatory variables, the x_t's, and the error terms, the e_t's, are not correlated.

Knowing the value of an observation's explanatory variable does not help us predict the value of that observation's error term.

17.1.3   Estimation Procedures Embedded within the Ordinary Least Squares (OLS) Estimation Procedure

The ordinary least squares (OLS) estimation procedure includes three important estimation procedures:

• Values of the regression parameters, β_x and β_{Const}:

$$b_x = \frac{\sum_{t=1}^{T}(y_t - \overline{y})(x_t - \overline{x})}{\sum_{t=1}^{T}(x_t - \overline{x})^2} \quad \text{and} \quad b_{Const} = \overline{y} - b_x\overline{x}$$

• Variance of the error term's probability distribution, Var[e]:

$$\text{EstVar}[e] = \frac{SSR}{\text{Degrees of freedom}}$$

• Variance of the coefficient estimate's probability distribution, Var[b_x]:

$$\text{EstVar}[b_x] = \frac{\text{EstVar}[e]}{\sum_{t=1}^{T}(x_t - \overline{x})^2}$$

When the standard ordinary least squares (OLS) regression premises are met:

• Each estimation procedure is unbiased; that is, each estimation procedure does not systematically underestimate or overestimate the actual value.

• The ordinary least squares (OLS) estimation procedure for the coefficient value is the best linear unbiased estimation procedure (BLUE).

Crucial point: When the ordinary least squares (OLS) estimation procedure performs its calculations, it implicitly assumes that the standard ordinary least squares (OLS) regression premises are satisfied.

In chapter 16 we focused on the first standard ordinary least squares (OLS) premise. We will now turn our attention to the second, error term/error term independence premise. We begin by examining precisely what the premise means. Subsequently, we investigate what problems do and do not emerge when the premise is violated and finally what can be done to address the problems that do arise.

17.1.4   Covariance and Independence

We introduced covariance to quantify the notions of correlation and independence. On the one hand, if two variables are correlated, their covariance is nonzero. On the other hand, if two variables are independent their covariance is 0. A scatter diagram allows us to illustrate how covariance is related to independence and correlation. To appreciate why, consider the equation we use to calculate covariance:

$$\text{Cov}[x, y] = \frac{(x_1 - \overline{x})(y_1 - \overline{y}) + (x_2 - \overline{x})(y_2 - \overline{y}) + \ldots + (x_N - \overline{x})(y_N - \overline{y})}{N} = \frac{\sum_{t=1}^{N}(x_t - \overline{x})(y_t - \overline{y})}{N}$$

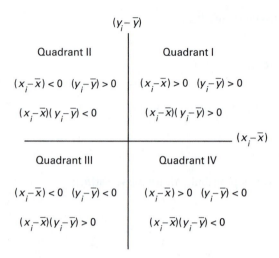

Figure 17.1
Scatter diagram and covariance

Focus on one term in the numerator the covariance term, $(x_t - \bar{x})(y_i - \bar{y})$; consider its sign in each of the four quadrants (see figure 17.1).

· First quadrant. Dow growth rate is greater than its mean and Nasdaq growth is greater than its mean; the product of the deviations is positive in the first quadrant:

$$(x_t - \bar{x}) > 0 \quad \text{and} \quad (y_t - \bar{y}) > 0 \rightarrow (x_t - \bar{x})(y_t - \bar{y}) > 0$$

· Second quadrant. Dow growth rate is less than its mean and Nasdaq growth is greater than its mean; the product of the deviations is negative in the second quadrant:

$$(x_t - \bar{x}) < 0 \quad \text{and} \quad (y_t - \bar{y}) > 0 \rightarrow (x_t - \bar{x})(y_t - \bar{y}) < 0$$

· Third quadrant. Dow growth rate is less than its mean and Nasdaq growth is less than its mean; the product of the deviations is positive in the third quadrant:

$$(x_t - \bar{x}) < 0 \quad \text{and} \quad (y_t - \bar{y}) < 0 \rightarrow (x_t - \bar{x})(y_t - \bar{y}) > 0$$

· Fourth quadrant. Dow growth rate is greater than its mean and Nasdaq growth is less than its mean; the product of the deviations is negative in the fourth quadrant:

$$(x_t - \bar{x}) > 0 \quad \text{and} \quad (y_t - \bar{y}) < 0 \rightarrow (x_t - \bar{x})(y_t - \bar{y}) < 0$$

Recall that we used precipitation in Amherst, the Nasdaq growth rate, and the Dow Jones growth rate to illustrate independent and correlated variables in chapter 1.

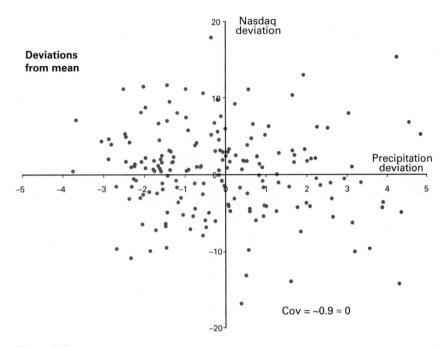

Figure 17.2
Precipitation versus Nasdaq growth

Precipitation in Amherst and the Nasdaq growth rate are independent; knowing one does not help us predict the other. Figure 17.2 shows that the scatter diagram points are distributed relatively evenly throughout the four quadrants thereby suggesting that the covariance is approximately 0. However, the Dow Jones growth rate and the Nasdaq growth rate are not independent; they are correlated. Most points on figure 17.3 are located in the first and third quadrants; consequently most of the covariance terms are positive resulting in a positive covariance.

17.2   What Is Autocorrelation (Serial Correlation)?

Autocorrelation (serial correlation) is present whenever the value of one observation's error term allows us to predict the value of the next. When this occurs, one observation's error term is correlated with the next observation's; the error terms are correlated, and the second premise, the error term/error term independence premise, is violated. The following equation models autocorrelation:

Autocorrelation model:

$$e_t = \rho e_{t-1} + v_t,$$

where v_t's are independent.

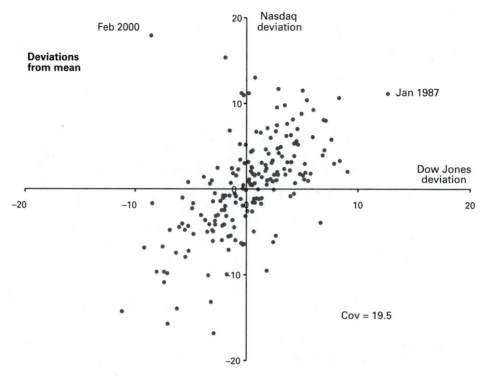

Figure 17.3
Dow Jones growth versus Nasdaq growth

The Greek letter "rho" is the traditional symbol that is used to represent autocorrelation. When rho equals 0, no autocorrelation is present; when rho equals 0, the ρe_{t-1} term disappears and the error terms, the e's, are independent because the v_t's are independent. However, when rho does not equal 0, autocorrelation is present.

$$\rho = 0 \qquad\qquad\qquad \rho \neq 0$$

$$\downarrow \qquad\qquad\qquad\qquad \downarrow$$

$$e_t = v_t \qquad\qquad e_t \text{ depends on } e_{t-1}$$

$$\downarrow \qquad\qquad\qquad\qquad \downarrow$$

No autocorrelation   Autocorrelation present

We will now turn to the Econometrics Lab to illustrate this.

Econometrics Lab 17.1: The Error Terms and Autocorrelation

[To access this online material, go to http://mitpress.mit.edu/westhoffeconometrics and select Lab 17.1.]

We can use a simulation to illustrate autocorrelation. We begin with selecting .0 in the "rho" list (figure 17.4). Focus on the e_{t-1} versus e_t scatter diagram (figure 17.5). You will observe that this scatter diagram looks very much like the Amherst precipitation–Nasdaq scatter diagram (figure 17.2), indicating that the two error terms are independent; that is, does knowing e_{t-1} not help us to predict e_t? Next specify rho to equal 0.9. Now the scatter diagram (figure 17.6) will look much more like the Dow Jones–Nasdaq scatter diagram (figure 17.3), suggesting that for the most part, when e_{t-1} is positive e_t will be positive also, or alternatively when e_{t-1} is negative, e_t will be negative also; this illustrates positive autocorrelation.

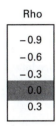

Rho

Figure 17.4
Rho list

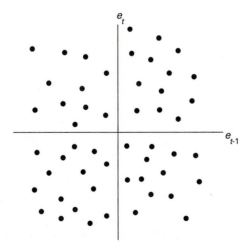

Figure 17.5
$\rho = 0$

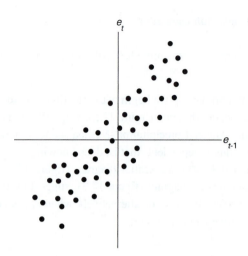

Figure 17.6
$\rho = 0.9$

17.3   Autocorrelation and the Ordinary Least Squares (OLS) Estimation Procedure: The Consequences

17.3.1   The Mathematics

Now let us explore the consequences of autocorrelation. Just as with heteroskedasticity, we will focus on two of the three estimation procedures embedded within the ordinary least squares (OLS) estimation procedure:

· Value of the coefficient.

· Variance of the coefficient estimate's probability distribution.

Question: Are these estimation procedures still unbiased when autocorrelation is present?

Ordinary Least Squares (OLS) Estimation Procedure for the Coefficient Value
Begin by focusing on the coefficient value. Previously we showed that the estimation procedure for the coefficient value was unbiased by

· applying the arithmetic of means

and

· recognizing that the means of the error terms' probability distributions equal 0 (since the error terms represent random influences).

Let us quickly review. First recall the arithmetic of means:

Mean of a constant plus a variable: $\text{Mean}[c + x] = c + \text{Mean}[x]$

Mean of a constant times a variable: $\text{Mean}[cx] = c\,\text{Mean}[x]$

Mean of the sum of two variables: $\text{Mean}[x + y] = \text{Mean}[x] + \text{Mean}[y]$

To keep the algebra straightforward, we focused on a sample size of 3.

Equation for coefficient estimate:

$$b_x = \beta_x + \frac{\sum_{t=1}^{T}(x_t - \overline{x})e_t}{\sum_{t=1}^{T}(x_t - \overline{x})^2} = \beta_x + \frac{(x_1 - \overline{x})e_1 + (x_2 - \overline{x})e_2 + (x_3 - \overline{x})e_3}{(x_1 - \overline{x})^2 + (x_2 - \overline{x})^2 + (x_3 - \overline{x})^2}$$

Now some algebra obtains[1]

$$\text{Mean}[b_x] = \text{Mean}\left[\beta_x + \frac{(x_1 - \overline{x})e_1 + (x_2 - \overline{x})e_2 + (x_3 - \overline{x})e_3}{(x_1 - \overline{x})^2 + (x_2 - \overline{x})^2 + (x_3 - \overline{x})^2}\right]$$

Applying $\text{Mean}[c + x] = c + \text{Mean}[x]$

$$= \beta_x + \text{Mean}\left[\frac{(x_1 - \overline{x})e_1 + (x_2 - \overline{x})e_2 + (x_3 - \overline{x})e_3}{(x_1 - \overline{x})^2 + (x_2 - \overline{x})^2 + (x_3 - \overline{x})^2}\right]$$

Rewriting the fraction as a product

$$= \beta_x + \text{Mean}\left[\left(\frac{1}{(x_1 - \overline{x})^2 + (x_2 - \overline{x})^2 + (x_3 - \overline{x})^2}\right)\left((x_1 - \overline{x})e_1 + (x_2 - \overline{x})e_2 + (x_3 - \overline{x})e_3\right)\right]$$

Applying $\text{Mean}[cx] = c\,\text{Mean}[x]$

$$= \beta_x + \frac{1}{(x_1 - \overline{x})^2 + (x_2 - \overline{x})^2 + (x_3 - \overline{x})^2}\,\text{Mean}\left[\left((x_1 - \overline{x})e_1 + (x_2 - \overline{x})e_2 + (x_3 - \overline{x})e_3\right)\right]$$

Applying $\text{Mean}[x + y] = \text{Mean}[x] + \text{Mean}[y]$

$$= \beta_x + \frac{1}{(x_1 - \overline{x})^2 + (x_2 - \overline{x})^2 + (x_3 - \overline{x})^2}\left[\text{Mean}[(x_1 - \overline{x})e_1] + \text{Mean}[(x_2 - \overline{x})e_2] + \text{Mean}[(x_3 - \overline{x})e_3]\right]$$

Applying $\text{Mean}[cx] = c\,\text{Mean}[x]$

$$= \beta_x + \frac{1}{(x_1 - \overline{x})^2 + (x_2 - \overline{x})^2 + (x_3 - \overline{x})^2}\left[(x_1 - \overline{x})\text{Mean}[e_1] + (x_2 - \overline{x})\text{Mean}[e_2] + (x_3 - \overline{x})\text{Mean}[e_3]\right]$$

---

1. Recall that to keep the algebra straightforward, we assume that the explanatory variables are constants. By doing so, we can easily apply the arithmetic of means. Our results are unaffected by this assumption.

Since Mean$[e_1]$ = Mean$[e_2]$ = Mean$[e_3]$ = 0

= β_x

What is the critical point here? We have not relied on the error term/error term independence premise to show that the estimation procedure for the coefficient value is unbiased. Consequently we suspect that the estimation procedure for the coefficient value will continue to be unbiased in the presence of autocorrelation.

Ordinary Least Squares (OLS) Estimation Procedure for the Variance of the Coefficient Estimate's Probability Distribution

Next consider the estimation procedure for the variance of the coefficient estimate's probability distribution used by the ordinary least squares (OLS) estimation procedure:

The strategy involves two steps:

• First, we used the adjusted variance to estimate the variance of the error term's probability distribution: EstVar$[e]$ = SSR/Degress of freedoms.

• Second, we applied the equation relating the variance of the coefficient estimates probability distribution and the variance of the error term's probability distribution: $\text{Var}[b_x] = \text{Var}[e]\Big/\sum_{t=1}^{T}(x_t - \bar{x})^2$.

Step 1: Estimate the variance of the error term's probability distribution from the available information – data from the first quiz

Step 2: Apply the relationship between the variances of coefficient estimate's and error term's probability distributions

$\downarrow$ $\downarrow$

$$\text{EstVar}[e] = \frac{SSR}{\text{Degrees of freedom}} \qquad \text{Var}[b_x] = \frac{\text{Var}[e]}{\sum_{t=1}^{T}(x_t - \bar{x})^2}$$

$$\text{EstVar}[b_x] = \frac{\text{EstVar}[e]}{\sum_{t=1}^{T}(x_t - \bar{x})^2}$$

Unfortunately, when autocorrelation is present, the second step is not justified. To understand why, recall the arithmetic of variances:

Variance of a constant times a variable: Var$[cx]$ = c^2 Var$[x]$

Variance of the sum of a constant and a variable: Var$[c + x]$ = Var$[x]$

Variance of the sum of two variables: Var$[x + y]$ = Var$[x]$ + Var$[y]$ + Cov$[x, y]$

Focus on the variance of the sum of two variables:

Var$[x + y]$ = Var$[x]$ + Var$[y]$ + Cov$[x, y]$

Since the covariance of independent variables equals 0, we can simply ignore the covariance terms when calculating the sum of independent variables. However, if two variables are not independent, their covariance does not equal 0. Consequently, when calculating the variance of the sum of two variables that are not independent we cannot ignore their covariance.

$$\text{Var}[x + y] = \text{Var}[x] + \text{Var}[y] + \text{Cov}[x, y]$$

x and y independent $\qquad\qquad\qquad\qquad$ x and y not independent

$\downarrow$ $\qquad\qquad\qquad\qquad\qquad\qquad\qquad$ $\downarrow$

$\text{Cov}[x, y] = 0$ $\qquad\qquad\qquad\qquad\qquad$ $\text{Cov}[x, y] \neq 0$

$\downarrow$ $\qquad\qquad\qquad\qquad\qquad\qquad\qquad$ $\downarrow$

Can ignore covariance $\qquad\qquad\qquad\qquad$ Cannot ignore covariance

$\downarrow$

$$\text{Var}[x + y] = \text{Var}[x] + \text{Var}[y]$$

Next apply this to the error terms when autocorrelation is absent and when it is present:

When autocorrelation is absent $\qquad\qquad$ When autocorrelation is present

$\downarrow$ $\qquad\qquad\qquad\qquad\qquad\qquad\qquad$ $\downarrow$

The error terms are independent $\qquad\qquad$ The error terms not independent

$\downarrow$ $\qquad\qquad\qquad\qquad\qquad\qquad\qquad$ $\downarrow$

We can ignore the error term covariances $\qquad$ We cannot ignore the error term covariances

We will now review our derivation of the relationship between the variance of the coefficient estimate's probability distribution and the variance of the error term's probability distribution, $\text{Var}[b_x] = \text{Var}[e] \big/ \sum_{t=1}^{T} (x_t - \bar{x})^2$, to illustrate the critical role played by the error term/error term independence premise. We began with the equation for the coefficient estimate:

Equation for coefficient estimate:

$$b_x = \beta_x + \frac{\sum_{t=1}^{T}(x_t - \bar{x})e_t}{\sum_{t=1}^{T}(x_t - \bar{x})^2} = \beta_x + \frac{(x_1 - \bar{x})e_1 + (x_2 - \bar{x})e_2 + (x_3 - \bar{x})e_3}{(x_1 - \bar{x})^2 + (x_2 - \bar{x})^2 + (x_3 - \bar{x})^2}$$

Then we applied a little algebra:[2]

$$\text{Var}[b_x] = \text{Var}\left[\beta_x + \frac{(x_1 - \bar{x})e_1 + (x_2 - \bar{x})e_2 + (x_3 - \bar{x})e_3}{(x_1 - \bar{x})^2 + (x_2 - \bar{x})^2 + (x_3 - \bar{x})^2}\right]$$

Applying $\text{Var}[c + x] = \text{Var}[x]$

---

2. Recall that to keep the algebra straightforward, we assume that the explanatory variables are constants. By doing so, we can apply the arithmetic of variances easily. Our results are unaffected by this assumption.

$$= \mathrm{Var}\left[\frac{(x_1 - \bar{x})e_1 + (x_2 - \bar{x})e_2 + (x_3 - \bar{x})e_3}{(x_1 - \bar{x})^2 + (x_2 - \bar{x})^2 + (x_3 - \bar{x})^2}\right]$$

Rewriting the fraction as a product

$$= \mathrm{Var}\left[\left(\frac{1}{(x_1 - \bar{x})^2 + (x_2 - \bar{x})^2 + (x_3 - \bar{x})^2}\right)\left((x_1 - \bar{x})e_1 + (x_2 - \bar{x})e_2 + (x_3 - \bar{x})e_3\right)\right]$$

Applying $\mathrm{Var}[cx] = c^2\,\mathrm{Var}[x]$

$$= \frac{1}{\left[(x_1 - \bar{x})^2 + (x_2 - \bar{x})^2 + (x_3 - \bar{x})^2\right]^2}\,\mathrm{Var}\left[\left((x_1 - \bar{x})e_1 + (x_2 - \bar{x})e_2 + (x_3 - \bar{x})e_3\right)\right]$$

Error term/error term independence premise: The error terms are independent, $\mathrm{Var}[x + y] = \mathrm{Var}[x] + \mathrm{Var}[y]$

$$= \frac{1}{\left[(x_1 - \bar{x})^2 + (x_2 - \bar{x})^2 + (x_3 - \bar{x})^2\right]^2}\left[\mathrm{Var}[(x_1 - \bar{x})e_1] + \mathrm{Var}[(x_2 - \bar{x})e_2] + \mathrm{Var}[(x_3 - \bar{x})e_3]\right]$$

Applying $\mathrm{Var}[cx] = c^2\,\mathrm{Var}[x]$

$$= \frac{1}{\left[(x_1 - \bar{x})^2 + (x_2 - \bar{x})^2 + (x_3 - \bar{x})^2\right]^2}\left[(x_1 - \bar{x})^2\,\mathrm{Var}[e_1] + (x_2 - \bar{x})^2\,\mathrm{Var}[e_2] + (x_3 - \bar{x})^2\,\mathrm{Var}[e_3]\right]$$

Error term equal variance premise: The error term variance is identical, $\mathrm{Var}[e_1] = \mathrm{Var}[e_2] = \mathrm{Var}[e_3] = \mathrm{Var}[e]$.

Factoring out the $\mathrm{Var}[e]$

$$= \frac{1}{\left[(x_1 - \bar{x})^2 + (x_2 - \bar{x})^2 + (x_3 - \bar{x})^2\right]^2}\left[(x_1 - \bar{x})^2 + (x_2 - \bar{x})^2 + (x_3 - \bar{x})^2\right]\mathrm{Var}[e]$$

Simplifying

$$= \frac{\mathrm{Var}[e]}{(x_1 - \bar{x})^2 + (x_2 - \bar{x})^2 + (x_3 - \bar{x})^2}$$

Generalizing

$$= \frac{\mathrm{Var}[e]}{\sum_{t=1}^{T}(x_t - \bar{x})^2}$$

Focus on the fourth step. When the error term/error term independence premise is satisfied, that is, when the error terms are independent, we can ignore the covariance terms when calculating the variance of a sum of variables:

$$\text{Var}[e] = \frac{1}{\left[(x_1 - \bar{x})^2 + (x_2 - \bar{x})^2 + (x_3 - \bar{x})^2\right]^2} \text{Var}\left[((x_1 - \bar{x})e_1 + (x_2 - \bar{x})e_2 + (x_3 - \bar{x})e_3)\right]$$

Error term/error term independence premise: The error terms are independent: $\text{Var}[x + y] = \text{Var}[x] + \text{Var}[y]$.

When autocorrelation is present, however, the error terms are not independent and the covariance terms cannot be ignored. Therefore, when autocorrelation is present, the fourth step is invalid:

$$\text{Var}[b_x] = \frac{1}{\left[(x_1 - \bar{x})^2 + (x_2 - \bar{x})^2 + (x_3 - \bar{x})^2\right]^2}\left[\text{Var}[(x_1 - \bar{x})e_1] + \text{Var}[(x_2 - \bar{x})e_2] + \text{Var}[(x_3 - \bar{x})e_3]\right]$$

Consequently, in the presence of autocorrelation, the equation we used to describe the relationship between the variances of the probability distribution for the error term and the probability distribution coefficient estimate is no longer valid:

The procedure used by the ordinary least squares (OLS) to estimate the variance of the coefficient estimate's probability distribution is flawed.

Step 1:   Estimate the variance of the error term's probability distribution from the available information—data from the first quiz

Step 2:   Apply the relationship between the variances of coefficient estimate's and error term's probability distributions

$$\downarrow \qquad\qquad\qquad \downarrow$$

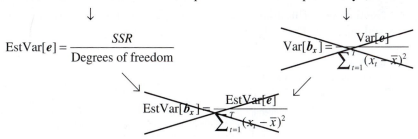

The equation that the ordinary least squares (OLS) estimation procedure uses to estimate the variance of the coefficient estimate's probability distribution is flawed when autocorrelation is present. Consequently, how can we have faith in the variance estimate?

17.3.2   Our Suspicions

Let us summarize. After reviewing the algebra, we suspect that when autocorrelation is present, the ordinary least squares (OLS) estimation procedure for the

• coefficient value will still be unbiased;

• variance of the coefficient estimate's probability distribution may be biased.

17.3.3   Confirming Our Suspicions

We will use a simulation to confirm our suspicions (shown in table 17.1 and figure 17.7).

Econometrics Lab 17.2: The Ordinary Least Squares (GLS) Estimation Procedure and Autocorrelation

[To access this online material, go to http://mitpress.mit.edu/westhoffeconometrics and select Lab 17.2.]

Autocorrelation model: $e_t = \rho e_{t-1} + v_t$ V_t's are independent

As a benchmark, we begin by specifying rho to equal .0; consequently no autocorrelation is present. Click **Start** and then after many, many repetitions click **Stop**. As we observed before, both the estimation procedure for the coefficient value and the estimation procedure for the variance of coefficient estimate's probability distribution are unbiased. When the ordinary least squares (OLS) standard regression premises are met, all is well. But, what happens when autocorrelation is present and the error term/error term independence premise is violated? To investigate this, we set rho to equal .6. Click **Start** and then after many, many repetitions click **Stop**. There is both good news and bad news:

• **Good news:**   The ordinary least squares (OLS) estimation procedure for the coefficient value is still unbiased. The average of the estimated values equals the actual value, 2.

Table 17.1
Autocorrelation simulation results

Sample size 30		Is OLS estimation procedure for the coefficient's value unbiased?		Is OLS estimation procedure for the variance of the of the coefficient estimate's probability distribution unbiased?	
		Actual coefficient value $\downarrow$	Estimate of coefficient value $\downarrow$	Variance of the estimated coefficient values $\downarrow$	Estimate of the variance for coefficient estimate's probability distribution $\downarrow$
Rho	Estim proc	**Actual value of β_x**	**Mean (average) of the estimated values, b_x, from all repetitions**	**Variance of the estimated coefficient values, b_x, from all repetitions**	**Average of estimated variances, $EstVar[b_x]$, from all repetitions**
0	OLS	2.0	≈2.0	≈0.22	≈0.22
0.6	OLS	2.0	≈2.0	≈1.11	≈0.28

Rho

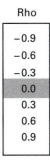

−0.9
−0.6
−0.3
0.0
0.3
0.6
0.9

Figure 17.7
Specifying rho

· **Bad news:** The ordinary least squares (OLS) estimation procedure for the variance of the coefficient estimate's probability distribution is biased. The average the actual variance of the estimated coefficient values equals 1.11 while the average of the estimated variances equals 0.28.

Just as we feared, when autocorrelation is present, the ordinary least squares (OLS) calculations to estimate the variance of the coefficient estimates are flawed.

When the estimation procedure for the variance of the coefficient estimate's probability distribution is biased, all calculations based on the estimate of the variance will be flawed also; that is, the standard errors, t-statistics, and tail probabilities appearing on the ordinary least squares (OLS) regression printout are unreliable. Consequently we will use an example to explore how we account for the presence of autocorrelation.

17.4 Accounting for Autocorrelation: An Example

We can account for autocorrelation by applying the following steps:

Step 1: Apply the ordinary least squares (OLS) estimation procedure. Estimate the model's parameters with the ordinary least squares (OLS) estimation procedure.

Step 2: Consider the possibility of autocorrelation.

· Ask whether there is reason to suspect that autocorrelation may be present.

· Use the ordinary least squares (OLS) regression results to "get a sense" of whether autocorrelation is a problem by examining the residuals.

· Use the Lagrange multiplier approach by estimating an artificial regression to test for the presence of autocorrelation.

· Estimate the value of the autocorrelation parameter, ρ.

Step 3: Apply the generalized least squares (GLS) estimation procedure.

· Apply the model of autocorrelation and algebraically manipulate the original model to derive a new, tweaked model in which the error terms do not suffer from autocorrelation.

• Use the ordinary least squares (OLS) estimation procedure to estimate the parameters of the tweaked model.

Time series data often exhibit autocorrelation. We will consider monthly consumer durables data:

Consumer durable data: Monthly time series data of consumer durable consumption and income statistics 2004 to 2009.

$ConsDur_t$ Consumption of durables in month t (billions of 2005 chained dollars)

$Cons_t$ Consumption in month t (billions of 2005 chained dollars)

Inc_t Disposable income in month t (billions of 2005 chained dollars)

Project: Assess the effect of disposable income on the consumption of consumer durables.

These particular start and end dates were chosen to illustrate the autocorrelation phenomenon clearly.

[To access this online material, go to http://mitpress.mit.edu/westhoffeconometrics and select Consumption and Disposable Income.]

We will focus on a traditional Keynesian model to explain the consumption of consumer durables:

Model: $ConsDur_t = \beta_{Const} + \beta_I Inc_t + e_t$

Economic theory suggests that higher levels of disposable income increase the consumption of consumer durables:

Theory:

$\beta_I > 0$

Higher disposable income increases the consumption of durables.

Step 1:   Apply the ordinary least squares (OLS) estimation procedure (table 17.2).

We now formulate the null and alternative hypotheses:

H_0: $\beta_I = 0$ Higher disposable income does not affect the consumption of durables

H_1: $\beta_I > 0$ Higher disposable income increases the consumption of durables

As always, the null hypothesis challenges the evidence; the alternative hypothesis is consistent with the evidence. Next we calculate Prob[Results IF H_0 true].

Prob[Results IF H_0 true]: What is the probability that the *Inc* coefficient estimate from one repetition of the experiment will be 0.087 or more, if H_0 were true (i.e., if the per capita income has no effect on the Internet use, if β_I actually equals 0)?

Table 17.2
OLS consumer durable regression results

Ordinary least squares (OLS)				
Dependent variable: *ConsDur*				
Explanatory variable(s):	Estimate	SE	*t*-Statistic	Prob
Inc	0.086525	0.016104	5.372763	0.0000
Const	290.7887	155.4793	1.870273	0.0656
Number of observations	72			

Estimated equation: *EstConsDur* = 290.8 + 0.087*Inc*

Interpretation of estimates:

b_{Inc} = 0.087: A $1 increase in real disposable income increases the real consumption of durable goods by $0.087

Critical result: The *Inc* coefficient estimate equals 0.087. This evidence, the positive sign of the coefficient estimate, suggests that higher disposable income increases the consumption of consumer durables thereby supporting the theory.

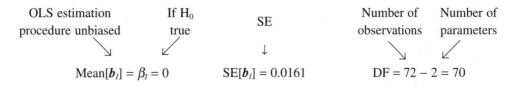

OLS estimation   If H_0 SE   Number of   Number of
procedure unbiased   true   observations   parameters

$\text{Mean}[b_I] = \beta_I = 0$ $\text{SE}[b_I] = 0.0161$ $\text{DF} = 72 - 2 = 70$

Econometrics Lab 17.3: Calculating Prob[Results IF H_0 true]

[To access this online material, go to http://mitpress.mit.edu/westhoffeconometrics and select Lab 17.3.]

To emphasize that the Prob[Results IF H_0 true] depends on the standard error we will use the Econometrics Lab to calculate the probability. The following information has already been entered:

Mean = 0   Value = 0.087

Standard error = 0.0161   Degrees of freedom = 70

Click **Calculate**.

Prob[Results IF H_0 true] = <0.0001

We use the standard error provided by the ordinary least squares (OLS) regression results to compute the Prob[Results IF H_0 true].

We can also calculate the Prob[Results IF H_0 true] by using the tails probability reported in the regression printout. Since this is a one-tailed test, we divide the tails probability by 2:

$$\text{Prob[Results IF } H_0 \text{ true]} = \frac{<0.0001}{2} \approx <0.0001$$

Based on the 1 percent significance level, we would reject that null hypothesis. We would reject the hypothesis that disposable income has no effect on the consumption of consumer durables use.

There may a problem with this, however. The equation used by the ordinary least squares (OLS) estimation procedure to estimate the variance of the coefficient estimate's probability distribution assumes that the error term/error term independence premise is satisfied. Our simulation revealed that when autocorrelation is present and the error term/error term independence premise is violated, the ordinary least squares (OLS) estimation procedure estimating the variance of the coefficient estimate's probability distribution can be flawed. Recall that the standard error equals the square root of the estimated variance. Consequently, if autocorrelation is present, we may have entered the wrong value for the standard error into the Econometrics Lab when we calculated Prob[Results IF H_0 true]. When autocorrelation is present the ordinary least squares (OLS) estimation procedure bases it computations on a faulty premise, resulting in flawed standard errors, t-statistics, and tails probabilities. Consequently we should move on to the next step.

Step 2:   Consider the possibility of autocorrelation.

Unfortunately, there is reason to suspect that autocorrelation may be present. We would expect the consumption of durables are not only influenced by disposable income, but also by the business cycle:

• When the economy is strong, consumer confidence tends to be high; consumers spend more freely and purchase more than "usual." When the economy is strong the error term tends to be positive.

• When the economy is weak, consumer confidence tends to be low; consumers spend less freely and purchase less than "usual." When the economy is weak the error term tends to be negative.

We know that business cycles tend to last for many months, if not years. When the economy is strong, it remains strong for many consecutive months; hence, when the economy is strong we would expect consumers to spend more freely and for the error term to be positive for many consecutive months. On the other hand, when the economy is weak, we would expect consumers to spend less freely and the error term to be negative for many consecutive months.

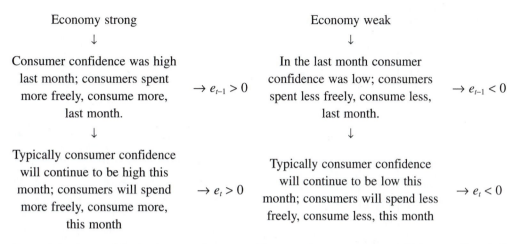

As a consequence of the business cycle we would expect the error term to exhibit some "inertia." Positive error terms tend to follow positive error terms; negative error terms tend to follow negative error terms. So we suspect that the error terms are not independent; instead, we suspect that the error terms will be positively correlated, positive autocorrelation. How can we "test" our suspicions?

Of course, we can never observe the error terms themselves. We can, however, use the residuals to estimate the error terms:

Error term $\quad\quad\quad\quad\quad$ Residual
$\downarrow$ $\quad\quad\quad\quad\quad\quad\quad\quad$ $\downarrow$

$$y_t = \beta_{Const} + \beta_x x_t + e_t \quad\quad\quad Res_t = y_t - Est_t$$
$$\downarrow \quad\quad\quad\quad\quad\quad\quad\quad\quad \downarrow$$
$$e_t = y_t - (\beta_{Const} + \beta_x x_t) \quad\quad Res_t = y_t - (b_{Const} + b_x x_t)$$

We can think of the residuals as the estimated errors. Since the residuals are observable we use the residuals as proxies for the error terms. Figure 17.8 plots the residuals.

The residuals are plotted consecutively, one month after another. As we can easily see, a positive residual is typically followed by another positive residual; a negative residual is typically followed by a negative residual. "Switchovers" do occur, but they are not frequent. This suggests that positive autocorrelation is present. Most statistical software provides a very easy way to look at the residuals.

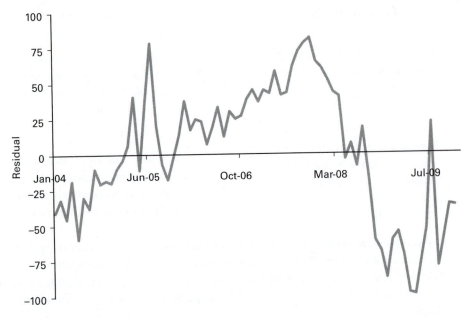

Figure 17.8
Plot of the residuals

Getting Started in EViews

- First, run the regression.
- In the Equation window, click **View**.
- Click **Actual**, **Fitted**, **Residual**.
- Click **Residual Graph**.

It is also instructive to construct a scatter diagram (figure 17.9) of the residuals versus the residuals lagged one month. Most of the scatter diagram points lie in the first and third quadrants. The residuals are positively correlated.

Since the residual plots suggest that our fears are warranted, we now test the autocorrelation model more formally. While there are many different approaches, we will focus on the Lagrange multiplier (LM) approach, which uses an artificial regression to test for autocorrelation.[3] We will proceed by reviewing a mathematical model of autocorrelation.

---

3. The Durbin–Watson statistic is the traditional method of testing for autocorrelation. Unfortunately, the distribution of the Durbin–Watson statistic depends on the distribution of the explanatory variable. This makes hypotheses testing with the Durbin–Watson statistic more complicated than with the Lagrange multiplier test. Consequently we will focus on the Lagrange multiplier test.

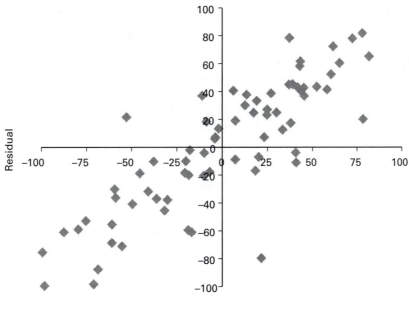

Figure 17.9
Scatter diagram of the residuals

Autocorrelation model: $e_t = \rho e_{t-1} + v_t$

where v_t's are independent,

$$\rho = 0 \qquad\qquad\qquad \rho \neq 0$$

$$\downarrow \qquad\qquad\qquad\qquad \downarrow$$

$$e_t = v_t \qquad\qquad e_t \text{ depends on } e_{t-1}$$

$$\downarrow \qquad\qquad\qquad\qquad \downarrow$$

No autocorrelation   Autocorrelation present

In this case we believe that ρ is positive. A positive rho provides the error term with inertia. A positive error term tends to follow a positive error term and a negative error term tends to follow a negative term. But also note that there is a second term, v_t. The v_t's are independent; they represent random influences that affect the error term also. It is the v_t's that "switch" the sign of the error term.

Now we combine the original model with the autocorrelation model:

Original model: $y_t = \beta_{Const} + \beta_x x_t + e_t$ e_t's are unobservable

Autocorrelation model: $e_t = \rho e_{t-1} + v_t$ v_t's are independent

Ordinary least squares (OLS) estimate: $Esty_t = b_{Const} + b_x x_t$

Residuals: $Res_t = y_t - Esty_t$ Res_t's are observable

Res_t = y_t $-$ $Esty_t$ Substituting for y_t,
$$y_t = \beta_{Const} + \beta_x x_t + e_t$$

$\downarrow$

= β_{Const} + $\beta_x x_t$ + e_t $-$ $Esty_t$ Substituting for e_t,
$$e_t = \rho e_{t-1} + v_t$$

$\downarrow$

= β_{Const} + $\beta_x x_t$ + $\rho e_{t-1} + v_t$ $-$ $Esty_t$ Substituting for $Esty_t$,
$$Esty_t = b_{Const} + b_x x_t$$

$\downarrow$

= β_{Const} + $\beta_x x_t$ + $\rho e_{t-1} + v_t$ $-$ $(b_{Const} + b_x x_t)$

Rearranging terms

= $(\beta_{Const} - b_{Const})$ + $(\beta_x - b_x)x_t$ + ρe_{t-1} + v_t Cannot observe e_{t-1} use Res_{t-1} instead

$\downarrow$

= $(\beta_{Const} - b_{Const})$ + $(\beta_x - b_x)x_t$ + ρRes_{t-1} + v_t

NB: Since the v_t's are independent, we need not worry about autocorrelation here.
Most statistical software allows us to easily assess this model (table 17.3).

Getting Started in EViews

- First, run the regression.
- In the Equation window, click **View**.
- Click **Residual Diagnostics**.
- Click **Serial Correlation LM Test**.
- Change the number of Lags to include from 2 to 1.

Critical result: The *Resid(−1)* coefficient estimate equals 0.8394. The positive sign of the coefficient estimate suggests that an increase in last period's residual increases this period's residual. This evidence suggests that autocorrelation is present.

Now we formulate the null and alternative hypotheses:

Table 17.3
Lagrange multiplier test results

Lagrange multiplier (LR)				
Dependent variable: *Resid*				
Explanatory variable(s):	Estimate	SE	*t*-Statistic	Prob
Inc	−0.002113	0.008915	−0.237055	0.8133
Const	19.96027	86.07134	0.231904	0.8173
Resid(−1)	0.839423	0.066468	12.62904	0.0000
Number of observations	72			
Presample missing value lagged residuals set to zero				

H_0: $\rho = 0$ No autocorrelation present

H_1: $\rho > 0$ Positive autocorrelation present

The null hypothesis challenges the evidence by asserting that no autocorrelation is present. The alternative hypothesis is consistent with the evidence.

Next we calculate Prob[Results IF H_0 true].

Prob[Results IF H_0 true]: What is the probability that the coefficient estimate from one regression would be 0.8394 or more, if the H_0 were true (i.e., if no autocorrelation were actually present, if ρ actually equals 0)?

Using the tails probability reported in the regression printout obtains

Prob[Results IF H_0 True] <0.0001

Autocorrelation appears to be present; accordingly, we will now return to the autocorrelation model to estimate the parameter, ρ.

Autocorrelation model: $e_t = \rho e_{t-1} + v_t$

where v_t's are independent,

$\rho = 0$ $\rho \neq 0$

↓   ↓

$e_t = v_t$ e_t depends on e_{t-1}

↓   ↓

No autocorrelation   Autocorrelation present

In practice there are a variety of ways to estimate ρ. We will discuss what is perhaps the most straightforward. Since the error terms are unobservable, we "replace" the error terms with the residuals:

Table 17.4
Regression results—Estimating ρ

	Ordinary least squares (OLS)			
Dependent variable: *Residual*				
Explanatory variable(s):	Estimate	SE	*t*-Statistic	Prob
ResidualLag	0.839023	0.064239	13.06089	0.0000
Number of observations	71			

Estimated equation: $Residual = 0.0890 ResidualLag$

Critical result: The *ResidualLag* coefficient estimate equals 0.8390; that is, the estimated value of ρ equals 0.8390.

Model:
$$e_t = \rho e_{t-1} + v_t$$
$$\downarrow \qquad \downarrow$$
$$Res_t = \rho Res_{t-1} + v_t$$

where v_t's are independent. Note that there is no constant in this model (table 17.4).

Estimate of $\rho = Est\rho = 0.8390$

Getting Started in EViews

• Run the original regression; EViews automatically calculates the residuals and places them in the variable **resid**.

• EViews automatically modifies *Resid* every time a regression is run. Consequently we will now generate two new variables before running the next regression to prevent a "clash:"

residual = resid

residuallag = residual(−1)

• Now specify **residual** as the dependent variable and **residuallag** as the explanatory variable; do not forget to "delete" the constant.

Step 3: Apply the generalized least squares (GLS) estimation procedure.

Strategy: Our strategy for dealing with autocorrelation will be similar to our strategy for dealing with heteroskedasticity. Algebraically manipulate the original model so that the problem of autocorrelation is eliminated in the new model. That is, tweak the original model so that the error terms in the tweaked model are independent.

We can accomplish this with a little algebra. We begin with the original model and then apply the autocorrelation model:

Original model: $y_t = \beta_{Const} + \beta_x x_t + e_t$

Autocorrelation model: $e_t = \rho e_{t-1} + v_t$

where v_t's are independent.
Original model for period t:

$$y_t = \beta_{Const} + \beta_x x_t + e_t$$

Original model for period $t - 1$:

$$y_{t-1} = \beta_{Const} + \beta_x x_{t-1} + e_{t-1}$$

Multiplying by ρ,

$$\rho y_{t-1} = \rho\beta_{Const} + \rho\beta_x x_{t-1} + \rho e_{t-1}$$

Rewrite the equations for y_t and by ρy_{t-1}:

$$y_t = \beta_{Const} + \beta_x x_t + e_t$$

$$\rho y_{t-1} = \rho\beta_{Const} + \rho\beta_x x_{t-1} + \rho e_{t-1}$$

Subtracting

$$y_t - \rho y_{t-1} \;=\; \beta_{Const} - \rho\beta_{Const} \;+\; \beta_x x_t - \rho\beta_x x_{t-1} + e_t - \rho e_{t-1}$$

$$\downarrow \qquad \text{Factoring out } \beta_x$$

$$y_t - \rho y_{t-1} \;=\; \beta_{Const} - \rho\beta_{Const} \;+\; \beta_x(x_t - \rho x_{t-1}) + e_t - \rho e_{t-1}$$

$$\downarrow \qquad \text{Substituting for } e_t$$

$$y_t - \rho y_{t-1} \;=\; \beta_{Const} - \rho\beta_{Const} \;+\; \beta_x(x_t - \rho x_{t-1}) + \rho e_{t-1} + v_t - \rho e_{t-1}$$

$$\downarrow \qquad \text{Simplifying}$$

$$(y_t - \rho y_{t-1}) = (\beta_{Const} - \rho\beta_{Const}) + \beta_x(x_t - \rho x_{t-1}) + v_t$$

In the tweaked model:

New dependent variable: $y_t - \rho y_{t-1}$

New explanatory variable: $x_t - \rho x_{t-1}$

Critical point: In the tweaked model, v_t's are independent; hence we need not be concerned about autocorrelation in the tweaked model.

Now let us run the tweaked regression for our example; using the estimate of ρ, we generate two new variables:

New dependent variable: $AdjConsDur_t = y_t - Est\rho y_{t-1}$

$$AdjConsDur_t = ConsDur_t - 0.8390 ConsDur_{t-1}$$

Table 17.5
GLS regression results—Accounting for autocorrelation

Ordinary least squares (OLS)				
Dependent variable: *AdjConsDur*				
Explanatory variable(s):	Estimate	SE	*t*-Statistic	Prob
AdjInc	0.040713	0.028279	1.439692	0.1545
Const	118.9134	44.43928	2.675861	0.0093
Number of observations	71			

Estimated equation: $EstAdjConsDur = 118.9 + 0.041Inc$

Interpretation of estimates:

$b_{AdjInc} = 0.041$: A \$1 increase in real disposable income increases the real consumption of durable goods by \$0.041

Critical result: The *Inc* coefficient estimate equals 0.041. This evidence, the positive sign of the coefficient estimate, suggests that higher disposable income increases the consumption of consumer durables thereby supporting the theory.

New explanatory variable: $AdjInc_t = x_t - Est\rho x_{t-1}$
$$AdjInc_t = Inc_t - 0.8390Inc_{t-1}$$

Then we estimate the tweaked model (table 17.5):

We now review of null and alternative hypotheses:

H_0: $\beta_I = 0$ Higher disposable income does not affect the consumption of durables

H_1: $\beta_I > 0$ Higher disposable income increases the consumption of durables

Then, using the tails probability, we calculate Prob[Results IF H_0 true]:

$$\text{Prob[Results IF } H_0 \text{ true]} = \frac{0.1545}{2} \approx 0.0772$$

After accounting for autocorrelation, we cannot reject the null hypothesis at the 1 or 5 percent significance levels.

Let us now compare the disposable income coefficient estimate in last regression, the generalized least squares (GLS) regression that accounts for autocorrelation, with the disposable income coefficient estimate in the ordinary least squares (OLS) regression that does not account for autocorrelation (table 17.6). The most striking differences are the calculations that are based on the estimated variance of the coefficient probability distribution: the coefficient's standard error, *t*-statistic, and tails probability. The standard error nearly doubles when we account for autocorrelation. This is hardly surprising. The ordinary least squares (OLS) regression calculations are based on the premise that the error terms are independent. Our analysis suggests that this is not true. The general least squares (GLS) regression accounts for error term correlation. The standard

Table 17.6
Coefficient estimate comparison

	β_t Coefficient estimate	Standard error	t-Statistic	Tails probability
Ordinary least squares (OLS)	0.087	0.016	5.37	<0.0001
Generalized least squares (GLS)	0.041	0.028	1.44	0.1545

Table 17.7
Autocorrelation simulation results

Sample size: 30		Actual value of β_x	Mean (average) of the estimated values, b_x, from all repetitions	Variance of the estimated coefficient values, b_x, from all repetitions
Rho	Estim proc			
0.6	OLS	2.0	≈ 2.0	≈ 1.11
0.6	GLS	2.0	≈ 2.0	≈ 1.01

error, t-statistic, and tails probability in the general least squares (GLS) regression differ substantially.

17.5   Justifying the Generalized Least Squares (GLS) Estimation Procedure

We will now use a simulation to illustrate that the generalize least squares (GLS) estimation procedure indeed provides "better" estimates than the ordinary least squares (OLS) estimation procedure. While both procedures provide unbiased estimates of the coefficient's value, only the generalized least squares (GLS) estimation procedure provides an unbiased estimate of the variance.

Econometrics Lab 17.4: Generalized Least Squares (GLS) Estimation Procedure

[To access this online material, go to http://mitpress.mit.edu/westhoffeconometrics and select Lab 17.4.]

As before, choose a rho of 0.6; by default the ordinary least squares (OLS) estimation procedure is chosen. Click **Start** and then after many, many repetitions click **Stop**. When the ordinary least squares (OLS) estimation procedure is used, the variance of the estimated coefficient values equals about 1.11. Now specify the generalized least squares (GLS) estimation procedure by clicking GLS. Click **Start** and then after many, many repetitions click **Stop**. When the generalized least squares (GLS) estimation procedure is used, the variance of the estimated coefficient values is less, 1.01. Consequently the generalized least squares (GLS) estimation procedure provides more reliable estimates (table 17.7).

Table 17.8
OLS regression results—Robust standard errors

Ordinary least squares (OLS)				
Dependent variable: *ConsDur*				
Explanatory variable(s):	Estimate	SE	*t*-Statistic	Prob
Inc	0.086525	0.028371	3.049804	0.0032
Const	290.7887	268.3294	1.083701	0.2822
Number of observations	72			

Estimated equation: $EstConsDur = 290.8 + 0.087Inc$

Interpretation of estimates:

$b_{Inc} = 0.087$: A \$1 increase in real disposable income increases the real consumption of durable goods by \$0.087.

17.6   Robust Standard Errors

Like heteroskedasticity, two issues emerge when autocorrelation is present:

• The standard error calculations made by the ordinary least squares (OLS) estimation procedure are flawed.

• While the ordinary least squares (OLS) for the coefficient value is unbiased, it is not the best linear unbiased estimation procedure (BLUE).

As before, robust standard errors address the first issue arising when autocorrelation is present. Newey–West standard errors provide one such approach that is suitable for both autocorrelation and heteroskedasticity. This approach applies the same type of logic that we used to motivate the White approach for heteroskedasticity, but it is more complicated. Consequently we will not attempt to motivate the approach here. Statistical software makes it easy to compute Newey–West robust standard errors (table 17.8).[4]

[To access this online material, go to http://mitpress.mit.edu/westhoffeconometrics and select Consumption and Disposable Income.]

Getting Started in EViews

• Run the ordinary least squares (OLS) regression.

• In the Equation window, click **Estimate** and **Options**.

• In the Coefficient covariance matrix box select HAC (Newey–West) from the dropdown list.

• Click **OK**.

---

4. While it is beyond the scope of this textbook, it can be shown that while this estimation procedure is biased, the magnitude of the bias diminishes and approaches zero as the sample size approaches infinity.

Chapter 17 Review Questions

1. In words, what is autocorrelation?

2. When autocorrelation is present, are all the standard ordinary least (OLS) premises satisfied? If not, which one(s) is violated?

3. Suppose that autocorrelation is present in a regression.

    a. What is the "good news?"

    b. What is the "bad news?"

4. When autocorrelation is present, what strategy do we use to account for it?

Chapter 17 Exercises

Petroleum consumption data for Massachusetts: Annual time series data of petroleum consumption and prices for Massachusetts from 1970 to 2004.

PetroCons$_t$	Consumption of petroleum for observation t (1,000s of gallons)
PetroConsPC$_t$	Per capita consumption of petroleum for observation t (gallons)
Pop$_t$	Population for observation t (persons)
PriceReal$_t$	Real price of petroleum for observation t (1982–84 dollars per gallon)
Year$_t$	Year

1. Consider the following linear model:

$$PetroConsPC_t = \beta_{Const} + \beta_P PriceReal_t + e_t$$

    a. Develop a theory regarding how the explanatory variable influences the dependent variable. What does your theory imply about the sign of each coefficient?

    b. Using the ordinary least squares (OLS) estimation procedure, estimate the value of each coefficient. Interpret the coefficient estimates. What are the critical results?

[To access this online material, go to http://mitpress.mit.edu/westhoffeconometrics and select Petroleum Consumption—Mass.]

    c. Formulate the null and alternative hypotheses.

    d. Calculate Prob[Results IF H$_0$ true] and assess your theory.

2. Consider the possibility of autocorrelation.

[To access this online material, go to http://mitpress.mit.edu/westhoffeconometrics and select Petroleum Consumption—Mass.]

a. Time series data often exhibit autocorrelation. Consequently plot the residuals. Does the plot of the residuals possible suggest the presence of autocorrelation?

b. Use the Lagrange multiplier approach by estimating an artificial regression to test for the presence of autocorrelation.

c. Estimate the value of the autocorrelation parameter, ρ.

3. Apply the generalized least squares (GLS) estimation procedure.

[To access this online material, go to http://mitpress.mit.edu/westhoffeconometrics and select Petroleum Consumption—Mass.]

a. Apply the model of autocorrelation and algebraically manipulate the original model to derive a new, tweaked model in which the error terms do not suffer from autocorrelation.

b. Use the ordinary least squares (OLS) estimation procedure to estimate the parameters of the tweaked model.

4. How, if at all, does accounting for autocorrelation affect the assessment of your theory?

Crime data for California: Annual time series data of crime and economic statistics for California from 1989 to 2008.

$CrimesAll_t$ Crimes per 100,000 persons in year t

$IncPC_t$ Per capita disposable personal income in year t (1982–84 dollars)

$UnemRate_t$ Unemployment rate in year t (percent)

$State_t$ Name of state t

5. Apply the ordinary least squares (OLS) estimation procedure.

a. Consider the following linear model:

$$CrimesAll_t = \beta_{Const} + \beta_I IncPC_t + \beta_{Un} UnemRate_t + e_t$$

Develop a theory regarding how the explanatory variable influences the dependent variable. What does your theory imply about the sign of each coefficient?

b. Using the ordinary least squares (OLS) estimation procedure, estimate the value of each coefficient. Do the signs of the coefficient estimates lend support for your theory?

[To access this online material, go to http://mitpress.mit.edu/westhoffeconometrics and select Crime in California.]

c. Formulate the null and alternative hypotheses.

d. Calculate Prob[Results IF H_0 true] and assess your theory.

6. Consider the possibility of autocorrelation.

[To access this online material, go to http://mitpress.mit.edu/westhoffeconometrics and select Crime in California.]

a. Time series data often exhibit autocorrelation. Consequently plot the residuals. Does the plot of the residuals possible suggest the presence of autocorrelation?

b. Use the Lagrange multiplier approach by estimating an artificial regression to test for the presence of autocorrelation.

c. Estimate the value of the autocorrelation parameter, ρ.

7. Apply the generalized least squares (GLS) estimation procedure.

[To access this online material, go to http://mitpress.mit.edu/westhoffeconometrics and select Crime in California.]

a. Apply the model of autocorrelation and algebraically manipulate the original model to derive a new, tweaked model in which the error terms do not suffer from autocorrelation.

b. Use the ordinary least squares (OLS) estimation procedure to estimate the parameters of the tweaked model.

8. How, if at all, does accounting for autocorrelation affect the assessment of your theories?

18 Explanatory Variable/Error Term Independence Premise, Consistency, and Instrumental Variables

Chapter 18 Prep Questions

1. Consider the following model:

$$y_t = \beta_{Const} + \beta_x x_t + e_t, \qquad t = 1, 2, \ldots, T$$

where

y_t = dependent variable

e_t = error term

x_t = explanatory variable

T = sample size

Suppose that the actual constant equals 6 and the actual coefficient equals 1/2:

$$\beta_{Const} = 6, \quad \beta_x = \frac{1}{2}$$

Also suppose that the sample size is 6. The following table reports the value of the explanatory variable and the error term for each of the six observations:

Observation	x_t	e_t
1	2	4
2	6	2
3	10	3
4	14	-2
5	18	-1
6	22	-4

   a. On a sheet of graph paper place x on the horizontal axis and e on the vertical axis.

   i. Plot a scatter diagram of x and e.

   ii. As x_t increases, does e_t typically increase or decrease?

   iii. Is e_t positively or negatively correlated with x_t?

   b. Immediately below this graph construct a second graph with x on the horizontal axis and y on the vertical axis.

   i. Plot the line depicting the actual equation, the line representing the actual constant and the actual coefficient:

$$y = 6 + \frac{1}{2}x$$

ii. Fill in the following blanks for each observation t:

Observation	x_t	e_t	y_t
1	2	4	_____
2	6	2	_____
3	10	3	_____
4	14	−2	_____
5	18	−1	_____
6	22	−4	_____

iii. Plot the x and y values for each of the six observations.

c. Based on the points you plotted in your second graph, "eyeball" the best fitting line and sketch it in.

d. How are the slope of the line representing the actual equation and the slope of the best fitting line related?

2. Recall the poll Clint conducted to estimate the fraction of the student population that supported him in the upcoming election for class president. He used the following approach:

Random sample technique: Write the name of each individual in the population on a 3×5 card.

Perform the following procedure 16 times:

· Thoroughly shuffle the cards.

· Randomly draw one card.

· Ask that individual if he/she is voting for Clint and record the answer.

· Replace the card.

Calculate the fraction of the sample supporting Clint.

   Now consider an alternative approach. You are visiting Clint in his dorm room when he asks you to conduct the poll. Instead of writing the name of each individual on a 3×5 card, you simply leave Clint's room and ask the first 16 people you run into how he/she will vote:

Nonrandom Sample Technique:

· Leave Clint's dorm room and ask the first 16 people you run into if he/she is voting for Clint.

· Calculate the fraction of the sample supporting Clint.

Use the Econometrics Lab to simulate the two sampling techniques (figure 18.1).

[To access this online material, go to http://mitpress.mit.edu/westhoffeconometrics and select Lab 18P.2.]

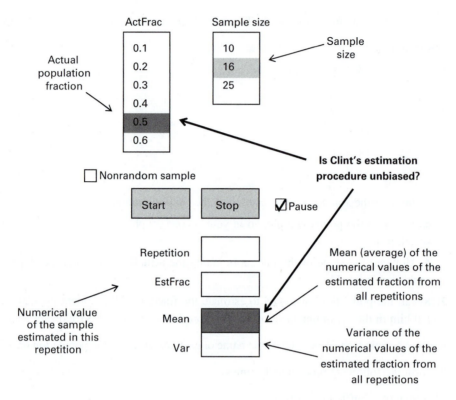

Figure 18.1
Opinion Poll simulation

a. Answer the questions posed in the lab, and then fill in the following blanks:

After many, many repetitions

Sampling technique	Population fraction	Sample size	Mean (average) of estimates	Magnitude of bias	Variance of estimates
Random	0.50	16	_____	_____	_____
Nonrandom	0.50	16	_____	_____	_____
Nonrandom	0.50	25	_____	_____	_____
Nonrandom	0.50	100	_____	_____	_____

Focus on the nonrandom sampling technique.

b. What happens to the mean of the estimated fraction as the sample size increases?

c. Explain why your answer to part b "makes sense." To do so, consider the following questions:

i. Compared to the general student population, are the students who live near Clint more likely to be Clint's friends?

ii. Compared to the general student population, are the students who live near Clint more likely to vote for him?

iii. Would the nonrandom sampling technique bias the poll in Clint's favor?

iv. What happens to the magnitude of the bias as the sample size increases? Explain.

d. As the sample size increases, what happens to the variance of the estimates?

18.1 Review

18.1.1 Regression Model

We begin by reviewing the basic regression model:

$$y_t = \beta_{Const} + \beta_x x_t + e_t, \qquad t = 1, 2, \ldots, T$$

where

y_t = dependent variable

e_t = error term

x_t = explanatory variable

T = sample size

The error term is a random variable that represents random influences:

$$\text{Mean}[e_t] = 0$$

18.1.2 The Standard Ordinary Least Squares (OLS) Premises

Recall the standard ordinary least squares (OLS) regression premises:

• **Error term equal variance premise:**   The variance of the error term's probability distribution for each observation is the same; all the variances equal Var[e]:

$$\text{Var}[e_1] = \text{Var}[e_2] = \ldots = \text{Var}[e_T] = \text{Var}[e]$$

• **Error term/error term independence premise:**   The error terms are independent: Cov[e_i, e_j] = 0.

Knowing the value of the error term from one observation does not help us predict the value of the error term for any other observation.

• **Explanatory variable/error term independence premise:**   The explanatory variables, the x_t's, and the error terms, the e_t's, are not correlated.

Knowing the value of an observation's explanatory variable does not help us predict the value of that observation's error term.

18.1.3   Estimation Procedures Embedded within the Ordinary Least Squares (OLS) Estimation Procedure

The ordinary least squares (OLS) estimation procedure includes three important estimation procedures:

• Values of the regression parameters, β_x and β_{Const}:

$$b_x = \frac{\sum_{t=1}^{T}(y_t - \overline{y})(x_t - \overline{x})}{\sum_{t=1}^{T}(x_t - \overline{x})^2} \quad \text{and} \quad b_{Const} = \overline{y} - b_x\overline{x}$$

• Variance of the error term's probability distribution, Var[e]:

$$\text{EstVar}[e] = \frac{SSR}{\text{Degrees of freedom}}$$

• Variance of the coefficient estimate's probability distribution, Var[b_x]:

$$\text{EstVar}[b_x] = \frac{\text{EstVar}[e]}{\sum_{t=1}^{T}(x_t - \overline{x})^2}$$

When the standard ordinary least squares (OLS) regression premises are met:

• Each estimation procedure is unbiased; that is, each estimation procedure does not systematically underestimate or overestimate the actual value.

• The ordinary least squares (OLS) estimation procedure for the coefficient value is the best linear unbiased estimation procedure (BLUE).

Crucial point: When the ordinary least squares (OLS) estimation procedure performs its calculations, it implicitly assumes that the standard ordinary least squares (OLS) regression premises are satisfied.

18.2   Taking Stock and a Preview: The Ordinary Least Squares (OLS) Estimation Procedure

The ordinary least square (OLS) estimation procedure is economist's most widely used estimation procedure. When contemplating the use of this procedure, we should keep two issues in mind: Is the ordinary least squares (OLS) estimation procedure for the coefficient value unbiased? If unbiased, is the ordinary least squares (OLS) estimation procedure reliable in the following two ways:

• Can the calculations for the standard errors be trusted?

• Is the ordinary least square (OLS) estimation procedure for the coefficient value the most reliable, the best linear unbiased estimation procedure (BLUE)?

In the previous two chapters we showed that the violation the first two standard ordinary least squares (OLS) premises, the error term equal variance premise and the error term/error term independence premise, does not cause the ordinary least squares (OLS) estimation procedure for the coefficient value to be biased. This was good news. We then focused on the reliability issue. We learned that the standard error calculations could not be trusted and that the ordinary least squares (OLS) estimation procedure was not the best linear unbiased estimation procedure (BLUE). In this chapter we turn our attention to the third premise, explanatory variable/error term independence. Unfortunately, violation of the third premise does cause the ordinary least squares (OLS) estimation procedure for the coefficient value to be biased. The explanatory variable/error term independence premise determines whether or not the ordinary least squares (OLS) estimation procedure is unbiased or biased. Figure 18.2 summarizes the roles played by the three standard premises.

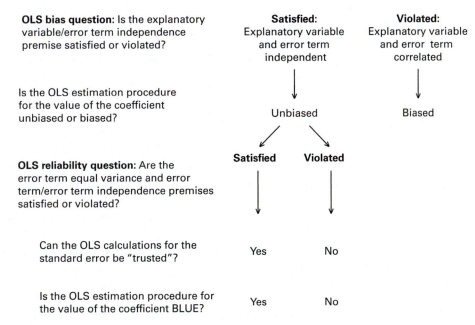

Figure 18.2
OLS bias and reliability flow diagram

This chapter begins by explaining why bias results when the explanatory variable/error term independence premise is violated. Next we introduce a new property that is used to describe estimation procedures, consistency. Typically, consistency is considered to be not as desirable as is being unbiased, but in some cases, estimation procedures that are biased sometimes meet the consistency standard. We close the chapter by introducing one such procedure: the Instrumental Variables (IV) estimation procedure.

18.3   A Closer Look at the Explanatory Variable/Error Term Independence Premise

We begin by using a simulation to illustrate the explanatory variable/error term independence premise:

· **Explanatory variable/error term independence premise:**   The explanatory variables, the x_t's, and the error terms, the e_t's, are not correlated. Knowing the value of an observation's explanatory variable does not help us predict the value of that observation's error term.

Econometrics Lab 18.1: Explanatory Variable/Error Term Independence and Correlation

[To access this online material, go to http://mitpress.mit.edu/westhoffeconometrics and select Lab 18.1.]

Initially the explanatory variable/error term correlation coefficient equals 0. Be certain that the Pause checkbox is checked. Then click the **Start** button. Note that the blue points indicate the observations with low x values, the black points the observations medium x values, and the red points the observations with high x values. Click the **Start** button a few more times to convince yourself that this is always true. Now clear the Pause checkbox and click **Start**. After many, many repetitions, click **Stop**. Note that the scatter diagram points are distributed more or less evenly across the graph as shown in figure 18.3.

Since the points are spread evenly, knowing the value of the explanatory variable, x_t, does not help us predict the value of the error term, e_t. The explanatory variable and the error term are independent: the explanatory variable/error term independence premise is satisfied. The value of x, low, medium, or high, does not affect the mean of the error terms. The mean is approximately 0 in each case (figure 18.4).

Next we select 0.60 in the Corr X&E list. Consequently the explanatory variable and error term are now positively correlated. After many, many repetitions we observe that the explanatory variable and the error term are no longer independent. The scatter diagram points are no longer spread evenly; a pattern emerges. As illustrated in figure 18.5, as the value of explanatory variable rises, the error term tends to rise also:

· When the value of the explanatory variable is low, the error term is typically negative. The mean of the low x value error terms is negative (figure 18.6).

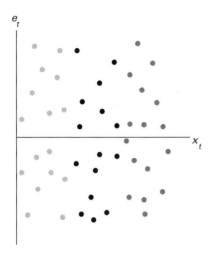

Figure 18.3
Scatter diagram—Corr X&E = 0

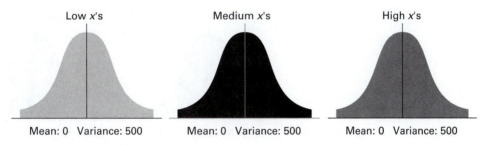

Low *x*'s	Medium *x*'s	High *x*'s
Mean: 0 Variance: 500	Mean: 0 Variance: 500	Mean: 0 Variance: 500

Figure 18.4
Error term probability distributions—Corr X&E = 0

• When the value of the explanatory variable is high and the error term is typically positive. The mean of the high *x* value error terms is positive (figure 18.6).

Last, we select −0.60 in the Corr X&E list. Again, the scatter diagram points are not spread evenly (figure 18.7). The explanatory variable and error term are now negatively correlated. As the value of explanatory variable rises, the error term falls:

• When the value of the explanatory variable is low, the error term is typically positive. The mean of the low *x* value error terms is positive.

• When the value of the explanatory variable is high, the error term is typically negative. The mean of the high *x* value error terms is negative.

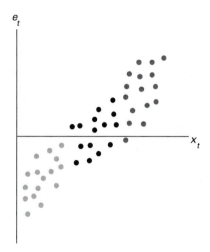

Figure 18.5
Scatter diagram—Corr X&E = 0.6

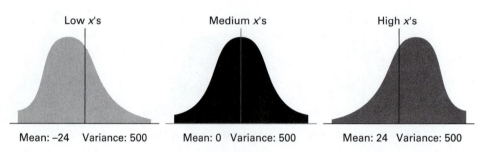

Figure 18.6
Error term probability distributions—Corr X&E = 0.6

We will proceed by explaining geometrically why correlation between the explanatory variables and error terms biases the ordinary least squares (OLS) estimation procedure for coefficient value. Then we will use a simulation to confirm our logic.

18.4   Explanatory Variable/Error Term Correlation and Bias

18.4.1   Geometric Motivation

Focus attention on figure 18.8. The line in the lower two graphs represent the actual relationship between the dependent variable, y_t, and the explanatory variable, x_t:

$$y_t = \beta_{Const} + \beta_x x_t$$

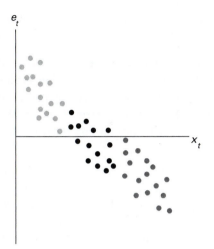

Figure 18.7
Corr X&E = −0.6

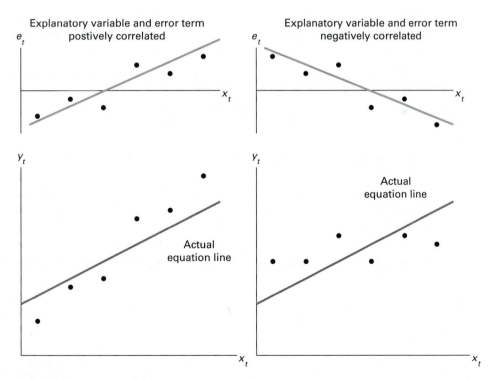

Figure 18.8
Explanatory variable/error term correlation

β_{Const} is the actual constant and β_x the actual coefficient. Now we will examine the left and right panels:

• Left panels of figure 18.8:   The explanatory variable, x_t, and error term, e_t, are positively correlated as illustrated in the top left scatter diagram. The e_t tends to be low for low values of x_t and high for high values of x_t. Now consider the bottom left scatter diagram in which the x_t's and y_t's are plotted. When the explanatory variable and the error term are positively correlated, the scatter diagram points tend to lie below the actual equation line for low values of x_t and above the actual equation line for high values of x_t.

• Right panels of figure 18.8:   The explanatory variable, x_t, and error term, e_t, are negatively correlated as illustrated in the top right scatter diagram. The e_t tends to be tends to be high for low values of x_t and low for high variables of x_t. Now consider the bottom right scatter diagram in which the x_t's and y_t's are plotted. When the explanatory variable and the error term are negatively correlated, the scatter diagram points tend to lie above the actual regression line for low values of x_t and below the actual regression line for high values of x_t.

In figure 18.9 we have added the best fitting line for each of the two panels:

• Left panels of figure 18.9:   When the explanatory variable and error terms are positively correlated the best fitting line is more steeply sloped that the actual equation line; consequently the ordinary least squares (OLS) estimation procedure for the coefficient value is biased upward.

• Right panels of figure 18.9:   When the explanatory variable and error terms are negatively correlated the best fitting line is less steeply sloped than the actual equation line; consequently, the ordinary least squares (OLS) estimation procedure for the coefficient value is biased downward.

18.4.2   Confirming Our Suspicions

Based on our logic we would expect the ordinary least squares (OLS) estimation procedure for the coefficient value to be biased whenever the explanatory variable and the error term are correlated.

Econometrics Lab 18.2: Ordinary Least Squares (OLS) and Explanatory Variable/Error Term Correlation

[To access this online material, go to http://mitpress.mit.edu/westhoffeconometrics and select Lab 18.2.]

We can confirm our logic using a simulation. As a base case, we begin with 0.00 specified in the Corr X&E list; the explanatory variables and error terms are independent. Click **Start** and then after many, many repetitions click **Stop**. The simulation confirms that no bias results whenever the explanatory variable/error term independence premise is satisfied.

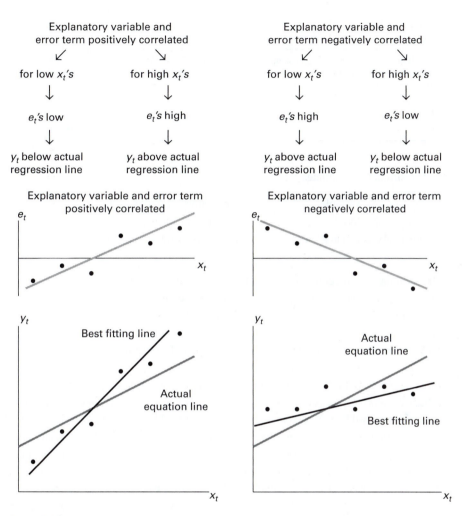

Figure 18.9
Explanatory variable/error term correlation with best fitting line

Now, specify 0.30 in the Corr X&E list; the explanatory variable and error terms are positively correlated. Click **Start** and then after many, many repetitions click **Stop**. The average of the estimated coefficient values, 6.1, exceeds the actual value, 2.0; the ordinary least squares (OLS) estimation procedure for the coefficient value is biased upward whenever the explanatory variable and error terms are positively correlated. By selecting -0.6 from the "Corr X&E" list, we can show that downward bias results whenever the explanatory variable and error terms are negatively correlated. The average of the estimated coefficient values, -2.1, is less than the actual value, 2.0 (table 18.1).

Table 18.1
Explanatory variable/error term correlation—Simulation results

Estimation procedure	Corr X&E	Sample size	Actual coef	Mean of coef ests	Magnitude of bias	Variance of coef ests
OLS	0.00	50	2.0	≈2.0	≈0.0	≈4.0
OLS	0.30	50	2.0	≈6.1	≈4.1	≈3.6
OLS	−0.30	50	2.0	≈−2.1	≈4.1	≈3.6

The simulation validates our logic:

Explanatory variable and error term positively correlated	Explanatory variable and error term negatively correlated
↓	↓
OLS estimation procedure for the coefficient value is biased upward	OLS estimation procedure for the coefficient value is biased downward

18.5   Estimation Procedures: Small and Large Sample Properties

Explanatory variable/error term correlation creates a problem for the ordinary least squares (OLS) estimation procedure. Positive correlation causes upward bias and negative correlation causes downward bias. What can we do in these cases? Econometricians respond to this question very pragmatically by adopting the philosophy that "half a loaf is better than none." In general, we use different estimation procedures that, while still biased, may meet an arguably less demanding criterion called consistency. In most cases, consistency is not as desirable as is being unbiased; nevertheless, if we cannot find an unbiased estimation procedure, consistency proves to be better than nothing. After all, "half a loaf is better than none." To explain the notion of consistency, we begin by reviewing what it means for an estimation procedure to be unbiased (figure 18.10).

Unbiased: An estimation procedure is unbiased whenever the mean (center) of the estimate's probability distribution equals the actual value.

Mean of the estimate's probability distribution = Actual value

An unbiased estimation procedure does not systematically underestimate or overestimate the actual value. The relative frequency interpretation of probability provides intuition. If the experiment were repeated many, many times the average of the numerical values of the estimates will equal the actual value:

Mean (average) of the estimates = Actual value after many, many repetitions

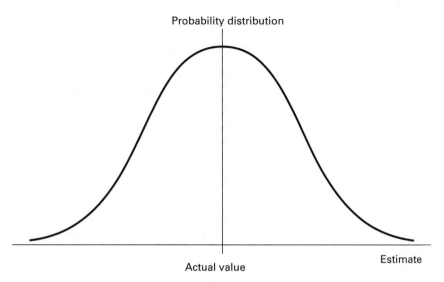

Figure 18.10
Unbiased estimation procedures and the probability distribution of estimates

Being unbiased is a **small sample property** because the size of the sample plays no role in determining whether or not an estimation procedure is unbiased.

Consistent: Consistency is a **large sample property**; the size sample plays a critical role here. Also both the mean and variance of the estimate's probability distribution are important when deciding if an estimation procedure is consistent.

Mean of the estimate's probability distribution: Consistency requires the mean to either

• equal the actual value:

Mean[*Est*] = Actual value

or

• approach the actual value as the sample size approaches infinity:

Mean[*Est*] → Actual value

as

Sample size → ∞

That is, either the

• estimation procedure must be unbiased

or

· magnitude of the bias must diminish as the sample size becomes larger.

Variance of the estimate's probability distribution: Consistency requires the variance to diminish as the sample size becomes larger; more specifically, the variance must approach 0 as the sample size approaches infinity:

Variance[*Est*] $\rightarrow$ 0

as

Sample size $\rightarrow \infty$

Figure 18.11 illustrates the relationship between the two properties of estimation procedures. Figure 18.12 provides a flow diagram, a "roadmap," that we can use to determine the properties of an estimation procedure.

To illustrate the distinction between these two properties of estimation procedures we will consider three examples:

· Unbiased and consistent.

· Unbiased but not consistent.

· Biased and consistent.

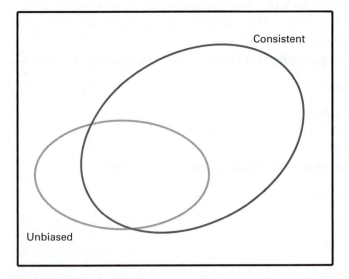

Figure 18.11
Unbiased and consistent estimation procedures

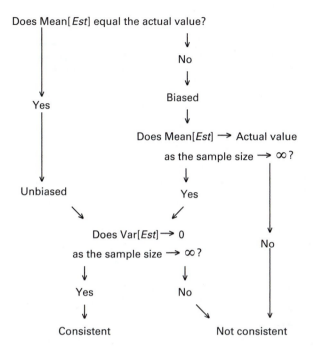

Figure 18.12
Determining the properties of an estimation procedure

18.5.1   Unbiased and Consistent Estimation Procedure

When the standard ordinary least squares (OLS) premises are met the ordinary least squares (OLS) estimation procedure is not only unbiased, but also consistent. We will use our Econometrics Lab to illustrate this.

Econometrics Lab 18.3: Ordinary Least Squares (OLS) Estimation Procedure

[To access this online material, go to http://mitpress.mit.edu/westhoffeconometrics and select Lab 18.3.]

This estimation procedure is unbiased and consistent (table 18.2). After many, many repetitions:

• The average of the estimated coefficient values equals the actual value, 2.0, suggesting that the estimation procedure is unbiased.

• The variance of the estimated coefficient values appears to be approaching 0 as the sample size increases.

Table 18.2
Unbiased and consistent estimation procedure

Estimation procedure	Corr X&E	Sample size	Actual coef	Mean of coef ests	Magnitude of bias	Variance of coef ests
OLS	0.00	3	2.0	≈2.0	≈0.0	≈2.50
OLS	0.00	6	2.0	≈2.0	≈0.0	≈1.14
OLS	0.00	10	2.0	≈2.0	≈0.0	≈0.67
OLS	0.00	100	2.0	≈2.0	≈0.0	≈0.07
OLS	0.00	250	2.0	≈2.0	≈0.0	≈0.03

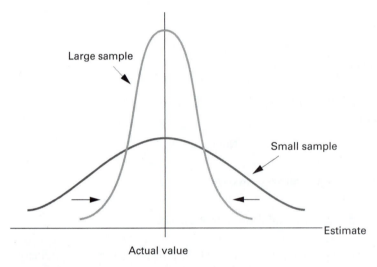

Figure 18.13
OLS estimation procedure—Probability distributions

When the standard ordinary least squares (OLS) premises are met, the ordinary least squares (OLS) estimation procedure provides us with the best of all possibilities; it is both unbiased and consistent (figure 18.13).

18.5.2   Unbiased but Inconsistent Estimation Procedure

The Any Two estimation procedure that we introduced in chapter 6 provides us with an example of an estimation procedure that is unbiased but not consistent. Let us review the Any Two estimation procedure. First we construct a scatter diagram plotting the explanatory variable on the horizontal axis and the dependent variable on the vertical axis. Then we choose any two points at random and draw a straight line connecting these points. The coefficient estimate equals the slope of this line (figure 18.14).

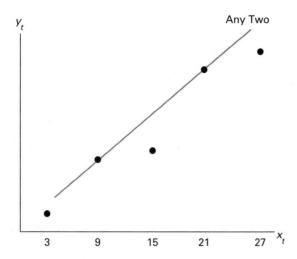

Figure 18.14
Any Two estimation procedure

Table 18.3
Any Two estimation procedure

Estimation procedure	Sample size	Actual coef	Mean of coef ests	Magnitude of bias	Variance of coef ests
Any Two	3	2.0	≈2.0	≈0.0	≈7.5
Any Two	6	2.0	≈2.0	≈0.0	≈17.3
Any Two	10	2.0	≈2.0	≈0.0	≈31.0

Econometrics Lab 18.4: Any Two Estimation Procedure

[To access this online material, go to http://mitpress.mit.edu/westhoffeconometrics and select Lab 18.4.]

As table 18.3 reports the Any two estimation procedure is unbiased but not consistent. After many, many repetitions:

• The average of the estimated coefficient values equals the actual value, 2.0, suggesting that the estimation procedure is unbiased.

• The variance of the estimated coefficient values increases as the sample size increases (figure 18.15); consequently the estimation procedure is not consistent.

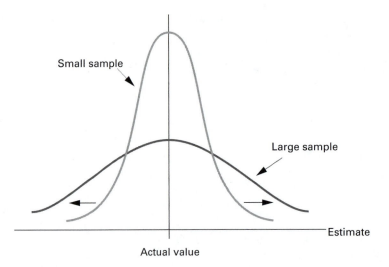

Figure 18.15
Any Two estimation procedure—Probability distributions

18.5.3   Biased but Consistent Estimation Procedure

To illustrate an estimation procedure that is biased, but consistent, we will revisit the opinion poll conducted by Clint. Recall that Clint used a random sampling procedure to poll the population.

Random Sampling Procedure
Write the name of each individual in the population on a 3 × 5 card. Perform the following procedure 16 times:

- Thoroughly shuffle the cards.
- Randomly draw one card.
- Ask that individual if he/she supports Clint and record the answer.
- Replace the card.

Calculate the fraction of the sample supporting Clint. This estimation procedure proved to be unbiased.

But now consider an alternative approach. Suppose that you are visiting Clint in his dorm room and he asks you to conduct the poll. Instead of taking the time to write the name of each individual on a 3 × 5 card, you simply leave Clint's room and ask the first 16 people you run into how he/she will vote.

Nonrandom Sampling Procedure

Leave Clint's dorm room.

- Ask the first 16 people you run into if he/she is voting for Clint.
- Calculate the fraction of the sample supporting Clint.

Why do we call this a nonrandom sampling technique? Compared to the general student population:

- Are the students who live near Clint more likely to be a friend of Clint?
- Consequently, are the students who live near Clint more likely to vote for Clint?

Since your starting point is Clint's dorm room, it is likely that you will poll students who are Clint's friends. They will probably be more supportive of Clint than the general student population, will they not? Consequently we would expect this nonrandom polling technique to be biased in favor of Clint. We will use a simulation to test our logic.

Econometrics Lab 18.5: Biased but Consistent Estimation Procedure

[To access this online material, go to http://mitpress.mit.edu/westhoffeconometrics and select Lab 18.5.]

Observe that you can select the sampling technique by checking or clearing the Nonrandom Sample checkbox (see figure 18.16). Begin by clearing the Nonrandom Sample checkbox to choose the random sampling technique; this provides us with a benchmark. Click **Start** and then after many, many repetitions click **Stop**. As before, we observe that the estimation procedure is unbiased. Convince yourself that the random sampling technique is also consistent by increasing the sample size from 16 to 25 and to 100.

Next specify the nonrandom technique that we just introduced by checking the "Nonrandom Sample" checkbox. You walk out of Clint's dorm room and poll the first 16 people you run into. Click **Start** and then after many, many repetitions click **Stop**. The simulation results confirm our logic. The nonrandom polling technique biases the poll results in favor of Clint. But now what happens as we increase the sample size from 16 to 25 and then to 100?

We observe that while the nonrandom sampling technique is still biased, the magnitude of the bias declines as the sample size increases (table 18.4). As the sample size increases from 16 to 25 to 100, the magnitude of the bias decreases from 0.06 to 0.04 to 0.01. This makes sense, does it not? As the sample size becomes larger, you will be farther and farther from Clint's dorm room, which means that you will be getting larger and larger portion of your sample from the general student population rather than Clint's friends. Furthermore the variance of the estimates also decreases as the sample size increases. This estimation procedure is biased but consistent. After many, many repetitions:

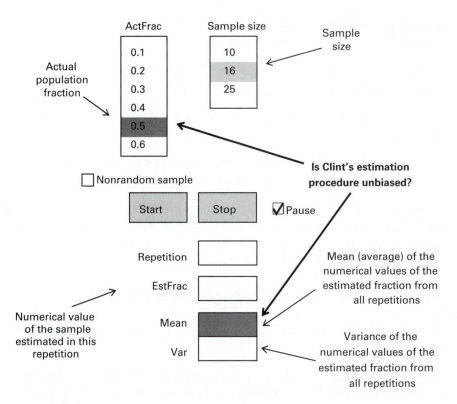

Figure 18.16
Opinion Poll simulation

Table 18.4
Opinion Poll simulation—Random and nonrandom samples

Sampling technique	Population fraction	Sample size	After many, many repetitions		
			Mean (average) of estimates	Magnitude of bias	Variance of estimates
Random	0.50	16	≈0.50	≈0.00	≈0.016
Random	0.50	25	≈0.50	≈0.00	≈0.010
Random	0.50	100	≈0.50	≈0.00	≈0.0025
Nonrandom	0.50	16	≈0.56	≈0.06	≈0.015
Nonrandom	0.50	25	≈0.54	≈0.04	≈0.010
Nonrandom	0.50	100	≈0.51	≈0.01	≈0.0025

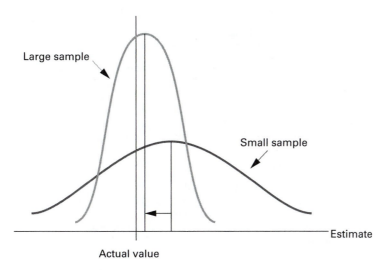

Figure 18.17
Nonrandom sample estimation procedure—Probability distributions

• The average of the estimates appears to be approaching the actual value, 0.5.

• The variance of the estimated coefficient values appears to be approaching 0 as the sample size increases (figure 18.17).

18.6 The Ordinary Least Squares (OLS) Estimation Procedure, and Consistency

We have shown that when the explanatory variable/error term independence premise is violated, the ordinary least squares (OLS) estimation procedure for the coefficient estimate is biased. But might it be consistent?

Econometrics Lab 18.6: Ordinary Least Squares (OLS) Estimation Procedure and Consistency

[To access this online material, go to http://mitpress.mit.edu/westhoffeconometrics and select Lab 18.6.]

Clearly, the magnitude of the bias does not diminish as the sample size increases (table 18.5). The simulation demonstrates that when the explanatory variable/error term independence premise is violated, the ordinary least squares (OLS) estimation procedure is neither unbiased nor consistent. This leads us to a new estimation procedure, the instrumental variable (IV) estimation procedure. Like ordinary least squares, the instrumental variables will prove to be biased when the explanatory variable/error term independence premise is violated, but it has an advantage: under certain conditions, the instrumental variable (IV) estimation procedure is consistent.

Table 18.5
Explanatory variable/error term correlation—Simulation results

Estimation procedure	Corr X&E	Sample size	Actual coef	Mean of coef ests	Magnitude of bias	Variance of coef ests
OLS	0.30	50	2.0	≈ 6.1	≈ 4.1	≈ 3.6
OLS	0.30	100	2.0	≈ 6.1	≈ 4.1	≈ 1.7
OLS	0.30	150	2.0	≈ 6.1	≈ 4.1	≈ 1.2

Original model:

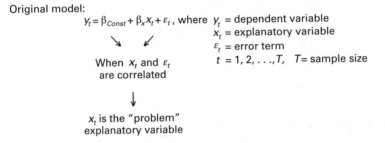

$y_t = \beta_{Const} + \beta_x x_t + \varepsilon_t$, where y_t = dependent variable
x_t = explanatory variable
ε_t = error term
$t = 1, 2, \ldots, T,$ T = sample size

When x_t and ε_t are correlated

x_t is the "problem" explanatory variable

Figure 18.18
"Problem" explanatory variable

18.7   Instrumental Variable (IV) Estimation Procedure: A Two Regression Procedure

18.7.1   Motivation of the Instrumental Variables Estimation Procedure

In some situations the instrumental variable estimation procedure can mitigate, but not completely remedy, cases where the explanatory variable and the error term are correlated (figure 18.18). When an explanatory variable, x_t, is correlated with the error term, ε_t, we will refer to the explanatory variable as the "problem" explanatory variable. The correlation of the explanatory variable and the error term creates the bias problem for the ordinary least squares (OLS) estimation procedure.

We begin by searching for another variable called an instrument. Traditionally, we denote the instrument by the lower case Roman letter z, z_t. An effective instrument must possess two properties. A "good" instrument, z_t, must be

• correlated with the "problem" explanatory variable, x_t, and

• independent of the error term, ε_t.

We use the instrument to provide us with an estimate of the "problem" explanatory variable. Then this estimate is used as a surrogate for the "problem" explanatory variable. The estimate of the "problem" explanatory variable, rather than the "problem" explanatory variable itself, is used to explain the dependent variable.

18.7.2   Mechanics

Choose a "good" instrument: A "good" instrument, z_t, must have be

• correlated with the "problem" explanatory variable, x_t, and
• uncorrelated with the error term, ε_t.

Instrumental Variables (IV) Regression 1:   Use the instrument, z_t, to provide an "estimate" of the problem explanatory variable, x_t.

• Dependent variable: "Problem" explanatory variable, x_t.
• Explanatory variable: Instrument, z_t.
• Estimate of the "problem" explanatory variable: $Estx_t = a_{Const} + a_z z_t$, where a_{Const} and a_z are the estimates of the constant and coefficient in this regression, IV Regression 1.

Instrumental Variables (IV) Regression 2:   In the original model, replace the "problem" explanatory variable, x_t, with its surrogate, $Estx_t$, the estimate of the "problem" explanatory variable provided by the instrument, z_t, from IV Regression 1.

• Dependent variable: Original dependent variable, y_t.
• Explanatory variable: Estimate of the "problem" explanatory variable based on the results from IV Regression 1, $Estx_t$.

18.7.3   The "Good" Instrument Conditions

Let us now provide the intuition behind why a "good" instrument, z_t, must satisfy the two conditions mentioned above.

Instrument/"Problem" Explanatory Variable Correlation

The instrument, z_t, must be correlated with the "problem" explanatory variable, x_t. To understand why, focus on IV Regression 1. We are using the instrument to create a surrogate for the "problem" explanatory variable in IV Regression 1:

$$Estx_t = a_{Const} + a_z z_t$$

The estimate, $Estx_t$, will be a good surrogate only if it is a good predictor of the "problem" explanatory variable, x_t. This will occur only if the instrument, z_t, is correlated with the "problem" explanatory variable, x_t.

Instrument/Error Term Independence

The instrument, z_t, must be independent of the error term, ε_t. Focus on IV Regression 2. We begin with the original model and then replace the "problem" explanatory, x_t, variable with its surrogate, $Estx_t$:

$$y_t = \beta_{Const} + \beta_x x_t + \varepsilon_t$$

$$\downarrow \qquad \text{Replace "problem" with surrogate}$$

$$= \beta_{Const} + \beta_x Estx_t + \varepsilon_t$$

where $Estx_t = a_{Const} + a_z z_t$ from IV Regression 1.

   To avoid violating the explanatory variable/error term independence premise in IV Regression 2, the surrogate for the "problem" explanatory variable, $Estx_t$, must be independent of the error term, ε_t. The surrogate, $Estx_t$, is derived from the instrument, z_t, in IV Regression 1:

$$Estx_t = a_{Const} + a_z z_t$$

Consequently, to avoid violating the explanatory variable/error term independence premise, the instrument, z_t, and the error term, ε_t, must be independent.

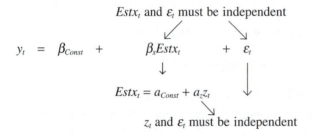

18.7.4   Justification of the Instrumental Variables Estimation Procedure

As we will see, while instrumental variable estimation procedure will not solve the problem of bias, it can mitigate it. We will use a simulation to illustrate that while the instrumental variable (IV) estimation procedure is still biased, it is consistent when "good" instrument conditions are satisfied (figure 18.19).

Econometrics Lab 18.7: Instrumental Variables (IV) Estimation Procedure and Consistency

[To access this online material, go to http://mitpress.mit.edu/westhoffeconometrics and select Lab 18.7.]

Two new correlation lists appear in this simulation: Corr X&Z and Corr Z&E. The two new lists reflect the two conditions required for a good instrument:

• The Corr X&Z list specifies the correlation coefficient for the explanatory variable and the instrument. To be a "good" instrument the explanatory variable and the instrument must be correlated. The default value is 0.50.

• The Corr Z&E specifies the correlation coefficient for the instrument and error term. To be a "good" instrument the instrument and error term must be independent. The default value is 0.00; that is, the instrument and error term are independent.

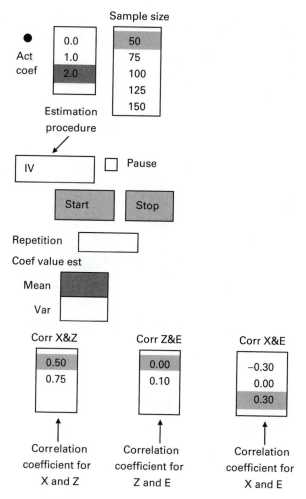

Figure 18.19
Instrumental Variables simulation

The default values meet the "good" instrument conditions.

Also note that in the Corr X&E list the value 0.30 is specified. The correlation coefficient for the explanatory variable and error term equals 0.30. The explanatory variable/error term independence premise is violated. Last, IV is selected indicating that the instrumental variable (IV) estimation procedure we just described will be used to estimate the value of the explanatory variable's coefficient.

We will now illustrate that while the instrumental variable (IV) estimation procedure is still biased, it is consistent. To do so, click **Start** and then after many, many repetitions click **Stop**.

Table 18.6
IV estimation procedure—"Good" instrument conditions satisfied

Estimation procedure	Correlation coefficients			Sample size	Actual coef	Mean of coef ests	Magnitude of bias	Variance of coef ests
	X&Z	Z&E	X&E					
IV	0.50	0.00	0.30	50	2.0	≈1.61	≈0.39	≈20.3
IV	0.50	0.00	0.30	100	2.0	≈1.82	≈0.18	≈8.7
IV	0.50	0.00	0.30	150	2.0	≈1.88	≈0.12	≈5.5

Table 18.7
IV estimation procedure—A better instrument

Estimation procedure	Correlation coefficients			Sample size	Actual coef	Mean of coef ests	Magnitude of bias	Variance of coef ests
	X&Z	Z&E	X&E					
IV	0.50	0.00	0.30	150	2.0	≈1.88	≈0.12	≈5.5
IV	0.75	0.00	0.30	150	2.0	≈1.95	≈.005	≈2.3

Subsequently we increase the sample size from 50 to 100 and then again from 100 to 150. Table 18.6 reports the simulation results.

Both bad news and good news emerge:

Bad news: The instrumental variable estimation is biased. The mean of the estimates for the coefficient of the explanatory variable does not the actual value we specified, 2.0.

Good news: As we increase the sample size,

• the mean of the coefficient estimates gets closer to the actual value

and

• the variance of the coefficient estimates becomes smaller.

This illustrates the fact that the instrumental variable (IV) estimation procedure is consistent.

Next we will use the lab to illustrate the importance of the "good" instrument conditions. First, let us see what happens when we improve the instrument by making it more highly correlated with the problem explanatory variable. We do this by increasing the correlation coefficient of the explanatory variable and the instrument from 0.50 to 0.75 in the Corr X&Z list (table 18.7).

The magnitude of the bias decreases; also the variance of the coefficient estimates also decreases. A more highly correlated instrument provides a better estimate of the "problem" explanatory variable in IV Regression 1 and hence is a better instrument.

Table 18.8
IV estimation procedure—Instrument correlated with error term

Estimation procedure	Correlation coefficients			Sample size	Actual coef	Mean of coef ests	Magnitude of bias	Variance of coef ests
	X&Z	Z&E	X&E					
IV	0.75	0.10	0.30	50	2.0	≈3.69	≈1.69	≈6.8
IV	0.75	0.10	0.30	100	2.0	≈3.74	≈1.74	≈3.2
IV	0.75	0.10	0.30	150	2.0	≈3.76	≈1.76	≈2.1

Last, let us use the lab to illustrate the important role that the independence of the error term and the instrument plays by specifying 0.10 from the Corr Z&E list; the instrument and the error term are no longer independent (table 18.8). As we increase the sample size from 50 to 100 to 150, the magnitude of the bias does not decrease. The instrumental variable (IV) estimation procedure is no longer consistent when the instrument is correlated with the error term; the explanatory variable/error term independence premise is violated in IV Regression 2.

Chapter 18 Review Questions

1. What are the ramifications for the ordinary least squares (OLS) estimation procedure for the value of the coefficient if the explanatory variable and error term are

   a. positively correlated?

   b. negatively correlated?

   c. independent?

2. How does the problem resulting from explanatory variable/error term correlation differ from the problems caused by heteroskedasticity or autocorrelation?

3. When is an estimation procedure unbiased?

4. When is an estimation procedure consistent?

5. Must an unbiased estimation procedure be consistent? Explain.

6. Must a consistent estimation procedure be unbiased? Explain.

7. What are the two "good" instrument conditions? Why is each important?

Chapter 18 Exercises

1. Random Sampling Procedure

Write the name of each individual in the population on a 3 × 5 card. Perform the following procedure T times (T equals the sample size):

· Thoroughly shuffle the cards.

· Randomly draw one card.

· Ask that individual if he/she supports Clint and record the answer.

· Replace the card.

Calculate the fraction of the sample supporting Clint.

Since there is little time to conduct the poll only 16 individuals can be sampled if Clint uses the random polling procedure.

[To access this online material, go to http://mitpress.mit.edu/westhoffeconometrics and select Lab 18E.1.]

The Nonrandom Sample box is cleared; hence the random sampling procedure described above will be used. By default the actual fraction supporting Clint, *ActFrac*, equals 0.5; also the From–To values are specified as 0.45 and 0.55. Click the **Start** button and then after many, many, repetitions click **Stop**.

    a. What does the mean of the estimates equal?

    b. What does the variance of the estimates equal?

    c. What percent of the repetitions fall within 0.05 of the actual fraction, *ActFrac*?

2. Nonrandom Sampling Procedure

Leave Clint's dorm room.

· Ask the first T individuals encountered if he/she supports Clint and record the answer (T equals the sample size).

· Calculate the fraction of the sample supporting Clint.

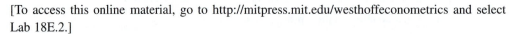

[To access this online material, go to http://mitpress.mit.edu/westhoffeconometrics and select Lab 18E.2.]

The Nonrandom Sample box is checked; hence the nonrandom sampling procedure described above will be used. As in problem 1, the sample size equals 16, the actual fraction supporting Clint, *ActFrac*, equals 0.5, and the From–To values are specified as 0.45 and 0.55. Click the **Start** button and then after many, many, repetitions click **Stop**.

    a. What does the mean of the estimates equal?

    b. What is the magnitude of the bias?

    c. What does the variance of the estimates equal?

    d. What percent of the repetitions fall within 0.05 of the actual fraction, *ActFrac*?

3. Compare your answers to problems 1 and 2. When the sample size is the same which sampling procedure is more reliable?

4. Clearly, the nonrandom polling procedure requires less "setup." It is not necessary to write the name of each student on a separate card, and so forth. Consequently, with the nonrandom procedure, there is time to poll more students. In the following simulation the sample size has been raised from 16 to 25 to account for this.

[To access this online material, go to http://mitpress.mit.edu/westhoffeconometrics and select Lab 18E.4.]

Click the **Start** button and then after many, many, repetitions click **Stop**.

    a. What does the mean of the estimates equal?

    b. What is the magnitude of the bias?

    c. What does the variance of the estimates equal?

    d. What percent of the repetitions fall within .05 of the actual fraction, *ActFrac*?

5. Compare your answers to problems 1 and 4. Is an unbiased estimation procedure always better than a biased one? Explain.

19 Measurement Error and the Instrumental Variables Estimation Procedure

19.7   Justifying the Instrumental Variable (IV) Estimation Procedure

Chapter 19 Prep Questions

1. Suppose that a physics assignment requires you to measure the amount of time it takes a one pound weight to fall six feet. You conduct twenty trials in which you use a very accurate stop watch to measure how long it takes the weight to fall.

a. Even though you are very careful and conscientious would you expect the stop watch to report precisely the same amount of time on each trial? Explain.

Suppose that the following equation describes the relationship between the measured elapsed time and the actual elapsed time:

$$yMeasured_t = yActual_t + v_t$$

where

$yMeasured_t$ = measured elapsed time

$yActual_t$ = actual elapsed time

and where v_t is a random variable. v_t represents the random influences that cause your measurement of the elapsed time to deviate from the actual elapsed time. The random influences cause you to click the stop watch a little early or a little late.

b. Recall that you are careful and conscientious in attempting to measure the elapsed time.

i. In approximately what portion of the trials would you overestimate the elapsed time; that is, in approximately what portion of the trials would you expect v_t to be positive?

ii. In approximately what portion of the trials would you underestimate the elapsed time; that is, in approximately what portion of the trials would you expect v_t to be negative?

iii. Approximately what would the mean (average) of v_t equal?

2. Economists distinguish between permanent income and annual income. Loosely speaking, permanent income equals what a household earns per year "on average;" that is, permanent income can be thought of as the "average" of annual income over an entire lifetime. In some years, annual income is more than its permanent income, but in other years, it is less. The difference between the household's annual income and permanent income is called transitory income:

$$IncTrans_t = IncAnn_t - IncPerm_t$$

where

$IncAnn_t$ = household's annual income

$IncPerm_t$ = household's permanent income

$IncTrans_t$ = household's transitory income

or equivalently,

$$IncAnn_t = IncPerm_t + IncTrans_t$$

Since permanent income equals what a household earns "on average," the mean of transitory income equals 0. Microeconomic theory teaches that households base their consumption decisions on their "permanent" income.

Theory: Additional permanent income increases consumption.

Consider the following model to assess the theory:

Model: $Cons_t = \beta_{Const} + \beta_{IncPerm}IncPerm_t + e_t$

Theory: $\beta_{IncPerm} > 0$

When we attempt to gather data to access this theory, we immediately encounter a difficulty. Permanent income cannot be observed. Only annual income data are available to assess the theory. So, while we would like to specify permanent income as the explanatory variable, we have no choice. We must use annual disposable income.

   a. Can you interpret transitory income as measurement error? Hint: What is the mean (average) of transitory income?

   b. Now represent transitory income, $IncTrans_t$, by u_t:

$$IncAnn_t - IncPerm_t + u_t$$

Express the model in terms of annual income.

   c. What is the equation for the new error term?

   d. Will the new error term and the explanatory variable, $IncAnn_t$, be correlated?

   e. What are the econometric ramifications of using the ordinary least squares (OLS) estimation procedure to estimate the permanent income coefficient, $\beta_{IncPerm}$, using annual income as the explanatory variable?

19.1   Introduction to Measurement Error

Two types of measurement error can be present:

• Dependent variable
• Explanatory variable

We will argue that dependent variable measurement error does not lead to bias. However, whenever explanatory variable measure error exists, the explanatory variable and error term will be correlated resulting in bias. We consider dependent variable measurement error first. Before doing so, we will describe precisely what we mean by measurement error.

19.1.1   What Is Measurement Error?

Suppose that a physics assignment requires you to measure the amount of time it takes a one pound weight to fall six feet. You conduct twenty trials in which you use a very accurate stop watch to measure how long it takes the weight to fall.

Question: Will your stop watch report the same amount of time on each trial?

Answer: No. Sometimes reported times will be lower than other reported times. Sometimes you will be a little premature in clicking the stop watch button. Other times you will be a little late.

It is humanly impossible to measure the actual elapsed time perfectly. No matter how careful you are, sometimes the measured value will be a little low and other times a little high. This phenomenon is called measurement error.

19.1.2   Modeling Measurement Error

We can model measurement error with the following equation:

$yMeasured_t = yActual_t + v_t$

Recall that $yActual_t$ equals the actual amount of time elapsed and $yMeasured_t$ equals the measured amount of time; v_t represents measurement error. Sometimes v_t will be positive when you are a little too slow in clicking the stop watch button; other times v_t will be negative when you click the button a little too soon. v_t is a random variable; we cannot predict the numerical value of v_t beforehand. What can we say about v_t? We can describe its distribution. Since you are conscientious in measuring the elapsed time, the mean of v_t's probability distribution equals 0:

$Mean[v_t] = 0$

Measurement error does not systematically increase or decrease the measured value of y_t. The measured value of y_t, $yMeasured_t$, will not systematically overestimate or underestimate the actual value.

19.2   The Ordinary Least Squares (OLS) Estimation Procedure and Dependent Variable Measurement Error

We begin with the equation specifying the actual relationship between the dependent and explanatory variables:

Actual relationship: $yActual_t = \beta_{Const} + \beta_{xActual}xActual_t + e_t$

But now suppose that as a consequence of measurement error, the actual value of the dependent variable, $yActual_t$, is not observable. You have no choice but to use the measured value, $yMeasured_t$. Recall that the measured value equals the actual value plus the measurement error random variable, v_t:

$$yMeasured_t = yActual_t + v_t$$

where v_t is a random variable with mean 0: $\text{Mean}[v_t] = 0$. Solving for $yActual_t$:

$$yActual_t = yMeasured_t - v_t$$

Let us apply this to the actual relationship:

$$yActual_t \quad = \beta_{Const} + \beta_{xActual}xActual_t + \quad e_t$$
$$\downarrow \qquad\qquad\qquad\qquad\qquad\qquad \text{Substituting for } yActual_t$$
$$yMeasured_t - v_t = \beta_{Const} + \beta_{xActual}xActual_t + \quad e_t$$
$$\qquad\qquad\qquad\qquad\qquad\qquad \text{Rearranging terms}$$
$$yMeasured_t \quad = \beta_{Const} + \beta_{xActual}xActual_t + e_t + v_t$$
$$\downarrow \quad \text{Letting } \varepsilon_t = e_t + v_t,$$
$$yMeasured_t \quad = \beta_{Const} + \beta_{xActual}xActual_t + \quad \varepsilon_t$$

ε_t represents the error term in the regression that you will actually be running. Will this result in bias? To address this issue consider the following question:

Question: Are the explanatory variable, $xActual_t$, and the error term, ε_t, correlated?

To answer the question, suppose that the measurement error term, v_t, were to increase:

$$v_t \text{ up}$$
$$\swarrow \qquad \searrow \quad \varepsilon_t = e_t + v_t$$
$$xActual_t \text{ unaffected} \quad \leftrightarrow \quad \varepsilon_t \text{ up}$$

The value of the explanatory variable, $xActual_t$, is unchanged while the error term, ε_t, increases. Hence the explanatory variable and error term ε_t are independent; consequently no bias should result.

Econometrics Lab 19.1: Dependent Measurement Error

[To access this online material, go to http://mitpress.mit.edu/westhoffeconometrics and select Lab 19.1.]

We use a simulation to confirm our logic (figure 19.1). First we consider our base case, the no measurement error case. The YMeas Err checkbox is cleared indicating that no dependent variable measurement error is present. Consequently no bias should result. Be certain that the Pause

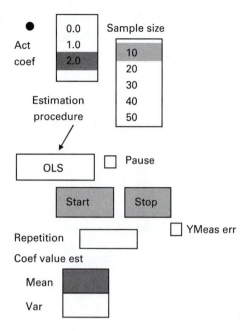

Figure 19.1
Dependent variable measurement error simulation

checkbox is cleared and click Start. After many, many repetitions, click Stop. The ordinary least squares (OLS) estimation procedure is unbiased in this case; the average of the estimated coefficient values and the actual coefficient value both equal 2.0. When no measurement error is present, all is well.

Now we will introduce dependent variable measurement error by checking the YMeas Err checkbox. The YMeas Var list now appears with 20.0 selected; the variance of the measurement error's probability distribution, $Var[v_t]$, equals 20.0. Click **Start** and then after many, many repetitions click **Stop**. Again, the average of the estimated coefficient values and the actual coefficient value both equal 2.0. Next select from 20.0 to 50.0 to 80.0 from the YMeas Var list and repeat the process.

The simulation confirms our logic (table 19.1). Even when dependent variable measurement error is present, the average of the estimated coefficient values equals the actual coefficient value. Dependent variable measurement error does not lead to bias.

What are the ramifications of dependent variable measurement error? The last column of table 19.1 reveals the answer. As measurement error variance increases, the variance of the estimated coefficient values and hence the variance of the coefficient estimate's probability distribution increases. As the variance of the dependent variable measurement error term increases, we introduce "more uncertainty" into the process and hence, the ordinary least squares (OLS) estimates become less reliable.

Table 19.1
Dependent variable measurement error simulation results

		Sample size = 10		
Type of measurement error	YMeas var	Actual coef value	Mean (average) of the estimated coef values	Variance of estimated coef values
None		2.0	≈2.0	≈1.7
Dep Vbl	20.0	2.0	≈2.0	≈1.8
Dep Vbl	50.0	2.0	≈2.0	≈2.0
Dep Vbl	80.0	2.0	≈2.0	≈2.2

19.3   The Ordinary Least Squares (OLS) Estimation Procedure and Explanatory Variable Measurement Error

To investigate explanatory variable measurement error we again begin with the equation that describes the actual relationship between the dependent and explanatory variables:

Actual relationship: $yActual_t = \beta_{Const} + \beta_{xActual}xActual_t + e_t$

Next suppose that we cannot observe the actual value of the explanatory variable; we can only observe the measured value. The measured value equals the actual value plus the measurement error random variable, u_t:

$xMeasured_t = xActual_t + u_t$

where

u_t is a random variable with mean 0: Mean$[u_t] = 0$. Solving for $yActual_t$:

$xActual_t = xMeasured_t - u_t$

Now we apply this to the actual relationship:

$$yActual_t = \beta_{Const} + \beta_{xActual}xActual_t + e_t$$

$\downarrow$ Substituting for $xActual_t$

$$= \beta_{Const} + \beta_{xActual}(xMeasured_t - u_t) + e_t$$

$\downarrow$ Multiplying

$$= \beta_{Const} + \beta_{xActual}xMeasured_t - \beta_{xActual}u_t + e_t$$

Rearranging terms

$$= \beta_{Const} + \beta_{xActual}xMeasured_t + e_t - \beta_{xActual}u_t$$

$\downarrow$ Letting $\varepsilon_t = e_t - \beta_{xActual}u_t$,

$$yActual_t = \beta_{Const} + \beta_{xActual}xMeasured_t + \varepsilon_t$$

ε_t is the error term in the regression that we will actually be running.

Recall what we learned about correlation between the explanatory variable and error term (figure 19.2):

Explanatory variable and error term positively correlated	Explanatory variable and error term uncorrelated	Explanatory variable and error term negatively correlated
$\downarrow$	$\downarrow$	$\downarrow$
OLS estimation procedure for the coefficient value is biased upward	OLS estimation procedure for the coefficient value is unbiased	OLS estimation procedure for the coefficient value is biased downward

Are the explanatory variable, $xMeasured_t$, and the error term, ε_t, correlated? The answer to the question depends on the sign of the actual coefficient. Consider the three possibilities:

• $\beta_{xActual} > 0$: When the actual coefficient is positive, negative correlation exists; consequently, the ordinary least squares (OLS) estimation procedure for the coefficient value would be biased downward. To understand why, suppose that u_t increases:

$$u_t \text{ up}$$

$$xMeasured_t = xActual_t + u_t \quad \nearrow \quad \searrow \quad e_t = e_t - \beta_{xActual}u_t \quad \beta_{xActual} > 0$$

$$xMeasured_t \text{ up} \quad \leftrightarrow \quad \varepsilon_t \text{ down}$$

$$\searrow \qquad \swarrow$$

$$\text{Negative explanatory variable/error}$$
$$\text{term correlation}$$

$$\downarrow$$

$$\text{OLS biased downward}$$

• $\beta_{xActual} < 0$: When the actual coefficient is negative, positive correlation exists; consequently the ordinary least squares (OLS) estimation procedure for the coefficient value would be biased upward. To understand why, suppose that u_t increases:

$$u_t \text{ up}$$

$$xMeasured_t = xActual_t + u_t \quad \nearrow \quad \searrow \quad e_t = e_t - \beta_{xActual}u_t \quad \beta_{xActual} > 0$$

$$xMeasured_t \text{ up} \quad \leftrightarrow \quad \varepsilon_t \text{ up}$$

$$\searrow \qquad \swarrow$$

$$\text{Positive explanatory variable/error}$$
$$\text{term correlation}$$

$$\downarrow$$

$$\text{OLS biased upward}$$

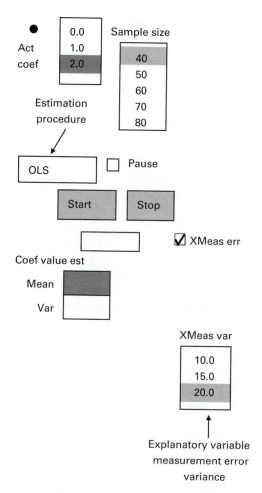

Figure 19.2
Explanatory variable measurement error simulation

- $\beta_{xActual} = 0$: When the actual coefficient equals 0, no correlation exists; consequently no bias results. To understand why, suppose that u_t increases:

$$u_t \text{ up}$$

$$xMeasured_t = xActual_t + u_t \quad\swarrow\qquad\searrow\quad e_t = e_t - \beta_{xActual}u_t \quad \beta_{xActual} > 0$$

$$xMeasured_t \text{ up} \quad\leftrightarrow\quad \varepsilon_t \text{ unaffected}$$

$$\searrow\qquad\swarrow$$

$$\text{No explanatory variable/error}$$
$$\text{term correlation}$$

$$\downarrow$$

$$\text{OLS unbiased}$$

19.3.1   Summary: Explanatory Variable Measurement Error Bias

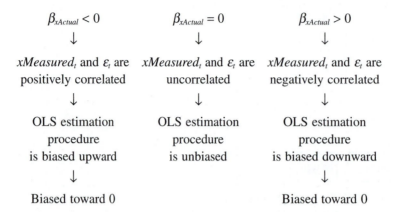

$\beta_{xActual} < 0$	$\beta_{xActual} = 0$	$\beta_{xActual} > 0$
↓	↓	↓
$xMeasured_t$ and ε_t are positively correlated	$xMeasured_t$ and ε_t are uncorrelated	$xMeasured_t$ and ε_t are negatively correlated
↓	↓	↓
OLS estimation procedure is biased upward	OLS estimation procedure is unbiased	OLS estimation procedure is biased downward
↓		↓
Biased toward 0		Biased toward 0

Econometrics Lab 19.2: Explanatory Variable Measurement Error

[To access this online material, go to http://mitpress.mit.edu/westhoffeconometrics and select Lab 19.2.]

We will use a simulation to check our logic. This time we check the XMeas Err checkbox. The XMeas Var list now appears with 20.0 selected; the variance of the measurement error's probability distribution, Var[u_t], equals 20.0. Then we select various values for the actual coefficient. In each case, click **Start** and then after many, many repetitions click **Stop**. The simulation results are reported in table 10.2 (table 19.2).

The simulation results confirm our logic. When the actual coefficient is positive and explanatory variable measurement error is present, the ordinary least squares (OLS) estimation procedure for the coefficient value is biased downward. When the actual coefficient is negative and explanatory variable measurement error is present, upward bias results. Last, when the actual coefficient is zero, no bias results even in the presence of explanatory variable measurement error.

Table 19.2
Explanatory variable measurement error simulation results

		Sample size = 40		
Type of measurement error	XMeas var	Actual coef value	Mean (average) of the estimated coef values	Magnitude of bias
Exp Vbl	20.0	2.0	≈1.11	≈0.89
Exp Vbl	20.0	1.0	≈0.56	≈0.44
Exp Vbl	20.0	−1.0	≈−0.56	≈0.44
Exp Vbl	20.0	0.0	≈0.00	≈0.00

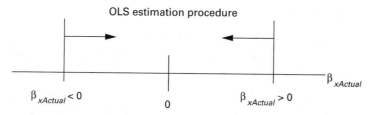

Figure 19.3
Effect of explanatory variable measurement error

19.3.2   Explanatory Variable Measurement Error: Attenuation (Dilution) Bias

The simulations reveal an interesting pattern. While explanatory variable measurement error leads to bias, the bias never appears to be strong enough to change the sign of the mean of the coefficient estimates. In other words, explanatory variable measurement error biases the ordinary least squares (OLS) estimation procedure for the coefficient value toward 0. This type of bias is called **attenuation** or **dilution bias** (figure 19.3).

Why does explanatory variable measurement error cause attenuation bias? Even more basic, why does explanatory variable measurement error cause bias at all? After all, the chances that the measured value of the explanatory variable will be too high equal the chances it will be too low. Why should this lead to bias? To appreciate why, suppose that the actual value of the coefficient, $\beta_{xActual}$, is positive. When the measured value of the explanatory variable, $xMeasured_t$, rises it can do so for two reasons:

- the actual value of explanatory variable, $xActual_t$, rises

or

- the value of the measurement error term, u_t, rises.

Consider what happens to $yActual_t$ in each case:

$$xMeasured_t \text{ up} \quad \nearrow \quad \begin{array}{l} xActual_t \text{ up} \quad \rightarrow \quad yActual_t \text{ up} \\ \qquad\qquad \text{or} \\ u_t \text{ up} \qquad\quad \rightarrow \quad yActual_t \text{ unchanged} \end{array}$$

So we have two possibilities:

• First case: The actual value of the dependent variable rises since the actual value of the explanatory variable has risen. In this case the estimation procedure will estimate the value of the coefficient estimate "correctly."

• Second case: The actual value of the dependent variable remains unchanged since the actual value of the explanatory variable is unchanged. In this case the estimation procedure would estimate the value of the coefficient to be 0.

Taking into account both cases, we conclude that the estimation procedure will understate the effect that the actual value of the explanatory variable has on the dependent variable. Overall, the estimation procedure will understate the actual value of the coefficient.

19.3.3   Might the Ordinary Least Squares (OLS) Estimation Procedure Be Consistent?

Econometrics Lab 19.3: Consistency and Explanatory Variable Measurement Error

[To access this online material, go to http://mitpress.mit.edu/westhoffeconometrics and select Lab 19.3.]

We have already shown that when explanatory variable measurement error is present and the actual coefficient is nonzero, the ordinary least squares (OLS) estimation procedure for the coefficient value is biased. But perhaps it is consistent. Let us see by increasing the sample size (table 19.3).

The bias does not lessen as the sample size is increased. Unfortunately, when explanatory variable measurement error is present and the actual coefficient is nonzero, the ordinary least squares (OLS) estimation procedure for the coefficient value provides only bad news:

• **Bad news:**   The ordinary least squares (OLS) estimation procedure is biased.

• **Bad news:**   The ordinary least squares (OLS) estimation procedure is not consistent.

Table 19.3
OLS estimation procedure, measurement error, and consistency

Estimation procedure	XMeas var	Sample size	Actual coef	Mean of coef ests	Magnitude of bias	Variance of coef ests
OLS	20	40	2.0	≈1.11	≈0.89	≈0.2
OLS	20	50	2.0	≈1.11	≈0.89	≈0.2
OLS	20	60	2.0	≈1.11	≈0.89	≈0.1

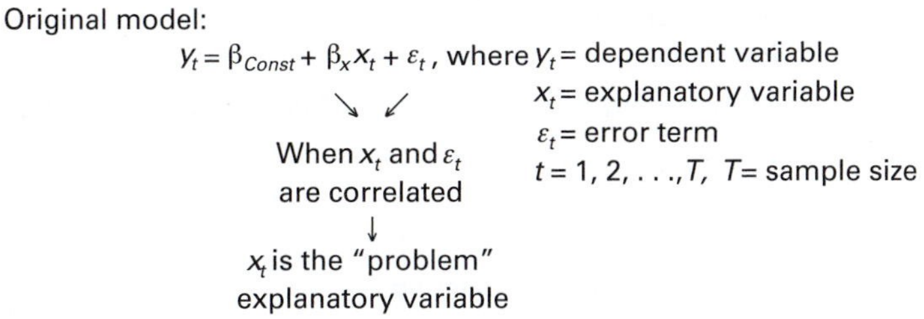

Original model:
$$Y_t = \beta_{Const} + \beta_x x_t + \varepsilon_t, \text{ where } y_t = \text{dependent variable}$$

x_t = explanatory variable

When x_t and ε_t are correlated

ε_t = error term

$t = 1, 2, \ldots, T,\ T$ = sample size

↓

x_t is the "problem" explanatory variable

Figure 19.4
The "problem" explanatory variable

19.4   Instrumental Variable (IV) Estimation Procedure: A Two Regression Procedure

Recall that the instrumental variable estimation procedure addresses situations in which the explanatory variable and the error term are correlated (figure 19.4).

When an explanatory variable, x_t, is correlated with the error term, ε_t, we will refer to the explanatory variable as the "problem" explanatory variable. The correlation of the explanatory variable and the error term creates the bias problem for the ordinary least squares (OLS) estimation procedure. The instrumental variable estimation procedure can mitigate, but not completely remedy the problem. Let us briefly review the procedure and motivate it.

19.4.1   Mechanics

Choose a "good" instrument: A "good" instrument, z_t, must be

• correlated with the "problem" explanatory variable, x_t, and

• uncorrelated with the error term, ε_t.

Instrumental variables (IV) Regression 1:   Use the instrument, z_t, to provide an "estimate" of the problem explanatory variable, x_t.

• Dependent variable: "Problem" explanatory variable, x_t.

• Explanatory variable: Instrument, z_t.

• Estimate of the "problem" explanatory variable: $Estx_t = a_{Const} + a_z z_t$, where a_{Const} and a_z are the estimates of the constant and coefficient in this regression, IV Regression 1.

Instrumental variables (IV) Regression 2:   In the original model, replace the "problem" explanatory variable, x_t, with its surrogate, $Estx_t$, the estimate of the "problem" explanatory variable provided by the instrument, z_t, from IV Regression 1.

• Dependent variable: Original dependent variable, y_t.

• Explanatory variable: Estimate of the "problem" explanatory variable based on the results from IV Regression 1, $Estx_t$.

19.4.2   The "Good" Instrument Conditions

Let us now provide the intuition behind why a "good" instrument, z_t, must satisfy the two conditions: instrument/"problem" explanatory variable correlation and instrument/error term independence.

Instrument/"Problem" Explanatory Variable Correlation

The instrument, z_t, must be correlated with the "problem" explanatory variable, x_t. To understand why, focus on IV Regression 1. We are using the instrument to create a surrogate for the "problem" explanatory variable in IV Regression 1:

$$Estx_t = a_{Const} + a_z z_t$$

The estimate, $Estx_t$, will be a good surrogate only if it is a good predictor of the "problem" explanatory variable, x_t. This will occur only if the instrument, z_t, is correlated with the "problem" explanatory variable, x_t.

Instrument/Error Term Independence

The instrument, z_t, must be independent of the error term, ε_t. Focus on IV Regression 2. We begin with the original model and then replace the "problem" explanatory, x_t, variable with its surrogate, $Estx_t$:

$$y_t = \beta_{Const} + \beta_x x_t \quad + \varepsilon_t$$
$$\downarrow \qquad\qquad \text{Replace "problem" with surrogate}$$
$$= \beta_{Const} + \beta_x Estx_t + \varepsilon_t$$

where $Estx_t = a_{Const} + a_z z_t$ from IV Regression 1.

To avoid violating the explanatory variable/error term independence premise in IV Regression 2, the surrogate for the "problem" explanatory variable, $Estx_t$, must be independent of the error term, ε_t. The surrogate, $Estx_t$, is derived from the instrument, z_t, in IV Regression 1:

$$Estx_t = a_{Const} + a_z z_t$$

Consequently, to avoid violating the explanatory variable/error term independence premise, the instrument, z_t, and the error term, ε_t, must be independent.

$$Estx_t \text{ and } \varepsilon_t \text{ must be independent}$$
$$\nearrow \qquad\qquad \searrow$$
$$y_t \;=\; \beta_{Const} \;+\; \beta_x Estx_t \;+\; \varepsilon_t$$
$$\downarrow \qquad\qquad\qquad |$$
$$Estx_t = a_{Const} + a_z z_t$$
$$\searrow \qquad\quad \searrow$$
$$z_t \text{ and } \varepsilon_t \text{ must be independent}$$

19.5   Measurement Error Example: Annual, Permanent, and Transitory Income

19.5.1   Definitions and Theory

Economists distinguish between permanent income and annual income. Loosely speaking, permanent income equals what a household earns per year "on average;" that is, permanent income can be thought of as the "average" of annual income over an entire lifetime. In some years, the household's annual income is more than its permanent income, but in other years, it is less. The difference between the household's annual income and permanent income is called transitory income:

$$IncTrans_t = IncAnn_t - IncPerm_t$$

where

$IncAnn_t$ = households's annual income

$IncPerm_t$ = household's permanent income

$IncTrans_t$ = household's transitory income

or equivalently,

$$IncAnn_t = IncPerm_t + IncTrans_t$$

Since permanent income equals what the household earns "on average," the mean of transitory income equals 0.

Microeconomic theory teaches that households base their consumption decisions on their "permanent" income. We are going to apply the permanent income consumption theory to health insurance coverage:

Theory: Additional permanent per capita disposable income within a state increases health insurance coverage within the state.

Project: Assess the effect of permanent income on health insurance coverage.

We consider a straightforward linear model:

Model: $Covered_t = \beta_{Const} + \beta_{IncPerm}IncPermPC_t + e_t$

Theory: $\beta_{IncPerm} > 0$

where

$Covered_t$ = percent of individuals with health insurance in state t

$IncPermPC_t$ = per capita permanent disposable income in state t

When we attempt to gather data to access this theory, we immediately encounter a difficulty. Permanent income cannot be observed. Only annual income data are available to assess the theory.

Health insurance data: Cross-sectional data of health insurance coverage, education, and income statistics from the 50 states and the District of Columbia in 2007.

$Covered_t$ Adults (25 and older) covered by health insurance in state t (percent)

$IncAnnPC_t$ Per capita annual disposable income in state t (thousands of dollars)

HS_t Adults (25 and older) who completed high school in state t (percent)

$Coll_t$ Adults (25 and older) who completed a four year college in state t (percent)

$AdvDeg_t$ Adults (25 and older) who have an advanced degree in state t (percent)

[To access this online material, go to http://mitpress.mit.edu/westhoffeconometrics and select Health Insurance.]

While we would like to specify permanent income as the explanatory variable, permanent income is unobservable. We have no choice. We must use annual disposable income as the explanatory variable. Using the ordinary least squares (OLS) estimation procedure to estimate the parameters (table 19.4).

   Now construct the null and alternative hypotheses:

H_0: $\beta_{IncPerm} = 0$ Disposable income has no effect on health insurance coverage

H_1: $\beta_{IncPerm} > 0$ Additional disposable income increases health insurance coverage

Table 19.4
Health insurance OLS regression results

Ordinary least squares (OLS)				
Dependent variable: *Covered*				
Explanatory variable(s):	Estimate	SE	*t*-Statistic	Prob
IncAnnPC	0.226905	0.104784	2.165464	0.0352
Const	78.56242	3.605818	21.78768	0.0000
Number of observations	51			

Estimated equation: *EstCovered* = 78.6 + .23*IncAnnPC*

Interpretation of estimates:

   $b_{IncAnnPC} = 0.23$: A $1,000 increase in annual per capita disposable income increases the state's health insurance coverage by 0.23 percentage points

Critical result: The *IncAnnPC* coefficient estimate equals 0.23. The positive sign of the coefficient estimate suggests that increases in disposable income increase health insurance coverage. This evidence supports the theory.

Since the null hypothesis is based on the premise that the actual value of the coefficient equals 0, we can calculate the Prob[Results IF H_0 true] using the tails probability reported in the regression printout:

$$\text{Prob[Results IF } H_0 \text{ true]} = \frac{0.0352}{2} = 0.0176$$

19.5.2 Might the Ordinary Least Squares (OLS) Estimation Procedure Suffer from a Serious Econometric Problem?

Might this regression suffer from a serious econometric problem, however? Yes. Annual income equals permanent income plus transitory income; transitory income can be viewed as measurement error. Sometimes transitory income is positive, sometimes it is negative, on average it is 0:

$$IncAnnPC_t \quad = \quad IncPermPC_t \quad + \quad IncTransPC_t$$
$$\downarrow$$
$$\text{Measurement}$$
$$\text{error}$$
$$\downarrow$$
$$IncAnnPC_t \quad = \quad IncPermPC_t \quad + \quad u_t$$

where $\text{Mean}[u_t] = 0$, or equivalently,

$$IncPermPC_t = IncAnnPC_t - u_t$$

As a consequence of explanatory variable measurement error the ordinary least squares (OLS) estimation procedure for the coefficient will be biased downward. To understand why we begin with our model and then do a little algebra:

$$Covered_t = \beta_{Const} + \quad \beta_{IncPerm}IncPermPC_t \quad + \quad e_t$$
$$\downarrow \qquad\qquad\qquad \text{Substituting for } IncPermPC_t$$
$$= \beta_{Const} + \quad \beta_{IncPerm}(IncAnnPC_t - u_t) \quad + \quad e_t$$
$$\downarrow \qquad\qquad\qquad \text{Multiplying}$$
$$= \beta_{Const} + \beta_{IncPerm}IncAnnPC_t - \beta_{IncPerm}u_t + \quad e_t$$
$$\qquad\qquad\qquad\qquad \text{Rearranging terms}$$
$$= \beta_{Const} + \quad \beta_{IncPerm}IncAnnPC_t \quad + e_t - \beta_{IncPerm}u_t$$
$$\downarrow \qquad \text{Letting } \varepsilon_t = \beta_{IncPerm}u_t$$
$$Covered_t = \beta_{Const} + \quad \beta_{IncPerm}IncAnnPC_t \quad + \quad \varepsilon_t$$

where $\beta_{IncPerm} > 0$. Theory suggests that $\beta_{IncPerm}$ is positive; consequently we expect the new error term, ε_t, and the explanatory variable, $IncAnnPC_t$, to be negatively correlated.

$$IncAnnPC_t = IncPermPC_t + u_t \quad \nearrow^{u_t \text{ up}} \searrow \quad \varepsilon_t = e_t - \beta_{IncPerm}u_t \quad \beta_{IncPerm} > 0$$

$$IncAnnPC_t \text{ up} \quad \leftrightarrow \quad \varepsilon_t \text{ down}$$

$$\searrow \qquad \swarrow$$

Negative explanatory variable/error
term correlation

$$\downarrow$$

OLS biased downward

$IncAnnPC_t$ is the "problem" explanatory variable because it is correlated with the error term, ε_t. The ordinary least squares (OLS) estimation procedure for the coefficient value is biased toward 0. We will now show how we can use the instrumental variable (IV) estimation procedure to mitigate the problem.

19.6   Instrumental Variable (IV) Approach

19.6.1   The Mechanics

Choose an instrument: In this example we use percent of adults who completed high school, HS_t, as our instrument. In doing so, we believe that it satisfies the two "good" instrument conditions. We believe that high school education, HS_t,

· is positively correlated with the "problem" explanatory variable, $IncAnnPC_t$

and

· is uncorrelated with the error term, ε_t.

Instrumental Variables (IV) Regression 1
· **Dependent variable:**   "Problem" explanatory variable, $IncAnnPC$.
· **Explanatory variable:**   Instrument, the correlated variable, HS.

We can motivate IV Regression 1 by devising a theory to explain permanent income. Our theory is very straightforward, state per capita permanent income depends on percent of state residents who are high school graduates:

$$IncPermPC_t = \alpha_{Const} + \alpha_{HS}HS_t + e_t$$

Table 19.5
Health insurance IV Regression 1 results

	Ordinary least squares (OLS)			
Dependent variable: *IncAnnPC*				
Explanatory variable(s):	Estimate	SE	*t*-Statistic	Prob
HS	0.456948	0.194711	2.346797	0.0230
Const	−5.274762	16.75975	−0.314728	0.7543
Number of observations	51			
Estimated equation: *EstIncAnnPC* = −5.27 + 0.457*HS*				

where

HS_t = percent of adults (25 and over) who completed high school in state t

Theory: As a state has a greater percent of college graduates, its per capita permanent income increase; hence $\alpha_{HS} > 0$.

But, again, we note that permanent income is not observable, only annual income is. Consequently we have no choice but to use annual per capita income as the dependent variable (table 19.5).

[To access this online material, go to http://mitpress.mit.edu/westhoffeconometrics and select Health Insurance.]

What are the ramifications of using annual per capita income as the dependent variable? We can view annual per capita income as permanent per capita income with measurement error. What do we know about dependent variable measurement error? Dependent variable does not lead to bias; only explanatory variable measurement error creates bias. Since annual income is the dependent variable in IV Regression 1, the ordinary least squares (OLS) estimation procedure for the regression parameters will not be biased.

Instrumental Variables (IV) Regression 2
• **Dependent variable:**   Original dependent variable, *Covered*.

• **Explanatory variable:**   Estimate of the "problem" explanatory variable based on the results from IV Regression 1, *EstIncAnnPC*.

Use the estimates of IV Regression 1 to create a new variable, the estimated value of per capita disposable income based on the completion of high school (table 19.6):

$EstIncAnnPC = -5.27 + 0.457HS$

Table 19.6
Health insurance IV Regression 2 results

Ordinary least squares (OLS)				
Dependent variable: *Covered*				
Explanatory variable(s):	Estimate	SE	*t*-Statistic	Prob
EstIncAnnPC	1.387791	0.282369	4.914822	0.0000
Const	39.05305	9.620730	4.059260	0.0002
Number of observations	51			

Estimated equation: *EstCovered* = 39.05 + 1.39*EstIncAnnPC*

Interpretation of estimates:

$b_{EstIncAnnPC} = 1.39$: A \$1,000 increase in annual per capita disposable income increases the state's health insurance coverage by 1.39 percentage points

Critical result: The *EstIncAnnPC* coefficient estimate equals 1.39. The positive sign of the coefficient estimate suggests that increases in permanent disposable income increase health insurance coverage. This evidence supports the theory.

Table 19.7
Comparison of OLS and IV Regression results

	$\beta_{IncPerm}$ estimate	Standard error	*t*-Statistic	Tails probability
Ordinary least squares (OLS)	0.23	0.105	2.17	0.0352
Instrumental variable (IV)	1.38	0.282	4.91	<0.0001

19.6.2   Comparison of the Ordinary Least Squares (OLS) and the Instrumental Variables (IV) Approaches

Now review the two approaches that we used to estimate of the effect of permanent income on health insurance coverage: the ordinary least squares (OLS) estimation procedure and the instrumental variable (IV) estimation procedure.

• First, we used annual disposable income as the explanatory variable and applied the ordinary least squares (OLS) estimation procedure. We estimated that a \$1,000 increase in per capita disposable income increases health insurance coverage by 0.23 percentage points. But we believe that an explanatory variable measurement error problem is present here.

• Second, we used an instrumental variable (IV) approach, which resulted in a higher estimate for the impact of permanent income. We estimated that a \$1,000 increase in per capita disposable income increases health insurance coverage by 1.39 percentage points.

These results are consistent with the notion that the ordinary least squares (OLS) estimation procedure for the coefficient value is biased downward whenever explanatory variable measurement error is present (table 19.7).

19.6.3   "Good" Instrument Conditions Revisited

IV Regression 1 allows us to assess the first "good" instrument condition.

Instrument/"problem" explanatory variable correlation: The instrument, HS_t, must be correlated with the "problem" explanatory variable, $IncAnnPC_t$.

We are using the instrument to create a surrogate for the "problem" explanatory variable in IV Regression 1:

$$EstIncAnnPC_t = -5.27 + 0.457HS_t$$

The estimate, $EstIncAnnPC_t$, will be a "good" surrogate only if the instrument, HS_t, is correlated with the "problem" explanatory variable, $IncAnnPC_t$; that is, only if the estimate is a good predictor of the "problem" explanatory variable.

The sign of the HS_t coefficient is positive supporting our view that annual income and high school education are positively correlated. Furthermore, the coefficient is significant at the 5 percent level and nearly significant at the 1 percent level. So it is reasonable to judge that the instrument meets the first condition.

Next focus on the second "good" instrument condition:

Instrument/error term independence: The instrument, HS, and the error term, ε_t, must be independent. Otherwise, the explanatory variable/error term independence premise would be violated in IV Regression 2.

Recall the model that IV Regression 2 estimates:

$$Covered_t \;=\; \beta_{Const} \;+\; \beta_{IncPerm}EstAnnIncPC_t \;+\; \varepsilon_t$$

Question: Are $EstAnnIncPC_t$ and ε_t independent?

$$EstIncAnnPC_t = -5.27 + 0.457HS_t, \qquad\qquad \varepsilon_t = e_t - \beta_{IncPerm}u_t$$

Answer: Only if HS_t and ε_t are independent.

The explanatory variable/error term independence premise will be satisfied only if the instrument, HS_t, and the new error term, ε_t, are independent. If they are correlated, then we have gone "from the frying pan into the fire." It was the violation of this premise that created the problem in the first place. There is no obvious reason to believe that they are correlated. Unfortunately, there is no way to confirm this empirically, however. This can be the "Achilles heel" of the instrumental variable (IV) estimation procedure. Finding a good instrument can be very tricky.

19.7   Justifying the Instrumental Variable (IV) Estimation Procedure

Claim: While the instrumental variable (IV) estimation procedure for the coefficient value in the presence of measurement is biased, it is consistent.

Econometrics Lab 19.4: Consistency and the Instrumental Variable (IV) Estimation Procedure

While this claim can be justified rigorous, we will avoid the mathematics by using a simulation.

[To access this online material, go to http://mitpress.mit.edu/westhoffeconometrics and select Lab 19.4.]

Focus your attention on figure 19.5. Since we wish to investigate the properties of the instrumental variable (IV) estimation procedure, IV is selected in the estimation procedure box. Next note the XMeas Var List. Explanatory variable measurement error is present. By default, the

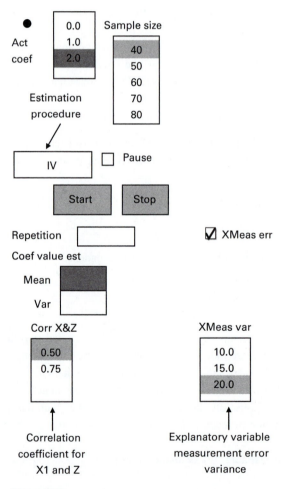

Figure 19.5
Instrumental variable measurement error simulation

Table 19.8
Measurement error, IV estimation procedure, and consistency

Estimation procedure	XMeas var	Sample size	Actual coef	Mean of coef ests	Magnitude of bias	Variance of coef ests
IV	20	40	2.0	≈2.24	≈0.24	≈8.7
IV	20	50	2.0	≈2.21	≈0.21	≈5.4
IV	20	60	2.0	≈2.17	≈0.17	≈3.4

variance of the probability distribution for the measurement error term, $Var[u_t]$, equals 20.0. In the Corr X&Z list .50 is selected; the correlation coefficient between the explanatory variable and the instrument is .50.

Initially, the sample size is 40. Click **Start** and then after many, many repetitions click **Stop**. The average of the estimated coefficient values equals 2.24. Next increase the sample size from 40 to 50 and repeat the process. Do the same for a sample size of 60. As table 19.8 reports, the average of the estimated coefficient values never equals the actual value; consequently the instrumental variable (IV) estimation procedure for the coefficient value is biased. But also note that the magnitude of the bias decreases as the sample size increases. Also the variance of the estimates declines as the sample size increases.

Table 19.8 suggests that when explanatory variable measurement error is present, the instrumental variable (IV) estimation procedure for the coefficient value provides both good news and bad news:

• **Bad news:**   The instrumental variable (IV) estimation procedure for the coefficient value is still biased; the average of the estimated coefficient values does not equal the actual value.

• **Good news:**   The instrumental variable (IV) estimation procedure for the coefficient value is consistent.

As the sample size is increased,

• the magnitude of the bias diminishes and
• the variance of the estimated coefficient values decreases.

Chapter 19 Review Questions

1. Suppose that dependent variable measurement error is present.
   a. What problem does not result? In words, explain why.
   b. What problem does result? Explain why.
2. What problem results when explanatory variable measurement error is present? Explain why.
3. When explanatory variable measurement error is present:

a. Is the ordinary least squares (OLS) estimation procedure appropriate? Explain.

b. In what way is the instrumental variable (IV) estimation procedure not better than the ordinary least squares (OLS) estimation procedure? In what way is the instrumental variable (IV) estimation procedure better?

Chapter 19 Exercises

Reconsider the following model to explain scores on a final exam:

$$ExamScore_t = \beta_{Const} + \beta_{Prob}ProbScores_t + \beta_{Sat}SATScores_t + e_t$$

where

$ExamScore_t$ = student t's score on the final exam

$ProbScores_t$ = sum of student t's score on the semester's problem sets

$SATScores_t$ = sum of student t's math and verbal SAT scores

Suppose that we wish to publish the results of our analysis along with the data. As a consequence of privacy concerns, we wish to prevent "outsiders" from connecting an individual student's exam, problem set, and SAT scores.

1. Randomize the student $SATScores$. More specifically, for each student flip a coin:

- If the coin lands heads, add 10 points to that student's $SATScores$.
- If the coin lands tails, subtract 10 points from that student's $SATScores$.

Use the randomized values in the analysis instead of the actual values. What are the econometric consequences of this approach?

2. Randomize the student $ProbScores$. More specifically, for each student flip a coin:

- If the coin lands heads, add 10 points to that student's $ProbScores$.
- If the coin lands tails, subtract 10 points from that student's $ProbScores$.

Use the randomized values in the analysis instead of the actual values. What are the econometric consequences of this approach?

3. Randomize the student $ExamScore$. More specifically, for each student flip a coin:

- If the coin lands heads, add 10 points to that student's $ExamScore$.
- If the coin lands tails, subtract 10 points from that student's $ExamScore$.

Use the randomized values in the analysis instead of the actual values. What are the econometric consequences of this approach?

Health insurance data: Cross-sectional data of health insurance coverage, education, and income statistics from the 50 states and the District of Columbia in 2007.

$Covered_t$ Percent of adults (25 and older) with health insurance in state t

$IncAnnPC_t$ Per capita annual disposable income in state t (thousands of dollars)

HS_t Percent of adults (25 and older) who completed high school in state t

$Coll_t$ Percent of adults (25 and older) who completed a four year college in state t

$AdvDeg_t$ Percent of adults (25 and older) who have an advanced degree in state t

4. Consider the same theory and model that we used in the chapter:

Theory: Additional permanent per capita disposable income within a state increases health insurance coverage within the state.

$$Covered_t = \beta_{Const} + \beta_{IncPerm}IncPermPC_t + e_t$$

where

$Covered_t$ = percent of individuals with health insurance in state t

$IncPermPC_t$ = per capita permanent disposable income in state t

Repeat part of what was done in this chapter: use the ordinary least squares (OLS) estimation procedure to estimate the value of the $IncPermPC$ coefficient. You have no choice but to use $IncAnnPC_t$ as the explanatory variable since $IncPermPC_t$ is not observable. Does the sign of the coefficient lend support for your theory?

[To access this online material, go to http://mitpress.mit.edu/westhoffeconometrics and select Health Insurance.]

5. Use the instrumental variable (IV) estimation procedure to estimate the coefficient of $IncPermPC_t$. But instead of using the percentage of adults who completed high school, HS, as the instrument use the percentage of adults who completed a four year college, $Coll$, as the instrument.

[To access this online material, go to http://mitpress.mit.edu/westhoffeconometrics and select Health Insurance.]

    a. Compute the IV Regression 1 results.

    b. Compute the IV Regression 2 results.

6. How, if at all, does the instrumental variable (IV) procedure affect the assessment of your theory?

Judicial data: Cross-sectional data of judicial and economic statistics for the fifty states in 2000.

JudExp_t   State and local expenditures for the judicial system per 100,000 persons in state *t*

CrimesAll_t   Crimes per 100,000 persons in state *t*

GdpPC_t   Per capita real per capita GDP in state *t* (2000 dollars)

Pop_t   Population in state *t* (persons)

UnemRate_t   Unemployment rate in state *t* (percent)

State_t   Name of state *t*

Year_t   Year

7. Consider the following linear model explaining judicial expenditures:

$$JudExp_t = \beta_{Const} + \beta_{Crimes}CrimesAll_t + \beta_{GDP}GdpPC_t + e_t$$

    a. Develop a theory regarding how each explanatory variable influences the dependent variable. What does your theory imply about the sign of each coefficient?

    b. Using the ordinary least squares (OLS) estimation procedure, estimate the value of each coefficient using the Judicial Data. Interpret the coefficient estimates. What are the critical results?

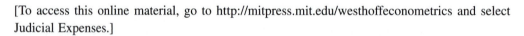

[To access this online material, go to http://mitpress.mit.edu/westhoffeconometrics and select Judicial Expenses.]

8. Many believe that measurement error is present in crime rate statistics. Use instrumental variable (IV) estimation procedure to account for the measurement error.

[To access this online material, go to http://mitpress.mit.edu/westhoffeconometrics and select Judicial Expenses.]

    a. Explain why *UnemRate_t* may be an appropriate instrument for *CrimesAll_t*.

    b. Using *UnemRate_t* as the instrument, compute the IV Regression 1 results.

    c. Compute the IV Regression 2 results.

9. How, if at all, does the instrumental variable (IV) procedure affect the assessment of your theory?

20 Omitted Variables and the Instrumental Variable Estimation Procedure

Chapter 20 Prep Question

1. Consider two regression models:

$$y_t = \beta_{Const} + \beta_{x1}x1_t + \beta_{x2}x2_t + e_t$$

and

$$y_t = \beta_{Const} + \beta_{x1}x1_t + \varepsilon_t$$

    a. Express the second model's error term, ε_t, in terms as a function of the first model's terms.

Assume that

• the coefficient β_{x2} is positive

and

• the explanatory variables, $x1_t$ and $x2_t$, are positively correlated.

    b. Will the explanatory variable, $x1_t$, and the second model's error term, ε_t, be correlated? If so, how?

    c. Focus on the second model. Suppose that the ordinary least squares (OLS) estimation procedure were used to estimate the parameters of the second model. Would the ordinary least squares estimation (OLS) estimation procedure for the value of β_{x1} be biased? If so, how?

Omitted explanatory variables example—2008 presidential election data: Cross-sectional data of election, population, and economic statistics from the 50 states and the District of Columbia in 2008.

$AdvDeg_t$	Percent adults who have advanced degrees in state t
$Coll_t$	Percent adults who graduated from college in state t
HS_t	Percent adults who graduated from high school in state t
$PopDen_t$	Population density of state t (persons per square mile)
$RealGdpGrowth_t$	GDP growth rate for state t in 2008 (percent)
$UnemTrend_t$	Change in the unemployment rate for state t in 2008 (percent)
$VoteDemPartyTwo_t$	Percent of the vote received in 2008 received by the Democratic party in state t based on the two major parties (percent)

2. Consider the following model explaining the vote received by the Democratic Party in the 2008 presidential election:

$$\begin{aligned}VoteDemPartyTwo_t &= \beta_{Const} + \beta_{PopDen}PopDen_t + \beta_{Lib}Liberal_t + e_t \\ &= \beta_{Const} + \beta_{PopDen}PopDen_t + (\beta_{Lib}Liberal_t + e_t) \\ &= \beta_{Const} + \beta_{PopDen}PopDen_t + \varepsilon_t\end{aligned}$$

The variable $Liberal_t$ reflects the "liberalness" of the electorate in state t. On the one hand, if the electorate is by nature liberal in state t, the $Liberal_t$ would be high; on the other hand, if the electorate is conservative the $Liberal_t$ would be low.

a. Express the second model's error term, ε_t, in terms as a function of the first model's terms.

Assume that

· the coefficient β_{Lib} is positive

and

· the explanatory variables $PopDen_t$ and $Liberal_t$ are positively correlated.

b. Will the explanatory variable $PopDen_t$ and the second model's error term, ε_t, be correlated? If so, how?

c. Focus on the second model. Suppose that the ordinary least squares (OLS) estimation procedure were used to estimate the parameters of the second model. Would the ordinary least squares estimation (OLS) estimation procedure for the value of β_{Lib} be biased? If so, how?

3. What does the correlation coefficient of $PopDen_t$ and $Coll_t$ equal?

20.1 Revisit Omitted Explanatory Variable Bias

We will briefly review our previous discussion of omitted explanatory variables that appears in chapter 14. Then we will show that omitted explanatory variable phenomenon can also be analyzed in terms of explanatory variable/error term correlation.

20.1.1 Review of Our Previous Explanation of Omitted Explanatory Variable Bias

In chapter 14 we argued that omitting an explanatory variable from a regression will bias the ordinary least squares (OLS) estimation procedure for the coefficient value whenever two conditions are met. Bias results if the omitted variable

· influences the dependent variable;
· is correlated with an included variable.

When these two conditions are met, the ordinary least squares (OLS) procedure to estimate the coefficient of the included explanatory variable captures two effects:

· **Direct effect:**   The effect that the included explanatory variable actually has on the dependent variable.

· **Proxy effect:**   The effect that the omitted explanatory variable has on the dependent variable because the included variable is acting as a proxy for the omitted variable.

Recall the goal of multiple regression analysis:

Goal of multiple regression analysis: Multiple regression analysis attempts to sort out the individual effect that each explanatory variable has on the dependent variable.

Consequently we want the coefficient estimate of the included variable to capture only the direct effect and not the proxy effect. Unfortunately, the ordinary least squares (OLS) estimation procedure fails to do this when the omitted variance influences the dependent variable and when it is also correlated with an included variable.

To illustrate this, we considered a model with two explanatory variables, $x1$ and $x2$:

Model: $y_t = \beta_{Const} + \beta_{x1}x1_t + \beta_{x2}x2_t + e_t$

For purposes of illustration, assume that the coefficients are positive and that the explanatory variables are positively correlated:

- $\beta_{x1} > 0$ and $\beta_{x2} > 0$.
- $x1_t$ and $x2_t$ are positively correlated.

What happens when we omit the explanatory variable $x2_t$ from the regression?
The two conditions necessary for the omitted variable bias are satisfied:

- Since β_{x2} is positive, the omitted variable influences the dependent variable.
- Since $x1_t$ and $x2_t$ are positively correlated, the omitted variable is correlated with an included variable.

An increase in $x1_t$ directly affects y_t, causing y_t to increase; this is the direct effect we want to capture. But the story does not end here when $x2_t$ is omitted. Since the two explanatory variables are positively correlated, an increase in $x1_t$ is typically accompanied by an increase in $x2_t$, which in turn leads to an additional increase in y_t:

When the explanatory variable $x2_t$ is omitted from a regression, the ordinary least squares (OLS) estimation procedure for the value of $x1_t$'s coefficient, β_{x1}, is biased upward because it reflects not only the impact of $x1_t$ itself (direct effect) but also the impact of $x2_t$ (proxy effect).

20.1.2 Omitted Explanatory Variable Bias and the Explanatory Variable/Error Term Independence Premise

We can also use what we learned in chapter 18 about correlation between the explanatory variable and error term to explain why bias occurs. When we omit the explanatory variable $x2_t$ from the regression, the error term of the new equation, ε_t, includes not only the original error term, e_t, but also the "omitted variable term," $\beta_{x2}x2_t$:

$$y_t = \beta_{Const} + \beta_{x1}x1_t + \beta_{x2}x2_t + e_t$$
$$= \beta_{Const} + \beta_{x1}x1_t + (\beta_{x2}x2_t + e_t)$$
$$= \beta_{Const} + \beta_{x1}x1_t + \varepsilon_t$$

where $\varepsilon_t = \beta_{x2}x2_t + e_t$.

Recall that

- $\beta_{x2} > 0$.
- $x1_t$ and $x2_t$ are positively correlated.

The new error term, ε_t, includes the "omitted variable term," $\beta_{x2}x2_t$. Therefore the included explanatory variable, $x1_t$, and the new error term, ε_t, are positively correlated:

- Since $x1_t$ and $x2_t$ are positively correlated, when $x1_t$ increases, $x2_t$ typically increases also.
- Since β_{x2} is positive when $x1_t$ increases, $\beta_{x2}x2_t$ and the new error term, ε_t, increases also, the new error term will typically increase.

$$x1_t \text{ and } x2_t$$
$$\text{positively correlated}$$

Included variable $x1_t$ up	$\longrightarrow$	Typically omitted variable $x2_t$ up	
$\downarrow$		$\downarrow$	$\varepsilon_t = \beta_{x2}x2_t + e_t$
$x1_t$ up		ε_t up $\beta_{x2} > 0$	

$$x1_t \text{ and } \varepsilon_t \text{ positively correlated}$$

What did we learn about the consequence of correlation between the explanatory variable and error term? When the explanatory variable and error term are positively correlated, the ordinary least squares (OLS) estimation procedure for the value of $x1_t$'s coefficient is biased upward.

$x1_t$ and ε_t positively correlated

$$\downarrow$$

OLS estimation procedure for
  the value of $x1$'s coefficient
      is biased upward

When $x2_t$ is omitted, $x1_t$ becomes a "problem" explanatory variable because it is correlated with the new error term. Our two analyzes arrive at the same conclusion.

20.2   The Ordinary Least Squares Estimation Procedure, Omitted Explanatory Variable Bias, and Consistency

When an omitted explanatory variable causes the ordinary least squares (OLS) estimation procedure to be biased, might the procedure still be consistent? We will use a simulation to address this question (figure 20.1).

Econometrics Lab 20.1: Ordinary Least Squares, Omitted Variables, and Consistency

[To access this online material, go to http://mitpress.mit.edu/westhoffeconometrics and select Lab 20.1.]

By default, the actual value of $x1_t$ coefficient, Coef1, equals 2.0 and the actual value of the $x2_t$ coefficient, Coef2, equals 4.0. The correlation coefficient for the explanatory variables $x1_t$ and $x2_t$ equals 0.60; the explanatory variables are positively correlated. Furthermore the Only X1 option is selected; the explanatory variable $x2_t$ is omitted. The included explanatory variable, $x1_t$, will be positively correlated with the error term. $x1_t$ becomes a "problem" explanatory variable.

Initially, the sample size equals 50. Click **Start** and then after many, many repetitions click **Stop**. The mean of the coefficient estimates for the explanatory variable $x1$ equals 4.4. Our logic is confirmed; upward bias results. Nevertheless, to determine if the ordinary least squares (OLS) estimation procedure might consistent we increase the sample size from 50 to 100 and once more from 100 to 150. As table 20.1 reports, the mean of the coefficient estimates remains at 4.4.

Unfortunately, the ordinary least squares (OLS) estimation procedure proves to be not only biased but also not consistent whenever an explanatory variable is omitted that

• affects the dependent variable

and

• is correlated with an included variable.

What can we do?

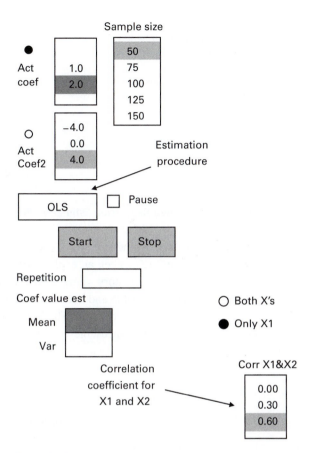

Figure 20.1
OLS omitted variable simulation

Table 20.1
Ordinary least squares: Bias and consistency

Estimation procedure	Corr X1&X2	Actual coef2	Sample size	Actual coef	Mean of coef1 ests	Magnitude of bias	Variance of coef1 ests
OLS	0.60	4.0	50	2.0	≈4.4	≈2.4	≈6.6
OLS	0.60	4.0	100	2.0	≈4.4	≈2.4	≈3.2
OLS	0.60	4.0	150	2.0	≈4.4	≈2.4	≈2.1

Original model:
$$Y_t = \beta_{Const} + \beta_x x_t + \varepsilon_t, \text{ where } y_t = \text{dependent variable}$$

$x_t = $ explanatory variable

$\varepsilon_t = $ error term

When x_t and ε_t $t = 1, 2, \ldots, T,\ \ T = $ sample size

are correlated

$\downarrow$

x_t is the "problem"
explanatory variable

Figure 20.2
"Problem" explanatory variable

20.3   Instrumental Variable Estimation Procedure: A Two Regression Estimation Procedure

The instrumental variable (IV) estimation procedure can deal with situations when the explanatory variable and the error term are correlated (figure 20.2). When an explanatory variable, x_t, is correlated with the error term, ε_t, we refer to the explanatory variable as the "problem" explanatory variable. The correlation of the explanatory variable and the error term creates the bias problem for the ordinary least squares (OLS) estimation procedure. The instrumental variable estimation procedure can mitigate, but not completely remedy these cases. Let us briefly review the procedure and motivate it.

20.3.1   Mechanics

Choose a "good" instrument: A "good" instrument, z_t, must have two properties:

- Correlated with the "problem" explanatory variable, x_t, and
- Uncorrelated with the error term, ε_t.

Instrumental variables (IV) Regression 1:   Use the instrument, z_t, to provide an "estimate" of the problem explanatory variable, x_t.

- Dependent variable: "Problem" explanatory variable, x_t.
- Explanatory variable: Instrument, z_t.
- Estimate of the "problem" explanatory variable: $Estx_t = a_{Const} + a_z z_t$, where a_{Const} and a_z are the estimates of the constant and coefficient in this regression, IV Regression 1.

Instrumental variables (IV) Regression 2:   In the original model, replace the "problem" explanatory variable, x_t, with its surrogate, $Estx_t$, the estimate of the "problem" explanatory variable provided by the instrument, z_t, from IV Regression 1.

- Dependent variable: Original dependent variable, y_t.
- Explanatory variable: Estimate of the "problem" explanatory variable based on the results from IV Regression 1, $Estx_t$.

20.3.2   The "Good" Instrument Conditions

Let us again provide the intuition behind why a "good" instrument, z_t, must satisfy the two conditions:

Instrument/"problem" explanatory variable correlation: The instrument, z_t, must be correlated with the "problem" explanatory variable, x_t. To understand why, focus on IV Regression 1. We are using the instrument to create a surrogate for the "problem" explanatory variable in IV Regression 1:

$$Estx_t = a_{Const} + a_z z_t$$

The estimate, $Estx_t$, will be a good surrogate only if it is a good predictor of the "problem" explanatory variable, x_t. This will occur only if the instrument, z_t, is correlated with the "problem" explanatory variable, x_t.

Instrument/error term independence: The instrument, z_t, must be independent of the error term, ε_t. Focus on IV Regression 2. We begin with the original model and then replace the "problem" explanatory, x_t, variable with its surrogate, $Estx_t$:

$$y_t = \beta_{Const} + \beta_x x_t + \varepsilon_t$$
$$\downarrow \qquad\qquad \text{Replace "problem" with surrogate}$$
$$= \beta_{Const} + \beta_x Estx_t + \varepsilon_t$$

where $Estx_t = a_{Const} + a_z z_t$ from IV Regression 1.

   To avoid violating the explanatory variable/error term independence premise in IV Regression 2, the surrogate for the "problem" explanatory variable, $Estx_t$, must be independent of the error term, ε_t. The surrogate, $Estx_t$, is derived from the instrument, z_t, in IV Regression 1:

$$Estx_t = a_{Const} + a_z z_t$$

Consequently, to avoid violating the explanatory variable/error term independence premise the instrument, z_t, and the error term, ε_t, must be independent.

$$\textit{Estx}_t \text{ and } \varepsilon_t \text{ must be independent}$$
$$y_t \quad = \quad \beta_{Const} \quad + \quad \beta_x Estx_t \quad + \quad \varepsilon_t$$
$$\downarrow$$
$$Estx_t = a_{Const} + a_z z_t$$
$$z_t \text{ and } \varepsilon_t \text{ must be independent}$$

20.4   Omitted Explanatory Variables Example: 2008 Presidential Election

2008 presidential election data: Cross-sectional data of election, population, and economic statistics from the 50 states and the District of Columbia in 2008.

$AdvDeg_t$	Percent adults who have advanced degrees in state t
$Coll_t$	Percent adults who graduated from college in state t
HS_t	Percent adults who graduated from high school in state t
$PopDen_t$	Population density of state t (persons per square mile)
$RealGdpGrowth_t$	GDP growth rate for state t in 2008 (percent)
$UnemTrend_t$	Change in the unemployment rate for state t in 2008 (percent)
$VoteDemPartyTwo_t$	Percent of the vote received in 2008 received by the Democratic party in state t based on the two major parties (percent)

[To access this online material, go to http://mitpress.mit.edu/westhoffeconometrics and select Presidential Election—2008.]

Now we introduce a model to explain the Democratic vote:

Model: $VoteDemPartyTwo_t = \beta_{Const} + \beta_{PopDen}PopDen_t + \beta_{Lib}Liberal_t + e_t$

The variable $Liberal_t$ reflects the "liberalness" of the electorate in state t. On the one hand, if the electorate is by nature liberal in state t, the $Liberal_t$ would be high; on the other hand, if the electorate is conservative, the $Liberal_t$ would be low. The theories described below suggest that coefficients both $Liberal_t$ and $PopDen_t$ would be positive:

· **Population density theory:**   States with high population densities have large urban areas which are more likely to vote for the Democratic candidate, Obama; hence $\beta_{PopDen} > 0$.

· **"Liberalness" theory:**   Since the Democratic party is more liberal than the Republican party, a high "liberalness" value would increase the vote of the Democratic candidate, Obama; hence $\beta_{Lib} > 0$.

Unfortunately, we do not have any data to quantify the "liberalness" of a state; according, $Liberal$ must be omitted from the regression (table 20.2).

Question: Might the ordinary least squares (OLS) estimation procedure suffer from a serious econometric problem?

Since the "liberalness" variable is unobservable and must be omitted from the regression, the explanatory variable/error term premise would be violated if the included variable, $PopDen_t$, is correlated with the new error term, ε_t.

Table 20.2
Democratic vote OLS regression results

Ordinary least squares (OLS)				
Dependent variable: *VoteDemPartyTwo*				
Explanatory variable(s):	Estimate	SE	*t*-Statistic	Prob
PopDen	0.004915	0.000957	5.137338	0.0000
Const	50.35621	1.334141	37.74431	0.0000
Number of observations	51			

Estimated equation: *VoteDemPartyTwo* = 50.3 + 0.005*PopDen*

Interpretation of estimates:

$b_{EstPopDen} = 0.005$: A 1 person increase in a state's population density increases the state's Democratic vote by 0.005 percentage points; that is, a 100 person increase in a state's population density increases the state's Democratic vote by 0.5 percentage points

Critical result: The *EstPopDen* coefficient estimate equals 0.005. The positive sign of the coefficient estimate suggests that increases in a state with a higher population density will have a greater Democratic vote. This evidence supports the theory.

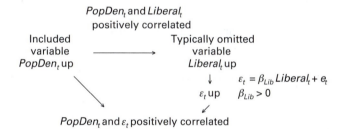

Figure 20.3
PopDen—A "problem" explanatory variable

$$VoteDemPartyTwo_t = \beta_{Const} + \beta_{PopDen}PopDen_t + \beta_{Lib}Liberal_t + e_t$$
$$= \beta_{Const} + \beta_{PopDen}PopDen_t + (\beta_{Lib}Liberal_t + e_t)$$
$$= \beta_{Const} + \beta_{PopDen}PopDen_t + \varepsilon_t$$

where $\varepsilon_t = \beta_{Lib}Liberal_t + e_t$. We have good reason to believe that they will be correlated because we would expect $PopDen_t$ and $Liberal_t$ to be correlated. States that tend to elect liberal representatives and senators then to have high population densities. That is, we suspect that $PopDen_t$ and $Liberal_t$ are positively correlated (figure 20.3). Consequently the included explanatory variable, $PopDen_t$, and the error term, ε_t, will be positively correlated. The ordinary least squares (OLS) estimation procedure for the value of the coefficient will be biased upward.

To summarize, when the explanatory variable *Liberal* is omitted, as it must be, *PopDen* becomes a "problem" explanatory variable become it is correlated with the error term, ε_t. Now we will apply the Instrumental Variable (IV) estimation procedure to understand how the instrument variable estimation procedure can address the omitted variable problem.

20.5   Instrument Variable (IV) Application: 2008 Presidential Election

20.5.1   The Mechanics

Choose an instrument: In this example we will use the percent of college graduates, $Coll_t$, as our instrument. In doing so, we believe that it satisfies the two "good" instrument conditions; that is, we believe that the percentage of high school graduates, $Coll_t$, is

· positively correlated with the "problem" explanatory variable, $PopDen_t$

and

· uncorrelated with the error term, $\varepsilon_t = \beta_{Lib}Liberal_t + e_t$. Consequently we believe that the instrument, $Coll_t$, is uncorrelated with the omitted variable, $Liberal_t$.

Instrumental variables (IV) Regression 1 (table 20.3):

· **Dependent variable:**   "Problem" explanatory variable, $PopDen$.
· **Explanatory variable:**   Instrument, $Coll$.

Instrumental variables (IV) Regression 2 (table 20.4):

· **Dependent variable:**   Original dependent variable, $VoteDemPartyTwo$.
· **Explanatory variable:**   Estimate of the "problem" explanatory variable based on the results from IV Regression 1, $EstPopDen$.

Table 20.3
Democratic vote IV Regression 1 results

Ordinary least squares (OLS)				
Dependent variable: *PopDen*				
Explanatory variable(s):	Estimate	SE	*t*-Statistic	Prob
Coll	149.3375	28.21513	5.292816	0.0000
Const	−3,676.281	781.0829	−4.706647	0.0000
Number of observations	51			
Estimated equation: $EstPopDen = -3{,}676.3 + 149.3Coll$				

Table 20.4
Democratic vote IV Regression 2 results

Ordinary least squares (OLS)				
Dependent variable: *VoteDemPartyTwo*				
Explanatory variable(s):	Estimate	SE	*t*-Statistic	Prob
EstPopDen	0.009955	0.001360	7.317152	0.0000
Const	48.46247	1.214643	39.89852	0.0000
Number of observations	51			

Estimated equation: *VoteDemPartyTwo* = 48.5 + 0.010*EstPopDen*

Interpretation of estimates:

$b_{EstPopDen}$ = 0.010: A 1 person increase in a state's population density increases the state's Democratic vote by 0.010 percentage points; that is, a 100 person increase in a state's population density increases the state's Democratic vote by 1.0 percentage points

Critical result: The *EstPopDen* coefficient estimate equals 0.010. The positive sign of the coefficient estimate suggests that increases in a state with a higher population density will have a greater Democratic vote. This evidence supports the theory.

Table 20.5
Correlation matrices *Coll* and *PopDen*

	Correlation matrix	
	Coll	*PopDen*
Coll	1.000000	0.603118
PopDen	0.603118	1.000000

20.5.2   Good Instrument Conditions Revisited

IV Regression 1 allows us to assess the first "good" instrument condition.

Instrument/"problem" explanatory variable correlation: The instrument, $Coll_t$, must be correlated with the "problem" explanatory variable, $PopDen_t$. We are using the instrument to create a surrogate for the "problem" explanatory variable in IV Regression 1:

$$EstPopDen = -3,676.3 + 149.3Coll$$

The estimate, $EstPopDen_t$, will be a "good" surrogate only if the instrument, $Coll_t$, is correlated with the "problem" explanatory variable, $PopDen_t$; that is, only if the estimate is a good predictor of the "problem" explanatory variable. Table 20.5 reports that the correlation coefficient for $Coll_t$ and $PopDen_t$ equals 0.60. Furthermore the IV Regression 1 results appearing in table 20.3 suggest that the instrument, $Coll_t$, will be a good predictor of the "problem" explanatory variable, $PopDen_t$. Clearly, the coefficient estimate is significant at the 1 percent level. So it is reasonable to judge that the instrument meets the first condition.

Next focus on the second "good" instrument condition:

Instrument/error term independence: The instrument, $Coll_t$, and the error term, ε_t, must be independent. Otherwise, the explanatory variable/error term independence premise would be violated in IV Regression 2.

Recall the model that IV Regression 2 estimates:

$$VoteDemPartyTwo_t \quad = \quad \beta_{Const} \quad + \quad \beta_{PopDen}EstPopDen_t \quad + \quad \varepsilon_t$$

Question: Are $EstPopDen_t$ and ε_t independent?

$$EstPopDen_t = -3{,}676.3 + 149.3Coll_t, \qquad \varepsilon_t = \beta_{Lib}Liberal_t + e_t$$

Answer: Only if $Coll_t$ and $Liberal_t$ are independent.

The explanatory variable/error term independence premise will be satisfied only if the surrogate, $EstPopDen_t$, and the error term, ε_t, are independent. $EstPopDen_t$ is a linear function of $Coll_t$ and ε_t is a linear function of $PopDen_t$:

• $EstPopDen_t = -560.9 + 28.13Coll_t$

and

• $\varepsilon_t = \beta_{Lib}Liberal_t + e_t$

Hence the explanatory variable/error term independence premise will be satisfied only if the instrument, $Coll_t$, and the omitted variable, $Liberal_t$, are independent. If they are correlated, then we have gone "from the frying pan into the fire." It was the violation of this premise that created the problem in the first place. Unless we were to believe that liberals are better educated than conservatives, and vice versa, it is not unreasonable to believe that education and political leanings are independent. Many liberals are highly educated and many conservatives are highly educated. Unfortunately, there is no way to confirm this empirically. This can be the "Achilles heel" of the instrumental variable (IV) estimation procedure. When we choose an instrument, it must be uncorrelated with the omitted variable. Since there is no way to assess this empirically, we are implicitly assuming that the second good instrument condition is satisfied when we use the instrumental variables estimation procedure to address the omitted explanatory variables problem.

20.6 Justifying the Instrumental Variable (IV) Approach: A Simulation

We claim that while the instrumental variable (IV) estimation procedure for the coefficient value is still biased when an omitted explanatory variable problem exists, it will be consistent when we use a "good" instrument.

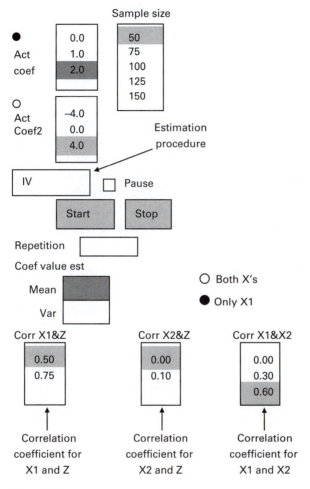

Figure 20.4
IV omitted variable simulation

Econometrics Lab 20.2: Instrumental Variables—Omitted Variables: Good Instrument

While this claim can be justified rigorous, we will avoid the complicated mathematics by using a simulation (figure 20.4).

[To access this online material, go to http://mitpress.mit.edu/westhoffeconometrics and select Lab 20.2.]

The model upon which this simulation is based on the following model:

$$y_t = \beta_{Const} + \beta_{x1}x1_t + \beta_{x2}x2_t + e_t$$

The Only X1 button is selected; hence, only the first explanatory variable will be included in the analysis. The model becomes

$$y_t = \beta_{Const} + \beta_{x1}x1_t + \beta_{x2}x2_t + e_t$$
$$= \beta_{Const} + \beta_{x1}x1_t + (\beta_{x2}x2_t + e_t)$$
$$= \beta_{Const} + \beta_{x1}x1_t + \varepsilon_t$$

where $\varepsilon_t = \beta_{x2}x2_t + e_t$. The second explanatory variable, $x2$, is omitted.

As before the values for the actual coefficients of the two explanatory variables are 2.0 and 4.0. Since the Only X1 button is selected, the explanatory variable, $x2$, is omitted and only the first explanative variable, $x1$, is included. The correlation coefficient of the two explanatory variables equals 0.60. The included and omitted variables are positively correlated.

Since the instrumental variable (IV) estimation procedure, IV, is specified, the Corr X1&Z and Corr X2&Z lists appear. These lists concern the instrumental variable, z. Recall that to be a good instrument two conditions must be met:

• included "problem" explanatory variable must be correlated so that the instrument acts as a good surrogate for the "problem" explanatory variable.

• error term must be independent so that we do not violate the explanatory variable/error term independence premise.

The Corr X1&Z list specifies the correlation coefficient of the included explanatory variable, $x1$, and the instrument, z. This correlation indicates how good a surrogate the instrument will be. An increase in correlation means that the instrument should become a better surrogate. By default, this correlation coefficient equals .50. The Corr X2&Z list specifies the correlation coefficient of the omitted explanatory variable, $x2$, and the instrument, z. Recall how the omitted variable, $x2$, and the error term, ε_t, are related:

$$y_t = \beta_{Const} + \beta_{x1}x1_t + \varepsilon_t$$

where $\varepsilon_t = \beta_{x2} x2_t + e_t$. By default, .00 is selected from the Corr X2&Z list. Hence the instrument, z, and the error term, ε_t, are independent. The second condition required for a "good" instrument is also satisfied. Initially, the sample size equals 50. Then we increase from 50 to 100 and subsequently from 100 to 150. Table 20.6 reports results from this simulation:

Both bad news and good news emerge:

• **Bad news:** The instrumental variable estimation is biased. The mean of the estimates for the coefficient of the first explanatory variable, $x1$, does not equal the actual value we specified, 2.

• **Good news:** As we increase the sample size, the mean of the coefficient estimates gets closer to the actual value and the variance of the coefficient estimates becomes smaller. This illustrates the fact that the instrumental variable (IV) estimation procedure is consistent.

Table 20.6
IV estimation procedure—Biased but consistent

Estimation procedure	Correlation coefficients			Sample size	Actual coef1	Mean of coef1 ests	Magnitude of bias	Variance of coef1 ests
	X1&Z	X2&Z	X1&X2					
IV	0.50	0.00	0.60	50	2.0	≈1.81	≈0.19	≈32.6
IV	0.50	0.00	0.60	100	2.0	≈1.89	≈0.11	≈14.5
IV	0.50	0.00	0.60	150	2.0	≈1.94	≈0.06	≈9.2

Table 20.7
IV estimation procedure—Improved instrument

Estimation procedure	Correlation coefficients			Sample size	Actual coef1	Mean of coef1 ests	Magnitude of bias	Variance of coef1 ests
	X1&Z	X2&Z	X1&X2					
IV	0.50	0.00	0.60	150	2.0	≈1.94	≈0.06	≈9.2
IV	0.75	0.00	0.60	150	2.0	≈1.97	≈0.03	≈3.9

Next let us see what happens when we improve the instrument by making it more correlated with the included "problem" explanatory variable. We do this by increasing the correlation coefficient of the included explanatory variable, $x1$, and the instrument, z, from 0.50 to 0.75 when the sample size equals 150 (table 20.7). The magnitude of the bias decreases and the variance of the coefficient estimates also decreases. We now have a better instrument.

Econometrics Lab 20.3: Instrumental Variables—Omitted Variables: Bad Instrument

[To access this online material, go to http://mitpress.mit.edu/westhoffeconometrics and select Lab 20.3.]

Last, let us use the lab to illustrate the important role that the independence of the error term, ε_t, and the instrument, z, plays:

$$\beta_t = \beta_{x2}x2_t + e_t$$

By specifying 0.10 from the Corr X2&Z list the error term, ε_t, and the instrument, z, are no longer independent (table 20.8). As we increase the sample size from 50 to 100 to 150, the magnitude of the bias does not decrease. The instrumental variable (IV) estimation procedure is no longer consistent. This illustrates the "Achilles heel" of the instrument variable (IV) estimation procedure.

Table 20.8
IV estimation procedure—Instrument correlated with omitted variable

Estimation procedure	Correlation coefficients			Sample size	Actual coef1	Mean of coef1 ests	Magnitude of bias	Variance of coef1 ests
	X1&Z	X2&Z	X1&X2					
IV	0.50	0.10	0.60	50	2.0	≈2.63	≈0.63	≈31.1
IV	0.50	0.10	0.60	100	2.0	≈2.70	≈0.70	≈13.7
IV	0.50	0.10	0.60	150	2.0	≈2.73	≈0.73	≈8.7

Chapter 20 Review Questions

1. In generally, what are the two conditions that a "good" instrument must meet?

2. More specifically, when an omitted variable issue arises, a "good" instrument must satisfy two conditions.

   a. The instrument and the included "problem" explanatory variable:

      i. How must the instrument be related to the included "problem" explanatory variable? Explain.

      ii. Can we determine whether this condition is met? If so, how?

   b. The instrument and the omitted variable:

      i. How must the instrument be related to the omitted explanatory variable? Explain.

      ii. Can we determine whether this condition is met? If so, how?

Chapter 20 Exercises

[To access this online material, go to http://mitpress.mit.edu/westhoffeconometrics and select Presidential Election—2008.]

Consider the following model explaining the vote received by the Democratic Party in the 2008 presidential election:

$$VoteDemPartyTwo_t = \beta_{Const} + \beta_{UnTrend}UnemTrend_t + \beta_{PopDen}PopDen_t + \beta_{Lib}Liberal_t + e_t$$

where

$AdvDeg_t$	Percent adults who have advanced degrees in state t
$UnemTrend_t$	Change in the unemployment rate for state t in 2008 (percent)
$PopDen_t$	Population density of state t (persons per square mile)
$Liberal_t$	"Liberalness" of the electorate in state t

Recall that $\beta_{PopDen} > 0$ and $\beta_{Lib} > 0$.

1. Focus on the unemployment trend.

a. How do you believe a state's unemployment trend affected the Democrat vote in the 2008 presidential election?

b. What does this suggest about the sign of $\beta_{UnTrend}$?

2. Since no measures of state "liberalness" are included in the data, what problems, if any, might concern you when using the ordinary least squares (OLS) estimation procedure to calculate this estimate? Explain.

3. As a consequence of the troublesome issues arising from using the ordinary least squares (OLS) estimation procedure use the instrumental variable (IV) estimation procedure to estimate the effect of population density. Consider using the *AdvDeg* variable as an instrument. To be a "good" instrument, what conditions must the *AdvDeg* variable meet?

4. Use the instrumental variable (IV) estimation procedure with *AdvDeg* as the instrument to estimate the effect of population density. (To do so, you cannot use the two-stage estimation procedure. You must run the two instrumental variables regressions: IV Regression 1 and IV Regression 2.)

[To access this online material, go to http://mitpress.mit.edu/westhoffeconometrics and select Presidential Election—2008.]

a. What are your results for IV Regression 1?

b. What are your results for IV Regression 2?

5. Assess whether or not *AdvDeg* meets the "good" instrument conditions.

Consider the following model explaining the vote received by the Democratic Party in the 2008 presidential election:

$$VoteDemPartyTwo_t = \beta_{Const} + \beta_{GdpGth} \, RealGdpGrowth_t + \beta_{PopDen} PopDen_t + \beta_{Lib} Liberal_t + e_t$$

where

$AdvDeg_t$	Percent adults who have advanced degrees in state t
$RealGdpGrowth_t$	GDP growth rate for state t in 2008 (percent)
$PopDen_t$	Population density of state t (persons per square mile)
$Liberal_t$	"Liberalness" of the electorate in state t

Recall that $\beta_{PopDen} > 0$ and $\beta_{Lib} > 0$.

6.

a. First focus on the growth rate of real GDP.

i. How do you believe a state's GDP growth rate affected the Democrat vote in the 2008 presidential election?

ii. What does this suggest about the sign of β_{GdpGth}?

b. Next focus on population density.

i. How do you believe a state's population density affected the Democrat vote in the 2008 presidential election?

ii. What does this suggest about the sign of β_{PopDen}?

c. Last focus on "liberalness."

i. How do you believe a state's "liberalness" affected the Democrat vote in the 2008 presidential election?

ii. What does this suggest about the sign of β_{Lib}?

7. Since no measures of state "liberalness" are included in the data, What problems, if any, might concern you when using the ordinary least squares (OLS) estimation procedure to calculate this estimate? Explain.

8. As a consequence of the troublesome issues arising from using the ordinary least squares (OLS) estimation procedure use the instrumental variable (IV) estimation procedure to estimate the effect of population density. Consider using the *AdvDeg* variable as an instrument. To be a "good" instrument, what conditions must the *AdvDeg* variable meet?

9. Use the instrumental variable (IV) estimation procedure with *AdvDeg* as the instrument to estimate the effect of population density. (To do so, you cannot use the two-stage estimation procedure. You must run the two instrumental variables regressions: IV Regression 1 and IV Regression 2.)

[To access this online material, go to http://mitpress.mit.edu/westhoffeconometrics and select Presidential Election—2008.]

a. What are your results for IV Regression 1?

b. What are your results for IV Regression 2?

10. Assess whether or not *AdvDeg* meets the "good" instrument conditions.

21 Panel Data and Omitted Variables

Chapter 21 Preview Questions

1. Fill in each of the following blanks with a Yes or a No:

	Satisfied:	**Violated:**
OLS bias question: Is the explanatory variable/error term independence premise satisfied or violated?	Explanatory variable and error term independent	Explanatory variable and error term correlated

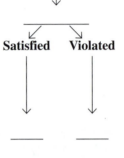

Is the OLS estimation procedure for the value of the coefficient unbiased or biased?

OLS reliability question: Are the error term equal variance and error term/error term independence premises satisfied or violated?

Can the OLS calculations for the standard error be "trusted?"

Is the OLS estimation procedure for the value of the coefficient BLUE?

2. Suppose that there are three college students enrolled in a small math class: Jim, Peg, and Tim. A quiz is given weekly. Each student's quiz score for the first ten weeks of the semester is reported below along with the number of minutes the student studied and his/her math SAT score from high school.

Student	Week	Quiz score	Math SAT	Minutes studied	Student	Week	Quiz score	Math SAT	Minutes studied
Jim	1	18	720	13	Peg	1	31	760	27
Jim	2	20	720	17	Peg	2	32	760	23
Jim	3	24	720	19	Peg	3	28	760	21
Jim	4	16	720	23	Peg	4	22	760	23
Jim	5	8	720	13	Peg	5	22	760	27
Jim	6	18	720	15	Peg	6	31	760	19
Jim	7	27	720	17	Peg	7	26	760	25
Jim	8	15	720	13	Peg	8	24	760	25
Jim	9	14	720	17	Peg	9	25	760	17
Jim	10	11	720	13	Peg	10	24	760	19
Tim	1	15	670	17	Tim	6	12	670	17
Tim	2	5	670	11	Tim	7	12	670	19
Tim	3	14	670	21	Tim	8	17	670	13
Tim	4	13	670	15	Tim	9	11	670	11
Tim	5	14	670	13	Tim	10	10	670	9

Panel data (also called longitudinal data) combines time series and cross-sectional information. A time series refers to data for a single entity in different time periods. A cross section refers to data for multiple entities in a single time period. In this example, data from the ten weeks represent the time series; that is, the ten weeks provide data from ten different time periods. The data from the three students represent the cross section; that is, the three students provide data for three different entities, Jim, Peg, and Tim.

Our assignment is to assess the effect of studying on the students' math quiz scores:

Assignment: Assess the effect of studying on quiz scores.

Consider the following model:

$$MathScore_t^i = \beta_{Const} + \beta_{Sat}MathSat_t^i + \beta_{Mins}MathMins_t^i + e_t^i$$

where

$MathScore_t^i =$ quiz score for student i in week t

$MathSat_t^i =$ math SAT score for student i in week t

$MathMins_t^i =$ minutes studied student i in week t

Focus on the superscripts and subscripts of the variables:

- The subscript t denotes time; that is, t equals the week: 1, 2, . . . , or 10.
- The superscript i denotes the individual student; that is, i equals Jim, Peg, or Tim.

Let us now take a closer look at the data. The math SAT scores are from high school. Jim's SAT score in high school equaled a constant 720. Similarly Peg's is a constant 760 and Tim's is a constant 670:

$MathSat_t^{Jim} = 720$ for $t = 1, 2, . . . , 10$

$MathSat_t^{Peg} = 760$ for $t = 1, 2, . . . , 10$

$MathSat_t^{Tim} = 670$ for $t = 1, 2, . . . , 10$

This allows us to simplify the notation. Since the *MathSat* variable only depends on the student and does not depend on the week, we can drop the time subscript t for the *MathSat* variable, but of course we must retain the individual student superscript i to denote the student:

$$MathScore_t^i = \beta_{Const} + \beta_{Sat}MathSat^i + \beta_{Mins}MathMins_t^i + e_t^i$$

a. Develop a theory regarding how each explanatory variable influences the dependent variable. What does your theory imply about the sign of each coefficient?

Privacy concerns did not permit the college to release student SAT data. Consequently, you have no choice but to omit *MathSat* from your regression.

b. Do high school students who receive high SAT math scores tend to study more or less than those students who receive low scores?

c. Would you expect *MathSat* and *MathMins* to be correlated?

d. Would you expect the ordinary least squares (OLS) estimation procedure for the value of the *MathMins* coefficient to be biased? Explain.

21.1   Taking Stock: Ordinary Least Squares (OLS) Estimation Procedure

This chapter does not introduce any new concepts. It instead applies the concepts that we already learned to a new situation. We begin by reviewing the concepts we will be using. First recall the standard ordinary least squares (OLS) premises:

21.1.1   Standard Ordinary Least Squares (OLS) Premises

· **Error term equal variance premise:**   The variance of the error term's probability distribution for each observation is the same; all the variances equal Var[*e*]:

$$\text{Var}[e_1] = \text{Var}[e_2] = \ldots = \text{Var}[e_T] = \text{Var}[e]$$

· **Error term/error term independence premise:**   The error terms are independent: $\text{Cov}[e_i, e_j] = 0$.

Knowing the value of the error term from one observation does not help us predict the value of the error term for any other observation.

· **Explanatory variable/error term independence premise:**   The explanatory variables, the x_t's, and the error terms, the e_t's, are not correlated.

Knowing the value of an observation's explanatory variable does not help us predict the value of that observation's error term.

The ordinary least square (OLS) estimation procedure is economist's most widely used estimation procedure (figure 21.1). When contemplating the use of this procedure, we should keep two questions in mind:

OLS bias question: Is the ordinary least squares (OLS) explanatory variable/error term independence premise satisfied; that is, are the model's error term and explanatory variable independent or correlated?

· If independent, the ordinary least squares (OLS) estimation procedure for the coefficient value will be unbiased, and we should pose the second reliability question.

· If correlated, the ordinary least squares (OLS) estimation procedure for the coefficient value will be biased, in which case we should consider an alternative procedure in an effort to calculate better estimates.

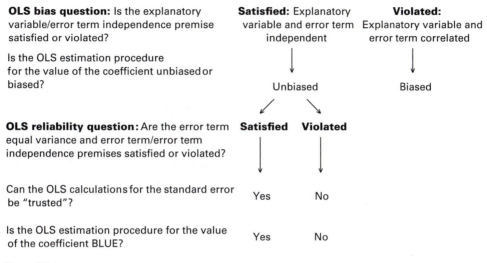

Figure 21.1
Ordinary least squares (OLS) bias summary

OLS reliability question: Are the ordinary least square (OLS) error term equal variance premise and the error term/error term independence premises satisfied; that is, is the variance of the probability distribution for each observation's error term the same and are the error terms independent from each other?

• If satisfied, the ordinary least squares (OLS) estimation procedure calculation of the coefficient's standard error, t-statistic, and tails probability will be "sound" and the ordinary least squares (OLS) estimation procedure is the best linear unbiased estimation procedure (BLUE). In some sense, we cannot find a better linear estimation procedure and hence we should be pleased.

• If violated, the ordinary least squares (OLS) estimation procedure calculation of the coefficient's standard error, t-statistic, and tails probability will be flawed and the ordinary least squares (OLS) estimation procedure is not the best linear unbiased estimation procedure (BLUE). In this case, we can use a generalized least squares (GLS) estimation by tweaking the original model in a way that eliminates the problem or calculate robust standard errors.

21.2   Preview: Panel Data Examples and Strategy

In this chapter we apply what we have learned to panel data (also called longitudinal data), situations in which have time series data for a number of cross sections. We use three artificially generated examples to show how the use of panel data techniques can mitigate some of the difficulties encountered when using the ordinary least squares (OLS) estimation procedure. These examples are designed to illustrate the issues clearly. All three examples involve the score students receive in their college classes:

· **Math class panel data:**   Three students comprise the entire enrollment of a math class. Each week a quiz is given. The quiz score earned by each student is collected from the first ten weeks of the course. Also the number of minutes each student studied for each week's quiz and each student's math SAT score from high school is available.

· **Chemistry class panel data:**   Two students are enrolled in an advanced undergraduate chemistry course. Each week a lab report is due. The score earned by each student is collected from the first ten labs along with the number of minutes each student devoted to the lab. Each week a different graduate student grades both lab reports submitted by the two students.

· **Studio art class panel data:**   Three students are randomly selected from a heavily enrolled studio art class. Each week each student submits an art project. The score earned by each student is collected from the first ten weeks of the course along with the number of minutes each student devoted to the project.

We have data describing the performance of a number of students over a number of weeks. This is what we mean by panel data. Cross-sectional and time series information are combined. In our cases the students comprise the cross sections and the weeks the time series. As we will learn, the existence of panel data can sometimes allow us to account for omitted variables.

21.3   First Differences and Fixed Effects (Dummy Variables)

Suppose that there are three college students enrolled in a small math class: Jim, Peg, and Tim. A quiz is given weekly. Each student's quiz score for the first ten weeks of the semester is reported below along with the number of minutes the student studied and his/her math SAT score from high school.

Math quiz score data: Artificially constructed panel data for 3 students during the first 10 weeks of a math class (table 21.1):

$MathScore_t^i$ Quiz score for student i in week t

$MathSat_t^i$ Math SAT score for student i in week t

$MathMins_t^i$ Minutes studied student i in week t

$Week_t^i$ Week

$DumJim_t^i$ 1 if student i is Jim; 0 otherwise

$DumPeg_t^i$ 1 if student i is Peg; 0 otherwise

$DumTim_t^i$ 1 if student i is Tim; 0 otherwise

 [To access this online material, go to http://mitpress.mit.edu/westhoffeconometrics and select Panel Data—Math.]

Table 21.1
Math quiz panel data

Student	Week	Quiz score	Math SAT	Minutes studied	Student	Week	Quiz score	Math SAT	Minutes studied
Jim	1	18	720	13	Peg	1	31	760	27
Jim	2	20	720	17	Peg	2	32	760	23
Jim	3	24	720	19	Peg	3	28	760	21
Jim	4	16	720	23	Peg	4	22	760	23
Jim	5	8	720	13	Peg	5	22	760	27
Jim	6	18	720	15	Peg	6	31	760	19
Jim	7	27	720	17	Peg	7	26	760	25
Jim	8	15	720	13	Peg	8	24	760	25
Jim	9	14	720	17	Peg	9	25	760	17
Jim	10	11	720	13	Peg	10	24	760	19
Tim	1	15	670	17	Tim	6	12	670	17
Tim	2	5	670	11	Tim	7	12	670	19
Tim	3	14	670	21	Tim	8	17	670	13
Tim	4	13	670	15	Tim	9	11	670	11
Tim	5	14	670	13	Tim	10	10	670	9

Panel data combines time series and cross-sectional information. A time series refers to data from a single entity in different time periods. A cross section refers to data for multiple entities in a single time period. In this example, data from the ten weeks represent the time series; that is, the ten weeks provide data from ten different time periods. The data from the three students represent the cross section; that is, the three students provide data for three different entities. Our assignment is to assess the effect of studying on the students' math quizzes:

Project: Assess the effect of studying on math quiz scores.

21.3.1   Math Quiz Score Model

Consider the following model:

$$MathScore_t^i = \beta_{Const} + \beta_{Sat}MathSat_t^i + \beta_{Mins}MathMins_t^i + e_t^i$$

First focus on the superscripts and subscripts of the variables:[1]

---

1 Traditionally both the cross section and time are identified as subscripts. To reduce the possibility of confusion, however, we use a superscript to identify the cross section so that there is only a single subscript, the subscript identifying the time period.

• The subscript t denotes time period, the week; that is, t equals 1, 2, . . . , or 10.

• The superscript i denotes the cross section, the individual student; that is, i equals Jim, Peg, or Tim.

Let us now take a closer look at the data. The math SAT scores are from high school. Jim's SAT score from high school equaled a constant 720. Similarly Peg's is a constant 760 and Tim's is a constant 670:

$$MathSat_t^{Jim} = 720 \quad \text{for } t = 1, 2, \ldots, 10$$
$$MathSat_t^{Peg} = 760 \quad \text{for } t = 1, 2, \ldots, 10$$
$$MathSat_t^{Tim} = 670 \quad \text{for } t = 1, 2, \ldots, 10$$

This allows us to simplify the notation. Since the SAT data for our three college students are from high school, the *MathSat* variable only depends on the student and does not depend on the week. We can drop the time subscript t for the *MathSat* variable, but we must, of course, retain the individual student superscript i to denote the student:

$$MathScore_t^i = \beta_{Const} + \beta_{Sat}MathSat^i + \beta_{Mins}MathMins_t^i + e_t^i$$

For clarity, let us apply this to each of the three students:

• For Jim, i = Jim,

$$MathScore_t^{Jim} = \beta_{Const} + \beta_{Sat}MathSat^{Jim} + \beta_{Mins}MathMins_t^{Jim} + e_t^{Jim}$$

• For Peg, i = Peg,

$$MathScore_t^{Peg} = \beta_{Const} + \beta_{Sat}MathSat^{Peg} + \beta_{Mins}MathMins_t^{Peg} + e_t^{Peg}$$

• For Tim, i = Tim,

$$MathScore_t^{Tim} = \beta_{Const} + \beta_{Sat}MathSat^{Tim} + \beta_{Mins}MathMins_t^{Tim} + e_t^{Tim}$$

The model's implicit assumptions now become apparent:

• β_{Const} is the same for each student.

• β_{Sat} is the same for each student. This implies that the effect of math SAT scores on quiz scores is identical for each student

• $\beta_{MathMins}$ is the same for each student. This implies that the effect of minutes studied on quiz scores is identical for each student; that is, each student receives the same number of additional points for each additional minute studied.

Theory: The theory concerning how math SAT scores and studying affect quiz scores is straightforward. Both coefficients should be positive:

$\beta_{Sat} > 0$:   Higher math SAT scores increase a student's quiz score

$\beta_{Mins} > 0$:   Studying more increases a student's quiz score

Table 21.2
Math quiz pooled OLS regression results—*MathSAT* and *MathMins* explanatory variables

Ordinary least squares (OLS)				
Dependent variable: *MathScore*				
Explanatory variable(s):	Estimate	SE	*t*-Statistic	Prob
MathSat	0.117932	0.028331	4.162589	0.0003
MathMins	0.431906	0.214739	2.011305	0.0544
Const	−73.54375	18.05883	−4.072454	0.0004
Number of observations	30			

Estimated equation: *EstMathScore* = −73.54 + 0.118*MathSat* + 0.43*MathMins*

Interpretation of estimates:

$b_{MathSat}$ = 0.118: A 100 point increase in a student's math SAT score increases his/her quiz score by 11.8 points

$b_{MathMins}$ = 0.43: A 10 minute increase in studying increases a student's math quiz score by 4.3 points

21.3.2 Ordinary Least Squares (OLS) Pooled Regression

We begin pooling the data and using the ordinary least squares (OLS) estimation procedure to estimate the parameters of the model. We run a regression in which each week of student data represents one observation. This is called a **pooled regression** because we merge the weeks and students together. No distinction is made between a specific student (cross section) or a specific week (time). In a pooled regression every week of data for each student is treated the same (table 21.2).

Now apply the estimates to each of the three students:

Jim: *MathSat^{Jim}* = 720

$$
\begin{aligned}
EstMathScore^{Jim} &= -73.54 + 0.118 MathSat + 0.43 MathMins \\
&= -73.54 + \ 0.118 \times 720 \ + 0.43 MathMins \\
&= -73.54 + \quad 84.96 \quad + 0.43 MathMins \\
&= \qquad\quad 11.42 \quad\ \ + 0.43 MathMins
\end{aligned}
$$

Peg: *MathSat^{Peg}* = 760

$$
\begin{aligned}
EstMathScore^{Peg} &= -73.54 + 0.118 MathSat + 0.43 MathMins \\
&= -73.54 + \ 0.118 \times 760 \ + 0.43 MathMins \\
&= -73.54 + \quad 89.68 \quad + 0.43 MathMins \\
&= \qquad\quad 16.14 \quad\ \ + 0.43 MathMins
\end{aligned}
$$

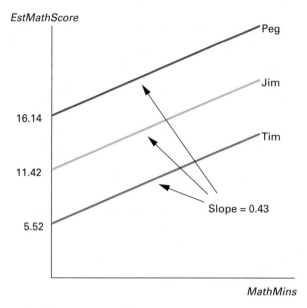

Figure 21.2
Estimates of math scores with math SAT explanatory variable

Tim: *MathSat*^{Tim} = 670

$$
\begin{aligned}
EstMathScore^{Tim} &= -73.54 + 0.118MathSat + 0.43MathMins \\
&= -73.54 + \ 0.118 \times 670 \ + 0.43MathMins \\
&= -73.54 + \qquad 79.06 \qquad + 0.43MathMins \\
&= \qquad\quad 5.52 \qquad\quad + 0.43MathMins
\end{aligned}
$$

When we plot the estimated equations the three students have different intercepts, but all have the same slope (figure 21.2). This is a consequence of our model's assumption regarding the effect of studying:

$$MathScore_t^i = \beta_{Const} + \beta_{Sat}MathSat^i + \beta_{Mins}MathMins_t^i + e_t^i$$

We have implicitly assumed that the effect of studying reflected by the coefficient β_{Mins} is the same for each student.

Now let us introduce a twist. What if privacy concerns did not permit the college to release student SAT data? In this case we must omit *MathSat* from our pooled regression (table 21.3). What are the ramifications of omitting *MathSat* from this regression?

Table 21.3
Math quiz pooled OLS regression results—*MathMins* explanatory variable only

Ordinary least squares (OLS)				
Dependent variable: *MathScore*				
Explanatory variable(s):	Estimate	SE	*t*-Statistic	Prob
MathMins	1.017235	0.204204	4.981467	0.0000
Const	0.594368	3.754613	0.158303	0.8754
Number of observations	30			

Estimated equation: *EstMathScore* = 0.59 + 1.02*MathMins*

Interpretation of estimates:

$b_{MathMins}$ = 1.02: A 10 minute increase in studying increases a student's quiz score by 10.2 points

$$MathScore_t^i = \beta_{Const} + \beta_{Sat}MathSat^i + \beta_{Mins}MathMins_t^i + e_t^i$$

Switch the $\beta_{Sat}MathSat^i$ and $\beta_{Mins}MathMins_t^i$ terms

$$= \beta_{Const} + \beta_{Mins}MathMins_t^i + \beta_{Sat}MathSat^i + e_t^i$$

$$= \beta_{Const} + \beta_{Mins}MathMins_t^i + \beta_{Sat}MathSat^i + e_t^i$$

$$= \beta_{Const} + \beta_{Mins}MathMins_t^i + \varepsilon_t^i$$

where $\varepsilon_t^i = \beta_{Sat}MathSat^i + e_t^i$. The *MathSat* term becomes "folded" into the new error term.

Will the ordinary least squares (OLS) estimation procedure for the coefficient value be unbiased? The OLS bias question cited at the start of the chapter provides the answer:

OLS bias question: Is the ordinary least squares (OLS) explanatory variable/error term independence premise satisfied; that is, are the model's error term and explanatory variable independent or correlated?

More specifically, we need to determine whether or not the model's explanatory variable, *MathMins_t^i*, and error term, ε_t^i, are correlated. To do so, suppose that *MathSat^i* rises. Recall the definition of ε_t^i:

$$\varepsilon_t^i = \beta_{Sat}MathSat^i + e_t^i$$

ε_t^i will rise also. What would happen to *MathMins_t^i*? Consider the following question:

Question: Do high school students who receive high SAT math scores tend to study more or less than those students who receive low scores?

Typically students earning higher SAT scores tend to study more. Hence *MathMins_t^i* would typically rise also. The explanatory variable, *MathMins_t^i*, and the error term, ε_t^i, are positively correlated. The ordinary least squares (OLS) estimation procedure for the value of the coefficient

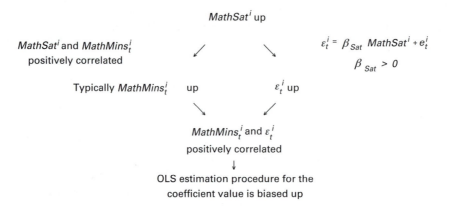

Figure 21.3
Math quiz scores and bias

is biased upward (figure 21.3). When the explanatory variable *MathSat* is omitted and the ordinary least squares (OLS) estimation procedure is used to estimate the value of the *MathMin*'s coefficient, upward bias results.

What can we do? We will now introduce two approaches we can take to address this problem:

· First differences
· Dummy variable/fixed effects

21.3.3 First Differences

To explain the first differences approach, focus on the first student, Jim. Apply the model to week t and the previous week, week $t - 1$:

For week t: $\quad MathScore_t^{Jim} = \beta_{Const} + \beta_{Sat}MathSat^{Jim} + \beta_{Mins}MathMins_t^{Jim} + e_t^{Jim}$

For week $t - 1$: $\quad MathScore_{t-1}^{Jim} = \beta_{Const} + \beta_{Sat}MathSat^{Jim} + \beta_{Mins}MathMins_{t-1}^{Jim} + e_{t-1}^{Jim}$

First subtract. The first two terms are the right-hand side, β_{Const} and $\beta_{Sat}MathSat^{Jim}$, subtract out leaving us with the following expression:

$$
\begin{aligned}
MathScore_t^{Jim} - MathScore_{t-1}^{Jim} &= \beta_{Mins}MathMins_t^{Jim} - \beta_{Mins}MathMins_{t-1}^{Jim} + e_t^{Jim} - e_{t-1}^{Jim} \\
&= \beta_{Mins}(MathMins_t^{Jim} - \beta_{Mins}MathMins_{t-1}^{Jim}) + (e_t^{Jim} - e_{t-1}^{Jim})
\end{aligned}
$$

By computing first differences, we have eliminated the omitted variable, $MathSat^{Jim}$, from the equation because $MathSat^{Jim}$ is the same for all weeks.

Table 21.4
Math quiz first difference OLS regression results

Ordinary least squares (OLS)				
Dependent variable: *DifMathScore*				
Explanatory variable(s):	Estimate	SE	*t*-Statistic	Prob
DifMathMins	0.262500	0.226398	1.159463	0.2568
Number of observations	27			
Estimated equation: *EstDifMathScore* = 0.26*DifMathMins*				
Interpretation of estimates:				
$b_{DifMathMins}$ = 0.26: A 10 minute increase in studying increases a student's math quiz score by 2.6 points				

Using similar logic for Jones and Smith obtains

$$MathScore_t^{Peg} - MathScore_{t-1}^{Peg} = \beta_{Mins}MathMins_t^{Peg} - \beta_{Mins}MathMins_{t-1}^{Peg} + e_t^{Peg} - e_{t-1}^{Peg}$$

$$MathScore_t^{Tim} - MathScore_{t-1}^{Tim} = \beta_{Mins}MathMins_t^{Tim} - \beta_{Mins}MathMins_{t-1}^{Tim} + e_t^{Tim} - e_{t-1}^{Tim}$$

We can now generalize this by using the superscript *i* to represent the students:

$$MathScore_t^i - MathScore_{t-1}^i = \beta_{Mins}MathMins_t^i - \beta_{Mins}MathMins_{t-1}^i + e_t^i - e_{t-1}^i$$

Next generate two new variables and use the ordinary least squares (OLS) estimation procedure to estimate the parameters of the first differences model (table 21.4):

DifMathScore = MathScore − MathScore(−1)

DifMathMins = MathMins − MathMins(−1)

Note that this approach relies on one critical assumption:

First differences critical assumption: For each student (cross section) the omitted variable must equal the same value in each week (time period). That is, from week to week:

- *MathSat^{Jim}* does not vary.
- *MathSat^{Peg}* does not vary.
- *MathSat^{Tim}* does not vary.

In fact math SAT scores do not vary for a student from week to week because students take their math SAT's in high school, not while they are in college. But, if the math SAT scores for a student were to vary from week to week, our logic would fail because the *MathSat* term for that student would not subtract out when we calculated the first differences. So we have satisfied the critical assumption in this case.

21.3.4   Cross-sectional Fixed Effects (Dummy Variables)

Again, begin by focusing on Jim. Because $MathSat^{Jim}$ does not vary from week to week, we can "fold" the $MathSat^{Jim}$ term into Jim's constant.

$$MathScore_t^{Jim} = \beta_{Const} + \beta_{Cat}MathSat^{Jim} + \beta_{Mins}MathMins^{Jim} + e_t^{Jim}$$

$$\downarrow \qquad MathSat^{Jim} = 720$$

$$= \beta_{Const} + \beta_{Sat} \times 720 + \beta_{Mins}MathMins^{Jim} + e_t^{Jim}$$

$$\searrow \quad \swarrow \qquad \text{Leting } \alpha_{Const}^{Jim} = \beta_{Const} + \beta_{Sat} \times 720$$

$$= \quad \alpha_{Const}^{Jim} \qquad +\beta_{Mins}MathMins^{Jim} + e_t^{Jim}$$

Using the same logic for Peg and Tim obtains

$$MathScore_t^{Peg} = \alpha_{Const}^{Peg} + \beta_{Mins}MathMins^{Peg} + e_t^{Peg}$$

$$MathScore_t^{Tim} = \alpha_{Const}^{Tim} + \beta_{Mins}MathMins^{Tim} + e_t^{Tim}$$

We now have three separate equations: one for Jim, one for Peg, and one for Tim. We can represent for the three equations concisely introducing three dummy variables:

$DumJim^i = 1$ if the student is Jim (if $i = $ Jim); 0 otherwise
$DumPeg^i = 1$ if the student is Peg (if $i = $ Peg); 0 otherwise
$DumTim^i = 1$ if the student is Tim (if $i = $ Tim); 0 otherwise

and using them in the following model:

$$MathScore_t^i = \alpha_{Const}^{Jim}DumJim^i + \alpha_{Const}^{Peg}DumPeg^i + \alpha_{Const}^{Tim}DumTim^i + \beta_{Mins}MathMins^i + e_t^i$$

To convince yourself that the "concise" model is equivalent to the three separate equations, consider each student individually:

For Jim, $i = Jim$ $DumJim^i = 1$ $DumPeg^i = 0$ $DumTim^i = 0$

$$MathScore_t^{Jim} = \quad \alpha_{Const}^{Jim} \quad + \quad 0 \quad + \quad 0 \quad + \beta_{Mins}MathMins^{Jim} + e_t^{Jim}$$

For Peg, $i = Peg$ $DumJim^i = 0$ $DumPeg^i = 1$ $DumTim^i = 0$

$$MathScore_t^{Jim} = \quad 0 \quad + \quad \alpha_{Const}^{Peg} \quad + \quad 0 \quad + \beta_{Mins}MathMins^{Peg} + e_t^{Peg}$$

For Tim, $i = Tim$ $DumJim^i = 0$ $DumPeg^i = 0$ $DumTim^i = 1$

$$MathScore_t^{Jim} = \quad 0 \quad + \quad 0 \quad + \quad \alpha_{Const}^{Tim} \quad + \beta_{Mins}MathMins^{Tim} + e_t^{Tim}$$

Table 21.5
Math quiz OLS regression results—*MathMins* and cross-sectional dummy variable explanatory variables

	Ordinary least squares (OLS)			
Dependent variable: *MathScore*				
Explanatory variable(s):	Estimate	SE	*t*-Statistic	Prob
MathMins	0.327305	0.231771	1.412189	0.1698
DumJim	11.86313	3.948825	3.004217	0.0058
DumPeg	19.10292	5.410950	3.530419	0.0016
DumTim	7.521354	3.645812	2.063012	0.0492
Number of observations	30			

Estimated equation: $EstMathScore = 11.86DumJim + 19.10DumPeg + 7.52\ DumTim + 0.33MathMins$
    Jim: $EstMathScore = 11.86 + 0.33MathMins$
    Peg: $EstMathScore = 19.10 + 0.33MathMins$
    Tim: $EstMathScore = 7.52 + 0.33MathMins$

Interpretation of estimates:

$b_{MathMins} = 0.33$: A 10 minute increase in studying increases a student's quiz score by 3.3 points

Next we use the ordinary least squares (OLS) estimation procedure to estimate the parameters of our "concise" model (table 21.5). Let us plot the estimated equations for each student (figure 21.4). The dummy variable coefficient estimates are just the intercepts of the estimated equations. Jim's intercept is 11.86, Peg's 19.10, and Tim's 7.72.

Statistical software makes it easy for us to do this. See table 21.6.

Getting Started in EViews

- Click on **MathScore** and then while holding the \<Ctrl\> key down, click on **MathMins**.
- Double click the highlighted area.
- Click the **Panel Options** tab.
- In the Effects Specification box, select **Fixed** from the Cross Section dropdown box.
- Click **OK**.

Question: What does the estimate of the constant, 12.83, represent?

Answer: The average of Jim's, Peg's, and Tim's intercepts.

$$\text{Average of the intercepts} = \frac{11.86 + 19.10 + 7.52}{3} = \frac{38.48}{3} = 12.83$$

Statistical software allows us to obtain the individual fixed effects intercepts.

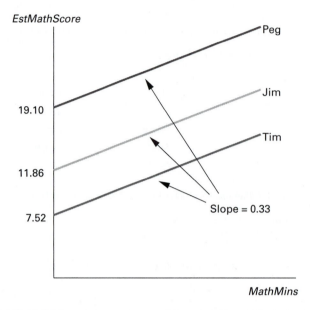

Figure 21.4
Estimates of math scores with dummy cross-sectional variables

Getting Started in EViews

- First, estimate the cross-sectional fixed effects.
- Click **View**.
- Click **Fixed/Random Effects**.
- Click **Cross Section Effects**.

The intercept for each group equals the constant from the regression results (table 21.6) plus the effect value from table 21.7:

Intercept for Jim: Cross ID 1 $12.83 - 0.97 = 11.86$

Intercept for Peg: Cross ID 2 $12.83 + 6.27 = 19.10$

Intercept for Tim: Cross ID 3 $12.83 - 5.31 = 7.52$

These are just the dummy variable coefficient estimates, the intercepts of the estimated equations.

The dummy/fixed effects approach relies on the same critical assumption as did the first difference approach:

Table 21.6

Math quiz cross-sectional fixed effects regression results

	Fixed effects (FE)			
Dependent variable: *MathScore*				
Explanatory variable(s):	Estimate	SE	*t*-Statistic	Prob
MathMins	0.327305	0.231771	1.412189	0.1698
Const	12.82913	4.184080	3.066178	0.0050
Number of observations	30			
Cross sections	3			
Periods	10			

Estimated equation: *EstMathScore* = 12.83 + 0.33*MathMins*

Interpretation of estimates:

$b_{MathMins}$ = 0.33: A 10 minute increase in studying increases a student's math quiz score by 3.3 points

Table 21.7

Math quiz cross-sectional fixed effects

Cross ID	Fixed effect
1	−0.966005
2	6.273785
3	−5.307779

Cross-sectional dummy variable/fixed effects critical assumption: For each student (cross section) the omitted variable must equal the same value in each week (time period). That is, from week to week:

- *MathSat*^{Jim} does not vary.
- *MathSat*^{Peg} does not vary.
- *MathSat*^{Tim} does not vary.

If the math SAT scores for a student were to vary from week to week our logic would fail because the *MathSat* term for that student could not be folded into that student's constant. But, since the SAT scores are from high school, they do not vary.

21.4   Period Fixed Effects (Dummy Variables)

Next we consider a second scenario in which two students, Ted and Sue, are enrolled in an advanced undergraduate chemistry course. Each week a lab report is due.

Table 21.8
Chemistry lab panel data

Student	Week	*LabMins*	*LabScore*	Student	Week	*LabMins*	*LabScore*
Ted	1	63	83	Sue	1	63	83
Ted	2	64	92	Sue	2	64	92
Ted	3	70	82	Sue	3	70	82
Ted	4	80	95	Sue	4	80	95
Ted	5	71	85	Sue	5	71	85
Ted	6	78	96	Sue	6	78	96
Ted	7	68	86	Sue	7	68	86
Ted	8	67	96	Sue	8	67	96
Ted	9	80	89	Sue	9	80	89
Ted	10	63	90	Sue	10	63	90

Chemistry lab score data: Artificially constructed panel data for 2 students during the first 10 weeks of a chemistry class.

$LabScore_t^i$ Chemistry lab score for student i in week t

$LabMins_t^i$ Minutes devoted to lab by student i in week t

$Week_t$ Week

[To access this online material, go to http://mitpress.mit.edu/westhoffeconometrics and select Panel Data—Chemistry.]

The scores of the two students and the time each devoted to each lab each week are given in table 21.8.

Each week the lab reports of the two students are graded by one of 10 graduate students in the small chemistry department. Each week a different graduate student grades the lab reports of the two undergraduates; the undergraduate students do not know which graduate student will be doing the grading beforehand. In the first week, both Ted's and Sue's lab reports are graded by one graduate student; in the second week, Ted's and Sue's reports are graded by a second graduate student; and so on. Our assignment is to use this information to assess the effect that time devoted to the lab each week has on the score that week's lab report receives.

Project: Assess the effect of time devoted to lab on the lab report score.

21.4.1 Chemistry Lab Score Model

We begin by formulating a model:

$$LabScore_t^i = \beta_{Const} + \beta_{GG}GraderGenerosity_t^i + \beta_{LabMins}LabMins_t^i + e_t^i$$

where

$GraderGenerosity_t^i$ = generosity of the grader for student i in week t

We apply the model to each student individually:

$$LabScore_t^{Ted} = \beta_{Const} + \beta_{GG}GraderGenerosity_t^{Ted} + \beta_{LabMins}LabMins_t^{Ted} + e_t^{Ted}$$

$$LabScore_t^{Sue} = \beta_{Const} + \beta_{GG}GraderGenerosity_t^{Sue} + \beta_{LabMins}LabMins_t^{Sue} + e_t^{Sue}$$

Again, we should be aware of the model's implicit assumptions:

• β_{Const} is the same for each student.

• β_{GG} is the same for each student. The grader does not "play favorites." The graduate student applies the same grading standards to each student.

• $\beta_{LabMins}$ is the same for each student. This implies that the effect of time devoted to the lab on the lab score is identical for each student.

Recall that in a given week the same graduate student grades each student's lab report. Therefore we can drop the student superscript in the $GraderGenerosity$ variable:

$$LabScore_t^{Ted} = \beta_{Const} + \beta_{GG}GraderGenerosity_t + \beta_{LabMins}LabMins_t^{Ted} + e_t^{Ted}$$

$$LabScore_t^{Sue} = \beta_{Const} + \beta_{GG}GraderGenerosity_t + \beta_{LabMins}LabMins_t^{Sue} + e_t^{Sue}$$

We apply this to each week:

Week 1 ($t = 1$): $LabScore_1^{Ted} = \beta_{Const} + \beta_{GG}GraderGenerosity_1 + \beta_{LabMins}LabMins_1^{Ted} + e_1^{Ted}$

$LabScore_1^{Sue} = \beta_{Const} + \beta_{GG}GraderGenerosity_1 + \beta Lab_{Mins}LabMins_1^{Sue} + e_1^{Sue}$

Week 2 ($t = 2$): $LabScore_2^{Ted} = \beta_{Const} + \beta_{GG}GraderGenerosity_2 + \beta_{LabMins}LabMins_2^{Ted} + e_2^{Ted}$

$LabScore_2^{Sue} = \beta_{Const} + \beta_{GG}GraderGenerosity_2 + \beta Lab_{Mins}LabMins_2^{Sue} + e_2^{Sue}$

$\vdots$

Week 10 ($t = 10$): $LabScore_{10}^{Ted} = \beta_{Const} + \beta_{GG}GraderGenerosity_{10} + \beta_{LabMins}LabMins_{10}^{Ted} + e_{10}^{Ted}$

$LabScore_{10}^{Sue} = \beta_{Const} + \beta_{GG}GraderGenerosity_{10} + \beta Lab_{Mins}LabMins_{10}^{Sue} + e_{10}^{Sue}$

Generalizing obtains

$$LabScore_t^i = \beta_{Const} + \beta_{LabMins}LabMins_t^i + \beta_{GG}GraderGenerosity_t + e_t^i$$

where

i = Ted, Sue

$t = 1, 2, \ldots, 10$

Table 21.9
Chemistry lab pooled OLS regression results

Ordinary least squares (OLS)				
Dependent variable: *LabScore*				
Explanatory variable(s):	Estimate	SE	*t*-Statistic	Prob
LabMins	0.513228	0.174041	2.948883	0.0086
Const	52.67196	12.58013	4.186916	0.0006
Number of observations	20			

Estimated equation: *EstLabScore* = 52.7 + 0.51*LabMins*

Interpretation of estimates:

$b_{LabMins} = 0.51$: A 10 minute increase devoted to the lab increases a student's lab score by 5.1 points

21.4.2   Ordinary Least Squares (OLS) Pooled Regression

We begin by using the ordinary least squares (OLS) estimation procedure in a pooled regression to estimate the parameters. We include all ten weeks for each of the two students in a single regression; consequently, we include a total of twenty observations. But we have a problem: the explanatory variable *GraderGenerosity* is unobservable. We must omit it from the regression (table 21.9).

What are the ramifications of omitting *GraderGenerosity* from the regression?

$$LabScore_t^i = \beta_{Const} + \beta_{GG}GraderGenerosity_t + \beta_{LabMins}LabMins_t^i + e_t^i$$

Switching the *GraderGenerosity$_t$* and *LabMins$_t^i$* terms

$$= \beta_{Const} + \beta_{LabMins}LabMins_t^i + \beta_{GG}GraderGenerosity_t + e_t^i$$

$$= \beta_{Const} + \beta_{LabMins}LabMins_t^i + (\beta_{GG}GraderGenerosity_t + e_t^i)$$

$$= \beta_{Const} + \beta_{LabMins}LabMins_t^i + \varepsilon_t^i$$

where $\varepsilon_t^i = \beta_{GG}GraderGenerosity_t + e_t^i$. The *GraderGenerosity$_t$* term becomes "folded" into the new error term, e_t^i.

Will the ordinary least squares (OLS) estimation procedure for the coefficient value be unbiased? The OLS bias question cited earlier in the chapter provides the answer:

OLS bias question: Is the ordinary least squares (OLS) explanatory variable/error term independence premise satisfied; that is, are the model's error term and explanatory variable independent or correlated?

To answer this question, suppose the grader in week *t* is unusually generous. Then *GraderGenerosity$_t$* and the new error term, e_t^i, would rise. Ted and Sue would not know about the grader's generosity until after the lab report was returned. Consequently the number of minutes devoted

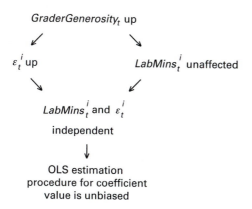

Figure 21.5
Chemistry lab scores and bias

to the lab, $LabMins_t^i$, would be unaffected. The explanatory variable, $LabMins_t^i$ and the new error term, e_t^i are independent. The ordinary least squares (OLS) estimation procedure for the value of the coefficient is unbiased (figure 21.5).

Now let us move on to the OLS reliability question:

OLS reliability question: Are the ordinary least square (OLS) error term equal variance premise and the error term/error term independence premises satisfied; that is, is the variance of the probability distribution for each observation's error term the same and are the error terms independent of each other?

In fact the error terms are not independent. We would expect Ted's error term in a particular week to be correlated with Sue's error term in that week. The reason stems from the fact that a different graduate student grades the each week's lab reports. Naturally some graduate students will award more partial credit than others. For example, on the one hand, if a generous graduate student grades the lab reports in the first week we would expect the error terms of both students to be positive. On the other hand, if the first week's reports are graded by a very demanding graduate student, we would expect the error terms of both students to be negative.

How might be get a sense of whether or not this type of correlation is present in this case? Recall that while the error terms are unobservable we can think of the residuals as the estimated error terms. Table 21.10 reports on the residuals. The residuals appear to confirm our suspicions. The sign of the residuals is always the same. Figure 21.6 plots a scatter diagram of Ted's and Sue's residuals. Each point on the scatter diagram represents on specific week.

The scatter diagram points fall in the first and third quadrants. On the one hand, when the residual of one student is positive, the residual for the other student is positive also. On the other hand, when the residual of one student is negative, the residual for the other student is negative. The scatter diagram suggests that our suspicions about error term/error term correlation are warranted.

Table 21.10
Chemistry lab OLS residuals

Week	Ted's residual	Sue's residual
1	3.30	1.30
2	6.48	3.35
3	−6.60	−3.14
4	1.27	2.30
5	−4.11	−3.60
6	−2.01	−2.57
7	−1.57	−1.16
8	8.94	0.27
9	−4.73	−7.03
10	4.99	4.32

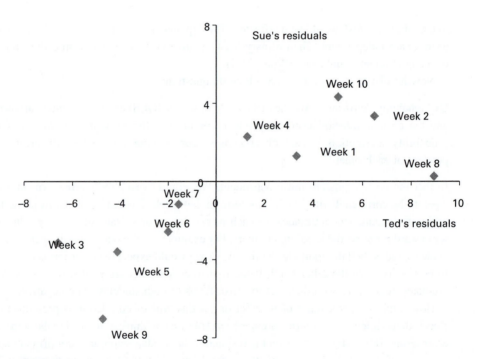

Figure 21.6
Scatter diagram of Ted's and Sue's chemistry lab OLS residuals

21.4.3 Period Fixed Effects (Dummy Variables)

To understand how period fixed effects can address this issue, recall the original model:

Week 1 ($t = 1$): $LabScore_1^{Ted} = \beta_{Const} + \beta_{GG}GraderGenerosity_1 + \beta_{LabMins}LabMins_1^{Ted} + e_1^{Ted}$

$\qquad\qquad\qquad LabScore_1^{Sue} = \beta_{Const} + \beta_{GG}GraderGenerosity_1 + \beta Lab_{Mins}LabMins_1^{Sue} + e_1^{Sue}$

Week 2 ($t = 2$): $LabScore_2^{Ted} = \beta_{Const} + \beta_{GG}GraderGenerosity_2 + \beta_{LabMins}LabMins_2^{Ted} + e_2^{Ted}$

$\qquad\qquad\qquad LabScore_2^{Sue} = \beta_{Const} + \beta_{GG}GraderGenerosity_2 + \beta Lab_{Mins}LabMins_2^{Sue} + e_2^{Sue}$

$$\vdots$$

Week 10 ($t = 10$): $LabScore_{10}^{Ted} = \beta_{Const} + \beta_{GG}GraderGenerosity_{10} + \beta_{LabMins}LabMins_{10}^{Ted} + e_{10}^{Ted}$

$\qquad\qquad\qquad\quad LabScore_{10}^{Sue} = \beta_{Const} + \beta_{GG}GraderGenerosity_{10} + \beta Lab_{Mins}LabMins_{10}^{Sue} + e_{10}^{Sue}$

Now focus on week 1. We can fold the constant grader generosity term into the constant for that week:

Week 1 ($t = 1$): $LabScore_1^{Ted} = \beta_{Const} + \beta_{GG}GraderGenerosity_1 + \beta_{LabMins}LabMins_1^{Ted} + e_1^{Ted}$

$\qquad\qquad\qquad\qquad\qquad \searrow \quad \swarrow \qquad$ Fold into constant

$\qquad\qquad LabScore_1^{Ted} = \qquad \alpha_1 \qquad\qquad\qquad\quad + \beta_{LabMins}LabMins_1^{Ted} + e_1^{Ted}$

$\qquad\qquad LabScore_1^{Sue} = \beta_{Const} + \beta_{GG}GraderGenerosity_1 + \beta_{LabMins}LabMins_1^{Sue} + e_1^{Sue}$

$\qquad\qquad\qquad\qquad\qquad \searrow \quad \swarrow \qquad$ Fold into constant

$\qquad\qquad LabScore_1^{Sue} = \qquad \alpha_1 \qquad\qquad\qquad\quad + \beta_{LabMins}LabMins_1^{Sue} + e_1^{Sue}$

Using the same logic for the other weeks obtains

Week 2 ($t = 2$): $LabScore_2^{Ted} = \alpha_2 + \beta_{LabMins}LabMins_2^{Ted} + e_2^{Ted}$

$\qquad\qquad\qquad LabScore_2^{Sue} = \alpha_2 + \beta_{LabMins}LabMins_2^{Sue} + e_2^{Sue}$

$$\vdots$$

Week 10 ($t = 10$): $LabScore_{10}^{Ted} = \alpha_{10} + \beta_{LabMins}LabMins_{10}^{Ted} + e_{10}^{Ted}$

$\qquad\qquad\qquad\quad LabScore_{10}^{Sue} = \alpha_{10} + \beta_{LabMins}LabMins_{10}^{Sue} + e_{10}^{Sue}$

For each week we have folded the generosity of the grader into the constant. In each week the constant is identical for both students because the same graduate grades both lab reports. We now have ten new constants for each week, one constant for each of the ten weeks. Period fixed effects estimates the values of parameters. Statistical software makes it easy to compute these estimates (table 21.11).

Table 21.11
Chemistry lab time period fixed effects regression results

	Period fixed effects (FE)			
Dependent variable: *LabScore*				
Explanatory variable(s):	Estimate	SE	*t*-Statistic	Prob
LabMins	0.366178	0.116859	3.133509	0.0121
Const	63.26684	8.434896	7.500607	0.0000
Number of observations	20			
Cross sections	2			
Periods	10			
Estimated equation: *EstLabScore* = 63.27 + 0.37*LabMins*				
Interpretation of estimates:				
$b_{LabMins} = 0.37$: A 10 minute increase devoted to the lab increases a student's lab score by 3.7 points				

Getting Started in EViews

- Click on **MathScore** and then, while holding the <Ctrl> key down, click on **MathMins**.
- Double click the highlighted area.
- Click the **Panel Options** tab.
- In the Effects specification box, select **Fixed** from the Period dropdown box.
- Click **OK**.

Question: What does the estimate of the constant, 63.27, represent?

Answer: The average of the weekly time constants.

Statistical software allows us to obtain the estimates of each week's constant (table 21.12).

Getting Started in EViews

- First, estimate the cross-sectional fixed effects.
- Click **View**.
- Click **Fixed/Random Effects**.
- Click **Period Effects**.

The period fixed effects suggest that the graduate student who graded the lab reports for week 9 was the toughest grader and the graduate student who graded for week 8 was the most generous.

Period dummy variable/fixed effects critical assumption: For each week (time period) the omitted variable must equal the same value for each student (cross section).

Table 21.12
Chemistry lab period fixed effects

Period ID	Fixed effect
1	3.171238
2	4.466844
3	−4.948602
4	2.805060
5	−4.082423
6	−3.251531
7	−1.448602
8	4.819041
9	−5.814780
10	4.283755

21.5   Cross-sectional Random Effects

Thus far we have been considering the cases in which we had data for all the students in the course. In reality this is not always true, however. For example, in calculating the unemployment rate, the Bureau of Labor Statistics conducts a survey that acquires data from approximately 60,000 American households. Obviously there are many more than 60,000 households in the United States.

We will now consider a scenario to gain insights into such cases. Suppose that there are several hundred students enrolled in a studio art course at a major university. Each week a studio art project is assigned. At the beginning of the semester, three students were selected randomly from all those enrolled: Bob, Dan, and Kim.

Art project score data: Artificially constructed panel data for 3 students during the first 10 weeks of a studio art class.

$ArtScore_t^i$ Studio art project score for student i in week t

$ArtMins_t^i$ Minutes devoted to studio art project by student i in week t

$Week_t^i$ Week

The scores of the three students and the time each devoted to the project each week are reported in table 21.13:

[To access this online material, go to http://mitpress.mit.edu/westhoffeconometrics and select Panel Data—Art.]

Our assignment is to use information from the randomly selected students to assess the effect that time devoted to the project each week has on the score that week's project receives:

Project: Assess the effect of time devoted to project on the project score.

Table 21.13
Studio art panel data

Student	Week	*ArtScore*	*ArtMins*	Student	Week	*ArtScore*	*ArtMins*
Bob	1	13	35	Dan	1	17	55
Bob	2	17	42	Dan	2	11	57
Bob	3	19	33	Dan	3	21	61
Bob	4	23	45	Dan	4	15	58
Bob	5	13	31	Dan	5	13	54
Bob	6	15	42	Dan	6	17	62
Bob	7	17	35	Dan	7	19	61
Bob	8	13	37	Dan	8	13	53
Bob	9	17	35	Dan	9	11	50
Bob	10	13	34	Dan	10	9	55
Kim	1	27	53	Kim	6	19	43
Kim	2	23	53	Kim	7	25	56
Kim	3	21	49	Kim	8	25	50
Kim	4	23	48	Kim	9	17	44
Kim	5	27	53	Kim	10	19	48

21.5.1 Art Project Model

We begin by formulating a model:

$$ArtMins_t^i = \beta_{Const} + \beta_{AnIQ}ArtIQ^i + \beta_{Mins}ArtMins_t^i + e_t^i$$

where

$ArtIQ^i$ = innate artistic talent for student i

i = Bob, Dan, Kim

t = 1, 2, . . . , 10

Again, we should be aware of two implicit assumptions made by this model:

• β_{Const} is the same for each student.

• $\beta_{ArtMins}$ is the same for each student. This implies that the effect of minutes studied on art project scores is identical for each student; that is, each student receives the same number of additional points for each additional minute devoted to the project.

The $ArtIQ^i$ variable, innate artistic talent, requires explanation. Clearly, $ArtIQ$ is an abstract concept and is unobservable. Therefore, we must omit it from the regression. Nevertheless, we do know that different students possess different quantities of innate artistic talent. Figure 21.7 illustrates this notion.

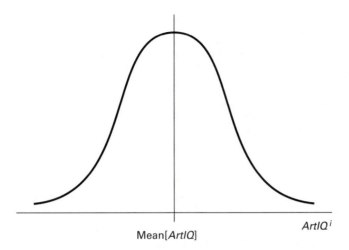

Figure 21.7
Probability distribution of *ArtIQ* random variable

Since our three students were selected randomly, define a random variable, v^i, to equal the amount by which a student's innate artistic talent deviates from the mean:

$$ArtIQ^i = \text{Mean}[\textbf{ArtIQ}] + v^i$$

where v^i is a random variable. Since the three students were chosen randomly, the mean of v^i's probability distribution equals 0:

$$\text{Mean}[v^i] = 0$$

Next let us incorporate our specification of $ArtIQ^i$ to the model:

$$ArtScore_t^i = \beta_{Const} + \beta_{ArtIQ}ArtIQ^i + \beta_{Mins}ArtMins_t^i + e_t^i$$

$$= \beta_{Const} + \beta_{ArtIQ}(\text{Mean}[\textbf{ArtIQ}] + v^i) + \beta_{Mins}ArtMins_t^i + e_t^i$$

$$= \beta_{Const} + \beta_{ArtIQ}\text{Mean}[\textbf{ArtIQ}] + \beta_{ArtIQ}v^i + \beta_{Mins}ArtMins_t^i + e_t^i$$

Fold the Mean[**ArtIQ**] term into the constant:
Let $\alpha_{Const} = \beta_{Const} + \beta_{ArtIQ}\text{Mean}[\textbf{ArtIQ}]$

$$= \alpha_{Const} + \beta_{ArtIQ}v^i + \beta_{Mins}ArtMins_t^i + e_t^i$$

Rearrange terms

$$= \alpha_{Const} + \beta_{Mins}ArtMins_t^i + \beta_{ArtIQ}v^i + e_t^i$$

$$= \alpha_{Const} + \beta_{Mins}ArtMins_t^i + \varepsilon_t^i$$

where $\varepsilon_t^i = \beta_{ArtIQ}v^i + e_t^i$ and

ε_t^i represents random influences for student i in week t.

Table 21.14
Studio art pooled OLS regression results

	Ordinary least squares (OLS)			
Dependent variable: *ArtScore*				
Explanatory variable(s):	Estimate	SE	*t*-Statistic	Prob
ArtMins	0.403843	0.345388	1.169242	0.2522
Const	40.57186	6.350514	6.388752	0.0000
Number of observations	30			

Estimated equation: *EstArtScore* = 40.6 + 0.40*ArtMins*
Interpretation of estimates:
$b_{ArtMins} = 0.40$: A 10 minute increase in studying increases a student's art project score by 4.0 points

21.5.2   Ordinary Least Squares (OLS) Pooled Regression

We begin with a pooled regression by using the ordinary least squares (OLS) estimation procedure to estimate model's parameters (table 21.14):

Interpretation: $EstArtScore = 40.57 + 0.40ArtMins$

$b_{Mins} = 0.40$

We estimate that a ten-minute increase devoted to an art project increases a student's score by 4 points. Will the ordinary least squares (OLS) estimation procedure for the coefficient value be unbiased? The OLS bias question cited earlier in the chapter provides the answer:

OLS bias question: Is the ordinary least squares (OLS) explanatory variable/error term independence premise satisfied; that is, are the model's error term and explanatory variable independent or correlated?

Recall the model that we are using (figure 21.8):

$$ArtMins_t^i = \alpha_{Const} + \beta_{Mins}ArtMins_t^i + \varepsilon_t^i$$

where

$$\varepsilon_t^i = \beta_{ArtIQ}v^i + e_t^i$$
$$ArtIQ^i = \text{Mean}[\textbf{ArtIQ}] + v^i$$

When v^i increases both innate artistic ability, $ArtIQ^i$, and the model's error term, ε_t^i, increases. Therefore the correlation or lack thereof between innate artistic ability, $ArtIQi$, and the amount of time devoted to the project, $ArtMins_t^i$, determines whether or not the ordinary least squares (OLS) estimation procedure for the coefficient value is biased or unbiased.

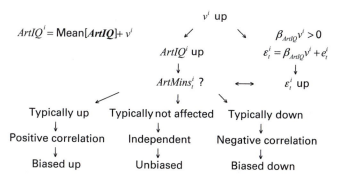

Figure 21.8
Studio art projects and bias

It is unclear how the amount a time students devote to their studio art projects will be correlated with their innate artistic ability. It could be argued that students with more artistic ability will be more interested in studio art and hence would devote more time to their art projects. However, highly talented students may only spend a little time on their projects because they only need to spend a few minutes to get a good score.

The random effects (RE) estimation procedure is only appropriate when the omitted explanatory variable and the included explanatory variable are independent. Consequently we will now assume that innate artistic ability, $ArtIQ^i$, and the time devoted to studio art projects, $ArtMins^i_t$, are independent so to motivate the rationale of the random effects (RE) estimation procedure. Since we are assuming independence, we can move on to pose the OLS reliability question:

OLS reliability question: Are the ordinary least square (OLS) error term equal variance premise and the error term/error term independence premises satisfied; that is, is the variance of the probability distribution for each observation's error term the same and are the error terms independent?

In fact the error terms are not independent. To understand why, note that the error term, ε^i_t, in this model is interesting; it has two components: $\varepsilon^i_t = \beta_{ArtIQ}v^i + e^i_t$. The first term, $\beta_{ArtIQ}v^i$, reflects innate artistic talent of each randomly selected student:

- Bob's deviation from the innate artistic talent mean: v^{Bob}
- Dan's deviation from the innate artistic talent mean: v^{Dan}
- Kim's deviation from the innate artistic talent mean: v^{Kim}

The second term, e^i_t, represents the random influences of each student's weekly quiz.

It is instructive to illustrate the error terms:

Individual	Week	$\varepsilon_t^i = \beta_{ArtIQ}v^i + e_t^i$
Bob	1	$\beta_{ArtIQ}v^{Bob} + e_1^{Bob}$
Bob	2	$\beta_{ArtIQ}v^{Bob} + e_2^{Bob}$
$\vdots$	$\vdots$	$\vdots$
Bob	10	$\beta_{ArtIQ}v^{Bob} + e_{10}^{Bob}$
Dan	1	$\beta_{ArtIQ}v^{Dan} + e_1^{Dan}$
Dan	2	$\beta_{ArtIQ}v^{Dan} + e_2^{Dan}$
$\vdots$	$\vdots$	$\vdots$
Dan	10	$\beta_{ArtIQ}v^{Dan} + e_{10}^{Dan}$
Kim	1	$\beta_{ArtIQ}v^{Kim} + e_1^{Kim}$
Kim	2	$\beta_{ArtIQ}v^{Kim} + e_2^{Kim}$
$\vdots$	$\vdots$	$\vdots$
Kim	10	$\beta_{ArtIQ}v^{Kim} + e_{10}^{Kim}$

Each of Bob's error terms has a common term, $\beta_{ArtIQ}v^{Bob}$. Similarly each of Dan's error terms has and common error term, $\beta_{ArtIQ}v^{Dan}$, and each of Kim's error terms has a common term, $\beta_{ArtIQ}v^{Kim}$. Consequently the error terms are not independent. Since the error term/error term independence premise is violated, the standard error calculations made by the ordinary least squares (OLS) estimation procedure are flawed; furthermore the ordinary least square estimation procedure for the coefficient value is not the best linear unbiased estimation procedure (BLUE).

To check our logic, we would like to analyze the error terms to determine if they appear to be correlated, but the error terms are not observable. We can exam the residuals, however. Recall that the residuals can be thought of as the estimated error terms (figure 21.9). The residuals indeed suggested that the error term/error term independence premise is violated.

21.5.3 Cross-sectional Random Effects

The random effects estimation procedure exploits this error term pattern to calculate "better" estimates (table 21.15).

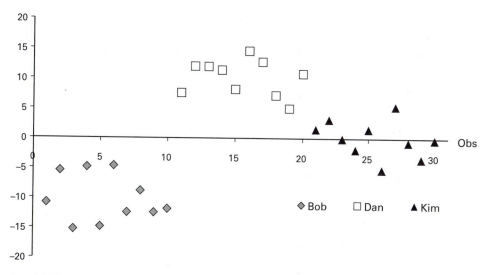

Figure 21.9
Art class ordinary least squares (OLS) residuals

Table 21.15
Studio art cross-sectional random effects regression results

Period random effects (RE)				
Dependent variable: *ArtScore*				
Explanatory variable(s):	Estimate	SE	*t*-Statistic	Prob
ArtMins	0.813260	0.167838	4.845507	0.0000
Const	33.31153	8.687413	3.834459	0.0007
Number of observations	30			
Cross sections	3			
Periods	10			

Estimated equation: *EstArtScore* = 33.31 + 0.81*LabMins*
Interpretation of estimates:

$b_{ArtMins}$ = 0.81: A 10 minute increase devoted to the lab increases a student's art project score by 8.1 points

Getting Started in EViews

- Click on **ArtScore** and then, while holding the <Ctrl> key down, click on **ArtMins**.
- Double click the highlighted area.
- Click the **Panel Options** tab.
- In the Effects Specification box, select **Random** from the Cross Section dropdown box.
- Click **OK**.

The intuition behind all this is that we can exploit the additional information about the error terms to improve the estimation procedure. Additional information is a "good thing." It is worth noting that we adopted the same strategy when we studied heteroskedasticity and autocorrelation (chapters 16 and 17). When the error terms are not independent we can exploit that information to improve our estimate beyond what the ordinary least squares (OLS) estimation procedure provides. In this case we used the random effects estimation procedure to do so.

21.6   Random Effects Critical Assumptions

For each student (cross section) the omitted variable must equal the same value in each week (time period). That is, from week to week:

- $ArtIQ^{Bob}$ does not vary.
- $ArtIQ^{Dan}$ does not vary.
- $ArtIQ^{Kim}$ does not vary.

The omitted variable and the included variable(s) are independent.

Chapter 21 Review Questions

1. What is the critical assumption that the first differences estimation procedure makes?

2. What is the critical assumption that the cross section fixed effects (FE) estimation procedure makes?

3. What is the critical assumption that the period fixed effects (FE) estimation procedure makes?

4. What is the critical assumption that the random effects (RE) estimation procedure makes?

5. What is the intuition behind our treatment of heteroskedasticity and autocorrelation? How is the random effects estimation procedure similar?

Chapter 21 Exercises

Beer consumption data: Panel gasoline data of beer consumption, beer prices, and income statistics for fifty states and the District of Columbia from 1999 to 2007:

$BeerPC_t^i$ Per capita beer consumption in state i during year t (12 oz cans)

$Price_t$ Real price of beer in year t (1982–84 dollars per 12 oz can)

$IncPC_t^i$ Per capita real disposable income in state i during in year t (thousands of chained 2005 dollars)

1. Consider the following linear model of beer consumption:

$$BeerPC_t^i = \beta_{Const} + \beta_P Price_t + \beta_I IncPC_t^i + e_t^i$$

a. Develop a theory regarding how each explanatory variable influences the dependent variable. What does your theory imply about the sign of each coefficient?

b. Using the ordinary least squares (OLS) estimation procedure to estimate the parameters without fixed or random effects, estimate the value of each coefficient. Interpret the coefficient estimates. What are the critical results?

[To access this online material, go to http://mitpress.mit.edu/westhoffeconometrics and select Beer Consumption.]

c. Formulate the null and alternative hypotheses.

d. Calculate Prob[Results IF H_0 true] and assess your theory.

2. Introduce cross-sectional fixed effects to estimate the parameters.

[To access this online material, go to http://mitpress.mit.edu/westhoffeconometrics and select Beer Consumption.]

a. Interpret the coefficient estimates. What are the critical results?

b. Calculate Prob[Results IF H_0 true] and assess your theories.

c. What effect does the introduction of cross section fixed effects have on the results?

d. Can you justify the inclusion of fixed effects? Explain. Hint: Consider the state of Utah.

Internet and TV data: Panel data of Internet, TV, economic, and political statistics for 208 countries from 1995 to 2002.

$UsersInternet_t^i$	Internet users per 1,000 people in country i during year t
$UsersTV_t^i$	Television users per 1,000 people in country i during year t
$Year_t^i$	Year
$CapitaHuman_t^i$	Literacy rate in country i during year t (percent of population 15 and over)
$CapitaPhysical_t^i$	Telephone mainlines per 10,000 people in country i during year t
$GdpPC_t^i$	Per capita real GDP in country i during year t (1,000's of "international" dollars)
$AuthPC_t^i$	The Freedom House measure of political authoritarianism in country i during year t normalized to a 0 to 10 scale. 0 represents the most democratic rating and 10 the most authoritarian. During the 1995 to 2002 period, Canada and the United States had a 0 rating; Iraq and the Democratic Republic of Korea (North Korea) rated 10.

Consider the following log-linear model of Internet use:

$$\text{Log } (UsersInternet_t^i) = \beta_{Const} + \beta_{Year}Year_t^i + \beta_{CapHum}CapitaHuman_t^i + \beta_{CapPhy}CapitaPhysical_t^i$$

$$+ \beta_{GDP}GdpPC_t^i + \beta_{Auth}Auth_t^i + e_t^i$$

3. Use the ordinary least squares (OLS) estimation procedure to estimate the parameters without fixed or random effects. Interpret the coefficient estimate of *Year*.

[To access this online material, go to http://mitpress.mit.edu/westhoffeconometrics and select Internet and TV Use—1995–2002.]

4. Do not include the variable *Year* as an explanatory variable. Instead introduce period fixed effects.

[To access this online material, go to http://mitpress.mit.edu/westhoffeconometrics and select Internet and TV Use—1995–2002.]

a. Are the coefficient estimates of *CapitalHuman*, *CapitalPhysical*, *GdpPC*, and *Auth* qualitatively consistent with the estimates that you obtained in the previous exercise when the variable *Year* was included and period fixed effects were not specified?

b. Examine the estimates of the period fixed effects coefficients. Are they qualitatively consistent with the coefficient estimate for the variable year that you obtained when period fixed effects were not specified?

Motor fuel consumption data for Arkansas, Massachusetts, and Washington: Panel data relating to motor fuel consumption for Arkansas, Massachusetts, and Washington from 1973 to 2007. These three states were chosen randomly from the fifty states and the District of Columbia.

$MotorFuelPC_t^i$	Per capita motor fuel consumption in state *i* during year *t* (gallons)
$Price_t^i$	Real price of gasoline in state *i* during year *t* (1982–84 dollars per gallon)
$IncPC_t^i$	Per capita real disposable income in state *i* during year *t* (thousands of chained 2005 dollars)
$PopDen_t^i$	Population density in state *i* during year *t* (persons per square mile)
$UnemRate_t^i$	Unemployment rate in state *i* during year *t* (percent)

5. Consider the following linear model of motor fuel consumption:

$$MotorFuelPC_t^i = \beta_{Const} + \beta_P Price_t + e_t^i$$

a. Develop a theory regarding how the explanatory variable influences the dependent variable. What does your theory imply about the sign of each coefficient?

b. Using the ordinary least squares (OLS) estimation procedure to estimate the parameters without fixed or random effects, estimate the value of each coefficient. Interpret the coefficient estimate. What is the critical result?

[To access this online material, go to http://mitpress.mit.edu/westhoffeconometrics and select Motor Fuel Consumption.]

    c. Formulate the null and alternative hypotheses.

    d. Calculate Prob[Results IF H_0 true] and assess your theory.

    e. Examine the residuals. Do they suggest that the random effect approach may be appropriate? Explain.

6. Introduce cross section random effects to estimate the parameters.

[To access this online material, go to http://mitpress.mit.edu/westhoffeconometrics and select Motor Fuel Consumption.]

    a. Interpret the coefficient estimates. What are the critical results?

    b. Calculate Prob[Results IF H_0 true] and assess your theory.

    c. What effect does the introduction of cross-sectional random effects have on the results?

22 Simultaneous Equations Models—Introduction

Chapter 22 Prep Questions

1. This question requires slogging through much high school algebra, so it is not very exciting. While tedious, it helps us understand simultaneous equations models. Consider the following two equations that model the demand and supply of beef:

Demand model: $Q_t^D = \beta_{const}^D + \beta_P^D P_t + \beta_I^D Inc_t + e_t^D$

Supply model: $Q_t^S = \beta_{const}^S + \beta_P^S P_t + \beta_{FP}^S FeedP_t + e_t^S$

where

Q_t^D = quantity of beef demanded in period t

Q_t^S = quantity of beef supplied in period t

P_t = price of beef in period t

Inc_t = disposable income in period t

$FeedP_t$ = price of cattle feed in period t

Let

Q_t = equilibrium quantity in period t: $Q_t^D = Q_t^S = Q_t$

Using algebra, solve for P_t and Q_t in terms of $FeedP_t$ and Inc_t:

a. Strategy to solve for P_t:

- Substitute Q_t for Q_t^D and Q_t^S.
- Subtract the supply model equation from the demand model equation.
- Solve for P_t.

b. Strategy to solve for Q_t:

- Substitute Q_t for Q_t^D and Q_t^S.
- Multiply the demand model equation by β_P^S and the supply model equation by β_P^D.
- Subtract the new equation for the supply model from the new equation for the demand model.
- Solve for Q_t.

2. Next, we express equations for P_t and Q_t in terms of the following α's:

$Q_t = \alpha_{Conts}^Q + \alpha_{FP}^Q FeedP_t + \alpha_I^Q Inc_t + \varepsilon_t^Q$

$P_t = \alpha_{Conts}^P + \alpha_{FP}^P FeedP_t + \alpha_I^P Inc_t + \varepsilon_t^P$

Compare these two equations for Q_t and P_t with the two equations for Q_t and P_t in problem 1. Express α_{FP}^Q, α_I^Q, α_{FP}^P, and α_I^P in terms of the β's appearing in problem 1:

a. $\alpha_{FP}^Q =$ _____ $\alpha_I^Q =$ _____ $\alpha_{FP}^P =$ _____ $\alpha_I^P =$ _____

Now consider the following ratios of α's.

b. What does $\alpha_{FP}^Q / \alpha_{FP}^P$ equal?

c. What does α_I^Q / α_I^P equal?

3. In words answer the following questions:

   a. What is the goal of multiple regression analysis?

   b. What is the interpretation of each coefficient in the regression model?

   Consider the following multiple regression model:

   General regression model: $y_t = \beta_{Const} + \beta_{x1}x1_t + \beta_{x2}x2_t + e_t$

   Since the actual parameters of the model, the β's, are unobservable, we estimate them. The estimated parameters are denoted by italicized Roman b's:

   $Esty = b_{Const} + b_{x1}x1 + b_{x2}x2$

   In terms of the estimated coefficients, b_{x1} and/or b_{x2}, what is the expression for the estimated change in y?

   c. If $x1$ changes by $\Delta x1$ while $x2$ constant: $\Delta y =$

   d. If $x2$ changes by $\Delta x2$ while $x1$ constant: $\Delta y =$

   e. Putting parts c and d together, if both $x1$ and $x2$ change: $\Delta y =$

4. Consider the following model of the US beef market:

   Demand model: $Q^D = 100{,}000 - 10{,}000P + 150Inc$

   Supply model: $Q^S = 190{,}000 + 5{,}000P - 6{,}000FeedP$

   Equilibrium: $Q^D = Q^S = Q$

   where

   Q = quantity of beef (millions of pounds)

   P = real price of beef (cents per pound)

   Inc = real disposable income (billions of dollars)

   $FeedP$ = real price of cattle feed (cents per pounds of corn cobs)

   Use algebra to solve for the equilibrium price and quantity. That is,

   a. Express the equilibrium price, P, in terms of $FeedP$ and Inc.

   b. Express the equilibrium quantity, Q, in terms of $FeedP$ and Inc.

   These two equations are called the reduced form (RF) equations.

5. Suppose that *FeedP* equals 40 and *Inc* equals 4,000.

   a. What are the numerical values of the equilibrium price and quantity?

   b. On a sheet of graph paper, plot the demand and supply curves to illustrate the equilibrium.

6. Assume that you did not know the equations for the demand and supply models. But you do know the reduced form (RF) equations that you derived in part a.

   a. Suppose that *Inc* were to rise from 4,000 to 6,000 while *FeedP* remains constant at 40. Using the reduced form (RF) equations calculate the new equilibrium price and quantity.

   • Will the demand curve shift? Explain.

   • Will the supply curve shift? Explain.

   • On a sheet of graph paper, plot the demand curve(s), the supply curve(s), and the two equilibria.

   • Based on the numerical values of the two equilibria can you calculate the slope of the supply curve? Explain.

   • Based on the numerical values of the two equilibria can you calculate the price coefficient of the demand model? Explain.

   b. Instead, suppose that *FeedP* were to rise from 40 to 60 while *Inc* remains constant at 4,000. Using the reduced form (RF) equations calculate the new equilibrium price and quantity.

   • Will the demand curve shift? Explain.

   • Will the supply curve shift? Explain.

   • On a sheet of graph paper, plot the demand curve(s), the supply curve(s), and the two equilibria.

   • Based on the numerical values of the two equilibria can you calculate the price coefficient of the demand model? Explain.

   • Based on the numerical values of the two equilibria can you calculate the price coefficient of the supply model? Explain.

22.1   Review: Explanatory Variable/Error Term Correlation

Demand and supply curves are arguably the economist's most widely used tools. They provide one example of simultaneous equations models. Unfortunately, as we will shortly show, the ordinary least squares (OLS) estimation procedure is biased when it is used to estimate the parameters of these models. To illustrate this, we begin by reviewing the effect that explanatory variable/error term correlation has on the ordinary least squares (OLS) estimation procedure. Then we focus on a demand/supply model to explain why the ordinary least squares (OLS) estimation procedure leads to bias.

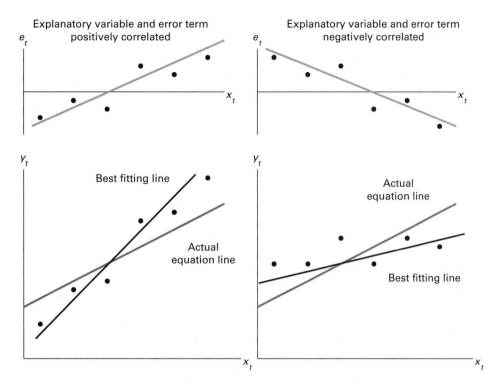

Figure 22.1
Explanatory variable and error term correlation

Explanatory variable/error term correlation (figure 22.1) leads to bias. On the one hand, when the explanatory variable and error term are positively correlated, the best fitting line is more steeply sloped than the actual equation line; consequently the ordinary least squares (OLS) estimation procedure for the coefficient value is biased upward. On the other hand, when the explanatory variable and error term are negatively correlated, the best fitting line is less steeply sloped than the actual equation line; consequently, the ordinary least squares (OLS) estimation procedure for the coefficient value is biased downward.

Explanatory variable and error term are positively correlated	Explanatory variable and error term are negatively correlated
↓	↓
OLS estimation procedure for coefficient value biased upward	OLS estimation procedure for coefficient value biased downward

22.2   Simultaneous Equations: Demand and Supply

Consider the market for a good such as food or clothing. The following two equations describe a standard demand/supply model of the market for the good:

Demand model: $Q_t^D = \beta_{Const}^D + \beta_P^D P_t +$ Other demand factors $+ e_t^D$

Supply model: $Q_t^S = \beta_{Const}^S + \beta_P^S P_t +$ Other supply factors $+ e_t^S$

where

P_t = price of the good

Q_t^D = quantity of the good demanded

e_t^D = error term in the demand equation

Q_t^S = quantity of the good supplied

e_t^S = error term in the supply equation

First, focus on our notation. The superscripts denote the models:

- **Superscript D—Demand model:** Q_t^D equals the quantity demand. β_{Const}^D, β_P^D, and e_t^D refer to the parameters and error term of the demand model.
- **Superscript S—Supply model:** Q_t^S equals the quantity supplied. β_{Const}^S, β_P^S, and e_t^s refer to the parameters and the error term of the supply model.

The parameter subscripts refer to the constants and explanatory variable coefficients of the models.

- **Subscript $Const$—Constant:** β_{Const}^D and β_{Const}^S are the constants of the demand model and the supply model.
- **Subscript P—Price coefficient:** β_P^D and β_P^S are the price coefficients of the demand model and the supply model.

The quantity of a good demanded is determined by the good's own price and other demand factors such as income, the price of substitutes, the price of and complements. Similarly the quantity of a good supplied is determined by the good's own price and other supply factors such as wages and raw material prices.

The market is in equilibrium whenever the quantity demanded equals the quantity supplied:

$$Q_t^D = Q_t^S = Q_t$$

Both the quantity, Q_t, and the price, P_t, are determined simultaneously as depicted by the famous demand/supply diagram reproduced in figure 22.2.

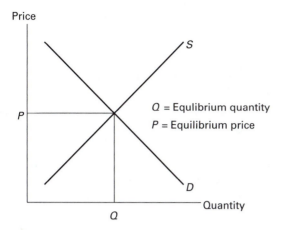

Figure 22.2
Demand/supply model

22.2.1 Endogenous versus Exogenous Variables

In a simultaneous equations model, it is important to distinguish between endogenous and exogenous variables. Endogenous variables are variables whose values are determined "within" the model. In the demand/supply model, the quantity and the price, as determined by the intersection of the supply and demand curves, are endogenous; that is, both quantity and price are determined simultaneously "within" the model. Conversely, exogenous variables are determined "outside" the model; in the context of the model, the values of exogenous variables are taken as given. The model does not attempt to explain how the values of exogenous variables are determined. For example, when considering the demand and supply models for beer, we are not trying to explain the effect of the other demand and supply factors; that is, we are not trying to explain how income, the price of wine, wages, and the price of hops are determined. Income, the price of wine, wages, and the price of hops would all be exogenous variables, so we would take them as given.

Endogenous variables: Variables determined "within" the model; namely price and quantity

Exogenous variables: Variables determined "outside" the model; namely other demand and supply factors

22.2.2 Single Equation versus Simultaneous Equations Models

In single equation models, there is only one endogenous variable, the dependent variable itself; all explanatory variables are exogenous. For example, in the following single model the dependent variable is consumption and the explanatory variable income:

$$Cons_t = \beta_{Const} + \beta_I Inc_t + e_t$$

The model only attempts to explain how consumption is determined. The dependent variable, consumption, is the only endogenous variable. The model does not attempt to explain how income is determined; that is, the values of income are taken as given. All explanatory variables, in this case only income, are exogenous.

In a simultaneous equations model, while the dependent variable is endogenous, an explanatory variable can be either endogenous or exogenous. In the demand/supply model, quantity, the dependent variable, is an endogenous; quantity is determined "within" the model. Price is both an endogenous variable and an explanatory variable. Price is determined "within" the model, and it is used to explain the quantity demanded and the quantity supplied.

What are the consequences of endogenous explanatory variables for the ordinary least squares (OLS) estimation procedure?

Claim: Whenever an explanatory variable is also an endogenous variable, the ordinary least squares (OLS) estimation procedure for the value of its coefficient is biased.

We will now use the demand and supply models to justify this claim.

22.2.3   Demand Model

When the ordinary least squares (OLS) estimation procedure is used to estimate the demand model, the good's own price and the error term are positively correlated; accordingly, the ordinary least squares (OLS) estimation procedure for the value of the price coefficient will be biased upward (figure 22.3). Let us now show why.

Demand model: $Q_t^D = \beta_{Const}^D + \beta_P^D P_t + \text{Other demand factors} + e_t^D$

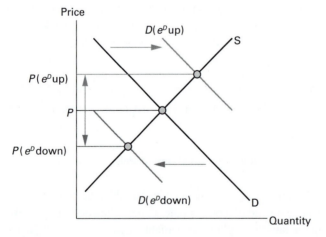

Figure 22.3
Effect of the demand error term

Ordinary Least Squares (OLS) Estimation Procedure: Our Suspicions

When the error term, e_t^D, rises the demand curve shifts to the right resulting in a higher price; on the other hand, when the error, e_t^D, falls the demand curve shifts to the left resulting in a lower price. In the demand model, the price, P_t, and the error term, e_t^D, are positively correlated. Since the good's own price is an explanatory variable, bias results:

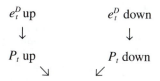

e_t^D up e_t^D down

↓   ↓

P_t up P_t down

↘   ↙

Explanatory variable and
error term positively correlated

↓

OLS estimation procedure for
coefficient value biased upward

Confirming Our Suspicions

The ordinary least squares (OLS) estimation procedure for the value of the price coefficient in the demand model should be biased upward (figure 22.4). We will check our logic with a simulation.

Econometrics Lab 22.1: Simultaneous Equations—Demand Price Coefficient

[To access this online material, go to http://mitpress.mit.edu/westhoffeconometrics and select Lab 22.1.]

We are focusing on the demand model; hence, the Dem radio button is selected. The lists immediately below the Dem radio button specify the demand model. The actual constant equals 30, the actual price coefficient equals –4, and so forth. XCoef represents an "other demand factor," such as income.

Be certain that the Pause checkbox is cleared. Click **Start** and then after many, many repetitions click **Stop**. The average of the estimated demand price coefficient values is –2.6, greater than the actual value, –4.0 (table 22.1). This result suggests that the ordinary least squares (OLS) estimation procedure for the value of the price coefficient is biased upward. Our Econometrics Lab confirms our suspicions.

But even though the ordinary least squares (OLS) estimation procedure is biased, it might be consistent, might it not? Recall the distinction between an unbiased and a consistent estimation procedure:

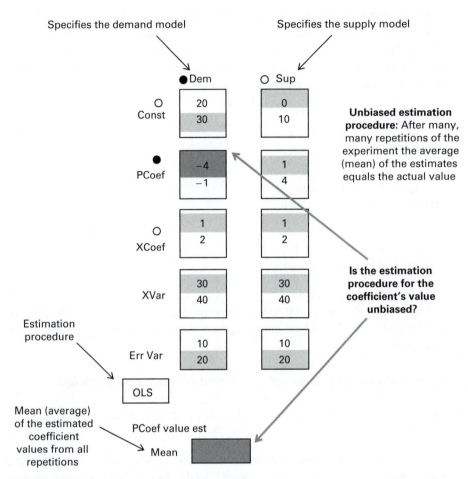

Figure 22.4
Simultaneous equations simulation

Table 22.1
Simultaneous equations simulation results—Demand

Estimation procedure	Sample size	Actual coef value	Mean (average) of estimated coef values	Magnitude of bias
OLS	20	−4.0	≈−2.6	≈1.4

Table 22.2
Simultaneous equations simulation results—Demand

Estimation procedure	Sample size	Actual coef value	Mean (average) of estimated coef values	Magnitude of bias
OLS	20	−4.0	≈−2.6	≈1.4
OLS	30	−4.0	≈−2.6	≈1.4
OLS	40	−4.0	≈−2.6	≈1.4

Unbiased: The estimation procedure does not systematically underestimate or overestimate the actual value; that is, after many, many repetitions the average of the estimates equals the actual value.

Consistent but biased: As consistent estimation procedure can be biased. But, as the sample size, as the number of observations, grows:

• The magnitude of the bias decreases. That is, the mean of the coefficient estimate's probability distribution approaches the actual value.

• The variance of the estimate's probability distribution diminishes and approaches 0.

How can we use the simulation to investigate this possibility? Just increase the sample size. If the procedure is consistent, the average of the estimated coefficient values after many, many repetitions would move closer and closer to −4.0, the actual value, as we increase the sample size. That is, if the procedure is consistent, the magnitude of the bias would decrease as the sample size increases. (Also the variance of the estimates would decrease.) So let us increase the sample size from 20 to 30 and then to 40. Unfortunately, we observe that a larger sample size does not reduce the magnitude of the bias (table 22.2).

When we estimate the value of the price coefficient in the demand model, we find that the ordinary least squares (OLS) estimation procedure fails in two respects:

Bad news: The ordinary least squares (OLS) estimation procedure is biased.

Bad news: The ordinary least squares (OLS) estimation procedure is not consistent.

22.2.4   Supply Model

We will now use the same line of reasoning to show that the ordinary least squares (OLS) estimation procedure for the value of the price coefficient in the supply model is also biased (figure 22.5).

Supply model: $Q_t^S = \beta_{Const}^S + \beta_P^S P_t + \text{Other supply factors} + e_t^S$

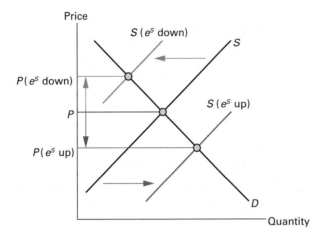

Figure 22.5
Effect of the supply error term

Ordinary Least Squares (OLS) Estimation Procedure: Our Suspicions

On the one hand, when the error term, e_t^S, rises, the supply curve shifts to the right, resulting in a lower price; on the other hand, when the error term, e_t^S, falls, the supply curve shifts to the left, resulting in a higher price. In the supply model, the price, P_t, and the error term, e_t^S, are negatively correlated:

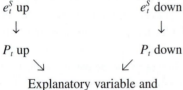

e_t^S up e_t^S down
↓   ↓
P_t up P_t down
↘   ↙
Explanatory variable and
error term negatively correlated
↓
OLS estimation procedure for
coefficient value biased downward

The ordinary least squares (OLS) estimation procedure for the value of the price coefficient in the supply model should be biased downward. Once again, we will use a simulation to confirm our logic.

Confirming Our Suspicions

Econometrics Lab 22.2: Simultaneous Equations—Supply Price Coefficient

[To access this online material, go to http://mitpress.mit.edu/westhoffeconometrics and select Lab 22.2.]

Table 22.3
Simultaneous equations simulation results—Supply

Estimation procedure	Sample size	Actual coef value	Mean (average) of estimated coef values	Magnitude of bias
OLS	20	1.0	≈−0.4	≈1.4
OLS	30	1.0	≈−0.4	≈1.4
OLS	40	1.0	≈−0.4	≈1.4

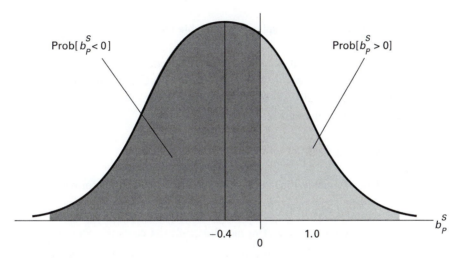

Figure 22.6
Probability distribution of price coefficient estimate

We are now focusing on the supply curve; hence, the Sup radio button is selected. Note that the actual value of the supply price coefficient equals 1.0. Be certain that the Pause checkbox is cleared. Click **Start** and then after many, many repetitions click **Stop**. The average of the estimated coefficient values is −1.4, less than the actual value, 1.0. This result suggests that the ordinary least squares (OLS) estimation procedure for the value of the price coefficient is biased downward, confirming our suspicions.

But might the estimation procedure be consistent? To answer this question increase the sample size from 20 to 30 and then from 30 to 40. The magnitude of the bias is unaffected. Accordingly, it appears that the ordinary least squares (OLS) estimation procedure for the value of the price coefficient is not consistent either (table 22.3).

When estimating the price coefficient's value in the supply model, the ordinary least squares (OLS) estimation procedure fails in two respects (figure 22.6):

Bad news: The ordinary least squares (OLS) estimation procedure is biased.

Bad news: The ordinary least squares (OLS) estimation procedure is not consistent.

The supply model simulations illustrate a problem even worse than that encountered when estimating the demand model. In this case the bias can be so severe that the mean of the coefficient estimate's probability distribution has the wrong sign. To gain more intuition, suppose that the probability distribution is symmetric. Then the chances that the coefficient estimate would have the wrong sign are greater than the chances that it would have the correct sign when using the ordinary least squares (OLS) estimation procedure. This is very troublesome, is it not?

22.2.5   Summary: Endogenous Explanatory Variable Problem

We have used the demand and supply models to illustrate that an endogenous explanatory variable creates a bias problem for the ordinary least squares (OLS) estimation procedure. Whenever an explanatory variable is also an endogenous variable, the ordinary least squares (OLS) estimation procedure for the value of its coefficient is biased.

22.3   An Example: The Market for Beef

Beef market data: Monthly time series data relating to the market for beef from 1977 to 1986.

Q_t	Quantity of beef in month t (millions of pounds)
P_t	Real price of beef in month t (1982–84 cents per pound)
Inc_t	Real disposable income in month t (billions of 2005 dollars)
$ChickP_t$	Real price of whole chickens in month t (1982–84 cents per pound)
$FeedP_t$	Real price of cattle feed in month t (1982–84 cents per pounds of corn cobs)

22.3.1   Demand and Supply Models

We begin by describing the endogenous and exogenous variables:

Endogenous variables: Both the quantity of beef and the price of beef, Q_t and P_t, are endogenous variables; they are determined within the model.

Exogenous Variables:

• Disposable income is an "Other demand factor"; disposable income, Inc_t, is an exogenous variable that affects demand. Since beef is regarded as a normal good, we expect that households would demand more beef when income rises.

• The price of chicken is also an "Other demand factor"; the price of chicken, $ChickP_t$, is an exogenous variable that affects demand. Since chicken is a substitute for beef, we expect that households would demand more beef when the price of chicken rises.

• The price of cattle feed is an "Other supply factor"; the price of cattle feed, $FeedP_t$, is an exogenous variable that affects supply. Since cattle feed is an input to the production of beef, we expect that firms would produce less when the price of cattle feed rises.

Now let us formalize the simultaneous equations demand/supply model that we will investigate:

Demand model: $Q_t^D = \beta_{Const}^D + \beta_P^D P_t + \beta_I^D Inc_t + e_t^D$

Supply model: $Q_t^S = \beta_{Const}^S + \beta_P^S P_t + \beta_{FP}^S FeedP_t + e_t^S$

Equilibrium: $Q_t^D = Q_t^S = Q_t$

Endogenous variables: Q_t and P_t

Exogenous variables: $FeedP_t$ and Inc_t

Project: Estimate the beef market demand and supply parameters.

22.3.2 Ordinary Least Squares (OLS) Estimation Procedure

Let us begin by using the ordinary least squares (OLS) procedure to estimate the parameters.

[To access this online material, go to http://mitpress.mit.edu/westhoffeconometrics and select Market for Beef.]

As reported in table 22.4, the estimate of the demand model's price coefficient is negative, −364.4, suggesting that higher prices decrease the quantity demanded. The result is consistent with economic theory suggesting that the demand curve is downward sloping.

Table 22.4
OLS regression results—Demand model

Ordinary least squares (OLS)				
Dependent variable: Q				
Explanatory variable(s):	Estimate	SE	t-Statistic	Prob
P	−364.3646	18.29792	−19.91290	0.0000
Inc	23.74785	0.929082	25.56056	0.0000
$Const$	155,137.0	4,731.400	32.78882	0.0000
Number of observations	120			

Estimated equation: $EstQ^D = 155,137 - 364.4P + 23.75Inc$

Interpretation of estimates:

$b_P^D = -364.4$: A 1 cent increase in the price of beef decreases the quantity demanded by 364.4 million pounds

$b_I^D = 23.75$: A 1 billion dollar increase in real disposable income increases the quantity of beef demanded by 23.75 million pounds

Table 22.5
OLS regression results—Supply model

Ordinary least squares (OLS)				
Dependent variable: Q				
Explanatory variable(s):	Estimate	SE	t-Statistic	Prob
P	−231.5487	41.19843	−5.620328	0.0000
$FeedP$	−700.3695	119.3941	−5.866031	0.0000
$Const$	272,042.7	7,793.872	34.90469	0.0000
Number of observations	120			

Estimated equation: $EstQ^S = 272{,}043 - 231.5P + 700.1FeedP$

Interpretation of estimates:

$b_P^S = -231.5$: A 1 cent increase in the price of beef decreases the quantity supplied by 231.5 million pounds

$b_{FP}^S = -700.1$: A 1 cent increase in cattle feed decreases the quantity of beef supplied by 700.1 million pounds

As reported in table 22.5, the estimate of the supply model's price coefficient is negative, −231.5, suggesting that higher prices decrease the quantity supplied. Obviously this result is not consistent with economic theory. This result suggests that the supply curve is downward sloping rather than upward sloping. But what have we just learned about the ordinary least squares (OLS) estimation procedure. The ordinary least squares (OLS) estimation procedure for the price coefficient estimate of the supply model will be biased downward. This could explain our result, could it not?

22.3.3   Reduced Form (RF) Estimation Procedure: The Mechanics

We will now describe an alternative estimation procedure, the reduced form (RF) estimation procedure. We will show that while this new procedure does not "solve" the bias problem, it mitigates it. More specifically, while the procedure is still biased, it proves to be consistent. In this way, the new procedure is "better than" ordinary least squares (OLS). We begin by describing the mechanics of the reduced form (RF) estimation procedure.

We have argued that the ordinary least squares (OLS) estimation procedure leads to bias because an endogenous variable, in our case the price, is an explanatory variable. The reduced form (RF) approach begins by using algebra to express each endogenous variable only in terms of the exogenous variables. These new equations are called the reduced form (RF) equations.

Intuition: Since bias results from endogenous explanatory variables, algebraically manipulate the simultaneous equations model to express each endogenous variable only in terms of the exogenous variables. Then use the ordinary least squares (OLS) estimation procedure to estimate the parameters of these newly derived equations, rather than the original ones.

The reduced form (RF) approach involves three steps:

Step 1:   Derive the reduced form (RF) equations from the original models.

• The reduced form (RF) equations express each endogenous variable in terms of the exogenous variables only.

• Algebraically solve for the original model's parameters in terms of the reduced form (RF) parameters.

Step 2:   Use ordinary least squares (OLS) estimation procedure to estimate the parameters of the reduced form (RF) equations.

Step 3:   Calculate coefficient estimates for the original models using the derivations from step 1 and estimates from step 2.

Step 1: Derive the Reduced Form (RF) Equations from the Original Models

We begin with the supply and demand models:

Demand model: $Q_t^D = \beta_{Const}^D + \beta_P^D P_t + \beta_I^D Inc_t + e_t^D$

Supply model: $Q_t^S = \beta_{Const}^S + \beta_P^S P_t + \beta_{FP}^S FeedP_t + e_t^S$

Equilibrium: $Q_t^D = Q_t^S = Q_t$

Endogenous variables: Q_t and P_t

Exogenous variables: $FeedP_t$ and Inc_t

There are six parameters of the demand and supply models: β_{Const}^D, β_P^D, β_I^D, β_{Const}^S, β_P^S, and β_{FP}^S. We wish to estimate the values of these parameters.

The reduced form (RF) equations express each endogenous variable in terms of the exogenous variables. In this case we wish to express Q_t in terms of $FeedP_t$ and Inc_t and P_t in terms of $FeedP_t$ and Inc_t. The appendix at the end of this chapter shows that how elementary, yet laborious, algebra can be used to derive the following reduced form (RF) equations for the endogenous variables, Q_t and P_t:

$$Q_t = \frac{\beta_P^S \beta_{Const}^D - \beta_P^D \beta_{Const}^S}{\beta_P^S - \beta_P^D} - \frac{\beta_P^D \beta_{FP}^S}{\beta_P^S - \beta_P^D} FeedP_t + \frac{\beta_P^S \beta_I^D}{\beta_P^S - \beta_P^D} Inc_t + \frac{\beta_P^S e_t^D - \beta_P^D e_t^S}{\beta_P^S - \beta_P^D}$$

$$P_t = \frac{\beta_{Const}^D - \beta_{Const}^S}{\beta_P^S - \beta_P^D} - \frac{\beta_{FP}^S}{\beta_P^S - \beta_P^D} FeedP_t + \frac{\beta_I^D}{\beta_P^S - \beta_P^D} Inc_t + \frac{e_t^D - e_t^S}{\beta_P^S - \beta_P^D}$$

Now let us make an interesting observation about the reduced form (RF) equations. Focus first on the ratio of the feed price coefficients and then on the ratio of the income coefficients. These ratios equal the price coefficients of the original demand and supply models, β_P^D and β_P^S:

Feed price coefficients in the   Income coefficients in the
reduced form (RF) equations   reduced form (RF) equations

$\downarrow$ $\downarrow$

Ratio of feed price   Ratio of income
coefficients equals the   coefficients equals the
price coefficient of   price coefficient of
the demand model   the supply model

$\downarrow$ $\downarrow$

$$-\frac{-\dfrac{\beta_P^D\beta_{FP}^S}{\beta_P^S - \beta_P^D}}{-\dfrac{\beta_{FP}^S}{\beta_P^S - \beta_P^D}} = \beta_P^D \qquad\qquad \frac{\dfrac{\beta_P^S\beta_I^D}{\beta_P^S - \beta_P^D}}{\dfrac{\beta_I^D}{\beta_P^S - \beta_P^D}} = \beta_P^S$$

We will formalize this observation by expressing all the parameters of the original simultaneous equations model (the constants and coefficients of the demand and supply models, the β's) in terms of the parameters of the reduced form (RF) model (the constants and coefficients of the reduced form equations. To do so, let α represent the parameters, the constants and coefficients, of the reduced form (RF) equations:

$$Q_t = \alpha_{Const}^Q + \alpha_{FP}^Q FeedP_t + \alpha_I^Q Inc_t + \varepsilon_t^Q$$

$$P_t = \alpha_{Const}^P + \alpha_{FP}^P FeedP_t + \alpha_I^P Inc_t + \varepsilon_t^P$$

First, consider the notation we use in the reduced form (RF) equations. Superscripts refer to the reduced form (RF) equation:

• **Superscript Q—Quantity reduced form (RF) equation:** α_{Const}^Q, α_{FP}^Q, α_I^Q, and ε_t^Q are the parameters and error term of the quantity reduced form (RF) equation.

• **Superscript P—Price reduced form (RF) equation:** α_{Const}^P, α_{FP}^P, α_I^P, and ε_t^P are the parameters and the error term of the price reduced form (RF) equation.

The parameter subscripts refer to the constants and coefficients of each reduced form (RF) equation:

• **Subscript $Const$—Reduced form (RF) constants:** α_{Const}^Q and α_{Const}^P, are the constants of the quantity and price reduced form (RF) equations.

• **Subscript FP—Reduced form (RF) feed price coefficients:** α_{FP}^Q and α_{FP}^P are the feed price coefficients of the quantity and price reduced form (RF) equations.

• **Subscript I—Reduced form (RF) income coefficients:** α_I^Q and α_I^P are the income coefficients of the quantity and price reduced form (RF) equations.

There are six parameters of the reduced form (RF) equations: α_{Const}^Q, α_{FP}^Q, α_I^Q, α_{Const}^P, α_{FP}^P, and α_I^P.

By comparing the two sets of reduced form (RF) equations, we can express each of the reduced form (RF) parameter, each α, in terms of the parameters of the original demand and supply models, the β's. We have six equations:

$$\alpha_{Const}^{Q} = \frac{\beta_{P}^{S}\beta_{Const}^{D} - \beta_{P}^{D}\beta_{Const}^{S}}{\beta_{P}^{S} - \beta_{P}^{D}}, \quad \alpha_{FP}^{Q} = -\frac{\beta_{P}^{D}\beta_{FP}^{S}}{\beta_{P}^{S} - \beta_{P}^{D}}, \quad \alpha_{I}^{Q} = \frac{\beta_{P}^{S}\beta_{I}^{D}}{\beta_{P}^{S} - \beta_{P}^{D}}$$

$$\alpha_{Const}^{P} = \frac{\beta_{Const}^{D} - \beta_{Const}^{S}}{\beta_{P}^{S} - \beta_{P}^{D}}, \quad \alpha_{FP}^{P} = -\frac{\beta_{FP}^{S}}{\beta_{P}^{S} - \beta_{P}^{D}}, \quad \alpha_{I}^{P} = \frac{\beta_{I}^{D}}{\beta_{P}^{S} - \beta_{P}^{D}}$$

There are six parameters of the original demand and supply models: β_{Const}^{D}, β_{P}^{D}, β_{I}^{D}, β_{Const}^{S}, β_{P}^{S}, and β_{FP}^{S}. That is, we have six unknowns, the β's. We have six equations and six unknowns. We can solve for the unknowns by expressing the β's in terms of the α's. For example, we can solve for price coefficients of the original demand and supply models, β_{P}^{D} and β_{P}^{S}:

Feed price coefficients in the reduced form (RF) equations: Ratio of α_{FP}^{Q} to α_{FP}^{P} equals β_{P}^{D}

Income coefficients in the reduced form (RF) equations: Ratio of α_{I}^{Q} to α_{I}^{P} equals β_{P}^{S}

$$\downarrow$$

$$\frac{\alpha_{FP}^{Q}}{\alpha_{FP}^{P}} = \frac{-\dfrac{\beta_{P}^{D}\beta_{FP}^{S}}{\beta_{P}^{S} - \beta_{P}^{D}}}{-\dfrac{\beta_{FP}^{S}}{\beta_{P}^{S} - \beta_{P}^{D}}} = \beta_{P}^{D}$$

$$\frac{\alpha_{I}^{Q}}{\alpha_{I}^{P}} = \frac{\dfrac{\beta_{P}^{S}\beta_{I}^{D}}{\beta_{P}^{S} - \beta_{P}^{D}}}{\dfrac{\beta_{I}^{D}}{\beta_{P}^{S} - \beta_{P}^{D}}} = \beta_{P}^{S}$$

$$\downarrow$$

$$\frac{\alpha_{FP}^{Q}}{\alpha_{FP}^{P}} = \beta_{P}^{D}$$

$$\frac{\alpha_{I}^{Q}}{\alpha_{I}^{P}} = \beta_{P}^{S}$$

These coefficients reflect the "slopes" of the demand and supply curves.[1]

Step 2: Use Ordinary Least Squares (OLS) to Estimate the Reduced Form Equations

We use the ordinary least squares (OLS) estimation procedure to estimate the α's (see tables 22.6 and 22.7).

[To access this online material, go to http://mitpress.mit.edu/westhoffeconometrics and select Market for Beef.]

Estimate of $\alpha_{FP}^{Q} = \alpha_{FP}^{Q} = -332.00$ Estimate of $\alpha_{I}^{Q} = \alpha_{I}^{Q} = 17.347$

Estimate of $\alpha_{FP}^{Q} = \alpha_{FP}^{Q} = 1.0562$ Estimate of $\alpha_{I}^{P} = \alpha_{I}^{P} = 0.018825$

---

1. The coefficients do not equal the slope of the demand curve, but rather the reciprocal of the slope. They are the ratio of run over rise instead of rise over run. This occurs as a consequence of the economist's convention of placing quantity on the horizontal axis and price on the vertical axis. To avoid the awkwardness of using the expression "the reciprocal of the slope" repeatedly, we will place the word slope within quotes to indicate that it is the reciprocal.

Table 22.6
OLS regression results—Quantity reduced form (RF) equation

Ordinary least squares (OLS)				
Dependent variable: Q				
Explanatory variable(s):	Estimate	SE	t-Statistic	Prob
FeedP	−331.9966	121.6865	−2.728293	0.0073
Inc	17.34683	2.132027	8.136309	0.0000
Const	138,725.5	13,186.01	10.52066	0.0000
Number of observations	120			

Estimated equation: $EstQ = 138,726 − 332.00 FeedP + 17.347 Inc$

Interpretation of estimates:

$a_{FP}^Q = -332.00$: A 1 cent increase in the price of cattle feed decreases the quantity of beef by 332.00 million pounds

$a_I^Q = 17.347$: A 1 billion dollar increase in real disposable income increases the quantity of beef by 17.347 million pounds

Table 22.7
OLS regression results—Price reduced form (RF) equation

Ordinary least squares (OLS)				
Dependent variable: P				
Explanatory variable(s):	Estimate	SE	t-Statistic	Prob
FeedP	1.056242	0.286474	3.687044	0.0003
Inc	0.018825	0.005019	3.750636	0.0003
Const	33.02715	31.04243	1.063936	0.2895
Number of observations	120			

Estimated equation: $EstP = 33.037 + 1.0562 FeedP + 0.018825 Inc$

Interpretation of estimates:

$a_{FP}^P = 1.0562$: A 1 cent increase in the price of cattle feed increases the price of beef by 1.0562 cents

$a_I^P = 17.347$: A 1 billion dollar increase in real disposable income increases the price of beef by 0.018825 cents

Table 22.8 summarizes the reduced form (RF) coefficient estimates.

Let us now take a brief aside to show that the reduced form (RF) estimates are consistent with the standard demand/supply analysis for the beef market.

• **Feed price reduced form (RF) estimates:** Since cattle feed is an input for beef production, an increase in the feed price shifts the supply curve for beef to the left. As figure 22.7 illustrates, the equilibrium quantity falls and the equilibrium price rises.

The feed price coefficient estimate in the quantity reduced form (RF) equation is negative, −332.00. The negative estimate suggests that an increase in feed prices reduces the quantity. The

Table 22.8
Reduced form (RF) coefficient estimates

	Quantity reduced form (RF) coefficient estimate	Price reduced form (RF) coefficient estimate
Feed price	−332.00	1.0562
Income	17.347	0.018825

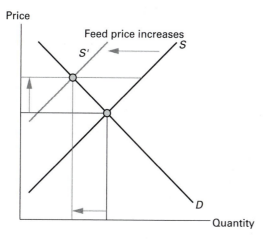

Figure 22.7
Demand/supply analysis—An increase in feed price

feed price estimate in the price reduced form (RF) equation is positive, 1.0562. This suggests that an increase in the feed price increases the price of beef.

Feed price increases
↙   ↘
Quantity   Price
falls   rises

The feed price coefficient estimates are consistent with the standard demand/supply analysis.

• **Income reduced form (RF) estimates:**   Since beef is generally regarded as a normal good, an increase in income shifts the demand curve for beef to the right. As figure 22.8 illustrates, the equilibrium quantity and price both increase.

The income coefficient estimates in both the quantity and price reduced form (RF) regression are positive, 17.347 and .018825. The positive estimates suggest that an increase in income cause both the quantity and the price of beef to rise.

Price

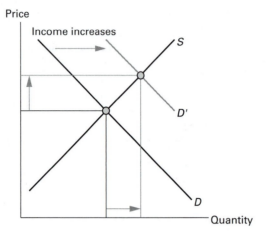

Figure 22.8
Demand/supply analysis—An increase in income

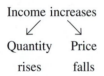

The income coefficient estimates are consistent with the standard demand/supply analysis.

We now return to complete step 3 of the reduced form (RF) estimation procedure.

Step 3: Calculate Coefficient Estimates for the Original Model Using the Derivations and Estimates from Steps 1 and 2

We will use the reduced form (RF) coefficient estimates from step 2 to estimate the price coefficients of the demand and supply models, β_P^D and β_P^S, the "slopes" of the supply and demand curves. To do so, we apply the equations for β_P^D and β_P^S that we derived in step 1.

	Demand curve price coefficient	Supply curve price coefficient

From step 1:

$$\beta_P^D = \frac{\alpha_{FP}^Q}{\alpha_{FP}^P} \qquad\qquad \beta_P^S = \frac{\alpha_I^Q}{\alpha_I^P}$$

$$\downarrow \qquad\qquad\qquad\qquad \downarrow$$

$$\text{Estimate of } \beta_P^D = b_P^D = \frac{a_{FP}^Q}{a_{FP}^P} \qquad \text{Estimate of } \beta_P^S = b_P^S = \frac{a_I^Q}{a_I^P}$$

From step 2:
$$a_{FP}^Q = -332.00 \qquad\qquad a_I^Q = 17.347$$
$$a_{FP}^P = 1.0562 \qquad\qquad\quad a_I^P = 0.018825$$

$$\downarrow \qquad\qquad\qquad\qquad \downarrow$$

$$b_P^D = \frac{a_{FP}^Q}{a_{FP}^P} = \frac{-332.00}{1.0562} = -314.3 \qquad b_P^S = \frac{a_I^Q}{a_I^P} = \frac{17.347}{0.018825} = 921.5$$

22.3.4 Comparing Ordinary Least Squares (OLS) and Reduced Form (RF) Estimates

We will now compare the ordinary least squares (OLS) and reduced form (RF) estimates of the price coefficients (table 22.9). The supply curve price coefficient is the most obvious difference. The ordinary least squares (OLS) estimate is negative while the reduced form (RF) estimate is positive. In view of our upward sloping supply curve theory, this result is comforting. Unlike the ordinary least squares (OLS) estimates, the signs of the reduced form (RF) price coefficient estimates are consistent not only with our theory of demand, but also our theory of supply. Consequently we will now show that the reduced form (RF) estimation procedure is "better" than the ordinary least squares (OLS) estimation procedure when estimating simultaneous equations models.

22.4 Justifying the Reduced Form (RF) Estimation Procedure

Previously, we used the simultaneous equations simulation to show that the ordinary least squares (OLS) estimation procedure was neither unbiased nor consistent when estimating the values of

Table 22.9
Comparing OLS and RF price coefficient estimates

	Estimated demand curve price coefficient b_P^D	Estimated supply curve price coefficient b_P^S
Ordinary least squares (OLS)	−364.4	−231.5
Reduced form (RF)	−314.3	921.5

Table 22.10
Simultaneous equations simulation results

Estimation procedure	Sample size	Demand price coefficient			Supply price coefficient		
		Actual coef value	Mean of estimated coef values	Variance of estimated coef values	Actual coef value	Mean of estimated coef values	Variance of estimated coef values
RF	20	−4.0	≈−4.3	≈5.4	1.0	≈1.3	≈5.3

the price coefficients. Now, we will use this simulation to investigate the properties of the reduced form (RF) estimation procedure. It would be wonderful if the reduced form (RF) approach were unbiased. Failing that, might the reduced form (RF) approach be consistent? While we could address these issues rigorously, we will avoid the complex mathematics by using a simulation.

Econometrics Lab 22.3: Reduced From (RF) Estimation Procedure

[To access this online material, go to http://mitpress.mit.edu/westhoffeconometrics and select Lab 22.3.]

Note that the reduced form (RF), rather than the ordinary least squares (OLS), estimation procedure is now selected. Also the Dem radio button is selected initially; the demand model is being analyzed. Be certain that the Pause checkbox is cleared. Click **Start** and then after many, many repetitions click **Stop**. Next select the Sup radio button and repeat the process to analyze the supply model.

Table 22.10 reports the reduced form (RF) results for a sample size of 20. The results suggest that reduced form (RF) estimation procedures for the price coefficients are biased. The averages of the estimated price coefficient values after many, many repetitions do not equal the actual values for either the demand or supply models. The average of the demand price coefficient estimates equals −4.3 while the actual value equals −4.0; similarly the averate of the supply price coefficient estimates equals 1.3 while the actual value equals 1.0.

But perhaps that unlike the ordinary least squared (OLS) estimation procedure, the reduced form (RF) approach might be consistent. To address this question, we increase the sample size, first from 20 to 30 and then from 30 to 40 (table 22.11). As the sample size becomes larger, bias is still present but the magnitude of the bias diminishes for both the demand and supply price coefficients. Furthermore the variances also fall. The simulation illustrates that while the reduced form (RF) estimation procedure for the price coefficient value is still biased, it is consistent.

We can conclude that the reduced form (RF) estimation procedure for the coefficient value of an endogenous explanatory variable provides both good news and bad news:

Bad news: The reduced form (RF) estimation procedure for the coefficient value is biased.

Table 22.11
Simultaneous equations simulation results

Estimation procedure	Sample size	Demand price coefficient			Supply price coefficient		
		Actual coef value	Mean of estimated coef values	Variance of estimated coef values	Actual coef value	Mean of estimated coef values	Variance of estimated coef values
RF	20	−4.0	≈−4.3	≈5.4	1.0	≈1.3	≈5.3
RF	30	−4.0	≈−4.2	≈1.2	1.0	≈1.2	≈1.2
RF	40	−4.0	≈−4.1	≈0.6	1.0	≈1.1	≈0.6

Good news: The reduced form (RF) estimation procedure for the coefficient value is consistent.

22.5 Two Paradoxes

Let us reexamine how we obtained the estimates for the price coefficients of the demand and supply models:

$$b_P^D = \frac{a_{FP}^Q}{a_{FP}^P} = \frac{-332.00}{1.0562} = -314.3, \quad b_P^S = \frac{a_I^Q}{a_I^P} = \frac{17.347}{0.018825} = 921.5$$

These equations for the two price coefficient estimates appear paradoxical at first glance:

• The demand model's price coefficient, b_P^D, depends on the reduced form (RF) coefficients of feed price, a_{FP}^Q and a_{FP}^P. But a_{FP}^Q and a_{FP}^P tell us something about supply, not demand. They tell us how the feed price, a variable that shifts the supply curve, affects the equilibrium quantity and price.

• Similarly the supply model's price coefficient, b_P^S, depends on the reduced form (RF) coefficients of income, a_I^Q and a_I^P. But a_I^Q and a_I^P tell us something about demand, not supply. They tell us how income, a variable that shifts the demand curve, affects the equilibrium quantity and price.

22.6 Resolving the Paradoxes: Coefficient Interpretation Approach

22.6.1 Review: Goal of Multiple Regression Analysis and the Interpretation of the Coefficients

Now let us review two key concepts:

• **Goal of multiple regression analysis:** Multiple regression analysis attempts to sort out the individual effect that each explanatory variable has on the dependent variable.

• **Interpretation of coefficients:**   Each explanatory variable's coefficient reveals the individual impact which that explanatory variable has on the dependent variable; that is, each explanatory variable's coefficient tells us how changes in that explanatory variable affect the dependent variable while all other explanatory variables remain constant.

Consider a general regression model with two explanatory variables:

$$y_t = \beta_{Const} + \beta_{x1}x1_t + \beta_{x2}x2_t + e_t$$

where

y_t = value of the dependent variable for observation t

$x1_t$ = value of the explanatory variable 1 for observation t

$x2_t$ = value of the explanatory variable 2 for observation t

Since the actual parameters of the model, the β's are unobservable, we estimate them:

$$Esty = b_{Const} + b_{x1}x1 + b_{x2}x2$$

The coefficient estimates attempt to separate out the individual effect that each explanatory variable has on the dependent variable. To explain what this means, focus on the estimate of the first explanatory variable's coefficient, b_{x1}. It estimates the change in the dependent variable resulting from a change in the explanatory variable 1 while all other explanatory variables remain constant. More formally,

$$\Delta y = b_{x1}\Delta x1 \quad \text{or} \quad b_{x1} = \frac{\Delta y}{\Delta x1}$$

where

$\Delta x1$ = change in explanatory variable 1

Δy = estimated change in dependent variable

while all other explanatory variables remain constant. A little algebra explains why. We begin with the equation estimating our model:

$$Esty = b_{Const} + b_{x1}x1 + b_{x2}x2$$

Now increase the explanatory variable 1 by $\Delta x1$ while keeping all other explanatory variables constant. Δy estimates the resulting change in the dependent variable.

	From		To
Price:	$x1$	$\rightarrow$	$x1 + \Delta x1$
Quantity:	$Esty$	$\rightarrow$	$Esty + \Delta y$

All other explanatory variables remain constant. In the equation estimating our model, substitute

$$\frac{Esty + \Delta y}{\text{for } Esty} \quad \text{and} \quad \frac{x1 + \Delta x1}{\text{for } x1}$$

$$Esty \quad = \quad b_{Const} \quad + \quad b_{x1}x1 \quad + \quad b_{x2}x2 \qquad \text{Substituting}$$
$$\downarrow \qquad\qquad\qquad \downarrow$$

$$Esty + \Delta y \quad = \quad b_{Const} \quad + \quad b_{x1}(x1 + \Delta x1) \quad + \quad b_{x2}x2 \quad \text{Multiplying through by } b_{x1}$$
$$\downarrow$$

$$Esty + \Delta y \quad = \quad b_{Const} \quad + \quad b_{x1}x1 + b_{x1}\Delta x1 \quad + \quad b_{x2}x2$$

Return to the original equation:

$$Esty = b_{Const} + b_{x1}x1 + b_{x2}x2$$

Subtract the equations:

$$\Delta y = 0 + b_{x1}\Delta x1 + 0$$

Simplify:

$$\Delta y = b_{x1}\Delta x1$$

Divide through by $\Delta x1$:

$$\frac{\Delta y}{\Delta x1} = b_{x1}$$

while all other explanatory variables remain constant.

Using the same logic, we can interpret the estimate of the second explanatory variable's coefficient, b_{x2}, analogously:

$$\Delta y = b_{x2}\Delta x2 \quad \text{or} \quad b_{x2} = \frac{\Delta y}{\Delta x2}$$

while all other explanatory variables remain constant. b_{x2} allows us to estimate the change in the dependent variable when explanatory variable 2 changes while all other explanatory variables remain constant.

What happens when both explanatory variables change simultaneously?

The total estimated change in the quantity demanded equals the sum of the individual changes:

Total estimated change in quantity demanded resulting from a change in

		Explanatory variable 1		Explanatory variable 2
		$\downarrow$		$\downarrow$
Δy	$=$	$b_{x1}\Delta x1$	$+$	$b_{x2}\Delta x2$

Each term estimates the change in the dependent variable resulting from a change in each individual explanatory variable. We will now apply the interpretation of the coefficient estimates to resolve the paradoxes.

We will resolve the paradoxes by applying the interpretation of the coefficient estimates:

- First, to the original simultaneous equations models.
- Second, to the reduced form (RF) equations.

22.6.2 Paradox: Demand Model Price Coefficient Depends on the Reduced Form (RF) Feed Price Coefficients

We will first explain why the price coefficient estimate of the demand model, b_P^D, is determined by the reduced form (RF) feed price coefficient estimates, a_{FP}^Q and a_{FP}^P.

Recall the demand model:

Memand model: $Q_t^D = \beta_{Const}^D + \beta_P^D P_t + \beta_I^D Inc_t + e_t^D$

The following equation estimates the quantity demanded:

$EstQ^D = b_{Const}^D + b_P^D P + b_I^D Inc$

Interpret the price coefficient estimate, b_P^D. The price coefficient estimate of the demand model estimates the change in the quantity of beef demanded when price of beef changes while income remains constant.

$$\Delta Q^D = b_P^D \Delta P$$

while income remains constant. Solving for b_P^D obtains

$$b_P^D = \frac{\Delta Q^D}{\Delta P}$$

while income remains constant. Since income remains constant, the demand curve does not shift; hence, b_P^D is just the estimated "slope" of the demand curve for beef (figure 22.9).

Next consider the reduced form (RF) equations that estimate the quantity and price:

$EstQ = 138{,}726 - 332.00 FeedP + 17.347 Inc$

$EstP = 33.027 + 1.0562 FeedP + 0.018825 Inc$

Suppose that the feed price decreases while income remains constant. As shown in figure 22.10, the decrease in feed prices shifts the supply curve for beef to the right.

Now interpret the feed price coefficients in the reduced form (RF) equations:

- The feed price coefficient of the quantity reduced form (RF) equation estimates the change in the beef quantity of beef when the feed price changes while income remains constant:

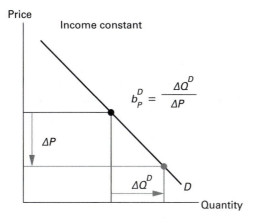

Figure 22.9
"Slope" of demand curve

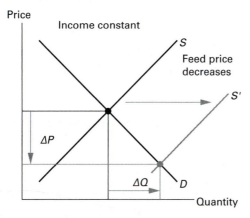

Figure 22.10
Feed price decreases and income remains constant

$$\Delta Q = -332.00 \Delta FeedP$$

while income remains constant.

• The feed price coefficient of the quantity reduced form (RF) equation estimates the change in the beef price when the feed price changes:

$$\Delta P = 1.0562 \Delta FeedP$$

while income remains constant. Divide ΔQ by ΔP. While income remains constant:

$$\frac{\Delta Q}{\Delta P} = \frac{-332.00\Delta FeedP}{1.0562\Delta FeedP} = \frac{-332.00}{1.0562} = -314.3$$

while income remains constant.

Next recognize that Q represents the quantity of beef demanded. The change in the feed price causes the supply curve to shift, but the demand curve remains stationary because income has remained constant. As figure 22.10 illustrates, we are moving from one point on the demand curve to another point on the same demand curve. This movement represents a change in the quantity of beef demanded, Q^D:

$$\frac{\Delta Q^D}{\Delta P} = -314.3$$

We now can appreciate why the "slope" of the demand curve for beef is estimated by the reduced form (RF) feed price coefficients. Changes in the feed price cause the supply curve for beef to shift. When the demand curve remains stationary, changes in the feed price move the equilibrium from one point on the demand curve to another point on the same demand curve. Consequently the feed price coefficients of the reduced form (RF) equations estimate how the quantity and price change as we move along the demand curve because they are based on the premise that income remains constant and therefore the demand curve remains stationary. The reduced form (RF) feed price coefficients provide us with the information we need to calculate the "slope" of the demand curve for beef.

22.6.3   Paradox: Supply Model Price Coefficient Depends on the Reduced Form (RF) Income Coefficients

We will use similar logic to explain why is the price coefficient estimate of the supply model, β_P^S, is determined by the reduced form (RF) income coefficient estimates, a_I^Q and a_I^P. Recall the supply model:

Supply model: $Q_t^S = \beta_{Const}^S + \beta_P^S P_t + \beta_{FP}^S FeedP_t + e_t^S$

The following equation estimates the quantity supplied:

Begin by focusing on the supply model estimated equation:

$EstQ^S = b_{Const}^S + b_P^S P + b_{FP}^S FeedP$

Interpret the price coefficient estimate, b_P^S. The price coefficient estimate of the supply model estimates the change in the quantity of beef supplied when price of beef changes while the feed price remains constant:

$\Delta Q^S = b_P^S \Delta P$

while feed price remains constant. Solving for b_P^S:

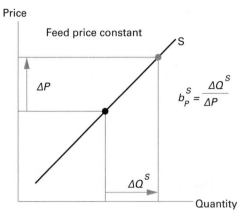

Figure 22.11
"Slope" of supply curve

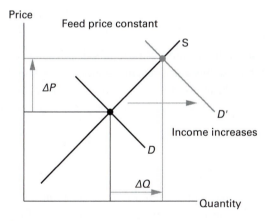

Figure 22.12
Income increases and feed price remains constant

$$b_P^S = \frac{\Delta Q^S}{\Delta P}$$

while feed price remains constant. Since the feed price is constant, the supply curve does not shift; hence, b_P^S is just the estimated "slope" of the supply curve for beef (figure 22.11).

Once again, consider the reduced form (RF) equations that estimate the quantity and price:

$$EstQ = 138{,}726 - 332.00FeedP + 17.347Inc$$

$$EstP = 33.027 + 1.0562FeedP + 0.018825Inc$$

Suppose that income increases and feed price remains constant. As shown in figure 22.12, the demand curve will shift to the right.

Now interpret the income coefficients in the reduced form (RF) equations:

• The income coefficient of the quantity reduced form (RF) equation estimates the change in beef quantity when income changes while feed prices remain constant:

$$\Delta Q = 17.347 \Delta Inc$$

while feed price remains constant.

• The income coefficient of the price reduced form (RF) equation estimates the change in the beef price changes income changes while feed prices remain constant:

$$\Delta P = 0.018825 \Delta Inc$$

while feed price remains constant. Dividing ΔQ by ΔP, we have

$$\frac{\Delta Q}{\Delta P} = \frac{17.347 \Delta Inc}{018825 \Delta Inc} = \frac{17.347}{018825} = 921.5$$

while feed price remains constant.

Next recognize that this Q represents the quantity of beef supplied. The change in income causes the demand curve to shift, but the supply curve remains stationary because the feed price has remained constant. As figure 22.12 illustrates, we move from one point on the supply curve to another point on the same supply curve. This movement represents a change in the quantity of beef supplied, Q^S:

$$\frac{\Delta Q^S}{\Delta P} = 921.5$$

We can appreciate why the "slope" of the supply curve for beef is determined by the reduced form (RF) income coefficients. Changes in income cause the demand curve for beef to shift. When the supply curve remains stationary, changes in income move the equilibrium from one point on the supply curve to another point on the same supply curve. Consequently the income coefficients of the reduced form (RF) equations estimate how the quantity and price change as we move along the supply curve because they are based on the premise that the feed price remains constant and therefore the supply curve remains stationary. The reduced form (RF) income coefficients provide us with the information we need to calculate the "slope" of the supply curve for beef.

22.7   The Coefficient Interpretation Approach: A Bonus

We now have developed some intuition regarding why the estimated "slope" of the demand curve depends on the feed price reduced form (RF) coefficient estimates and why the estimated "slope" of the supply curve depends on the income reduced form (RF) coefficient estimates. The coefficient interpretation approach provides intuition and also gives us a bonus. The coefficient interpretation approach provides us with a simple way to derive the relationships between the estimated "slopes" of the demand and supply curves and the reduced form (RF) estimates. Compare the algebra we just used to express the estimated "slopes" of the demand and supply curves with the algebra used in the appendix to this chapter.

Chapter 22 Review Questions

1. What is the distinction between endogenous and exogenous variables?

2. How do simultaneous equations models differ from single equation models?

3. In a simultaneous equations model, is the ordinary least squares (OLS) estimation procedure for the value of an endogenous explanatory variable's coefficient

    a. unbiased?

    b. consistent?

4. Consider a reduced form (RF) equation:

    a. What type of variable is the dependent variable, endogenous or exogenous?

    b. What type of variable are the explanatory variables, endogenous or exogenous?

5. In a simultaneous equations model, is the reduced form (RF) estimation procedure for the value of a coefficient for an endogenous explanatory variable

    a. unbiased?

    b. consistent?

6. What paradoxes arise when using the reduced form (RF) estimation procedure to estimate the price coefficients of the demand/supply simultaneous equations model? Resolve the paradoxes.

Chapter 22 Exercises

Beef market data: Monthly time series data relating to the market for beef from 1977 to 1986.

Q_t Quantity of beef in month t (millions of pounds)

P_t Real price of beef in month t (1982–84 cents per pound)

Inc_t Real disposable income in month t (billions of 2005 dollars)

$ChickP_t$ Real price of whole chickens in month t (1982–84 cents per pound)

$FeedP_t$ Real price of cattle feed in month t (1982–84 cents per pounds of corn cobs)

Consider the linear model of the beef market we used in class:

Demand model: $Q_t^D = \beta_{Const}^D + \beta_P^D P_t + \beta_I^D Inc_t + e_t^D$

Supply model: $Q_t^S = \beta_{Const}^S + \beta_P^S P_t + \beta_{FP}^S FeedP_t + e_t^S$

Equilibrium: $Q_t^D = Q_t^S = Q_t$

and the reduced form (RF) estimates:

$EstQ = 138{,}726 - 332.00FeedP + 17.347Inc$

$EstP = 33.027 + 1.0562FeedP + 0.018825Inc$

1. Focus on the linear demand model.

   a. In words, interpret the *Inc* coefficient estimate, b_I^D. Express this more mathematically by filling in the following blanks:

   $b_I^D =$ _____ while _____ remains constant

   b. Consider the price reduced form (RF) estimates: $EstP = 33.027 + 1.0562FeedP + 0.018825Inc$

   i. What equation estimates the change in the price, ΔP, when both income changes by ΔInc and the feed price changes by$\Delta FeedP$?

   ii. When the "while" condition cited in part a is satisfied, how must the change in income, ΔInc, and the change in feed prices, $\Delta FeedP$, be related? Solve the equation for $\Delta FeedP$?

   c. Consider the quantity reduced form (RF) estimates: $EstQ = 138{,}726 - 332.00FeedP + 17.347Inc$

   i. What equation estimates change in the quantity, ΔQ, when both income changes by ΔInc and the feed price changes by $\Delta FeedP$?

   ii. Substitute in your answer to part b(ii). Then recall your answer to part a to calculate the numerical value of b_I^D.

2. Focus on the original supply model.

   a. In words, interpret the *FeedP* coefficient estimate, b_{FP}^S. Express this more mathematically by filling in the following blanks:

   $b_{FP}^S =$ _____ while _____ remains constant

   b. Consider the price reduced form (RF) estimates: $EstP = 33.027 + 1.0562FeedP + .018825Inc$

   i. What equation estimates the change in the price, ΔP, when both income changes by ΔInc and the feed price changes by $\Delta FeedP$?

ii. When the "while" condition cited in part a is satisfied, how must the change in income, ΔInc, and the change in feed prices, $\Delta FeedP$, be related? Solve the equation for ΔInc.

c. Consider the quantity reduced form (RF) estimates: $EstQ = 138{,}726 - 332.00 FeedP + 17.347 Inc$

i. What equation estimates change in the quantity, ΔQ, when both income changes by ΔInc and the feed price changes by $\Delta FeedP$?

ii. Substitute in your answer to part b(ii). Then recall your answer to part a to calculate the numerical value of b_{FP}^S.

Now consider a different model describing the beef market: a constant elasticity model. The log version of this model is

Demand model: $\log(Q_t^D) = \beta_{Const}^D + \beta_P^D \log(P_t) + \beta_I^D \log(Inc_t) + e_t^D$

Supply model: $\log(Q_t^S) = \beta_{Const}^S + \beta_P^S \log(P_t) + \beta_{FP}^s \log(FeedP_t) + e_t^S$

Equilibrium: $\log(Q_t^D) = \log(Q_t^S) = \log(Q_t)$

3. What are the reduced form (RF) equations for this model?

4. Estimate the parameters for the reduced form (RF) equations.

[To access this online material, go to http://mitpress.mit.edu/westhoffeconometrics and select Market for Beef.]

a. Focus on the quantity reduced form (RF) regression. Use the regression results to estimate the change in the log of the quantity, $\Delta \log(Q)$, when the log of the feed price changes by $\Delta \log(FeedP)$ and the log of income changes by $\Delta \log(Inc)$:

$\Delta \log(Q) =$

b. Focus on the price reduced form (RF) regression. Use the regression results to estimate the change in the log of the price, $\Delta \log(P)$, when the log of the feed price changes by $\Delta \log(FeedP)$ and the log of income changes by $\Delta \log(Inc)$:

$\Delta \log(P) =$

5. Focus on the original demand and supply models:

a. Use the parameters of the reduced form (RF) equations to estimate the own price elasticity of demand. Interpret the estimate.

b. Use the parameters of the reduced form (RF) equations to estimate the own price elasticity of supply. Interpret the estimate.

Chicken market data: Monthly time series data relating to the market for chicken from 1980 to 1985.

Q_t Quantity of chicken in month t (millions of pounds)

P_t Real price of whole chickens in month t (cents per pound 1982–84 = 100)

$FeedP_t$ Real price chicken formula feed in month t (cents per pound)

Inc_t Real disposable income in month t (billions of 2005 dollars)

$PorkP_t$ Real price of pork in month t (cents per pound)

Consider the following linear model of the chicken market:

Demand model: $Q_t^D = \beta_{Const}^D + \beta_P^D P_t + \beta_I^D Inc_t + e_t^D$

Supply model: $Q_t^S = \beta_{Const}^S + \beta_P^S P_t + \beta_{FP}^s FeedP_t + e_t^S$

Equilibrium: $Q_t^D = Q_t^S = Q_t$

6. What are the reduced form (RF) equations for this model?

7. Estimate the parameters for the reduced form (RF) equations.

[To access this online material, go to http://mitpress.mit.edu/westhoffeconometrics and select Market for Chicken.]

a. Focus on the quantity reduced form (RF) regression. Use the regression results to estimate the change in the quantity, ΔQ, when the feed price changes by $\Delta FeedP$ and income changes by ΔInc:

$\Delta Q =$

b. Focus on the price reduced form (RF) regression. Use the regression results to estimate the change in the price, ΔP, when the feed price changes by $\Delta FeedP$ and income changes by ΔInc:

$\Delta P =$

8. Focus on the original demand model:

a. Use the parameters of the reduced form (RF) equations to estimate the price coefficient of demand, β_P^D.

b. Use the parameters of the reduced form (RF) equations to estimate the price coefficient of demand, β_P^S.

Crime and police data: Annual time series data of US crime and economic statistics from 1988 to 2007.

Crime_t   Violent crimes per 100,000 persons in year *t*

PoliceExp_t   Per capita police expenditures in year *t* (2005 dollars)

UnemRate_t   Unemployment rate in year *t* (percent)

GdpPC_t   Per capita GDP in year *t* (2005 dollars)

PovRate_t   Individuals below the poverty level in year *t* (percent)

Consider the following simultaneous equations model of crime and police expenditures

Crime model: $Crime_t = \beta^C_{Const} + \beta^C_P PoliceExp_t + \beta^C_U UnemRate_t + e^C_t$

Police expenditure model: $PoliceExp_t = \beta^P_{Const} + \beta^P_C Crime_t = \beta^P_G GdpPC_t + e^P_t$

9. Focus on the crime model:

a. What is your theory concerning how police expenditures should affect violent crime? What does you theory suggest about the sign of the police expenditure coefficient, β^C_P?

b. What is your theory concerning how the employment rate should affect violent crime? What does you theory suggest about the sign of the unemployment rate coefficient, β^C_P?

10. Focus on the police expenditure model:

a. What is your theory concerning how violent crime should affect police expenditures? What does you theory suggest about the sign of the violent crime coefficient, β^P_C?

b. What is your theory concerning how per capita GDP should affect police expenditures? What does you theory suggest about the sign of the per capita GDP coefficient, β^P_C?

11. What are the reduced form (RF) equations for this model?

12. Estimate the parameters for the reduced form (RF) equations.

[To access this online material, go to http://mitpress.mit.edu/westhoffeconometrics and select Crime in US.]

a. Focus on the crimes reduced form (RF) regression. Use the regression results to estimate the change in the crime rate, $\Delta Crimes$, when the unemployment rate changes by $\Delta UnemRate$ and per capita GDP changes by $\Delta GdpPC$:

b. Focus on the police expenditure reduced form (RF) regression. Use the regression results to estimate the change in police expenditures, $\Delta PoliceExp$, when the unemployment rate changes by $\Delta UnemRate$ and per capita GDP changes by $\Delta GdpPC$:

13. Focus on the original crime model:

a. In words, interpret the *PoliceExp* coefficient estimate, b^C_P. Express this more mathematically.

b. Use your answers to exercises 12a and 12b to calculate the value of b^C_P.

14. Focus on the original police expenditure model:

    a. In words, interpret the *Crimes* coefficient estimate, b_C^P. Express this more mathematically.

    b. Use your answers to exercises 12a and 12b to calculate the value of b_C^P.

Appendix 22.1: Algebraic Derivation of the Reduced Form Equations

Demand model: $Q_t^D = \beta_{Const}^D + \beta_P^D P_t + \beta_I^D Inc_t + e_t^D$

Supply model: $Q_t^S = \beta_{Const}^S + \beta_P^S P_t + \beta_{FP}^s FeedP_t + e_t^S$

Equilibrium: $Q_t^D = Q_t^S = Q_t$

Strategy to Derive the Reduced Form (RF) Equation for P$_t$

- Substitute Q_t for Q_t^D and Q_t^S.
- Subtract the supply model equation from the demand model equation.
- Solve for P_t.

$$Q_t^D = \beta_{Const}^D + \beta_P^D P_t + \qquad\qquad + \beta_I^D Inc_t \qquad + e_t^D$$

$$Q_t^S = \beta_{Const}^S + \beta_P^S P_t + \beta_{FP}^s FeedP_t + \qquad\qquad + e_t^S$$

Substitute

$$Q_t = \beta_{Const}^D + \beta_P^D P_t + \qquad\qquad + \beta_I^D Inc_t \qquad + e_t^D$$

$$Q_t = \beta_{Const}^S + \beta_P^S P_t + \beta_{FP}^s FeedP_t + \qquad\qquad + e_t^S$$

Subtract

$$0 = \beta_{Const}^D - \beta_{Const}^S + \beta_P^D P_t - \beta_P^S P_t - \beta_{FP}^s FeedP_t + \beta_I^D Inc_t \quad + e_t^D - e_t^S$$

Solve

$$\beta_P^S P_t - \beta_P^D P_t = \beta_{Const}^D - \beta_{Const}^S + \qquad\qquad - \beta_{FP}^s FeedP_t + \beta_I^D Inc_t \quad + \beta_t^D - e_t^S$$

$$(\beta_P^S - \beta_P^D)P_t = \beta_{Const}^D - \beta_{Const}^S + \qquad\qquad - \beta_{FP}^s FeedP_t + \beta_I^D Inc_t \quad + \beta_t^D - e_t^S$$

$$P_t = \frac{\beta_{Const}^D - \beta_{Const}^S}{\beta_P^S - \beta_P^D} + \qquad - \frac{\beta_{FP}^s FeedP_t}{\beta_P^S - \beta_P^D} + \frac{\beta_I^D Inc_t}{\beta_P^S - \beta_P^D} + \frac{e_t^D - e_t^S}{\beta_P^S - \beta_P^D}$$

Strategy to Derive the Reduced Form (RF) Equation for Q$_t$

- Substitute Q_t for Q_t^D and Q_t^S.
- Multiply the demand model equation by β_P^S and the supply model equation by β_P^D.

- Subtract the new equation for the supply model from the new equation for the demand model.
- Solve for Q_t.

$$Q_t^D = \beta_{Const}^D \qquad + \beta_P^D P_t \qquad + \qquad + \beta_I^D Inc_t \quad + e_t^D$$

$$Q_t^S = \beta_{Const}^S \qquad + \beta_P^S P_t \qquad + \beta_{FP}^s FeedP_t \quad + \qquad + e_t^s$$

Substitute

$$Q_t = \beta_{Const}^D \qquad + \beta_P^D P_t \qquad + \qquad + \beta_I^D Inc_t \quad + e_t^D$$

$$Q_t = \beta_{Const}^S \qquad + \beta_P^S P_t \qquad + \beta_{FP}^s FeedP_t \quad + \qquad + e_t^s$$

Multiply

$$\beta_P^S Q_t = \beta_P^S \beta_{Const}^D \qquad + \beta_P^S \beta_P^D P_t \qquad + \qquad + \beta_P^S \beta_I^D Inc_t + \beta_P^S e_t^D$$

$$\beta_P^D Q_t = \beta_P^D \beta_{Const}^S \qquad + \beta_P^D \beta_P^S P_t \qquad + \beta_P^D \beta_{FP}^S FeedP_t \quad + \qquad + \beta_P^D e_t^S$$

Subtract

$$\beta_P^S Q_t - \beta_P^D Q_t = \beta_P^S \beta_{Const}^D - \beta_P^D \beta_{Const}^S \quad + \beta_P^S \beta_P^D P_t - \beta_P^D \beta_P^S P_t - \beta_P^D \beta_{FP}^S FeedP_t \quad + \beta_P^S \beta_I^D Inc_t + \beta_P^S e_t^D - \beta_P^D e_t^S$$

Solve

$$(\beta_P^S - \beta_P^D) Q_t = \beta_P^S \beta_{Const}^D - \beta_P^D \beta_{Const}^S \quad + \qquad - \beta_P^D \beta_{FP}^S FeedP_t \quad + \beta_P^S \beta_I^D Inc_t + \beta_P^S e_t^D - \beta_P^D e_t^S$$

$$Q_t = \frac{\beta_P^S \beta_{Const}^D - \beta_P^D \beta_{Const}^S}{\beta_P^S - \beta_P^D} + \qquad - \frac{\beta_P^D \beta_{FP}^S FeedP_t}{\beta_P^S - \beta_P^D} + \beta_P^S \beta_I^D Inc_t + \frac{\beta_P^S e_t^D - \beta_P^D e_t^S}{\beta_P^S - \beta_P^D}$$

23 Simultaneous Equations Models—Identification

Chapter 23 Prep Questions

Beef market data: Monthly time series data relating to the market for beef from 1977 to 1986.

Q_t Quantity of beef in month t (millions of pounds)

P_t Real price of beef in month t (1982–84 cents per pound)

Inc_t Real disposable income in month t (thousands of chained 2005 dollars)

$ChickP_t$ Real price of whole chickens in month t (1982–84 cents per pound)

$FeedP_t$ Real price of cattle feed in month t (1982–84 cents per pounds of corn cobs)

Consider the model for the beef market that we used in the last chapter:

Demand model: $Q_t^D = \beta_{Const}^D + \beta_P^D P_t + \beta_I^D Inc_t + e_t^D$

Supply model: $Q_t^S = \beta_{Const}^S + \beta_P^S P_t + \beta_{FP}^S FeedP_t + e_t^s$

Equilibrium: $Q_t^D = Q_t^S = Q_t$

Endogenous variables: Q_t and P_t

Exogenous variables: $FeedP_t$ and Inc_t

1. We will now introduce another estimation procedure for simultaneous equations models, the two-stage least squares (TSLS) estimation procedure:

First stage: Use the exogenous explanatory variable(s) to estimate the endogenous explanatory variable(s).

• **Dependent variable:**   The endogenous explanatory variable(s), the "problem" explanatory variable(s).

• **Explanatory variable(s):**   All exogenous variables.

Second stage: In the original model, replace the endogenous explanatory variable with its estimate.

• **Dependent variable:**   Original dependent variable.

• **Explanatory variable(s):**   First-stage estimate of the endogenous explanatory variable and the relevant exogenous explanatory variables.

Naturally, begin by focusing on the first stage.

First stage: Use the exogenous explanatory variable(s) to estimate the endogenous explanatory variable(s).

• **Dependent variable:**   The endogenous explanatory variable(s), the "problem" explanatory variable(s). In this case the price of beef, P_t, is the endogenous explanatory variable.

- **Explanatory variable(s):** All exogenous variables. In this case the exogenous variables are *FeedP$_t$* and *Inc$_t$*.

Using the ordinary least squares (OLS) estimation procedure, what equation estimates the "problem" explanatory variable, the price of beef?

[To access this online material, go to http://mitpress.mit.edu/westhoffeconometrics and select Market for Beef.]

EstP = _____

Generate a new variable, *EstP*, that estimates the price of beef based on the first stage.

2. Next consider the demand model:

Demand model: $Q_t^D = \beta_{Const}^D + \beta_P^D P_t + \beta_I^D Inc_t + e_t^D$

and the second stage of the two-stage least squares (TSLS) estimation procedure:

Second stage: In the original model, replace the endogenous explanatory variable with its estimate.

- **Dependent variable:** Original dependent variable. In this case the original explanatory variable is the quantity of beef, Q_t.
- **Explanatory variable(s):** First-stage estimate of the endogenous explanatory variable and the relevant exogenous explanatory variables. In this case the estimate of the price of beef and income, *EstP$_t$* and *Inc$_t$*.

[To access this online material, go to http://mitpress.mit.edu/westhoffeconometrics and select Market for Beef.]

  a. Using the ordinary least squares (OLS) estimation procedure, estimate the *EstP* coefficient of the demand model.

  b. Compare the two-stage least squares (TSLS) coefficient estimate for the demand model with the estimate computed using the reduced form (RF) estimation procedure in chapter 22.

3. Now consider the supply model:

Supply model: $Q_t^S = \beta_{Const}^S + \beta_P^S P_t + \beta_{FP}^S FeedP_t + e_t^S$

and the second stage of the two-stage least squares (TSLS) estimation procedure:

Second stage: In the original model, replace the endogenous explanatory variable with its estimate.

- **Dependent variable:** Original dependent variable. In this case the original explanatory variable is the quantity of beef, Q_t.

• **Explanatory variable(s):** First-stage estimate of the endogenous explanatory variable and the relevant exogenous explanatory variables. In this case the estimate of the price of beef and income, $EstP_t$ and $PFeed_t$.

[To access this online material, go to http://mitpress.mit.edu/westhoffeconometrics and select Market for Beef.]

   a. Using the ordinary least squares (OLS) estimation procedure, estimate the $EstP$ coefficient of the supply model.

   b. Compare the two-stage least squares (TSLS) coefficient estimate for the supply model with the estimate computed using the reduced form (RF) estimation procedure in chapter 22.

4. Reconsider the following simultaneous equations model of the beef market and the reduced form (RF) estimates:

Demand and Supply Models

Demand model: $Q_t^D = \beta_{Const}^D + \beta_P^D P_t + \beta_I^D Inc_t + e_t^D$

Supply model: $Q_t^S = \beta_{Const}^S + \beta_P^S P_t + \beta_{FP}^S FeedP_t + e_t^S$

Equilibrium: $Q_t^D = Q_t^S = Q_t$

Endogenous variables: Q_t and P_t

Exogenous variables: $FeedP_t$ and Inc_t

Reduced Form (RF) Estimates

Quantity reduced form (RF) estimates: $EstQ = a_{Const}^Q + a_{FP}^Q FeedP + a_I^Q Inc$

Price reduced form (RF) estimates: $EstP = a_{Const}^P + a_{FP}^P FeedP + a_I^P Inc$

   a. Focus on the reduced form (RF) estimates for the income coefficients:

   i. The reduced form (RF) income coefficient estimates, a_I^Q and a_I^P, allowed us to estimate the "slope" of which curve?

   ____ Demand   ___Supply

   ii. If the reduced form (RF) income coefficient estimates were not available, would we be able to estimate the "slope" of this curve?

   b. Focus on the reduced form (RF) estimates for the feed price coefficients:

   i. The reduced form (RF) feed price coefficient estimates of these coefficients, a_{FP}^Q and a_{FP}^P, allowed us to estimate the "slope" of which curve?

___ Demand   ___Supply

ii. If the reduced form (RF) feed price coefficient estimates were not available, would we be able to estimate the "slope" of this curve?

23.1   Review

23.1.1   Demand and Supply Models

For the economist, arguably the most important example of a simultaneous equations model is the demand/supply model:

Demand model: $Q_t^D = \beta_{Const}^D + \beta_P^D P_t + \beta_I^D Inc_t + e_t^D$

Supply model: $Q_t^S = \beta_{Const}^S + \beta_P^S P_t + \beta_{FP}^S FeedP_t + e_t^S$

Equilibrium: $Q_t^D = Q_t^S = Q_t$

Endogenous variables: Q_t and P_t

Exogenous variables: $FeedP_t$ and Inc_t

Project: Estimate the beef market demand and supply parameters.

It is important to emphasize the distinction between endogenous and exogenous variables in a simultaneous equations model. Endogenous variables are variables whose values are determined "within" the model. In the demand/supply example, both quantity and price are determined simultaneously "within" the model; the model is explaining both the equilibrium quantity and the equilibrium price as depicted by the intersection of the supply and demand curves. Conversely, exogenous are determined "outside" the context of the model; the values of exogenous variables are taken as given. The model does not attempt to explain how the values of exogenous variables are determined.

• **Endogenous variables:**   Variables determined "within" the model: Quantity and Price.
• **Exogenous variables:**   Variables determined "outside" the model.

Unlike single regression models, an endogenous variable can be an explanatory variable in simultaneous equations models. In the demand and supply models the price is such a variable. Both the quantity demanded and the quantity supplied depend on the price; hence the price is an explanatory variable.

Furthermore the price is determined "within" the model; the price is an endogenous variable. The price is determined by the intersection of the supply and demand curves. The traditional demand/supply graph clearly illustrates that both the quantity, Q_t, and the price, P_t, are endogenous, both are determined "within" the model (figure 23.1).

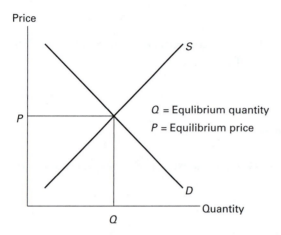

Figure 23.1
Demand/supply model

23.1.2   Ordinary Least Squares (OLS) Estimation Procedure

In the last chapter we learned why simultaneous equations cause a problem for the ordinary least squares (OLS) estimation procedure:

Simultaneous equations and bias: Whenever an explanatory variable is also an endogenous variable, the ordinary least squares (OLS) estimation procedure for the value of the explanatory variable's coefficient is biased.

   In the demand/supply model, the price is an endogenous explanatory variable. When we used the ordinary least squares (OLS) estimation procedure to estimate the value of the price coefficient in the demand and supply models, we observed that a problem emerged. In each model, price and the error term were correlated resulting in bias; the price is the "problem" explanatory variable (figure 23.2).

   So where did we go from here? We explored the possibility that the ordinary least squares (OLS) estimation procedure might be consistent. After all, is not "half a loaf" better than none? We took advantage of our Econometrics Lab to address this issue. Recall the distinction between an unbiased and a consistent estimation procedure:

Unbiased: The estimation procedure does not systematically underestimate or overestimate the actual value; that is, after many, many repetitions the average of the estimates equals the actual value.

Consistent but biased: As consistent estimation procedure can be biased. But as the sample size, as the number of observations, grows:

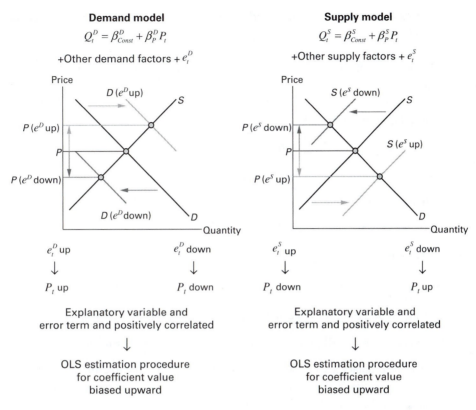

Figure 23.2
Correlation of price and error terms

- The magnitude of the bias decreases. That is, the mean of the coefficient estimate's probability distribution approaches the actual value.

- The variance of the estimate's probability distribution diminishes and approaches 0.

Unfortunately, the Econometrics Lab illustrates the sad fact that the ordinary least squares (OLS) estimation procedure is neither unbiased nor consistent.

We then considered an alternative estimation procedure: the reduced form (RF) estimation procedure. Our Econometrics Lab taught us that while the reduced form (RF) estimation procedure is biased, it is consistent. That is, as the sample size grows, the average of the coefficient estimates gets "closer and closer" to the actual value and the variance grew smaller and smaller. Arguably, when choosing between two biased estimates, it is better to use the one that is consistent. This represents the econometrician's pragmatic, "half a loaf is better than none" philosophy. We will now quickly review the reduced form (RF) estimation procedure.

Reduced Form (RF) Estimation Procedure—One Way to Cope with Simultaneous Equations Models

We begin with the simultaneous equations model and then constructed the reduced form (RF) equations:

Demand and Supply Models

Demand model: $Q_t^D = \beta_{Const}^D + \beta_P^D P_t + \beta_I^D Inc_t + e_t^D$

Supply model: $Q_t^S = \beta_{Const}^S + \beta_P^S P_t + \beta_{FP}^S FeedP_t + e_t^S$

Equilibrium: $Q_t^D = Q_t^S = Q_t$

Endogenous variables: Q_t and P_t

Exogenous variables: $FeedP_t$ and Inc_t

Reduced Form (RF) Estimates

Quantity reduced form (RF) estimates: $EstQ = a_{Const}^Q + a_{FP}^Q FeedP + a_I^Q Inc$

Price reduced form (RF) estimates: $EstP = a_{Const}^P + a_{FP}^P FeedP + a_I^P Inc$

We use the ordinary least squares (OLS) estimation procedure to estimate the reduced form (RF) parameters (tables 23.1 and 23.2) and then use the ratio of the reduced form (RF) estimates to estimate the "slopes" of the demand and supply curves.

[To access this online material, go to http://mitpress.mit.edu/westhoffeconometrics and select Market for Beef.]

Table 23.1
OLS regression results—Quantity reduced form (RF) equation

Ordinary least squares (OLS)				
Dependent variable: Q				
Explanatory variable(s):	Estimate	SE	t-Statistic	Prob
FeedP	−331.9966	121.6865	−2.728293	0.0073
Inc	17.34683	2.132027	8.136309	0.0000
Const	138,725.5	13,186.01	10.52066	0.0000
Number of observations	120			

Estimated equation: $EstQ = 138{,}726 - 332.00 FeedP + 17.347 Inc$
$a_{FP}^Q = -332.00, \quad a_I^Q = 17.347$

Table 23.2
OLS regression results—Price reduced form (RF) equation

Ordinary least squares (OLS)				
Dependent variable: P				
Explanatory variable(s):	Estimate	SE	t-Statistic	Prob
$FeedP$	1.056242	0.286474	3.687044	0.0003
Inc	0.018825	0.005019	3.750636	0.0003
$Const$	33.02715	31.04243	1.063936	0.2895
Number of observations	120			

Estimated equation: $EstP = 33.037 - 1.0562FeedP + 0.018825Inc$

$a_{FP}^P = 1.0562, \quad a_I^P = 0.018825$

Estimated "slope"
of the demand curve

$\downarrow$

Ratio of reduced form (RF)
feed price
coefficient estimates

$\downarrow$

Estimate of $\beta_P^D = b_P^D = \dfrac{a_{FP}^Q}{a_{FP}^P}$

$= \dfrac{-332.00}{1.0562} = -314.3$

Estimated "slope"
of the supply curve

$\downarrow$

Ratio of reduced form (RF)
income
coefficient estimates

$\downarrow$

Estimate of $\beta_P^S = b_P^S = \dfrac{a_I^Q}{a_I^P}$

$= \dfrac{17.347}{0.018825} = 921.5$

23.2 Two-Stage Least Squares (TSLS): An Instrumental Variable (IV) Two-Step Approach—A Second Way to Cope with Simultaneous Equations Models

Another way to estimate simultaneous equations model is the **two-stage least squares (TSLS) estimation procedure**. As the name suggests, the procedure involves two steps. As we will see, two-stage least squares (TSLS) uses a strategy that is similar to the instrumental variable (IV) approach.

First stage: Use the exogenous explanatory variable(s) to estimate the endogenous explanatory variable(s).

• **Dependent variable:** The endogenous explanatory variable(s), the "problem" explanatory variable(s).

- **Explanatory variable(s):**   All exogenous variables.

Second stage: In the original model, replace the endogenous explanatory variable with its estimate.

- **Dependent variable:**   Original dependent variable.

- **Explanatory variables:**   First-stage estimate of the endogenous explanatory variable and the relevant exogenous explanatory variables.

We will now illustrate the two-stage least squares (TSLS) approach by considering the beef market.

Beef market data: Monthly time series data relating to the market for beef from 1977 to 1986.

Q_t Quantity of beef in month t (millions of pounds)

P_t Real price of beef in month t (1982–84 cents per pound)

Inc_t Real disposable income in month t (thousands of chained 2005 dollars)

$ChickP_t$ Real price of whole chickens in month t (1982–84 cents per pound)

$FeedP_t$ Real price of cattle feed in month t (1982–84 cents per pounds of corn cobs)

Consider the model for the beef market that we used in the last chapter:

Demand model: $Q_t^D = \beta_{Const}^D + \beta_P^D P_t + \beta_I^D Inc_t + e_t^D$

Supply model: $Q_t^S = \beta_{Const}^S + \beta_P^S P_t + \beta_{FP}^S FeedP_t + e_t^S$

Equilibrium: $Q_t^D = Q_t^S = Q_t$

Endogenous variables: Q_t and P_t

Exogenous variables: $FeedP_t$ and Inc_t

The strategy for the first stage is similar to the strategy used by instrumental variable (IV) approach. The endogenous explanatory variable is the source of the bias; consequently the endogenous explanatory variable is the "problem" explanatory variable. In the first stage the endogenous explanatory variable is the dependent variable. The explanatory variables are all the exogenous variables. In our example, price is the endogenous explanatory variable; consequently price becomes the dependent variable in the first stage. The exogenous variables, income and feed price, are the explanatory variables.

23.2.1   First Stage: Exogenous Explanatory Variable(s) Used to Estimate the Endogenous Explanatory Variable(s)

- **Dependent variable:**   The endogenous explanatory variable(s), the "problem" explanatory variable(s). In this case the price of beef, P_t, is the endogenous explanatory variable.

Table 23.3
OLS regression results—TSLS first-stage equation

Ordinary least squares (OLS)				
Dependent variable: P				
Explanatory variable(s):	Estimate	SE	t-Statistic	Prob
FeedP	1.056242	0.286474	3.687044	0.0003
Inc	0.018825	0.005019	3.750636	0.0003
Const	33.02715	31.04243	1.063936	0.2895
Number of observations	120			
Estimated equation: $EstP = 33.027 + 1.0562 FeedP + 0.018825 Inc$				

- **Explanatory variable(s):** All exogenous variables. In this case the exogenous variables are $FeedP_t$ and Inc_t.

[To access this online material, go to http://mitpress.mit.edu/westhoffeconometrics and select Market for Beef.]

Using these regression results we estimate the price of beef based on the exogenous variables, income and feed price (table 23.3).

The strategy for the second stage is also similar to the instrumental variable (IV) approach. We return to the original model and replace the endogenous explanatory variable with its estimate from stage 1. The dependent variable is the original dependent variable, quantity. The explanatory variables are stage 1's estimate of the price and the relevant exogenous variables. In our example we have two models, one for demand and one for supply; accordingly we first apply the second stage to demand and then to supply.

23.2.2 Second Stage: In the Original Model, the Endogenous Explanatory Variable Replaced with Its Estimate

Demand Model

- **Dependent variable:** Original dependent variable. In this case the original explanatory variable is the quantity of beef, Q_t.

- **Explanatory variables:** First-stage estimate of the endogenous explanatory variable and the relevant exogenous explanatory variables. In this case the estimate of the price of beef and income, $EstP_t$ and Inc_t.

We estimate the "slope" of the demand curve to be −314.3 (table 23.4).

Table 23.4
OLS regression results—TSLS second-stage demand equation

Ordinary least squares (OLS)				
Dependent variable: Q				
Explanatory variable(s):	Estimate	SE	t-Statistic	Prob
EstP	−314.3312	115.2117	−2.728293	0.0073
Inc	23.26411	2.161914	10.76089	0.0000
Const	149,106.9	16,280.07	9.158860	0.0000
Number of observations	120			
Estimated equation: $EstQ^D = 149{,}107 - 314.3EstP + 23.26Inc$				
$b_P^D = -314.3, \quad b_P^I = 23.26$				

Table 23.5
OLS regression results—TSLS second-stage supply equation

Ordinary least squares (OLS)				
Dependent variable: Q				
Explanatory variable(s):	Estimate	SE	t-Statistic	Prob
EstP	921.4783	113.2551	8.136309	0.0000
FeedP	−1305.262	121.2969	−10.76089	0.0000
Const	108,291.8	16,739.33	6.469303	0.0000
Number of observations	120			
Estimated equation: $EstQ^S = 108{,}292 + 921.5EstP - 1{,}305.3\ FeedP$				
$b_P^S = 921.5, \quad b_{FP}^S = -1{,}305.3$				

Supply Model

• **Dependent variable:**   Original dependent variable. In this case the original explanatory variable is the quantity of beef, Q_t.

• **Explanatory variables:**   First-stage estimate of the "problem" explanatory endogenous variable and any relevant exogenous explanatory variable. In this case the estimated of the price of beef and income, $EstP_t$, and $PFeed_t$.

We estimate the "slope" of the demand curve to be 921.5 (table 23.5).

23.3   Comparison of Reduced Form (RF) and Two-Stage Least Squares (TSLS) Estimates

Compare the estimates from the reduced form (RF) approach with the estimates from the two-stage least squares (TSLS) approach (table 23.6). The estimates are identical. In this case the

Table 23.6
Comparison of reduced form (RF) and two-stage least squares (TSLS) price coefficient estimates

	Price coefficient estimates: Estimated "slope" of	
	Demand curve (b_P^D)	Supply curve (b_P^S)
Reduced form (RF)	−314.3	921.5
Two-stage least squares (TSLS)	−314.3	921.5

Table 23.7
TSLS regression results—Demand model

Two-stage least squares (TSLS)				
Dependent variable: Q				
Instrument(s): *FeedP* and *Inc*				
Explanatory variable(s):	Estimate	SE	*t*-Statistic	Prob
P	−314.3188	58.49828	−5.373129	0.0000
Inc	23.26395	1.097731	21.19276	0.0000
Const	149,106.5	8,266.413	18.03763	0.0000
Number of observations	120			

Estimated equation: $EstQ^D = 149{,}107 − 314.3EstP + 23.26Inc$

$b_P^D = −314.3, \quad b_I^D = 23.26$

reduced form (RF) estimation procedure and the two-stage least squares (TSLS) estimation procedure produce identical results.

23.4   Software and Two-Stage Least Squares (TSLS)

Many statistical packages provide an easy way to apply the two-stage least squares (TSLS) estimation procedure so that we do not need to generate the estimate of the endogenous explanatory variable ourselves (tables 23.7 and 23.8).

Table 23.8
TSLS regression results—Supply model

Two-stage least squares (TSLS)				
Dependent variable: Q				
Instrument(s): *FeedP* and *Inc*				
Explanatory variable(s):	Estimate	SE	*t*-Statistic	Prob
P	921.4678	348.8314	2.641585	0.0094
FeedP	−1,305.289	373.6098	−3.493723	0.0007
Const	108,292.0	51,558.51	2.100372	0.0378
Number of observations	120			

Estimated equation: $EstQ^S = 108{,}292 + 921.5 EstP - 1{,}305.3\ FeedP$
$b_P^S = 921.5, \quad b_{FP}^S = -1{,}305.3$

Getting Started in EViews

EViews makes it very easy for us to use the two-stage least squares (TSLS) approach. EViews does most of the work for us eliminating the need to generate a new variable:

- In the Workfile window, highlight all relevant variables: **q p feedp income**.

- Double click on one of the highlighted variables and click Open Equation.

- In the Equation Estimation window, click the Method drop down list and then select TSLS—Two-Stage Least Squares (TSNLS and ARIMA).

- In the Instrument List box, enter the exogenous variables: **feedp income**.

- In the Equation Specification box, enter the dependent variable followed by the explanatory variables (both exogenous and endogenous) for each model:

  · To estimate the demand model, enter **q p income**.

  · To estimate the supply model, enter **q p feedp**.

[To access this online material, go to http://mitpress.mit.edu/westhoffeconometrics and select Market for Beef.]

Note that these are the same estimates that we obtained when we generated the estimates of the price on our own.

23.5 Identification of Simultaneous Equations Models: The Order Condition

23.5.1 Taking Stock

Let us step back for a moment to review our beef market model.

Demand and Supply Models

Demand model: $Q_t^D = \beta_{Const}^D + \beta_P^D P_t + \beta_I^D Inc_t + e_t^D$

Supply model: $Q_t^S = \beta_{Const}^S + \beta_P^S P_t + \beta_{FP}^S FeedP_t + e_t^S$

Equilibrium: $Q_t^D = Q_t^S = Q_t$

Endogenous variables: Q_t and P_t

Exogenous variables: $FeedP_t$ and Inc_t

Reduced Form (RF) Estimates

Quantity reduced form (RF) estimates: $EstQ = a_{Const}^Q + a_{FP}^Q FeedP + a_I^Q Inc$

Price reduced form (RF) estimates: $EstP = a_{Const}^P + a_{FP}^P FeedP + a_I^P Inc$

We can use the coefficient interpretation approach to estimate the "slopes" of the demand and supply in terms of the reduced form (RF) estimates (figure 23.3).[1]

Intuition: Critical Role of the Exogenous Variable Absent from the Model

In each model there is one exogenous variable absent and one endogenous explanatory variable. This one to one correspondence allows us to estimate the coefficient of the endogenous explanatory variable, price.

- Demand model: $Q_t^D = \beta_{Const}^D + \beta_P^D P_t + \beta_I^D Inc_t + e_t^D$

  Changes in the feed price, the exogenous variable absent from the demand model, allow us to estimate the "slope" of the demand curve. The intuition is that the supply curve shifts while the demand curve remains stationary. Consequently the equilbria "trace out" the stationary demand curve.

- Supply model: $Q_t^S = \beta_{Const}^S + \beta_P^S P_t + \beta_{FP}^S FeedP_t + e_t^S$

  Changes in income, the exogenous variable absent from the demand model, allow us to estimate the "slope" of the supply curve. The intuition is that the demand curve shifts while the supply curve remains stationary. Consequently the equilibria "trace out" the stationary supply curve.

Key point: In each case, changes in the exogenous variable absent in the model allow us to estimate the value of the price coefficient, the model's endogenous explanatory variable.

---

1. Again, recall that the coefficients do not equal the slope of the demand curve, but rather the reciprocal of the slope. They are the ratio of run over rise instead of rise over run. This occurs as a consequence of the economist's convention of placing quantity on the horizontal axis and price on the vertical axis. To avoid the awkwardness of using the expression "the reciprocal of the slope" repeatedly, we will place the word slope within double quotes to indicate that it is the reciprocal.

Suppose that *FeedP* increases while *Inc* remains constant:

$$\Delta Q = a_{FP}^Q \Delta FeedP$$

$$\Delta P = a_{FP}^P \Delta FeedP$$

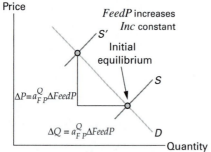

Changes in the feed price shift the supply curve, but not the demand curve

↓

We are moving from one equilibrium to another on the same demand curve. This movement represents a change in

the quantity of beef demanded, Q^D

↓

Estimated "slope" of demand curve:

$$b_P^D = \frac{\Delta Q}{\Delta P} = \frac{a_{FP}^Q \Delta FeedP}{a_{FP}^P \Delta FeedP} = \frac{a_{FP}^Q}{a_{FP}^P}$$

↓

The exogenous variable absent in the demand model, *FeedP*, allows us to estimate the "slope" of the demand curve

Suppose that *Inc* increases while *FeedP* remains constant:

$$\Delta Q = a_I^Q \Delta Inc$$

$$\Delta P = a_I^P \Delta Inc$$

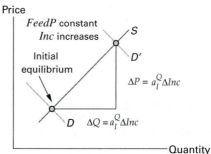

Changes in the income shift the demand curve, but not the supply curve

↓

We are moving from one equilibrium to another on the same supply curve. This movement represents a change in

the quantity of beef supplied, Q^S

↓

Estimated "slope" of supply curve:

$$b_P^S = \frac{\Delta Q}{\Delta P} = \frac{a_I^Q \Delta Inc}{a_I^P \Delta Inc} = \frac{a_I^Q}{a_I^P}$$

↓

The exogenous variable absent in the supply model, *Inc*, allows us to estimate the "slope" of the supply curve

Figure 23.3
Reduced form (RF) and coefficient interpretation approach—Identified

Order Condition

The order condition formalizes this relationship:

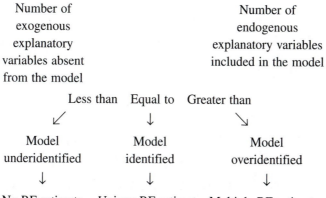

Number of exogenous explanatory variables absent from the model		Number of endogenous explanatory variables included in the model
Less than	Equal to	Greater than
↙	↓	↘
Model underidentified	Model identified	Model overidentified
↓	↓	↓
No RF estimate	Unique RF estimate	Multiple RF estimates

The reduced form estimation procedure for our beef market example is identified. For both the demand model and the supply model, the number of exogenous variable absent from the model equaled the number of endogenous explanatory variables in the model:

Exogenous variables: *FeedP* and *Inc*.
A total of two exogenous explanatory variables.

Demand model				**Supply model**			
Exogenous explanatory		Endogenous explanatory		Exogenous explanatory		Endogenous explanatory	
variables included	variables **absent**	variables **included**		variables included	variables **absent**	variables **included**	
1	2 − 1 = 1	1		1	2 − 1 = 1	1	
1	**equal to**	**1**		**1**	**less than**	**1**	
	↓				↓		
	Unique RF estimate				Unique RF estimate		

23.5.2   Underidentification

We will now illustrate the **underidentification** problem. Suppose that no income information was available. Obviously, if we have no income information, we cannot include *Inc* as an explanatory variable in our models:

Demand and Supply Models

Demand model: $Q_t^D = \beta_{Const}^D + \beta_P^D P_t + \beta_I^D Inc_t + e_t^D$

Supply model: $Q_t^S = \beta_{Const}^S + \beta_P^S P_t + \beta_{FP}^S FeedP_t + e_t^S$

Equilibrium: $Q_t^D = Q_t^S = Q_t$

Endogenous variables: Q_t and P_t

Exogenous variables: $FeedP_t$ and ~~Inc_t~~

Reduced Form (RF) Estimates

Quantity reduced form (RF) estimates: $EstQ = a_{Const}^Q + a_{FP}^Q FeedP + a_I^Q Inc$

Price reduced form (RF) estimates: $EstP = a_{Const}^P + a_{FP}^P FeedP + a_I^P Inc$

Let us now apply the order condition by comparing the number of absent exogenous variables and endogenous explanatory variables in each model:

Exogenous variable: *Feed*.
A total of one exogenous explanatory variable.

Demand model				Supply model		
Exogenous explanatory		Endogenous explanatory		Exogenous explanatory		Endogenous explanatory
variables included	variables **absent**	variables **included**		variables included	variables **absent**	variables **included**
1	$1 - 0 = 1$	1		1	$1 - 1 = 0$	1
	1 equal to	**1**			**0** less than	**1**
	↓				↓	
	Unique RF estimate				No RF estimate	

The order condition suggests that we should

• be able to estimate the coefficient of the endogenous explanatory variable, P, in the demand model and

• not be able to estimate the coefficient of the endogenous explanatory variable, P, in the supply model.

The coefficient interpretation approach explains why. We can still estimate the "slope" of the demand curve by calculating the ratio of the reduced form (RF) feed price coefficient estimates, a_{FP}^Q and a_{FP}^P, but we cannot estimate the "slope" of the supply curve since we cannot estimate the

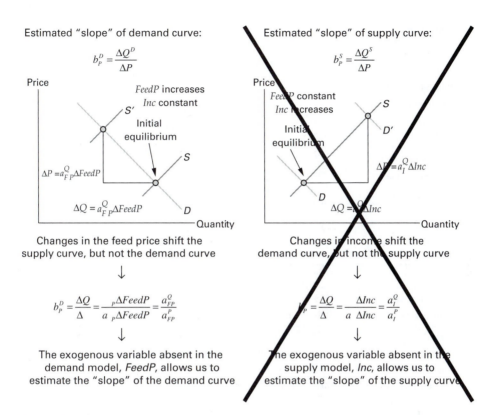

Estimated "slope" of demand curve:

$$b_P^D = \frac{\Delta Q^D}{\Delta P}$$

Estimated "slope" of supply curve:

$$b_P^S = \frac{\Delta Q^S}{\Delta P}$$

Changes in the feed price shift the supply curve, but not the demand curve

↓

$$b_P^D = \frac{\Delta Q}{\Delta} = \frac{{}_P \Delta FeedP}{a {}_P \Delta FeedP} = \frac{a_{FP}^Q}{a_{FP}^P}$$

↓

The exogenous variable absent in the demand model, *FeedP*, allows us to estimate the "slope" of the demand curve

Changes in income shift the demand curve, but not the supply curve

↓

$$b_P = \frac{\Delta Q}{\Delta} = \frac{\Delta Inc}{a \ \Delta Inc} = \frac{a_I^Q}{a_I^P}$$

↓

The exogenous variable absent in the supply model, *Inc*, allows us to estimate the "slope" of the supply curve

Figure 23.4
Reduced form (RF) and coefficient interpretation approach—Underidentified

reduced for (RF) income coefficients. We will use the coefficient estimate approach to explain this phenomenon to take advantage of the intuition it provides (figure 23.4).

There is both good news and bad news when we have feed price information but no income information:

Good news: On the one hand, since we still have feed price information, we have information about supply curve shifts. The shifts in the supply curve cause the equilibrium quantity and price to move along the demand curve. In other words, shifts in the supply curve "trace out" the demand curve; hence we can still estimate the "slope" of the demand curve.

Bad news: On the other hand, since we have no income information, we have no information about demand curve shifts. Without knowing how the demand curve shifts we have no idea how the equilibrium quantity and price move along the supply curve. In other words, we cannot "trace out" the supply curve; hence we cannot estimate the "slope" of the supply curve.

To use the reduced form (RF) approach to estimate the "slope" of the demand curve, we first use ordinary least squares (OLS) to estimate the parameters of the reduced form (RF) equations (tables 23.9 and 23.10).

Table 23.9
OLS regression results—Quantity reduced form (RF) equation

Ordinary least squares (OLS)				
Dependent variable: Q				
Explanatory variable(s):	Estimate	SE	t-Statistic	Prob
FeedP	−821.8494	131.7644	−6.237266	0.0000
Const	239,158.3	5,777.771	41.39283	0.0000
Number of observations	120			
Estimated equation: $EstQ = 239{,}158 − 821.85 FeedP$				
$a_{FP}^{Q} = −821.85$				

Table 23.10
OLS regression results—Price reduced form (RF) equation

Ordinary least squares (OLS)				
Dependent variable: P				
Explanatory variable(s):	Estimate	SE	t-Statistic	Prob
FeedP	0.524641	0.262377	1.999571	0.0478
Const	142.0193	11.50503	12.34411	0.0000
Number of observations	120			
Estimated equation: $EstP = 142.0 + 0.52464 FeedP$				
$a_{FP}^{P} = 0.52464$				

 [To access this online material, go to http://mitpress.mit.edu/westhoffeconometrics and select Market for Beef.]

Then we can estimate the "slope" of the demand curve by calculating the ratio of the feed price estimates:

$$\text{Estimated "slope" of the demand curve} = b_P^D = \frac{a_{FP}^{Q}}{a_{FP}^{P}} = \frac{-821.85}{0.52464} = -1{,}566.5$$

Now let us use the two-stage least squares (TSLS) estimation procedure to estimate the "slope" of the demand curve (table 23.11). In both cases the estimated "slope" of the demand curve is −1,566.5.

When we try to use two-stage least squares (TSLS) to estimate the "slope" of the supply curve the statistical software will report an error. We are asking the statistical software to do the impossible.

Similarly an underidentification problem would exist if income information was available, but feed price information was not.

Table 23.11
TSLS regression results—Demand model

Two-stage least squares (TSLS)				
Dependent variable: Q				
Instrument(s): *FeedP*				
Explanatory variable(s):	Estimate	SE	*t*-Statistic	Prob
P	−1,566.499	703.8335	−2.225667	0.0279
Const	46,1631.4	115,943.8	3.981510	0.0001
Number of observations	120			
Estimated equation: $EstQ = 461{,}631 - 1{,}566.5P$				
$b_P^D = -1{,}566.5$				

Demand and Supply Models

Demand model: $Q_t^D = \beta_{Const}^D + \beta_P^D P_t + \beta_I^D Inc_t + e_t^D$

Supply model: $Q_t^S = \beta_{Const}^S + \beta_P^S P_t + \beta_{FP}^S \cancel{FeedP}_t + e_t^S$

Equilibrium: $Q_t^D = Q_t^S = Q_t$

Endogenous variables: Q_t and P_t

Exogenous variables: $\cancel{FeedP}_t$ and Inc_t

Reduced Form (RF) Estimates

Quantity reduced form (RF) estimates: $EstQ = a_{Const}^Q + a_{FP}^Q \cancel{FeedP} + a_I^Q Inc$

Price reduced form (RF) estimates: $EstP = a_{Const}^P + a_{FP}^P \cancel{FeedP} + a_I^P Inc$

Again, let us now apply the order condition by comparing the number of absent exogenous variables and endogenous explanatory variables in each model:

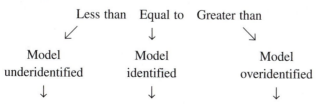

Exogenous variable: *Inc.*
A total of one exogenous explanatory variable.

Demand model			Supply model		
Exogenous explanatory variables included	variables **absent**	Endogenous explanatory variables **included**	Exogenous explanatory variables included	variables **absent**	Endogenous explanatory variables **included**
1	$1 - 1 = 0$	1	1	$2 - 1 = 1$	1
	0 less than	**1**		**1** equal to	**1**
	↓			↓	
	No			Unique	
	RF estimate			RF estimate	

The order condition suggests that we should

• be able to estimate the coefficient of the endogenous explanatory variable, P, in the supply model and

• not be able to estimate the coefficient of the endogenous explanatory variable, P, in the demand model.

The coefficient interpretation approach explains why (figure 23.5).

Again, there is both good news and bad news when we have income information, but no feed price information:

Good news: Since we have income information, we still have information about demand curve shifts. The shifts in the demand curve cause the equilibrium quantity and price to move along the supply curve. In other words, shifts in the demand curve "trace out" the supply curve; hence we can still estimate the "slope" of the supply curve.

Bad news: On the other hand, since we have no feed price information, we have no information about supply curve shifts. Without knowing how the supply curve shifts we have no idea how the equilibrium quantity and price move along the demand curve. In other words, we cannot "trace out" the demand curve; hence we cannot estimate the "slope" of the demand curve.

To use the reduced form (RF) approach to estimate the "slope" of the supply curve, we first use ordinary least squares (OLS) to estimate the parameters of the reduced form (RF) equations (tables 23.12 and 23.13).

[To access this online material, go to http://mitpress.mit.edu/westhoffeconometrics and select Market for Beef.]

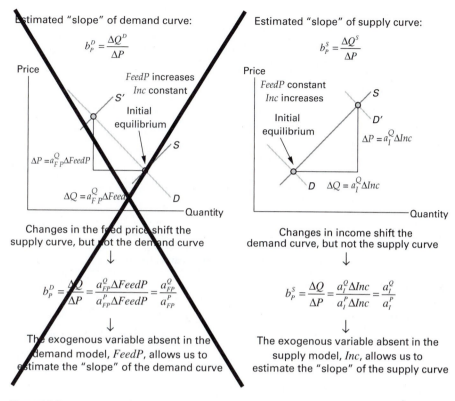

Estimated "slope" of demand curve:

$$b_P^D = \frac{\Delta Q^D}{\Delta P}$$

Estimated "slope" of supply curve:

$$b_P^S = \frac{\Delta Q^S}{\Delta P}$$

FeedP increases
Inc constant

S'

Initial
equilibrium

S

$\Delta P = a_{FP}^Q \Delta FeedP$

$\Delta Q = a_{FP}^Q \Delta Feed$

D

Changes in the feed price shift the
supply curve, but not the demand curve

↓

$$b_P^D = \frac{\Delta Q}{\Delta P} = \frac{a_{FP}^Q \Delta FeedP}{a_{FP}^P \Delta FeedP} = \frac{a_{FP}^Q}{a_{FP}^P}$$

↓

The exogenous variable absent in the
demand model, *FeedP*, allows us to
estimate the "slope" of the demand curve

FeedP constant
Inc increases

S

Initial
equilibrium

D'

$\Delta P = a_I^Q \Delta Inc$

D $\Delta Q = a_I^Q \Delta Inc$

Changes in income shift the
demand curve, but not the supply curve

↓

$$b_P^S = \frac{\Delta Q}{\Delta P} = \frac{a_I^Q \Delta Inc}{a_I^P \Delta Inc} = \frac{a_I^Q}{a_I^P}$$

↓

The exogenous variable absent in the
supply model, *Inc*, allows us to
estimate the "slope" of the supply curve

Figure 23.5
Reduced form (RF) and coefficient interpretation approach—Underidentified

Table 23.12
OLS regression results—Quantity reduced form (RF) equation

Ordinary least squares (OLS)				
Dependent variable: Q				
Explanatory variable(s):	Estimate	SE	*t*-Statistic	Prob
Inc	20.22475	1.902708	10.62946	0.0000
Const	111,231.3	8,733.000	12.73690	0.0000
Number of observations	120			

Estimated equation: $EstQ = 111{,}231 + 20.225 Inc$

$a_I^Q = 20.225$

Table 23.13
OLS regression results—Price reduced form (RF) equation

Ordinary least squares (OLS)				
Dependent variable: P				
Explanatory variable(s):	Estimate	SE	t-Statistic	Prob
Inc	0.009669	0.004589	2.107161	0.0372
Const	120.4994	21.06113	5.721413	0.0000
Number of observations	120			
Estimated equation: $EstP = 120.5 + 0.009669Inc$				
$a_I^P = 0.009669$				

Table 23.14
TSLS regression results—Supply equation

Two-stage least squares (TSLS)				
Dependent variable: Q				
Instrument(s): *Inc*				
Explanatory variable(s):	Estimate	SE	t-Statistic	Prob
P	2091.679	1169.349	1.788756	0.0762
Const	−140,814.8	192,634.8	−0.730994	0.4662
Number of observations	120			
Estimated equation: $EstQ = -140,815 + 2,091.7P$				
$b_P^S = 2,091.7$				

Then we can estimate the "slope" of the supply curve by calculating the ratio of the income estimates:

$$\text{Estimated "slope" of the supply curve} = b_P^S = \frac{a_I^Q}{a_I^P} = \frac{20.225}{0.009669} = 2,091.7$$

Once again, two-stage least squares (TSLS) provide the same estimate (table 23.14).

Also when we try to use two-stage least squares (TSLS) to estimate the "slope" of the demand curve the statistical software will report an error.

Conclusion: When a simultaneous equations model is underidentified, we cannot estimate all its parameters. For those parameters we can estimate, however, the reduced form (RF) estimation procedure and the two-stage least squares (TSLS) estimation procedures are equivalent.

23.5.3   Overidentification

While an underidentification problem arises when too little information is available, an **overidentification** problem arises when, in some sense, too much information is available. To illustrate this, suppose that in addition to the feed price and income information, the price of chicken is also available. Since beef and chicken are substitutes, the price of chicken would appear as an exogenous explanatory variable in the demand model. The simultaneous equations model and the reduced form (RF) estimates would change:

Demand and Supply Models

Demand model: $Q_t^D = \beta_{Const}^D + \beta_P^D P_t + \beta_I^D Inc_t + \beta_{CP}^D ChickP_t + e_t^D$

Supply model: $Q_t^S = \beta_{Const}^S + \beta_P^S P_t + \beta_{FP}^S FeedP_t + \qquad + e_t^S$

Equilibrium: $Q_t^D = Q_t^S = Q_t$

Endogenous variables: Q_t and P_t

Exogenous variables: $FeedP_t$, Inc_t, and $ChickP_t$

Reduced Form (RF) Estimates

Quantity reduced form (RF) estimates: $EstQ = a_{Const}^Q + a_{FP}^Q FeedP + a_I^Q Inc + a_{CP}^Q ChickP$

Price reduced form (RF) estimates: $EstP = a_{Const}^P + a_{FP}^P FeedP + a_I^P Inc + a_{CP}^P ChickP$

Let us now apply the order condition by comparing the number of absent exogenous variables and endogenous explanatory variables in each model:

Exogenous variables: *FeedP*, *Inc*, and *ChickP*
A total of three exogenous explanatory variables.

Demand model			Supply model		
Exogenous explanatory variables included	variables **absent**	Endogenous explanatory variables **included**	Exogenous explanatory variables included	variables **absent**	Endogenous explanatory variables **included**
1	$3 - 2 = 1$	1	1	$3 - 1 = 2$	1
	1 equal to	**1**		**2** greater than	**1**
	↓			↓	
	Unique RF estimate			Multiple RF estimates	

Estimated "slope" of supply curve:

$$b_P^S = \frac{\Delta Q^S}{\Delta P}$$

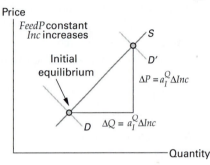

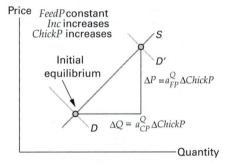

Changes in income shift the demand curve, but not the supply curve

↓

Changes in the chicken price shift the demand curve, but not the supply curve

↓

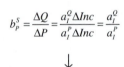

$$b_P^S = \frac{\Delta Q}{\Delta P} = \frac{a_I^Q \Delta Inc}{a_I^P \Delta Inc} = \frac{a_I^Q}{a_I^P}$$

$$b_P^S = \frac{\Delta Q}{\Delta P} = \frac{a_{CP}^Q \Delta ChickP}{a_{CP}^P \Delta ChickP} = \frac{a_{CP}^Q}{a_{CP}^P}$$

↓

↓

The exogenous variable absent in the supply model, *Inc*, allows us to estimate the "slope" of the supply curve

The exogenous variable absent in the supply model, *ChickP*, allows us to estimate the "slope" of the supply curve

Figure 23.6
Reduced form (RF) and coefficient interpretation approach—Overidentified

The order condition suggests that we should

• be able to estimate the coefficient of the endogenous explanatory variable, *P*, in the demand model and

• encounter some complications when estimating the coefficient of the endogenous explanatory variable, *P*, in the supply model. In fact, the reduced form (RF) estimation procedure provides multiple estimates.

We will now explain why the multiple estimates result (figure 23.6). We have two exogenous factors that shift the demand curve: income and the price of chicken. Consequently there are two ways to "trace out" the supply curve. There are now two different ways to use the reduced form (RF) estimates to estimate the "slope" of the supply curve:

Ratio of the reduced form (RF)   Ratio of the reduced form (RF)
income coefficients   chicken feed coefficients

$\downarrow$ $\downarrow$

Estimated "slope"   Estimated "slope"
of supply curve: of supply curve:

$\downarrow$ $\downarrow$

$$b_P^S = \frac{a_I^Q}{a_I^P}$$ $$b_P^S = \frac{a_{CP}^Q}{a_{CP}^P}$$

We will go through the mechanics of the reduced form (RF) estimation procedures to illustrate the overidentification problem. First we use the ordinary least squares (OLS) to estimate the reduced form (RF) parameters (tables 23.15 and 23.16).

Table 23.15
OLS regression results—Quantity reduced form (RF) equation

Ordinary least squares (OLS)				
Dependent variable: Q				
Explanatory variable(s):	Estimate	SE	t-Statistic	Prob
FeedP	−349.5411	135.3993	−2.581558	0.0111
Inc	16.86458	2.675264	6.303894	0.0000
ChickP	47.59963	158.4147	0.300475	0.7644
Const	138,194.2	13,355.13	10.34765	0.0000
Number of observations	120			

Estimated equation: $EstQ = 138{,}194 - 349.54 FeedP + 16.865 Inc + 47.600 ChickP$

$a_{FP}^Q = -349.54, \quad a_I^Q = 16.865, \quad a_{CP}^Q = 47.600$

Table 23.16
OLS regression results—Price reduced form (RF) equation

Ordinary least squares (OLS)				
Dependent variable: P				
Explanatory variable(s):	Estimate	SE	t-Statistic	Prob
FeedP	0.955012	0.318135	3.001912	0.0033
Inc	0.016043	0.006286	2.552210	0.0120
ChickP	0.274644	0.372212	0.737870	0.4621
Const	29.96187	31.37924	0.954831	0.3416
Number of observations	120			

Estimated equation: $EstP = 29.96 + 0.95501 FeedP + 0.016043 Inc + 0.27464 ChickP$

$a_{FP}^P = 0.95501, \quad a_I^P = 0.95501, \quad a_{CP}^P = 0.27464$

[To access this online material, go to http://mitpress.mit.edu/westhoffeconometrics and select Market for Beef.]

Then we use the reduced form (RF) estimates to compute the estimates for the "slopes" of the demand and supply curves:

Estimated "slope" of demand curve	Estimated "slope" of the supply curve	Estimated "slope" of the supply curve
↓	↓	↓
Ratio of reduced form (RF) feed price coefficient estimates	Ratio of reduced form (RF) income coefficient estimates	Ratio of reduced form (RF) chicken price coefficient estimates
↓	↓	↓

$$b_P^D = \frac{a_{FP}^Q}{a_{FP}^P} = \frac{-349.54}{0.95501} = -366.0 \quad b_P^S = \frac{a_I^Q}{a_I^P} = \frac{16.865}{0.016043} = 1051.2 \quad b_P^S = \frac{a_{CP}^Q}{a_{CP}^P} = \frac{47.600}{0.27464} = 173.3$$

The reduced form (RF) estimation procedure produces two different estimates for the "slope" for the supply curve. This is what we mean by overidentification.

23.5.4   Overidentification and Two-Stage Least Squares (TSLS)

While reduced form (RF) estimation procedure cannot resolve the overidentification problem, two-stage least squares (TSLS) approach can. The two-squares least squares estimation procedure provides a single estimate of the "slope" of the supply curve. The following regression printout reveals this (tables 23.17 and 23.18).

Table 23.17
TSLS regression results—Demand model

Two-stage least squares (TSLS)			
Dependent variable: Q			
Instrument(s): *FeedP*, *Inc*, and *ChickP*			
Explanatory variable(s):	Estimate	SE	*t*-Statistic	Prob
---	---	---	---	---
P	−366.0071	68.47718	−5.344950	0.0000
Inc	22.73632	1.062099	21.40697	0.0000
ChickP	148.1212	86.30740	1.716205	0.0888
Const	149,160.5	7,899.140	18.88313	0.0000
Number of observations	120			

Estimated equation: $EstQ^D = 149,160 - 366.0EstP + 22.74Inc$
$b_P^D = -366.0, \quad b_I^D = 22.74, \quad b_{CP}^D = 22.74$

Table 23.18
TSLS regression results—Supply model

Two-stage least squares (TSLS)				
Dependent variable: Q				
Instrument(s): *FeedP*, *Inc*, and *ChickP*				
Explanatory variable(s):	Estimate	SE	*t*-Statistic	Prob
P	893.4857	335.0311	2.666874	0.0087
FeedP	−1,290.609	364.0891	−3.544761	0.0006
Const	112,266.0	49,592.54	2.263769	0.0254
Number of observations	120			

Estimated equation: $EstQ^S = 112{,}266 + 893.5 EstP - 1{,}290.6 FeedP$

$b_P^S = 893.5, \quad b_{FP}^S = -1{,}290.6$

Table 23.19
Comparison of RF and TSLS estimates

	Price coefficient estimates: Estimated "slope" of	
	Demand curve (b_P^D)	Supply curve (b_P^S)
Reduced form (RF)	−366.0	
Based on income coefficients		1,051.2
Based on chicken price coefficients		173.3
Two-stage least squares (TSLS)	−366.0	893.5

[To access this online material, go to http://mitpress.mit.edu/westhoffeconometrics and select Market for Beef.]

The estimated "slope" of the demand curve is −366.0. This is the same estimate as computed by the reduced form (RF) estimation procedure. Two-stage least squares (TSLS) provides a single estimate for the "slope" of the supply curve:

$$b_P^S = 893.5$$

Table 23.19 compares the estimates that result when using the two different estimation procedures. Note that on the one hand, the demand model is not overidentified. Both the reduced form (RF) estimation procedure and the two-stage least squares (TSLS) estimation procedure provide the same estimate for the "slope" of the demand curve. On the other hand, the supply model is overidentified. The reduced form (RF) estimation procedure provides two estimates for the "slope" of the supply curve; the two-stage least squares (TSLS) estimation procedure provides only one.

23.6   Summary of Identification Issues

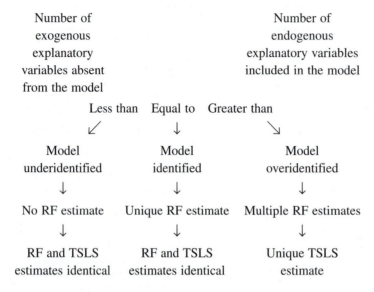

Number of exogenous explanatory variables absent from the model

Number of endogenous explanatory variables included in the model

Less than	Equal to	Greater than
↙	↓	↘
Model underidentified	Model identified	Model overidentified
↓	↓	↓
No RF estimate	Unique RF estimate	Multiple RF estimates
↓	↓	↓
RF and TSLS estimates identical	RF and TSLS estimates identical	Unique TSLS estimate

Chapter 23 Review Questions

1. What does it mean for a simultaneous equations model to be underidentified?

2. What does it mean for a simultaneous equations model to be overidentified?

3. Compare the reduced form (RF) estimation procedure and the two-stage least squares (TSLS) estimation procedure:

    a. When will the two procedures produce identical results?

    b. When will the two procedures produce different results? How do the results differ?

Chapter 23 Exercises

Consider the data we used in class to analyze the beef market:

Beef market data: Monthly time series data relating to the market for beef from 1977 to 1986.

Q_t Quantity of beef in month t (millions of pounds)

P_t Real price of beef in month t (1982–84 cents per pound)

Inc_t Real disposable income in month t (thousands of chained 2005 dollars)

$ChickP_t$ Real price of whole chickens in month t (1982–84 cents per pound)

$FeedP_t$ Real price of cattle feed in month t (1982–84 cents per pounds of corn cobs)

Consider the following constant elasticity model describing the beef market:

Demand model: $\log(Q_t^D) = \beta_{Const}^D + \beta_P^D \log(P_t) + \beta_I^D \log(Inc_t) + \beta_{CP}^D \log(ChickP) + e_t^D$

Supply model: $\log(Q_t^S) = \beta_{Const}^S + \beta_P^S \log(P_t) + \beta_{FP}^S \log(FeedP_t) + \qquad + e_t^S$

Equilibrium: $\log(Q_t^D) = \log(Q_t^S) = \log(Q_t)$

1. Suppose that there were no data for the price of chicken and income; that is, while you can include the variable *FeedP* in your analysis, you cannot use the variables *Inc* and *ChickP*.

[To access this online material, go to http://mitpress.mit.edu/westhoffeconometrics and select Market for Beef.]

a. Consider the reduced form (RF) estimation procedure:

i. Can we estimate the own price elasticity of demand, β_P^D? If not, explain why not. If so, does the reduced form (RF) estimation procedure provide a single estimate? What is (are) the estimate (estimates)?

ii. Can we estimate the own price elasticity of supply, β_P^S? If not, explain why not. If so, does the reduced form (RF) estimation procedure provide a single estimate? What is (are) the estimate (estimates)?

b. Consider the two-stage least squares (TSLS) estimation procedure:

i. Can we estimate the own price elasticity of demand, β_P^D? If so, what is (are) the estimate (estimates)?

ii. Can we estimate the own price elasticity of supply, β_P^S? If so, what is (are) the estimate (estimates)?

2. Suppose instead that there were no data for the price of feed; that is, while you can include the variables *Inc* and *ChickP* in your analysis, you cannot use the variable *FeedP*.

[To access this online material, go to http://mitpress.mit.edu/westhoffeconometrics and select Market for Beef.]

a. Consider the reduced form (RF) estimation procedure:

i. Can we estimate the own price elasticity of demand, β_P^D? If not, explain why not. If so, does the reduced form (RF) estimation procedure provide a single estimate? What is (are) the estimate (estimates)?

ii. Can we estimate the own price elasticity of supply, β_P^S? If not, explain why not. If so, does the reduced form (RF) estimation procedure provide a single estimate? What is (are) the estimate (estimates)?

b. Consider the two-stage least squares (TSLS) estimation procedure:

i. Can we estimate the own price elasticity of demand, β_P^D? If so, what is (are) the estimate (estimates)?

ii. Can we estimate the own price elasticity of supply, β_P^S? If so, what is (are) the estimate (estimates)?

3. Last suppose that you can use all the variables in your analysis.

[To access this online material, go to http://mitpress.mit.edu/westhoffeconometrics and select Market for Beef.]

a. Consider the reduced form (RF) estimation procedure:

i. Can we estimate the own price elasticity of demand, β_P^D? If not, explain why not. If so, does the reduced form (RF) estimation procedure provide a single estimate? What is (are) the estimate (estimates)?

ii. Can we estimate the own price elasticity of supply, β_P^S? If not, explain why not. If so, does the reduced form (RF) estimation procedure provide a single estimate? What is (are) the estimate (estimates)?

b. Consider the two-stage least squares (TSLS) estimation procedure:

i. Can we estimate the own price elasticity of demand, β_P^D? If so, what is (are) the estimate (estimates)?

ii. Can we estimate the own price elasticity of supply, β_P^S? If so, what is (are) the estimate (estimates)?

Chicken market data: Monthly time series data relating to the market for chicken from 1980 to 1985.

Q_t	Quantity of chicken in month t (millions of pounds)
P_t	Real price of whole chickens in month t (1982–84 cents per pound)
$FeedP_t$	Real price chicken formula feed in month t (1982–84 cents per pound)
Inc_t	Real disposable income in month t (thousands of chained 2005 dollars)
$PorkP_t$	Real price of pork in month t (1982–84 cents per pound)

Consider the following constant elasticity model describing the chicken market:

Demand model: $\log(Q_t^D) = \beta_{Const}^D + \beta_P^D \log(P_t) + \beta_I^D \log(Inc_t) + \beta_{PP}^D \log(PorkP) + e_t^D$

Supply model: $\log(Q_t^S) = \beta_{Const}^S + \beta_P^S \log(P_t) + \beta_{FP}^S \log(FeedP_t) + \qquad\qquad + e_t^S$

Equilibrium: $\log(Q_t^D) = \log(Q_t^S) = \log(Q_t)$

4. Suppose that there were no data for the price of pork and income; that is, while you can include the variable *FeedP* in your analysis, you cannot use the variables *Inc* and *PorkP*.

[To access this online material, go to http://mitpress.mit.edu/westhoffeconometrics and select Market for Chicken.]

a. Consider the reduced form (RF) estimation procedure:

i. Can we estimate the own price elasticity of demand, β_P^D? If not, explain why not. If so, does the reduced form (RF) estimation procedure provide a single estimate? What is (are) the estimate (estimates)?

ii. Can we estimate the own price elasticity of supply, β_P^S? If not, explain why not. If so, does the reduced form (RF) estimation procedure provide a single estimate? What is (are) the estimate (estimates)?

b. Consider the two-stage least squares (TSLS) estimation procedure:

i. Can we estimate the own price elasticity of demand, β_P^D? If so, what is (are) the estimate (estimates)?

ii. Can we estimate the own price elasticity of supply, β_P^S? If so, what is (are) the estimate (estimates)?

5. Suppose instead that there were no data for the price of feed; that is, while you can include the variables *Inc* and *PorkP* in your analysis, you cannot use the variable *FeedP*.

[To access this online material, go to http://mitpress.mit.edu/westhoffeconometrics and select Market for Chicken.]

a. Consider the reduced form (RF) estimation procedure:

i. Can we estimate the own price elasticity of demand, β_P^D? If not, explain why not. If so, does the reduced form (RF) estimation procedure provide a single estimate? What is (are) the estimate (estimates)?

ii. Can we estimate the own price elasticity of supply, β_P^S? If not, explain why not. If so, does the reduced form (RF) estimation procedure provide a single estimate? What is (are) the estimate (estimates)?

b. Consider the two-stage least squares (TSLS) estimation procedure:

i. Can we estimate the own price elasticity of demand, β_P^D? If so, what is (are) the estimate (estimates)?

ii. Can we estimate the own price elasticity of supply, β_P^S? If so, what is (are) the estimate (estimates)?

6. Last suppose that you use all the variables in your analysis.

[To access this online material, go to http://mitpress.mit.edu/westhoffeconometrics and select Market for Chicken.]

a. Consider the reduced form (RF) estimation procedure:

i. Can we estimate the own price elasticity of demand, β_P^D? If not, explain why not. If so, does the reduced form (RF) estimation procedure provide a single estimate? What is (are) the estimate (estimates)?

ii. Can we estimate the own price elasticity of supply, β_P^S? If not, explain why not. If so, does the reduced form (RF) estimation procedure provide a single estimate? What is (are) the estimate (estimates)?

b. Consider the two-stage least squares (TSLS) estimation procedure:

i. Can we estimate the own price elasticity of demand, β_P^D? If so, what is (are) the estimate (estimates)?

ii. Can we estimate the own price elasticity of supply, β_P^S? If so, what is (are) the estimate (estimates)?

In general, compare the reduced form (RF) estimation procedure and the two-stage least squares (TSLS) estimation procedure.

7. When the reduced form (RF) estimation procedure provides no estimate for a coefficient, how many estimates does the two-stage least squares (TSLS) estimation procedure provide?

8. When the reduced form (RF) estimation procedure provides a single estimate for a coefficient, how many estimates does the two-stage least squares (TSLS) estimation procedure provide? How are the estimates related?

9. When the reduced form (RF) estimation procedure provides multiple estimates for a coefficient, how many estimates does the two-stage least squares (TSLS) estimation procedure provide?

24 Binary and Truncated Dependent Variables

Chapter 24 Prep Questions

2004 Electoral College data: Cross-sectional data from the 2004 presidential election for the fifty states.

$PopDen_t$ Population density of state t in 2004 (persons per square mile)

$Unem_t$ Unemployment rate in 2004 of state t (percent)

$WinDem1_t$ 1 if Democrats won state t in 2004; 0 if Republicans won state t

Consider the following model explaining the winning party in each state:

Model: $WinDem1_t = \beta_{Const} + \beta_{Den}PopDen_t + e_t$

1. Devise a theory regarding how the population density of a state affects voting behavior. That is, as a state's population density increases thereby becoming more urban will a state become more or less likely to vote Democratic? What does your theory suggest about the sign of the coefficient for $PopDen_t$?

2. Construct a scatter diagram to illustrate the relationship between *PopDen* and *WinDem1* by plotting Plot *PopDen* on the horizontal axis and *WinDem1* on the vertical axis.

[To access this online material, go to http://mitpress.mit.edu/westhoffeconometrics and select Electoral College—2004.]

    a. What does the scatter diagram suggest about your theory?

    b. What feature of this scatter diagram is different from the scatter diagrams we have seen previously?

3. Use the ordinary least squares (OLS) estimation procedure to estimates the model's parameters.

[To access this online material, go to http://mitpress.mit.edu/westhoffeconometrics and select Electoral College—2004.]

    a. What equation estimates the effect of *PopDen* on *WinDem1*?

    b. What is the estimated value of *WinDem1* for

        i. Alaska?

        ii. Florida?

        iii. Maryland?

        iv. Massachusetts?

        v. Rhode Island?

        vi. New Jersey?

Salaries and hitting performance of American League hitters: Cross-sectional 2011 salary and 2010 performance data for all hitters on Major League rosters at the opening of the 2011 season.

Salary$_t$	Salary of player t in 2011 (thousands of dollars)
AtBats$_t$	At bats of player t in 2010
BatAvg$_t$	Batting average of player t in 2010
NameFirst$_t$	Player t's first name
NameLast$_t$	Player t's last name
OnBasePct$_t$	On base percentage of player t in 2010
SlugAvg$_t$	Slugging average of player t in 2010
Team$_t$	Player t's team

Consider the following model explaining salaries of Major League hitters:

Model: $Salary_t = \beta_{Const} + \beta_{OBP}OnBasePct_t + e_t$

4. Devise a theory regarding how on base percentage affects salary. What does you theory suggest about the sign of the coefficient for *OnBasePct$_i$*?

5. Construct a scatter diagram to illustrate the relationship between *OnBasePct* and *Salary* by plotting *OnBasePct* on the horizontal axis and *Salary* on the vertical axis.

[To access this online material, go to http://mitpress.mit.edu/westhoffeconometrics and select MLB Hitter Salaries—2011.]

a. What does the scatter diagram suggest about your theory?

b. In 2011 Major League Baseball's collective bargaining agreement with the players' union requires teams to pay each Major League player at least $414,000. How is the minimum salary reflected on the scatter diagram?

6. Use the ordinary least squares (OLS) estimation procedure to estimate the model's parameters.

[To access this online material, go to http://mitpress.mit.edu/westhoffeconometrics and select MLB Hitter Salaries—2011.]

a. What equation estimates the effect of *OnBasePct* on *Salary*?

b. What is the estimated value of *Salary* when

i. *OnBasePct* equals .400?

ii. *OnBasePct* equals .300?

iii. *OnBasePct* equals .200?

c. Do all the estimated values make sense?

24.1 Introduction

We will now consider two special problems that the dependent variable can create when using the ordinary least squares (OLS) estimation procedure:

• The first arises when the dependent variable is binary, that is, when the dependent variable can only take on two values such as Yes/No or True/False. In this case one of the two possibilities is represented with a 0 and the other with a 1; that is, the dependent variable is a dummy variable.

• The second problem arises when the dependent variable can never be greater than a specific value and/or less than a specific value. For example, in the United States the legal wage an employee can be paid cannot fall below the Federal minimum wage in most states and occupations. Currently the federally mandated minimum wage is $7.25 per hour.

We will now show that whenever either of these problems is present, the ordinary least squares (OLS) estimation procedure can produce erroneous results.

24.2   Binary Dependent Variables

24.2.1   Electoral College: Red and Blue States

The number of votes a state receives in the Electoral College equals the number of congress-people the state sends to Washington: the number of Representatives plus the number of Senators, two.[1] With the exception of two states, Maine and Nebraska, all a state's electoral votes are awarded to the presidential candidate receiving the most votes. We will focus on the 2004 presidential election in which the Democrat, John Kerry, challenged the incumbent Republican, George W. Bush.[2]

Project: Assess the effect of state population density on state Electoral College winner.

2004 Electoral College data: Cross-sectional data from the 2004 presidential election for the fifty states.

$PopDen_t$ Population density of state t in 2004 (persons per square mile)

$Unem_t$ Unemployment rate in 2004 of state t (percent)

$WinDem1_t$ 1 if Democrats won state t in 2004; 0 if Republicans won state t

[To access this online material, go to http://mitpress.mit.edu/westhoffeconometrics and select Electoral College—2004.]

Table 24.1 reports on the winner of each state's electoral votes along with each state's population density. Note that the table ranks the states in order of their population density. As you can see, the Republicans won all of the eleven least densely populated states. The Democrats won all of the seven most densely populated states. The Republicans and Democrats split the states in the middle. This observation allows us to formulate a theory:

Theory: The party winning a state's Electoral College vote depends on the state's population density; as a state becomes more densely populated, the Democrats rather than the Republicans become more likely to win.

To assess the theory we begin by constructing a scatter diagram (figure 24.1). Each point represents one state. The dependent variable y which equals 1 whenever the Democrats win and 0 whenever the Republicans win. The dependent variable $WinDem1$ is a binary variable, a dummy variable; $WinDem1$ takes on only one of two values, either 0 or 1:

---

1. The District of Columbia has three votes even though it has no (voting) members of Congress. Consequently the District of Columbia was not included in our analysis, although its inclusion would not affect our conclusions.

2. While Maine and Nebraska do not have a "winner take all" system, in 2004 all of the state's electoral votes were won by a single party in each of these states. The Democrats won all of Maine's electoral votes and the Republicans won all of Nebraska's votes.

Table 24.1
2004 Electoral College winners by state

State	Population density (persons per sq mi)	Winner	State	Population density (persons per sq mi)	Winner
Alaska	1.2	Rep	Washington	92.8	Dem
Wyoming	5.2	Rep	Wisconsin	101.4	Dem
Montana	6.4	Rep	Louisiana	103.0	Rep
North Dakota	9.2	Rep	Kentucky	104.1	Rep
South Dakota	10.2	Rep	South Carolina	139.4	Rep
New Mexico	15.6	Rep	Tennessee	143.3	Rep
Idaho	16.8	Rep	New Hampshire	144.1	Dem
Nevada	21.2	Rep	Georgia	153.8	Rep
Nebraska	22.7	Rep	Indiana	173.1	Rep
Utah	29.7	Rep	North Carolina	174.9	Rep
Kansas	33.4	Rep	Michigan	177.6	Dem
Oregon	37.3	Dem	Virginia	188.3	Rep
Maine	42.4	Dem	Hawaii	194.9	Dem
Colorado	44.3	Rep	Illinois	227.8	Dem
Arizona	50.6	Rep	California	228.4	Dem
Oklahoma	51.1	Rep	Pennsylvania	275.2	Dem
Arkansas	52.6	Rep	Ohio	279.5	Rep
Iowa	52.7	Rep	Florida	321.0	Rep
Mississippi	61.5	Rep	New York	408.7	Dem
Minnesota	63.8	Dem	Delaware	422.3	Dem
Vermont	66.9	Dem	Maryland	566.6	Dem
West Virginia	74.9	Rep	Connecticut	717.3	Dem
Missouri	83.4	Rep	Massachusetts	821.3	Dem
Texas	85.6	Rep	Rhode Island	1,025.0	Dem
Alabama	88.8	Rep	New Jersey	1,162.0	Dem

$WinDem1_t = 1$ if the Democrats win in state t

       $= 0$ if the Republicans win in state t

The scatter diagram appears to support our theory. As the population density increases, states tend to support Democrats rather than Republicans. All states whose population density was less than 35 persons per square mile voted Republican while all states whose population density was greater than 400 persons per square mile voted Democrat. States whose population density was between 35 and 400 persons per square mile were split. Next we will formulate a model to assess the theory.

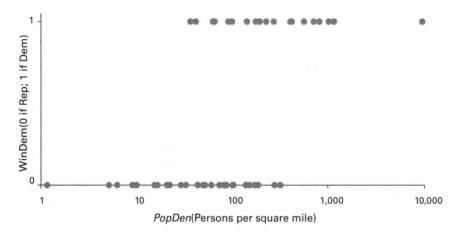

Figure 24.1
Scatter diagram—Population density versus election winner

24.2.2   Linear Probability Model

The linear probability model is just the "standard" linear specification. The dependent variable, $WinDem1_t$, is the winning party indicated by a 0 or 1 and the explanatory variable is population density, $PopDen$:

$$WinDem1_t = \beta_{Const} + \beta_{Den}PopDen_t + e_t$$

Interpretation of the Dependent Variable

The dependent variable $WinDem1_t$ can be interpreted as the probability of Democrats winning. On the one hand, if the Democrats actually win in a state, then the probability of the Democrats winning is 1; therefore, if the Democrats win, $WinDem1_t$ equals 1. On the other hand, if the Republicans actually win in a state, then the probability of the Democrats winning is 0; therefore, if the Republicans win, $WinDem1_t$ equals 0. Using the ordinary least squares (OLS) estimation procedure, we can estimate the model's parameters (table 24.2).

[To access this online material, go to http://mitpress.mit.edu/westhoffeconometrics and select Electoral College—2004.]

We now formulate out null and alternative hypotheses:

H_0: $\beta_{Den} = 0$ Population density has no effect on the election outcome.

H_1: $\beta_{Den} > 0$ An increase in population density increases the probability of a Democrat win.

Table 24.2
OLS regression results—2004 presidential election

Ordinary least squares (OLS)				
Dependent variable: *WinDem1*				
Explanatory variable(s):	Estimate	SE	*t*-Statistic	Prob
PopDen	0.001001	0.000236	4.247280	0.0001
Const	0.192315	0.074299	2.588406	0.0127
Number of observations	50			

Estimated equation: $EstWinDem1 = 0.192 + 0.001PopDen$

Interpretation of estimates:

$b_{PopDen} = 0.001$: When a state's population density increases by 100, the probability that the state votes Democratic increases by 0.1

Critical result: The estimate of *PopDen*'s coefficient is positive. As a state becomes more densely populated, it is more likely to vote Democratic. This lends support to our theory.

Intrinsic Problems with the Linear Probability Model

Using these results we can estimate the probability that the Democrats will win a particular state:

$$EstWinDen = 0.192 + 0.001PopDen$$

Using this equation let us calculate estimates for some selected states:

State	PopDen	EstWinDem1
Alaska	1.2	$0.192 + 0.001 \times 1.2 = 0.192 + 0.001 = 0.193$
Florida	321.0	$0.192 + 0.001 \times 321.0 = 0.192 + 0.321 = 0.513$
Maryland	566.6	$0.192 + 0.001 \times 566.6 = 0.192 + 0.567 = 0.759$

These estimates for the probability of the Democrats winning each state appear to be reasonable. Alaska's population density is very low, and we estimate that the probability of a Democrat win is low also, only 0.193. Florida's population density falls in the middle, between 35 and 400; we estimate that the probability of a Democrat win in Florida is about half. Maryland's population density is high, above 400; we estimate that the probability of a Democrat win in Maryland is high also, 0.759.

Let us calculate probability estimates for Massachusetts, Rhode Island, and New Jersey:

State	PopDen	EstWinDem1
Massachusetts	821.3	$0.192 + 0.001 \times 821.3 = 0.192 + 0.821 = 1.013$
Rhode Island	1,025.0	$0.192 + 0.001 \times 1,025.0 = 0.192 + 1.025 = 1.217$
New Jersey	1,162.0	$0.192 + 0.001 \times 1,162.0 = 0.192 + 1.162 = 1.354$

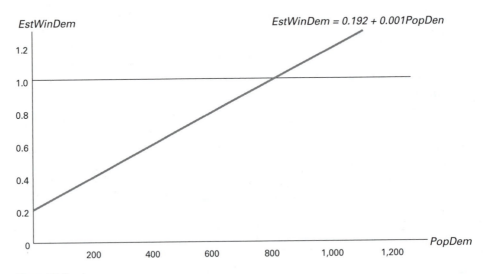

Figure 24.2
Scatter diagram—Population density versus winning party with linear best fitting line

The probability estimates for these states are nonsensical. Remember that a probability cannot be less than 0 or greater than 1. On the one hand, if the probability of an event equals 0, that event cannot occur. On the other hand, if the probability of an event equal 1, the event will occur with certainty. An event cannot be more certain than certain. A probability of 1.013 or 1.217 or 1.354 simply does not make sense.

It is easy to understand why the linear probability model produces the nonsensical results; just graph the best fitting line (figure 24.2). The probability model is linear; consequently, the slope of the best fitting line is a constant, 0.001. Since the slope is a positive constant, the estimated probability will exceed 1 whenever the population density is large enough.

24.2.3   Probit Probability Model: Correcting the Linear Model's Intrinsic Problems

Stretched S-shaped versus Straight Regression Lines
How can we remedy this problem? Instead of a linear (straight) best fitting line, perhaps we should use a "stretched S-shaped" best fitting line, to account for the fact that the probability can never be less than 0 or greater than 1. The stretched S-shaped regression line never falls below 0 and never rises above 1 (figure 24.3). What are the ramifications of a stretched S-shaped regression line? The stretched S-shaped line means that the change in probability resulting from a change in population density varies with population density:

• When population density is "small," a change in population density results in only a small change in probability; for example, when the population density falls from 400 to 200, the estimated probability of a Democratic win falls, but by only a little. When the population density

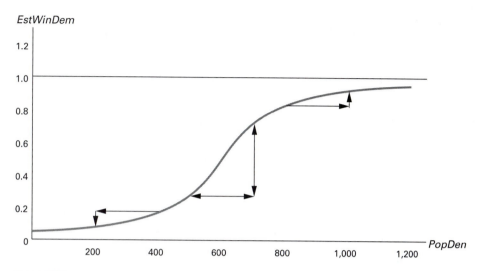

Figure 24.3
Scatter diagram—Population density versus winning party with stretched S-shaped best fitting line

is low initially we would expect the probability of a Democratic win to be low already. Therefore any subsequent decrease in population density must reduce the estimated probability only by a small amount; otherwise, a nonsensical negative probability would result.

• When the population density is "large," a change in the population density results in only a small change in probability; for example, when the population density rises from 800 to 1,000, the estimated probability of being a Democratic win rises, but by only a little. When the population density is high initially we would expect the probability of being a Democratic win to be high already. Therefore any subsequent increase in the population density must raise the estimated probability only by a small amount; otherwise, a nonsensical probability exceeding 1 would result.

• When the population density is "moderate" a change in the population results in a large change in probability; for example, the change in the estimated probability of being a Democratic win is large in the 500 to 700 range.

Simple Probit Example Data

The probit approach is arguably the most frequently used procedure to construct a stretched S-shaped regression line.[3] For pedagogical purposes we will consider a hypothetical example including only four states to illustrate how this is done. To simplify the notation, we let x_t equal

---

3. Any procedure that is used frequently is logit. While the probit and logit procedures do not produce identical results, rarely do the results differ in any substantial way.

776 Chapter 24

Table 24.3
Party affiliation—Simple probit example data

State	$x = PopDen$ (persons/sq mi)	Winning party	$y = WinDem1$ (Dem = 1, Rep = 0)
1	100	Rep	0
2	450	Dem	1
3	550	Rep	0
4	900	Dem	1

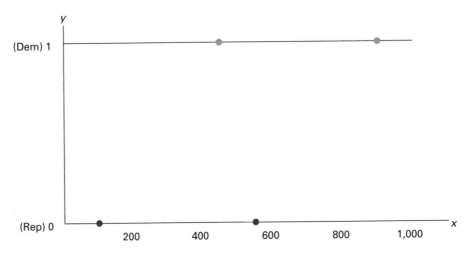

Figure 24.4
Scatter diagram—Simplified example

the population density, $PopDen_t$, and y_t equal the dummy variable representing the winning party, $WinDem1_t$, (Table 24.3).

The first state votes Republican and has a population density of 100 persons per square mile. The second state votes Democratic and has a population density of 450. The third state votes Republican and has a population density of 550. The fourth state votes Democratic and has a population density of 900. The scatter diagram appears in Figure 24.4:

Constructing the Stretched S-shaped Line Using the Normal Distribution
As we continue, we want to find the best fitting stretched S-shaped regression line. But how do we construct a stretched S-shaped regression line (figure 24.5)? The probit model utilizes the normal distribution to construct the line. Recall that the normal distribution's z equals the number of standard deviations a value is from the distribution's mean. The probit model involves two steps:

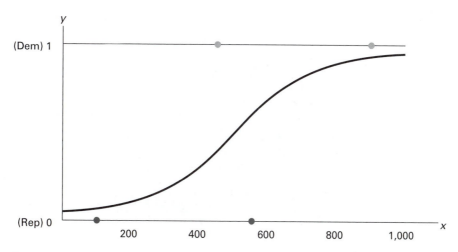

Figure 24.5
Scatter diagram—Simplified example with stretched S-shaped best fitting line

Step 1:   We transform population density into a z using a transformation function.

Step 2:   We apply the normal distribution to the z to compute the probability of the state will vote Republican and Democratic.

The easiest way to understand how the probit model works is to use an example. Let us begin by considering one possible transformation function: $z = -2 + 0.004x$. For the moment, do not worry about why we are using this particular transformation function. We simply wish to show how the probit estimation procedure constructs its stretched S-shaped lines.

Begin by calculating the probability that state 1 votes Democratic. Its population density, x_t, equals 100, we simply plug it into the transformation function:

$$z = -2 + 0.004x = -2 + 0.004 \times 100 = -2 + 0.4 = -1.6$$

Next we turn to the normal distribution to calculate the probability of the Democrats and Republicans winning in the state. We can use the Econometrics Lab to do so (figure 24.6).

[To access this online material, go to http://mitpress.mit.edu/westhoffeconometrics and select Lab 24.1a.]

A z value of −1.6 is already entered for us, so we just click **Calculate**.

The area to the left of −1.6 is 0.0548; hence the probability of the Democrats winning in state 1 equals 0.0548. The area to the right and the probability of the Republicans winning is 0.9452.

Let us perform the same calculation for state 2. Since its population density, x_t, equals 450, z equals −0.2:

$$z = -2 + 0.004x = -2 + 0.004 \times 450 = -2 + 1.8 = -0.2$$

Apply the normal distribution (figure 24.7).

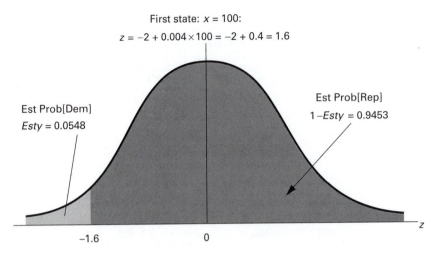

First state: $x = 100$:
$z = -2 + 0.004 \times 100 = -2 + 0.4 = 1.6$

Est Prob[Dem]
$Esty = 0.0548$

Est Prob[Rep]
$1 - Esty = 0.9453$

-1.6 0 z

Prob[Dem] = $Esty$ = 0.0548
Prob[Rep] = 1 $- Esty$ = 0.9452

Figure 24.6
x equals 100

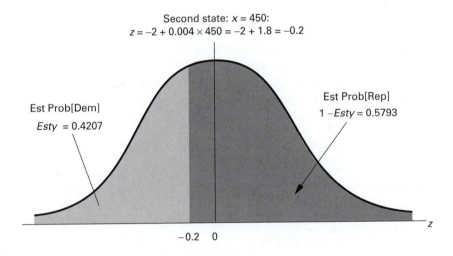

Second state: $x = 450$:
$z = -2 + 0.004 \times 450 = -2 + 1.8 = -0.2$

Est Prob[Dem]
$Esty = 0.4207$

Est Prob[Rep]
$1 - Esty = 0.5793$

-0.2 0 z

Prob[Dem] = $Esty$ = 0.4207
Prob[Rep] = 1 $- Esty$ = 0.5793

Figure 24.7
x equals 450

Table 24.4
Simple probit example probability calculations

State	Win party	Actual Y	x	$z = -2 + 0.004x$		Est Prob[Dem] Esty	Est Prob[Rep] $1 - Esty$	Prob of actual y
1	Dem	0	100	$-2 + 0.004 \times 100 =$	-1.6	0.0548	0.9452	0.9452
2	Rep	1	450	$-2 + 0.004 \times 450 =$	-0.2	0.4207	0.5793	0.4207
3	Dem	0	550	$-2 + 0.004 \times 550 =$	0.2	0.5793	0.4207	0.4207
4	Rep	1	900	$-2 + 0.004 \times 900 =$	1.6	0.9452	0.0548	0.9452

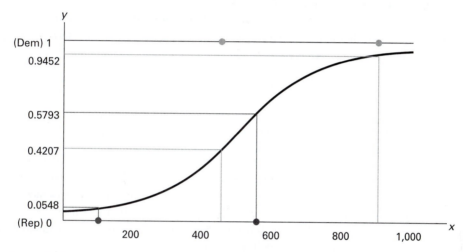

Figure 24.8
Scatter diagram—Population density versus winning party with stretched S-shaped best fitting line

[To access this online material, go to http://mitpress.mit.edu/westhoffeconometrics and select Lab 24.1b.]

The probability of the Democrats winning in state 2 equals 0.4207; the probability of the Republicans winning equals 0.5793.

Table 24.4 reports on the probabilities for the four states (plotted in figure 24.8). The transformation function, $z = -2 + 0.004x$, obtains the four probabilities:

• First state votes Republican equals 0.9452.

• Second state votes Democratic equals 0.4207.

• Third state votes Republican equals 0.4207.

• Fourth state votes Democratic equals 0.9452.

Now let us calculate the probability of the actual result, that is, the probability that the first state votes Republican and the second state votes Democratic and the third state votes Republican and the fourth state votes Democratic; this equals the product of the individual probabilities:

Prob[1st Rep and 2nd is Dem and 3rd is Rep and 4th is Dem]

$$= \frac{\text{Prob}}{[\text{1st Rep}]} \times \frac{\text{Prob}}{[\text{2nd Dem}]} \times \frac{\text{Prob}}{[\text{3rd Rep}]} \times \frac{\text{Prob}}{[\text{4th Dem}]}$$

$$= 0.9452 \times 0.4207 \times 0.4207 \times 0.9452 = 0.1582$$

Maximum Likelihood Estimation Procedure

So we understand how the probit estimation procedure constructs its stretched S-shaped line. But how do we choose the transformation function, the equation that "transforms" population density into z? That is, how do we decide if

$$z = -2 + 0.004x$$

is better or worse than

$$z = -2 + 0.005x \quad \text{or} \quad z = -3 + 0.004x \quad \text{or} \quad z = -3 + 0.003x \quad \text{or} \quad \dots$$

The answer is that we choose the equation that maximizes the likelihood of obtaining the actual result. That is, choose the equation that maximizes the likelihood that the first state votes Republican, the second Democratic, the third Republican, and the fourth Democratic.

We already calculated this probability for the transformation function $z = -2 + 0.004x$; it equals 0.1582. Obviously the search for the "best" transformation function could be very time-consuming. Our Econometrics Lab can help, however.

Econometrics Lab 24.2: Probit Estimation Procedure

[To access this online material, go to http://mitpress.mit.edu/westhoffeconometrics and select Lab 24.2.]

We can specify different constants and coefficients by moving the slide bars (figure 24.9). The simulation quickly calculates the probability of obtaining the actual results for the transformation functions with different constants and coefficients.

Initially, a constant of −2.00 and a coefficient of 0.004 are selected, the values we used to explain the construction of the stretched S-shaped line. Note that the probabilities we calculated and those calculated by the lab are identical. But let us try some other constants and coefficients. Table 24.5 reports on several different transformation functions:

It looks like a constant of −2.00 and coefficient of 0.004 is the best. That is, the transformation function $z = -2 + 0.004x$ maximizes the probability of obtaining the actual results. Fortunately, computational techniques have been devised to estimate the best transformation functions quickly. Statistical software uses such algorithms (table 24.6).

Constant Coefficient

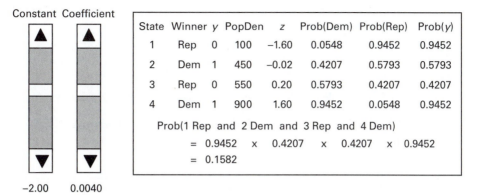

State	Winner	y	PopDen	z	Prob(Dem)	Prob(Rep)	Prob(y)
1	Rep	0	100	−1.60	0.0548	0.9452	0.9452
2	Dem	1	450	−0.02	0.4207	0.5793	0.5793
3	Rep	0	550	0.20	0.5793	0.4207	0.4207
4	Dem	1	900	1.60	0.9452	0.0548	0.9452

Prob(1 Rep and 2 Dem and 3 Rep and 4 Dem)
= 0.9452 x 0.4207 x 0.4207 x 0.9452
= 0.1582

−2.00   0.0040

Figure 24.9
Probit Calculation Lab

Table 24.5
Simple probit example—Econometric Lab calculations

Constant	Coefficient	Prob[1st Rep and 2nd Dem and 3rd Rep and 4th Dem]
−2.00	0.0040	0.1582
−2.00	0.0039	0.1277
−2.00	0.0041	0.1278
−2.05	0.0040	0.1278
−1.95	0.0040	0.1278

Table 24.6
Probit results—Simple probit example

	Probit			
Dependent variable: y				
Explanatory variable(s):	Estimate	SE	z-Statistic	Prob
x	0.004014	0.003851	1.042327	0.2973
Const	−2.006945	2.068016	−0.970469	0.3318
Number of observations	4			

[To access this online material, go to http://mitpress.mit.edu/westhoffeconometrics and select Probit Example.]

Getting Started in EViews

In EViews, after double clicking on variables selected for the regression, y and x:

· In the Equation Estimation window, click on the **Method** dropdown list.
· Select **BINARY**.
· Click **OK**.

These results are consistent with our simulation results. The maximum likelihood transformation is:

$$z = -2 + 0.004x$$

Now we will apply the Probit estimation procedure to the 2004 election results using EViews (table 24.7). Using the probit estimates we can calculate the probabilities for a few selected states (table 24.8).

Table 24.7
Probit results—2004 presidential election

	Probit			
Dependent variable: *WinDem1*				
Explanatory variable(s):	Estimate	SE	z-Statistic	Prob
PopDen	0.005729	0.002030	2.821456	0.0048
Const	−1.186613	0.326697	−3.632150	0.0003
Number of observations	50			

Table 24.8
Probit estimates—2004 presidential election

State	PopDen	$z = -1.187 + 0.00573PopDen$		Est Prob[Dem]	Est Prob[Rep]
Alaska	1.2	$-1.187 + 0.00573 \times 1.2$ =	−1.180	0.119	0.881
Indiana	173.1	$-1.187 + 0.00573 \times 173.1$ =	−0.195	0.423	0.577
Florida	321.0	$-1.187 + 0.00573 \times 321.0$ =	0.652	0.743	0.257
New York	408.7	$-1.187 + 0.00573 \times 408.7$ =	1.155	0.876	0.124

24.3   Truncated (Censored) Dependent Variables

We will now consider a second example in which the ordinary least squares (OLS) estimation procedure falters. The problem arises whenever the dependent variable cannot take on a value that is greater than or less than a specific value. Our example considers the salaries of Major League Baseball hitters at the beginning of the 2011 season.

Project: Assess the impact of a hitter's the previous season's performance on his salary.

Salaries and hitting performance of Major League hitters: Cross-sectional 2011 salary and 2010 performance data for all hitters on Major League rosters at the opening of the 2011 season.

$Salary_t$	Salary of player t in 2011 (thousands of dollars)
$AtBats_t$	At bats of player t in 2010
$BatAvg_t$	Batting average of player t in 2010
$NameFirst_t$	Player t's first name
$NameLast_t$	Player t's last name
$OnBasePct_t$	On base percentage of player t in 2010
$SlugAvg_t$	Slugging average of player t in 2010
$Team_t$	Player t's team

[To access this online material, go to http://mitpress.mit.edu/westhoffeconometrics and select MLB Hitter Salaries—2011]

First examine the salaries of the twenty-five highest paid hitters (table 24.9). Next consider the let us examine the salaries of the twenty-five lowest paid hitters (table 24.10). As table 24.10 shows, no player earns less than $414,000. This is dictated by the collective bargaining agreement negotiated by Major League Baseball and the Major League Baseball Player's Union. The minimum salary a team could pay to a Major League player in 2011 was $414,000. Consequently player salaries are said to be **truncated** or **censored**, their value cannot fall below $414,000.

We will now investigate the theory that a hitter's performance in 2010 affects his salary in 2011.[4] On the one hand, if a hitter does well in 2010, he will be able to negotiate a high salary in 2011; on the other hand, if his 2010 performance was poor, a low salary would results. More specifically, we will focus on the effect that on base percentage has on salary:

Theory: An increase in a hitter's on base percentage in 2010 increases his 2011 salary.

---

4. For purposes of illustration we are ignoring the existence of multiyear contracts.

Table 24.9
Salaries of the twenty-five highest paid MLB hitters in 2011

NameLast	NameFirst	Team	Salary ($1,000)
Rodriguez	Alex	NYY	32,000
Wells	Vernon	LAA	26,643
Teixeira	Mark	NYY	23,125
Mauer	Joe	MIN	23,000
Helton	Todd	COL	20,275
Cabrera	Miguel	DET	20,000
Howard	Ryan	PHI	20,000
Beltran	Carlos	NYM	19,325
Lee	Carlos	HOU	19,000
Soriano	Alfonso	CHN	19,000
Hunter	Torii	LAA	18,500
Bay	Jason	NYM	18,125
Suzuki	Ichiro	SEA	18,000
Holliday	Matt	STL	16,318
Young	Michael	TEX	16,175
Fielder	Prince	MIL	15,500
Utley	Chase	PHI	15,286
Morneau	Justin	MIN	15,000
Crawford	Carl	BOS	14,857
Jeter	Derek	NYY	14,729
Ramirez	Aramis	CHN	14,600
Pujols	Albert	STL	14,508
Fukudome	Kosuke	CHN	14,500
Wright	David	NYM	14,250
Beltre	Adrian	TEX	14,000

We begin by considering a simple linear model relating on base percent and salary:

Model: $Salary_t = \beta_{Const} + \beta_{OBP}OnBasePct_t + e_t$

where

$Salary_t$ = salary of player t in 2011 (thousands of dollars)

$OnBasePct_t$ = on base percentage of player t in 2010

Theory: $\beta_{OBP} > 0$

To assess this model, first construct a scatter diagram (figure 24.10).

The rectangular points on the scatter diagram represent the eighteen players who earn the minimum salary of $414,000; the triangular points represent all other players. The on base

Table 24.10
Salaries of the twenty-five lowest paid MLB hitters in 2011

NameLast	NameFirst	Team	Salary ($1,000)
Freese	David	STL	416
Wilson	Bobby	LAA	416
Greene	Tyler	STL	416
Espinosa	Danny	WAS	415
Ramos	Wilson	WAS	415
Hoffpauir	Jarrett	SND	415
Mangini	Matt	SEA	415
Baxter	Mike	SND	414
Bocock	Brian	PHI	414
Bourjos	Peter	LAA	414
Brown	Domonic	PHI	414
Conger	Hank	LAA	414
Cousins	Scott	FLA	414
Craig	Allen	STL	414
Descalso	Daniel	STL	414
Duda	Lucas	NYM	414
Dyson	Jarrod	KAN	414
Francisco	Juan	CIN	414
Freeman	Freddie	ATL	414
Hayes	Brett	FLA	414
Hicks	Brandon	ATL	414
Morel	Brent	CHA	414
Morrison	Logan	FLA	414
Nickeas	Mike	NYM	414
Trumbo	Mark	LAA	414

percentage of all but two of these players falls below the average on base percentage of all MLB hitters, 0.323. Consequently it is reasonable to believe that without the minimum salary imposed by the collective bargaining agreement the salaries of most of these players would fall below $414,000. In other words, the collective bargaining agreement is truncating salaries. To understand why truncated variables create problems for the ordinary least squares (OLS) estimation procedure we begin by estimating the model's parameters by using ordinary least square (OLS) estimation procedure (table 24.11).

[To access this online material, go to http://mitpress.mit.edu/westhoffeconometrics and select MLB Hitter Salaries—2011.]

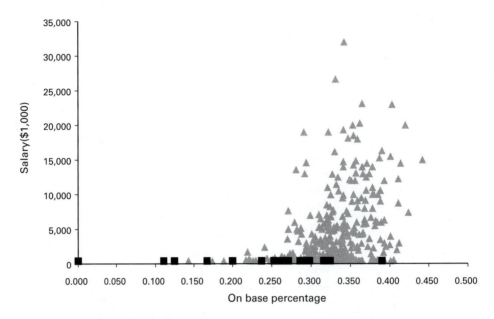

Figure 24.10
Scatter diagram—On base percentage versus salary

Table 24.11
OLS regression results—MLB salaries

Ordinary least squares (OLS)				
Dependent variable: *Salary*				
Explanatory variable(s):	Estimate	SE	*t*-Statistic	Prob
OnBasePct	37,964.84	4,885.038	7.771657	0.0000
Const	−8,372.006	1,593.313	−5.254463	0.0000
Number of observations	401			

Estimated equation: $EstSalary = -8{,}370 + 37{,}960 OnBasePct$

Interpretation of estimates:

$b_{OnBasePct} = 37{,}960$: A 0.001 point increase in on base percentage increases salary by $37,960

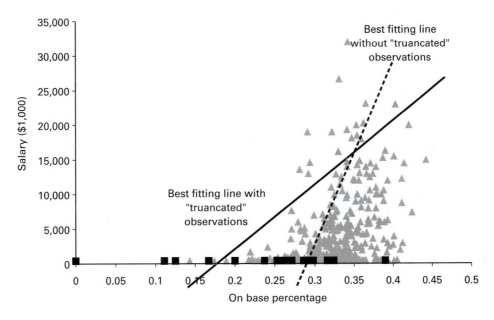

Figure 24.11
Scatter diagram—On base percentage versus salary and best fitting lines

24.3.1 Ordinary Least Squares (OLS) Estimation Procedure

The ordinary least squares (OLS) estimates suggest that a 0.001 point increase in on base percentage increases salary by $37,960. This in fact understates the actual effect of on base percentage, how salaries would be affected by on base percentage if Major League Baseball would not be artificially constrained by the $414,000 minimum salary (figure 24.11). Without baseball's minimum wage, it is reasonable to believe that the "truncated" points would be lower and, consequently, the best filling line would be steeper.

24.3.2 Tobit Estimation Procedure

The Tobit estimation procedure accounts for the truncation of the dependent variable. It takes advantage of all the available information, but treats "truncated" observations differently than the "nontruncated" ones (table 24.12). While we will not delve into the mathematics underlying the Tobit estimation procedure, we will show that software packages allow us to apply the procedure easily.

Table 24.12
Tobit results—MLB salaries

	Tobit			
Dependent variable: *Salary*				
Explanatory variable(s):	Estimate	SE	*z*-Statistic	Prob
OnBasePct	47,800.87	5,502.369	8.687325	0.0000
Const	−11,732.32	1,802.921	−6.507397	0.0000
Number of observations	401			
Left (lower) censoring value	414			

Estimated equation: *EstSalary* = −11,730 + 47,800*OnBasePct*

Interpretation of estimates:

$b_{OnBasePct}$ = 47,800: A 0.001 point increase in on base percentage increases salary by $47,800

Table 24.13
Comparison of ordinary least squares (OLS) and tobit results

Estimation procedure	Estimate of β_{OBP}
OLS	37,960
Tobit	47,800

Getting Started in EViews

- As usual, select the dependent and explanatory variables and then double click on one of the selected variables.

- In the Equation Estimation window, click on the **Method** dropdown list;

- Select **CENSORED**.

- By default, the left (lower) censoring value is 0. This value should be changed to 414, the minimum wage, for Major League players.

- Click **OK**.

[To access this online material, go to http://mitpress.mit.edu/westhoffeconometrics and select MLB Hitter Salaries—2011.]

Now let us compare the two estimates (table 24.13). The Tobit estimate of the *OnBasePct* coefficient is 47,800 as opposed to the ordinary least squares (OLS) estimate of 37,960. This is consistent with the scatter diagram appearing in figure 24.11.

Chapter 24 Review Questions

1. How do we interpret the dependent variable when it is a binary (dummy) variable?

2. What problem arises with the ordinary least squares (OLS) estimation procedure when the dependent variable is a binary variable? Explain.

3. Does the probit estimation procedure address the problem that arises with the ordinary least squares (OLS) estimation procedure when the dependent variable is a binary variable? Explain.

4. What problem can arise with the ordinary least squares (OLS) estimation procedure when the dependent variable is truncated?

Chapter 24 Exercises

2004 Electoral College data: Cross-sectional data from the 2004 presidential election for the fifty states.

$PopDen_t$ Population density of state t in 2004 (persons per square mile)

$Unem_t$ Unemployment rate in 2004 of state t (percent)

$WinDem1_t$ 1 if Democrats won state t in 2004; 0 if Republicans won state t

Generate a new variable, $WinRep1_t$:

$WinRep1_t = 1$ if Republicans won state t in 2004

$\qquad = 0$ if Democrats won state t

1. Consider the following model explaining the winning party in each state:

Model: $WinRep1_t = \beta_{Const} + \beta_{Den}PopDen_t + e_t$

a. Develop a theory regarding how population density influences the probability of a Republican victory. What does your theory imply about the sign of population density coefficient?

b. Using the ordinary least squares (OLS) estimation procedure, estimate the value of the population density coefficient using the 2004 Electoral College data. Interpret the coefficient estimates. What is the critical result?

[To access this online material, go to http://mitpress.mit.edu/westhoffeconometrics and select Electoral College—2004.]

c. Formulate the null and alternative hypotheses.

d. Calculate Prob[Results IF H_0 true] and assess your theory.

e. Compare the ordinary least squares (OLS) equation we computed earlier in the chapter estimating *WinDem1* with the equation you just computed estimating *WinRep1*. Are these two equations consistent? That is, do the two equations suggest that the effect of population density on the winning party in a state is the same? Explain.

2. Use the probit estimation procedure to analyze the effect that *PopDen* has on *WinRep1*. Compare the probit estimates we computed earlier in the chapter estimating *WinDem1* with the probit estimates you just computed estimating *WinRep1*. Are the estimates consistent?

2008 Electoral College data: Cross-sectional data from the 2008 presidential election for the fifty states.

PopDen$_t$ Population density of state t in 2008 (persons per square mile)

Unem2007$_t$ Unemployment rate in 2007 of state t (percent)

Unem2008$_t$ Unemployment rate in 2008 of state t (percent)

UnemTrend$_t$ Unemployment rate trend state t (percent); that is, *Unem2008$_t$* − *Unem2007$_t$*

WinDem1$_t$ 1 if Democrats won state t in 2008; 0 if Republicans won state t

3. Use the probit estimation procedure to analyze the effect of population density in the 2008 presidential election. For the moment, assume that population density is the only explanatory variable affecting the election results.

    a. Use the probit estimation procedure to find the maximum likelihood transformation. What is the critical result?

[To access this online material, go to http://mitpress.mit.edu/westhoffeconometrics and select Electoral College—2008.]

    b. Formulate the null and alternative hypotheses.

    c. Calculate Prob[Results IF H$_0$ true] and assess your theory.

4. Use the probit estimation procedure to analyze the effect of the unemployment trend in the 2008 presidential election. Suppose that the unemployment trend, rather than population density, is the only explanatory variable affecting the election results.

    a. Develop a theory regarding how the unemployment trend influences the probability of a Democratic victory.

    b. Use the probit estimation procedure to find the maximum likelihood transformation. What is the critical result?

[To access this online material, go to http://mitpress.mit.edu/westhoffeconometrics and select Electoral College—2008.]

    c. Formulate the null and alternative hypotheses.

    d. Calculate Prob[Results IF H$_0$ true] and assess your theory.

5. Use the probit estimation procedure to analyze the effect of both the population density and the unemployment trend in the 2008 presidential election in a single model.

   a. Use the probit estimation procedure to find the maximum likelihood transformation. What is the critical result?

[To access this online material, go to http://mitpress.mit.edu/westhoffeconometrics and select Electoral College—2008.]

Compare your probit estimates in exercises 3 and 4 with the ones you just computed.

   b. Are the critical results the same?

   c. How do the estimate values and their significances differ?

Degree day and temperature data for Charlestown, SC: Daily time series data of degree days and high temperatures for Charlestown, SC, in 2001.

$HeatDegDays_t$ Number of heating degree days on day t (degrees Fahrenheit)

$HighTemp_t$ High temperature on day t (degrees Fahrenheit)

Heating degree days only consider those days in which heat is required; that is, when temperatures are high and cooling rather than heating is required, the value of heating degree days is 0. Consequently heating degree days is a truncated or censored variable—truncated at 0.

Consider the following model:

Model: $HeatDegDays_t = \beta_{Const} + \beta_{HT}HighTemp_t$

6. Devise a theory to explain the number of degree days based on the high temperature. What does your theory suggest about the sight of the coefficient for $HighTemp$?

7. Construct a scatter diagram to illustrate the relationship between $HighTemp$ and $HeatDegDays$ by plotting $HighTemp$ on the horizontal axis and $HeatDegDays$ on the vertical axis. Does the scatter diagram lend support to your theory?

[To access this online material, go to http://mitpress.mit.edu/westhoffeconometrics and select Charleston SC Degree Days.]

8. Use the ordinary least squares (OLS) estimation procedure to analyze the effect of the high temperature on heating degree days.

[To access this online material, go to http://mitpress.mit.edu/westhoffeconometrics and select Charleston SC Degree Days.]

   a. Estimate the value of the high temperature coefficient. Interpret the coefficient estimate. What is the critical result?

   b. Formulate the null and alternative hypotheses.

c. Calculate Prob[Results IF H_0 true] and assess your theory.

9. Use the Tobit estimation procedure to estimate the model's parameters.

[To access this online material, go to http://mitpress.mit.edu/westhoffeconometrics and select Charleston SC Degree Days.]

a. How do the ordinary least squares (OLS) and the Tobit estimates differ?

b. Explain these results.

25 Descriptive Statistics, Probability, and Random Variables—A Closer Look

Chapter 25 Outline

Chapter 25 Prep Questions

1. Consider a deck of cards that contains only 3 red cards and 2 black cards.

   a. Draw one card from the deck. What is the probability that the card drawn is

      i. red?

      ii. black?

   b. Do not replace the first card drawn. Draw a second card from the deck. If the first card drawn is red, what is the probability that the second card drawn is

      i. red?

      ii. black?

   c. If the first card drawn is black, what is the probability that the second card drawn is

      i. red?

      ii. black?

2. Monty Hall was the host of the popular TV game show "Let's Make a Deal." Use our lab to familiarize yourself with the game.

[To access this online material, go to http://mitpress.mit.edu/westhoffeconometrics and select Lab 25P.2.]

Click **Play** and follow the instructions. Play the game a dozen times or so. How frequently did you win?

3. Let v be a discrete random variable.

   a. What is the equation for the mean of v, Mean[v]?

   b. What is the equation for the variance of v, Var[v]?

4. In words, what does it mean for two random variables to be independent?

25.1   Descriptive Statistics: Other Measures of the Distribution Center

In chapter 1 we introduced the mean as a measure of the distribution center. While the mean is the most commonly cited measure of the center, two others are also useful: mode and median. We will now introduce them by considering the distribution of American family sizes. Table 25.1 provides data for the sizes of American families in 2008. We begin by constructing a histogram to illustrate the data visually (figure 25.1).

In total, there were approximately 224,703,000 adult Americans in 2008. The mean family size for American adults in 2008 was 2.76. Now we will introduce two other measures of the distribution center, the mode and the median.

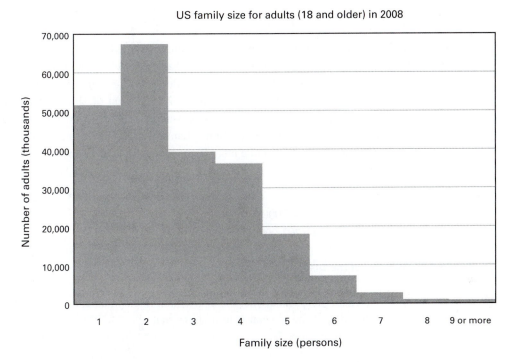

Figure 25.1
Histogram of family size—2008

Table 25.1
Family sizes—2008

Family size (persons)	Number of adults (thousands)	Percent of adults (%)
1	51,565	22.9
2	67,347	30.0
3	39,432	17.5
4	36,376	16.2
5	18,074	8.0
6	7,198	3.2
7	2,784	1.2
8	1,028	0.5
9 or more	899	0.4

Source: *US Census Bureau Current Population Survey, Annual Social and Economic Supplement, 2008*

25.1.1   Measure of the Distribution Center: Mode

The **mode** is the most frequently occurring data value. It is easy to determine the mode from the histogram; the mode corresponds to the highest bar. In our case, the mode is 2 persons. As table 25.1 reports, 30.0 percent of all American adults were members of two person families. The second most frequent was one person families; 20.5 percent of all American adults were members of one person families. If you chose one American adult at random, he/she would be more likely to be a member of a two person family than any other family size. Be aware, however, that while a family size of two would be more likely than any other family size, the probability that a randomly selected adult would be a member of a two person family would be less than one-half, only 0.30:

$$\text{Prob[Family size} = 2] = \frac{67,347,000}{244,703,000} = 0.30$$

25.1.2   Measure of the Distribution Center: Median

The **median** is the data value that divides the distribution in the middle, that is, into two "equal" parts. One way to think of the median is to imagine that all 224,703,000 American adults are lined up in order of increasing family size. The median family size is the family size of the 112,351,500th American in the line, the American in the middle (figure 25.2).

In 2008 the median family size was 2. At least half (22.9 + 30.0 = 52.9 percent) of all American adults were members of families including 2 or fewer persons and at least half (30.0 + 17.5 + 16.2 + 13.3 = 77.0 percent) were members of families including 2 or more persons.

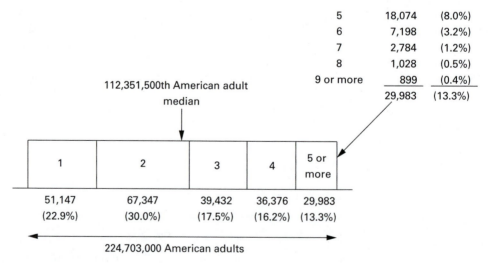

Figure 25.2
Americans adults lined up in order of family size

Table 25.2
Preferred level of aid assumption

Number of persons in family	Preferred level of federal aid per family (dollars)	Percent of adults (%)
1	$2,000	22.9
2	4,000	30.0
3	6,000	17.5
4	8,000	16.2
5	10,000	8.0
6	12,000	3.2
7	14,000	1.2
8	16,000	0.5
9 or more	18,000	0.4

The median voter theorem provides one example of how important the median can be. To appreciate why, suppose that each family's preferred level of federal aid for education depends on its size. To make this illustration more concrete, assume that table 25.2 reports on the preferred level of Federal aid for each family size. While these preferred aid numbers are hypothetical, they do attempt to capture one realistic feature of family preferences. That is, as a family has more children, it typically supports more aid for education because the family will gain more benefits from that aid.

The median voter theorem states that in a majority rule voting process, the preferences of the median voter, the voter in the middle, will win whenever the median's preference is pitted against any other alternative. In this case, the preferences of the 2 person family, the median, will win. The preferred aid level of the median voter, $4,000, will win. To understand why, we will consider two elections, one in which $4,000 is pitted against a proposal greater than $4,000 and a second in which $4,000 is pitted against a proposal that is less than $4,000.

• **$4,000 versus a proposal greater than $4,000:** Suppose that the median voter's choice, $4,000, is pitted against a proposal that is greater than $4,000. Clearly, all adult members of 2 person families will vote for $4,000 since $4,000 is their preferred choice. Although $4,000 is not the preferred choice of 1 person families, $4,000 is closer to their preferred $2,000 choice than a proposal that is greater than $4,000. Hence adult members of 1 person families will vote for $4,000 also. Now let us count the votes. Adult members of 1 and 2 person families will vote for $4,000 which constitutes a majority of the votes, 52.9 percent to be exact. $4,000 will defeat any proposal that is greater than $4,000.

• **$4,000 versus a proposal less than $4,000:** Suppose that the median voter's choice, $4,000, is pitted against a proposal that is less than $4,000. As before, all adult members of 2 person families will vote for $4,000 since $4,000 is their preferred choice. Although $4,000 is not the preferred choice of 3, 4, 5, 6, 7, 8, and 9 or more person families, $4,000 is closer to their preferred choice than a proposal that is less than $4,000. Hence adult members of these families will vote for $4,000 also. Adult members of 2, 3, 4, 5, 6, 7, 8, and 9 or more person families will vote for $4,000, which constitutes a majority of the votes, 77.0 percent to be exact. $4,000 will defeat any proposal that is less than $4,000.

The median family's preferred level of aid, $4,000, will defeat any proposal that is greater than $4,000 and any proposal that is less.

25.1.3   Relationship between the Mean and Median

Recall that the mean is the average. The mean describes the average characteristic of the population. For example, per capita income describes the income earned by individuals on average; batting average describes the hits per official at bat a baseball player gets. In our family size example, the mean equals 2.76. On average, the typical American adult resides in a family of 2.76 persons.

For our family size example, the median, 2, was less than the mean, 2.76. To understand why this occurs look at the histogram again. Its right-hand tail is longer than its left-hand tail. When we calculate the median, we find that a family of 4 persons has the same impact as a family of 9. If suddenly quintuples were born to a family of 4, making it a family of 9, the median would not be affected. However, the mean would be affected. With the birth of the quintuples, the mean would rise. Consequently, since the right-hand tail of the distribution is longer than the left-hand tail, the mean is greater than the median because the high values have a greater impact on the mean than they do on the median.

25.2   Event Trees: A Tool to Calculate Probabilities

Event trees are simple but useful tools we can employ to calculate probabilities. We will use the following experiment to introduce event trees:

Experiment 25.1: A Standard Deck of 52 Cards

- Shuffle the 52 cards thoroughly.
- Draw one card and record its color—red or black.
- Replace the card.

An event tree visually illustrates the mutually exclusive outcomes (events) of a random process. In figure 25.3 there are two such outcomes: either the card is red or it is black. The circle represents the event of the random process, the card draw. There are two branches from the circle: one representing a red card and one a black card. The ends of the two branches represent mutually exclusive events—two events that cannot occur simultaneously. A card cannot

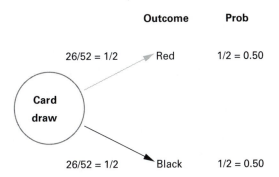

Figure 25.3
Card draw event tree for one draw

be both red and black. The event tree reports the probabilities of a red or black card. The "standard" deck of cards contains 13 spades, 13 hearts, 13 diamonds, and 13 clubs. 26 of the 52 cards are red, the hearts and diamonds; 26 of the 52 cards are black, the spades and clubs.

• What are the chances the card drawn will be red? Since 26 of the 52 cards are red, there are 26 chances in 52 or 1 chance in 2 that the card will be red. The probability that the card will be red equals 26/52 or 1/2.

• What are the chances the card drawn will be black? Similarly, since 26 of the 52 cards are black, there are 26 chances in 52 or 1 chance in 2 that the card will be black. The probability that the card will be black is 26/52 or 1/2.

The probability is 1/2 that we will move along the red branch and 1/2 that we will move along the black branch.

There are two important features of this event tree that are worth noting. First, we can only wind up at the end of one of the branches because the card drawn cannot be both red and black; stated more formally, red and black are mutually exclusive events. Second, we must wind up at the end of one branch because the card drawn must be either red or black. This means that the probabilities of the branch ends must sum to 1.0. We have now introduced the general characteristics of event trees:

• We cannot wind up at the end of more than one event tree branch; consequently the ends of each event tree branch represent mutually exclusive events.

• We must wind up at the end of one event tree branch; consequently the sum of the probabilities of the event tree branches equals 1.0.

Econometrics Lab 25.1: Card Draw Simulation—A Standard Deck of 52 Cards

The Card Draw simulation permits us to study this experiment.

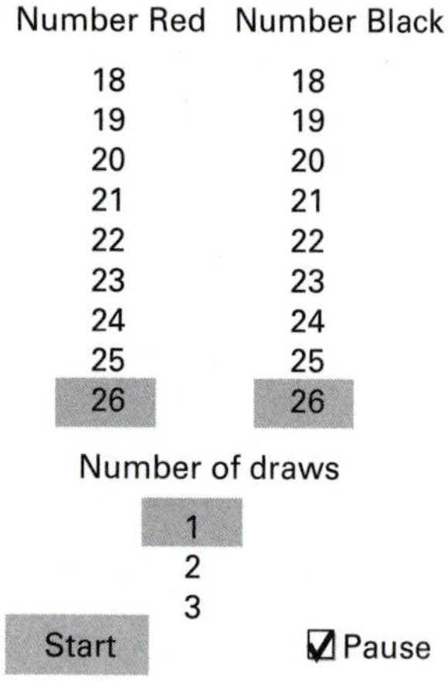

Number Red   Number Black

Number Red	Number Black
18	18
19	19
20	20
21	21
22	22
23	23
24	24
25	25
26	26

Number of draws

1
2
3

Start   ☑ Pause

Figure 25.4
Card Draw simulation

[To access this online material, go to http://mitpress.mit.edu/westhoffeconometrics and select Lab 25.1.]

In the simulation we select the number of red cards and the number of black cards to include in our deck. We can also specify the number of cards to be drawn from the deck. In this case, we include 26 red cards and 26 black cards in the deck; we draw one card from the deck. The relative frequencies of red and black cards are reported. Since the Pause checkbox is checked, the simulation will pause after each repetition. Click **Start**. Was a red or black card drawn? Now the Start button becomes the Continue button. Click **Continue** to run the second repetition. Is the simulation calculating the relative frequency of red and black cards correctly? Click the Continue button a few more times to convince yourself that the simulation is calculating relative frequencies correctly. Now uncheck the Pause checkbox and click **Continue**. After many, many repetitions, click **Stop**. Observe that the relative frequencies of red and black cards will be about 0.500, equal to the probabilities. The simulation illustrates the relative frequency interpretation of probability (figure 25.4):

Relative frequency interpretation of probability: When the experiment is repeated many, many times, the relative frequency of an outcome equals its probability.

We now wish to illustrate the usefulness of event trees when analyzing more complicated random processes. Unfortunately, the arithmetic can become cumbersome when experimenting with a standard deck of 52 cards. To keep the arithmetic straightforward, we will proceed with a smaller deck of cards, a nonstandard deck of cards consisting of only 3 red cards and 2 black cards.

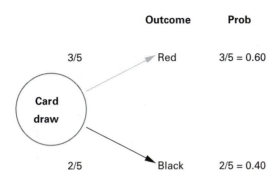

Figure 25.5
Card draw event tree for one draw

Experiment 25.2: A Deck of 5 Cards—3 Red Cards and 2 Black Cards

- Shuffle the 5 cards thoroughly.
- Draw one card and record its color—red or black.
- Replace the card.

Since 3 of the 5 cards are red, the probability of drawing a red card is 3/5; since 2 of the 5 cards are black, the probability of drawing a black card is 2/5. Like our first card draw, the new event tree possesses two properties (figure 25.5):

- We cannot wind up at the end of more than one event tree branch; consequently the ends of each event tree branch represent mutually exclusive events.
- We must wind up at the end of one event tree branch; consequently the sum of the probabilities of the event tree branches equals 1.0.

Econometrics Lab 25.2: Card Draw Simulation—Draw One Card from a Deck of 3 Red Cards and 2 Black Cards

Again, we will use a simulation this experiment to illustrate the relative frequency notion of probability.

[To access this online material, go to http://mitpress.mit.edu/westhoffeconometrics and select Lab 25.2.]

By default, the deck includes 3 red cards and 2 black cards. Click **Start** and then after many, many repetitions click **Stop**. The relative frequency of red cards is about 0.600 and the relative frequency of black card is about 0.400. Once again, see that the probabilities we calculated equal the relative frequencies when the experiment is repeated many times (figure 25.6).

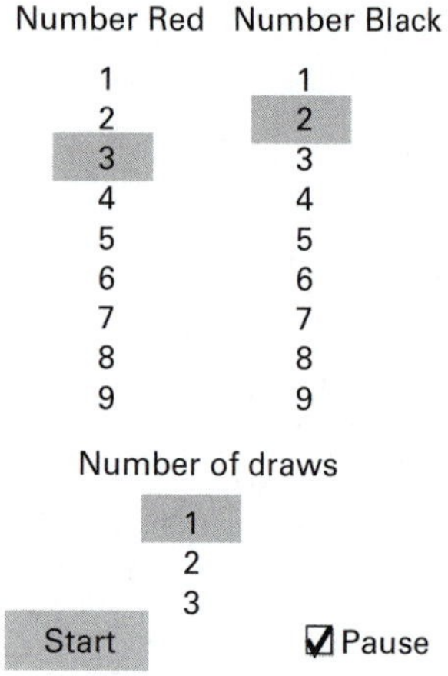

Number Red   Number Black

1   1
2   2
3   3
4   4
5   5
6   6
7   7
8   8
9   9

Number of draws

1
2
3

Start   ☑ Pause

Figure 25.6
Card Draw simulation

Experiment 25.3: Card Draw Simulation—Draw Two Cards from a Deck of 3 Red Cards and 2 Black Cards without Replacement

Thus far we have been only drawing one card from the deck. Now consider an experiment in which we draw two cards from our small deck.

- Shuffle the 5 cards thoroughly.
- Draw one card and record its color—red or black.
- Do not replace the card.
- Draw a second card and record its color—red or black.
- Replace both cards.

The event tree now looks a little more complicated because it must illustrate both the first and second draws (figure 25.7).

   Since the first card drawn is not replaced, the probabilities of obtaining a red and black card on the second draw depend on whether a red or black card was drawn on the first draw. If a red card is drawn on the first draw, two red cards and two black cards remain in the deck; consequently on the second draw

- there are two chances in four of drawing a red card. The probability of drawing a red card is 1/2:

$$\text{Prob}[\text{2nd is red IF 1st is red}] = \frac{1}{2} = 0.50$$

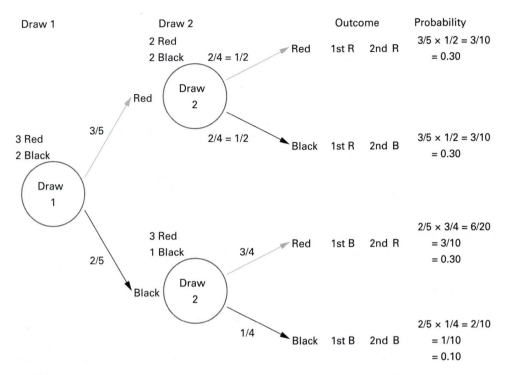

Draw 1

Draw 2

Outcome

Probability

2 Red
2 Black   2/4 = 1/2   →Red   1st R   2nd R   3/5 × 1/2 = 3/10
= 0.30

Draw
2

Red

3/5

2/4 = 1/2   →Black   1st R   2nd B   3/5 × 1/2 = 3/10
= 0.30

3 Red
2 Black

Draw
1

2/5

3 Red
1 Black   3/4   →Red   1st B   2nd R   2/5 × 3/4 = 6/20
= 3/10
= 0.30

Black   Draw
2

1/4   →Black   1st B   2nd B   2/5 × 1/4 = 2/10
= 1/10
= 0.10

Figure 25.7
Card draw event tree for two draws

- there are two chances in four of drawing a black card. The probability of drawing a black card is 1/2:

$$\text{Prob}[2\text{nd is red IF 1st is black}] = \frac{1}{2} = 0.50$$

If a black card is drawn on the first draw, 3 red cards and 1 black card remain in the deck; consequently on the second draw

- there are three chances in four of drawing a red card. The probability of drawing a red card is 3/4:

$$\text{Prob}[2\text{nd is red IF 1st is black}] = \frac{3}{4} = 0.75$$

- there is one chance in four of drawing a black card. The probability of drawing a black card is 1/4:

$$\text{Prob}[2\text{nd is red IF 1st is red}] = \frac{1}{4} = 0.25$$

After the two draws are complete, there are four possible outcomes (events) as indicated by the end of each event tree branch:

- A red card in the first draw and a red card in the second draw.
- A red card in the first draw and a black card in the second draw.
- A black card in the first draw and a red card in the second draw.
- A black card in the first draw and a black card in the second draw.

These four outcomes (events) are mutually exclusive. The probability of winding up at the end of a branch equals the product of the probabilities of each limb of the branch.

For example, consider Prob[1st is red AND is 2nd red] by focusing on the top branch of the event tree:

Prob[1st is red AND 2nd is red]

$$= \text{Prob}[\text{1st is red}] \times \text{Prob}[\text{2nd is red IF 1st is red}]$$

$$= \frac{3}{5} \times \frac{1}{2}$$

$$= \frac{3}{5} \times \frac{1}{2} = \frac{3}{10} = 0.30$$

As figure 25.7 indicates, when the first card is drawn there are 3 chances in 5 that we will move along the Draw 1 red limb; the probability of drawing a red card on the first draw is 3/5. Since the first card drawn is not replaced only 4 cards now remain, 2 of which are red. So there is 1 chance in 2 that we will continue along the Draw 1's Draw 2 red limb; if the first card drawn is a red card, the probability of drawing a red card on the second draw is 1/2. We will use the relative frequency interpretation of probability to confirm that the probability of a red card on the first draw and a red card on the second draw equals the product of these two probabilities. After many, many repetitions of the experiment:

- In the first draw, a red card will be drawn in 3/5 of the repetitions.
- For these repetitions, the repetitions in which a red card is drawn, a red card will be drawn in 1/2 of the second draws.
- Overall, a red card will be drawn in the first and second draws in $\frac{3}{5} \times \frac{1}{2} = \frac{3}{10} = 0.30$ of the repetitions.

Next consider Prob[1st is red AND 2nd is black] by focusing on the second branch from the top.

Prob[1st is red AND 2nd is black]

$$= \text{Prob}[\text{1st is red}] \times \text{Prob}[\text{2nd is red IF 1st is red}]$$

$$= \qquad \frac{3}{5} \qquad \times \qquad \frac{1}{2}$$

$$= \frac{3}{5} \times \frac{1}{2} = \frac{3}{10} = 0.30$$

The probability of a red card in the first draw is 3/5. Of the 4 cards now remaining, 2 are black. Therefore, the probability of a black card in the second draw is 1/2. The probability of a red card on the first draw and a black card on the second is the product of the two probabilities.

Using the same logic, we can calculate the probability of winding up at the end of the other two event tree branches:

Prob[1st is black AND 2nd is red]

$$= \text{Prob}[\text{1st is black}] \times \text{Prob}[\text{2nd is red IF 1st is black}]$$

$$= \qquad \frac{2}{5} \qquad \times \qquad \frac{3}{4}$$

$$= \frac{2}{5} \times \frac{3}{4} = \frac{3}{10} = 0.30$$

and

Prob[1st is black AND 2nd is black]

$$= \text{Prob}[\text{1st is black}] \times \text{Prob}[\text{2nd is black IF 1st is black}]$$

$$= \qquad \frac{2}{5} \qquad \times \qquad \frac{1}{4}$$

$$= \frac{2}{5} \times \frac{1}{4} = \frac{1}{10} = 0.10$$

Once again, note that our new event tree exhibits the general event tree properties:

• We cannot wind up at the end of more than one event tree branch; consequently the ends of each event tree branch represent mutually exclusive events.

• We must wind up at the end of one event tree branch; consequently the sum of the probabilities of the event tree branches equals 1.

Econometrics Lab 25.3: Card Draw Simulation—Draw Two Cards from a Deck of 3 Red Cards and 2 Black Cards without Replacement

We can use our Card Draw simulation to illustrate the relative frequency interpretation of probability.

[To access this online material, go to http://mitpress.mit.edu/westhoffeconometrics and select Lab 25.3.]

The relative frequency of each outcome mirrors the probability of that outcome.

25.3   Calculating the Probability of a Combination of Different Outcomes

Event trees facilitate the calculation of a combination of different outcomes. Since the ends of each event tree branch represent mutually exclusive events, we add the probabilities of each outcome. For example, suppose that we want to calculate the probability that a black card is drawn on the second draw. As the event tree in figure 25.7 illustrates, there are two different ways of this event occurring:

• A red card could be drawn on the first draw.
• A black card could be drawn on the first draw.

Focusing on the second and fourth event tree branches from the top:

Prob[2nd is black]

   = Prob[1st is red AND 2nd is black] + Prob[1st is black AND 2nd is black]

   =   0.30   + 0.10

   =   0.40

The probability of drawing a black card on the second draw equals 0.40.

Similarly we can calculate the probability that the second card drawn is red by focusing on the first and third event tree branches from the top:

Prob[2nd is red]

   = Prob[1st is red AND 2nd is red] + Prob[1st is black AND 2nd is red]

   =   0.30   + 0.30

   =   0.60

The probability of drawing a red card on the second draw equals 0.60.

Similarly suppose that we wish to know the probability of drawing two reds cards or two black cards:

Prob[2 reds OR 2 blacks]

   = Prob[1st is red AND 2nd is red] + Prob[1st is black AND 2nd is black]

   =   0.30   + 0.10

   =   0.40

The probability of drawing two reds cards or two black cards equals 0.40. We simply sum the probabilities of the appropriate branch ends.

25.4 Nonconditional, Joint, and Conditional Probabilities

It is important to distinguish between conditional, joint, and nonconditional probabilities:

- **Conditional probability:**   The probability that an event will occur if another event occurs.
- **Joint probability:**   The probability that two events will occur together.
- **Nonconditional probability:**   The probability that an event will occur without any information about other events.

To understand the distinction better, consider our last experiment and two possible events:

- Drawing a black card on the first draw: 1st is black.
- Drawing a red card on the second draw: 2nd is red.

The probability that the second card will be red if the first card is black, Prob[2nd is red IF 1st is black], is a conditional probability. The probability that first card is black and the second card is red, Prob[1st is black AND 2nd is red], is a joint probability. The probability of drawing a red card on the second draw without any additional information, Prob[2nd is red], is a nonconditional probability.

We have already computed these probabilities by using the event tree appearing in figure 25.7:

$$\text{Conditional probability: } \text{Prob}\left[\text{2nd is red IF 1st is black}\right] = \frac{3}{4} = 0.75$$

$$\text{Joint probability: } \text{Prob}\left[\text{1st is black AND 2nd is red}\right] = \frac{3}{10} = 0.30$$

Nonconditional probability: Prob[2nd is red] = 0.60

Event trees are useful because they facilitate the calculation of all three types of probabilities. First, event trees report the conditional probabilities and then the joint probabilities. Then, since the ends of the branches represent mutually exclusive events, we can compute the nonconditional probabilities by summing the joint probabilities. Table 25.3 summarizes all three types of probabilities.

25.5 Conditional/Joint Probability Relationship

The joint, conditional, and nonconditional probabilities are related. We have in fact already used this relationship to calculate the probabilities:

Table 25.3
Conditional, joint, and nonconditional probabilities without replacement

Conditional probabilities	Joint probabilitites	Nonconditional probabilities
Prob[2nd R IF 1st R] = $\frac{1}{2}$ = 0.50	Prob[1st R AND 2nd R] = $\frac{3}{10}$ = 0.30	Prob[1st R] = $\frac{3}{5}$ = 0.60
Prob[2nd B IF 1st R] = $\frac{1}{2}$ = 0.50	Prob[1st R AND 2nd B] = $\frac{3}{10}$ = 0.30	Prob[2nd R] = $\frac{3}{5}$ = 0.60
Prob[2nd R IF 1st B] = $\frac{3}{4}$ = 0.75	Prob[1st B AND 2nd R] = $\frac{3}{10}$ = 0.30	Prob[1st B] = $\frac{2}{5}$ = 0.40
Prob[2nd B IF 1st B] = $\frac{1}{4}$ = 0.25	Prob[1st B AND 2nd B] = $\frac{1}{10}$ = 0.10	Prob[2nd B] = $\frac{2}{5}$ = 0.40

$$\text{Prob}\left[\text{1st is black AND 2nd is red}\right] = \text{Prob}\left[\text{1st is black}\right] \times \text{Prob}\left[\text{2nd is red IF 1st is black}\right]$$

$$= \quad \frac{2}{5} \quad \times \quad \frac{3}{4}$$

$$= \frac{2}{5} \times \frac{3}{4} = \frac{3}{10} = 0.30$$

The probability of drawing a black card on the first draw and a red card on the second draw equals the probability of drawing a black card on the first times the probability of drawing a red card on the second draw if black is drawn first.

We can generalize this relationship between joint and conditional probabilities by specifying events A and B as follows:

- A = Drawing a black card on the first draw: 1st is black.

- B = Drawing a red card on the second draw: 2nd is red.

Substituting A for 1st is black and B for 2nd is red:

Prob[1st is black AND 2nd is red] = Prob[1st is black] × Prob[2nd is red IF 1st is black]

$$\searrow \quad \swarrow \qquad\qquad \downarrow \qquad\qquad\qquad \searrow \quad \swarrow$$

$$\text{Prob}[A \text{ and } B] \quad = \quad \text{Prob}[A] \quad \times \quad \text{Prob}[B \text{ IF } A]$$

We can rewrite this equation in its more common form[1]:

$$\text{Prob}[B \text{ IF } A] = \frac{\text{Prob}[A \text{ AND } B]}{\text{Prob}[A]}$$

---

1. Frequently the following symbols are used instead of the words OR, AND, and IF:

- Prob[A OR B] can be denoted as Prob[$A \cup B$] .

- Prob[A AND B] can be denoted as Prob[$A \cap B$].

- Prob[A IF B] can be denoted as Prob[$A \mid B$].

25.6 The Monty Hall Problem: Mathematicians Eat "Humble Pie"

To illustrate the value of event trees and the conditional/joint probability relationship, consider a mathematical controversy that erupted in the popular press during 1990. The controversy involved the game show "Let's Make a Deal." On the show, a contestant is presented with three closed doors, numbered 1, 2, and 3. One of the doors has a valuable prize behind it. A "dud" is behind the other two doors. The real prize has been randomly placed behind one of the three doors. Monty Hall, the emcee, knows where the prize is located. Monty asks the contestant to choose one of the three doors after which he opens one of the three doors. In deciding which door to open, Monty adheres to two rules. He never opens the door that

- the contestant chose;

- contains the prize.

Monty always opens one of the doors containing a dud. He then gives the contestant the opportunity to change his/her mind and switch doors. Should the contestant stay with the door he/she chose initially or should the contestant switch?

In September 1990 Marilyn vos Salant, a columnist for *Parade Magazine*, wrote about the contestant's choice. She claimed that the contestant should always switch. This created a firestorm of ridicule from academic mathematicians, some of whom were on the faculty of this country's most prestigious institutions. *The New York Times* even reported the controversy on the front page of its Sunday, July 21, 1991, edition stating that several thousand letters criticized Ms. Salant's advice.[2] Two typical responses were:

- Robert Sachs, George Mason University: "You blew it! Let me explain: If one door is shown to be a loser, that information changes the probability of either remaining choice—neither of which has any reason to be more likely—to 1/2. As a professional mathematician, I'm very concerned with the general public's lack of mathematical skills. Please help by confessing your error and, in the future, being more careful."

- E. Ray Bobo, Georgetown University: "How many irate mathematicians are needed to get you to change your mind?"

Much to the embarrassment of many mathematicians, Ms. Salant's advice was eventually proved correct. One of them, Dr. Sachs, had the grace to apologize:

I wrote her another letter, telling her that after removing my foot from my mouth, I'm now eating humble pie. I vowed as penance to answer all the people who wrote to castigate me. It's been an intense professional embarrassment.

This incident teaches us a valuable lesson. As Persi Diaconis, a mathematician from Harvard University, stated: "Our brains are just not wired to do probability problems very well. . . ." That

---

2. John Tierney, *The New York Times,* Sunday, July 21, 1991, pp. 1 and 20.

is why event trees are so useful. We will now use event trees to analyze the Monty Hall problem and show how many mathematicians would have avoided embarrassment had they applied this simple, yet powerful tool.

Suppose that you are a contest appearing on the "Let's Make a Deal" stage. The prize has already been placed behind one of the doors. There is an equal chance of the prize being behind each door. The probability that it is behind any one door is one out of three, 1/3. We begin by drawing the event tree that appears in figure 25.8.

You now choose one of the doors. Suppose you choose door numbered 3. Recall Monty's rules: Monty never opens the door that

- the contestant choses;
- contains the prize.

Since you chose door 3, we do not have worry about Monty opening door 3 as a consequence of Monty's first rule. Monty will now open either door 1 or door 2. Keeping in mind Monty's second rule:

- If the prize is behind door 1, he would open door 2:

Prob[Monty opens door 1 IF prize behind door 1] = 0

Prob[Monty opens door 2 IF prize behind door 1] = 1

- If the prize is behind door 2, he would open door 1:

Prob[Monty opens door 1 IF prize behind door 2] = 1

Prob[Monty opens door 2 IF prize behind door 2] = 0

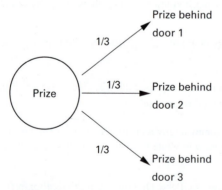

Figure 25.8
Event tree before you choose a door

• If the prize is behind door 3, he will randomly choose to open either door 1 or door 2; the chances are 50-50 he will open door 1 and 50-50 he will open door 2:

$$\text{Prob}[\text{Monty opens door 1 IF prize behind door 3}] = \frac{1}{2}$$

$$\text{Prob}[\text{Monty opens door 2 IF prize behind door 3}] = \frac{1}{2}$$

Figure 25.9 extends the event tree we drew in figure 25.8 to account for the fact that you chose door 3. Let us explain how we extended the top branch of the event tree. As shown in both figures 25.8 and 25.9, the probability that the prize is behind door 1 is 1/3. Now, if the prize is behind door 1, the probability that Monty will open door 1 is 0, and hence the probability that he will open door 2 is 1 as indicated in figure 25.9. Using similar logic, we can now extend the other branches.

Before opening a door Monty pauses for a commercial break so you have time to consider your strategy. Using the event tree, it is easy to calculate the joint probabilities. From top to bottom of figure 25.9:

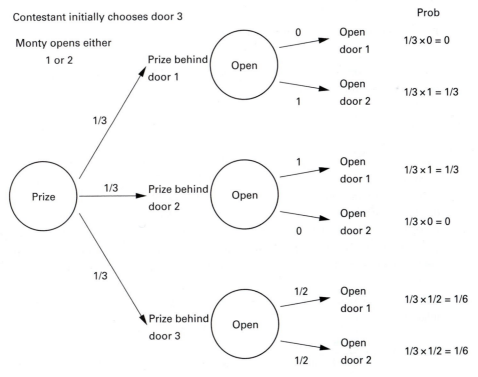

Figure 25.9
Event tree after you choose door 3

Prob[Monty opens door 1 AND Prize behind door 1] = 0

Prob[Monty opens door 2 AND Prize behind door 1] $= \dfrac{1}{3}$

Prob[Monty opens door 1 AND Prize behind door 2] $= \dfrac{1}{3}$

Prob[Monty opens door 2 AND Prize behind door 2] = 0

Prob[Monty opens door 1 AND Prize behind door 3] $= \dfrac{1}{6}$

Prob[Monty opens door 2 AND Prize behind door 3] $= \dfrac{1}{6}$

Also the event tree allows us to calculate the nonconditional probabilities of which door Monty will open. Since you choose door 3, Monty will open either door 1 or door 2:

• Prob[Monty opens door 1]:   Counting from the top of figure 25.9, focus on the ends of branches 1, 3, and 5:

$$\text{Prob[Monty opens door 1]} = 0 + \frac{1}{3} + \frac{1}{6} = \frac{1}{2}$$

• Prob[Monty opens door 2]:   Counting from the top of figure 25.9, focus on the ends of branches 2, 4, and 6:

$$\text{Prob[Monty opens door 2]} = \frac{1}{3} + 0 + \frac{1}{6} = \frac{1}{2}$$

Note that these two nonconditional probabilities sum to 1 because we know that Monty always opens one of the two doors that you did not choose.

Now we are in a position to give you some advice. We know that Monty will open door 1 or door 2 as soon as the commercial ends. First, consider the possibility that Monty opens door. 1. If so, door 1 will contain a dud. In this case the prize is either behind door 2 or door 3. We can calculate the probability that the prize is behind door 2 and the probability that the prize is behind door 3 if Monty were to open door 1 by applying the conditional/joint probability relationship:

• Prob[Prize behind door 2 IF Monty opens door 1]: Begin with the conditional/joint probability relationship

$$\text{Prob}[B \text{ IF } A] = \frac{\text{Prob}[A \text{ AND } B]}{\text{Prob}[A]}$$

We will apply this relationship by letting

A = Monty opens door 1

B = Prize behind door 2

Substituting Monty opens door 1 for A and Prize behind door 2 for B gives

Prob[Prize behind door 2 IF Monty opens door 1]

$$= \frac{\text{Prob[Monty opens door 1 AND Prize behind door 2]}}{\text{Prob[Monty opens door 1]}}$$

We have already calculated these probabilities with the help of the event tree:

$$\text{Prob[Monty opens door 1 AND Prize behind door 2]} = \frac{1}{3}$$

$$\text{Prob[Monty opens door 1]} = \frac{1}{2}$$

Now we plug in:

Prob[Prize behind door 2 IF Monty opens door 1]

$$= \frac{\text{Prob[Monty opens door 1 AND Prize behind door 2]}}{\text{Prob[Monty opens door 1]}}$$

$$= \frac{1/3}{1/2} = \frac{2}{3}$$

$$\text{Prob[Prize behind door 2 IF Monty opens door 1]} = \frac{2}{3}$$

• Prob[Prize behind door 3 IF Monty opens door 1]: We use the same logic. Begin with the conditional/joint probability relationship

$$\text{Prob}[B \text{ IF } A] = \frac{\text{Prob}[A \text{ AND } B]}{\text{Prob}[A]}$$

Next apply this relationship by letting

A = Monty opens door 1

B = Prize behind door 3

Substituting Monty opens door 1 for A and Prize behind door 3 for B gives

Prob[Prize behind door 3 IF Monty opens door 1]

$$= \frac{\text{Prob[Monty opens door 1 AND Prize behind door 3]}}{\text{Prob[Monty opens door 1]}}$$

We have already calculated these probabilities:

$$\text{Prob[Monty opens door 1 AND Prize behind door 3]} = \frac{1}{6}$$

$$\text{Prob[Monty opens door 1]} = \frac{1}{2}$$

Now we plug in:

Prob[Prize behind door 2 IF Monty opens door 1]

$$= \frac{\text{Prob[Monty opens door 1 AND Prize behind door 3]}}{\text{Prob[Monty opens door 1]}}$$

$$= \frac{1/6}{1/2} = \frac{1}{3}$$

$$\text{Prob[Prize behind door 3 IF Monty opens door 1]} = \frac{1}{3}$$

If Monty opens door 1 after you have chosen door 3,

the probability that the prize is behind door 2 is $\frac{2}{3}$ and

the probability that the prize is behind door 3 is $\frac{1}{3}$.

Therefore, if Monty opens door 1, you should switch from door 3 to door 2.

Next consider the possibility that Monty opens door 2. If so, door 2 will contain a dud. In this case the prize is either behind door 1 or door 3. We can calculate the probability that the prize is behind door 1 and the probability that the prize is behind door 3 if Monty were to open door 2 by applying the conditional/joint probability relationship:

• Prob[Prize behind door 1 IF Monty opens door 2]: Conditional/joint probability relationship

$$\text{Prob}[B \text{ IF } A] = \frac{\text{Prob}[A \text{ AND } B]}{\text{Prob}[A]}$$

We will apply this relationship by letting

A = Monty opens door 2

B = Prize behind door 1

By the same logic as before,

$$\text{Prob}[\text{Prize behind door 1 IF Monty opens door 2}] = \frac{2}{3}$$

• Calculating Prob[Prize behind door 3 IF Monty opens door 2]: Conditional/joint probability relationship

$$\text{Prob}[B \text{ IF } A] = \frac{\text{Prob}[A \text{ AND } B]}{\text{Prob}[A]}$$

We will apply this relationship by letting

A = Monty opens door 2

B = Prize behind door 3

By the same logic as before,

$$\text{Prob}[\text{Prize behind door 3 IF Monty opens door 2}] = \frac{1}{3}$$

If Monty opens door 2 after you have chosen door 3,

the probability that the prize is behind door 1 is $\frac{2}{3}$ and

the probability that the prize is behind door 3 is $\frac{1}{3}$.

Therefore, if Monty opens door 2, you should switch from door 3 to door 1.

So let us summarize. If Monty opens door 1, you should switch. If Monty opens door 2, you should switch. Regardless of which door Monty opens, you should switch doors. Ms. vos Salant is correct and all her academic critics should be eating "humble pie."

What is the intuition here? Before you make your initial choice, you know that the probability that the prize lies behind door 3 equals 1/3. Furthermore you know that after you make your choice, Monty will open neither the door you chose nor the door that contains the prize. Therefore, when Monty actually opens a door, you will be given no additional information that is relevant to door 3. Without any additional information about door 3, it should not affect the probability that the prize lies behind door 3. This is precisely what our calculations showed.

Econometrics Lab 25.4: Monty Hall Simulation

We will use a simulation to confirm our conclusion that switching is the better strategy.

[To access this online material, go to http://mitpress.mit.edu/westhoffeconometrics and select Lab 25.4.]

Click **Start Simulation** and then after many, many repetitions click **Stop**. The simulation reports the winning percentage for both the no switch and switch strategies. No switch winning frequency equals 0.3333 . . . and the switch winning percentages equals 0.6666. . . . The results are consistent with the probabilities that we just calculated.

25.7   Correlation

We begin with correlated events presenting both verbal and rigorous definitions. Then, we extend the notion of correlation to random variables.

25.7.1   Correlated Events

Definition
Two events are **correlated** whenever the occurrence of one event helps up predict the other; more specifically, two events are correlated when the occurrence of one event either increases or decreases the probability of the other. Formally, events A and B are correlated whenever

$$\text{Prob}[B \text{ IF } A] \neq \text{Prob}[B]$$

The conditional probability of an event B does not equal its nonconditional probability. When events A and B are correlated, event A is providing additional information that causes us to modify our assessment of event B's likelihood. To illustrate what we mean by correlation, review experiment 25.3:

Experiment 25.3: Card Draw Simulation—Draw Two Cards from a Deck of 3 Red Cards and 2 Black Cards without Replacement

- Shuffle the 5 cards thoroughly.
- Draw one card and record its color—red or black.
- Do not replace the card.
- Draw a second card and record its color—red or black.
- Replace both cards.

It is easy to show that the two events, second card drawn is red and first card drawn is black in experiment 25.3, are correlated. Refer to the event tree appearing in figure 25.7 to compute the nonconditional probability that the second card drawn is red. Since the ends of each event tree branch represent mutually exclusive events, we can calculate the combination of different outcomes by adding the probabilities of ending up at the appropriate branches. As the event tree in figure 25.7 illustrates, there are two different ways to draw a red card on the second draw:

• A red card could be drawn on the first draw: first is red.

• A black card could be drawn on the first draw: first is black.

Consequently the probability of drawing a red card on the second draw equals 0.60:

Prob[2nd is red] + Prob[1st is red AND 2nd is red] + Prob[1st is black AND 2nd is red]

$$= \qquad 0.30 \qquad + \qquad 0.30$$

$$= \qquad 0.60$$

Recall that the conditional probability of drawing a red card on the second draw if the first card drawn is black. As illustrated in figure 25.7,

$$\text{Prob}\left[\text{2nd is red IF 1st is black}\right] = \frac{3}{4} = 0.75$$

Consequently the conditional and nonconditional probabilities are not equal:

Prob[2nd is red IF 1st is black] ≠ Prob[2nd is red]

Therefore the events are correlated. This is intuitive, is it not? If we know that we have drawn a black card on the first draw and we do not replace it, there will be fewer black cards remaining in the deck. Consequently we will be more likely to draw a red card on the second draw.

Correlated Events and Joint Probability

When two events are correlated their joint probability will not equal the product of the nonconditional probabilities; that is, if A and B are correlated, then

Prob[A AND B] ≠ Prob[A] × Prob[B]

We can illustrate this with our example. We know that the events 1st is black and 2nd is red are correlated. Let

A = 1st is black, B = 2nd is red

Now let us review the probabilities:

Prob[1st is black AND 2nd is red] = 0.30

Prob[1st is black] = 0.40,   Prob[2nd is red] = 0.60

Prob[1st is black] × Prob[2nd is red] = 0.40 × 0.60 = 0.24

Clearly, 0.30 ≠ 0.24:

Prob[1st is black AND 2nd is red] ≠ Prob[1st is black] × Prob[2nd is red]

25.7.2   Correlated Random Variables and Covariance

We will now extend the notions of correlation to random variables. Continuing on with experiment 25.3, let

v_1 = number of black cards drawn in the first draw

v_2 = number of black cards drawn in the second draw

v_1 can take on two possible values, 0 and 1. Similarly v_2 can take on two possible values, 0 and 1.

Let us modify figure 25.7 by adding v_1 and v_2 to the event tree describing experiment 25.3 as shown in figure 25.10. Using the event tree, we can calculate the conditional, joint, and nonconditional probabilities for the random variables v_1 and v_2 (table 25.4). In the absence of

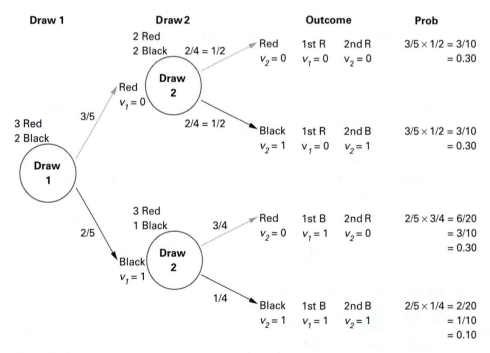

Figure 25.10
Event tree for two draws without replacement

Table 25.4
Conditional, joint, and nonconditional probabilities without replacement

Conditional probabilities	Joint probabilitites	Nonconditional probabilities
$\text{Prob}[v_2 = 0 \text{ IF } v_1 = 0] = \dfrac{1}{2} = 0.50$	$\text{Prob}[v_1 = 0 \text{ AND } v_2 = 0] = \dfrac{3}{10} = 0.30$	$\text{Prob}[v_1 = 0] = \dfrac{3}{5} = 0.60$
$\text{Prob}[v_2 = 1 \text{ IF } v_1 = 0] = \dfrac{1}{2} = 0.50$	$\text{Prob}[v_1 = 0 \text{ AND } v_2 = 1] = \dfrac{3}{10} = 0.30$	$\text{Prob}[v_2 = 0] = \dfrac{3}{5} = 0.60$
$\text{Prob}[v_2 = 0 \text{ IF } v_1 = 1] = \dfrac{3}{4} = 0.75$	$\text{Prob}[v_1 = 1 \text{ AND } v_2 = 0] = \dfrac{3}{10} = 0.30$	$\text{Prob}[v_1 = 1] = \dfrac{2}{5} = 0.40$
$\text{Prob}[v_2 = 1 \text{ IF } v_1 = 1] = \dfrac{1}{4} = 0.25$	$\text{Prob}[v_1 = 1 \text{ AND } v_2 = 1] = \dfrac{1}{10} = 0.10$	$\text{Prob}[v_2 = 1] = \dfrac{2}{5} = 0.40$

information about v_1, the nonconditional probabilities are relevant. The nonconditional probability that v_2 will equal

0 is 0.60: $\text{Prob}[v_2 = 0] = 0.60$

1 is 0.40: $\text{Prob}[v_2 = 1] = 0.40$

On the one hand, if we know that v_1 equals 0, the probabilities change; the conditional probability that v_2 will now equal

0 is 0.50: $\text{Prob}[v_2 = 0 \text{ IF } v_1 = 0] = 0.50$

1 is 0.50: $\text{Prob}[v_2 = 1 \text{ IF } v_1 = 0] = 0.50$

On the other hand, if we know that v_1 equals 1, the conditional probability that v_2 will now equal

0 is 0.75: $\text{Prob}[v_2 = 0 \text{ IF } v_1 = 1] = 0.75$

1 is 0.25: $\text{Prob}[v_2 = 1 \text{ IF } v_1 = 1] = 0.25$

The random variables v1 and v2 are correlated. Knowing the value of v1 helps us predict the value of v2 because the value of v1 affects v2's probability distribution. In this case, v1 and v2 are negatively correlated; an increase in the value of v1 from 0 to 1, increases the likelihood that v2 will be lower

$$v_1 = 0 \qquad \longrightarrow \qquad v_1 = 1$$

$\text{Prob}[v_2 = 0 \text{ IF } v_1 = 0] = 0.50 \qquad \text{Prob}[v_2 = 0 \text{ IF } v_1 = 1] = 0.75$

$\text{Prob}[v_2 = 1 \text{ IF } v_1 = 0] = 0.50 \qquad \text{Prob}[v_2 = 1 \text{ IF } v_1 = 1] = 0.25$

Now recall that covariance is a measure of correlation. If two variables are correlated, their covariance not equal 0. Let us now calculate the covariance of the random variables of v_1 and v_2 to illustrate this fact. The equation for the covariance is

$$\text{Cov}[v_1, v_2] = \sum_{\text{All } v_1} \sum_{\text{All } v_2} (v_1 - \text{Mean}[v_1])(v_2 - \text{Mean}[v_2])\text{Prob}[v_1 \text{ AND } v_2]$$

First, calculate the means of v_1 and v_2:

$$\text{Mean}[v_1] = \sum_{\text{All } v_1} v_1 \text{Prob}[v_1] \qquad\qquad \text{Mean}[v_2] = \sum_{\text{All } v_2} v_2 \text{Prob}[v_2]$$

$$= 0 \times 0.60 + 1 \times 0.40 \qquad\qquad\qquad = 0 \times 0.60 + 1 \times 0.40$$

$$= 0.4 \qquad\qquad\qquad\qquad\qquad\qquad = 0.4$$

Now, focusing on the equation for covariance, obtain

v_1	v_2	$(v_1 - \text{Mean}[v_1])$	$(v_2 - \text{Mean}[v_2])$	$\text{Prob}[v_1 \text{ AND } v_2]$	Product
0	0	$0 - 0.4 = -0.4$	$0 - 0.4 = -0.4$	0.30	$-0.4 \times -0.4 \times 0.30 = 0.0480$
0	1	$0 - 0.4 = -0.4$	$1 - 0.4 = 0.6$	0.30	$-0.4 \times 0.6 \times 0.30 = -0.0720$
1	0	$1 - 0.4 = 0.6$	$0 - 0.4 = -0.4$	0.30	$0.6 \times -0.4 \times 0.30 = -0.0720$
1	1	$1 - 0.4 = 0.6$	$1 - 0.4 = 0.6$	0.10	$0.6 \times 0.6 \times 0.10 = \underline{0.0360}$

$$\text{Cov}[v_1, v_2] = -0.0600$$

The covariance is negative because v_1 and v_2 are negatively correlated. An increase in v_1, increases the probability that v_2 will be lower.

25.8   Independence

As with correlation we begin with independent events presenting both verbal and rigorous definitions. Then we extend the notion of independence to random variables.

25.8.1 Independent Events

Definition
Two events are **independent** (uncorrelated) whenever the occurrence of one event does not help us predict the other. For example, the total points scored in the Super Bowl and the relative humidity in Santiago, Chile, on Super Bowl Sunday are independent events. Knowing the value of one would not help us predict the other. Two events are independent when the occurrence of one event does not affect the likelihood that the other event will occur. Formally, event B is independent of event A independent whenever

$$\text{Prob}[B \text{ IF } A] = \text{Prob}[B]$$

The occurrence of event A does not affect the chances that event B will occur.

Independence and Joint Probability
The joint probability of two independent events equals the product of the nonconditional probabilities:

If Prob[B IF A] = Prob[B], then Prob[A AND B] = Prob[A] $\times$ Prob[B]

To justify this, begin with the conditional/joint probability relationship:

$$\text{Prob}[B \text{ IF } A] = \frac{\text{Prob}[A \text{ AND } B]}{\text{Prob}[A]}$$

Multiply both sides of the equation by Prob[A]:

Prob[A] $\times$ Prob[B IF A] = Prob[A AND B]

$$\downarrow$$

Since B is independent of A, Prob[B IF A] = Prob[B]

Prob[A] $\times$ Prob[B] = Prob[A AND B]

Independent Events and Symmetry

The notion of independence is symmetric; when the probability of event B is unaffected by event A, the probability of event A is unaffected by event B:

If Prob[B IF A] = Prob[B], then Prob[A IF B] = Prob[A]

To justify this, apply the conditional/joint probability relationship to Prob[A IF B]:

$$\text{Prob}[A \text{ IF } B] = \frac{\text{Prob}[B \text{ AND } A]}{\text{Prob}[B]}$$

Prob[B AND A] = Prob[A AND B]

$$= \frac{\text{Prob}[A \text{ AND } B]}{\text{Prob}[B]}$$

Since Prob[B IF A] = Prob[B], Prob[A AND B] = Prob[A] $\times$ Prob[B]

$$= \frac{\text{Prob}[A] \times \text{Prob}[B]}{\text{Prob}[B]}$$

$$= \text{Prob}[A]$$

25.8.2   Independent Random Variables and Covariance

Two random variables are independent if the probability distribution of each is unaffected by the value of the other:

Prob[v_2 IF v_1] = Prob[v_2]

And hence, after applying the logic we used with independent events, the joint probability equals the product of the nonconditional probabilities:

$\text{Prob}[v_1 \text{ AND } v_2] = \text{Prob}[v_1] \times \text{Prob}[v_2]$

We can show that when two random variables are independent their covariance will equal 0:

$$\text{Cov}[v_1, v_2] = \sum_{\text{All } v_1} \sum_{\text{All } v_2} (v_1 - \text{Mean}[v_1])(v_2 - \text{Mean}[v_2])\text{Prob}[v_1 \text{ AND } v_2]$$

If v_1 and v_2 are independent,

$$= \sum_{\text{All } v_1} \sum_{\text{All } v_2} (v_1 - \text{Mean}[v_1])(v_2 - \text{Mean}[v_2])\text{Prob}[v_1] \times \text{Prob}[v_2]$$

Rearranging factors

$$= \sum_{\text{All } v_1} \sum_{\text{All } v_2} (v_1 - \text{Mean}[v_1])\text{Prob}[v_1] \times (v_2 - \text{Mean}[v_2])\text{Prob}[v_2]$$

Rearranging terms

$$= \sum_{\text{All } v_1} (v_1 - \text{Mean}[v_1])\text{Prob}[v_1] \times \sum_{\text{All } v_2} (v_2 - \text{Mean}[v_2])\text{Prob}[v_2]$$

Now focus on $\sum_{\text{All } v_2} (v_2 - \text{Mean}[v_2])\text{Prob}[v_2]$. By applying the equation for the mean, we can show that $\sum_{\text{All } v_2} (v_2 - \text{Mean}[v_2])\text{Prob}[v_2] = 0$:

$$\sum_{\text{All } v_2} (v_2 - \text{Mean}[v_2])\text{Prob}[v_2]$$

Simplifying algebra

$$= \sum_{\text{All } v_2} v_2 \text{Prob}[v_2] - \sum_{\text{All } v_2} \text{Mean}[v_2]\text{Prob}[v_2]$$

Simplifying algebra

$$= \sum_{\text{All } v_2} v_2 \text{Prob}[v_2] - \sum_{\text{All } v_2} \text{Mean}[v_2]\text{Prob}[v_2]$$

$$\downarrow \qquad\qquad\qquad\qquad\qquad \text{Mean}[v_2] = \sum_{\text{All } v_2} v_2 \text{Prob}[v_2]$$

$$= \text{Mean}[v_2] - \sum_{\text{All } v_2} \text{Mean}[v_2]\text{Prob}[v_2]$$

$$\downarrow \qquad\qquad\qquad\qquad\qquad \text{Simplifying algebra}$$

$$= \text{Mean}[v_2] - \text{Mean}[v_2]\sum_{\text{All } v_2} \text{Prob}[v_2]$$

$$\downarrow \qquad\qquad\qquad\qquad\qquad \sum_{\text{All } v_2} \text{Prob}[v_2] = 1$$

$$= \text{Mean}[v_2] - \text{Mean}[v_2]$$

$$= 0$$

Returning to the covariance equation:

$$\text{Cov}[v_1, v_2] = \sum_{\text{All } v_1} (v_1 - \text{Mean}[v_1])\text{Prob}[v_1] \times \sum_{\text{All } v_2} (v_2 - \text{Mean}[v_2])\text{Prob}[v_2]$$
$$= \sum_{\text{All } v_1} (v_1 - \text{Mean}[v_1])\text{Prob}[v_1] \times 0$$
$$= 0$$

We have shown that when the random variables v_1 and v_2 are independent their covariance equals 0.

To illustrate two independent random variables, let us modify experiment 25.3 by replacing the card drawn after the first draw:

Experiment 25.4: Card Draw Simulation—Draw Two Cards from a Deck of 3 Red Cards and 2 Black Cards with Replacement

- Shuffle the 5 cards thoroughly.
- Draw one card and record its color—red or black.
- Replace the card.
- Draw a second card and record its color—red or black.
- Replace the card.

As before, our random variable equals the number of black cards drawn:

v_1 = number of black cards drawn in the first draw

v_2 = number of black cards drawn in the second draw

v_1 can take on two possible values, 0 and 1. Similarly v_2 can take on two possible values, 0 and 1.

Let us begin by constructing the event tree (figure 25.11). Using the event tree, we can calculate the conditional, joint, and nonconditional probabilities for the random variables v_1 and v_2 (table 25.5). In the absence of information about v_1, the nonconditional probabilities are relevant; the nonconditional probability that v_2 will equal

0 is 0.60: $\text{Prob}[v_2 = 0] = 0.60$

1 is 0.40: $\text{Prob}[v_2 = 1] = 0.40$

But what happens if we know that v_1 equals 0? The conditional probabilities tell us that nothing changes. The probability that v_2 will equal

0 is 0.60: $\text{Prob}[v_2 = 0 \text{ IF } v_1 = 0] = 0.60$

1 is 0.40: $\text{Prob}[v_2 = 1 \text{ IF } v_1 = 0] = 0.40$

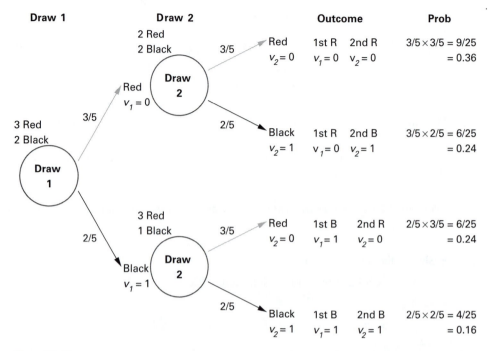

Figure 25.11
Event tree for two draws with replacement

Table 25.5
Conditional, joint, and nonconditional probabilities with replacement

Conditional probabilities	Joint probabilitites	Nonconditional probabilities
$\text{Prob}[v_2 = 0 \text{ IF } v_1 = 0] = \dfrac{3}{5} = 0.60$	$\text{Prob}[v_1 = 0 \text{ AND } v_2 = 0] = \dfrac{9}{25} = 0.36$	$\text{Prob}[v_1 = 0] = \dfrac{3}{5} = 0.60$
$\text{Prob}[v_2 = 1 \text{ IF } v_1 = 0] = \dfrac{2}{5} = 0.40$	$\text{Prob}[v_1 = 0 \text{ AND } v_2 = 1] = \dfrac{6}{25} = 0.24$	$\text{Prob}[v_2 = 0] = \dfrac{3}{5} = 0.60$
$\text{Prob}[v_2 = 0 \text{ IF } v_1 = 1] = \dfrac{3}{5} = 0.60$	$\text{Prob}[v_1 = 1 \text{ AND } v_2 = 0] = \dfrac{6}{25} = 0.24$	$\text{Prob}[v_1 = 1] = \dfrac{2}{5} = 0.40$
$\text{Prob}[v_2 = 1 \text{ IF } v_1 = 1] = \dfrac{2}{5} = 0.40$	$\text{Prob}[v_1 = 1 \text{ AND } v_2 = 1] = \dfrac{4}{25} = 0.16$	$\text{Prob}[v_2 = 1] = \dfrac{2}{5} = 0.40$

However, if we know that v_1 equals 1, the probability that v_2 will now equal

0 is 0.60: Prob[$v_2 = 0$ IF $v_1 = 1$] = 0.60

1 is 0.40: Prob[$v_2 = 1$ IF $v_1 = 1$] = 0.40

Knowing the value of v_1 does not help us predict the value of v_2 because it does not affect v_2's probability distribution. In this case, v_1 and v_2 are independent.

Let us now calculate the covariance of these random variables to show that their covariance equals 0. The equation for the covariance is

$$\text{Cov}[v_1, v_2] = \sum\nolimits_{\text{All } v_1} \sum\nolimits_{\text{All } v_2} (v_1 - \text{Mean}[v_1])(v_2 - \text{Mean}[v_2])\text{Prob}[v_1 \text{ AND } v_2]$$

First, calculate the means of v_1 and v_2:

$$\text{Mean}[v_1] = \sum\nolimits_{\text{All } v_1} v_1 \text{Prob}[v_1] \qquad \text{Mean}[v_2] = \sum\nolimits_{\text{All } v_2} v_2 \text{Prob}[v_2]$$
$$= 0 \times 0.60 + 1 \times 0.40 \qquad\qquad = 0 \times 0.60 + 1 \times 0.40$$
$$= 0.4 \qquad\qquad\qquad\qquad = 0.4$$

Now, focusing on the equation for covariance, obtain

v_1	v_2	$(v_1 - \text{Mean}[v_1])$	$(v_2 - \text{Mean}[v_2])$	Prob[v_1 AND v_2]	Product
0	0	$0 - 0.4 = -0.4$	$0 - 0.4 = -0.4$	0.36	$-0.4 \times -0.4 \times 0.36 = 0.0576$
0	1	$0 - 0.4 = -0.4$	$1 - 0.4 = 0.6$	0.24	$-0.4 \times 0.6 \times 0.24 = -0.0576$
1	0	$1 - 0.4 = 0.6$	$0 - 0.4 = -0.4$	0.24	$0.6 \times -0.4 \times 0.24 = -0.0576$
1	1	$1 - 0.4 = 0.6$	$1 - 0.4 = 0.6$	0.16	$0.6 \times 0.6 \times 0.16 = \underline{0.0576}$

$$\text{Cov}[v_1, v_2] = 0.0000$$

When v_1 and v_2 are independent, the covariance equals 0.

25.9 Summary of Correlation and Independence

25.9.1 Correlation

Correlated Events

• **Definition:** Two events are correlated whenever the occurrence of one event helps up predict the other; more specifically, whenever the occurrence of one event either increases or decreases the probability of the other:

Prob[B IF A] $\neq$ Prob[B]

• **Correlated events and joint probability:**   Two events are correlated whenever their joint probability will not equal the product of the nonconditional probabilities:

$$\text{Prob}[B \text{ IF } A] \neq \text{Prob}[B]$$
$$\downarrow$$

$$\text{Prob}[A \text{ AND } B] \neq \text{Prob}[A] \times \text{Prob}[B]$$

• **Correlated random variables and covariance:**   Two variables are correlated whenever their covariance does not equal 0.

$$\text{Cov}[v_1, v_2] \neq 0$$

25.9.2   Independence

Independent Events

• **Definition:**   Two events are independent (uncorrelated) whenever the occurrence of one event does not help us predict the other; more specifically, whenever the occurrence of one event does not increase or decrease the probability of the other:

$$\text{Prob}[B \text{ IF } A] = \text{Prob}[B]$$

• **Independent events and joint probability:**   The joint probability of two independent events equals the product of the nonconditional probabilities:

$$\text{Prob}[B \text{ IF } A] = \text{Prob}[B]$$
$$\downarrow$$

$$\text{Prob}[A \text{ AND } B] = \text{Prob}[A] \times \text{Prob}[B]$$

• **Independent events and symmetry:**   When the probability of event B is unaffected by event A, the probability of event A is unaffected by event B:

$$\text{Prob}[B \text{ IF } A] = \text{Prob}[B]$$
$$\downarrow$$

$$\text{Prob}[A \text{ IF } B] = \text{Prob}[A]$$

• **Independent random variables and covariance:**   Two variables are independent whenever their covariance equals 0:

$$\text{Cov}[v_1, v_2] = 0$$

25.10   Describing Probability Distributions of Continuous Random Variables

Integral calculus allows us to extend the equations for the mean and variance of discrete random variables to continuous random variables. Since knowledge of integral calculus is not needed for most econometric analysis, we will include only the definition for those students who have been exposed to the integral calculus:

Distribution center: $\text{Mean}[v] = \int_{\text{All } v} v \text{Prob}[v] dv$

Distribution spread: $\text{Var}[v] = \int_{\text{All } v} (v - \text{Mean}[v])^2 \text{Prob}[v] dv$

Correlation: $\text{Var}[v_1, v_2] = \int_{\text{All } v} (v_1 - \text{Mean}[v_1])(v_2 - \text{Mean}[v_2]) \text{Prob}[v_1 \text{ AND } v_2] dv$

Chapter 25 Review Questions

1. Consider the measures of the center that we introduced. Define the

   a. mean.

   b. mode.

   c. median.

2. What can you conclude about the distribution when the mean is greater than the median?

3. What is an event tree?

4. Explain the differences between nonconditional, conditional, and joint probabilities.

5. Consider two independent random variables.

   a. In words, what does it mean for two random variables to be independent?

   b. What will the covariance equal for two random variables?

Chapter 25 Exercises

1. Focus on thirty students who enrolled in an economics course during a previous semester.

Student SAT data: Cross-sectional data of student math and verbal high school SAT scores from a group of 30 students.

SatMath$_t$ Math SAT score for student t

SatVerbal$_t$ Verbal SAT score for student t

SexM1$_t$ 1 if student t is male; 0 if female

Student	SatMath	SatVerbal	SexM1	Student	SatMath	SatVerbal	SexM1
1	670	760	0	16	680	580	1
2	780	700	0	17	750	730	1
3	720	700	0	18	630	610	1
4	770	750	0	19	700	730	1
5	610	620	0	20	730	650	1
6	790	770	0	21	760	730	1
7	740	800	0	22	650	650	1
8	720	710	0	23	800	800	1
9	700	680	0	24	680	750	1
10	750	780	0	25	800	740	1
11	800	750	1	26	800	770	1
12	770	690	1	27	770	730	1
13	790	750	1	28	750	750	1
14	700	620	1	29	790	780	1
15	730	700	1	30	780	790	1

 [To access this online material, go to http://mitpress.mit.edu/westhoffeconometrics and select Student SAT.]

a. Construct a histogram for the data variable *SatVerbal*.

b. What are the mean, mode, and median for *SatVerbal*?

c. How does your histogram help you explain why the mean and median are related as they are?

2. Two cab companies, Yellow Cab and Orange Cab, serve a small town. There are 900 Yellow cabs and 100 Orange cabs. A cab strikes a color-blind pedestrian. After striking the pedestrian, the cab immediately leaves the scene of the accident. The victim knows that a cab struck him, but his color blindness makes him unable to report on the hue of the cab.

a. Based on this information, draw an event tree to determine the probability that the guilty cab was Yellow and the probability that the guilty cab was Orange?

A judge must find one of the cab companies liable for the damage done to the pedestrian.

b. Based on the available information, which cab company should the judge find guilty? Explain.

3. Reconsider the cab liability issue described in question 2. An eyewitness has just come forward who reports that he saw the accident. Irrefutable documentation has proven that the probability of the eyewitness being correct is 0.8 and the probability of being incorrect is 0.2.

a. Extend the event tree you constructed in question 2 to reflect two possibilities: the possibility that the eyewitness will report that a Yellow cab was guilty and that an Orange cab was guilty.

b. Using your event tree, determine the following joint probabilities:

Prob[Yellow guilty AND Yellow reported] =

Prob[Yellow guilty AND Orange reported] =

Prob[Orange guilty AND Orange reported] =

Prob[Orange guilty AND Yellow reported] =

c. Using your event tree, calculate the following probabilities:

Prob[Yellow reported] =

Prob[Orange reported] =

d. Using the conditional/joint probability relationship, compute the following conditional probabilities:

Prob[Yellow guilty IF Yellow reported] =

Prob[Yellow guilty IF Orange reported] =

Prob[Orange guilty IF Orange reported] =

Prob[Orange guilty IF Yellow reported] =

e. Should the judge, a very busy individual, take the time to hear the eyewitness's testimony? Explain.

f. Your event tree reflects two pieces of information: the relative number of Yellow and Orange cabs and the reliability of eyewitness testimony. Intuitively, how do these two pieces of information explain you results?

4. This problem comes from a "Car Talk Puzzler: Attack of the Bucolic Plague."[3]

RAY: This puzzler came to us a while ago—January 1999, to be precise. It's from Professor Bruce Robinson at the University of Tennessee in Knoxville. Of course, I had to make a few modifications . . .

TOM: He won't even want to be associated with it, once you're finished.

RAY: I'm sure he'll send us an email asking to have his name expunged.

_____

3. This problem was the "Car Talk Puzzler" on June 7, 2004.

Here it is:

• A dreaded new disease is sweeping across the countryside. It's called "The Bucolic Plague." If you're afflicted with it, you begin wandering around the woods aimlessly, until you finally collapse and die. The remedy is to lock yourself in the bathroom for two or three days, until the urge passes.

• A test has been developed that can detect whether you have the disease. The test is 99 percent accurate. That is, if you have the disease, there is a 99 percent chance that the test will detect it. If you don't have the disease, the test will be 99 percent accurate in saying that you don't.

• In the general population, 0.1 percent of the people have the disease—that's one-tenth of one percent.

• You decide to go for the test. You get your results: positive.

Should you lock yourself in the bathroom and ask for a constant supply of magazines, or should you not be worried? And, the real question is, what is the probability that you actually have the Bucolic Plague?

a. First, suppose that you have not been tested yet. Consider the fact that 0.1 percent of the general population has the disease. Assuming that you are typical, what is the probability that you have the disease? Draw the appropriate event tree to illustrate this.

b. Now, you have been tested, but you have not yet received the test results. Extend your event tree to account for the possibility of a positive or negative result.

i. Using your event tree, determine the following joint probabilities:

Prob[You have the disease AND You test positive]

Prob[You have the disease AND You test negative]

Prob[You do not have the disease AND You test positive]

Prob[You do not have the disease AND You test negative]

ii. Using your event tree, calculate the following probabilities:

Prob[You test positive]

Prob[You test negative]

iii. Using the conditional/joint probability relationship, compute the following conditional probabilities:

Prob[You have the disease IF You test positive]

Prob[You have the disease IF You test negative]

Prob[You do not have the disease IF You test positive]

Prob[You do not have the disease IF You test negative]

    c. Based on your answers to part b, should you be overly concerned?

    d. Your event tree reflects two pieces of information: the incidence of the disease in the general population and the reliability of the test. Intuitively, how do these two pieces of information explain your results?

5. Suppose that the producer of "Let's Make a Deal" changes the way in which the "prize door" is selected. Instead of randomly placing the prize behind one of the three doors, the following procedure is used:

• First, the contestant chooses two doors rather one.

• Second, Monty opens one of the two doors the contestant had chosen. The door Monty opens never contains the prize.

• Third, Monty gives the contestant the opportunity to stay with unopened door that he/she initially chose or switch to the other unopened door.

Suppose that the contestant initially chooses doors 1 and 2. Monty uses the following rules to decide which door to open:

• If the prize is behind door 1, he would open door 2.

• If the prize is behind door 2, he would open door 1.

• If the prize is behind door 3, he would choose either to open door 1 or door 2 randomly; that is, if the prize is behind door 3, the chances are 50-50 he will open door 1 and 50-50 he will open door 2.

    a. Draw the event tree describing which door Monty will open.

    b. Calculate the following conditional probabilities:

        i. Prob[Prize behind door 2 IF Monty opens door 1]

        ii. Prob[Prize behind door 3 IF Monty opens door 1]

        iii. Prob[Prize behind door 1 IF Monty opens door 2]

        iv. Prob[Prize behind door 3 IF Monty opens door 2]

    c. After Monty opens a door, would you advise the contestant to stay with the unopened door he/she chose initially or switch to the other unopened door, door 3?

5. Suppose that the producer of "Let's Make a Deal" changes the way in which the "prize door" is selected. Instead of randomly placing the prize behind one of the three doors, the following procedure is used:

• Thoroughly shuffle a standard deck of fifty-two cards.

• Randomly draw one card, note its color, and replace the card.

- Thoroughly shuffle the deck again.
- Randomly draw a second card, note its color, and replace the card.

After the two cards are drawn, the producer uses the following rules to decide where to place the prize:

- If both cards drawn are red, the prize door is 1.
- If both cards drawn are black, the prize door is 3.
- If one card drawn is red and one black, the prize door is 2.

   a. Which door is most likely to hide the prize?

   b. Suppose that you initially choose this door, the door most likely to hide the prize. After Monty opens a door that does not include the prize, should you switch?

26 Estimating the Mean of a Population

Chapter 26 Objectives

26.9   Normal Distribution and the Student t-Distribution

26.10   Tying Up a Loose End: Degrees of Freedom

Chapter 26 Prep Questions

1. Apply the arithmetic of means to show that

$$\text{Mean}\left[\frac{1}{T}(v_1 + v_2 + \ldots + v_T)\right] = ActMean$$

whenever $\text{Mean}[v_i] = ActMean$ for each i; that is,

$\text{Mean}[v_1] = \text{Mean}[v_2] = \ldots = \text{Mean}[v_T] = ActMean$ for $i = 1, 2, \ldots, T$

2. Apply the arithmetic of variances to show that

$$\text{Var}\left[\frac{1}{T}(v_1 + v_2 + \ldots + v_T)\right] = \frac{ActVar}{T}$$

whenever

- $\text{Var}[v_i] = ActVar$ for each i; that is,

$\text{Var}[v_1] = \text{Var}[v_2] = \ldots = \text{Var}[v_T] = ActVar$ for $i = 1, 2, \ldots, T$

and

- the v_i's are independent; that is, all the covariances equal 0.

3. Consider an estimate's probability distribution:

  a. Why is the mean of the probability distribution important? Explain.

  b. Why is the variance of the probability distribution important? Explain.

4. Consider a random variable. When additional uncertainty is present how is the spread of does the random variable's probability distribution affected? How is the variance affected?

26.1   Estimation Procedure for the Population Mean

Last summer our friend Clint was hired by the consumer group to analyze a claim made by the Key West Tourist Bureau. The tourist bureau claims that the average low temperature in Key West during the winter months is 65 degrees Fahrenheit (rounded to the nearest degree). Clint has been hired to assess this claim.

The consumer group has already compiled the high and low high temperatures for each winter day from the winter of 2000–2001 to the winter of 2008–2009, 871 days in total.

12-1-2000	12-2-2000	12-3-2000	. . .	2-28-2009
66.90	69.10	69.80		69.10

Figure 26.1
Clint's 871 cards

Key West winter weather data: Time series data of daily high and low temperatures in Key West, Florida, during the winter months (December, January, and February) from the 2000–2001 winter to the 2008–2009 winter.

$Year_t$ Year of observation t

$Month_t$ Month of observation t

Day_t Day of observation t

$High_t$ Precipitation for observation t

Low_t Precipitation for observation t

Clint has recorded the low temperature for each day on a 3×5 card (figure 26.1).

Since we can access statistical software, we can use the software to calculate the actual average low temperature and the actual variance in the winter months.

[To access this online material, go to http://mitpress.mit.edu/westhoffeconometrics and select Key West Winters.]

$$ActMeanAll871 = \frac{66.90 + 69.10 + 69.80 + \ldots + 69.10}{871} = 64.56$$

$$ActVarAll871 = \frac{(66.90 - 64.56)^2 + (69.10 - 64.56)^2 + (69.80 - 64.56)^2 + \ldots + (69.10 - 64.56)^2}{871}$$
$$= 43.39$$

In fact the claim of the Tourist Bureau is justified. The average low temperature in Key West was 64.56 which when rounded to the nearest whole number equals 65. But Clint has a problem. He does not have access to any statistical software, however. He does not have the time to sum all 871 observations to calculate the mean. It would take him a long time to do so. Instead, he adopts the econometrician's philosophy to assess the Tourist Bureau's claim:

Econometrician's philosophy: If you lack the information to determine the value directly, estimate the value to the best of your ability using the information you do have.

Clint samples the population of all 871 days by performing the following experiment:

12-2-2001		2-15-2008		1-22-2004		1-23-2001
69.10		66.20		54.00		55.90

Figure 26.2
Four cards Clint randomly selects

Experiment 26.1: Using Clint's 871 Cards

Perform the following procedure four times:

- Thoroughly shuffle the cards.
- Randomly draw one card.
- Record the low reported on the card drawn; call it v_i.
- Replace the card.

Use the average of the low for the four days sampled to estimate the mean:

$$EstMean = \frac{v_1 + v_2 + v_3 + v_4}{4}$$

Clint draws the following four cards (figure 26.2). Clint uses these four values to estimate the mean of the population:

$$EstMean = \frac{69.10 + 66.20 + 54.00 + 55.90}{4} = \frac{245.20}{4} = 61.30$$

Project: Assess the reliability of a sample mean.

Can Clint expect his estimated mean to equal the actual mean? Unfortunately, he cannot. The following simulation clearly illustrates this.

Econometrics Lab 26.1: Estimating the Population Mean

[To access this online material, go to http://mitpress.mit.edu/westhoffeconometrics and select Lab 26.1.]

By default, a sample size of 4 is selected (figure 26.3) and the Pause checkbox is checked. Click the Start button and compare the numerical value of the estimated mean with the actual mean from the first repetition of the experiment. Are they equal? Click the Continue button a few times and compare the estimated and actual means for each of the subsequent repetitions. We can draw two conclusions:

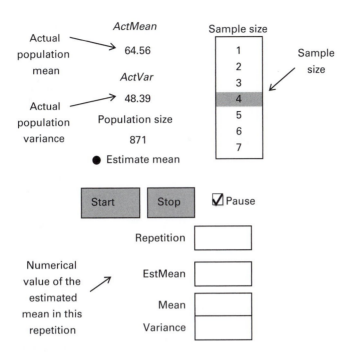

Figure 26.3
Opinion Poll simulation

• We cannot expect the numerical value of the estimated mean to equal the actual population mean.

• We cannot predict the numerical value of the estimated mean before the experiment is conducted; hence the estimated mean is a random variable.

So where does this leave Clint? He knows that in all likelihood his estimate, 61.30, does not equal the actual population mean. But perhaps he could get some sense of how likely it is for his estimate to be "close" to the actual value. Recall that Clint faced the same problem when assessing the reliability of his opinion poll. He wanted to know how likely it was that his opinion poll results were close to the actual fraction of the population supporting him for class president. As with Clint's opinion poll, we will use the general properties of Clint's estimation procedure to assess the reliability of one specific application of the procedure:

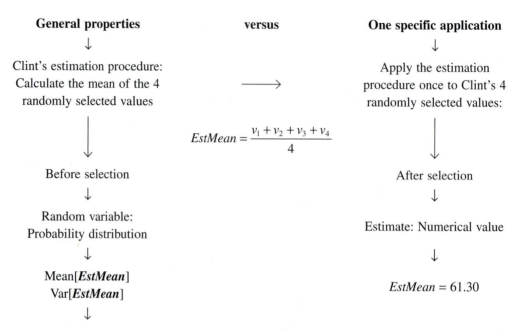

| General properties | versus | One specific application |

Mean and variance describe the center and spread of the estimate's probability distribution

The estimated mean, *EstMean*, is a random variable. While we cannot determine the value of a random variable before the experiment is conducted, we can often describe a random variable's probability distribution. Our next goal is to do just that. We will describe the probability distribution of the estimated mean, *EstMean*, by deriving the equations for its mean and variance. The mean describes the probability distribution's center and the variance describes the probability distribution's spread. We will use the same strategy that we used when studying opinion polls. First we will consider a very simple and unrealistic experiment in which only one card is drawn. Then we will apply the arithmetic of means and variances to generalize the results for sample sizes greater than one.

Experiment 26.2: Write Each Day's Low on a 3 × 5 Card

- Thoroughly shuffle the cards.
- Randomly draw one card.
- Record the low written on the card drawn.
- Replace the card.

Let v equal the recorded value:

v = the low temperature recorded on the card drawn

We will now derive the equation for the mean and variance of v's probability distribution.

26.2   Estimated Mean's Probability Distribution

26.2.1   Measure of the Probability Distribution's Center: Mean

Recall the formula for the mean (expected value) of a random variable:

$$\text{Mean}[v] = \sum_{\text{All } v} v \,\text{Prob}[v]$$

To apply this formula to our experiment, we will calculate the probability of drawing a specific card from Clint's deck of 871 cards (figure 26.4).

What is the probability of drawing the card for December 1, 2000? Since there are 871 cards in the well-shuffled deck, there is one chance in 871 of drawing the December 1, 2000, card. Thus the probability of drawing the December 1, 2000, card is 1/871. What is the probability of drawing the card for December 2, 2000? By the same logic, the probability of drawing the December 2, 2000, card is 1/871. Clearly, the probability of drawing the card for any specific day from a well-shuffled deck of 871 cards is 1/871:

$$\text{Prob}[12\text{-}1\text{-}2000] = \text{Prob}[12\text{-}2\text{-}2000] = \ldots = \text{Prob}[2\text{-}28\text{-}2009] = \frac{1}{871}$$

Now we can apply the formula for the mean:

$$\text{Mean}[v] = \sum_{\text{All } v} v \,\text{Prob}[v]$$

$$= \underset{12\text{-}1\text{-}00}{66.90 \frac{1}{871}} + \underset{12\text{-}2\text{-}00}{66.10 \frac{1}{871}} + \ldots + \underset{2\text{-}28\text{-}09}{66.90 \frac{1}{871}}$$

Next let us do a little algebra:

Factoring out 1/871 from each term

$$= (66.90 + 66.10 + 69.80 + \ldots + 66.90)\frac{1}{871}$$

$$= \frac{66.90 + 69.10 + 69.80 + \ldots + 69.10}{871}$$

12-1-2000	12-2-2000	12-3-2000		2-28-2009
66.90	69.10	69.80	. . .	69.10

Figure 26.4
Clint's 871 cards

What does $\dfrac{66.90+69.10+69.80+\ldots+69.10}{871}$ equal? It equals the actual population mean, 64.56:

$$\text{Mean}[v] = ActMeanAll871 = 64.56$$

In words, the center of the random variable v's probability distribution, Mean[v], equals that actual mean of the population, 64.56.

26.2.2   Measure of the Probability Distribution's Spread: Variance

We can use the same strategy to show that the variance of the random variable v will equal the population variance. Review the formula for the variance of a random variable:

$$\text{Var}[v] = \sum_{\text{All } v}(v - \text{Mean}[v])^2\,\text{Prob}[v]$$

$$= \underset{\text{12-1-00}}{(66.90-64.56)^2\,\dfrac{1}{871}} + \underset{\text{12-2-00}}{(66.10-64.56)^2\,\dfrac{1}{871}} + \ldots + \underset{\text{2-28-09}}{(66.90-64.56)^2\,\dfrac{1}{871}}$$

Again, let us do a little algebra:

Factoring out 1/871 from each term

$$= \left[(66.90-64.56)^2 + (66.10-64.56)^2 + \ldots + (66.90-64.56)^2\right]\dfrac{1}{871}$$

$$= \dfrac{(66.90-64.56)^2 + (66.10-64.56)^2 + \ldots + (66.90-64.56)^2}{871}$$

What does $\dfrac{(66.90-64.56)^2 + (66.10-64.56)^2 + \ldots + (66.90-64.56)^2}{871}$ equal? It equals the actual population variance, 43.39:

$$\text{Var}[v] = ActVarAll871 = 43.39$$

In words, the spread of the random variable v's probability distribution, Var[v], equals the actual variance of the population, 43.39.

Next consider the general case where T cards are drawn from the deck and then apply the arithmetic of means and variances:

Experiment 26.3: Write Each Day's Low on a 3 × 5 Card

Perform the following procedure T times:

- Thoroughly shuffle the cards.
- Randomly draw one card.
- Record the amount of rainfall written on the card drawn; call it v_i.
- Replace the card.

Use the average of the T days sampled to estimate the mean:

$$EstMean = \frac{v_1 + v_2 + \ldots + v_T}{T}, \qquad \text{where } T = \text{sample size}$$

We can describe the probability distribution of the random variable *EstMean* by applying the arithmetic of means and variances to the estimate of the mean:

$$EstMean = \frac{v_1 + v_2 + \ldots + v_T}{T} = \frac{1}{T}(v_1 + v_2 + \ldots + v_T)$$

First we consider the mean. Keep in mind that the mean of each v equals the population mean, *ActMeanAll871*:

$$\text{Mean}[\boldsymbol{EstMean}] = \text{Mean}\left[\frac{1}{T}(v_1 + v_2 + \ldots + v_T)\right]$$

$$\text{Mean}[c\boldsymbol{x}] = c\,\text{Mean}[\boldsymbol{x}]$$

$$= \frac{1}{T}\text{Mean}\left[\boldsymbol{v}_1 + \boldsymbol{v}_2 + \ldots + \boldsymbol{v}_T\right]$$

$$\text{Mean}[\boldsymbol{x} + \boldsymbol{y}] = \text{Mean}[\boldsymbol{x}] + \text{Mean}[\boldsymbol{y}]$$

$$= \frac{1}{T}(\text{Mean}[\boldsymbol{v}_1] + \text{Mean}[\boldsymbol{v}_2] + \ldots + \text{Mean}[\boldsymbol{v}_T])$$

$$\text{Mean}[\boldsymbol{v}_1] = \text{Mean}[\boldsymbol{v}_2] = \ldots = \text{Mean}[\boldsymbol{v}_T] = ActMeanAll871$$

$$= \frac{1}{T}(ActMeanAll871 + ActMeanAll871 + \ldots + ActMeanAll871)$$

There are T *ActMeanAll871* terms

$$= \frac{1}{T}(T \times ActMeanAll871)$$

Simplifying

$$= ActMeanAll871$$

The terminology can be confusing: Mean[*EstMean*] is the mean of the estimated mean. To resolve this confusion, remember that the estimated mean, *EstMean*, is a random variable. Therefore, like any random variable, *EstMean* is described by its probability distribution. So Mean[*EstMean*] refers to the mean of *EstMean*'s probability distribution, the center of *EstMean*'s probability distribution. To emphasize this point, we will often follow the word "mean" with the word "center" in parentheses when referring to Mean[*EstMean*]; for example, Mean[*EstMean*] is the mean (center) of *EstMean*'s probability distribution.

Next we focus on the variance. Note that the variance of each v equals the population variance, *ActVarAll871*. Also note that since each card drawn is replaced, the probability distribution of v for one draw is not affected by the value of v on any other draw. The v's are independent; hence all the covariances equal 0:

$$\text{Var}[\textbf{\textit{EstMean}}] = \text{Var}\left[\frac{1}{T}(v_1 + v_2 + \ldots + v_T)\right]$$

$\text{Var}[c\textbf{\textit{x}}] = c^2\text{Var}[\textbf{\textit{x}}]$

$$= \frac{1}{T^2}\text{Var}[v_1 + v_2 + \ldots + v_T]$$

$\text{Var}[\textbf{\textit{x}} + \textbf{\textit{y}}] = \text{Var}[\textbf{\textit{x}}] + \text{Var}[\textbf{\textit{y}}]$ when x and y are independent. The covariances are all 0.

$$= \frac{1}{T^2}(\text{Var}[v_1] + \text{Var}[v_2] + \ldots + \text{Var}[v_T])$$

$\text{Var}[v_1] = \text{Var}[v_2] = \ldots = \text{Var}[v_T] = \textit{ActVarAll871}$

$$= \frac{1}{T^2}(\textit{ActVarAll871} + \textit{ActVarAll871} + \ldots + \textit{ActVarAll871})$$

There are T *ActVarAll871* terms

$$= \frac{1}{T^2}(T \times \textit{ActVarAll871})$$

Simplifying

$$= \frac{\textit{ActVarAll871}}{T}$$

Econometrics Lab 26.2: Checking the Equations

[To access this online material, go to http://mitpress.mit.edu/westhoffeconometrics and select Lab 26.2.]

By exploiting the relative frequency interpretation of probability, we can use a simulation to check our equations (figure 26.5). When we repeat this experiment many, many times, the distribution of the numerical values resulting from the experiments mirrors the probability distribution. We could keep track of the numerical value of the estimated mean for each repetition by hand. Then we could calculate the mean and variance of these numerical values. This would be a very laborious exercise, however. Fortunately, computers provide us with a quick, easy way to simulate the experiment. We need only specify one parameter: the sample size, in our case the number of cards drawn. Table 26.1 reports the results for three sample sizes, 1, 4, and 10.

Our simulation results confirm the equations we derived for the mean and variance. The equations reveal and the simulations confirm two important aspects of Clint's estimation procedure:

• The mean (center) of the estimated fraction's probability distribution, Mean[**EstMean**], equals the actual population mean:

Mean[**EstMean**] = ActMeanAll871

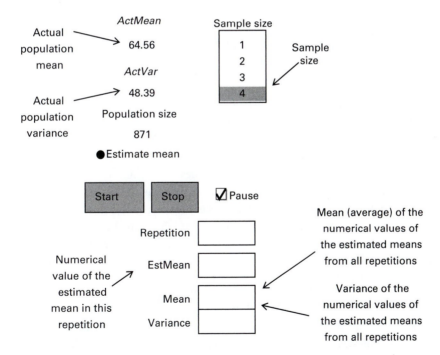

Figure 26.5
Opinion Poll simulation

Table 26.1
Checking our equations for the mean and variance

	Actual population mean = ActMeanAll871 = 64.56 Actual population variance = ActVarAll871 = 48.39			
	Equations		Simulation	
Sample size	Mean (Center) of *EstMean*'s probability distribution	Variance of *EstMean*'s probability distribution	Mean (average) of numerical values of *EstMean* from the experiments	Variance of numerical values of *EstMean* from the experiments
1	64.56	$\frac{48.39}{1} = 48.39$	≈ 64.56	≈48.39
4	64.56	$\frac{48.39}{4} = 12.10$	≈ 64.56	≈12.10
10	64.56	$\frac{48.39}{10} = 4.84$	≈ 64.56	≈4.84

• The variance of the estimated fraction's probability distribution, Var[**EstMean**], decreases as the sample size increases.

$$\text{Var}[\textbf{EstMean}] = \frac{ActVarAll871}{T}, \qquad \text{where } T = \text{sample size}$$

26.3 Taking Stock: What We Know versus What Clint Knows

It is important to keep in mind what we know versus what Clint knows. We know that the average of all the lows, the actual mean, equals 64.56 and the actual variance equals 43.39. We used a statistical package to compute these two statistics. Accordingly, we know that the Tourist Bureau's claim that the average winter low in Key West is 65 can be justified (at least to the nearest whole degree). Clint does not have access to a statistical package, however, and does not have the time to perform the arithmetic calculations needed to calculate the actual mean. Clint proceeds to estimate the mean winter low temperature by randomly selecting four days and calculating the average of the lows on these days. What does Clint know about his estimated mean, *EstMean*? Let us summarize what Clint knows:

• Clint cannot expect *EstMean* to equal the actual mean, *ActMeanAll871*.

• *EstMean* is a random variable. Even if Clint knew the actual mean, he could not predict with certainty the numerical value of *EstMean* before he randomly selected the four cards.

• *EstMean*, like any random variable, is described by its probability distribution. Clint can describe the center and spread of *EstMean*'s probability distribution by deriving the equations for its mean and variance (figure 26.6).

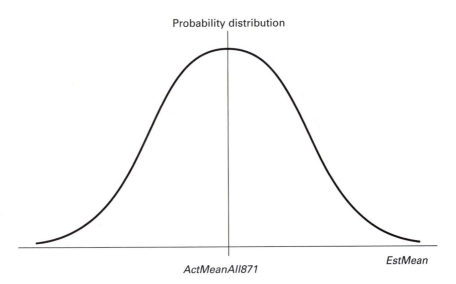

Figure 26.6
Probability distribution of *EstMean*

$$\text{Mean}[\textbf{\textit{EstMean}}] = ActMeanAll871$$

$$\text{Var}[\textbf{\textit{EstMean}}] = \frac{ActVarAll871}{T}$$

Even though Clint does not know the numerical value of the actual mean and actual variance, *ActMeanAll871* and *ActVarAll871*, he does know that the mean (center) of *EstMean*'s probability distribution equals *ActMeanAll871* and the variance equals $\dfrac{ActVarAll871}{T}$ whatever the values are.

26.4 Estimation Procedures: Importance of the Probability Distribution's Mean (Center) and Variance (Spread)

Let us review what we learned about estimation procedures (figure 26.7):

• **Importance of the probability distribution's mean:** Formally, an estimation procedure is unbiased whenever the mean (center) of the estimate's probability distribution equals the actual value. The relative frequency interpretation of probability provides intuition: if the experiment were repeated many, many times, the average of the numerical values of the estimates will equal the actual value. An unbiased estimation procedure does not systematically underestimate or overestimate the actual value. If the probability distribution is symmetric, the chances that the estimate calculated from one repetition of the experiment will be too high equal the chances that

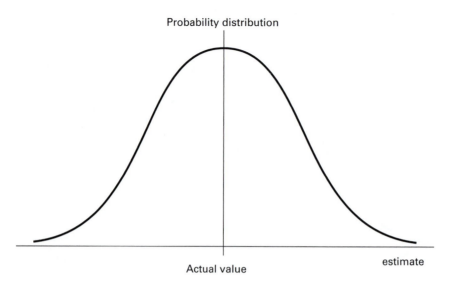

Figure 26.7
Probability distribution of estimates—Importance of the mean

the estimate will be too low. The fact that the mean (center) of *EstMean*'s probability distribution equals the population mean is good news for Clint. The procedure he used to estimate the population mean is unbiased, it does not systematically underestimate the actual population mean. Since the estimation procedure is unbiased, the variance of the estimate's probability distribution plays a critical role.

• **Importance of the probability distribution's variance:**   When the estimation procedure is unbiased, the probability distribution's variance (spread) reveals the estimate's reliability; the variance tells us how likely it is that the numerical value of the estimate calculated from one repetition of the experiment will be close to the actual value (figure 26.8).

26.5   Strategy to Estimate the Variance of the Estimated Mean's Probability Distribution

The variance of *EstMean*'s probability distribution is crucial in assessing the reliability of Clint's estimate. On the one hand, if the variance is small, Clint can be confident that his estimate is "close" to the actual population mean. On the other hand, if the variance is large, Clint must be skeptical. What does Clint know about the variance of *EstMean*'s probability distribution? He has already derived the equation for it:

$$\text{Var}[\textbf{\textit{EstMean}}] = \frac{ActVarAll871}{T}, \qquad \text{where } T = \text{sample size}$$

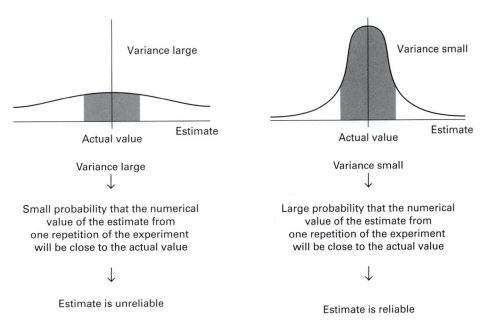

Figure 26.8
Probability distribution of estimates—Importance of the variance

The sample size equals 4. We know that the actual population variance equals 43.39; hence we know that the variance of the estimated mean's probability distribution, Var[**EstMean**], equals 10.85:

$$\text{Var}[\textbf{\textit{EstMean}}] = \frac{43.39}{4} = 10.85$$

Clint does not know the actual variance of the population, *ActVarAll871*, however. While he has the raw data needed to calculate *ActVarAll871*, he does not have time to do so—it takes longer to calculate the variance than the mean. So what should he do? Recall the econometrician's philosophy:

Econometrician's philosophy: If you lack the information to determine the value directly, estimate the value to the best of your ability using the information you do have.

Clint can estimate the population variance from the available information, his four randomly selected values for the low temperatures: 69.10, 66.20, 54.00, and 55.90. Then, he can modify the equation we derived for Var[**EstMean**] by replacing Var[**EstMean**] and *ActVarAll871* with their estimated versions:

$$\text{EstVar}[\textbf{\textit{EstMean}}] = \frac{EstVarAll871}{T}$$

where

EstVarAll871 = estimated population variance

T = sample size

Clint adopts a two-step strategy.

Step 1:   Clint estimates the variance of the population, *EstVarAll871*, the variance of all 871 observations.

Step 2:   Clint uses the estimate for the variance of population to estimate the variance for the estimated mean's probability distribution.

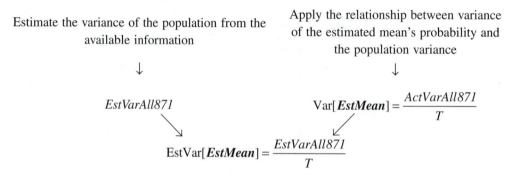

26.6   Step 1: Estimate the Variance of the Population

We will now describe three attempts to estimate the population variance using the Clint's four randomly selected values by calculating the following:

1. The variance of Clint's four numerical values based on the actual population mean.

2. The variance of Clint's four numerical values based on the estimated population mean.

3. The "adjusted" variance of Clint's four numerical values based on the estimated population mean.

While the first two attempts fail for different reasons, they provide the motivation for the third attempt, which succeeds. Therefore it is useful to explore the two failed attempts.

26.6.1   First Attempt: Variance of Clint's Four Numerical Values Based on the Actual Population Mean

The rationale is very simple. The variance is the average of the squared deviations from the mean. So why not just calculate the variance for the four values he has, 66.20, 62.60, 62.10, and 57.90, to estimate the variance of the entire population? Let us do that now:

Sample value	Actual population mean	Deviation from actual population mean $(v_i - ActMeanAll871)$	Deviation squared $(v_i - ActMeanAll871)^2$
69.10	64.56	$69.10 - 64.56 = 4.54$	20.6116
66.20	64.56	$66.20 - 64.56 = 1.64$	2.6896
54.00	64.56	$54.00 - 64.56 = -10.56$	111.5136
55.90	64.56	$55.90 - 64.56 = -8.66$	<u>74.9956</u>

Sum of squared deviations using actual population mean $= 209.8104$

Var[Clint's four values using actual population mean]

= Average of squared deviations using actual population mean

$$= \frac{\text{Sum of squared deviations using actual population mean}}{\text{Sample size}}$$

$$= \frac{209.8104}{4} = 69.94$$

The average of the squared deviations provides an estimate of the population's variance:

$EstVarAll871 = $ Var[Clint's four values using actual population mean] $= 69.94$

Note that the estimate obtained from Clint's sample, 69.94, does not equal the population variance, 43.39. This should not surprise us, however. We would never expect any estimate to achieve perfection. What then is the best we could hope for? We could hope that this estimation procedure would be unbiased; we could hope that the estimation procedure does not systematically underestimate or overestimate the actual value. This estimation procedure is in fact unbiased. We will use our simulation to illustrate this.

Econometrics Lab 26.3: First Attempt—Estimating the Population Variance

[To access this online material, go to http://mitpress.mit.edu/westhoffeconometrics and select Lab 26.3.]

Focus your attention on the lower left corner of the window. For the moment ignore the Divide By line. In the Use Mean line, note that the Act button is selected. This means that the actual population mean, 64.56, is used to calculate the deviations. Consequently our estimate of the variance is based on the actual population mean just as we did in our calculations above. Click **Start**. The values of the four cards selected are reported in figure 26.9. Calculate the variance of the four values based on the actual population mean, 64.56. Is the simulation calculating the estimated variance, *EstVar*, correctly? Next click **Continue**. Again, calculate the estimated variance. Is the simulation calculating it correctly? Also check to see if the simulation has calculated

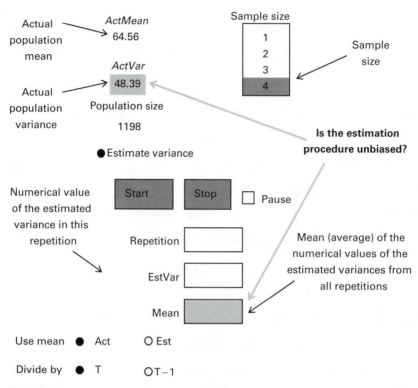

Figure 26.9
Opinion Poll simulation

the mean (average) of the variance estimates from the first two repetitions. Now uncheck the Pause checkbox; after many, many repetitions click **Stop**. Compare the mean (average) of the estimated variances with the actual population variance. Both equal 43.39. This suggests that the estimation procedure for the actual population variance is unbiased.

Does this help Clint? Unfortunately, it does not. Recall what Clint knows versus what we know. We know that the actual population mean equals 64.56, but Clint does not. Indeed, if he knew the population mean, he would not have to go through all of this trouble in the first place. So Clint must now try another tack.

26.6.2   Second Attempt: Variance of Clint's Four Numerical Values Based on the Estimated Population Mean

Since Clint does not know the actual population mean what can he do? He can use the estimate he calculated, 61.30, from the four randomly selected lows?

$$EstMean = \frac{69.10 + 66.20 + 54.00 + 55.90}{4} = \frac{245.20}{4} = 61.30$$

Sample value	Clint's estimate of actual population mean (EstMean)	Deviation from Clint's estimated mean $(v_i - EstMean)$	Deviation squared $(v_i - EstMean)^2$
69.10	61.30	$69.10 - 61.30 = 7.80$	60.8400
66.20	61.30	$66.20 - 61.30 = 4.90$	24.0100
54.00	61.30	$54.00 - 61.30 = -7.30$	53.2900
55.90	61.30	$55.90 - 61.30 = -5.40$	<u>29.1600</u>

Sum of squared deviations using estimated population mean $\quad = 167.3000$

Var[Clint's four values using estimated population mean]

= Average of squared deviations using estimated population mean

$= \dfrac{\text{Sum of squared deviations using estimated population mean}}{\text{Sample size}}$

$= \dfrac{167.3000}{4} = 41.825$

The average of the squared deviations based on Clint's estimated population mean provides an estimate of the actual population's variance that Clint can calculate:

$EstVarAll871$ = Var[Clint's four values using estimated population mean] = 41.825

Econometrics Lab 26.4: Second Attempt—Estimating the Population Variance

Hopefully this estimation procedure will be unbiased. Let us use a simulation to find out.

[To access this online material, go to http://mitpress.mit.edu/westhoffeconometrics and select Lab 26.4.]

Before clicking **Start**, note that Est is selected in the Use Mean line. Consequently, instead of calculating the deviation from the actual mean, the simulation will now calculate the deviation from the estimated mean. Now click **Start** and then after many, many repetitions click **Stop**. Compare the mean (average) of the estimated variances with the actual population variance. Unfortunately, they are not equal. The mean of the estimated variances equals 32.54 while the actual variance equals 43.39. This suggests that the estimation procedure for the actual population variance is biased downward; it systematically underestimates the variance of the population.

To explain why, note that when we use Clint's estimate of the population mean to calculate the sum of squared deviations, we obtain a lower sum than we did when we used the actual population mean:

Sum of squared deviations using actual population mean = 209.8104

Sum of squared deviations using estimated population mean = 167.3000

Is this just a coincidence? No, it is not. To understand why, we will ask a question: What value would minimize the sum of squared deviations of the 4 sample values? Let v_{VarMin} equal this value; that is,

$$v_{VarMin} \text{ minimizes } (v_1 - v_{VarMin})^2 + (v_2 - v_{VarMin})^2 + (v_3 - v_{VarMin})^2 + (v_4 - v_{VarMin})^2$$

where v_1, v_2, v_3, and v_4 equal the four sample values.

With a little calculus we can solve for v_{VarMin}, differentiate the sum of squared deviations with respect to v_{VarMin}, and then set the derivative equal to 0:

$$\frac{d[(v_1 - v_{VarMin})^2 + (v_2 - v_{VarMin})^2 + (v_3 - v_{VarMin})^2 + (v_4 - v_{VarMin})^2]}{dv_{VarMin}}$$

$$= -2(v_1 - v_{VarMin}) - 2(v_1 - v_{VarMin}) - 2(v_1 - v_{VarMin}) - 2(v_1 - v_{VarMin}) = 0$$

Now some algebra,

$$-2(v_1 - v_{VarMin}) - 2(v_2 - v_{VarMin}) - 2(v_3 - v_{VarMin}) - 2(v_4 - v_{VarMin}) = 0$$
$$(v_1 - v_{VarMin}) + (v_2 - v_{VarMin}) + (v_3 - v_{VarMin}) + (v_4 - v_{VarMin}) = 0$$
$$v_1 + v_2 + v_3 + v_4 - 4v_{VarMin} = 0$$
$$v_1 + v_2 + v_3 + v_4 = 4v_{VarMin}$$
$$\frac{v_1 + v_2 + v_3 + v_4}{4} = v_{VarMin}$$

What does $\frac{v_1 + v_2 + v_3 + v_4}{4}$ equal? It is just the estimated population mean. Using the estimate of the population mean to calculate the deviations from the mean minimizes the sum of squared deviations. The two sums are equal only if the estimate of the population mean equals the actual population mean:

	Only if the estimated mean equals the actual mean	
Sum of squared deviations based	↓	Sum of squared deviations based
on estimated population mean	=	on actual population mean

Typically the estimate of the population mean will not equal the actual population mean, however. Consequently the sum of squared deviations based on the estimate of the population mean will be less than the sum of squared deviations based on the population mean itself:

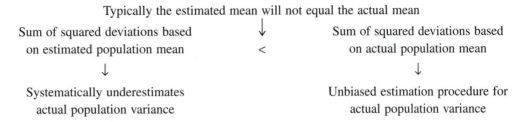

Typically the estimated mean will not equal the actual mean

Sum of squared deviations based on estimated population mean	↓ <	Sum of squared deviations based on actual population mean
↓		↓
Systematically underestimates actual population variance		Unbiased estimation procedure for actual population variance

Recall that the average of the sum of squared deviations based on the population mean provides an unbiased procedure for the population variance. Consequently, if Clint were to estimate the population variance by using the deviations from the estimated mean rather than the actual mean, he would systematically underestimate the variance of the population. So, let us make one last attempt.

26.6.3   Third Attempt: "Adjusted" Variance of Clint's Four Numerical Values Based on the Estimated Population Mean

How should Clint proceed? Fortunately, he has a way out. Clearly, Clint has no choice but to use the estimated population mean to calculate the sum of squared residuals. If he divides by 3 rather than 4, his estimation procedure will be unbiased. More generally, when the actual population mean is unknown and the estimated population mean must be used to calculate the deviations from the mean, we divide the sum of squared deviations by the sample size less 1 rather than by the sample size itself. In this case the sample size less 1 equals the **degrees of freedom**; there are 3 degrees of freedom. For the time being, do not worry about precisely what the degrees of freedom represent and why they solve the problem of bias. We will motivate the rationale later in this chapter. We do not wish to be distracted from Clint's efforts to assess the Tourist Bureau's claim at this time. So we will postpone the rationalization for now.

Let us now compute our "adjusted" estimate of the variance. Recall our calculations of the sum of squared deviations using the estimated population mean:

Sample value	Clint's estimate of actual population mean (EstMean)	Deviation from Clint's estimated mean $(v_i - EstMean)$	Deviation Squared $(v_i - EstMean)^2$
69.10	61.30	$69.10 - 61.30 = 7.80$	60.8400
66.20	61.30	$66.20 - 61.30 = 4.90$	24.0100
54.00	61.30	$54.00 - 61.30 = -7.30$	53.2900
55.90	61.30	$55.90 - 61.30 = -5.40$	29.1600

Sum of squared deviations using estimated population mean   = 167.3000

Now calculate the adjusted variance:

AdjVar[Clint's four values using estimated population mean]

= Adjusted average of squared deviations using estimated population mean

$$= \frac{\text{Sum of squared deviations using estimated population mean}}{\text{Sample size} - 1}$$

$$= \frac{167.3000}{4 - 1} = \frac{167.3000}{3} = 55.77$$

EstVarAll871 = AdjVar[Clint's four values using estimated population mean] = 55.77

Econometrics Lab 26.5: Third Attempt—Estimating the Population Variance

We will use a simulation to illustrate that the adjusted variance procedure is unbiased.

[To access this online material, go to http://mitpress.mit.edu/westhoffeconometrics and select Lab 26.5.]

Before clicking **Start**, note that Est is selected in the Use Mean line and $T - 1$ in the Divide By line. Consequently the simulation will now calculate the deviation from the estimated mean and then after summing the squared deviations, it will divide by the sample size less one, $T-1$, rather than the sample size itself, T.

Now click **Start** and then after many, many repetitions click **Stop**. Compare the mean (average) of the estimated variances with the actual population variance. They are equal. This suggests that our third estimation procedure for the population variance is unbiased. After many, many repetitions the adjusted average of the squared deviations equals the actual population variance.

26.7   Step 2: Use the Estimated Variance of the Population to Estimate the Variance of the Estimated Mean's Probability Distribution

At last we have an estimate for the population variance: *EstVarAll871* = 55.77

But why did Clint want to know the population variance in the first place? He will use his estimate of the population variance to estimate variance of the estimated mean's probability distribution, Var[***EstMean***]:

Estimate the variance of the population from the available information	Apply the relationship between variance of the estimated mean's probability and the population variance
↓	↓
EstVarAll871	$\text{Var}[\textbf{\textit{EstMean}}] = \dfrac{ActVarAll871}{T}$

$$\text{EstVar}[\textbf{\textit{EstMean}}] = \frac{EstVarAll871}{T}$$

Let us perform the calculation:

$$\text{EstVar}[\textbf{\textit{EstMean}}] = \frac{EstVarAll871}{T}$$

$$= \frac{55.77}{4} = 13.94$$

Recall that the standard deviation equals the square root of the variance. Consequently the estimated standard deviation equals the square root of the estimated variance. Furthermore the estimated standard deviation has been given a special name, it is called the standard error:

$$\text{SE} = \text{EstSD} = \sqrt{\text{EstVar}}$$

Now let us calculate the standard error, the estimated standard deviation of the estimated mean, *EstMean*'s, probability distribution:

$$\text{SE}[\textbf{\textit{EstMean}}] = \text{EstSD}[\textbf{\textit{EstMean}}] = \sqrt{\text{EstVar}[\textbf{\textit{EstMean}}]}$$

Since the estimated variance of the probability distribution equals 13.94,

$$\text{SE}[\textbf{\textit{EstMean}}] = \text{EstSD}[\textbf{\textit{EstMean}}] = \sqrt{13.94} = 3.73$$

26.8   Clint's Assessment of the Key West Tourist Bureau's Claim

Now, at last, Clint is in a position to assess the Tourist Bureau's claim that the average daily low temperature during winter was 65 in Key West. Hypothesis testing allows Clint to do so. Recall the steps involved in hypothesis testing:

Step 1:   Collect evidence.

Clint has already done this. By selecting four months randomly, Clint estimates the average low temperature to be 61.30.

$$\textit{EstMean} = \frac{69.10 + 66.20 + 54.00 + 55.90}{4} = \frac{245.20}{4} = 61.30$$

Critical result: The estimated mean is 61.30. This evidence, the fact that the estimated mean is less than 65, suggests that the Tourist Bureau's claim is not justified.

Step 2:   Play the cynic, challenge the evidence, and construct the null and alternative hypotheses.

Cynic's view: Despite the results the average low temperature is actually 65.

The null hypothesis adopts the cynical view by challenging the evidence; the cynic always challenges the evidence. The alternative hypothesis is consistent with the evidence.

H_0: $ActMeanAll871 = 65 \Rightarrow$ Actual mean is 65; cynic is correct.

H_1: $ActMeanAll871 < 65 \Rightarrow$ Actual mean is less than 65; cynic is incorrect.

Step 3:   Formulate the question to assess the null hypothesis and the cynic's view.

Question for the Cynic

• **Generic question:**   What is the probability that the result would be like the one obtained (or even stronger), if H_0 is true (if the cynic is correct)?

• **Specific question:**   The estimated mean was 61.30. What is the probability of obtaining an average low of 61.30 or less from four randomly selected days if the actual population mean of lows were 65 (if H_0 is true)?

Answer: Prob[Results IF cynic correct] or Prob[Results IF H_0 true]

The magnitude of this probability determines whether we reject or do not reject the null hypothesis; that is, the magnitude of this probability determines the likelihood that the cynic is correct and H_0 is true:

Prob[Results IF H_0 true] small   Prob[Results IF H_0 true] large

↓   ↓

Unlikely that H_0 is true   Likely that H_0 is true

↓   ↓

Reject H_0 Do not reject H_0

Step 4:   Use the general properties of the estimation procedure, the estimated mean's probability distribution, to calculate Prob[Results IF H_0 true].

When we assess Clint's poll, we used the normal distribution to calculate this probability. Unfortunately, we cannot use the normal distribution now. Instead, we must use a different distribution, the Student t-distribution. We will now explain why.

26.9   Normal Distribution and the Student t-Distribution

Recall that the variable z played a critical role in using the normal distribution:

$$z = \frac{\text{Value of random variable} - \text{Distribution mean}}{\text{Distribution standard deviation}}$$

= Number of standard deviations from the mean

In words, z equals the number of standard deviations the value lies from the mean. But Clint does not know what the actual variance and standard deviation of his probability distribution

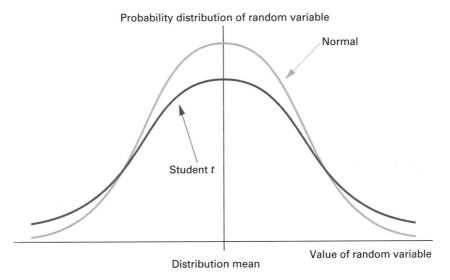

Figure 26.10
Normal and Student t-distributions

equals. That is why he had to estimate it. Consequently he cannot use the normal distribution to calculate probabilities.

When the standard deviation is not known and must be estimated, the Student t-distribution rather than the normal distribution must be used (figure 26.10). t equals the number of estimated standard deviations the value lies from the mean:

$$t = \frac{\text{Value of random variable} - \text{Distribution mean}}{\text{Estimated distribution standard deviation}}$$

$$= \text{Number of estimated standard deviations from the mean}$$

The estimated standard deviation is called the standard error; hence

$$t = \frac{\text{Value of random variable} - \text{Distribution mean}}{\text{Standard error}}$$

$$= \text{Number of standard errors from the distribution mean}$$

Since estimating the standard deviation introduces an additional element of uncertainty, the Student t-distribution is more "spread out" than the normal distribution.

Unfortunately, the Student t-table is more cumbersome than the normal distribution table. The right-hand tail probabilities not only depend on the value of t, the number of estimated standard deviations from the mean, but also on the degrees of freedom. We will exploit our Econometrics Lab to calculate the probability. Let us review the relevant information (figure 26.11):

Prob[Results IF H_0 true] = Prob[*EstMean* is 61.30 or less IF *ActMeanAll871* equals 65]

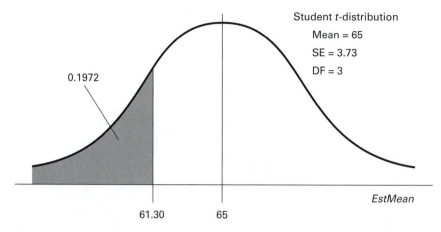

Figure 26.11
Probability distribution of *EstMean*

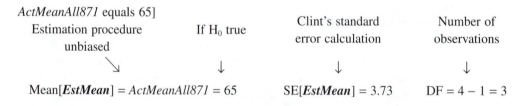

ActMeanAll871 equals 65] Estimation procedure unbiased	If H_0 true	Clint's standard error calculation	Number of observations
↘	↓	↓	↓
Mean[*EstMean*] = *ActMeanAll871* = 65		SE[*EstMean*] = 3.73	DF = 4 − 1 = 3

Econometrics Lab 26.6—Using the Student t-Distribution

[To access this online material, go to http://mitpress.mit.edu/westhoffeconometrics and select Lab 26.6.]

The following information has been entered:
Mean = 65

Standard error = 3.73

Value = 61.30

Degrees of freedom = 27

Click **Calculate**.

Using our Econometrics Lab, the probability that *EstMean* would be 61.30 or less if the actual population mean equals 65 is 0.1972; hence

Prob[Results IF H_0 true] ≈ 0.20

Now let us return to the fifth and last step in the hypothesis testing procedure.

Step 5:   Decide on the standard of proof, a significance level

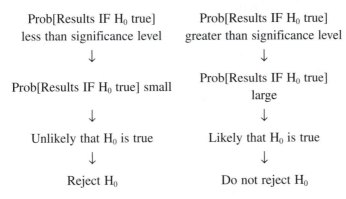

At the traditional significance levels used in academe (1, 5, and 10 percent), we cannot reject the null hypothesis that the average low is 65 and the tourist bureau's claims are justified. Consequently Clint fails to reject the null hypothesis; that is, he fails to reject the Tourist Bureau's claim that the average winter low temperature in Key West is 65.

26.10   Tying Up a Loose End: Degrees of Freedom

Earlier in this chapter we postponed our explanation of degrees of freedom because it would have interrupted the flow of our discussion. We will now return to the topic. In this case the degrees of freedom equal the sample size less one:

Degrees of freedom = Sample size − 1

We will now explain why we divided by the degrees of freedom, the sample size less one, rather than the sample size itself when estimating the variance. To do so, we will return to the basics and discuss a calculation we have been making since grade school.

Revisit Amherst precipitation in the twentieth century (table 26.2). Calculating the mean for June obtains

Table 26.2
Monthly precipitation in Amherst, MA, during the twentieth century

Year	Jan	Feb	Mar	Apr	May	Jun	Jul	Aug	Sep	Oct	Nov	Dec
1901	2.09	0.56	5.66	5.80	5.12	0.75	3.77	5.75	3.67	4.17	1.30	8.51
1902	2.13	3.32	5.47	2.92	2.42	4.54	4.66	4.65	5.83	5.59	1.27	4.27
⋮	⋮	⋮	⋮	⋮	⋮	⋮	⋮	⋮	⋮	⋮	⋮	⋮
2000	3.00	3.40	3.82	4.14	4.26	7.99	6.88	5.40	5.36	2.29	2.83	4.24

$$\text{Mean (average) for June} = \frac{0.75 + 4.54 + \ldots + 7.99}{100} = \frac{377.76}{100} = 3.78$$

Each of the 100 Junes in the twentieth century provides one piece of information that we use to calculate the average. To calculate an average, we divide the sum by the number of pieces of information. The key principle is how we calculate a mean or, in everyday language, an average:

Key principle:　To calculate a mean or an average, we divide the sum by the number of pieces of information.

$$\text{Mean (average)} = \frac{\text{Sum}}{\text{Number of pieces of information}}$$

Now focus on the variance. Recall that the variance equals the average of the squared deviations from the mean:

$$\text{Variance} = \text{Average of the squared deviations from the mean}$$

$$= \frac{\text{Sum of the squared deviations}}{\text{Number of pieces of information}}$$

In Clint's case the number of pieces of information available to estimate the variance equals 3, not 4; that is why we should divide by 3. To understand why, consider the first observation in isolation. Recall the first card Clint draws:

$$v_1 = 4.54$$

Based only on the first observation, the estimated population mean would equal 4.54; hence, when considering only the first observation, the deviation from the estimated mean, and the squared deviation would equal 0. More generally, when we consider only the first observation the deviation from the estimated mean and the squared deviation will always equal 0, despite which one of the 871 cards was drawn, the estimated mean would equal that value recorded on the card:

Considering first observation only

$$\downarrow$$

$$EstMean = v_1$$

$$\downarrow$$

$$v_1 - EstMean = 0$$

$$\downarrow$$

$$(v_1 - EstMean)^2 = 0$$

Based on only a single observation, the deviation and squared deviation will equal 0 regardless of what the actual population variance equals. Consequently the first observation provides no information when estimating the population variance. Only when the second observation is introduced would we begin to get some information about the actual population variance:

• On the one hand, if the actual population variance were large, then it would be likely for the value recorded on the second observation to be far from the first observation value; consequently the deviations from the estimated mean and squared deviations would be large.

• On the other hand, if the actual population variance were small, then it would be likely for the value recorded on the second observation to be close to the first observation value; consequently the deviations from the estimated mean and the squared deviations would be small.

Since the first observation in isolation provides no information about the variance, the number of pieces of information available to estimate the variance equals the sample size less one. The degrees of freedom equal the number of pieces of information that are available to estimate the variance.

Chapter 26 Review Questions

1. Consider an estimate's probability distribution:

    a. Why is the mean of the probability distribution important? Explain.

    b. Why is the variance of the probability distribution important? Explain.

2. Focus on the estimation procedure for the population mean. What is the equation for the

    a. mean of the estimate's probability distribution?

    b. variance of the estimate's probability distribution?

3. When estimating the population variance should we divide by the sample size or the sample size less 1? Explain.

4. What is the difference between the normal distribution and the Student t-distribution?

5. Why, when performing hypothesis tests involving the population mean, do we use the Student t-distribution rather than the normal distribution?

Chapter 26 Exercises

1. The large manufacturer of laptop computers claims that on average its laptops achieves 7 hours of battery life; that is, the manufacturer claims that the actual mean number of hours its laptop will operate without the battery begin recharged is 7:

Claim: *ActMeanAll* = 7.0

A consumer group has challenged the claim, however, asserting that the average is less than 7.0. You have been asked by the Consumer Protection Agency to investigate this claim. To do so you conduct the following experiment:

Experiment: Write the Serial Number of Each Laptop on a 3 × 5 Card

Perform the following procedure eight times:

- Thoroughly shuffle the cards.

- Randomly draw one card.

- Find the laptop with that serial number and determine its battery life, the number of the number of hours it will operate before needed a recharge.

- Replace the card.

Use the average of the eight laptops sampled to estimate the mean battery life:

$$EstMean = \frac{v_1 + v_2 + v_3 + v_8}{4}$$

The results of the experiment are reported below:

Laptop	Battery life (v_i)
1	8.9
2	6.4
3	6.2
4	6.7
5	7.5
6	5.3
7	6.4
8	6.2

a. What does the sum of the hours, $\sum_{t=1}^{8} v_t$, now equal? On average, what does the battery life of the eight laptops equal? What is the estimated mean, *EstMean*, for the battery life of all laptops produced?

b. Show that the sum of squared deviations from the estimated mean, *EstMean*, of the eight laptops you tested equals 8.12.

c. Estimate the variance for the battery life of all laptops produced by the manufacturer, the population?

d. Argue that the v_i's, the battery life of the laptops you tested, are independent random variables.

e. Estimate the variance of *EstMean*'s probability distribution. What is the estimated standard deviation; that is, what is the standard error?

2. Now, apply the information you compiled in problem 1 to assess the consumer group's complaint. We will use hypothesis testing to do so.

a. Play the cynic and construct the null and alternative hypotheses, H_0 and H_1.

b. If the null hypothesis were correct, what would the mean of *EstMean*'s probability distribution equal?

c. Formulate the question needed to assess the cynic's view and the null hypothesis, that is, compute Prob[Results IF H_0 true].

d. Using the Student t-distribution, calculate Prob[Results IF H_0 true]. Our Econometrics Lab includes software that allows you to calculate this probability easily. Access the lab using the following link and then fill in the blanks with the appropriate numbers:

[To access this online material, go to http://mitpress.mit.edu/westhoffeconometrics and select t-Distribution.]

Mean: _____

Standard error: _____

Value: _____

Degrees of freedom: _____

Prob[Results IF H_0 true] = _____

e. Assess the consumer manufacturer's claim.

3. Now suppose that the sample size were 64, eight times larger. That is, instead of randomly selecting eight cards, suppose that you randomly selected sixty-four laptops. Furthermore suppose that the battery life data just replicated the data from the first eight laptops. That is,

8 laptops achieved 8.9 hours

8 laptops achieved 6.4 hours

8 laptops achieved 6.2 hours

8 laptops achieved 6.7 hours

8 laptops achieved 7.5 hours

8 laptops achieved 5.3 hours

8 laptops achieved 6.4 hours

8 laptops achieved 6.2 hours

a. What would the sum of the hours for the sixty-four laptops, $\sum_{t=1}^{64} v_t$, equal? On average, what does the battery life of the sixty-four laptops equal? What is the estimated mean, *EstMean*, for the battery life of all laptops produced?

b. What would the sum of squared deviation from the estimated mean now equal?

c. Estimate the variance for number of hours of all laptops produced by the manufacturer, the population?

d. Estimate the variance of *EstMean*'s probability distribution. What is the estimated standard deviation; that is, what is the standard error?

e. Using the Student t-distribution, calculate Prob[Results IF H_0 true]. Access the lab using the following link and then fill in the blanks:

[To access this online material, go to http://mitpress.mit.edu/westhoffeconometrics and select t-Distribution.]

Mean: _____

Standard error: _____

Value: _____

Degrees of freedom: _____

Prob[Results IF H_0 true] = _____

f. Assess the consumer manufacturer's claim.

4. Now suppose that the sample size were 120, fifteen times larger than the original eight. Furthermore suppose that the battery life data just replicated the data from the first eight laptops. That is,

15 laptops achieved 8.9 hours

15 laptops achieved 6.4 hours

15 laptops achieved 6.2 hours

15 laptops achieved 6.7 hours

15 laptops achieved 7.5 hours

15 laptops achieved 5.3 hours

15 laptops achieved 6.4 hours

15 laptops achieved 6.2 hours

a. What would the sum of the hours for the 120 laptops, $\sum_{t=1}^{120} v_t$, now equal? On average, what does the battery life of the 120 laptops equal? What is the estimated mean, *EstMean*, for the battery life of all laptops produced?

b. What would the sum of squared deviation from the estimated mean now equal?

c. Estimate the variance for number of hours of all laptops produced by the manufacturer, the population?

d. Estimate the variance of *EstMean*'s probability distribution. What is the estimated standard deviation; that is, what is the standard error?

e. Using the Student *t*-distribution, calculate Prob[Results IF H_0 true]. Access the lab using the following link and then fill in the blanks:

[To access this online material, go to http://mitpress.mit.edu/westhoffeconometrics and select *t*-Distribution.]

Mean: _____

Standard error: _____

Value: _____

Degrees of freedom: _____

Prob[Results IF H_0 true] = _____

f. Assess the consumer manufacturer's claim.

5. Summarize you answers to the first three problems below:

Sample size	EstMean	Sum of squared deviations from EstMean	Variance estimate of population's probability distribution	Variance estimate of EstMean's probability distribution	Prob[Results IF H_0 true]
8	___	___	___	___	___
64	___	___	___	___	___
120	___	___	___	___	___

Using your intuition, explain why Prob[Results IF H_0 true] changes as the sample size increases.

6. Suppose that you had not learned about degrees of freedom and the Student t-distribution. Specifically, suppose that you used the sample size when estimating population variance and the normal distribution when calculating Prob[Results IF H_0 true]. Fill in the blanks had this been the case:

Sample size	EstMean	Sum of squared deviations from EstMean	Variance estimate of population's probability distribution	Variance estimate of EstMean's probability distribution	Prob[Results IF H_0 true]
8	____	____	_____	_____	_____
64	____	____	_____	_____	_____
120	____	____	_____	_____	_____

7. Compare your answers to problems 5 and 6. As the sample size increases does the use of the degrees of freedom and the Student t-distribution become more or less critical? Explain.

Index